The Shadow Warriors

The Shadow Warriors

O.S.S. and the Origins
of the C.I.A.

Bradley F. Smith

Basic Books, Inc., Publishers   New York

Library of Congress Cataloging in Publication Data

Smith, Bradley F.
  The shadow warriors.

  Bibliography: p. 478
  Includes index.
  1. World War, 1939–1945—Secret service—United
States. 2. United States. Office of Strategic
Services—History. 3. United States. Central
Intelligence Agency—History. I. Title.
D810.S7S554 1983   940.54′86′73   82–72407
ISBN 0–465–07756–0

To Lorenzo Brown and Family

Contents

Contents

Acknowledgments

AMONG the many people who helped in the course of the preparation of this volume, some must be singled out for special thanks.

Agnes F. Peterson, Merritt Robbins, and Jenny Wilkes read all, or portions, of the manuscript; Maggie and Leslie Smith gave me help with the research; Donald Belillo provided real hospitality; and John Toland and William Cunliffe gave me especially wise counsel.

For every manuscript reference there is at least one archivist who made the research possible. Those to whom I owe the greatest debt of gratitude are: William Cunliffe, John Taylor, Terri Hammett, William Lewis, Sally Marks, Kathy Nicastro, Tom Branigar, Denis Bilger, Robert Parks (in the various branches of the National Archives); James Miller (State Department); Nancy Bressler (Seeley Mudd Library, Princeton University); Charles Palm and Agnes F. Peterson (Hoover Institution); Mary Jo Pugh (Bentley Library, University of Michigan); John Jacob (George C. Marshall Foundation); Edmund Berkeley (Alderman Library, University of Virginia); Angela Raspin (British Library of Political and Economic Science); Marion Stewart (Churchill College Library, Cambridge).

Linda Carbone of Basic Books and Donna Lindeke also provided great assistance.

Above all I would like to express my thanks to those who, like the members of the J. H. Jebsen family, do not share my interpretation of events, but because of their respect for scholarship allowed me to quote from personal papers.

For permission to quote from material for which they have either the physical custody, the copyright, or both, I would like to thank:

Controller of Her Majesty's Stationery Office

The United States Government Printing Office

Master and Fellows of Churchill College Cambridge

Acknowledgments

The Library of Congress

The Seeley G. Mudd Manuscript Library, Princeton University

Michigan Historical Collections, Bentley Historical Library, University of Michigan

Rare Book and Manuscript Library, Columbia University

The Hoover Institution on War, Revolution and Peace

Manuscripts Department, University of Virginia Library

Appreciation for permission to publish extracts from published works is hereby made to David Dilks (ed.) and Cassell and Company, publishers of *The Diaries of Sir Alexander Cadogan*; B. G. Liddell Hart (ed.) and Harcourt Brace Jovanovich, Inc., publishers of *The Rommel Papers*; Kenneth Young (ed.) and Macmillan (London), publishers of *The Diaries of Sir Bruce Lockhart*; as well as for the opportunity to reprint from *The War Diary of Breckenridge Long: Selections from the Years 1939–1944*, selected and edited by Fred L. Israel, by permission of University of Nebraska Press, copyright © 1966 by the University of Nebraska Press; and from *The Price of Vision*, by John Morton Blum, copyright © 1973 by the Estate of Henry A. Wallace and John Morton Blum, reprinted by permission of Houghton Mifflin Company.

Prologue

DURING the evening of 15 April 1944, an eight-man Operations Group (O.G.) of the Office of Strategic Services (O.S.S.) left its base on the Italian island of Logasta in the central Adriatic and landed on the neighboring German-held Yugoslav island of Korcula. The O.S.S. men were met on the beach by Yugoslav partisans, who led them to their "secret cave," where the Americans were able to rest. On the following day, the partisans and O.S.S. men made preparations for an evening operation to ambush the Nazi patrol which made its rounds on the main road running through Korcula.[1]

The eight Americans left the cave along with twelve partisans early in the evening of 16 April for a two-hour march to the ambush spot. It was a pleasant hike, so effortless that at one point, "the lone partisana in the party held [up] the march for five minutes while she picked violets for her lapel." When the force reached the main road, its members leisurely set about establishing the ambush. Many of them were still "standing straight up" along the roadside "trying to decide which rock would offer the best protection" when, without warning, a Nazi motorcycle patrol roared around the corner. "The surprise was complete on both sides," and there was a moment of frozen shock until the partisan commander opened fire on the lead motorcycle. Swerving from side to side, the motorcycles accelerated, with their two drivers and three passengers ducking low to avoid being hit. The ambush team, though, had come quickly to life, firing everything from sten guns to old rifles, and "the whole hillside seemed to leap into flame." The motorcycles careened onto the shoulder of the road, one man fell out dead, and the other four scrambled for cover. Climbing up a low embankment, the Nazis' "broad backs" were fully exposed, and two were killed instantly. The remaining two managed to reach a clump of brush, where they dug in and began firing. As the O.S.S.–partisan force advanced, alternately firing and scurrying forward, the two Germans held on grimly, managing to inflict a leg wound on the lieutenant commanding the O.S.S. force. But the five-minute exchange of fire ended abruptly when the O.S.S.–partisan team closed in on the clump of bushes, hurled grenades, and poured in bursts of fire from automatic weapons.

The O.S.S. men had planned to give every Nazi a chance to surrender, and if "that generous offer" was refused, to use them "for target practice." But it had not worked out that way, for "all five of the enemy were now dead, or so close to dead that only a doctor could tell the difference." An O.S.S. man therefore went up to the five figures on the ground and "gave each one a burst from his Tommy gun" to make sure they were dead. An Austrian private was the last to die, muttering that "he was too young" and that "he wanted to live." The partisans, who had been "a little amazed" by the American idea of taking prisoners, moved in and stripped the bodies. One partisan berated a German corpse for having allowed himself to be shot through the legs, "thus ruining a perfectly new pair of boots."

Fifteen minutes after the firing began, the work by the roadside was finished. An improvised stretcher had been made for the wounded O.S.S. lieutenant, and the O.S.S.–partisan detachment began a long upward march into the mountains. "The trip to the cave was [a] nightmare, a five-hour horror that left the men fraught with exhaustion and the wounded lieutenant gibbering and whimpering with pain and agony." When the O.S.S. men finally reached the cave in the early hours of 17 April, the partisans did what they could to help the lieutenant. On 18 April, after O.S.S. attempts to contact home base failed, the Yugoslavs provided a small boat to take the eight Americans back to Logasta. There the O.S.S. group recuperated, the lieutenant's leg was treated, and reports (such as the one from which this account is taken) were written to help the American authorities improve their raiding techniques.

But there is one hitch to this tale of heroic resistance. On 17 April, the Nazis returned to the scene of the ambush, established a strict curfew in the area, burned several houses in a neighboring village, and took away twenty civilian hostages to be shot.

The incident of Korcula embodies many of the most significant features that characterized the Second World War. To be sure, the war had a generous supply of the traditional hell cited by General Sherman. Close-in infantry combat was still a decisive feature, leading G.I.s—like Billy Yanks, Doughboys, and Grunts—to fight, get wounded, and frequently die in conditions of surprise and torment. But the nature and form of warfare from 1939 to 1945 were also distinctly different from those of earlier conflicts. Mechanization had greatly increased since the last war. Even in small, isolated operations such as the one on Korcula, forces were mobile and had devastating fire power. Advanced technology and mechanization colored every aspect of the conflict, culminating in the strategic bombing and atomic horrors that cast such a shadow over our own day.

The war's impact on civilians was also a new phenomenon. Civilian casualties in previous modern conflicts generally had been incidental to front-line combat; in World War II, however, a focus on economic and ideological warfare brought civilians into the center of hostilities. The incident on Korcula, where the Nazis seem to have killed four civilians for every one of their dead soldiers, was repeated over and over again, especially in central eastern Europe and on the mainland of Asia. Thus, for combatants and civilians alike, war became more brutal, and incidents in which no quarter was given and savage reprisal was taken occurred on a scale previously unknown.

Sabotage, guerrilla attack, secret intelligence, and other forms of irregular warfare spread everywhere. By the war's end, no area of the globe, whether belligerent, neutral, or conquered, was immune to "shadow warfare." Along with the new focus on military technology and economic war, shadow warfare helped blur the line between safety and danger and revolutionized the rules of war. Thus, O.S.S. conceived of a Korcula raid, Ultra and Magic computers were put to work to unravel coded messages, German soldiers attacked in the Bulge wearing American uniforms, and civilians in every country were bombarded by open ("white") and disguised ("black") propaganda.

No country could be insulated from the effects of this war, not even the United States of America, which had long prided itself on its isolationist ability to hide behind oceans. The years 1939 to 1945 saw a steady and rapid increase in American productivity. By war's end, the United States accounted for nearly half of the world's industrial production (and much of its commercial agricultural output), while its huge armaments industry met not only America's far-flung martial needs but also those of many of its allies. During the same period, the United States created an enormous modern military force of 12 million men and women. United States equipment, money, and manpower reached into the most distant areas of the world. America's navy penetrated every ocean, and its ground and air units engaged in battle from North Africa to central China. O.S.S. Operational Groups (O.G.) and resistance support units (Special Operations— S.O.) fought and died in little-known backwaters such as Korcula and Saigon.

Prologue

The scale of operations and the astonishing range and speed of the changes made it impossible to turn back the clock when the war ended in 1945. Even the most determined isolationist was forced to recognize in the early Cold War era that the vast extension of American power and influence was irreversible. In 1947, Congress institutionalized the super-power status that World War II had bequeathed to the United States by creating, among other innovations, a large standing military machine— the Department of Defense—and a permanent shadow warfare organiza-tion—the Central Intelligence Agency (C.I.A.).

Of the many basic changes that World War II brought to the United States, normalizing shadow warfare as a part of government (in the form of the C.I.A.) has surely been among the most controversial. In the 1970s, in particular, conflicts over shadow warriors and their past and present actions raged through American public life. Many efforts were undertak-en to trace the C.I.A. back to its roots and much attention was focused on its immediate ancestor, O.S.S. Since William J. Donovan, the founder of this World War II centralized intelligence agency, was America's best-known champion of shadow warfare, it was only natural that those trou-bled by the C.I.A. should want to know more about Donovan's organiza-tion and its predecessor, the office of Coordinator of Information (C.O.I.). When observers realized that many of the C.I.A.'s most important offi-cials in its formative period—including Allen Dulles, Frank Wisner, Rich-ard Helms, and William Colby—were O.S.S. veterans, interest in the C.O.I.–O.S.S. heritage increased.

A spate of books quickly appeared on O.S.S. These accounts of espio-nage and covert adventure were supplemented by three "official" O.S.S. histories either written by C.I.A. men or released with the agency's bless-ing. A former O.S.S. official, Corey Ford, also brought forth a highly flattering biography of William Donovan. All these works tended to por-tray the O.S.S. director as a farsighted man who had produced a clear blueprint for shadow warfare. O.S.S. was depicted as the simple embodi-ment of the Donovan plan, and the C.I.A. was seen as the culminating achievement of his vision. Thus, the C.I.A. was provided a legitimatizing theoretical and historical ancestry.

The most influential book on American central intelligence history, written in the 1970s, R. Harris Smith's interesting and valuable *O.S.S.: The Secret History of America's First Central Intelligence Agency*, was, however, less sure that the C.I.A. fulfilled the promise of O.S.S. or grew naturally out of Donovan's plans. Like most writers on the subject, Smith's opinion of Donovan was high, but he concluded that the most important feature of O.S.S. was its attempt to embody American liberal idealism within its shadow warfare activities. The C.I.A. had gotten into trouble, in Smith's view, primarily because it had broken with what he saw as the idealistic tradition of Donovan's O.S.S. and had degenerated into an instrument of rightist repression.[2]

All these works—including Smith's book and those produced under C.I.A. auspices—had two limitations. They lacked documentary material necessary to systematically treat the evolution of O.S.S. because much of this rich source lode was widely scattered or still classified. Furthermore, in assuming that Donovan had a fixed plan that followed point by point between 1941 and 1945, they disregarded the effects of basic changes that shook the world and the manner of warfare in those years.

The present work moves further in regard to source material by using the Freedom of Information Act, British documentary sources, and pieces gathered from ninety manuscript collections. But its primary innovation is to break sharply with the view that the C.O.I.–O.S.S.–C.I.A. evolution can be understood best as the development of a clearly delineated Donovan plan that attained supreme fulfillment in the C.I.A. charter.

The evidence now available points to the view that Donovan and many of his contemporaries believed in the magic efficacy of irregular warfare because they misread the sources of Hitler's strength and gave too much credence to the power of a German fifth column. Their faith in shadow warfare was further nurtured by a similar gross overestimate of the effectiveness of British covert operations. Donovan did succeed in persuading Franklin Roosevelt to create the first American shadow warfare organization (C.O.I.) in 1941, but he was quickly compelled to revise his definition of intelligence and information to stay in touch with the changes that the war brought to the United States and the rest of the world.

Following Pearl Harbor, when the American government chose to establish its war-making system on a carefully planned mobilization of the nation's manpower and economic resources, Donovan's desire to emphasize the irregular and unpredictable was out of step with the main course of events. To survive at all, the C.O.I.–O.S.S. director had to subordinate his organization to the Joint Chiefs of Staff (J.C.S.) and search for opportunities to show that irregular warfare could usefully support regular military operations. O.S.S. embarked on hundreds of projects, constantly shifting and changing focus, while trying to prove to the generals and admirals that whatever current activity it was performing had value as "strategic intelligence" and "psychological warfare." Donovan's primary concern throughout was the promotion of his organization per se rather than of any O.S.S. flow chart or master plan.

Donovan's organization was preeminently a creature of the fast-moving times, which forced it to alter its shape as well as its spots. What existed at the end of the war was merely the last in a series of kaleidoscopic O.S.S. reformulations, staffed by a group of shadow warfare enthusiasts who identified with what had sold well, ignored what hadn't, and looked longingly for a chance to extend their activities into a postwar world where America's conventional armed forces were weak and Cold War dangers seemed to lurk everywhere. Therefore, the main line of continuity between C.O.I.–O.S.S. and the C.I.A. lies less in structural schemes and more in the wartime experiences of the organizations and the prominent people associated with them.

We will observe those experiences with a stress on four main phenomena: the factors that made Donovan and much of the Western world believers in shadow warfare in 1940–41; the processes that led C.O.I.–O.S.S. to settle on some kinds of subversive activities and eschew others; the areas and activities in which O.S.S. succeeded and thereby satisfied its "customers"; and some of the channels through which O.S.S. veterans directly contributed to the creation of the C.I.A.

Taken together, these factors (or experiences) were the central—if twisting—currents of development that shaped the American shadow warfare system during the Second World War. But that current was itself formed and moved along by the larger ebb and flow of an America surging within a storm-tossed world.

This then is unashamedly a history of the whole war, with American shadow warfare placed in the eye of the storm. To grasp the dynamics that moved both the current and the oceans, we must begin in May 1940, when the sea walls began to crumble and many Americans thought that the tempestuous world was about to flood in upon them in the form of a Nazi hurricane.

We all make an investment in falsehood.

ARTHUR MILLER

The Shadow Warriors

CHAPTER 1

Nazi Germany and the Birth of Anglo-American Shadow Warfare: 1940-41

Let us dwell for a moment on
those opening days of May 1940
and take a final glance at a West
that was never to be seen again.

JACQUES BENOIST-MECHIN
Sixty Days That Shook the West

The War in Europe and the German Fifth Column: 1940

AT 5:30 A.M. ON 10 MAY 1940, Adolf Hitler abruptly canceled the eight months of "phony war" during which the German and French armies had peacefully gazed at each other across the Maginot Line. While Gen. Wilhelm von Leeb's Army Group C continued its holding action in the south, two other large German army groups smashed across the borders of neutral Luxembourg, Belgium, and Holland. Gen. Gerd von Rundstedt's Army Group A, composed of forty-five divisions, including seven motorized (panzer), began to move steadily southwestward through the heavily wooded and lightly defended Ardennes region of Luxembourg and Belgium. Further to the north, Gen. Fedor von Bock's Army Group B hurled twenty-nine divisions, including three panzer, against the southern Netherlands and northern Belgium.

From the first moments of the assault, the dominant features of the western campaign of 1940 were manifest. The German forces in the two offensive army groups were deployed to create maximum concentration of force, with seventy-four divisions (one million men) attacking on a front fewer than 175 miles in width. The Luftwaffe, which had complete control of the air, acted as airborne artillery to clear the way for the advancing ground force while simultaneously striking deep into the Dutch and Belgian interior to disrupt Allied efforts to marshal support for the frontier defenders. The Belgians and Dutch were further paralyzed by German paratroop units. These forces, which never before had been extensively employed in combat, went to work with devastating effect. Civilians and military alike were often so stunned that the airborne units performed their assigned tasks virtually without opposition. At dozens of points they seized and held vital bridges over Holland's canals and rivers, thereby making possible the rapid advance of the main ground forces. Although thwarted in some large enterprises, such as an attack on Rotterdam's airport, the paratroop units carried through the single most stunning feat of the campaign. On 10 May, a tiny, specially trained force was dropped squarely on top of Belgium's main defensive bastion at Eben Emael—the greatest modern fort in the world at that time. The paratroopers drove explosive charges deep into the interior of the structure, and within minutes the fort was filled with noxious fumes and secondary explosions. The resulting capitulation of the garrison on the first day of the battle opened the heartland of Belgium to invasion and the shocking loss of Eben Emael made every Allied defender shudder at the threat posed by the German airborne forces.[1]

But it was not the paratroops or even the fury of the Luftwaffe that gave the Nazi attack its main striking power. Germany's ability to produce quick results lay in the organization of its ground forces. Hitler had been determined to avoid a war of attrition similar to that following the stalemate of 1914–18. To achieve mobility he and the Wehrmacht leadership had created armored divisions, which could concentrate enough force and move with sufficient flexibility to cut through moderately strong positions and drive into the enemy's rear. Once these units broke through, they ranged wide and deep, counting on surprise, air power, and a large force of follow-up infantry to solidify their gains. This form of lightning, or blitzkrieg, warfare depended on modern weaponry, efficient organization, and full coordination of air and ground units. Even more important for the blitzkrieg's success was the existence of a ruthless and determined political leader ready to use any means to secure initial surprise and aggressive combat commanders who would then exploit the opportunities that surprise provided.

In May 1940 Hitler had given the three neutral low countries no warning. The German Wehrmacht had made its final preparations and concentrations so stealthily that the defenders were caught completely unaware at the initial moment of assault. The attacking force also gained a minor advantage by the use of a single stratagem, or "dirty trick." In their earlier attacks on Poland in September 1939, and even more so on Norway and Denmark in March 1940, the Nazis had made fairly generous use of deception, such as hiding troops in what appeared to be innocent merchant ships and dressing German personnel in Polish uniforms. No such elaborate ruses were employed in May 1940. But a small German advance unit was outfitted in Dutch uniforms and sent forward to seize the bridges over the Maas on 10 May. In at least one foray this stratagem succeeded, but the German intelligence service (Abwehr) had not secured sufficient Dutch uniforms for the whole unit. Some of the men were therefore togged out in outfits that resembled carnival costumes—German uniforms dyed blue to look vaguely Dutch, with caps made of cardboard! Although the Dutch security forces had been stunned by the initial assault, they soon recovered and made rather short work of this disreputable band of invaders.[2]

While dirty tricks and propaganda were only peripheral factors in the speed and force of the Nazi assault, good German intelligence was vital. The Wehrmacht had acquired all the information it needed from Allied documents captured in Norway, supplemented by air observation, prisoner interrogation, and effective use of radio monitoring and decoding. Without having to depend much on spies, traitors, or luck, the Germans had worked out the complete Anglo–French, Dutch, and Belgian orders of battle prior to 10 May, and they also knew that in the event of a German attack on Belgium and Holland, the Anglo–French command intended to rush forces northward into Belgium (and if possible Holland) to build a defensive wall like that which had been created in 1914. Once the Allies moved into Belgium, their forces would be committed to an extended defensive perimeter and would have no additional strategic reserve.[3]

Musing on the campaign after the end of World War II, Gen. Siegfried Westphal remarked that if an army succeeds in breaking a stalemate and mounts a successful offensive, the defender will find that "he must follow where he is led." So it was in May 1940. When the Germans crossed into the low countries, the Allies immediately moved north, hoping to erect their defensive dam as quickly as possible. As the German offensive in Holland and Belgium gained momentum, the Allied forces redoubled their efforts to reach the north and dig in. However, the motorized Germans were too quick for them; hampered by lack of motorized transport, the Anglo-French forces were unable to gain a defensible line prior to the disintegration of the tiny Dutch army on 13–14 May. Von Bock's panzers, supported by waves of aircraft, flanked or pierced the best defensive positions before the Allied armies could be concentrated in force. While scrambling to find some kind of defensive line and man it, the northern Allied commanders learned to their horror that their immediate difficulties were nothing compared with the catastrophe that was developing further south.[4]

For despite the Allied shock and defeats occasioned by von Bock's invasion of Holland and northern Belgium, it was alas, not the main German offensive, but essentially a feint. While the world's attention had been fixed on von Bock's ferocious onslaught in the north, the advance units of von Rundstedt's Army Group A had been quietly working their way through southern Belgium and Luxembourg and had reached the French frontier. Behind the advance units came the full weight of the main German offensive force, seven panzer divisions, "like a great phalanx . . . densely closed up one behind the other." The armored column was so long that it extended "more than a hundred miles deep from head to tail" and initially trailed back from the German frontier to a point "fifty miles *east* of the Rhine." This was Hitler's hammer, and since the Luftwaffe had succeeded in preventing Allied aerial observers from catching a glimpse of it, the hammer fell with devastating force.[5]

By the third day of the campaign (12 May), von Rundstedt's lead units had cleared the Belgian forests and crossed the French frontier at a number of points. On 13 May, the decisive battle for the Meuse began with the main focus of the action at Sedan. After tank and artillery fire were concentrated on the French west bank positions, the full strength of the Luftwaffe was thrown in. To a German soldier, the attacking Stukas appeared like massed birds of prey: "They hurtle perpendicularly down. . . . Everything becomes blended together, along with the howling sirens of the Stukas in their dives, the bombs whistle and crack and burst. . . . All hell has broken loose." For one-and-a-half days the French troops held against this onslaught of bomb and shell, while German infantry and armor wiggled forward, around and about, searching for soft spots and gradually building up bridgeheads on the west bank. Then the German tanks began to slip behind the French defensive positions, and the cry,

"Tanks to the rear and to the left," echoed and reechoed through the French ranks. The artillery men were the first to crack, then riflemen and machine gunners got up and fled, and by 2:00 P.M. on 14 May the defensive works at Sedan were deserted. The fear of encirclement, the panic created by deep armored penetration, had become a collective nightmare for the French army. Soldiers who fled the battlefront claimed that "they had been pursued by formidable masses of tanks; some spoke of 400, others of 500, or even 5,000."[6]

The German victory on the Meuse decided the battle and the campaign. As French premier Paul Reynaud later told Churchill, "The hard point of the German lance" had gone through; the all-important defensive perimeter had been broken, and no strategic reserve remained. To the French commanders the debacle was "stupefying"; indeed, when the news of the German breakthrough reached the supreme French commander, Gen. Alphonse Georges, he merely collapsed into an armchair and "a sob" silenced him. German staff officers were equally "astonished" by what had happened, but front-line German commanders, such as Erwin Rommel, immediately grasped that with the Meuse behind them little or nothing stood between their panzers and the English Channel. Rejoicing that this "was not just a beautiful dream, it was reality," Rommel drove westward with redoubled energy.[7]

The Germans' one-week advance across northern France was delayed more by momentary fits of Hitlerian doubt than by the actions of the French and British armies. Once the German armor was given free rein west of the Meuse it simply outran the efforts of the Anglo-French command to erect defensive barriers. When the panzers encountered obstacles that they could not immediately reduce, the Luftwaffe was called in, allowing the tanks to swing around the flanks and move on. The deeper the penetrations, the more readily the French soldiers capitulated to tank forces that appeared where "they shouldn't have been." Repeatedly, the words that broke French morale were "Tanks, tanks. . . . We are outflanked." As at Sedan, it was deep armored penetration amid the confusion of land battle and the hell of air attack that undercut the French soldiers' willingness to resist. Writing immediately after the debacle, the great French historian Marc Bloch, who served as a soldier in both world wars, noted that "from the beginning to the end of the campaign, the Germans showed the same embarrassing skill in appearing where they ought not to have appeared." The Germans won so quickly and completely because, as Bloch noted, "They did not, in fact, play the game."[8]

Indeed they did not, and this allowed them to get what they wanted with blazing speed. On 21 May, the panzers reached the English Channel, just eleven days after the forces of von Bock and von Rundstedt had entered the low countries. The Allied armies were thereby cut in two and neither force was strong enough to sustain itself against the German armored power. In the north, the Allied expeditionary force in Belgium was caught between von Bock's Army Group B and the long arm of von Rundstedt's panzer armies moving up from the south. Dreadful scenes occurred in this "Flanders pocket" with French, Belgian, and British troops driven in upon each other, torn between the need to defend their positions by counterattack and the desire to save themselves by capitulation or flight to the Channel ports. The disorder of the Allied armies was compounded by the flood of refugees who took to the roads not only to escape from physical danger but also to do something that would allow them to break free from the shock and bewilderment that the blitzkrieg had wrought. "I don't understand," a dazed Belgian woman whispered to journalist William Shirer in late May as she and thousands of others crowded onto the roads, compounding the difficulties of the Allied armies.[9]

Under such conditions it was a near miracle that a third of a million men were evacuated from Dunkirk by 4 June. But it was an achievement of defeat, not of victory. Heavy equipment was left behind, as were the remnants of the Belgian army and a large portion of the French northern force. Further south, the rest of the French Army was drawn up behind the improvised Weygand Line, desperately hoping to shield central and southern France from the German armored onslaught. But on 5 June, when the attack on the Weygand Line began, the results were never in doubt despite a stiff and heroic French resistance. Once again, an overextended conventional defensive army was facing the Luftwaffe and a Wehrmacht assault force, which this time was far larger than that of the defenders. After four days of bitter fighting, the Weygand Line was shredded and German tanks again moved into open country. On 10 June, Benito Mussolini declared war on France, and four days later Hitler's army entered Paris. With the German armored units ranging freely, the fate of metropolitan France and of the Reynaud government was sealed. Marshal Henri Pétain replaced Reynaud as head of the French government on 16 June, and on the following day the marshal asked Hitler for an armistice.

In light of the scale and speed of the German triumph, the armistice terms that the Pétain government accepted on 22 June were surprisingly moderate. Hitler had decided that it was better to take three-fourths of the loaf than to impose terms so onerous that they would encourage the French to take their fleet to the colonies and thereby bolster Britain's willingness to fight. Although he could not forgo the chance to humiliate the French at the signing ceremony at Compiègne, the Führer hoped to end the war in the west by pacifying the French and luring Britain into a settlement based on German continental hegemony. It is now easy to see that Hitler's hope for an agreement with Britain was doomed to failure, but it is also easy to ignore the measure of success he attained in soothing defeated France. The German Army placed occupation troops only in the northern and Atlantic coastal regions. South and east of a line of demarcation, Pétain's government was allowed to exercise nominal authority from its capitol at Vichy. Clutching to an appearance of sovereignty, the Vichy government retained control of the fleet and a small army, held title to the colonies, and conducted the civil administration of France even in the German-occupied zone. Of course much of Vichy's theoretical independence was an illusion; Germany was too strong and too close. Nazi officials wandered about virtually at will in French territory and interfered in French business. Various clauses of the armistice agreement gave Hitler the means to exert whatever pressure he found appropriate on the French. But the maintenance of some form of French state, with the fatherly Pétain at its head, provided Frenchmen with an opportunity to begin the painful process of coming to terms with the events of May–June 1940.

All contemporaries agree that the speed and totality of the collapse had left people "dazed," with an inescapable "bruising sense of shock." The scale of the debacle that had turned one of the world's great powers into a wretched dwarf within forty-five days was truly breathtaking. The very language people used when expressing what they had seen and experienced denoted shock and incomprehension. As early as 16 May, a French liaison officer declared that "the situation is worse than anything we could have imagined." By the second week of June, General Maxime Weygand said that France had "come to the last quarter of an hour" and Pétain chorused that *"C'est la catastrophe."* Once the shooting stopped, Marc Bloch affirmed that France had "suffered such a defeat as no one would have believed possible," and some officers already wondered aloud whether France had "had her day like Athens, Rome, Spain or Portugal." Even after the end of the Second World War, this highly emotional language continued. William Langer was still verbally shuddering in 1948; a French general in 1969 characterized the collapse of the French Army as "the most important event of the twentieth century"; an American journalist who had been in France in 1940 declared three decades later that the defeat had been analogous to "the end of a world."[10]

Little wonder that, as Robert Paxton has noted, in the summer of 1940

Frenchmen began to turn "over the stones of their national life," searching "with morbid fascination" for the "crawling things, real or imaginary, that they believed festered there." Among the items that they should have found immediately were the backwardness and inefficiency of the French Army, an army whose armament, deployment, and leadership had been no match for the Wehrmacht. A French colonel, while visiting General Georges's headquarters on 19 May, had noted a good part of that story when he observed that confusion and inefficiency made the French general headquarters resemble "a rummage sale." Every British, Belgian, and French soldier in May and June 1940 who had been terrorized by panzers and pummeled by Stukas knew that he had been in a battle made unequal by poor armaments and faulty deployment.[11]

But attributing defeat to the mundane fact of military inadequacy did not, understandably, fulfill the need of the vanquished for answers. The reverberations of the debacle had gone too deep, the forces released were too powerful and ominous. Gazing at the flood of refugees in late May, Antoine de Saint Exupéry opined that "somewhere in the north of France a boot had scattered an anthill, and the ants were on the march," while a German officer observing similar refugees concluded that "everything has come on them as an act of God." To the tough men of Vichy, like Pierre Laval however, few of the causes of the defeat lay with boots, God, or the quality of the French officer corps. Laval and his colleagues believed that corruption, inefficiency, and divisions in the Third Republic bore most of the blame. "Parliamentary democracy lost the war," Laval told the Chamber of Deputies on 7 July 1940, adding that "it must give way to a new regime." Many in Vichy agreed that moral slackness and the "threat from the left" had been the real enemy. There were also those, like Pétain himself, who feared social disorder more than they feared the Germans. Such men opposed resorting to guerrilla warfare, or transferring the government to North Africa, not only because they quailed before the practical difficulties and the likely casualties, but because such moves would have threatened the preservation of law and order in France.[12]

These considerations were sufficient to bring much conservative and moderate support to Vichy, but they were not enough to satisfy completely the people of France. It was one thing to accept the proposition that Germany was strong; it was quite a different matter to embrace the notion that the Nazis had deserved to win. Whatever had happened in 1940, Western opinion—including nearly the complete spectrum of French opinion—remained unconvinced that Hitler represented the cause of moral virtue. No matter how disillusioning the cumulative effect of World War I, the Great Depression, and the frustrations of the 1930s had been, the belief that somehow justice *should* prevail had not been extinguished. Germans might be admired for their strength and efficiency, and Hitler might be held in awe for his determination, ability, and ruthlessness, but few in the West believed, much less felt, that Nazi Germany was on the side of righteousness. Paul Reynaud had come close to the popular view when, in the midst of the May–June 1940 catastrophe, he predicted that a Nazi victory "would be the Middle Ages again, but not illuminated by the mercy of Christ."[13]

When German victory became a reality in 1940, therefore, the folk ethos of the West was not inclined to find an explanation for it in Nazi moral strength but in a recognition of German efficiency and the power of Nazi immorality. The propaganda of the Third Reich had openly identified Nazism with the cause of ruthlessness and had prided itself on the clever and sometimes shady tricks with which the Nazi Party, its leader, and his state had gained their victories both at home and abroad. Toughness and triumph were what counted in the Nazi lexicon, and use of the unexpected was Hitler's trademark. He had proclaimed repeatedly that in foreign lands, as well as in Germany, his opponents were weak and splintered and that he had many secret sympathizers among them. In a Europe filled with doubt, deeply divided and uncertain on how or why things happened the way they did, a belief in the power of deceit and trickery was nearly universal. Ever since 1936, when Franco's Gen. Emilio Mola had boasted that he had a "fifth column" of sympathizers in Republican Madrid, the idea of a conspiratorial, centrally directed, Fascist underground "had smouldered on like a heath-fire" in the popular mind. The German attacks on Poland and Scandinavia—the suddenness of the assaults, the dirty tricks and military innovations employed, the rapid collapse of the defenders—all had increased the belief that dark forces were at work.[14]

Then came May–June 1940, and from the moment German forces crossed the frontiers of the low countries, the West was engulfed by tales of Nazi treachery and fifth column activity. Parachutists dressed as nuns were allegedly dropped in Holland; Nazi agents supposedly masquerading as Allied dispatch riders were said to have distributed false orders and spread confusion; "specially-trained and highly-paid Swiss and Belgians who could pass as Frenchmen" allegedly took to the telephone to issue false orders and undercut Allied morale. Hidden snipers were reported everywhere, and any unanticipated explosion was blamed on sabotage. Even the refugees who clogged the roads were attributed to the work of Nazi fifth column agitators who purportedly urged the masses on so they would be vulnerable to attack from the Luftwaffe. This operation was merely "an additional artist's touch from hell's academy, a splash of colour mixed on the Nazis' fiendish palette,"[15] according to Gen. Edward Spears, the British liaison officer with the French command who wrote ten years after the war.

The Germans certainly had used a small (and clumsy) deception operation to seize the Maas bridges. They also had attacked without warning, employed unconventional weapons such as paratroops, and propagandized via Berlin Radio to spread confusion and uncertainty among the Allies. There were, indeed, a handful of Abwehr intelligence agents in the west, mostly in Alsace, and small pockets of activist *Volksdeutschen* and Nazi sympathizers, who may have carried out isolated actions in support of the German forces. But at the time of the 1940 attack, France had been at war for eight months, and French security forces had gone to extreme lengths to intern or place under surveillance anyone remotely suspected of assisting the enemy. Thus, astute observers at the time, such as William Shirer, had good grounds to believe that the fifth column stories were grossly exaggerated and their conclusions have been borne out by every investigation of the German and Allied records carried out in the postwar period. The fifth column reports of 1940 were virtually all fantasies, and there is no hard evidence to support the belief that a German conspiratorial machine carried out "large-scale attacks from within" during the campaign. No centrally directed Nazi fifth column actually existed in the low countries or in France in 1940.[16]

Yet if belief in the existence of a fifth column rested on myth, fable, and mass delusion, this did not mean that it lacked power and importance. Fear of fifth column operations unleashed more confusion and disorder than any actual Nazi conspiracy could have done. An observer in the Netherlands during the battle caught the prevalent belief in dark, Nazi forces perfectly when he declared that the Germans "did not keep to any rules whatsoever." From there it was a small jump to conclude that every Allied reversal, every unforeseen or surprising event had been caused by Nazi efficiency, ruthlessness, and diabolical deception. In the popular mind, the Nazis became both supremely efficient and triumphantly immoral. When an Englishman sought to characterize German airborne forces in 1940, he used the suggestive phrase "the Trojan horse has become winged" to indicate that the weapon was not only surprising and effective but also in some way a dirty trick. Similarly, when the first French troops began to crack on the Meuse, some of them immediately concluded that they were victims of treachery. A French colonel who attempted to rally fleeing men as early as the fourth day of the campaign was met with the cry: "There's no use trying to fight. There's nothing we can do. We're lost! We've been betrayed."[17]

The word *betrayed* is most important here, because by the time the fighting on the continent ended in June 1940, the belief that the German victory had been aided greatly, perhaps even been caused, by the work of a centrally directed Nazi fifth column was firmly embedded in the minds of a large percentage of French officials. German intelligence officers might dismiss it as a fantasy and point to the absence of a French strategic reserve as the rather obvious cause of the French collapse, and a few Western leaders such as Churchill might emphasize on occasion that German machines, not traitorous marionettes, were the chief source of the West's misfortunes. For those Frenchmen apportioning the responsibility for the disaster, however, the fifth column myth was a highly convenient explanation. On 26 July 1940, for example, Gen. Henri Giraud (subsequently the American candidate for leadership of Free France at the time of the 1942 North African invasion) reported to Marshal Pétain that among the main causes of the French military disintegration was the fifth column, whose members "plied their trade admirably . . . sowed terror, propagated demoralization, encouraged desertion."[18]

Such exculpating observations by the defeated Allied generals constituted only one reason why the fifth column myth endured with such force in France. More important was the fact that the world had been turned upside down by the May–June campaign. An extended war, as in 1914–18, was supposed to have ended with the Allies victorious. Instead, Hitler had crushed France and conquered western Europe quickly and effortlessly, as if with a slap of his hand. What should have happened, failed miserably; what ought not to have happened, triumphed handsomely. The battle, which both Hitler and Paul Reynaud had predicted would determine Europe's "fate for hundreds of years," ended in such a way that the people of western Europe faced an eternity of Nazi occupation. For them it seemed easier to accept their plight as the product of Nazi deceit and treachery than as the result of a mundane series of military and strategic blunders. In the hearts and minds of the people of occupied Europe, the fifth column myth had become a necessary truth by June 1940.[19]

For those across the English Channel who, in the summer of 1940, confronted a much grimmer battle and a less certain future than they had anticipated, the fifth column myth also had a part to play. Britain had received a fearful drubbing on the continent in the course of the spring and early summer. Hitler had not only taken Norway, but had carried out his Scandinavian operation in the face of Britain's fleet. By May and June, all Britain's remaining continental allies were lost, a portion of her army and air force were destroyed, and the bulk of her heavy military equipment had been abandoned on the beaches of Dunkirk. With the Atlantic coast from Scandinavia to the Spanish border under German control, and the greatest concentration of air and armored force the world had ever seen in the hands of Adolf Hitler, a massive assault on Britain seemed imminent. "What is next then," Shirer asked in June, if not the "first invasion of England since 1066?" With the British army smaller, less well armed, and not markedly better led than the French Army had been, defensive prospects were indeed grim. The Royal Navy and Royal Air Force were formidable weapons, but by every other measure—population, arms production, resource bases, ground military power—Britain was far weaker than Germany. Britain had her empire and the trade of the world (if she obtained credit to buy), but Germany had Europe. What's more, through her connection with the Soviet Union as a result of the Nazi–Soviet pact of August 1939, Germany was able to avoid the major pressure of a British blockade. Momentum also lay with Hitler. Since the occupation of the Rhineland in 1936, every enterprise that he had attempted was successful. The Führer seemed to have become the guarantor of German victory; his judgment infallible, his power unbeatable. The events of May–June had silenced the remaining doubters and had convinced most of the world that Adolf Hitler had the determination and the means to achieve total victory, by fair means or foul.[20]

"It will ever live to the glory of this island," as Winston Churchill declared, that Britain did not buckle under the pressure and managed to beat back the Luftwaffe. A large share of the responsibility for that achievement must be credited to the customary reserve and grit of the British people. The London newspaper vendor's sign of 22 June 1940 proclaiming "French sign peace treaty: we're in the finals" symbolized the public mood and national character, as did Foreign Office Under Secretary Sir Alexander Cadogan's diary entry of 29 June, asserting "we have simply got to die at our posts—a far better fate than capitulating to Hitler as these damned Frogs have done."[21]

By maintaining a stance of grim combativeness and resistance to panic, Churchill left little room for defeatism. As he had told the French leaders in Paris on 31 May, even before the Dunkirk evacuation had succeeded, "We shall carry on with the war if every building in France and Great Britain is destroyed." When Britain stood alone, he brushed aside all doubts and reservations, proclaiming to the world that the British "would go on to the end," and would "defend our island whatever the cost may be."[22]

This fierce resolve acted as a barrier against the spread of fifth column hysteria in Britain, but it did not make the British government disbelieve in the existence of a German fifth column nor convince the British that such a phenomenon posed no serious threat. Reports of German fifth column activities in Scandinavia had left a noticeable mark on the British press as early as March–April 1940. The invasion of the low countries brought many refugees to the United Kingdom and greatly increased the number of fifth column reports. On the first day of the campaign (10 May 1940), the British Chiefs of Staff Committee held a worried discussion regarding the military dangers of German subversive and fifth column activity. Parachute and fifth column alerts soon followed, and on 13 May the authorities, who had interned some aliens in 1939, began an operation to intern every male alien in the British Isles. This tough program, which has led to serious postwar soul-searching about violation of traditional liberties in the United Kingdom, was a direct response to the German fifth column myth, not simply an overreaction to a real threat. Although the *Abwehr* had a handful of intelligence agents in the United Kingdom and would try to send in more (only to have them all turned into double agents by British counterintelligence, M.I. 5), there is no trace of evidence that in 1940 there was an organized German fifth column of aliens, refugees, or anyone else in Britain.[23]

So, although not allowed to run wild nor to undercut the morale of the population and its leaders, the fifth column myth was firmly established in Britain. Deep within the maze of departments and bureaus of the War Office and the Secret Intelligence Service (S.I.S.), there were some British officials who had been so convinced of its existence, and so entranced by its potentiality, that they sought to emulate the German fifth column even before the outbreak of war. A small propaganda office and two sabotage-subversive warfare sections (Section D, in the S.I.S. and Section GS [R] in the War Office) had been busily engaged since 1938 in creating plans for Allied subversive warfare operations. The Chamberlain government, determined to avoid a conflict if possible and extremely cautious in prosecuting it even after it began, was understandably less than enthusiastic about such revolutionary activities. The three offices were given a minimum of funds, personnel, and official encouragement. A few practitioners of sabotage managed to reach France in 1940 but, when the German attack came, they were not sufficiently organized to do anything except flee the panzers like everyone else. The Allies were as poor at what they thought was fifth column mimicry as at conventional warfare in the spring of 1940, and their sabotage activities came too little and too late.

The closest thing to a serious sabotage operation that the British had prepared in the winter of 1939–40 was a scheme to use their technicians to blow up oil fields in Rumania to cut the petroleum flow to Germany. Unfortunately, the arrangements had been made in conjunction with a group of Rumanian officials, and when the Bucharest government turned toward Berlin, the Germans learned the details of the plan. A flood of Nazi denunciations followed, including the usual accusations against the diabolical Secret Service, and all British technicians were dismissed from the oil fields. As a Foreign Office official who had been involved in the operation lamented a year and a half later, the most unfortunate aspect of the exposé was that "nearly all the German allegations" about this hare-brained plan to use oil technicians as saboteurs "were in substance true."[24]

The early fiascoes of the British subversive warfare sections were paralleled by failures in British secret intelligence operations. The S.I.S. (later Military Intelligence 6 [M.I. 6]) allowed two of its top agents to be ensnared and captured by Himmler's Security and Intelligence Service (S.D.) at Venlo on the Dutch–German border in late 1939, but the effectiveness of the organization's agent operations did not noticeably improve in the months that followed. The British Chiefs of Staff were still complaining as late as the fall of 1940 that S.I.S. agents did not provide useful intelligence. Part of the difficulty both for British intelligence and sabotage operations was that the flight of residents from the continent in May–June eliminated most of the contacts in or near German-occupied territory. It is also true that in the early stages of the war the intelligence services had become havens for the playboys and eccentrics of British upper-class life. The young *Sonnenkinder*, as Martin Green has called them—the dandies, naïfs, and rogues—had flocked to the S.I.S. and the new propaganda and sabotage sections, as if "to their own holiday camp." All contemporary accounts agree that, at least, up to the fall of France, the whole structure of British secret warfare was marked by appalling inefficiency and a playboy unreality. Some British officials felt pleased that the "entire Government machine on the foreign side, outside Number 10, was at the beginning of the war dominated by Old Etonians" because "coordination" was thereby made easier. But the fraternity atmosphere of the protected and pampered along with their concomitant belief that "there existed to every worthwhile experience a short-cut which, like the back way into their colleges, they alone knew how to take," facilitated cloak-and-dagger posing and spy novel heroics. It also provided ample operating room for tough Soviet moles like Kim Philby, without giving

Britain the stuff with which to wage a ruthless war of attrition.[25]

The 10 May attack on France and the low countries, coinciding with the resignation of Neville Chamberlain and the designation of Churchill as leader of a war cabinet, guaranteed that Britain's war-making system would be tightened and toughened. As General Spears remarked, playtime was over, "this indeed was war, the real thing." The old boys' network did not completely disappear and the *Sonnenkinder* were not all sent home, as the subsequent careers of such men as Guy Burgess and Anthony Blunt show only too well, but a new spirit and some brawny new leaders, including Lord Beaverbrook, Brendan Bracken, and Hugh Dalton, made their appearance. As the scale of the disaster on the continent became more obvious, the primary need was to build up air, sea, and ground defenses in the United Kingdom as quickly as possible. But, simultaneously, attention turned to the question of how Britain could strike back at Germany in the event that a "certain eventuality" (the surrender of France) eliminated the Allied ground force on the continent.[26]

Quite naturally, since this was Britain, first place was awarded to the sea—to the navy and the weapon of blockade. The "Dynamic Doctor," Hugh Dalton, was given the Ministry of Economic Warfare and told to wage blockade warfare with the same ruthlessness employed in World War I. A big, tough, Labour Party leader, who represented the Durham miners in Parliament while teaching at the London School of Economics, Dalton was "men" oriented, not very interested in theory, and lacking in "any great sense of organization." He was, in the words of one of his wartime aides, "immensely active, . . . often the reverse of easy" with "a rather elephantine way of endeavoring to ingratiate himself with people." Once the British government decided to wage ruthless warfare, Dalton was clearly its man. As he noted in his diary soon after his appointment, "It is not my duty to walk about with a watering-can, but rather to light the fires and let the F.O. extinguish them if they must."[27]

Yet even with a fighter like Dalton in charge, there was little hope that a British blockade could, on its own, seriously hurt Germany in 1940. Contrary to what London believed, the German economy was not severely stretched. Her industry had not been rigorously geared for war in 1939–40, she had suffered very minor casualties in the first campaigns, and her conquests had markedly improved her raw materials position. With the Soviet Union acting as a corridor through which she could obtain critical items, and the government in Berlin perfectly willing to grab anything in the occupied territories that it wanted (even if this entailed the starvation of the conquered populations), no British blockade could have broken German war-making power.

17

While the Chiefs of Staff in London failed to grasp the full strength of Germany's economic position and late in May 1940 declared that "upon the economic factor depends our only hope of bringing about the downfall of Germany," even they understood that more than a naval blockade would be necessary. In the chiefs' view, air attack on economic targets "and on German morale" would also be required, and in addition they asserted that London would have to foment "widespread revolt" in Germany's conquered territories.[28]

Through this thin wedge there gradually emerged the British government's long-term commitment to the strategic air offensive against Germany. Through the same wedge came a determination not only to accept as true the reality and power of the German fifth column but to copy it, improve upon it, and turn it back against the Germans as part of a three-pronged offensive of blockade, air attack, and subversion that could bring Germany to her knees. On 19 May, amid a long discussion on the horrors that the German fifth column had allegedly perpetrated in France and the low countries, the Chiefs of Staff began to consider what Britain could do to assist in the development of an anti-German fifth column on the continent. In the course of the following month, a number of extended and rambling discussions on this matter took place in various governmental departments and offices. No clear plan for action immediately emerged from the talks, however, and no one was able to come up with the name of a natural leader for an Allied fifth column. On 21 June, for example, Sir Alexander Cadogan conferred with Hugh Dalton "about sabotage" but "as usual" the two men were "without any idea of what we were to discuss" and merely "wasted half an hour."[29]

A general exploratory meeting ultimately took place on 1 July in the office of Lord Halifax to lay the groundwork for a British fifth column agency. In the course of the meeting, which numbered Dalton, Cadogan, Anthony Eden (then minister of war), and "C" (Sir Stewart Menzies, the Director of S.I.S.) among its participants, Dalton stressed that a fifth column agency should not be put under the authority of military intelligence because, in his view, "there was a clear distinction between 'war from without' and 'war from within.'" Subversive warfare could be better waged by civilians than soldiers, in the opinion of the minister of economic warfare, because "what we have in mind is not a military job at all" but one that "concerns trade unionists, Socialists, etc., the making of chaos and revolution." Certainly most of the others present were not as enthusiastic about revolution and chaos as Dalton claimed to be, but the group did agree that someone "armed with almost dictatorial powers" should be made "controller" for subversive operations.[30]

Given the divisions of opinion, it was probably best that the meeting of 1 July restricted itself to agreeing in principle that a centralized organization under the authority of an aggressive minister should be created to supplant the various existing sabotage units. The way was thereby cleared for Churchill to step in and select the title for the organization, name the minister of the crown who would lead it, and provide the slogan that would guide its activities. In mid-July the prime minister christened Britain's new fifth column organization the Special Operations Executive (S.O.E.), gave Minister of Economic Warfare Dalton the job of leading it, and told him that henceforth his duty was "to set Europe ablaze."

Both the slogan and the new chief of S.O.E. sounded determined and impressive in July 1940, but before a real instrument of war could emerge, an organization had to be created. To begin with, S.O.E. had to discover what it was actually supposed to do and how it was supposed to do it. For guidance Dalton tried to find assistance in the supposed efficacy of the German fifth column. As he told Lord Halifax, his new organization would be comparable "to the organizations which the Nazis themselves have developed so remarkably in almost every country in the world." In fact, as we now know, the Nazis had not created any such organizations and Dalton and his colleagues actually would be the first ones to take on the herculean task of trying to establish a centrally directed fifth column and subversive warfare system to operate across all of Europe.[31]

Since Section D of the S.I.S. and other groups had been perfecting special explosive devices and the like, S.O.E. would soon have an arsenal of what seemed to be the appropriate tools for its trade. But the essential fifth column ingredient—active populations in the occupied territories—was missing in 1940. The people were stunned and in general hopelessly resigned to a long period of German occupation. S.O.E. therefore had a long way to go in determining what a fifth column actually was and in discovering how to make it operate effectively in occupied Europe.

In the meantime, Britain faced such deadly peril that she could not wait to see if S.O.E. actually would pull a fifth column out of its hat. Hitler was massing the Luftwaffe across the English Channel and preparing for an invasion (Operation Sea Lion). German U-boat strength in the Atlantic was growing at an alarming rate, and the United Kingdom would soon face a life-and-death struggle to maintain her supply lines. On 10 May, Hitler had told both his soldiers on the western front and the people of continental Europe that "the hour has come for you." In a broadcast of 18 June, Churchill reminded his fellow countrymen that their hour had come as well. "What General Weygand has called the Battle of France is over," he said, and "the Battle of Britain is about to begin." In the prime minister's view, the outcome of that battle would decide whether Europe was to be slave or free, and he called on the British people to rise to the challenge and make it "their finest hour."[32]

With one eye cocked to the west—the only direction from which succor seemed likely to come—Churchill also stressed that more was at stake than the survival of Britain, or even the freedom of Europe. He predicted, as Reynaud had done before him, that if Britain failed and the Allied cause were totally defeated, then the whole world "including the United States . . . would sink into the abyss of a new Dark Age, made more sinister and perhaps more protracted by the lights of perverted science." To Churchill, as to virtually every European, it seemed obvious that Hitler's victory over France had destroyed the balance of power behind which America had hoped to shield herself from the full force of the war. If the Führer went on to crush the British fleet and defeat Britain, he would then, like a diabolical Moses, be able to part the waters that had for so long given security to the United States. In this summer in which so many bells were tolling, Churchill reminded the Americans that unless they roused themselves quickly from their isolationist slumber, they might awaken to find themselves alone in a very small world confronting a gigantic Nazi Germany.

The United States and the War: 1940

16 May: President Roosevelt requests $1 billion for defense
28 June: The Alien Registration (Smith) Act passes Congress
July: Republicans Frank Knox and Henry Stimson join Roosevelt's cabinet

Even without the prompting of Churchill's speeches, the United States reacted to Hitler's western offensive as if it had been struck by a thunderclap. Until May–June 1940, despite a general aversion to Hitler and sympathy for the populations of vanquished countries, Americans had felt removed from the direct impact of the war. They expected a repeat of the script that had seemed to work in 1914–17, believing that Britain and France would counterbalance Germany, thereby creating a protracted stalemate and ultimate victory. But then, as President Roosevelt told Congress on 31 May, there had come "the almost incredible events of the past two weeks," and American opinion reversed itself overnight. A 1939 poll had indicated that 82 percent of the population thought that France and Britain would defeat Germany; by June 1940, however, the majority of those questioned believed that Germany would win the war. Furthermore, for the first time, most Americans had swung over to the view that the war might actually threaten them directly. "Revolution seems not too strong a word," wrote Laurence Greene in the *New York Post* on 7 June, to describe "the change in American thought" from a "belief in security to a dread of tomorrow." On 1 June, *Time* publisher Henry Luce declared in a radio broadcast that if the United States could *"buy* an Allied victory in one year for $5 billion" then "we would be the luckiest people in the world."[33]

Stories alleging that the Nazis had used a deadly fifth column to gain their stunning victories in France and the low countries were widely circulated in the United States press and played a significant part in the rising sense of American vulnerablity. American press representatives in the war zone (including Edmund Taylor and Edgar Mowrer, who would later be associated with O.S.S.) sent back hair-raising tales about German subversive warfare. These were reinforced by countless similar dispatches from Allied reporters and news services as well as from stories told by hosts of refugees arriving in Britain and in various neutral havens from Sweden to the U.S.A. Even senior American diplomats, such as Ambassador William Bullitt in Paris, transmitted a steady stream of excited accounts of subversive acts allegedly perpetrated by German and communist fifth columns in France and Belgium. The vast majority of Americans, like most Europeans, accepted these reports as true. President Roosevelt cited fifth column dangers in his address to Congress on 16 May, and in a fireside radio chat of 26 May said: "We *know* [italics added] of new methods of attack. The Trojan Horse. The fifth column that betrays a nation unprepared for treachery. Spies, saboteurs and traitors are the actors in this new tragedy." That such statements reflected the new public temper is shown by the fact that, whereas in the whole of 1939 only 1,600 reports of alleged sabotage were made to the F.B.I., 2,900 such reports were received on a single day in May 1940![34]

A fifth column panic had struck America, and though its most feverish intensity was brief, it lingered long and had important consequences. One significant effect of the fear was an increased willingness among U.S. officials to cooperate with British security officers who wished to operate in North America. The Canadian millionaire William Stephenson arrived in New York in May to serve as British Security Coordinator (B.S.C.). Stephenson's official designation was chief of the M.I. 6 secret intelligence section in the United States, but the offices of the B.S.C. became headquarters for a broad range of British security and subversive warfare activities in the Western Hemisphere. In addition to establishing a formal intelligence gathering apparatus in 1940, Stephenson presided over the development of counterintelligence operations, propaganda activities, and an S.O.E. section at B.S.C. headquarters in New York. As we shall see below, he and the B.S.C. organization were to play important roles in developing support for Britain within the United States and also in encouraging and facilitating the creation of an American subversive warfare system. But at its inception, the B.S.C. was established primarily to deal with the possible threat of German subversion in the Western Hemisphere, and especially with the protection of British property and resources from subversive attack.

Since the British began their anti–fifth column campaign in the Americas at the very moment when Americans were most worried about subversive dangers, it is important to try to gauge whether Nazi subversive activity was extensive in the hemisphere at that time. From the vantage point of the 1980s, it is obvious that since the Nazis had not mounted a massive fifth column campaign in western Europe in 1940, they could hardly have developed such a campaign in America. In fact, Hitler had ordered Adm. Wilhelm Canaris, the chief of the Abwehr, not to carry out sabotage activities against the United States because he did not want to give the American government grounds for intervention. Furthermore, as a former B.S.C. official has recently conceded, the Führer had taken the additional step of ordering Canaris to refrain from attacking British property in the United States as well because he wished to avoid what had happened in World War I when foolish sabotage escapades by men like Franz von Papen had helped turn American opinion against Germany. Postwar surveys of the German records show that no sabotage actions ordered by the German government were carried out in the United States prior to Pearl Harbor, and only a handful of pathetically amateurish enterprises were attempted thereafter. No German planning papers pointing to an attack on the United States are extant, and German intelligence operations in North America were few in number, poorly organized, and generally ineffective.[35]

Regarding the southern half of the hemisphere, there were again no German plans to mount an invasion. Though Nazi covert operations were more extensive in the south, they were not markedly more effective. Some pro-Nazi organizations raised short-lived difficulties for a few Latin American governments, especially in Uruguay and Brazil, and German intelligence operatives were busier in the area than in North America. Not until after Pearl Harbor, however, did the Nazis make a vigorous effort to create an espionage network, and this activity, which was concentrated in Brazil, was carried out in such a clumsy manner that it was quickly quashed by the Anglo-American counterintelligence services. The only covert activities that the Germans carried out with any degree of energy and success in Latin America involved obtaining and shipping strategic raw materials through the British blockade, and doing whatever was possible to damage or undermine British commercial activities in the region. British operatives, directed primarily by the B.S.C. in New York, replied by carrying out a broad range of covert attacks on German business, government, and subversive organizations in Latin America. By late 1940, a kind of undeclared British–German economic war was being waged there, a war that the British, with the full backing of the United States, would win in a resounding manner.[36]

To sum up the situation, then, in the summer of 1940 there was no German fifth column in the United States, no danger of an imminent German attack on the Western Hemisphere, and no British property in the United States that was directly threatened by German sabotage. Of course, it is much easier to see this now, forty years later. In 1940, Britain had her back to the wall and was compelled to strike whenever possible at German trade while making every effort to gain the support of the United States. The British not only believed that their cause was just and that Americans were perversely blind to the dangers of Hitlerism, they were also convinced that a Nazi fifth column existed both in Europe and America. They therefore smote German business at every turn and simultaneously propagandized against the dangers of the Nazi fifth column with an easy conscience.

The British government was forced to pursue this course for two reasons: it was in a dire and desperate situation, and it was wary of the peculiar American response to the French collapse. Although just how the Americans managed to do so remained a mystery to the British, the people of the United States did not allow themselves to merge their shock, their sympathy for the Allies, and their fear of a fifth column into an effort to enter the war on Britain's side. The isolationist currents were still too strong and the legacy of disillusionment from the First World War too great for Americans to take this leap in June 1940. The United States was psychologically unready for war and, lacking large armed forces and modern equipment, practically unready as well. The "clouds of planes" that Paul Reynaud had asked America to send so that France could "hurl back the invader" simply did not exist in June 1940. The American navy was a formidable force, but neither it nor the army had an adequate modern air arm. The United States Army itself was smaller and less well equipped than even the Dutch Army, which General von Bock had smashed in a mere four days!

Therefore, the first lesson that Americans drew from the events of May–June 1940 was that the country needed to rearm immediately. In the first eight months of the war in Europe, President Roosevelt had been unable to move even modest military appropriations bills through Congress because of conservative and isolationist opposition. Then, on 16 May, as the panzers tore through France, the president asked for a $1 billion defense program, and in fewer than two weeks Congress gave it to him, with an additional half billion dollars thrown in for good measure. In subsequent months Congress approved $6.5 billion more for defense and unanimously approved a measure to increase the size of the American fleet by 70 percent. This special enthusiasm for strengthening the navy is a reminder that although this was "the most extensive peacetime preparedness campaign in American history," many of the old reservations about foreign entanglements and the dangers of standing armies had not lost their force. Everyone agreed that a powerful navy was necessary to prevent the United States from being "the next easy victim for the dictator nations," but there was little agreement on what, if anything, should be done after that.[37]

In May, a group led by prominent Republicans such as Henry Stimson, Grenville Clark, Robert Patterson, and Col. William Donovan drafted a universal military training bill, and in July Donovan and others spoke before the Senate's military affairs committee in favor of selective service. But there was deep resistance to the establishment of a peacetime draft, especially in the Midwest and in the conservative wing of the Republican Party, and the selective service bill failed to make rapid headway. Despite opinion polls indicating that the public overwhelmingly favored aid to Britain following the fall of France, serious obstacles still stood in the way of actually rendering such assistance. The American public and its congressional representatives had not abandoned their old love–hate relationship with the United Kingdom even at this late hour. On 4 July 1940 there was less twisting of the lion's tail than was customary on such occasions and more expressions of admiration for British grit and respect for her as the mother of parliaments. But the old suspicions of British imperialism, social arrogance, and alleged deviousness were still there. Mocking the speech of a British aristocrat could always produce derisive laughter in any American bar, and there was a deep fear that forces were afoot to draw America into the war to serve the financial interests of the City of London and the imperial needs of Whitehall. Congress was obsessed by the notion that the United States might be drawn into the conflict through the back door, as popular folk wisdom contended had happened in 1917. For ten years, the American public and many of its leaders had wallowed in the tale that a conspiracy of American munitions makers and British bankers had maneuvered the United States into World War I through the entangling "one-step-at-a-time" manipulations of men like the American ambassador to the Court of St. James, Walter Page, and Col. Edward House, President Wilson's confidential advisor.[38]

Such notions died hard, and even after the fall of France, Congress was unwilling to accept openly the proposition that American security was directly tied to the survival of Britain. To the congressional mind, hemispheric defense—including a vast expansion of United States military power—had to come first, while aid to Britain remained distinctly secondary. On 28 June, both houses approved, and the president signed, a measure requiring that no material owned by the American government should be delivered to any foreign country unless it had been certified as surplus by the chief of staff of the army or the chief of naval operations. In such an atmosphere, while American officials—including the president himself—were deeply concerned over the hemispheric dangers of an imaginary German fifth column, any move to give practical support to Britain required care and caution.[39]

President Roosevelt made an important opening move in the direction of aid to Britain, while at the same time broadening his political base in an election year, when he added two Republican Anglophile internationalists to his cabinet in mid-June of 1940. Citing the international emergency as his motive, he appointed the owner of the *Chicago Daily News*, Frank Knox, as secretary of the navy, and Henry Stimson, who had served every president since Theodore Roosevelt, as secretary of war. After stormy Senate hearings, which featured angry exchanges between isolationist Republican senators and internationalist Republicans like William Allen White and William Donovan, the appointments of Knox and Stimson were confirmed in early July. While putting their main effort into rebuilding American military strength, Knox and Stimson agreed that all available assistance should be extended to the United Kingdom. They found a firm ally for this program in Secretary of State Cordell Hull. After discussing the plight of the British with Hull in mid-July, Stimson noted in his diary that the secretary of state recognized "perfectly clearly that they are our last line of defense outside our own powers."[40]

Such clarity and forthrightness were possible in private discussions and diary entries, but with fewer than four months remaining prior to the election that would determine whether Franklin Roosevelt would serve an unprecedented third term, it behooved the president to move with extreme caution on the issue of aid to Britain. Privately, he seems to have been inclined to the belief that Britain had a chance to withstand a German assault and that it was in America's interest to play that chance and send aid, but the issue was far from simple. To begin with, talking about such a gamble made for poor election politics. Moreover, the president appears to have let doubts about Britain's chances of success stall a decision on whether to bend the law so that supplies, which America needed for its own rearmament, should be sent across the Atlantic.

Franklin Roosevelt was a shrewd and adroit political leader who was unwilling to walk blindly into an issue as complex and dangerous as this one. What he needed most was accurate information on Hitler's power and intentions, as well as a solid estimate of Britain's ability to withstand German air attack and a cross-channel invasion. In the atmosphere of 1940—when confusion, discouragement, and shock were compounded by a fear of fifth column hobgoblins—no intelligence service in the world had a precise picture of what was going on, nor of the comparative strengths of the two sides. As we have seen, although the British government knew it was in a very tight corner, it had badly overestimated Germany's vulnerability to blockade and air attack, and was seriously muddled about the potentialities of subversive warfare. For his part, Hitler was reluctant to accept the risk of a cross-channel invasion, and was eager to clutch at straws, nurturing a fantasy that Britain might sue for peace or hoping that Goering's Luftwaffe could so flatten the Royal Air Force (R.A.F.) and British morale that Operation Sealion would be akin to a late summer vacation outing.

Considering that Britain and Germany were the two countries on the spot and that they had well-established intelligence services, it is easy to understand why Roosevelt was cautious and uncertain. America was three thousand miles away from the conflict, virtually unarmed, and with no effective intelligence organization. The United States did not then, nor had it ever, possessed a central intelligence system. Many departments in the American government had small information gathering units, but most of these were focused on collecting domestic information. Various offices of the State Department and intelligence divisions of the military (the Office of Naval Intelligence or O.N.I., and the army's Military Intelligence Division, or M.I.D., and Military Intelligence Service, or M.I.S.) were keyed toward the acquisition of foreign intelligence, but all such operations were small, cautious, poorly funded, and hobbled by decades of bureaucratic infighting. Information was gathered from a great many sources through various channels, but it was seldom shared among departments, and there was no central point at which information was regularly concentrated for evaluation. Decentralization had not been viewed as a serious national liability because Americans were chary of anything that looked like concentrated military or secret operations. As long as the protective oceans, the fleet, and the capacity for quick mobilization did their work, it was assumed that there was little need to establish an early warning system or to accept the political hazards of setting up a European-type central intelligence service. Even as international crises increased in the 1930s, the White House and various governmental agencies filled in the most gaping informational holes by utilizing the services of special emissaries or travelers who volunteered their services. This old boys' network—operating on a sense of duty and of loyalty to government service rather than on secret funding—was what usually made such improvised informational systems possible. Men who had known each other during the First World War, especially those who had served in a section of military intelligence, were frequently willing to continue preparing reports during the journeys that they made abroad. Gen. Sherman Miles, who headed the M.I.D. in 1940, had been supplementing the work of the army's military attachés with "non-accredited, unpaid M.I.D. men" since the 1920s.[41]

In the Franklin Roosevelt years, special emissaries were more frequently dispatched openly to trouble spots, gathering first-hand information and reporting back to the State, War, and Navy departments or directly to the president himself. In both domestic and foreign affairs, Roosevelt delighted in skirting regular channels and establishing himself as the only person who had *all* the information on a given issue. By doing so, he was able to develop policies that transcended the limited knowledge and special interests of particular groups and agencies, and since he was preeminently an improviser and innovator, he depended on the special emissary as an essential element of his system of governing.

Consequently, in the summer of 1940, a steady flow of special observers and official representatives from the United States descended on London. No sooner had the German invasion in the west begun than the United States Army recalled its top British military specialist, Gen. Raymond E. Lee, from garrison duty and sent him back to London as a military attaché. Lee arrived in Britain on 21 June and immediately began to renew his connections in the British military and political hierarchy to gather information on Britain's military strength and gauge its readiness to fight to the finish. Shortly thereafter, the U.S. Army Air Corps ordered Lt. Col. (later General) Carl "Tooey" Spaatz to England to examine British and German bombing techniques. In mid-July, Col. William Donovan was sent over by Secretary of the Navy Knox and the president on a special mission that will be discussed more fully below. While Donovan was still in England, a high-level joint army–navy–army air corps investigatory team, comprised of the assistant chief of naval operations (Rear Adm. Robert Ghormley), the chief of the army's war plans division (Brig. Gen. George Strong), and the chief of the army air corps plans (Maj. Gen. Delos Emmons), was organized and sent to London, arriving within two weeks of Donovan's departure. In the fall of 1940, the president also sent Harry Hopkins to confer with Churchill, while Donovan returned for a second British survey during the same period. And continuing into early 1941, more Americans crossed the Atlantic, including special emissary Averell Harriman and John Winant, who replaced Joseph Kennedy as Ambassador to the Court of St. James. Supplementing this official coming and going were visits by highly respected private individuals, such as James Reston of the *New York Times* and David Bruce of the Red Cross (later to become O.S.S. chief in London). These men journeyed about the United Kingdom doing their respective jobs and also making general appraisals that were very welcome in high quarters in Washington.[42]

Such travelers comprised America's regular information gathering network as it functioned in 1940. The number of travelers was unusually large because the issue of British capability was of great importance, and neither the president nor the State Department trusted the judgment or reports of Ambassador Kennedy. Generally regarded in both Washington and London as difficult and a defeatist, Kennedy was a serious informational obstacle. Since he was also a power in the Democratic Party—not a man to antagonize on the eve of the crucial November 1940 elections—the president and the various agency chiefs made a special effort to get the necessary information by going around, rather than through, his office on Grosvenor Square. The British generally grasped what was going on and why, and did their best not only by welcoming their assorted transatlantic visiting cousins, but also by heavily utilizing their organizations in the United States to put information helpful to their cause into the hands of high American officials. As early as 18 June, for instance, summaries of the British daily situation report were cabled by the foreign secretary, Lord Halifax, to the embassy in Washington for direct transmission to the State Department and the president.[43]

To get Britain's story across to Americans and sustain the close personal contacts with United States officials that were essential for securing American assistance, British representatives did everything possible to democratize and "Americanize" their image. Under the leadership of the highly popular ambassador, Lord Lothian, much of the customary diplomatic formality was relaxed and the rigid rules governing liaison eased. This tendency toward friendly openness was especially obvious among British officials stationed in New York, such as those attached to the British purchasing mission. These men had to obtain the goodwill of numerous American business and government officials if they were to obtain needed supplies cheaply and quickly. American cooperation was also necessary to assure that such goods were handled expeditiously and as safely as possible on their voyage through the danger zone of U-boat activity in the North Atlantic. Here the work of the purchasing mission, under Arthur B. Purvis, lapped over into that of William Stephenson's B.S.C.

To do its main job of protecting British property as well as its subsidiary task of impeding German trade and attacking the chimerical German fifth column in the Americas, Stephenson first had to institute his own security arrangements and establish close relations with American police authorities. Much of the daily coordination work consisted of making portside security arrangements with the New York City Police Department, but relations with the F.B.I. were of much greater general significance. In early 1940, "C" had secured President Roosevelt's informal approval for contact to be established between the S.I.S. and J. Edgar Hoover's organization. Thus, when Stephenson was appointed chief of B.S.C. in May, the way had been cleared for him to bend every effort to gain Hoover's confidence and support. Stephenson (who would soon be known throughout the Anglo-American intelligence world as "Little Bill" to distinguish him from "Big Bill" Donovan) succeeded handsomely in convincing the difficult Hoover that cooperation with the British was possible and useful. A tough Canadian industrialist, who possessed a splendid combat record in the First World War and enjoyed the personal friendship and confidence of Winston Churchill, Stephenson was by all accounts, "shrewd, able and energetic." Exuding efficiency and confidence, without a trace of the proverbial British stuffiness, this no-nonsense man was well equipped to work with J. Edgar Hoover. Since both men were eager to pursue fifth columns in the Western Hemisphere—though Hoover never felt completely happy giving the Nazis pride of place over communists, his bête noire—a kind of hunters' comradeship developed between them. As soon as Hoover received Roosevelt's authorization to carry out counterintelligence and security operations in Latin America in June 1940, the F.B.I. and the B.S.C. formed a working relationship in the Western Hemisphere that functioned with minimal friction throughout late 1940 and all of 1941.[44]

Important though Stephenson's F.B.I. contacts were, his desire to promote Anglo-American cooperation extended much more broadly into a wide range of unorthodox activities. Like most British officials in America, he had the job of selling Britain and Britain's war effort, and this entailed making his organization seem as American as possible. More than one *Sonnenkind* (including Noel Coward) was refused a prominent post in B.S.C. because he was too much of a "beau" and might offend American sensitivities. Stephenson also conducted a large open—white—propaganda campaign to convince the American public and government officialdom that they should assist in striking at the peril posed by the German fifth column. Further beneath the surface, and going deeper still as the year 1940–41 progressed, B.S.C. made use of a section of Dalton's S.O.E. called Special Operations 1 (S.O. 1) to circulate disguised—black—propaganda designed to persuade Americans to go all out in their support of the United Kingdom. This operation, one of Stephenson's most important functions in the United States, was not in full operation in the summer of 1940 and therefore will be discussed in greater detail below, but it is important to note the extent to which the B.S.C. was an informational and propaganda agency as well as an organization busy with police and security questions.[45]

Subversive Dangers, Donovan, and Aid to Britain: July–December 1940

August–October: The Battle of Britain
September: Destroyer-for-bases deal sealed and American Selective Service established
October: Italy invades Greece
November: Franklin Roosevelt is elected to a third term

Given his duties and the circumstances he faced, Stephenson obviously needed to cultivate the goodwill of all those Americans who shaped policy, affected public opinion, and had access to those in high places. It was just about inevitable, then, that "Little Bill" Stephenson would draw close to "Big Bill" Donovan in the summer of 1940. Donovan possessed most, if not all, of the important credentials of influence and access so important to Stephenson and the British. These included a long career in New York State Republican politics—which gave him an important voice in the largest and most influential state. Not incidentally to Stephenson, New York was also the geographical center of B.S.C.'s operations. More significant, Donovan was a twenty-year veteran of national politics, and had served as assistant attorney general under Coolidge. His relations with the nominal head of the Republican Party, former president Herbert Hoover, were somewhat strained, but that did not greatly weaken his influence since a rather flawed image had clung to Hoover since the Depression.

Donovan knew men such as Henry Stimson well and was liked by them. He was also one of the two most highly decorated officers in American history due to his service as a colonel in World War I (only Douglas MacArthur equalled him in that department), and thus was a major propaganda asset in his own right. His public relations value and political importance were enhanced by an especially close friendship with Secretary of the Navy Frank Knox, the owner of the *Chicago Daily News*, who had been appointed to the cabinet in June 1940. The British were intent on befriending Knox and his close associates because the navy was the American military service whose close cooperation they needed most.

It must be stressed that Donovan was not just one more person who knew Knox fairly well. The new secretary of the navy regarded him as a close and trusted friend with whom he shared many ideas and in whom he had great confidence. When, in December 1939, Franklin Roosevelt first broached the possibility of adding the Republican Knox to his cabinet, the future secretary told Harold Ickes that it would be much easier for him to accept if another Republican were added at the same time. The man he suggested was William Donovan.[46]

As we have seen, Stimson—not Donovan—became Knox's fellow Republican in the cabinet, but Roosevelt was by no means unsympathetic to William Donovan. Many exaggerated accounts of the Roosevelt-Donovan relationship have created the impression that they were the closest of friends, or, as some would have it, old buddies. Donovan was not a personal crony of the president and did not belong to the inner White House circle. He never had the kind of political and personal intimacy with Roosevelt enjoyed by such men as Joe Daniels, Henry Morgenthau, or Harry Hopkins. But he did have a long association with the president. They attended Columbia University School of Law together and had crossed paths frequently in New York and Washington politics. Perhaps more to the point, they shared comparable personalities.[47]

Donovan and Franklin Roosevelt were activists, enthusiasts, doers—a legacy, perhaps, from growing up in the shadow of the dominant political figure of that generation, Theodore Roosevelt. Both were born and raised in upstate New York, and, although Franklin Roosevelt's personal connection with "Uncle Teddy" was more direct (as a distant nephew, but brought much closer by his marriage to Eleanor), both had been deeply affected by the Republican Roosevelt's style and values. Donovan was fifteen and Franklin Roosevelt sixteen, when the Rough Riders stormed up San Juan hill. Both possessed broad streaks of optimism and confidence about Americans' ability to accomplish virtually anything. They were also molded by the faith in America's democratic and liberal mission that

Theodore Roosevelt had so warmly espoused and dramatized. At the same time, like their mentor, they were Anglophiles. Franklin Roosevelt might on occasion grow misty eyed about his Dutch ancestors, and Donovan knew how to play New York Irish politics, but the two men's inclinations were pro-British despite some reservations about class rigidity and imperialism. Donovan, in particular, though he gained fame in the First World War as commander of the Irish-American "Fighting 69th," never showed "any particular fondness for the Irish Free State." It was the Anglo-American heritage with which both men identified, and like Theodore Roosevelt, they tended to see this heritage as the vessel that would make the virtues they prized manifest throughout the world.[48]

Along with optimism, energy, freedom, and a determination to get things done, Donovan and Franklin Roosevelt believed that courage could work wonders. Like Teddy before them, they were brave men. Franklin Roosevelt had refused to give up after early political defeat and a crippling attack of polio that could well have killed him, and had struggled back to become president. Colonel Donovan had shown a bravery and resolve in World War I that teetered on recklessness, and throughout his life he was unable to comprehend physical cowardice.

Thus the two men shared a common "Square Deal" and "Rough Rider" spirit. They also had the power builder's essential love of inside information and possession of an ear in another camp. Robert Murphy has noted Franklin Roosevelt's fascination with the inner doings of Catholic Church politics; Donovan's life shows his obvious relish at developing the reputation of super spy. Yet with all of these common features, Donovan was clearly more than a shadow of Roosevelt. "Big Bill" Donovan was a formidable character, universally regarded as "clever." Along with his energy, bravery, and great charm, he was more than quick enough to hold his own as a New York lawyer, and easily engendered intense loyalty and devotion from his many subordinates. Through travel and business he had cultivated contacts throughout the world and had made it a duty to study, and on occasion to directly examine, the international trouble spots of the late 1930s. In 1936 he toured the battlefront during the Italian invasion of Abyssinia and attempted in vain to convince the British government that the *Duce* would make short work of Ethiopia and its ancient and outmoded army. Foreign Minister Anthony Eden had not been impressed, though Donovan was soon proven right. He came away from the experience with a firm belief in the strength of rightist dictators (like most everyone else he overestimated the power of Fascist Italy), an increased awareness that the nature of warfare had substantially changed since 1918, and new contacts in Britain.[49]

Given his personality, values, experience, and connections, Donovan was a natural contact point for William Stephenson and the B.S.C. The two men were in many ways kindred spirits. Stephenson would eventually prove himself a far more effective administrator than Donovan, but in 1940 Donovan had what Stephenson needed most—interest in counterespionage, hostility to the Axis powers, sympathy for Britain, access to high places, and a willingness to undertake a "study" mission to the United Kingdom. "Prompted" by Stephenson, Donovan put together a travel plan in June 1940 that allowed him to play many roles while enjoying the status of an observer in wartime Britain. First, Frank Knox, in his capacity as owner of the *Chicago Daily News*, commissioned Donovan to represent the paper, at Knox's expense, on a project to obtain information on "the Fifth Column activities which had so helped the Germans in Norway, Holland, Belgium and France." To assist him in this task, Knox arranged for one of his paper's top correspondents, Edgar Mowrer, who had fled to Portugal from France just ahead of the panzers, to meet Donovan in London. As secretary of the navy, Knox also gave Donovan the assignment of determining whether closer intelligence collaboration could be established between the American O.N.I. and the British Admiralty. The president joined Knox in giving his blessing to Donovan's trip and broadened the colonel's mandate still further to include a general appraisal of Britain's ability to stand up against German air and invasion pressure to justify diverting a large measure of America's scarce defense material to the United Kingdom. Although a number of other individuals and agencies then jumped on the bandwagon and asked Donovan to study various specific aspects of the British war-making system, including production methods, supply problems, and the operation of her conscription law, his main attention was to be focused on counterintelligence and resistance to a fifth column.[50]

Important though Donovan's mission to Britain was in July 1940, some words of caution need to be added. Despite much subsequent exaggerated and loose comment, Donovan's trip was not analogous to a holy mission arranged by American internationalists to save Western civilization. And once Stephenson had made his initial suggestion, it owed little to British encouragement. The trip was primarily a hard-headed, ad hoc survey-and-coordination operation organized by Knox and approved by the president. The postwar assertions that Henry Stimson played a significant role in organizing the mission do not appear to be correct. Although Stimson's August diary contains entries praising Donovan's abilities and expressing interest in hearing his views upon his return from London, there is no indication that the secretary of war had a hand in arranging the trip. It is also not accurate to suggest that Donovan was Franklin Roosevelt's ace in the hole or that he had the only eyes and ears the president trusted. Donovan was not the first observer whom the White House had sent, and he would certainly not be the last.[51]

Still, he was a high-priority emissary, and once the necessary approvals had been secured, the mission went forward with unusual speed. On 10 July, Lord Lothian notified the Foreign Office that Donovan and Mowrer were coming to England to study German "Fifth Column methods" and that the colonel also had a secret mission. Presumably at the same time, Stephenson used his own channels to inform S.I.S. and Naval intelligence officials of Donovan's confidential intelligence liaison assignment. On the following day, the U.S. State Department cabled its officers in Portugal and England that Donovan would be flying to London via Lisbon to carry out a "survey of the British defense situation" for Secretary Knox. Although the cable declared that "the President has approved this trip," it nonetheless prompted two impassioned negative responses from Joe Kennedy. The ambassador claimed that although Donovan was "a man I know and like," he could not possibly obtain any information that was not already being secured by the embassy's attachés. Declaring that such missions as Donovan's were "the height of nonsense," he urged that it be canceled in the name of "good organization" and that Washington stop "sending Mowrers and Colonel Donovans over here." Under Secretary of State Sumner Welles immediately fired off a cable to London telling Kennedy that the mission was not an "individual matter" nor "an individual newspaper matter" but had been ordered by the secretary of the navy in his "official capacity." In the event that this was not enough to silence the ambassador, Welles also alerted the president in case a missile from the White House should be required. Though not satisfied and continuing privately to fuss and fume, Kennedy did not press further.[52]

Kennedy's opposition to the trip, which was known in the Foreign Office *before* Donovan arrived from America, further guaranteed the colonel a warm welcome, for the British tended to view the ambassador as injudicious and unfriendly. So, backed by the goodwill of Stephenson, Lothian, Roosevelt—and buoyed further in British eyes by Kennedy's opposition—Donovan was received with extreme cordiality and helpfulness in every corner from the moment of his arrival. On his first day in London (15 July), he met with Director of Naval Intelligence (D.N.I.), Adm. John Godfrey, while the public aspects of his mission were immediately taken in hand by Donovan's old friend Ronald Tree, who was serving as private secretary to Minister of Information Duff Cooper. While British officials helped Mowrer gather appropriately horrendous tales of German fifth column activities from various agencies, Donovan was free to talk with important British officials, analyze the situation, and take the measure of the United Kingdom at war. An unusual number of important doors were opened for him, and he was highly pleased by the spirit of friendly helpfulness with which he was received. He discussed military matters with high officials, including Gen. Alan Brooke, then commander in chief of Home Forces, and had a number of long discussions with naval intelligence officials.[53]

After three weeks of observation and a final set of conferences with the American military attachés in London, Donovan concluded that the R.A.F. and British resoluteness gave the United Kingdom a better than even chance of beating off a German attack. Despite the common portrayal of this in historical accounts as an idiosyncratic conclusion contrasting sharply with allegedly defeatist American attaché reports from London, Donovan seems to have been a trifle less optimistic about Britain's chances than was Gen. Raymond Lee and his attaché staff at Grosvenor Square. The chief value of Donovan's relatively optimistic conclusion, however, was that it reinforced the attaché reports and thus offset the effect of the doubters and pessimists who existed in Washington, in the American embassy in London, and in some quarters of British society as well. As we shall see, once back in Washington, Donovan worked unceasingly to advance Britain's cause in the eyes of the public and in the councils of the United States government. In this sense the trip was of great benefit to the United Kingdom, and British officials could feel well satisfied with it. The colonel had wanted to see the bright side and that was what his hosts had been most eager to show. He had not grasped how appallingly weak the British ground forces were (something on the order of 3 or 4 modern divisions against 150 German ones), and thus tended to be too optimistic about what could be accomplished once Germany was checked at the Channel. But he cannot be charged with falling completely for British public relations gimmicks, as some American observers were to do. To give one instance that took place a month after Donovan's journey, Gen. Delos Emmons, the air corps representative on the American military mission to the United Kingdom, was persuaded that Royal Air Forces Bomber Command was having remarkably good results in night bombing over Germany, due to its excellent bombsight. In fact, R.A.F. night bombing during this period was a total fiasco; losses in Bomber Command aircraft were extremely high, little damage of any kind was inflicted on the Germans, and most missions were unable to reach within 20 miles of their targets.[54]

Such exaggerated bagatelles as the imaginary success of Bomber Command were apparently not dangled before Donovan, or, if they were, did not impress him. In sizing up Britain's situation, he asked the right questions, and was provided with enough information to reach the right conclusion: the United Kingdom would win the air battle over Britain, but it would be a very close call.

The aspect of Donovan's mission concerned with gathering information on the German fifth column was also concluded in a manner satisfactory to all concerned. The British supplied Donovan and Mowrer with a generous stock of stories about Nazi villainy and deadly subversion. Since a large number of such tales was already available from American press sources and the B.S.C. in New York—and the existence of a centrally directed Nazi fifth column was in any case imaginary—on one level little actually had changed. But with both the British and Donovan firmly convinced that there actually was a Nazi fifth column and that awakening the American public to its dangers would increase American sympathy and support for the war effort, the acquisition of more on-the-spot material was deemed important.[55]

Donovan also performed the major intelligence job he had been sent to do. His talks with D.N.I. Admiral Godfrey and others went off successfully, and he was shown some secret information, but he did not gain entry to all Britain's intelligence secrets. He did not see vital information that was coming through from Polish and Czech intelligence channels, and he was not privy to the "Ultra secret"—the increasingly successful deciphering achievement attained by the staff of the Code and Cypher School at Bletchley Park in unraveling the mysteries of Germany's Enigma coding machines. Substantial but uneven Ultra progress had been made by July 1940, though the security risk of disclosure was so great that the project could not be bandied about before untested foreigners. There was also no reason or opportunity at this point to try to outline for Donovan a picture of Britain's plans for subversive warfare. The S.O.E. was only a few weeks old, and Dalton had not received his ministerial assignment for subversive warfare until Donovan was already in England. With nothing of consequence in hand, it was just too soon to flaunt British subversive warfare success—even to an observer who needed to be impressed. Dalton met Donovan on 2 August, just before the colonel returned to America, but the topics of conversation were the blockade and the European food crisis. The subject of subversive warfare and the existence of the S.O.E. did not arise, and it would be another eight months before Dalton would even confide to Donovan that he was the minister in charge of clandestine operations.[56]

Such matters as Ultra and S.O.E. had not been integral parts of Donovan's chief intelligence assignment, for he had been sent to discover whether naval intelligence cooperation was feasible. From his talks with Admiral Godfrey, he reached the conclusion that such cooperation was possible and that British defense and American security would benefit by providing Britain with copies of American consular reports from Vichy French ports. Such an example of specific, and limited, results of the Donovan mission have not been enough to satisfy some enthusiasts who have penned engrossing tales suggesting that Britain joyfully and open-handedly revealed all its intelligence and subversive warfare secrets to its visitor from across the sea. Aside from the fact that such accounts are simply wrong and that they grossly inflate the number of secrets Britain actually had at that time, they miss the main point, which was the effect of Donovan's visit on British officials. He had justified his initial warm welcome during his three weeks in the United Kingdom by showing himself to be extremely sympathetic to Britain and by demonstrating that he was a shrewd and diligent observer who could stick to the business at hand. His focus and apparent restraint impressed the British, who customarily had trouble getting the words "Yank" and "restraint" into the same sentence. In their future relations with Donovan, when they would have much more to tell, belief in his good judgment would stand the colonel in good stead.[57]

Having completed his various missions and stored up a fund of personal goodwill, Donovan returned home in early August. Once back in the United States, his most ambitious task was to spread the word that Britain would hold out and that sending essential materials to her would be a good security investment. He delivered this message to Secretary Knox and the president and also used various conferences and social occasions to spread the word. On 6 August, he discussed his observations with Secretary Stimson, emphasizing Britain's strengths as well as her crying need for rifles and destroyers. A week later, as the first stage of the German blitzkrieg rose to its full fury, he presented the same case to a select group of senators who had been invited to hear his message along with supporting speeches by Stimson and Under Secretary of War Robert Patterson. British observers in Washington reported to London that Donovan was "pressing everybody here vigorously to supply us with destroyers and other equipment" and rejoiced that they now had such a "a firm friend in the Republican camp." By 16 August President Roosevelt could tell Lord Lothian that he thought "the trick was done" on a destroyer-for-bases swap and that Knox and Donovan had "helped a lot" to put it through.

Donovan also believed that he had played an important role in the destroyer deal and, to put the icing on the cake, he spoke to the nation by radio on 17 August, urging aid for Britain and the establishment of a military draft in the United States.[58]

By all odds, despite the continuance of strong isolationist sentiment and the desire of some Washington observers to make the British pay dearly in political and economic concessions for every drop of assistance they received, Donovan had done yeoman service in helping to convince American opinion makers that generous assistance to Britain was in America's interest. He was equally successful in following through on his intelligence mission. The talks he had held with Admiral Godfrey opened the way for an exchange of Anglo-American naval intelligence, and despite the fact that the British were not enamored of General Strong, the U.S. Army's G-2 representative on the mid-August military mission to London, the talks with that mission led to a more general exchange of military intelligence. The arrangement was broadened again in early September when Roosevelt authorized American military and diplomatic authorities to make available to the British any "relevant" information and promised Stephenson "that he would be given every assistance in obtaining [the] information" that he desired. In late October 1940, Roosevelt also approved exchange of decoded Axis messages between British and American authorities.[59]

Donovan had helped set in motion the wheels leading to the development of initial intelligence cooperation between the two countries. That this development soon proved rather disappointing was not due to Donovan but to a British conclusion that the Americans had little useful information to give and that Washington's intelligence system was badly coordinated and leaky. London therefore took what it could get and stayed cautious about what it gave in return, especially regarding what Churchill would soon call those "golden eggs" that were being laid in increasingly greater numbers at Bletchley Park.

The impact of Donovan's effort to sell the American people on the dangers of the Nazi fifth column is more difficult to gauge, but it seems accurate to say that it was substantial. In the fall of 1940, the colonel joined with Edgar Mowrer to produce a series of syndicated articles on the fifth column, which were later published as a pamphlet with an introduction by Frank Knox. This collection of nightmare stories, which appeared under the title "Fifth Column Lessons for America," was cited after the war by a Dutch historian—who had himself earlier played a part in spreading fifth column tales—as a "typical and influential example" of the fifth column hysteria of late 1940. Even at a time when an able administrator like John J. McCloy could be selected assistant secretary of war, not primarily because of his overall ability but because Secretary Stimson thought he knew "more about subversive Germans in this country . . . than any other man," the pamphlet by Donovan and Mowrer still stands out as a horror. "Fifth Column Lessons for America" claimed that "no amount of genius" could have produced the stunning German victories of 1940 by conventional warfare alone. It was the fifth column, "organized by the Gestapo" and supported by an expenditure of "$200,000,000 annually" that made it all possible. Germany's subversive machinery had been honed to perfection, the pamphlet contended, and Hitler's determination to seize control of the whole world meant that America, "crippled by all sorts of civilized inhibitions," could expect no mercy. Although the authors granted that perhaps not every single person of German extraction in the United States was sympathetic to Hitler, there was a "German colony of several million strong," including "thousands" of domestic workers and "German waiters," who were happy to serve as "snoopers." Mowrer and Donovan found it "hard to believe" that many of the remaining German-Americans could not "be blackmailed into the most supine submission to the Gestapo." Unless America roused itself to action and dealt with this danger before being drawn into a war, the authors warned, disaster was inevitable. If the United States was engaged in an armed struggle with the Axis powers, they elaborated, "many" of those German-Americans in the huge Nazi fifth column would seize their opportunity and make every sacrifice "to destroy their own country, to sabotage its defenses, weaken its war effort, sink its ships, [and] kill its soldiers and sailors for the benefit of a foreign dictator and his alien political philosophy."[60]

With all due respect to the necessity of helping the American people rise out of their isolationist slumber, works such as "Fifth Column Lessons for America" were simply inflammatory exercises in hysteria and group hatred. In tracing William Donovan's rise to the position of roving ambassador and creator of the American subversive warfare system, it is necessary to remember that much of his domestic propaganda effort, culminating in the appearance of this pamphlet, used means that were themselves highly dangerous. In psychological warfare, whether employed at home in 1940 or abroad thereafter, William Donovan showed himself willing to take high risks and to use foul means as well as fair.

THE SHADOW WARRIORS

Donovan's Mission: December 1940–March 1941

November 1940–February 1941: The British Advance in North Africa
March 1941: The Lend-Lease Act

The appearance of "Fifth Column Lessons for America" suggests that by the fall of 1940, Donovan was hooked on the great game of secret missions, high policy, and international intrigue. The proposals then being bandied about Washington that the colonel might take a position in the army's training program or perhaps command one of the newly formed divisions failed to materialize because Donovan's imagination was flying elsewhere. In the late fall, he offered to help Britain secure bases in Ireland after an angry exchange between Eamon De Valera and Churchill had led to an impasse. When the British showed themselves less than enthusiastic about this potentially explosive suggestion—Lord Lothian, then in London, cabled the British embassy in Washington "please take no action pending my return . . . matter cannot suitably be dealt with by telegram"—Donovan turned his attention to the eastern Mediterranean. After his July–August trip, he had "enlarged" on the importance of this area in a discussion with the president and had subsequently "expounded" on the same subject to a group of admirals. The British had been engaged against the Italians in northern and eastern Africa since August 1940, and the situation became more serious when Mussolini invaded Greece in late October. In conjunction with Knox and Stephenson, Donovan therefore worked out a plan for a new survey trip that would take him to Britain and onward to the western and eastern Mediterranean in late 1940 and early 1941. This time the least secret task of the journey was to measure Britain's position at home and in the Mediterranean theater to see how the United States might be of practical assistance. The most secret portion of the mission was to acquaint himself with the subversive and counterintelligence organizations that the British had been developing since the summer.[61]

After securing presidential approval, as well as the "enthusiastic concurrence"of the British ambassador to the United States, Donovan completed his detailed plans. He intended to slip out of New York accompanied by Stephenson. First they were to fly to Bermuda so the colonel could examine the British security organization there, then go on to Lisbon and London. Following a few weeks of discussions and briefings in Britain, the plan was to travel to Vichy France, or at least to French North Africa, and then join with British officials for a survey of the Balkans and the Middle East. On the return journey, Donovan would come back through the Mediterranean, where he would discard his official robes and act as a representative of the *Chicago Daily News*.[62]

When told of this plan, Stimson thought it much too complicated and disapproved of mixing official and journalistic roles. Donovan and Stephenson, however, ignored him. Before they left New York, the press was already on Donovan's trail and managed to convert the journey into one of the best-published secret missions on record. The only really covert portion of the trip occurred during the stopover in Bermuda when Donovan was initiated into the wonders of an extensive British subversive control operation in which thousands of pieces of international mail were surreptitiously opened and examined. On the basis of these intercepts, British authorities were able to track much of the German commercial and covert activity in Latin America. Donovan also was shown material suggesting that an alleged Nazi fifth column was prepared to seize control of the southern half of the hemisphere. From Bermuda, Donovan and Stephenson went on to Lisbon, where they were met by an R.A.F. aircraft and taken directly to the United Kingdom.

In London, Donovan was warmly received as a staunch friend of the beleaguered British people, a man who had stood tall in their hour of greatest need. After careful self-examination, Foreign Office officials might confess that none of them really knew anything about Colonel Donovan, but they too joined in the festival of welcome. The prime minister was anxious to meet and talk with him, and a long private lunch was held on 18 December. In the following days Donovan discussed his views and plans with a number of British military and civilian officers, including friends and acquaintances from earlier visits. Although stressing the bond that united Britain and the United States—portraying the United Kingdom as the military shield of the democracies and America as their workshop and factory—he urged his hosts to be respectful of the vagaries of American public opinion and not to press President Roosevelt too hard even in the wake of his third-term election victory. Donovan even suggested to the head of the American section of the Foreign Office that, if Britain wanted to produce closer relations, it would some day have to settle the war debts from World War I—a notion that must have seemed to the British even more out of touch with the realities of 1940 than it does to us today.[63]

The mood and tone of British life had changed markedly between July and December 1940. Hitler's Luftwaffe had been checked, and although British authorities were not willing to tell this to Donovan, the Naval Intelligence Division (N.I.D.) had concluded, presumably on the basis of Ultra intercepts and aerial reconnaissance showing the withdrawal of German air and invasion support forces, that the threat of Operation Sealion had passed. For the time being, at least, the home islands were safe, but Britain was still standing alone, unevenly matched against Hitler's colossus, with no prospect of striking directly at Germany. As early as 4 September the Chiefs of Staff formally concluded that Britain would never be able to match German ground power. Careful studies had shown that even if British mobilization were stretched to the limit, she could not mount more than 90 modern divisions; the Germans by then had close to 150. Mercifully, the British did not realize that German economic and manpower resources, had not been seriously extended yet. Unable to "raise and land on the Continent an army comparable in size with that of Germany," the Chiefs of Staff decided to forgo the effort and to utilize instead a policy of "wearing down" the Axis. Blockade, air attack, and both psychological and fifth column warfare were to be employed until "numerically inferior forces" could "be used with a good chance of success" as "a striking force" to topple the Nazi regime.[64]

Although resting on an honest recognition of Britain's comparative weakness, this plan, based as it was on a mixture of myth, hope, and longshots, was not very cheering. Standing up to Goliath was one thing, but going into his dark cave armed with nothing but a slingshot, and what one hoped was a magic wand, was something else again. British leaders were therefore more tense and less tolerant of American delay and caution than they had been only six months earlier. They wanted help, and they wanted Americans to show belief in them by joining in the game of subversive and innovative warfare that Britain believed it had to play. Despite his occasional lapses on such issues as the repayment of war debts, William Donovan was as close to the perfect American as the British could hope to find. He not only had confidence in them, he had also been so primed by Stephenson and so entranced by his own anti–fifth column propaganda efforts, that he was prepared to believe in the effectiveness of their subversive warfare machine.

In December 1940 only the most benevolently inclined ally could be much impressed by Britain's shadow warfare system. Dalton had just begun to bring some order to the chaos; S.O.E. had been established and divided into a propaganda section, Special Operations 1 (S.O. 1), and a sabotage and resistance support section, Special Operations 2 (S.O. 2). The old sabotage organizations, such as Section D, had been absorbed or disbanded, and Dalton had appointed a new group of section chiefs and supervisors. S.O.E. representatives were dispatched in November to neutral cities such as Bern, and a limited S.O.E. communications network, dependent on S.I.S. and Foreign Office channels, was in operation by

December. Dalton had developed reasonably close relations with governments in exile and the Free French, and made use of their connections and intelligence organizations to make contact with possible resistance leaders in the occupied territories. The minister was "particularly attracted by the Poles" and, as Lord Gladwyn remarked, like most Englishmen Dalton had "a bad conscience as regards the Czechs" because of the Munich "sellout" in 1938. S.O.E. thus placed high hopes on potential Polish and Czech resistance, encouraged Polish efforts to recruit supporters everywhere (including the United States), and gave the exiled governments of these two countries top priority in subversive warfare planning. When the time came to test the possibility of infiltration by parachute in February 1941, after a series of disappointing attempts to carry out clandestine landings across the Channel by sea, the point selected for the experiment was Poland. S.O.E. thereby began its operational life with a commitment in a distant and barely accessible country, where resistance would produce few immediate results and where the effort to support such operations would place a heavy burden on the new organization.[65]

S.O.E. had a generous supply of difficulties without even considering its eastern European troubles. The Chiefs of Staff had approved the S.O.E. organizational plan in late August, and at the same time the Foreign Office also had formally accepted the new organization's existence. But S.O.E. was a late arrival and was viewed with suspicion by such old established organizations as S.I.S. and the Foreign Office as well as by other wartime agencies, including the Ministry of Information. Dalton and his staff spent much of their time trying to find the border of their new domain. Despite his early enthusiasm, Churchill was not of great assistance to them; he did not intervene frequently in his government's jurisdictional wars nor personally concern himself much with what S.O.E. was supposed to do. As Dalton noted in his diary after a talk with Churchill on 3 December 1940, "he is quite vague as to what we do and where." A measure of the vagueness within the top authorities' conception of S.O.E. is indicated by a Chiefs of Staff directive of 21 August that forbade the "use of officers or men wearing His Majesty's uniform" in any S.O.E. subversive activity. What a far cry this was from the hundreds of British Liaison Officers (B.L.O.s) who would later be employed with various resistance units and who would capture the public's imagination as the embodiment of what Allied subversive warfare was supposed to be![66]

The confusion outside S.O.E. increased the blur that prevailed within the young organization. Much of S.O.E.'s early history was dominated by Byzantine intrigue between various sections and section chiefs. Its dependence on men eager to act as adventurers opened the door to excess and folly, and Dalton's own desire for action led him to put aside some of his enthusiasm for trade unionists and leftist revolutionaries. By December 1940, the minister wrote in his diary that "there is no place, to-day, for stupid doctrinaire prejudices against 'Fascism' as such . . . we must offer, and quickly, a fair price to decent Italians who will get rid of M. [Mussolini] and his gang." When ideological opportunism failed to produce results against the German and Italian enemy, the buccaneer spirit in S.O.E. leaned toward ever more distant and farfetched projects. By early 1941, S.O.E. planners were trying to drum up support for an operation in the central Russian area of Kazan although Britain was not at war with the Soviet Union, and in March, though Britain was not yet at war with Japan either, S.O.E. was developing a scheme for a guerrilla warfare organization in China that would nominally be led by refugee Danish and Norwegian officers but was actually organized, supported, and directed by the British. An important feature of the latter plan was the use of guerrillas to spread rumors that would be circulated in China to undermine Japanese morale. One highly valued rumor, created by an erudite Asian scholar, contended that since 1941 was the year of the serpent, a negative sign "closely connected" with the Japanese sun goddess, all Japanese should be reminded that anything they attempted in the year 1941 "must be fatal for Japan." An organization that hoped to protect Britain's exposed colonial possessions from the advance of the third Axis power by using rumors so complicated that they required an accompanying explanatory glossary was capable of grasping at any mirage. When Donovan arrived in Britain in December 1940 S.O.E. officials courted him not only because they wanted to develop American proponents of subversive warfare but also because they, along with William Stephenson, actually thought he might be able to secure for their use the American diplomatic pouch in the Balkans, an area where S.O.E. had no effective system of communication. At a time when President Roosevelt was cloaking his every pro-British move in subterfuge to hold back the attacks of isolationists, such notions seem astonishing in their unreality and desperation.[67]

S.O.E.'s older secret sister, S.I.S., was not doing noticeably better with its secret agents than S.O.E. was with its guerrilla warfare and propaganda schemes. But the code and cipher operations of S.I.S. were yielding very valuable results by the end of 1940. The flow of Ultra decrypts had reached large proportions, especially regarding movements in the Mediterranean and the Balkans. Bletchley had been reading the French naval codes since July and as German armed might concentrated in southeastern Europe, the Enigma machines of the Luftwaffe, the Reich railroad administration, and various ground auxiliary forces spelled out the details of the new deployment. Though Bletchley was still not deciphering the main German naval or army codes very well—even if it had been, German ground forces depended chiefly on ground telecommunication rather than wireless—Ultra information showed that Britain was in for serious trouble in the eastern Mediterranean. Whatever the need to hold to the principle that the United Kingdom could not match German ground power, the threat to Britain's Mediterranean and Middle Eastern position could not be ignored. In addition, the old World War I memories of a Balkan front died hard, especially for Churchill, who pined for an opportunity to recoup the failure at Gallipoli.[68]

The Ultra decrypts unfortunately did not make clear to the British in December 1940 why Germany was concentrating massive force in the upper Balkans. The German preparations already seemed too large merely to rescue the Italian army from its farcical, and aborted, invasion of Greece. London was seized by the horrifying possibility that the Germans intended to slice right across the Balkans and on through Turkey, destroying the whole British Middle Eastern position and the lifeline to India at a single stroke. Actually, Hitler contemplated only a limited quick thrust into Greece, made possible by transit rights through Bulgaria, so he could stabilize the region and squelch British dreams of a Balkan front. The whole Balkan campaign was a nuisance and irritant to him, brought on by the folly of the Italians and the offensive fantasies of the British. Hitler's eye, and the concentration of his forces, was directed toward Operation Barbarossa, the invasion of Russia planned for May. The thrust into Greece would be a limited preparatory action, and even though the Germans would shore up the Italians in North Africa to prevent a disaster there as well, no Nazi invasion of the Middle East was being considered for 1941.

But the British would not realize the true focus of the German plans until the spring, when additional Ultra decrypts filled out the picture. In December 1940, Churchill was eyeing the Balkan and Middle Eastern situation with extreme concern. Britain's Mediterranean and imperial position were possibly at stake, and he was grasping for any straw. The only one seemingly available was the old idea that a Balkan front resting on an alliance of Bulgaria, Yugoslavia, and Turkey, firmly connected to Greece and Britain, could build a wall against a German advance and give Britain the basis for a return to the continent. The whole notion was, however, riddled with absurdities. The Balkan area did not get its reputation for conflict and intrigue for nothing; every country in the region was threatened by pressing internal ethnic and religious conflict and each government eyed its neighbors with intense suspicion. Bulgaria was as hostile to

Greece and Yugoslavia as ever, and all the Balkan states were nervous about the bumbling Italians, highly suspicious of the intentions of the Soviet Union, and quite rightly frightened into impotence by the reality of German power. A Balkan league tied to Britain was a political impossibility because everyone in the Balkans knew Germany was too strong and Britain too weak. But Churchill pressed ahead anyway, out of fear of a continued German advance on the Middle East, determined to use whatever influence and leverage Britain had in the region to move the Balkan states into a position of opposition to Germany. No longer would a position of cautious aloofness, such as that advocated by the regent of Yugoslavia, Prince Paul, satisfy London. The British government demanded not neutrality but alliance and dangled hints of the arrival of shipments of arms and invasion forces to encourage the Yugoslavs and Turks. Such efforts were not merely pointless. As some British official and semiofficial historians have recently suggested, to have "egged on" these small countries by promises of assistance that could not be fulfilled while encouraging them to oppose Nazi Germany with her "military record" and her "vastly superior armaments" was simply irresponsible. In light of the horror that an extended occupation and civil and guerrilla war would bring to the region in the following four years, London's pressure on the Balkan governments to become overt enemies of Nazi Germany in the spring of 1941 is one of the heavier ethical burdens that has weighed on Britain's official postwar conscience.[69]

Such considerations did not deter Churchill in late 1940 and early 1941, however. The Foreign Office was told in December 1940 to start putting the squeeze on the Balkan leaders, and the carrot of promised arms shipments together with the stick of British political and economic pressure were soon applied. Just as this was occurring, William Donovan arrived on the London scene. The Foreign Office initially was rather inclined to be circumspect with Donovan because of Secretary of State Hull's reported jealousy of him, but Churchill took the colonel to his ample bosom like a long lost friend. The prime minister saw in the visiting American a loyal champion of Britain and the perfect instrument through which to increase the pressure on the Balkan governments. Without fully opening his bag of Ultra tricks, Churchill instructed Donovan on the facts and issues involved in the Mediterranean situation as the British saw them and urged him to encourage the influential personalities with whom he came in contact in the eastern Mediterranean to throw off neutrality and join a Balkan and Middle Eastern group backed by Britain. Donovan raised no objections to the British estimate of the situation and became a willing and enthusiastic instrument through which London could increase its Balkan clout. The only cloud that arose to delay Donovan's Mediterranean mission was Vichy French suspicion of the colonel and a reluctance to allow him to travel through French territories. On 9 December, Pierre Laval sharply questioned the American chargé, Robert Murphy, on what Donovan was up to, and stories of Vichy doubts and German opposition were bandied about London for a number of weeks. The ax finally fell in early January when the Vichy government refused Donovan's request for a travel permit in French West and North Africa and in Vichy France itself. Other American observers, including Murphy himself and an M.I.D. agent, had to be employed to establish an American "survey" presence in North Africa, and Donovan was thereby free to pursue his main task for the American and British governments further east.[70]

The moral issues that hover over Donovan's Mediterranean journey are so serious, and the number of inflated tales purporting to tell what he did there are so numerous, that care must be used in surveying his activities from early January, when he reached Cairo, until his return to England in the first week of March. But there is no need to wander along the countless paths of interpretation and speculation that have appeared in print. We now have the reports that Donovan sent to Secretary Knox from Cairo and London, as well as the records of his conversations with Balkan leaders. Since United States Foreign Service officers were present during all of these conversations, except for one with Prince Paul (and we have Donovan's own notes of that talk), the documentation is unusually comprehensive. It is now a relatively simple matter to trace what Donovan did—and did not do—during his two months in the Mediterranean area. To begin, we should briefly chart the route of his travels. After spending the third week of January in Greece, he followed British advice and interrupted his stay there for a quick swing northward. He spent one day in Bulgaria, two in Yugoslavia, and then returned for an additional week in Greece, when he also surveyed the Albanian battlefront. After leaving Athens a second time, he spent the first week of February in Turkey and then went to Cairo. In the second week of February he made a swing through the Arab Middle East, including Iraq, but the French authorities would not let him enter Syria. Donovan then spent another short period in Cairo and under prompting from the British representatives in the Iberian peninsula and ultimately from Churchill as well, he made a rapid swing through Spain and Portugal at the end of February.[71]

The course of Donovan's travels immediately shows that previous accounts have misplaced the trip's emphasis. The focus of the mission was not primarily on the central Balkans. It was a Cairo–Greek–Middle East survey, with one short northern sortie. Although throughout his travels

Donovan contacted American diplomatic officials and was advised by them, the tour was arranged by the British and focused on British operations centers. Donovan was accompanied by a British staff officer, Lt. Col. Vivian Dykes, and though cursory attempts were made to render the British connection less blatant—Dykes wore civilian clothes and usually did not stay in the same hotel as the American—Donovan worked hard to display, rather than to hide, his ties to the British. Everywhere he went, his message was the same: the United States was solidly behind Great Britain. Furthermore, despite her enormous resources and her genuine concern for all people, Donovan asserted that America would withhold her favors not only from those who flirted with Nazis or Fascists, but also from those who failed to resist Axis pressure. Those countries that did not line up with Britain stood to lose American sympathy and all prospect of American assistance. Sometimes this message was presented subtly with only the hint of threat or promise; on other occasions it was put more boldly. Donovan promised the valiant Anglophile Greeks that he would do all he could to secure for them farm equipment and combat aircraft in America. In Belgrade and Ankara, he talked optimistically of the prospects of a Balkan front. In Baghdad, he told Iraqi leaders that Americans "were determined on one policy," namely, "aid to Britain in order to bring about the defeat of Germany." When the mufti nodded obliquely toward the Arab-Jewish question of Palestine, Donovan declared that such "side issues" did not interest the United States. "America would expect others to follow our policy," the colonel stressed to the Iraqis, and those who did not do so "could expect no help or sympathy from us either during the war or at the peace conference afterwards."[72]

British officials, quite naturally, were delighted with the colonel's efforts and showed their appreciation in many ways. Donovan was put up handsomely, encouraged, honored, and treated like a trusted friend. While in Athens he stayed at the British rather than the American legation, even when General Archibald P. Wavell (the British commander in chief in the Middle East) was there. Dispatches praising his efforts were filed by many British officials, including the new foreign secretary, Anthony Eden (Lord Lothian's death in December 1940 sent Lord Halifax to the United States as ambassador, and Eden to the Foreign Office). In addition, both to broaden Donovan's understanding and to give his reports to America as much pro-British coloration as possible, he was provided with a large number of interviews and briefing papers. Donovan's dispatches to Washington show the full mark of this information and reflect his admiration "for the superb job which the British have done in this area." His mission had convinced him that Germany's sole aim, the driving force that animated every action, was to defeat Great Britain. Every feint, every maneuver, whether in western Europe or the Balkans, was, in the colonel's opinion, directed solely to effect the overthrow of the United Kingdom. It therefore followed that the United States must support and assist the British at every threatened point.

Along with more military aid, Donovan felt that gestures of encouragement should be given to British sympathizers, which meant supplies to the Greeks and friendly praise for Anglophile Yugoslavs. Following the lead of Churchill and the British ambassador to Spain, Sir Samuel Hoare, the colonel believed that selective trade and even some economic assistance should be granted to encourage Franco to resist German pressure. In later years Donovan's O.S.S. would cause trouble for American officials in Spain by its anti-Franco activities (just as Sir Samuel was worrying about such actions by S.O.E. in 1941), but the appeasement of fascists did not trouble Donovan at all at the time of his Mediterranean journey. In February 1941, he saw the issue purely in terms of assisting Britain, and despite much talk of democracy, he was prepared to deal with nearly anyone who might improve the position of the United Kingdom.[73]

Given the dangerous corner in which Britain found herself, Donovan's desire to extend all possible aid to her has been understandable to the vast majority of observers, then and since. As every occupied area would discover to its sorrow, Nazi control would only offer assorted scenes in a common drama of suffering. The Nazis were dreadful, extremely powerful, at war with Britain, and poised to make a major move.

But it must be underscored that the Germans were not going to take either of the steps that Donovan, under British prompting, expected. They were not going to launch an attack on the British Isles, and they were not going into the Middle East. A limited thrust into Greece was imminent, and a massive thrust against Russia would soon follow. By February 1941, the British were convinced that Greece would be attacked but they were still uncertain that Russia would be Hitler's next target. Donovan, for his part, worried only about the threat to Britain and in his reports to Washington never raised the possibility of a German attack on Russia. Obviously, the British were not letting him in on all their secret thoughts, and he was so much under the influence of what they did tell him that he continued to believe England was the focus of all Germany's efforts. Again, given the circumstances prevailing in spring 1941, such a mistaken conclusion is certainly understandable. More disconcerting, however, is the fact that two years later Donovan was still circulating to intelligence associates the reports that he had made on this trip to illustrate his views on Mediterranean strategy. This suggests that the colonel never realized that he had missed the crucial point that Germany was then preparing to attack Russia.

In regard to other, less far-reaching blemishes on his travels, Donovan was quicker to recognize his errors than many subsequent writers have been. In Yugoslavia, for example, he discovered that using Knox's newspaper as a cover could cause him trouble, as Henry Stimson had earlier predicted. Prince Paul of Yugoslavia was so afraid that what he told Donovan might end up in the American press that the colonel repeatedly had to reassure the Regent on this point before he could get him to say anything at all. Donovan learned this lesson and never again used journalism as a cloak for his intelligence activities. Nor would he repeat the kind of sloppy error that he made soon after in Sofia. At an official reception there he momentarily slipped and left his wallet in the pocket of an overcoat which was hung in the waiting room. When the coat was recovered, the wallet was missing. An investigation followed, publicity and sarcastic comment followed that, and the incident left a small cloud over the rest of his Balkan travels. Again Donovan drew the obvious conclusion, did not repeat this kind of silly blunder, and in accordance with his forthright nature, later told the story on himself to emphasize to young intelligence operatives that one careless error could have serious consequences.[74]

Not satisfied with his frankness, however, some of Donovan's more zealous champions have claimed that the wallet incident was not really a blunder but a ruse through which false documents were planted on German intelligence. Others have asserted that Donovan was not the victim of an intelligence sting at all because the wallet was taken by a common thief. Now we know that both of these claims are false. On 15 February 1941 the wallet was recovered by the American Embassy in Sofia and at that time it still contained his passport, $150 in cash, a $15,000 National City Bank draft, and Donovan's letter of introduction from Frank Knox. But a list of questions—apparently on naval deployment matters, which an American admiral had asked Donovan to try to get answered during his trip, was missing. Donovan was not the victim of an ordinary robbery and he had not duped the Abwehr; he was stung by some country's intelligence service, most likely that of Bulgaria.[75]

Such incidents were, however, of only passing importance, because Donovan accomplished what he had set out to do. He surveyed the Mediterranean area, made an estimate of the situation, and used his journey to assist the British in every way possible. In the process, he charmed and impressed nearly everyone he met, from the American ambassador in Greece, who found him "friendly, well-bred and kind," to Sir Samuel Hoare who thought him "first class in every way." Donovan played no

part in preparing the coup which toppled the Yugoslav government shortly after his visit. Among his various meetings in Belgrade, he did have a
discussion with Gen. Dusan Simović, who later emerged as head of the
government which followed the coup, but all that happened during the
Donovan–Simović talk was a series of assurances by the Yugoslav general—stronger than those made by any other official in Belgrade—that Yugoslavia would fight if Hitler made *any* offensive move against Greece.
Such words were music to Donovan's ears, and he appears to have passed
on Simović's remarks to the British. Recent research has made it abun-
dantly clear that Donovan himself took no active part in preparing the
coup. The evidence is clear that Prince Paul brought his own downfall
when he gambled in March and tried to save his country by agreeing to
join the Tripartite pact. Though he made no military commitments and
still refused passage to German troops, various Yugoslav factions, aided
initially by S.O.E. and later by the British air force attachés in Belgrade,
overthrew the government on 26 March and put Simović in power. The
Simović government then tried to snuggle close with the British while
making various reassuring noises to the Germans. Hitler was infuriated by
the coup and immediately set in motion preparations to smash Yugoslavia
as well as Greece. The German invasion and rapid Allied defeat followed
in late April. The consequences were severe: the British were driven from
their continental toehold and the Balkans began a four-year period of
Nazi hell.[76]

Donovan deserves only limited credit or blame for what happened in
the Balkans. None of the specific acts that produced the disaster were
caused by him. As we have said, he did not create or even contribute to
the Yugoslav coup, and he did not play a direct part in Britain's decision
in early March to sharply increase her forces in Greece. It must be acknowledged that when Churchill urged his cabinet colleagues to send the
British army into Greece, he noted that since Donovan had tried to sell
the Americans on a Balkan front, Britain could not forsake Greece without it having a "bad effect in the United States." But this was a thin
causal thread and without it, the prime minister, who was determined to
act, would surely have found another supplemental supporting argument.
The real significance of Donovan's role in Balkan developments was his
work as a reinforcer of British policy. To the degree that the Balkan policy made the situation worse, some measure of responsibility falls to him.
Without British pressure, "peaceful" German occupation or a shaky satellite status would have fallen to every Balkan country. As it was, the British came first, which led to the panzers and the Luftwaffe. The British,
having quickly lost the battle, departed, and the Balkan people were left

to face the victorious Germans in the highly unpleasant role of defeated enemies. To the British and to Donovan, it appeared that they had simply gambled and lost; in retrospect it seems to have been more like irresponsible folly. Britain never had the strength to stop Hitler in the Balkans, and it is therefore difficult to ignore the point that Prince Paul made to America's ambassador to Yugoslavia, Arthur Lane, in late March 1941. "You big nations are hard," Paul said, "you talk of our honor, but you are far away."[77]

Such considerations apparently did not occur to William Donovan, however, who returned to London in early March 1941, satisfied with his survey and more supportive of Britain and her prospects than ever. His reception in London was in some respects even more cordial than it had been in July and December 1940. The colonel had established close American ties with British operations and procedures, and in a sense he was a foreign associate rather than a foreign observer. He had another meeting with Churchill, and, in what must be a nearly unprecedented opportunity for a foreigner, was allowed to address the operations and intelligence directors of the three service ministries on the subject of his Middle Eastern mission. Amid the various expressions of praise and gratitude extended to him by British officials, there was a handsome tribute from the prime minister, who personally thanked President Roosevelt for the "magnificent work done by Donovan" in the Middle East.[78]

Not everything went ahead with perfect smoothness in London, however. Some British officials were worried that extensive praise and encouragement of the colonel might ruffle feathers in jealous corners of the State Department, or even in the White House, thereby causing trouble for Britain. Others were concerned about vetting the colonel following his travels and briefings, a concern that became more pressing after Donovan surveyed a number of S.O.E. stations in the United Kingdom. Furthermore, the meeting that Donovan had with Hugh Dalton following his S.O.E. inspection tour did not go well. In the course of their discussion on 11 March, the colonel was told by Dalton that as minister of economic warfare he was the man in charge of S.O.E. In light of Donovan's close relations with Stephenson and his great interest in shadow warfare, this revelation should have turned the trick and brought the two men closer together. But it was not enough, because recommendations made by Donovan so raised Dalton's ire that he lost whatever faith he had in the colonel's judgment. The matter at issue was simple enough. While considering the stationing of American observers in Vichy North Africa to guarantee that nothing of military value imported into the region was allowed to trickle on to Germany, Donovan suggested to Dalton that some of the old conservative Republican diplomats would be good for the job. Dalton was horrified that Donovan would even consider that "Hooverites" would be suitable for such work. After the meeting, Dalton raged on in his diary about this "bloody hopeless" suggestion and refused to allow his assistants to use Donovan as a channel for communications with the White House on the subject of posting American observers in North Africa. A trivial incident on its face, surely, but since Donovan would soon be attempting to organize an American shadow warfare system in close cooperation with the British, and Dalton would remain as minister of economic warfare and S.O.E. chief for another year, it was not a good omen for the future.[79]

On balance, however, when Donovan returned to the United States in mid-March, all signs pointed to the conclusion that he had succeeded in everything he had attempted and had gained a substantial bonus in enhanced personal and political prestige. He had carried out special missions not only for the secretary of the navy and the president but for the British prime minister as well. Throughout Europe, he had been received as a man of great influence who hobnobbed with the mighty, and this picture was in large measure true. Before journeying to Ireland on the eve of his departure for Washington, for example, Donovan was told by Churchill that if he could move De Valera to open up Irish ports to the British, the Irish unity issue might be solvable. Contending that he favored a united Ireland but that the difficulties were enormous, Churchill confided to Donovan (according to a dispatch by the latter) that if the British secured use of the Irish ports in the battle of the Atlantic, Churchill would attempt to solve the matter of establishing a united Ireland by "using all his influence to do so." That Donovan failed to get De Valera to open the doors to the British fleet is not surprising in light of political conditions in Ireland then and since. But that Churchill would have said such things to the colonel is a measure of the amazing confidence with which he then regarded this man who was, after all, not only a foreigner, but a prominent Irish-American.[80]

In the United States, the returning William Donovan possessed even greater assets than that of having become a friend and confidant of top British leaders. He had surveyed critical areas in Europe, the Near East, and Africa; had seen the war at first hand; and had associated himself with Allied efforts to resist the Axis. At the point of his return to America, the ax had not yet fallen on Britain's Mediterranean policy and the British army was going into Greece, as Donovan had told Washington it would. The Germans were also massing forces in North Africa, and Donovan had likewise reported this in his dispatches. Rommel had not yet struck, and Operations 125 and Marita had not yet crushed Yugoslavia and Greece, driving the British from the Balkans.

In March 1941, Donovan was a partner with the British in a policy that still seemed to be promising, and he had seen more of the war than any other prominent figure in American public life. With his ability, charm, and connections thus enhanced by special knowledge and experience, it was inevitable that William J. Donovan would soon leave a significant mark on the defense and foreign policies of the United States.

CHAPTER 2

The Coordinator of
Information [C.O.I.] in 1941

> Although we are facing imminent peril, we are lacking an effective service for analyzing, comprehending, and appraising such information as we might obtain (or in some cases have obtained), relative to the intention of political enemies. . . . Even if we participate to no greater extent than we do now, it is essential that we set up a central enemy intelligence organization. . . .
>
> WILLIAM DONOVAN TO
> FRANKLIN D. ROOSEVELT
> *10 June 1941*

The Creation of C.O.I.: June–July 1941

UPON HIS ARRIVAL in the United States, Donovan first reported to Secretary of the Navy Knox and the president. As he had done following his first trip to Britain, he also gave a nationwide anti-isolationist radio address and spoke to various groups of government officials, including the officers of the War Department. He met with Henry Stimson on 16 March, and the two men "stood over the map for a long time talking in the way in which two old friends who are both interested in military affairs can do it." Stimson did not find that Donovan had anything "startlingly new" to say about the situation, but he felt that the colonel's report was "rather encouraging." Both Donovan and the secretary of war agreed that the time had come to take another step in aid to Britain by providing convoy protection for British shipping in the North Atlantic.[1]

The mood in the country and in Congress had tipped more strongly in favor of assisting Britain during the three months that Donovan had been out of the country. The Lend-Lease bill already had passed through Congress and been signed by the president when Donovan returned on 11 March. The struggle over Lend-Lease had sharpened the conflict between the isolationists (working chiefly through the America First Committee) on the one hand and those who favored more energetic opposition to the Axis and increased aid to Britain (such as the Century Group and the William Allen White Committee) on the other. In April 1941, a new broad-based pro-intervention group called the Fight for Freedom Committee was formed, and it drew heavily on the so-called eastern establishment for its support. Prominent internationalists and Anglophiles such as Dean Acheson, Joseph Alsop, John Winant, Henry Commager, Grenville Clark, as well as a large contingent of those who would later have important roles in William Donovan's intelligence enterprises were early members. Along with Donovan himself, Fight for Freedom members David Bruce, Allen Dulles, Whitney Shepardson, Corey Ford, Francis Miller, William Eddy, Conyers Read, and James P. Baxter would have parts in the Donovan intelligence story. Many voices were now speaking out, stressing the Axis threat and calling on the United States to enter the war and protect its security by saving Britain. Even such prudent figures as Allen Dulles had come to the point of declaring in mid-May that it was in America's best interest to act decisively and "rid the world of bandits." A new, more serious and determined mood prevailed—evidenced by moves ranging from increased arms production to more formidable security checks on new government employees or people being considered for sensitive posts.[2]

William Donovan fitted the new mood well. His foreign experience, knowledge, and resolve to support Britain and counter the Axis both in traditional battle and by means of shadow warfare made him something of a prophet whose time had come. He warned all and sundry, including F.D.R.'s confidant Harry Hopkins, of the dangers of Axis expansion into new areas, such as northwest Africa and Spain. Armed with British materials that he had acquired in London as well as from Stephenson, he painted a picture of mortal danger emanating from the German fifth column. At Donovan's request, an official of the Foreign Office, W. H. B. Mack, had prepared a memorandum on the threat of German subversive penetration of North Africa for the colonel to use as argumentative ammunition in America.

Mack's memorandum embodied the mood that prevailed in the Donovan circle in the spring of 1941. Granting that the German Armistice Commission in North Africa was in itself small and insignificant, Mack (who would later be political and psychological warfare adviser during Operation Torch) warned that the democracies should not be fooled by appearances. "Knowing German methods," he wrote, it was certain "that their numbers will multiply and that, termite-like, they will soon have spread over the whole of French North Africa." What's more, he added, once the Germans subvert North Africa, control of Spain and Portugal "will soon follow." True to their "usual form," the termites would gnaw their way south via Morocco and Dakar until west Africa—Britain's communications line with America—and the Cape of Good Hope route would all be "in deadly peril." The German fifth column myth was obviously still flourishing both in Britain and America in the spring of 1941.[3]

Donovan soon learned that while the American belief in the reality of a German fifth column peril had not diminished, the means by which the United States government was attempting to deal with this phantom danger were undergoing significant changes. In February, two F.B.I. officers had gone to England for counterintelligence training at S.I.S. London Office, and at that time American authorities were informed for the first time that Bletchley was producing a large flow of Ultra intelligence, including decoding of Abwehr messages. Throughout the same period, Anglo-American discussions continued on the establishment of a regular exchange of military missions between the two countries. When an understanding on such an exchange was finally reached at the end of March, it was also agreed that a full intelligence component would be included in each mission to arrange "full and prompt" provision of "pertinent information concerning war operations" between the two countries. By April 1941, British army and navy intelligence officers were on the job in Washington.[4]

The implementation of these arrangements on the American side was accompanied by sharp scuffles. In February, a jurisdictional struggle between the F.B.I. and the army's G-2 threatened to produce a cabinet-level clash among the War, Navy, and Justice departments over anti–fifth column measures and wartime plant security. Two months later, following the Balkan debacle, many G-2 officers showed themselves less than enthusiastic about close relations with Britain, since they were convinced that Germany was too strong for the United Kingdom. Stimson was angered by their gloomy reports and on 15 April ordered Gen. George Marshall to warn all those in G-2 that they must not repeat any statement that threatened to undercut the position of the Churchill government. As Stimson saw the world situation, the "success of the United States depended on the safety of the British fleet," and the safety of that fleet depended in turn "on the preservation of the Churchill government."[5]

Stimson had his way, and the G-2 doubters were silenced, but this was only possible because the secretary of war had the firm backing of a president who was now determined to push ahead with aid to Britain despite her dim prospects. On 11 April, with the panzers running loose in North Africa as well as in Yugoslavia and Greece, Roosevelt confided to director of the bureau of the budget, Harold Smith, that he was secretly developing plans to establish patrols in the Atlantic to protect British shipping. The president was moving forward with great stealth, as he loved to do, having shared the plan with only four members of the cabinet because, as he remarked, the rest of the group "could not keep their mouths shut."[6]

Roosevelt's furtive advance along the fringes of German power was not focused merely on the North Atlantic. He had also encouraged the development of an expanded American intelligence "presence" in French North Africa during the winter and spring of 1941. When in December 1940, Vichy France had refused Donovan entry to Morocco or Algeria, the Roosevelt administration employed a two-pronged program to establish American, anti-Axis influence there. Robert Murphy, the American chargé in Vichy, went to North Africa in January to size up the situation and work out an arrangement with the French and Spanish authorities whereby some American goods would be shipped into the region under supervision of American control officers stationed in Morocco, Algeria, and Tangier. After convincing himself that Axis influence in the region was weak, while pro-Allied and especially pro-American sentiment was strong, Murphy met with the French military commander in the region, General Weygand. Their understanding—the Murphy–Weygand agreement of 10 March 1941—established a limited trade and American observer system in North Africa. By May 1941, twelve American observers had been selected and sent to posts in North Africa to watch over imports and serve as American intelligence representatives in the region.[7]

Long before the observers actually reached Morocco and Algeria, however, another prong of the American intelligence thrust was already developing extensive information on North African conditions. Lt. Col. Robert Solborg of Army G-2, who would soon be one of the founding fathers of the C.O.I.–O.S.S., was sent on a tour of North Africa by the army and the State Department under the "soft" cover of an American businessman. First surveying conditions in Portugal and Spain, Solborg observed that although British intelligence was warning of an imminent German penetration of the Iberian peninsula, he could find no sign of it. Moving on to North Africa, where he remained form March through July, Solborg likewise concluded that the reports of German influence and power were exaggerated. The much feared German Armistice Commission included only fifty-three men, counting staff and technicians, while its weaponry consisted of sidearms and a mere "6 or 8 machine guns." Colonel Solborg, like Murphy, believed that the French in North Africa—who were equally poorly armed—were inclined toward the Allies and were enthusiastic about the prospect of United States support.[8]

During his travels, Solborg spoke to many prominent Frenchmen and attracted the attention of a group of junior military officers who claimed to speak for their commander, General Weygand. The young officers declared that if they received aid from the United States, they could turn North Africa to the Allied side. Weygand actually had no knowledge of this approach, but when Solborg's reports reached Washington, American authorities assumed that it had been made at the initiative of the French general. Some in Washington, such as Henry Stimson, viewed the idea of using American aid to entice Weygand to change sides with considerable skepticism, but since even de Gaulle supported such an arrangement with Weygand in this period, the enthusiasm of American officials, including Assistant Secretary of War John J. McCloy, is understandable.[9]

Solborg's arrangements ultimately led nowhere because the Germans learned that some dealings involving Solborg and Weygand, and contrary to their interests, were afoot. The leak may not first have come from the general cracking of State Department codes by the German cryptographic service, as has been suggested, because the Germans did not immediately have precise or accurate information on what had happened and did not file a protest against Solborg until long after he had left North Africa. In any event, when Weygand got wind of Solborg's activities, he was furious and henceforth refused to deal with American officials, although the economic arrangements and the twelve control officers were allowed to remain. Solborg was permitted to tour Dakar but was then directed by Washington to return to the United States in late July.[10]

This American intelligence venture in North Africa initiated a pattern of political intelligence dabbling with Vichy officials in the region that later would have serious consequences for American policy and its O.S.S. practitioners. But the Murphy–Solborg operations had also chalked up some successes. Quite accurate information on conditions had been obtained, and a machinery was established for keeping the intelligence picture current. The British were highly nervous about German intentions in northwest Africa at this time because Rommel was racing toward Egypt. Some in London still wished to make no exceptions to the blockade policy and others wanted nothing to do with Vichy collaborators. On balance, however, even the most convinced Vichy haters in London could see that an extensive American early warning system in French North Africa was clearly in Britain's as well as America's interest.

Spring 1941, however, was a trying time for the British and not a period in which they were inclined to look with tolerance on the modest activities of their transatlantic colleagues. By the end of April, Yugoslavia and Greece had capitulated, and in North Africa, Tobruk was encircled by Rommel's forces. A month later, though the Tobruk garrison continued to hold out, Rommel was on the Egyptian frontier; and German parachute forces further north had broken the British hold on Crete. Britain was cornered into a thin strip of the eastern Mediterranean, clinging to the Middle East and Egypt, with Malta as its only small beacon in an Axis sea. The heroic defense of Tobruk and the heavy casualties the British inflicted on the German airborne forces in Crete were bright spots. But the overall picture was dark and, with the bulk of German forces still not committed anywhere (though poised in the direction of the U.S.S.R.), the future looked even darker.

The British government was shaken by these developments, and in the assessment period that followed, special activities and shadow warfare, like other aspects of the British war machine, came in for sharp criticism. S.O.E. had received some inflated praise for its part in the Yugoslav coup, which established the pro-British Simović regime in Belgrade. But when the German blow fell, all the expansive plans for sabotage, assassination, and the blocking of the Danube showed themselves to be mere talk. S.O.E., along with every other mismatched Allied force in the Balkans, failed even to slow down the German advance, and its staff fled, leaving only one wireless set in the whole peninsula.

The scale of this calamity and the resulting sour mood in London led to accusations from without S.O.E. and reevaluation from within. General Wavell, with his back to the wall, had little patience for the swollen S.O.E. staffs in Cairo whose intrigues and wild plans failed to give him any significant help either in the Balkans or in North Africa. By late May, the general was complaining to Anthony Eden that S.O.E. Cairo was a "racket," and in mid-June he insisted that the operation be put under his control.[11]

Dalton was also dissatisfied with S.O.E. operations in the spring of 1941, and in his heavy-footed way he stomped about trying to improve matters. Actually, S.O.E. had begun to turn the corner in western Europe during the early summer, carrying out a successful joint raid with the R.A.F. on a French power transformer south of Bordeaux in June. The quality of its training, organization, and personnel had greatly improved and now featured such luminaries as D. W. Brogan and Hugh Seton Watson in its propaganda sections. But the old wild scheming and woolgathering had not been completely eradicated. Barraged with S.O.E. proposals to infiltrate Thailand, recruit Italian-Americans for secret sabotage units, and other such plans, the War Office was forced to step in on 18 June, just four days before the Nazi attack on Russia, to veto an S.O.E. proposal for the formation of a special Sudeten German and Russian "pioneer corps." Dalton and his staff rowed "violently" over what was wrong with S.O.E. The minister believed that there was too much paper shuffling, "too many business men," and "too many smooth-faced explanations." "The truth is," Dalton noted in his diary on 17 May, "the war is going rather badly and all these things are shown up sharply as a consequence."[12]

Annoyed and discouraged, British leaders again looked to the United States for succor in the early summer of 1941. Even organizations such as S.I.S., which was riding rather high since its Ultra decrypts had provided great assistance in the Balkan campaign, realized that more was needed and that a larger portion of America's vast resources had to be tapped for Britain's benefit. Despite the strong protest of a large group of Americans who were prepared to write Britain off, the Roosevelt administration had responded to the Balkan disaster by increasing assistance. In April, the United States occupied bases in Greenland; in July, it would do the same in Iceland. Both acts were intended to protect the shipment of lend-lease supplies to the United Kingdom.

In the late spring and early summer of 1941, large numbers of British officials arrived in America bent on furthering "cooperation," "coordination," and the shaping of American activities to meet Britain's needs. Included among them were intelligence men who wished to reform, centralize, and in other ways make efficient America's intelligence machinery. These men and their American counterparts were so numerous in Washington, New York, and London during this period that it is not possible to determine who managed to find the most appropriate channels and apply the right pressure to get the American intelligence reform movement moving more swiftly. Both the B.S.C. and N.I.D. have claimed responsibility for initiating the centralizing of American intelligence, and both contend that their efforts met with great success.

Such assertions need to be met with the reserve and quantities of salt appropriate to those who engage in postwar special pleading. Whatever the deficiencies in the American intelligence system, and there were many, the events of the preceding two years of European war had not been totally lost on American military leaders. Reform had started before June 1941, and pressure for change was growing within the system. Early in the war, attachés such as Col. Truman Smith, who from his post in Berlin was much impressed by the German war machine, had urged America to make many military reforms. The military attaché in London, Gen. Raymond E. Lee, who would later serve briefly as assistant chief of staff for G-2, was also pressing as early as April 1941 for the creation of a joint intelligence committee analogous to that of the British. In both these cases, foreign models played a part in the push for change, but it is noteworthy that neither was completely successful. The American military was not restructured along German lines, and when a formal American Joint Intelligence Committee was created after Pearl Harbor, it never attained the significance or power that the comparable committee held in Britain.[13]

British visitors who thought they could create basic changes in the American system in June 1941 also misjudged the complexity of the United States government and the shrewdness of its leader. William Stephenson might feel that he could get what he wanted through friendships with bosom companions of the president such as William Donovan, and Donovan himself might believe that Franklin Roosevelt's Anglophile enthusiasm, supplemented by Stephenson's and Donovan's arguments, could firmly win over the president. Conversely, Admiral Godfrey of the British D.N.I., and his associate Ian Fleming might conclude that Roosevelt was such a garrulous old fool that they could only pray for their cumulative brilliance to somehow penetrate his layers of ignorance and folly and strike a spark.

But all these estimates, in which Franklin Roosevelt was object, not subject, were wrong. As the president once told a young administrative assistant who pushed him too hard, it was not an accident that the American people had selected him and not the administrative assistant as president of the United States. Roosevelt was many things to many men, a rare blend of the most complicated qualities in the human species, but all would agree that he was a genius of applied politics. As one of Churchill's intimates once confided to a high S.I.S. official about to leave for Washington, the president was "first and foremost a politician," who, unlike "Winston," did not get lost among ideals and personalities. Roosevelt lived the art of the possible, bided his time, seized his opportunities, always kept his own counsel, and was never blindly drawn into any event or issue. He characteristically remarked to Budget Director Harold Smith in April 1941 that he had relished the lack of "rules and regulations" that prevailed when he was assistant secretary of the navy in World War I because in such an unstructured atmosphere "he got by with murder." With a nudge at Smith's bureaucratic fastidiousness, Roosevelt added that "he thought there ought to be considerable freedom of action now" as well.[14]

Not only did the president struggle to preserve his "freedom of action," he made use of it in many ways in 1940–41, including supplying Britain, increasing national defense measures, and expanding intelligence and counterintelligence operations. Roosevelt did not need outside pressure to convince him that it was difficult to secure adequate intelligence information from within the existing Washington departmental machinery, and he made a first move to meet the situation in February 1941. Stephenson, Admiral Godfrey, and other earnest advocates of presidential action on intelligence matters would probably have been shocked in June 1941 if they had known that Roosevelt had set up his own personal intelligence and research organization four months earlier. In the first part of February 1941, while Donovan was still abroad, the president secretly employed John Franklin Carter, a pro–New Deal newsman who wrote under the name of Jay Franklin, as a covert presidential investigator. Using special unvouchered funds made possible by the military appropriations act of 1940—the first time a president had had this opportunity—$10,000 was set aside to permit Carter to begin work.

The operation was hidden away under cover of the State Department, with Assistant Secretary Adolf Berle acting as paymaster. As Berle emphasized, though, the department was only "a post office" for the operation, which was actually "part of the personal staff of its creator," Franklin Roosevelt. Carter began to function immediately, hiring researchers and investigators, including Henry Field, the anthropologist. Initially concerned to determine the relative stability of various European governments, Carter's group expanded rapidly—as secret presidential investigatory groups seem to do—and soon went on to study the Middle East, population movements, and a wide assortment of other international and domestic security questions. The budgetary allotments for Carter's operation rose steadily into the hundreds of thousands of dollars, and his regular and special contract staff ultimately included hundreds of researchers and confidential sources of information, including German political scientist Robert Kempner in the former category and Ernst "Putzi" Hanfstaengel—the Führer's former piano player—in the latter. Although much of the work that Carter did for Roosevelt concerned partisan political matters, nothing remotely related to American security was outside his secret mandate. He sent reports to the president on everything from the loyalty of Japanese Americans to the alleged techniques of the Nazi fifth column. Some of his revelations were unintentionally comic, including a March 1941 discovery that Nazis were behind incidents in South Africa in which British soldiers "were spat upon by foul breathed women." But Carter also had some solid connections with American corporate executives, and he used them to secure information on conditions in Axis territories. A measure of the scale of his activity may be gained from the fact that eighteen boxes were required in the president's files to hold the finished reports received from Carter between March 1941 and April 1945.[15]

It must have been with an air of interest and mischievous satisfaction, therefore, that Roosevelt listened to Donovan, Godfrey, Stephenson, and the other intelligence enthusiasts in June 1941. He knew as much about the informational difficulties as they did, and was more aware than they could possibly be of the bloody political battle that would erupt if he tried to challenge the great information agency satraps in the War Department, the Navy Department, and the F.B.I. Precisely because he knew all this, he had already skipped around these obstacles by creating his own small secret intelligence agency. But since Donovan had political clout and British support, as well as boundless energy, the president had little to lose if he allowed him to have a go at pulling the informational services together.

In a memorandum setting out his ideas, which Donovan sent to Roosevelt on 10 June, the colonel put forward a number of suggestions combined in an unusual and rather peculiar manner. The memorandum emphasized the obvious point that in the dangerous international situation facing the United States there was a need for "strategic information"; that is, basic intelligence regarding the capabilities and intentions of the various powers. Contending that most of the necessary data were "scattered throughout the various departments of our government," Donovan urged that this material be pulled together, supplemented by additional information acquired "directly" and analyzed and interpreted by military officers and scholars.[16]

The memorandum then abruptly switched focus and raised the question of how radio propaganda could be used as a means of "psychological attack." Noting that radio had been "effectively employed by Germany," Donovan contended that the full use of radio "as a weapon . . . is still to be perfected." To attain this "perfection," planning based on accurate information would be necessary, and therefore, according to Donovan, a "coordinator of strategic information" office, which was needed for intelligence purposes, also would be required for the United States to exploit fully the potential of psychological warfare via radio.

Though vague in places, and peculiarly disjointed, what Donovan was suggesting to the president was the creation of an intelligence gathering and collating agency that emphasized modern methods of analysis and channeled its output to those American organizations that would be concerned with the use of radio in psychological warfare. Touching as it did on geopolitics and modern technology, the idea obviously had appeal for a president who loved geography, novelty, and the "big picture." It also contained audible echoes of the fifth column fears that reverberated throughout the era. Securing information that allowed "true" psychological warfare to counter "false" propaganda was felt by many to be the best method for countering the Axis subversive threat. By advocating the creation of an intelligence organization that aimed its informational efforts through psychological warfare, Donovan's scheme had the additional merit of appearing less threatening to the intelligence offices of the army, the navy, and the F.B.I.

Yet when all is said and done, despite much postwar praise for its innovativeness and breadth of vision, Donovan's 10 June proposal is still very curious. It started with a bang and ended with a whimper. After advocating very broad informational gathering and evaluation, the plan abruptly narrowed its focus to the limited kind of service provided to British propaganda agencies by a pair of small subsections of the ministry of information and S.O. 1. By combining two rather discordant activities—intelligence gathering based on secrecy and psychological warfare emphasizing publicity—the proposal invited confusion. It was not a plan for a central intelligence agency embracing all forms of intelligence; it did not make clear whether the proposed organization was to be an operating agency for intelligence collection or radio propaganda; and it said nothing about the kind of subversive warfare operations being carried out by the British S.O.E. Donovan's fertile and perceptive mind had grasped two compelling ideas about the state of the world and the war in 1941: that coordination of both strategic information and radio propaganda were important. With his boundless enthusiasm, though, he simply combined the two, selling them to the president with little consideration for their incompatibility or the organizational problems his plan would entail. In this, his first foray into the realm of American intelligence organization, Donovan revealed a basic characteristic that would mark all his subsequent activity. He was not a politician, an administrator, a bureaucrat, or a political artist but a prophetic observer of modern war, a seer, who sought to make his perceptions into flesh.

But Donovan was a shrewd character who understood how new programs were commonly created in the Roosevelt administration. After preparing his memorandum, he tried out his ideas on various high officials. Only after he had secured the verbal support of men such as Secretary of the Treasury Henry Morgenthau did he tackle the president himself. In a conference with Roosevelt in mid-June, Donovan waxed so eloquent that the president apparently thought the idea of creating a strategic information service was well worth a try. Following the talk, F.D.R. ordered a member of his staff, Ben Cohen, to "set this up *confidentially*." To a novice observer of Roosevelt's methods, such a directive might seem to have settled the matter, but Donovan knew that the serious struggle had probably just begun. He now had to sell a specific form of his plan to the White House staff and to the powerful officers of the executive departments, especially those in War and Navy.[17]

The beginning of his campaign went off smoothly. On 20 June, Henry Morgenthau reiterated his support for intelligence coordination and agreed to lend two treasury staff members to Donovan's new organization. The colonel wanted one of them to be Harry Dexter White, but the treasury secretary firmly refused this request. One cannot help reflecting on what might have happened had Morgenthau yielded to Donovan's entreaties and let White become one of the fathers of American central intelligence, for within a few years, every rightist in the United States would be denouncing Harry Dexter White as "pro-Communist" and a "dangerous" leftist. But Morgenthau held on to White, and subsequent scandal in the intelligence community was avoided. As his top recruit from Treasury, then, Donovan obtained a conservative former foreign service officer, John Wiley. When men like Wiley were combined with those Donovan secured from his legal, business, and Republican political associates, the result was a distinctly conservative leadership corps for the new strategic intelligence service.[18]

On the same day that Morgenthau reconfirmed his support for Donovan's plan, Secretary of the Navy Frank Knox also went to work on behalf of the colonel. Knox told Secretary of War Henry Stimson about the intelligence coordination proposal and declared that he personally favored it. Stimson replied that he was "inclined to favor it," too, simply because he "trusted Donovan." Two days later, after talking with the colonel and reading the 10 June memorandum, Stimson's favorable view was further strengthened. He thought that the intelligence coordination idea offered opportunities for "very useful service" and rejoiced that the president had "landed on a man" to head it for whom Stimson had "such respect and confidence." But then, in the third week of June, the secretaries of war and navy learned that the matter cut deeper than an easy understanding between old friends. Knox encountered serious opposition from his admirals and from O.N.I., while Stimson ran into bitter hostility to the plan from the "extremely angry" George C. Marshall, chief of staff of the army. Stimson tried to mollify Marshall by pointing to the intelligence benefits that could accrue from effective coordination. But the general saw Donovan's scheme as "an effort to supplant his responsibilities" and his "direct connection with the Commander-in-Chief" and was not pacified by Stimson's reassurances.[19] After consulting again in the late morning of 24 June, Stimson and Knox concluded that circular letters would have to be prepared to reassure the thirteen (!) federal agencies gathering intelligence information that Donovan's organization would not intrude on their respective turfs. But this conciliatory gesture came too late. The White House's Ben Cohen already had drafted an executive order for Donovan's office of Coordinator of Strategic Information that was studded with references to military intelligence functions and even proposed making Donovan a major general. British officials, who interestingly enough were immediately informed of the content of the draft, greeted the "good news" warmly—any form of American intelligence centralization was of benefit to them. But the draft executive order confirmed General Marshall's contention that Donovan was pointing toward a divided command of the military; and he redoubled his opposition to the scheme. This time, Stimson, when faced with a copy of the draft executive order, fully agreed with Marshall that the plan threatened to give "the President two Chiefs of Staff." The secretary of war told Cohen that he thought it was "bad planning" unless Donovan was "kept in a purely civilian capacity" and that he "disapproved completely of having him made a major general simultaneously with his assumption of this position of Coordinator of Information." Holding out some hope that "the thing might be worked out," Stimson told Cohen that the plan would have to be redrafted to guarantee that the organization was "kept purely civilian."[20]

Even so, the trick was not turned effortlessly because Cohen, who readily agreed to "take the military phrases out," was the least of the obstacles standing in the way of acceptance. Stimson managed to cool down Knox, who was "rampant on the subject . . . [of] immediate action on behalf of Donovan." On the other hand, he had trouble placating Marshall and others in the War Department who wanted no part of any C.O.I. plan. Three long sessions with the general (two of which were attended by Assistant Secretary McCloy also) were required before Marshall reluctantly agreed to go along—*if* an all-civilian form of the plan could be developed. To get the general to yield even to this degree, Stimson, who had come to feel that the whole matter was "troublesome" and a "nuisance," even had been forced to plead "how important it was for his own [Marshall's] sake that there should not be a sharp issue made on this." On 3 July a deal was finally struck in a meeting between McCloy, Stimson, and Donovan. The latter finally got his office for coordinating information, but it was to be completely civilian, and the executive order would include a provision guaranteeing that Donovan would not encroach on the intelligence functions of the army and navy.[21]

With this settled, a new draft executive order was prepared by Cohen and Budget Director Smith. It emphasized that C.O.I. would be a civilian information collection and analysis agency that would not "in any way interfere with or impair" the intelligence work of the armed forces. The order sidestepped the objections of various critics, such as Nelson Rockefeller (the Coordinator of Inter-American Affairs) who opposed giving Donovan a monopoly on foreign radio propaganda. No mention of psychological warfare or radio was therefore included in the order, and Donovan was left to depend on verbal support and indirect statements from the president as authorization for his subsequent propaganda endeavors. The new coordinator was successful in securing inclusion of an elastic clause in the executive order stating that when authorized by the president he could carry out "such supplementary activities as may facilitate the securing of information for national security not now available to the Government." However, he failed to get a similar statement into the White House press release announcing his appointment, which would have declared that he had authority "to undertake activities helpful in securing of defense information not available to the Government through existing departments and agencies." This phrase, which was originally in the press release, went too far for White House aides Steve Early and Harry Hopkins. But the "supplementary activities" passage of the executive order itself remained, and would soon spawn a bewildering range of projects in the fertile brain of William Donovan.[22]

The order establishing C.O.I. was officially promulgated on 11 July after the president had taken a short interval to reassure the fiery director of civilian defense, New York Mayor Fiorello LaGuardia, that Donovan would not be allowed to encroach on his control of domestic defense propaganda. This reassurance culminated in a letter to the mayor stating that the colonel would assume responsibility for "international broadcasts," a distinction that pleased LaGuardia for the moment and gave Donovan his only written, if indirect, authorization to enter the field of psychological warfare.[23]

The Foreign Information Service (F.I.S.)
and the Research and Analysis Branch (R. and A.)

The issuance of the C.O.I. order freed Donovan to put his great energy and grand inventiveness to work. Initially armed with $450,000 in unvouchered funds, he secured additional allotments totaling at least $1.7 million before Pearl Harbor and $12 million more in the first three months thereafter. Although critics would complain that this abundance of money made Donovan's people reckless and inefficient, the flow of unvouchered funds allowed the colonel to develop his organization rapidly, partly because less well-endowed domestic and foreign organizations were willing to smooth his path in return for a share of his largesse. Aside from administrative units, C.O.I. initially consisted of two main branches, the Foreign Information Service (F.I.S.) under playwright Robert Sherwood and the Research and Analysis Branch (R. and A.), which was supervised by a Board of Analysts and administratively directed by Dr. James P. Baxter III of Williams College. Immediately before Pearl Harbor, Donovan began to lay the basis for espionage and special operations (as we shall see below), but in its first five months of existence, the coordinator's organization accurately reflected its chartered emphasis of radio propaganda on the one hand and open information gathering and analysis on the other, as set forth in Donovan's memorandum to the president of 10 June 1941.[24]

F.I.S. began its activity by preparing guidelines for pro-Allied and anti-Axis radio propaganda programs and then moved on to acquire broadcasting time on shortwave radio stations. By the end of 1941, it was leasing substantial time and broadcasting a wide range of propaganda in English as well as in a number of foreign languages. In addition, an embryonic unit for monitoring and evaluating German radio broadcasts had been established. With ample money and Sherwood's and Donovan's extensive press and media contacts (made especially accessible through Frank Knox's influence), it was a relatively simple matter to assemble a team of high-level propaganda analysts and radio broadcasters. Since most other agencies of government lacked both the money and the highly skilled personnel available to the C.O.I., the latter's propaganda work easily outshone the others. An indication of what the shortage of specialists could mean to an informational organization is revealed by the experience of the Justice Department. None of the 155 foreign-language newspapers that Justice was screening for hints of subversive dangers in September 1941 was in Japanese because no one in the department could read the language![25]

However, ability and money were not enough in themselves to guarantee a smooth operating road for F.I.S. Tough F.I.S. propagandists, such as Edmund (*Strategy of Terror*) Taylor, were scornful of the moderation of "earnest and somewhat doctrinaire American Liberals" in the organization who desired to be mere "informationalists" and tell the story of America. Taylor and his fellow propagandists, a number of whom had been newsmen in Europe in 1940, wanted to take off the gloves and emulate Goebbels. Imbued with the reality of a Nazi fifth column, they sought to use radio as an instrument of aggressive subversive warfare without troubling much about morality or civil liberties. Disagreements between the informationalists and the propagandists kept the internal F.I.S. pot bubbling, but these were nothing compared with the troubles that F.I.S. had with neighboring departments and bureaus.[26]

The brashness of the F.I.S. newsmen caused difficulties for the information gathering branch of C.O.I. In October, R. and A. officials complained bitterly that O.N.I. and M.I.D. were keeping all C.O.I. people at arm's length because F.I.S. newshawks had been asking "embarrassing questions" of army and navy intelligence people over the phone with no regard for security. The two sides of C.O.I. were, after all, not very compatible—propaganda and intelligence simply do not mix—and the legitimate activities of each side cut against the other. F.I.S. ruffled even more feathers at the State Department, where officials believed that there was an inherent conflict between the F.I.S. propagandists and those in state responsible for the nation's foreign policy. Again, it was not simply a matter of personality, although as Berle wrote Sumner Welles in late July 1941 that if the department were to wait for Donovan to take the initiative in reducing jurisdictional troubles, "you will wait a long time." The core of the trouble, as Berle emphasized, was that in "cold fact" the line "between propaganda and foreign policy is nothing if not hazy" because one could "almost make foreign policy with . . . propaganda." The State Department wanted absolute control over the tone and content of the F.I.S. broadcasts but though it ultimately secured some measure of supervision, it never succeeded in creating full peace and tranquility between the two organizations.[27]

The fundamental difficulties that F.I.S. had with R. and A. and the State Department were compounded by jurisdictional conflicts with other newly created "defense" agencies, such as LaGuardia's civil defense organization, Rockefeller's Inter-American Affairs Office, and the Office of Facts and Figures, a government news service that was established under Archibald MacLeish in October 1941. F.I.S. and LaGuardia's group circled each other warily, trying to locate the line between domestic and foreign propaganda and competing for the attention of the commercial radio companies. However, LaGuardia's group, crippled by poor organization, erratic leadership, and the unpopularity of domestic propaganda in peacetime, never really got off the ground. F.I.S., therefore, was able to push forward rather effectively along this frontier. A similar advance was made in relation to the Office of Facts and Figures, a late arrival created three months after C.O.I. and unwelcome to rivals in the informational field as well as to the Bureau of the Budget. Created solely because of the president's enthusiasm and support, MacLeish understood that his organization was vulnerable and he went out of his way to court Donovan and Sherwood. Such a conciliatory rival was not much of a problem during the six weeks that remained before Pearl Harbor, and it was only in the period of rapid expansion occasioned by American entry into the war that F.I.S. and Facts and Figures really came to push and shove.[28]

As for the Inter-American Affairs Office, given the personalities of Rockefeller and Donovan, not to mention the jurisdictional overlap between Rockefeller's informational activities in Latin America and Donovan's claim to a monopoly on international radio propaganda, it was not necessary to wait for the outbreak of war to see fireworks. From the moment of F.I.S.'s birth, the two staffs haggled over propaganda policy, personnel, and shortwave radio time. Careful to appear conciliatory toward R. and A., Rockefeller had raised only relatively minor jurisdictional matters over F.I.S. in his talks with Donovan and Sherwood in early October. But in mid-October, deeply resenting Donovan's incursions into his sphere, Rockefeller launched a serious attack. Sherwood was then in Europe, and Rockefeller seized the opportunity to slip past Donovan and persuade Roosevelt that the terms of the C.O.I. foreign radio monopoly were improper because they clashed with the executive order granting his organization complete control of propaganda in Latin America. The president agreed that he had made an error, and with little or no explanation to Donovan, stripped C.O.I. of the right either to make propaganda broadcasts to Latin America or to determine the "line" to be used in such broadcasts.[29]

When he returned to Washington, Sherwood found "it difficult to understand" how this had happened and cited all the practical and policy problems that would result if two different organizations released what purported to be official American propaganda. Declaring that "history has broken into a gallop" that left little room for "childish bickering, puny jealousies, or backstairs intrigue," Sherwood urged Donovan to put the broad issues before Rockefeller and the president. But from all indications, Donovan failed to push the matter vigorously. At that moment, he was attempting to gain presidential approval for a vast expansion of his activities, carrying him much deeper into the domain of secret intelligence and special operations, and he probably considered it wise to give way gracefully on the Latin American radio issue in the hope of capturing bigger game. The decision seems to have soured relations between Sherwood and Donovan, but it should be noted that the colonel had no base of power except for his friendship with Knox and his access to the president, and he must have been reluctant to challenge such a man as Rockefeller in a standup battle for presidential favor. Donovan's capitulation on the Latin American radio issue was merely the first of a number of occasions on which he would sacrifice his earlier enthusiasms for his current ones while trying to avoid any move that might threaten his influence with Franklin Roosevelt.[30]

Yet F.I.S.'s loss in the battle over propaganda broadcasts should not obscure the extent of Sherwood's pre-Pearl Harbor achievement in creating an American foreign propaganda organization. He had ample money to do it, of course, but he and his staff also possessed a determination to "overcome our late start on the propaganda front by brute volume of communications world-wide regardless of business as usual." With this kind of drive and singleness of purpose, he not only achieved his main goal of putting American propaganda on the world map but also won the first lap in the race for dominance among the various branches of C.O.I. When C.O.I. prepared its budget request in November 1941 for the first half of 1942, the Bureau of the Budget approved an operational budget of $7 million. Of that amount, $4.7 million was to go to F.I.S. and the remaining $2.3 million was to be split between R. and A. and various special operations and overseas intelligence activities. Measured by the standard of operational budget size, which is the bottom line for most Washington bureaucrats, Sherwood and F.I.S. beat the rest of C.O.I. by a score of 2 to 1 in the period from July to December 1941. Since R. and A. operations were much cheaper than those of F.I.S. and the expensive forms of intelligence and special operations were only just beginning, these figures probably exaggerate the extent of Sherwood's relative triumph. Nevertheless, in light of the post-World War II tendency to see the significance of Donovan and C.O.I. exclusively in terms of intelligence and special operations, it should be recognized that it was the propaganda side of the colonel's original vision that scored first.[31]

In any American struggle for influence between propaganda and intelligence operations, the latter suffers from a number of handicaps. However distasteful propaganda may be to American sentiment, at least the United States has had extensive experience in using it, not only in national emergencies such as World War I and the Great Depression, but in the barrage that is daily released from advertising agencies. In contrast, many aspects of intelligence work had been completely nonexistent in the United States before 1941. Men summoned to Washington to take leading roles in R. and A. found such great uncertainty about priorites that "no one would or could enlighten us as to what we should do and how to go about it." In addition, intelligence gathering and analysis is a secret activity; its achievements are difficult to measure and because of their nature impossible to advertise. Intelligence successes cannot directly impress a society attuned to the neon sign and the paid commercial.[32]

Thus, it was inevitable that there would be uncertainty and hesitation in the early stages of the development of the R. and A. branch. To direct it, Donovan required a scholar with sufficiently high repute to attract specialists experienced in both administration and the ways of Washington to build an organization by cooperating with other government departments. After a month of searching, the colonel hit on the president of Williams College, Dr. James P. Baxter III, and in early August made him chief of R. and A. The basic plan was to create a ten-man Board of Analysts chaired by Baxter and composed of a naval officer, a military officer, and eight specialists (in addition to Baxter) who came from various fields of the social sciences and international affairs. All would need the requisite experience and breadth of vision to see their individual specialties in terms of a world picture. Another hundred or so researchers also were to be brought in to staff divisions and subsections organized around geographical or topical specializations, such as French history or special fields of psychology or geography. The research staff would be organized into four divisions, each one headed by a member of the Board of Analysts. The researchers were to sift through material acquired from government agencies and standard research depositories such as the Library of Congress and prepare factual papers on matters bearing on possible policy decisions. The original directives for R. and A. concentrated initial research on three topics: the intentions of Japan, the situation in Iberia and North Africa, and the problem of "our exposed right rear in South America." But the researchers were not to draw broad conclusions from their material; their work was to be narrow and "objective"—factual research (in the old-fashioned positivist sense) that left little room for interpretive comment or inferential conclusion. Any evaluations touching on policy alternatives were to be reserved solely for the Board of Analyst members, who, acting as an advisory body to the Director of C.O.I., would report to William Donovan, who would in turn, at his discretion, pass on such recommendations to the president.[33]

In mid-August 1941, Donovan and Baxter recruited members for the Board of Analysts. Some, such as William Langer, Coolidge Professor of History at Harvard, who was to serve as chief of the Special Information Division, were contacted jointly by Baxter and Donovan, while others were sought out by Baxter alone. Prospective board members were assured that they would be concerned primarily with interpretation and considerations of broad policy and that half of them would have no administrative assignment at all. Along with Langer and Baxter, the original board included five other academics—Joseph Hayden of Michigan, Calvin Hoover of Duke, Edwin Earle of Princeton, and Donald McKay and Edward Mason of Harvard. The board was rounded out by John Wiley, whom Donovan, as we have seen, secured from the Treasury Department, plus Lt. Col. J. T. Smith of the army, and Comdr. Francis C. Denebrink of the navy. The civilians were well known in their fields, came from prestigious institutions, tended to be politically conservative, and had some experience of government service. They were thus well suited to fill their first two assignments—the establishment of working relations with other government departments and the recruitment of research scholars. Despite some suspicion of the new organization from the research domains of older government agencies, the Board of Analysts did rather well in making contacts and smoothing the waters. By early November, it was receiving much assistance from Carter's organization, and although it had been unable to secure some Treasury reports it wanted, was rejoicing about the "splendid cooperation" it was getting from the State Department.[34]

Even more impressive achievements were made in the recruitment of R. and A. researchers from government agencies and the groves of academe. Many academics came because of a poor job market, but idealism and the attractive possibility of working under men with the academic stature of Langer, McKay, and Earle also played its part. By mid-October, men who would become well known for their government service—for example, R. A. Winnacker, Sherman Kent, and Ralph Bunche—were already at work in R. and A. Alongside them were many others who would leave significant marks on scholarship, including Norman O. Brown, Conyers Read, Walter Dorn, Arthur Marder, Eugene Anderson, Geroid Robinson, John K. Fairbank, and Charles Fahs.

However, the research assignments given to R. and A. personnel were not always very appropriate. Henry Cord Meyer, a central European specialist, was put to work on West African communications, and another authority on German questions, Gordon Craig, was subsequently also assigned to West African matters. We hope that Arthur Marder, the great expert on the British navy, was amused to find himself in charge of "Mediterranean (water)" and that Ralph Bunche, the only black in the group, did not suffer inordinately when he was assigned to handle "native problems all over the [British] Empire except India." On balance, though, despite some confusion and mismatching, R. and A., as a new and experimental organization, was notably successful in so quickly assembling a group of such breadth and quality.[35]

By mid-October 1941, a force of one hundred R. and A. scholars was at work, barracked because of space limitations at both the Library of Congress and the new C.O.I. headquarters. They soon were plugging away at specialized projects ranging from the "situation in Tangier" to "conditions in Thailand." Before the month ended, a "flow of material" in the form of internal C.O.I. papers called "R. and A. Reports" began to appear. The researchers were also put to work on "high priority" jobs, some of which were requested by outside agencies but most of which came from Donovan via the Board of Analysts. During the early months of C.O.I., the colonel asked for a large number of special studies on such matters as "the food situation in Europe" and conditions in the territories "just to the south" of North Africa. These projects were given special attention and, in contrast to the internal reports, were designated "R. and A. Memoranda," which meant that they were discussed and revised by the Board of Analysts and then given board serial numbers.[36]

At first glance R. and A. system appeared to be carrying out the three-stage procedure of the original plan, with the researchers researching, the analysts analyzing, and William Donovan feeding the results to the president. However, the grand scheme was actually aborted from the beginning, chiefly because of the close control initially exercised by the colonel. In those early pre-Pearl Harbor days, R. and A. was Donovan's pet and the branch was forced to follow wherever his imagination and enthusiasm led him. How anyone could have arranged projects in advance and carried out centrally directed evaluation for such an ebullient character is difficult to imagine. But the situation was made worse by the colonel's easy access to the president. Due to his own desire as well as the force of circumstances, Donovan had organized C.O.I. so that it was an agency that reported to the Oval Office rather than to a cabinet-level department of government. C.O.I. materials were not to be sent to the White House by mail or routing slips for, according to the procedural rules established by the colonel, every item had to be hand carried to the president's office, most frequently by Donovan himself. The colonel knew that to ensure his position he had to retain the president's favor, and to do that he had to be sensitive to every White House mood and whim. But in the age of Roosevelt, whims moved great distances with remarkable speed, and there was no way serious research could keep ahead of what might strike the president's fancy.[37]

Being dragged along in Wild Bill's wake as he chased after Franklin Roosevelt produced many basic difficulties for the R. and A. staff. Because Donovan's attention was keyed to the president and not to other departments of government, R. and A. work was pitched too high. Its reports and memoranda were forced to enter the deliberative process on policy at a very late stage. The War and State departments, which were suspicious of C.O.I., rarely drew R. and A. work into their systems of policy formulation. Since Donovan's interest was centered on distributing information only to the president, Langer and Baxter were primarily concerned with establishing good relations to *obtain* information rather than to distribute it. As a result, in the pre-Pearl Harbor period the established departments of government viewed C.O.I. as an intruder into their preserves, who only heightened the president's tendency toward light-hearted innovation and spur-of-the-moment decisions. Departmental hostility to R. and A. hardened in many quarters and only gradually softened again after Pearl Harbor when Donovan's enthusiasms led him elsewhere and R. and A. scholars were allowed to show their technical mettle.[38]

By that time, however, it was too late for the Board of Analysts to prove its worth, and the idea of centralized analysis died aborning. As long as Donovan personally dominated R. and A. operations, the board had no possibility of putting its stamp on things. They were a group of cautious men, concerned with rules and procedures, who liked to spend their mornings discussing policy matters and the ways of the world in an atmosphere akin to that of the Foreign Policy Association. But they were pulled this way and that, with priorities rising and falling according to the shifting focuses of Donovan and Roosevelt. In addition, the board found itself confronted with a bewildering range of new organizations and units, placed by Donovan either within its domain or along its fringes. One group was to produce still photographs. Another, under Donovan's old friend E. Edward "Ned" Buxton, was to interview travelers arriving in New York. In late 1941, under State Department prompting, the colonel organized a Foreign Nationalities Branch to measure the mood and mine the intelligence sources of the non-Asian foreign language groups within the United States. Individuals were dispatched on foreign missions seemingly willy-nilly. A representative of the Board of Analysts was dispatched to China, and Donovan's old London colleague, Edgar Mowrer was also sent to Asia. By the eve of Pearl Harbor, the colonel was toying with a project to survey general American opinion using the services of pollster

Elmo Roper, and by this time, too, he had discovered the cinema. Director John Ford had become a C.O.I. man and was leading a film team shooting pictures on current events in the hope of discovering what light Hollywood might throw on the questions of national policy.[39]

The Board of Analysts had to cope continually with this ever-changing Donovanesque free-for-all. It deliberated on whether to interview each representative who was to travel abroad and listened to returning representatives give oral reports that provided some new information but also added to the confusion. For example, Mowrer reported to the board after his six-week tour of Asia that most people in the Pacific area believed that "Japan would do nothing to provoke a major war" so long as Russia was not "liquidated." If Russia "holds," he predicted, "time is really on our side." The Mowrer report forecasting peace in Asia was given to the board on 21 November, and the final fifty-seven-page summary memorandum was completed on 3 December, just four days before the Japanese struck at Pearl Harbor![40]

One wonders if any group riding such a bewildering carrousel could have organized and subjected to effective analysis such varying pieces of inaccurate and accurate information. Certainly the Board of Analysts could not. Its members were totally cowed by the colonel, who shifted R. and A. members at will, told everyone what to do at daily 9:00 A.M. staff meetings, and even prohibited members of the board from speaking to the press. It was not so much that his administrative deficiencies caused trouble for the Board of Analysts—although these would soon be a problem for the whole C.O.I.–O.S.S. organization—but that he did not give it enough room and authority to do the job it had been created to do. The "gentleman's club" atmosphere on the board gradually came to dominate completely and soon crossed the line to farce. Donovan was invited to board meetings to hear members read memoranda aloud as if these were university seminars. In early 1942 the board concluded, after long deliberation, that it could not even decide such weighty questions as whether reports should be single- or double-spaced and this matter had to be referred to the colonel for decision.[41]

The systematic analysis function within C.O.I. was dead, and later efforts to bring it back by creating C.O.I.–O.S.S. planning groups all failed. R. and A., like every other information subsection of C.O.I. (and later of O.S.S.), became a data-feeding organization that developed information and then tried to find customers who would use it. As the Board of Analysts ossified and Donovan turned from R. and A. to other enthusiasms, the research organization lost its original raison d'être. During the post–Pearl Harbor period, the flow of R. and A. reports to the president gradually dwindled, and it is doubtful that he did more than leaf through some of those that found their way to the desk of his secretary, Grace Tully. From time to time, a particular R. and A. paper sparked Donovan's enthusiasm sufficiently for him to use it as the text for a session in the Oval Office, but after mid-1942 such occasions were rare indeed. R. and A. researchers were forced to find customers where they could—in some sections of M.I.S. and O.N.I., among various subcommittees of the military staffs, in the civil affairs division of the War Department (from mid-1942), in the State Department, and in various other branches of C.O.I.–O.S.S. itself. When there was no immediate demand, the researchers prepared reports on their own initiative (as approved by the R. and A. projects committee) hoping that someday someone might use such material in making policy decisions.[42]

Changes in Britain's Shadow Warfare System: July–December 1941

June: Germany invades Russia
July: Japanese begin occupying Indochina
August: The Atlantic Charter
September: Roosevelt issues order to shoot U-boats "on sight"

The original Donovan dream of creating an effective centralized structure to systematize and analyze important information was therefore an early casualty of the very nimble brain and active imagination that had created it. R. and A.'s needs were lost amid a jumble of events that moved so rapidly in late 1941 that Donovan's attention jumped first one way and then another. Japanese–American relations deteriorated when Japan penetrated French Indochina and the United States responded by slapping embargoes on scrap iron and petroleum shipments to Tokyo. Lines were being drawn, tensions were rising, and a general Asian war was a real threat, despite the views of a few false prophets like Edgar Mowrer.

In Europe, too, the stakes in the war rose immeasurably in 1941. Hitler's June attack on the Soviet Union (Operation Barbarossa) was not a limited, conventional, military operation but a showdown in which 500 to 600 divisions struggled for control of the Eurasian landmass. Hitler had gambled everything on his ability to deal the Russians such a massive and murderous initial blow that the Soviet regime would disintegrate and Germany would be able to rearrange the pieces of the Russian puzzle in any way it chose. Not only were three great army groups employed in the assault but behind the initial advance units came the S.S. murder squads (*Einsatzgruppen*) with orders to exterminate "Jews, Gypsies, and other undesirables."

What had happened in the German campaign in western Europe in the spring of 1940 had been shocking to the West and had released all the phantoms of fifth column hysteria. What the Nazis had done in Poland and the Balkans had also been startling, and the grim aftermath of repression and ghettoizing had been both dreadful and ominous. But what happened in Russia from June on was something far worse, for Hitler now showed his true stripes. He was not going east just to conquer but to exterminate the Slavs, Jews, and Communists who personified the hobgoblins of his racist nightmares. In eastern Europe, he would actually be what Paul Reynaud had feared he might be in the west, not just an old gentleman like the Kaiser but a new Ghengis Khan.

The scale of the attack and the issues at stake were so great that, as Hitler had said, it would make "the world hold its breath." The Soviets' border defenses went down under the first assault, but the Red Army retreated, regrouped, and formed new units, forcing the Germans to drive ever deeper and extend their supply lines ever further. The Soviet military structure was badly organized but determined and ruthless. It had the nucleus of a tank force that could match the Germans, and it was expanding its eastern industrial complex. As it became clear that the Nazi expedition was committed to pillage and mass murder, Russian public opinion rallied to the government. Hitler's war of extermination produced a near miracle and turned Joseph Stalin into a truly popular leader. The only choice for the Russian people now was between the glimmer of hope offered by a Soviet future and the certainty of destruction, slavery, and death at the hands of the Nazis. For Stalin, too, Hitler left only a narrow choice: either the Soviet leader would lose everything or, through determination and improvisation, would triumph over the greatest military power in the world and thereby leap into the front rank of world power.

No wonder that during the summer and fall of 1941 everyone in the West watched the struggle with nervous anticipation. The West did not really grasp that this was a systematic, genocidal war on the part of Germany, and it did not appreciate then, or since, the scale of Soviet suffering and achievement. But people in the United States, and even more so in Great Britain, realized that the length of the road they would have to travel to defeat Hitler would be determined primarily by the scale of resistance mounted by the Red Army and the Russian people. For Americans like Donovan, Stimson, and Roosevelt, who identified American security with the survival of the United Kingdom, nearly everything seemed to be hanging in the balance. The British government, seeing the eastern war as at least a respite from an immediate German attack on Britain and perhaps a salvation if the Russians could hold, tried to take advantage of the situation by mounting its own attacks on the Third Reich. Too weak on the ground even to confront the rear-guard units that the Germans had stationed in the west, the British turned their attention toward a North African offensive and tried to advance their cause at sea, in strategic bombing, and through various forms of shadow warfare.

Screwing up their political courage, British liaison missions were sent to Moscow to coordinate with the Russians. Among their number was an S.O.E. mission, commanded by Brig. George Hill, which hoped to arrange for combined subversive operations. Since the Russians had rather more important things on their minds, nothing much immediately came of these efforts, although the Soviets did send a Security Service (N.K.V.D.) mission to London as a counterpart to the S.O.E. unit, which was placed in Moscow.[43]

S.O.E. was further hampered in its relations with the Russians by a measure of inefficiency (Hill was sent by sea and did not reach Moscow until September) and a reluctance to cooperate wholeheartedly with people whom the British leaders only yesterday had considered to be the Bolshevik enemy. Hill was an odd choice to head a subversive warfare mission in the Soviet Union because he had been a British agent in Russia working against the Bolsheviks in 1919, and his deputy was a violently anti-Soviet Polish major named Turkouski, whom S.O.E. London insisted on sending despite Hill's objections. Even though Dalton and "C" grudgingly admitted that Communists in Germany and France might "be most potent on our side," they were not prepared to extend themselves very far to make use of them. When the Russians began to make overtures to establish full cooperation in both open and subversive propaganda operations, the head of S.O.E.'s subversive propaganda section, Rex Leeper, was, according to Dalton, "frightened out of his wits at the very idea." And while Hill was in Moscow trying to cooperate with the Soviets on subversive warfare operations, other sections of S.O.E. were secretly taking steps to mobilize a ragtag band of Armenians and Kurds to blow up the Caucasus oil fields in the event that the Wehrmacht got that far.[44]

If Britain was going to strike at the Germans in 1941, it would therefore have to be from somewhere other than Moscow. Yet the R.A.F. was still not producing serious damage in Germany, the British were barely hanging on in Egypt, and the struggle against the U-boat's was touch and go. Consequently, the main hope once again rested on shadow warfare. Ultra was by this point working quite smoothly, and S.I.S. was also having considerable success developing agent rings on the continent. S.O.E., too, had passed through the most trying stages of its infancy and was becoming really operational. Serious troubles still remained; rivalries with other departments were endemic and S.O.E. buccaneers still got into serious difficulties. A great scandal developed in S.O.E. Middle East during the summer and fall with revelations of "inefficiency, extravagance, and even corruption." Frank Nelson, the operational head of S.O.E., was himself forced to carry out an on-the-spot investigation in Cairo, and he ultimately purged the whole organization. There were also problems in Turkey and Spain, where Britain's ambassadors feared that reckless S.O.E. activities would push Madrid and Istanbul more heavily toward the Axis. Since S.O.E. was actually establishing secret weapons dumps in Turkey without the knowledge of the Turks or the British Ambassador, and since it had covertly recruited Spanish anti-Franco Republicans with the aim of arming them as a stay-behind force in the event of a German invasion of the Iberian peninsula, there was reason for Foreign Office concern.[45]

London was the scene of yet another bitter bureaucratic conflict involving S.O.E., which raged on through the fall of 1941. Dalton and Minister of Information Brendan Bracken were locked in a struggle for control of Britain's secret propaganda operations. With two such able and acid combatants in the field, the battle ranked as one of the most poisonously literate departmental struggles of all time. In September, a bargain was struck, or perhaps it would be more accurate to say that a compromise muddle was agreed to, whereby the Political Warfare Executive (P.W.E.) was established to handle foreign propaganda. The Ministry of Information (M.O.I.) was left in the domestic field, and for the time being S.O.E. kept a few of its fingers in overseas black propaganda operations.[46]

At a time in which British organizations were engaged in all kinds of operations, including the use of a million pounds in 1941 just to keep "the Iraqi tribes friendly," it is not surprising that some confusion developed regarding subversive warfare organization. Yet the scandals and squabbles did not mean that S.O.E. was impotent or simply a band of troublemakers. Despite the horror stories, Dalton's unit had become a serious organization in 1941, and there was truth along with poetic exaggeration in an S.O.E. official's boast in November that "a powerful anti-German fifth column" was being "maintained and expanded." Fifteen hundred men and women had passed through S.O.E.'s thirty-three training establishments by the fall. S.O.E. had its own small navy and R.A.F. units with adequate arms and means of delivery (though it would frequently demand more) to move a substantial number of agents to the continent. The main bottleneck to large-scale continental operations lay in a shortage of agents, a lack of promising places to send them, and a cautious attitude on the part of the British Chiefs of Staff.[47]

Resistance potential on the continent rose in 1941, spurred by the Communist parties that enthusiastically went over to anti-Nazi activism following Hitler's attack on Russia in June. But Nazi countermeasures had also increased, and the prospect of an anarchic war to the knife between the Germans and the resistance had little appeal for many conservatives in Britain and on the continent. S.O.E. worked with the governments in exile and the Free French movement, training agents, establishing resistance rings, and supplying some sabotage material, arms, and explosives. But the strongest exile groups, especially the Poles and the French, demanded a large measure of autonomy and did not always trust the intentions or effectiveness of S.O.E. and S.I.S. The British government, still nervous about German intentions, put intelligence considerations above those of special operations. S.I.S. had a higher priority than S.O.E. both for supplies and for air delivery, and the governments in exile in London were forced to try to work their passage by supplying information from their continental sources, who were not always informative or accurate.[48]

The British Chiefs of Staff concluded, therefore, that despite some S.O.E. successes here and there, the situation still was not ripe for large-scale resistance operations in western Europe. The most promising "secret armies" were presumed to be in central-eastern Europe—in Poland and Czechoslovakia—but the distance there was too great for effective supply. In western Europe only limited sabotage seemed possible due to the thin resistance organization, unsuitable terrain, and fear of German reprisal. In August 1941, the Chiefs of Staff ordered S.O.E. to deemphasize sabotage aid in central Europe, Scandinavia, and among "secret armies everywhere" and to concentrate instead on building up a sabotage organization in France and the low countries that could be of assistance to an Allied landing force when the day of invasion came. Such a policy was reasonable, prudent, and at the same time frustrating for S.O.E. and members of the resistance. It committed S.O.E. to a long, slow development which precluded premature action in the name of a far-off invasion that Britain obviously did not have the strength to mount on its own.[49]

The policy of going slow in western Europe was hard not only on the occupied populations and on S.O.E. but also on the impetuous Winston Churchill. He longed for action and sensed that Britain would have to do all in its limited power to encourage the Soviets to fight on. Temptation was therefore great to carry out action somewhere, and the venturesome spirits in S.O.E. scurried about trying to find suitable projects and operational locations. In late August, Dalton pondered how he could convince

Montague Norman, director of the Bank of England, to help with a plan to drop forged Reichmarks on Germany, but something more persuasive to bankers than counterfeiting was required. One possibility was giving encouragement to what in London was called the Yugoslav revolt.[50]

After the German conquest in April, groups of Yugoslav soldiers had gone into hiding, and the old Serbian patriotic organization of Chetniks had become more active. When the German and Italian occupation authorities later gave the collaborationist Croatian Ustachi regime license to carry out mass atrocities against the Serbs, popular resistance hardened, but the Chetnik and Serbian military resistance groups opted for a policy of preparation and waiting. After the Germans attacked the Soviet Union, however, Communists—under the direction of Tito—entered the picture. In accordance with Moscow's orders to use all means to help ease the pressure on the Soviet Union, the Communist partisans launched wholesale attacks on the Germans, Italians, and Ustachi. Faced with the reality of an actual resistance battle, some Chetnik commanders joined with the partisans, and for a moment in the fall of 1941 the movement took on the form of a broad popular revolt. However, when the Germans resorted to savage reprisal, most of the Chetnik and Serbian military officers recoiled and left the bitter and continuous resistance battle to Tito.[51]

Unfortunately, the British government misunderstood what had happened in Yugoslavia during the summer and fall of 1941. Under the impact of distorted reports that reached Cairo and were probably embroidered there by officials of the Yugoslav government in exile, British officials in S.O.E., the Foreign Office, and at Number 10 Downing Street concluded that it was not Communists, but royalist officers, supposedly under the command of Gen. Draža Mihajlović who had produced the "revolt." On the basis of this mistaken impression—Mihajlović had never been very active against the Germans and did not exercise overall command of the Chetniks or the varied bands of royalist officers—the BBC welcomed Mihajlović as the first popular hero of the resistance forces that would free Europe from Nazism. This was especially unfortunate. It enraged the Yugoslav Communists, who knew that Mihajlović was neither a resister nor a coordinator of the movement but a conservative Serbian willing to collaborate with the Italians and, as it turned out, the Germans too, to prevent communist or Croatian successes. British eulogizing of Mihajlović, which was echoed in the United States, only increased the bitterness of the struggles raging within Yugoslavia.

But Britain was in too great need of an area for shadow warfare to delay. After hesitating briefly—some leaders felt the Yugoslav "revolt" might be premature—British authorities, led by Churchill and S.O.E., decided to support what they believed was a successful national uprising. By November, Dalton was rejoicing that Britain was committed to aid Mihajlović and that "Juggery" had come "to the top of the bill in view of the continuance of the revolt." Eden even hoped that the Soviets would see from this that "we are doing everything possible to create the second front in the Balkans which they desire."[52]

Initially, the Soviets went along with the British view, apparently doubting Tito's claim that he was doing the work while Mihajlović was collaborating with the Italians. By the end of 1941, however, Tito convinced Moscow that he was telling the truth, and there followed a Soviet denunciation of Mihajlović and his British supporters. But London was hungry for some kind of victory, too concerned with the Balkans, and too tied to the Yugoslav government in exile to back off. S.O.E. and the Foreign Office stumbled more deeply into the morass, supporting Mihajlović and proclaiming that in the Balkans popular resistance and British support had finally joined hands in a venture to lead Europe out of Nazi slavery.[53]

C.O.I. and the British

The stories out of Yugoslavia, coupled with signs that Britain's secret warfare system now had more punch, could not help but exert a powerful influence on Anglophile American officials such as Donovan. The director of C.O.I. not only had hitched his wagon to Britain's star but also had, from mid-1940, maintained close contact with British shadow warfare organizations. As these organizations became more efficient and powerful, their enhanced strength was manifest in the Americas through the agency of Stephenson's B.S.C. In the summer of 1941, when S.I.S. and, even more so, S.O.E. were looking for places to flex their muscles and give the Germans a small pummeling, B.S.C. offered welcome opportunities. S.I.S. carried out ever more extensive intelligence and counterintelligence operations with the F.B.I. in the Western Hemisphere, and S.O.E. was also active attacking German organizations and shortwave transmitters in Bolivia, Peru, and Colombia. When Donovan's C.O.I. was created, B.S.C. was provided with a further opportunity to expand its activities, especially in the realm of subversive, and counter, propaganda. July 1941 saw an enormous expansion of S.O. 1's subversive black propaganda operations within B.S.C. as a great deal of money was suddenly made available. C.O.I. now provided extra cover, doors opened that previously had been closed to B.S.C., and it is possible, considering that C.O.I. funds were unvouchered and that the details of B.S.C. financing will be one of the last secrets of the universe to be revealed, that some of S.O. 1's funds in the summer of 1941 came from Donovan.[54]

S.O. 1 had two goals in its Western Hemisphere operations: the "destruction of enemy propaganda in the United States" and Latin America, and the "exploitation of American prestige and neutrality by directing ostensibly American propaganda toward the three Axis powers and enemy-occupied territories." To carry out these objectives, every possible form of attack and deception was employed. On the domestic American front, the British cultivated journalists friendly to Britain, such as Dorothy Thompson, Walter Winchell, and Edgar Mowrer. Pro-British, or anti-Nazi publications, including the *Nation* and the *New Republic*, were courted, and additional overt propaganda was released through a series of British front organizations such as the League of Human Rights, the Friends of Democracy, and Dorothy Thompson's Ring of Freedom. Cover for Latin American, and some North American, operations was provided by the legitimate press service, British Overseas Features, as well as by Britanova, a second press service created solely to distribute subversive propaganda and to provide cover for S.O.E. agents in Latin America. Stephenson used all these channels to attack those in the Western Hemisphere who voiced sympathy for the Axis or expressed opposition to American aid to Britain.[55]

Formidable though the British subversive propaganda operations were in American domestic life, the "ostensibly American propaganda" aimed at Europe was far more extensive and elaborate. B.S.C. took surreptitious control of a shortwave radio station in Boston, WRUL, which was owned by Rockefeller interests and was used heavily in peacetime for Christian Science broadcasts. S.O. 1 gradually assumed operational direction of the station, first by secretly subsidizing three of the commentators to the tune of $400 per month, and then by directly paying for certain foreign language broadcasts. In close cooperation with the Carter organization and C.O.I.'s propaganda arm (F.I.S.), S.O. 1 created the impression that these broadcasts were produced not by the British government but by devoted groups of Americans determined to support freedom and attack the Nazis. The Fight for Freedom Committee was used as cover for some broadcasts, and an additional grouping whose members included Dorothy Thompson, William Shirer, Walter Deuel, and Edmund Taylor, was created to exercise general direction over the broadcasts until the United States government took control of them. As an S.O. 1 report noted, although "all these people are anxious to cooperate in every way," they were not told that they were serving the British government as a front group nor that there were any "connections between themselves and us." So successful was this whole operation that B.S.C. subsequently took over two additional stations on the West Coast, and C.O.I. gradually developed further "freedom" broadcasting operations of its own.[56]

A second covert propaganda program centered in America but aimed primarily at Europe was the rumor or "whispering" campaign. Some of the rumors were developed by S.O. 1 in London and the remainder were created by B.S.C. teams who drew for inspiration on the censorship interceptions that British security men were making in Bermuda. Since S.O. 1 had "effective control" of the Overseas News Agency, its rumors (or "sibs," in propaganda parlance) were turned over to the "news" group, which in turn transformed them into stories for distribution to the Allied and neutral press. Once a "sib" had appeared in print, it was considered by S.O. 1 as a "come back," and extra efforts were then made to extend its life by replanting it in the British press through the work of such men as C. V. R. Thompson of the *Daily Express*.[57] Great care was lavished on the "sibs," each of which had to be approved by the Foreign Office and the War Office before release. Most of the rumors were what one would expect, tales that Hitler was going mad or that the Prussian military elite was turning against him. Some were unintentionally comical, such as one released in September 1941 claiming that Britain had let loose 1,000 huge Australian sharks off the coast of Tunis. After victory on land, sea, and in the air had eluded her, the United Kingdom was left to shark warfare, with even the sharks an imaginary propaganda ploy.[58]

It would be a mistake to dismiss the British rumor mill as mere froth, however. Whether it undermined Axis morale or gave heart to those in the occupied territories is impossible to establish, but it certainly helped blur the line between reality and illusion. This was not an unequivocally beneficial contribution because the muddling of public opinion led to some questionable moral results. A grim example of this phenomenon is a series of sibs planted in 1941 meant to undermine German morale by indicating the desperate measures she was forced to take because of her great losses. Included in the campaign were rumors alleging that the Germans were "reduced to" using Jewish blood for transfusions on the eastern front and that doctors on that front were required to wear masks because "so many of them are now Jews." Another British rumor, which continued as a "come back" in the United States press in 1942, claimed that the Germans had failed before Leningrad because of a typhus epidemic among the troops, which had originated in the Warsaw Ghetto. At a time when Hitler—unbeknown to the British—was gearing up for "the final solution of the Jewish question" (in which gas chambers would be disguised as delousing baths), false stories that could confuse the minds of the victims as well as the torturers may have had tragic consequences. The killers needed rationalizations such as typhus epidemics spread by Jews. And the last thing the intended victims needed was uncertainty about what was happening in the east and what German policy toward Jews actually was. The British did not intend to smooth the path to the gas chambers, of course, but in looking for easy ways to score victories over an opponent that outmatched them in conventional weaponry, they courted disasters. As other rumors suggest, they also may have lost sight of the moral dimension of their activities.[59]

In September 1941, another series of rumors was prepared to entice German civilians onto the railroads. These indicated that fares were scheduled to rise in late October, that the railroads soon would be closed to civilian traffic, and that wives should take advantage of special fares in early October to visit "wounded husbands in places like Vienna and Dresden." The purpose of the campaign was simple, if sinister: the R.A.F. was preparing to attack the German railroad network on 15 October, and if masses of civilians could be drawn onto the trains by rumors, the resulting congestion would produce more inviting targets and more casualties.[60]

One may contend that since Germany had started the war and had engaged in frightful deeds, all countermeasures were justified. Such may, or may not, be sufficient to excuse all the elements of the rumor campaigns. Whatever one's point of view, B.S.C.'s part in this subversive warfare campaign was not some playful idyll or diversion pursued by humorous literati in New York. It was a dirty business, in the mainstream of the total war horror, and when the rumors took root, they produced casualties among both enemy civilians and inhabitants of Germany's occupied territories.

Such considerations are important to our story, because C.O.I. was first drawn into close collaboration with the British shadow warfare services through its cooperation with B.S.C. propaganda mills. Postwar accounts have deemphasized the importance of this cooperation in 1940–41, choosing instead to stress the thin line connecting C.O.I. with S.O.E. guerrilla warfare and with S.I.S. secret agent operations. In reality, Sherwood and Donovan cut their eye teeth in shadow warfare by participating with the British in covert propaganda activities. Donovan's men worked closely with B.S.C. officials in determining the content and form of C.O.I. broadcasts to Europe and Asia. In August, some S.O. 1 officials in London wished Sherwood to take charge of the whole Anglo-American sib campaign, but this idea was vetoed by Dalton. In October Donovan developed a scheme to erect a shortwave transmitter in Singapore to broadcast British and United States propaganda and by November, the colonel wanted the British Ministry of Information to arrange for the distribution of C.O.I. posters in Spain and for the R.A.F. to drop American leaflets into occupied Europe. On the eve of Pearl Harbor, Donovan was toying with the notion of sending an R.A.F. bomber over Germany to release additional American propaganda broadsides right on Berlin.[61]

A number of London officials found Donovan's ideas "somewhat remarkable." Information Minister Bracken thought the colonel's leaflet-dropping schemes "more of a stunt than a serious propaganda effort," and he wondered aloud what Sir Samuel Hoare would do if British M.O.I. officials started "pasting American posters on hoardings throughout Spain." But B.S.C. continued to stand behind C.O.I. and, with some hesitancy, so did S.O.E. and S.I.S. Dalton struggled manfully to overcome his dislike for Americans in general and Donovan in particular and even tried to get the colonel to visit Britain again. When that failed, he cooperated with William Whitney, whom Donovan had sent over with Franklin Roosevelt's approval in November to head a C.O.I. mission in London. Dalton was relieved to find Whitney quite quick and keen "for an American," and despite the doubts of British visitors to America who thought Donovan was "still in the stratosphere" and his position "not very strong," Dalton authorized B.S.C. to keep supplying him with information from British sources.[62]

The S.O.E. and S.I.S. information that flowed into Donovan's hands via B.S.C. was one of his most important assets. Donovan was careful to pass on some select items to the president, and thus established himself as a channel through which current British information could reach Roosevelt. Much of the information was routine, including memoranda on commando actions and British operations in the Mediterranean. There were, in addition, reports derived from more secret sources, such as one of 17 November 1941 on German morale, which had been distilled from a quarter of a million letters screened by the British censor in Bermuda. It is unlikely that any of the reports from this period derived from Ultra intercepts of German Abwehr messages, although Donovan later would receive material from this source via B.S.C.[63]

A number of the British items sent in by Donovan touched on matters that troubled the president, including a survey of the political situation in Argentina. On occasion Roosevelt responded favorably to a particular report, as he did on 7 November 1941 when he thanked Donovan for a copy of British diplomat Robert Vansittart's denunciation of Germany's "Black Record" and suggested that it be "revised for an American public." However, most of the memoranda passed into White House files without noticeable comment, even when they were wrong or made surprising assertions. Thus a 17 November report on German morale was filled with wild claims that "despair" and "misery" were rampant in the Third Reich and predicted that "one major setback" would leave German morale and the regime hanging "dangerously in the balance." Such fantasies did not prompt a "Dear Bill" note from Roosevelt, nor was there a reply when Donovan passed on a memorandum from Whitney on 12 November quoting an astounding remark by Churchill to the effect that after the war "German and *Russian* [italics added] militarism must be destroyed." How anyone in a disarmed America and a beseiged Britain could have hoped to do any such thing in November 1941 boggles the imagination, but Franklin Roosevelt received the memorandum in silence.[64]

In part, Donovan hoped that his conduit role with Roosevelt would serve, as he told Lord Halifax, to "strengthen the president's hands" by giving him ammunition to defend his policies against the isolationists. As both Donovan and Halifax understood, the colonel's "immediate access to the President" was a great strength. Through the Donovan channel, the British could keep "the President fully informed of their problems and difficulties" and Roosevelt would thereby be able "to exercise a favourable influence with his own service departments." In addition to his Anglophile enthusiasms, Donovan played the British game because through the B.S.C. he received some information worth transmitting. The colonel loved to act the part of confidant and special informant standing just outside the normal channels of government. With great relish he provided information to Roosevelt from every conceivable source, including German officials, and on occasion used the phrase "hot off the wire" in dead seriousness to indicate that a press service item was up to date. He also prided himself on being an idea man and sent the president a steady stream of proposals, such as one to establish an American corporation in the Azores as cover for an espionage operation. Because he was constantly active and had a personal information gathering network extending from London to the Foreign Policy Association, and from Edmund Taylor to John Foster Dulles, the colonel's information was interesting and provocative.[65]

Franklin Roosevelt loved such people. He enjoyed the banter, the exchanges, and the excitement of new ideas percolating in an effervescent mind. The president found most bureaucrats tiresome and his mischievous temperament relished opportunities to skip around them. Prior to Pearl Harbor, when the war situation was serious but the United States itself was not fully extended, Roosevelt had time to play at world politics and toy with strategic gimmicks. Donovan did not enter the presidential circle at the level of Hopkins or Early, but he gradually became a kind of Oval Office playmate who Roosevelt liked to meet to trade ideas about war and the American defense system. He met with Donovan frequently in late 1941, allowed his son James to join Donovan's organization, suggested other people who might be useful to C.O.I., gave a sympathetic ear to the colonel's reports and proposals, and, in general, enjoyed himself.[66]

It was a time when anything and everything seemed possible. On behalf of C.O.I., James Roosevelt even proposed to the president in November 1941 that the United States government should deliver a bomberload of medical supplies to Mihajlović, who he called "a modern [Francis] Marion." Since Yugoslavia was by then under Nazi occupation, and it would be six more months before the British managed even to determine where Mihajlović actually was hiding in the Yugoslav mountains, a more harebrained notion would be hard to imagine. But this was the kind of proposal that resulted from the Oval Office war games, and such developments set men like Henry Stimson and Cordell Hull to grumbling about people who had access to that office and just what went on there.[67]

Those who oiled the regular machinery of government were generally suspicious of Franklin Roosevelt's freewheeling methods, and many of them adopted a similar reserve toward Donovan. The colonel was hyperactive, mercurial, and assertive. Furthermore, his assignment, by its very nature, necessitated an expansionist attitude. He had to keep shoving and probing, exploiting his access to the White House, to extend his range of activities until he reached at least the outer boundaries of informational coordination. He was a new kind of official in a new kind of war, and it was inevitable that he would make others nervous. If he had been rather calmer, or better at administration, or a Democrat, things would have gone easier. His charm and his war record helped some, but they were not enough to offset a feeling that he was difficult to handle. His nickname, "Wild Bill," had originally referred to his incomparable personal bravery in World War I, but in the Washington of late 1941, it gradually took on an additional shading indicating that Donovan was erratic and unpredictable.[68]

Given the increasing caution and suspicion toward him shown by the regular bureaucrats, Donovan quite naturally found it easier to work with the president's other shadow operations. John Franklin Carter and Donovan were drawn together on a number of projects concerned with possible Axis subversion in America. It was Carter who sparked a concerted campaign in November 1941 to deal with what he called "the West Coast

Japanese situation," and under the direction of the president he developed a multidepartmental program to arrest Japanese "suspects" on the West Coast. Donovan and Carter agreed that when the day for general arrests came, Carter and the regular military and police authorities would do the investigation and arrests while the colonel would have the task of reassuring "loyal Japanese-Americans," and telling other Americans that the government had everything in hand.[69]

But the regular officials could not simply relegate Donovan to some kind of ghetto for unorthodox organizations. The colonel's links to the president, Knox, Stimson, and the British were too important, and many of the men and the projects gathered around Donovan in C.O.I. were potentially too useful to be ignored. Some might sneer at the "professors" in R. and A., but informational research could be valuable, especially to the military and naval intelligence units, which were chronically short of funds and personnel. Robert Sherwood may not have been an administrator of dazzling ability (in fact, he may have been even worse than Donovan), but overseas propaganda was an instrument that could have important uses. Most regular officials shared Donovan's belief that the nature of war had been changed not only through new weaponry but also through strategies of deception and subversive warfare. The colonel easily convinced such American diplomats as Spruille Braden of the Nazi fifth column threat in Latin America, and the F.B.I. joined happily with B.S.C. in chasing elusive, and generally nonexistent, Nazi subversives in both North and South America. O.N.I. and M.I.D., together with the F.B.I., were equally willing to cooperate in the Carter–Donovan operation for arrest of subversive Japanese-Americans because they believed in the existence and the danger of fifth columns. Donovan might be a threat in the bureaucratic wars, and he often seemed to go a bridge too far, but he appeared to many regular American officials to be on the right track when it came to intelligence coordination and the need for waging subversive warfare.[70]

In August, when the colonel raised the idea of preparing an American force to wage guerrilla warfare, Stimson was sympathetic and noted in his diary that "we are likely to need that kind of fighting in any South American jungle country . . . to prevent the Germans from getting a foothold" there. The G-2 liaison officer with C.O.I., Maj. M. Preston Goodfellow, was also favorably inclined, and through his efforts Donovan secured the services of Lt. Col. Robert Solborg (who had carried out the North African mission). On 9 October, Solborg was put in charge of Special Operations, or "L" activities, and given the title of chief of operations and special activities in the office of C.O.I. Despite British encouragement for

Donovan to create his own "organization for S.O.E." activities, the colonel had no formal American sanction to establish a special operations unit, and he therefore moved cautiously. Solberg was sent to England in late October to survey the British subversive warfare setup and, since the S.O.E. school in Canada was only just being organized, to receive training in the S.O.E. schools in the United Kingdom. But Solborg did not return to the United States until late December, and in the meantime Donovan discussed possible guerrilla warfare projects—including a bizarre scheme to send American guerrila leadership teams into China, Indochina, and Mongolia—with various American agencies. Such notions were not welcomed by the State Department, which feared adverse Soviet reactions in northern China and doubted whether "any Americans would be able to teach the Chinese much in the field of guerrilla warfare." C.O.I.'s special operations organization had therefore not moved beyond the stage of aspiration for the future and a formal title for Solborg prior to American entry into the war on 8 December 1941.[71]

More headway had been made by that time, however, in expanding the C.O.I.'s activities into the realm of secret intelligence. The United States government had no centralized undercover agent system, and in the fall of 1941 this was causing concern to the military. The amount of "secret intelligence" that could be generated by attachés abroad was limited, and the supplementary information developed by various other "undercover" operations in the Treasury, State, and Justice departments was of marginal military value. The War and Navy departments were under great pressure from Britain and the White House to improve the organization and operation of their intelligence machinery. At the same time those holding positions of power in O.N.I. and M.I.D. were reluctant to move too rapidly into the innovative and sensitive aspects of intelligence. In the fall of 1941, the War and Navy departments found an ideal solution to one segment of their intelligence problem by suggesting that Donovan and C.O.I. be given a monopoly on the difficult and, to many Americans, shady intelligence activity of running undercover agents outside the Western Hemisphere. Since the colonel was in the good graces of Secretary Knox, the president, and the British, such a move would help quiet criticism of the American military intelligence setup, and with his enthusiasm and energy, Donovan might be able to get around the public opinion problem and come up with something useful.[72]

Indeed, Donovan moved into the realm of secret intelligence with his usual energy. On 10 October 1941 he informed the president that, with army and navy approval, he was taking over all responsibility for undercover intelligence operations. He also outlined what would be necessary to create a network of organizers and agents that could gather information in neutral countries and continue to function as a "stay behind" operation if such areas were overrun by the Axis. In mid-October the colonel acquired the services of Wallace Phillips, who had developed an undercover operation for O.N.I. In November, Phillips was made chief of the secret intelligence, or "K" section, of C.O.I. He controlled a handful of agents who had been placed in diplomatic missions, chiefly in Mexico, to gather information for the navy under State Department cover. This group formed the nucleus of the overseas cadre that Donovan hoped to expand quickly into a full-scale C.O.I. intelligence network. As the colonel told Phillips, although he wanted agents to be put in place who could later be used if necessary as sabotage operatives, secret intelligence and special operations were to be kept strictly separate from each other, and intelligence was to be given first priority. This was analogous to the British system in which S.I.S. and S.O.E. were sharply divided with priority given to S.I.S. In Britain, though, the two wings were placed under different ministers of the crown, while Donovan desired to keep them both inside C.O.I.[73]

In his memorandum to the president of 10 October, Donovan indicated that he intended to focus first on secret intelligence operations in North Africa. Vice consuls, who had been sent in to watch over American imports to the French colonies and ensure that this trade did not benefit the Axis, had been made partly responsible to Phillips and these men offered fertile ground for creation of a large espionage chain. Roosevelt did not veto this idea, but by instructing Donovan to check over his whole secret intelligence scheme with the State Department, he did signal the colonel that he had better move carefully. The vice consuls in North Africa, together with Carter's operatives, and the regular consular officers, were all under some measure of State Department authority and were all engaged in aspects of intelligence. Donovan understood the president's implicit warning of caution, and as Lord Halifax reported to London, the colonel was "proceeding slowly in the exercise of his power for the reason that too abrupt a call upon the state and service departments might result in raising an opposition within those departments and hampering his activities."[74]

In fact, Donovan proceeded so cautiously that at the time of Pearl Harbor his secret intelligence activities were little further advanced than the paper plans for C.O.I.'s special operations section. On 7 December 1941, C.O.I. was still primarily an organization made up of F.I.S. and R. and A. branches, each with its own special problems. R. and A.'s analysis function was already stillborn and F.I.S. was caught up in serious jurisdictional conflicts. Various small photographic and interview units were extant, secret intelligence ("K") had been authorized; the Foreign Nationalities Branch was still awaiting final approval; and ("L") was a label without an organization or formal authorization to back it up.

Then war came on 8 December 1941, and C.O.I. was suddenly presented with the task of proving that it could develop rapidly and make itself useful as part of the total war machine that had to be created.

CHAPTER 3

C.O.I. at War:
December 1941-June 1942

> The C.O.I. "is an amorphous group of
> activities which has developed out of the
> personality of Colonel Donovan."
>
> DAVID BOWES-LYON AND RITCHIE CALDER
> TO LONDON
> *14 April 1942*

The Post–Pearl Harbor Frenzy

December 1941: Wake, Guam, and Hong Kong Fall
February 1942: Singapore surrenders

COMING EIGHTEEN MONTHS after the fall of France, Pearl Harbor
was the second, and loudest, thunderclap to strike the American people
during the Second World War. Whatever the sins of omission, or commission, committed by the United States government prior to Pearl Harbor,
no one had foreseen an imminent assault on U.S. soil. The Japanese attack
on the Hawaiian islands stunned and momentarily bewildered the American population, but above all it drew them together like a tribal clan. The
long debates and discussions of neutrality, isolation, and pacifism ended

abruptly, and without need for a vote or a public opinion poll the people gave the government a mandate to enter the war, mobilize the country, and smash the Axis.

That reaction was in itself a decisive turning point in the war because it came to a country that had the capability (made reality within four years) of mobilizing 12 million men while simultaneously financing an enormous war and continuing to operate a civilian economy. Occurring at the very moment that Hitler's armies were stopped in front of Moscow, the American unity generated by Pearl Harbor proclaimed that the pendulum had swung to the Allied side. If East and West held together and managed their assets with even minimal ability, it seemed, they must win the war. Even Hitler, in his dark and murky way, appears to have sensed that this was really the beginning of the end. Checked by Stalin in the east, he declared war on the United States before the Americans had a chance to declare war on him and at the same time leapt into the pit of ultimate horror by beginning his full-scale "final solution of the Jewish question." Though Stalin, with the Nazis still at his throat, prudently declined to declare war on Japan (who reciprocated in kind by remaining at peace with the U.S.S.R.), for everyone else it was a war to the knife between all the Axis and all the Allies. The Germans had the initiative and the largest land forces at that moment, but the Allies had resources, manpower, and time on their side.

In the days immediately following 7 December 1941, it was difficult to keep all this in perspective. Americans were jolted by what had occurred at Pearl Harbor, had trouble accepting that it really had happened, and were unsure what was going to turn up next. Ballyhoo and nervous bravado characterized the first weeks of war. There was also suspicion that "subversives" had played a part in the Japanese success and that such shadow forces might produce further shocks and disasters. This reaction is quite understandable in a population that had been suckled on stories of Axis fifth columns. The press was full of scare stories, chronicling alleged acts of espionage and sabotage. The F.B.I. and other police forces gathered up "the usual suspects," often involving the wrong people and the wrong places in capers reminiscent of the Keystone Cops. Old and tainted war horses, including refugee German politicians Heinrich Brüning and Otto Strasser, were now listened to as if they were oracles when they confided to American officials that the United States needed "grim realism" and a willingness to "fight Hitler with his own weapons—propaganda, Fifth Column, and so on." Even a tough-headed observer like Hugh Dalton found it hard to keep a clear view of what was going on in the Western Hemisphere from his vantage point thousands of miles away in

London. On 1 February 1942, he mused in his diary that although the fifth column stories, especially from Latin America, might be "unreasonably" dramatic, "can one be sure and is one not running great risks in doing so little?"[1]

For the special intelligence and security organizations that Roosevelt had created in the course of 1941, the post–Pearl Harbor atmosphere provided a field day. John Franklin Carter immediately asked for more "operatives" and more money because he was busy checking "on certain groups in this country." As the Bureau of the Budget noted, the F.B.I. was even busier, for it was watching the same groups and Carter's "operatives" as well. Some of Donovan's people also rapidly entered into the business of keeping domestic "subversives" under surveillance. It was a · C.O.I. source who fed confidential information to the War Department on the efforts of Lindbergh and his friends to salvage something from the wreckage of the America First Movement. Donovan also explored schemes for using American workmen of Czech, Yugoslav, and Polish extraction, who were "trustworthy" because of "their hatred of Hitler," as informers to protect American defense factories against espionage and subversion. Donovan's labor surveillance ideas were so extreme that even the attorney general and J. Edgar Hoover thought they smacked of "vigilantism."[2]

Officials of C.O.I. were just as quick to make use of the new atmosphere to turn ostensibly foreign information gathering activities into measures for increasing domestic control. In early March 1942, Ralph Bunche of R. and A. proposed recruiting African students in the United States as espionage agents for use in their homelands—a suggestion that makes one wince, but was certainly within the mandate of a secret intelligence organization. Its limits were clearly exceeded, however, when John Wiley (who had just been made chief of the new C.O.I. Foreign Nationalities Branch, F.N.B.), seconded Bunche's suggestion and added that such African recruits could also "supply invaluable data on the extent of communist propaganda emanating from educated negroes in this country."[3]

Notions such as these seem to have contributed to Roosevelt's nervousness about the whole idea of F.N.B., which had been set up to gather information within the United States for use in waging war abroad, and in early 1942, the president restricted its activities somewhat. But pursuing subversives had by then become part of the government's calling. In April 1942, Donovan chalked up what must be close to a world's record in irregular and bizarre operations to control domestic subversion. The colonel arranged to receive information on alleged Axis agents and subversives from Eugene Dennis, secretary of the American Communist Party, and then, as he reported to the president, he "promptly" turned this information over to the F.B.I. "without disclosing the identity of our source!"[4]

When the Communist Party could give American government officials information on subversive dangers and a United States government agency could pass that information on to J. Edgar Hoover without telling him where it came from, anything was possible. Security had become everyone's business, and in early 1942 the president showed himself as gullible as anyone else. Reports passed on by Donovan to the effect that hoards of saboteurs were about to descend on American shores, where they would be received by "the widespread German SA and SS *Standarten*" which supposedly existed in the United States, were taken seriously by the White House. In the same period that a high State Department official contended that all radio announcers should be licensed "so that only loyal persons have an opportunity to make their voices heard," Edmund Taylor of C.O.I. recommended that the agency send teams of "reporter-propagandists" abroad who would be more "subject to discipline" than ordinary news people, and would report the news in ways most useful to the government.[5]

The basic rights and freedoms of all Americans were in peril at this time, but those of Japanese-Americans were the most threatened and the most seriously abridged. The "sneak" attack on Pearl Harbor and the subsequent rapid Japanese advance in Asia, when coupled with shock and humiliation, were enough to convince many government officials that all their troubles were the result of some heinous plan hatched by Japanese subversives. Three weeks after Pearl Harbor, for example, the liberal secretary of the interior, Harold Ickes, seriously suggested that the pattern of Japanese propaganda in the Philippines since Pearl Harbor had convinced him that the work of anti-American Filipino agitators had "for many years back . . . been inspired by the Japanese." In the same period, Donovan sent to the White House a number of "unconfirmed" newspaper reports that hoards of Japanese soldiers in disguise were lurking south of the border in Baja California just waiting for a chance to jump on San Diego.[6]

Yet in the rising tide of government repression of Japanese-Americans, culminating in the forced removal and internment of the whole West Coast Japanese-American population in April 1942, Donovan's organization played a modest and quite balanced role. Donovan worked hard to improve Hawaiian radio communications as a protection against renewed attack and an onslaught of subversive propaganda. When the Japanese internment order came, he prudently, if rather cynically, moved his West Coast Japanese-American translators to Colorado. (The navy did likewise with its translators.) But Donovan's personal involvement was chiefly as a funnel through which reports on what to do about Japanese-American "subversive dangers" reached the president. At least two of these reports, originating from prominent subordinates, were indeed genuine horrors. Atherton Richards wanted to turn the island of Hawaii into a work camp—an "obligatory rendezvous" for "doubtful Japanese," he called it. John Ford, who was in Hawaii making a C.O.I. film on Pearl Harbor, penned an outrage, which was passed to the president, saying he "honestly" believed that the majority of Japanese-Americans were "tainted" and deserved to have no mercy shown. He also was sure that the widely circulated figure of 600 Japanese agents on Oahu was much too low. Everywhere Ford looked, "most of the key positions" in Hawaii were held by "Japs," and he was ready to believe that the number of spies was really "triple that figure." Not everyone in C.O.I. agreed with such ravings. Men like Ford were seen by some of their colleagues as rather daft; Joseph Hayden once privately remarked, in expressing his doubts about the hotheads in C.O.I., "knowing Ford tells you a lot about this particular movie."[7]

Regarding the Japanese subversive scare, and other tense occasions, Donovan's role as purveyor of assorted information to the president probably worked to temper the atmosphere. On 15 December he forwarded to Roosevelt a series of comments by John Steinbeck that concluded that "there was no reason so far to suspect the loyalty of Japanese-American citizens." Steinbeck wanted to give the nisei the self-policing job of making the "loyal Japanese responsible for the disloyal." This idea would have made some Japanese-Americans shoulder a heavy burden of conflicting loyalties, but it was far less drastic than mass internment, and it rested on a belief in the fundamental patriotism of the vast majority of the Japanese-American people. In February 1942, Donovan sent the president an even more ardent defense of the view that the Japanese-American community was loyal and should be left in peace. This one came from a most surprising source, Gen. Ralph Van Deman, the chief of American military intelligence in World War I, and one of the fathers of the American anti-Communist crusade. Van Deman had caught wind of the government's internment plans. Stressing in a three-page memorandum that "so far the Pacific Coast has had little hysteria," he labeled the notion of mass removal unnecessary, impractical, and "about the craziest proposition that I have heard of yet."[8]

These restrained voices, as we know, were not heeded and the entire West Coast Japanese-American population was herded into internment camps in April 1942. But it must be emphasized that amid the fifth column paranoia, and despite the preparation of emergency prewar internment plans for a select group of Japanese-Americans by Donovan and Carter, their organizations kept much cooler heads on the issue than did most of the authorities in Washington or Sacramento. In February 1942, it was not a civil libertarian in the Justice Department but Curtis Munson of the Carter organization who warned Roosevelt that "we are drifting into a treatment of the Japanese corresponding to Hitler's treatment of Jews."[9]

However, Donovan did not do so well in regard to another controversial matter in the immediate post–Pearl Harbor period. America was not yet adequately prepared with modern weapons and trained forces to fight a successful war both in Europe and across the Pacific, and the United States was being whipped in 1942. The American people did not like it and wanted a dramatic counterattack. By April 1942, G-2 was pleading for a foreign and domestic propaganda campaign to discourage the clamor for an Allied offensive because it rested on "a misconception of military capabilities." But Donovan, who was supposed to be in charge of American foreign propaganda broadcasts, had no sympathy for such views. Defeat was simply intolerable to him, and instead of putting his energy into calming unreasonable public expectations, he used his role as "idea man" to recommend to the president a series of madcap schemes for offensive operations.[10]

Within ten days of the Japanese attack on Hawaii, the colonel urged Roosevelt to create an American air strike unit, "an independent force of cavalry under modern conditions," to bring immediate havoc to the Axis. He also told the president that it would be a good idea to repeat the British 1940 escapade at Oran by making a surprise attack on the Vichy French fleet. The colonel assumed that the French fleet would go over to the Germans sooner or later, so to his mind an Anglo-American raid on the French (when the Allies could net few other victories) would be beneficial "both from a morale and strategic standpoint." Undeterred by the overwhelming Japanese air and naval supremacy that resulted from Pearl Harbor, Donovan by mid-January was trying to persuade Roosevelt to use half the remaining American Pacific Fleet and a force of 10,000 to 15,000 American commandos (which did not exist) for an "out of the blue" strike against the Japanese home island of Hokkaido. In February, Donovan advised the White House that Alaska was the ideal place from which to attack Japan, leading Secretary Stimson to grumble two days later about Donovan's effort to "butt into" the army's project to build a road to Alaska (the Alkan highway).[11]

In this period of extreme national emergency, nothing was too outlandish for the colonel. He sent the president a memorandum on the wonders of using plywood for building pipelines and also urged him to sign a photograph for King Saud so C.O.I. emissaries to the Middle East would be able to spread word of the power and goodness of America throughout the British-dominated region. When Secretary of State Hull washed his hands of efforts to lure the Irish government into granting bases to the United States, Donovan, who had been dabbling with the Irish base question, took up the matter in earnest. Opening his effort on 3 January with the fawning remark that the president knew more about the Irish "than anyone else," he asked permission to play an aggressive hand under Roosevelt's direction. Even when the president replied that nothing should be done "at this time," Donovan returned in early February, forwarding a suggestion that Errol Flynn be sent to Ireland to act as a public relations and intelligence agent for C.O.I. Roosevelt was not keen on this idea either, despite the additional efforts of Wallace Deuel and Flynn himself to push the proposal. By late March, Donovan's Irish efforts finally petered out.[12]

No sooner had Ireland and Errol Flynn been sent out one door, however, then Ambassador William Bullitt and Otto of Habsburg (the pretender to the Austrian Imperial throne) were brought in through another. On 26 March, Donovan recommended to the president that Otto be received at the White House so he could present a scheme for contacting possible pro-Allied groups in Hungary. Since the Habsburgs were anathema to the Czechs and Yugoslavs as well as to the Soviets, the proposal was both silly and highly dangerous politically. Under Secretary of State Sumner Welles was horrified when he heard the idea, and State Department pressure soon forced Donovan to abandon the proposal, which he plaintively pleaded had been raised only as a favor to his friend William Bullitt.[13]

While considering these frequently bizarre post–Pearl Harbor schemes of Donovan, it is germane to remember that in such a game there is a catcher as well as a pitcher. Franklin Roosevelt thrived on genteel intrigue, and he was in an uncommonly delicate position in early 1942. The country was finally united for war, but Pearl Harbor had hardly been one of the administration's finest hours. There was a severe shortage of modern military equipment and an equal deficiency in trained fighting personnel. Proposals for miraculous triumphs were therefore very welcome, and the military as well as the president were willing to give an ear to virtually anything. When John Franklin Carter suggested in early January that Japan might literally be reduced to ashes by bombing her volcanoes, Army Air Corps Chief of Staff Gen. Henry "Hap" Arnold replied that he did "not feel that this suggestion can be dismissed without serious examination." Arnold promised the White House that as soon as opportunity permitted, the idea would be investigated and "given every consideration." In such an environment, it was easy for Roosevelt to give free rein to his imagination and that of William Donovan.[14]

The colonel knew how to play on the president's special loves. He sent maps, stamps, and reports on remote areas of the world to the White House, keyed to Roosevelt's interest in geography. The president, in return, sometimes told his thoughts to Donovan, and also requested the colonel's assistance in developing a number of peculiar notions. Within a week of Pearl Harbor, Roosevelt asked Donovan to help him find "some old law" that would allow the government to confiscate the property of American citizens who were "working for enemy governments." Franklin Roosevelt had such ample capacity for sustaining outlandish thoughts on his own that in 1944, two years after Donovan's original suggestion regarding Otto of Habsburg, the president was still considering the possibility of assisting a restoration in Hungary even though everyone else—including Donovan—had long abandoned such madness.[15]

Consequently, although Donovan certainly caused his own problems by intruding into the domains of other departments of the government to improve his position as idea man for the president, much of the responsibility for his behavior lay in the Oval Office. Even though the president gradually tired of the colonel's combativeness (in April 1942 he told Adolf Berle that he was considering putting Donovan "on some nice, quiet, isolated island where he could have a scrap with some Japs every morning before breakfast . . . [and] would be out of trouble and be entirely happy"), it is still true that the president wins the palm for the craziest idea that surfaced during the Roosevelt-Donovan exchanges of 1942. Soon after Pearl Harbor, the president received a memorandum from a Mr. Adams of Irwin, Pennsylvania, contending that the Japanese people were mortally afraid of bats. Mr. Adams recommended that the United States launch a "surprise attack" on Japan by dropping bats on the home islands, thereby "frightening, demoralizing and exciting the prejudices of the people of the Japanese Empire." On 9 February 1942, the president sent Adams's memorandum to Donovan together with a note stating that "this man is *not* a nut." While conceding that "it sounds like a perfectly wild idea," Roosevelt told the colonel that it was "worth your looking into." True to orders, Donovan recruited the curator of the division of mammals of the American Museum of Natural History, and also involved the army air corps, to work on the Adams proposal. Without anyone checking to see if the Japanese lived in mortal terror of bat attack—they apparently didn't—experiments in catapulting parachuted bats through space were carried on by the air corps and C.O.I.–O.S.S. for a number of years and were abandoned only when the uncooperative bats persisted in freezing to death in high-altitude aircraft.[16]

Compared with the bat project, the majority of C.O.I. reports were reasonable. William Langer of R. and A. tried to provide the president with periodic supplements to keep him current on C.O.I.'s more important studies, such as those concerned with German military manpower. Some of this material was of only marginal value for presidential decision making, but none of the R. and A. studies submitted by Donovan or Langer were frivolous.[17]

The Colonel also dispatched to the White House a bewildering range of intelligence and press reports on everything from India's willingness to resist the Japanese to a paper on the Society Islands prepared by Charles Nordoff of the popular writing team Nordoff and Hall. Some important and accurate reports were included, especially those derived from travelers just returned from Germany. One in particular, based on the experiences of an American banker who left Berlin in November 1941, correctly charted German conditions and even contained a description of the Jewish deportation process.[18]

Many of the documents that arrived on Roosevelt's desk over Donovan's signature had originated from British sources. The colonel was not quite as close to Stephenson as he had been before Pearl Harbor, but C.O.I. received much material from B.S.C., the British embassy, and the C.O.I. representative in London. A steady fortnightly flow of secret surveys of British public opinion prepared by the Home Office, together with regular reports from the Ministry of Economic Warfare, the B.S.C., the M.O.I., the P.W.E., and the British Joint Intelligence Committee (J.I.C.), reached the president via Donovan in the winter and spring of 1942. At a time when American intelligence gathering was poor, such British surveys were extremely useful, and indeed were a unique gesture in inter-Allied cooperation, considering they were provided by a government notoriously secretive about its intelligence operations.[19]

Donovan also supplied the president with material that came from British secret agents, the screenings of the British censor, and "the highest secret sources." Included among these items was one drawn from the letters of a German Catholic sister who chronicled the persecution of the German churches and mentioned the "terrible" conditions facing "non-aryans" and the "terrible things" which the Gestapo had done in Poland. Most of the reports drawn from such sources (one may have been derived from an Ultra decrypt of the French codes) were not on mortally important subjects, however, nor were they particularly accurate. An early 1942 report from the British censor pointed to a mythical German threat to invade Spain, and an item from a "highest secret source" grossly exaggerated the success of Laval's December 1941 effort to produce a full Vichy-German partnership.[20]

But such errors, and the fact that Donovan also sent Roosevelt reports that denigrated British prospects in the battle of Egypt and condemned her "reactionary" Greek policies, cannot gainsay that, next to the State Department, C.O.I. was the main channel through which useful British intelligence regularly reached the president. Roosevelt valued many of the items of British origin, including one woefully inaccurate appraisal of German intentions made by John Wheeler Bennett, and in some cases, such as Bennett's report, ordered that the material be used in developing American operational plans.[21]

This points up one of the major difficulties with the flow of material that Donovan sent to the White House. Much of it was simply incorrect. The Japanese were not preparing to run convoys to Chile, as he reported in April, and the Germans were not going to invade England or Spain, as he predicted in May. In addition to reports flawed by error, many of Donovan's proposals—such as one recommending that advertisements proclaiming the Four Freedoms be placed in Indian newspapers—were embarrassingly naive. Since the colonel insisted on continually sending Roosevelt statements made by hopelessly discredited characters, such as Otto Strasser, it must have been difficult even for the president to take a large portion of them seriously. No matter how much the president enjoyed the game, Donovan consistently went too far. He never provided evaluations with his reports, they frequently contradicted each other, and the many trivial bits of information he forwarded could only waste Roosevelt's time. Despite his great energy and playfulness, the president had more important things to do in the spring of 1942 than study items such as the subversive musical lyrics that Donovan's propaganda brain trust intended to direct at the sailors of the Vichy fleet.[22]

Many of Donovan's operational schemes for subversive warfare were also frequently bizarre or too clever by half. In January 1942, he thought it a grand idea to publicly announce that the Japanese intended to attack Singapore or the Panama Canal, and when they failed to do so, to proclaim that this "failure" was the turning point of the war. When the president referred Donovan's proposal to Adm. Ernest J. King and Gen. George Marshall, they replied on 21 January that the situation was so unstable that no point was really safe from Japanese attack, and that it was best not openly to invite the enemy to go in any direction. The military command in Washington was also not enthusiastic about Donovan's late December proposal to use "a man" he had in Manila to establish a "stay-behind" system in the Phillippines in the event of Japanese occupation. To implement such a plan, Gen. Douglas MacArthur's approval would have been necessary, and Washington had already decided that the general was not someone on whom one should try to press unwelcome suggestions. So C.O.I.'s Philippine underground program, though it had nominal presidential approval, remained stillborn in the president's files along with the colonel's plan to grab the Cape Verde Islands from Portugal and his scheme to undermine Fascist Italy by flooding the country with counterfeit currency.[23]

But some of Donovan's more orthodox operational suggestions did pay off, including one to transfer the California College in China to the Berkeley campus of the University of California, using supplemental C.O.I. funding. The $36,000 provided by C.O.I. for this purpose was one of the first occasions in which an American intelligence organization subsidized an academic institution to get the "various types of training and instruction" it desired—in this case mainly Chinese language classes—into a university curriculum.[24]

The Organizational Fate of C.O.I. and the Creation of O.S.S.

Colonel Donovan and C.O.I. did fairly well in some aspects of their effort to expand the scope of the organization's activities in the weeks immediately following Pearl Harbor. In the go-ahead atmosphere that then prevailed, every organization tried to stake out a wide zone of activity and authority. Jurisdictional conflicts inevitably occurred and old rivalries and jealousies were exacerbated. The State, War, and Navy departments were strongly opposed to "encroachment" on their turf by any of the emergency wartime bureaus and agencies. In January 1942, Assistant Secretary of State Berle confided to Carter that if Donovan was a "personal friend" of his he would be doing him a favor to "advise him" to concentrate on his propaganda and intelligence jobs "before reaching out for new fields" to conquer. State warned its consulates to apply great caution in use of C.O.I. propaganda materials because they were the work of amateurs and not always attuned to the sensitivities of the areas to which they were directed. A diplomat stationed in Liberia characterized the typical C.O.I. representative as a "Hollywood comic sleuth" who was "as confidential as a foghorn" in his "rousing game of cops and robbers."

Old, dour, foreign service hands like Breckenridge Long grumbled that one of the "most important things" that needed "to be controlled" during the war was Donovan.[25]

Nonetheless, the colonel established an effective program for censoring shortwave broadcasts, and C.O.I. spearheaded the creation of the Interdepartmental Committee for the Collection of Foreign Periodicals (I.D.C.), which by March was operating under the chairmanship of R. and A.'s William Langer. Donovan also succeeded in beating back efforts of those who contended that the economic work of R. and A. should be abolished because it overlapped with work done by the Board of Economic Warfare (B.E.W.), and he further managed to obtain a place for C.O.I. on the Censorship Board.[26]

Not all the bureaucratic skirmishes were won by C.O.I., and not all of the victories it did secure were achieved without cost. Donovan's reputation as a pushy and expansive man who hatched crazy ideas had not diminished. Some of his triumphs, such as the acquisition of a seat on the Censorship Board, were won because the White House staff thought it not "very important" and "it would please Donovan to give him the green light" on something. But C.O.I. was also becoming more efficient and professional, and the colonel succeeded quite well in using the emergency atmosphere of early 1942 to recruit able officials for his organization. Like every other agency chief in Washington, his life was made "miserable" by managerial job seekers, but he eluded most of the really atrocious candidates and put together a relatively efficient bureaucratic team. Secretary Knox continued to provide Donovan with strong backing, and Stimson noted in his diary in mid-January that he was "impressed" by the possibilities and "usefulness" of C.O.I.[27]

But the Donovan organization was nonetheless in a highly vulnerable position, spread thinly over a wide range of activities that bore directly on the war effort. Propaganda, intelligence, and subversive warfare were all important matters that would have to be developed in the course of America's rapid mobilization. Why they should be left in Donovan's hands, especially since little besides R. and A. and F.I.S. were anything but labels in early 1942, was not readily apparent. C.O.I. was simply a jumble of activities that had sprouted out of the colonel's personality. Despite the later efforts of many O.S.S. veterans and C.I.A. advocates to show that all C.O.I. activities were part of the Donovan master plan, there was neither rhyme nor reason to view this particular bundle of C.O.I. focuses as the rightful preserve of any special organization. The colonel's original proposal for one organization to handle information gathering and radio propaganda had never made much sense, and the pre-Pearl

Harbor bureaucratic wars and Donovan's enthusiasm and expansionism had not increased internal cohesion. C.O.I. was in the movie trade but was not allowed to touch domestic propaganda; it could do informational research but not formulate final analyses; it had a monopoly on secret intelligence operations but cooperated only minimally with M.I.D. and O.N.I. Such an odd agglomeration of limited activities cried out for partition and reorganization at a time when the United States had to concentrate its assets and produce a real military machine.

Donovan's organization survived, with only the marginal loss of F.I.S. in early 1942, because of three major factors: actions taken by the British, the hesitant but ultimately supportive role of the Chiefs of Staff of the U.S. Army and Navy, and a last-minute decision by the president. C.O.I.'s survival was a very close call, however, and to survey even briefly why it weathered the storm and lived on as O.S.S. after June 1942, we must look closely at these three factors.

The British Role

> March 1942: Japan closes the Burma Road into China; successful British commando raid on St. Nazaire

The Japanese attacks of December 1941 made in conjunction with that on Pearl Harbor produced a series of new defeats and humiliations for Britain. Hong Kong and the Southeast Asian colonies were lost, as were vital ships such as the *Repulse* and the *Prince of Wales*. The surrender of Singapore, where a large British defense force capitulated to a smaller Japanese offensive army, was probably the most bitter disgrace in the military history of the United Kingdom. All of these developments weakened Britain's military capabilities, shook the ground beneath the Churchill government and reinforced the impression of many observers that the United Kingdom had shown itself incapable of waging successful war against the Axis.

Offsetting these negative considerations, however, was the overwhelmingly positive fact that Pearl Harbor brought the United States into the war. In view of the special relationship that existed between London and Washington, Britain was now safe and could use its "seniority" in the war to guide the development and deployment of American forces in ways that would favor British interests. The United Kingdom had not achieved much in offensive operations since 1939, but it had added to its glory by struggling on alone through "one full year of mortal peril." By early 1942, Bomber Command was beginning to show its capacity for inflicting real damage on German-occupied territories of western Europe and on western Germany itself. The Battle of the Atlantic was still touch and go, and the U-boats had found a new happy hunting ground along the American coast after Pearl Harbor, but the long-range odds were on the side of the Allies. The first months of 1942 saw a new British drive into Libya, which Rommel would contain all too soon but which at its start looked promising.

Furthermore, Britain seemed to have mastered many of the mysteries of secret warfare. Possession and development of the Ultra secret was a clear plus for the United Kingdom. Her ability to read Luftwaffe, Abwehr, and other assorted codes was greatly enhanced by early 1942, and significant headway also had taken place in breaking German Navy and Army ciphers. Along with Ultra, which was known only to a narrow ring within Britain and to an even smaller circle in the United States, Britain possessed other instruments of shadow warfare, including the commandos; the propaganda machinery of P.W.E., M.O.I., and S.O. 1; and the resistance networks presided over by S.O.E. All of these added up to a machinery for conducting irregular warfare, which looked so highly formidable that it made a deep impression on world public opinion and on various political leaders from Hitler to William Donovan.

In actuality, once the romance and promotional exaggeration were discounted, the British special warfare system (with the exception of Ultra), was more potential than actual. Propaganda had not made a dent in German morale, and even the defeat before Moscow and America's entry into the war does not seem to have convinced a sizable portion of the German people that the war was lost. The Wehrmacht was still too strong, the luster of the early blitzkrieg victories still too dazzling, and the faith in Adolf Hitler still too intense to weaken German faith in a positive outcome of the war. The threat to Germany's continental hegemony from British Combined Operations also proved, as yet, to be hollow. Despite the best efforts of Lord Mountbatten and the great bravery of British commando units in limited operations such as that on St. Nazaire, the Germans showed in the spring of 1942 at Dieppe that they were more than a match for Britain's combined operations.

Although British authorities managed to keep knowledge of the fact from their American colleagues, everything was not well with their resistance support operations either. The bureaucratic war over control of subversive warfare had reached such proportions in London by February 1942 that British officials were "fighting each other instead of the enemy

... with such zest," Dalton wrote, "that we just don't deserve to win the war." P.W.E. and S.O.E. were at each other's throats and S.O.E.'s relations with S.I.S., the Foreign Office, and the War Office were also poor. In late February, as part of a general shuffling of cabinet posts, Churchill finally "just plunged," and without consulting anyone else, moved Dalton to the Board of Trade and brought in Lord Selborne, a conservative political ally of the prime minister, as minister of economic warfare. For a while government leaders considered either breaking up S.O.E. or transferring it from the Ministry of Economic Warfare to the War or Foreign office, but both options were allowed to slip by. Instead, Lord Selborne tried some internal reorganization, which was insufficient, however, and Foreign Office officials continued to be plagued by "interminable S.O.E. worries" while the system rattled on.[28]

Having failed to emasculate S.O.E., the War and Foreign offices did their best to make it harmless by imposing tight controls and restrictions. The Chiefs of Staff reiterated their insistence that all S.O.E. operations in Europe be supportive of "that day" when limited or full-scale invasion forces would attack the continent. Aid to resistance "secret armies" was to have second priority to a strengthening of sabotage and espionage organizations in France, the low countries, and Norway. Even sabotage operations were to be employed selectively so the main potential could be held in reserve to support the day of invasion. S.O.E. was thereby forced to try to organize a massive secret sabotage network with such a high pitch of discipline that it would follow orders perfectly, patiently carrying out only selected acts of sabotage while waiting for the real day of reckoning to arrive. This was not a happy situation for S.O.E., since the Germans were busy carrying out reprisals and trying to penetrate the resistance networks. Moreover, even after the Americans entered the war, years would go by before the Western powers would be capable of mounting a major invasion. But the Chiefs of Staff held to their policy of a slow, restrained resistance buildup, and since their services controlled the sources of weapons and the aircraft necessary to deliver them, the chiefs could make their demands stick.[29]

The Foreign Office also imposed restrictions on S.O.E., insisting in a "treaty" of 3 March 1942 that Selborne's organization should act only under Foreign Office supervision and control in "sensitive" areas such as the neutral territories and unoccupied (Vichy) France. Foreign Office officials did not consider even this limitation enough, since they believed Selborne to be "ponderous and tiresome (rather)," an easy mark for S.O.E. buccaneers who wanted to take big chances.[30]

The spring of 1942 indeed produced a fiesta of S.O.E. indiscretions.

There were political intrigues in Peru, complaints from the Turkish government, more arming of dissident Spaniards and Portuguese, and a delightful incident in Tangier in February when an S.O.E. arms smuggling enterprise literally blew up in public. S.O.E. might fairly maintain that it had been ordered by the Chiefs of Staff to expand activities in Turkey and North Africa, and officers of other British secret organizations might agree that the Foreign Office was too cautious and ambassadors in neutral countries were "ever-reluctant." But the Foreign Office believed that the primary aim of British policy was to keep the neutrals reasonably happy so as not to add them to the list of Britain's enemies, at a time when she was unable to cope successfully with the ones she already had. Parenthetically, we should note that one year later O.S.S. would get into similar trouble with the State Department and the U.S. Joint Chiefs of Staff in the same areas—the Iberian peninsula and Turkey—for the same reasons. The British Foreign Office dealt with the problem in the spring of 1942 (as the State Department would in 1943) by imposing ever more stringent controls. S.O.E. was compelled to keep the Foreign Office fully informed of all its activities, was not allowed to act in any neutral areas without Foreign Office approval, and was to do nothing in the Western Hemisphere, "where foreign policy issues predominate," except "in co-operation with an authority duly constituted by the United States Government." By early summer, P.W.E. had joined in the attack on S.O.E., and in September 1942 managed to wrest control of virtually all subversive propaganda activities from S.O. 1.[31]

Faced with these bureaucratic limitations, hampered by a shortage of airlift and equipment, and forced to focus on some distant "day" that the fainthearted in occupied Europe feared might never come, S.O.E. limped along. Its operations were most successful in France and Poland, two areas where S.O.E. depended heavily on exile groups—the de Gaulle Free French organization and the Polish government in exile. The ties with de Gaulle actually worsened S.O.E.'s standing with some British authorities, including the Chiefs of Staff, in the spring of 1942, because many were tempted by a wispy idea that a military deal could be made with Vichy that would require the exclusion of de Gaulle. Thus S.O.E. remained somewhat on the outs on French policy until London ultimately relinquished the dream of a Vichy deal in late summer.[32]

Regarding the Poles, S.O.E.'s first problem was that it did not have sufficient airlift to deliver adequate supplies to a movement that was mainly interested in organizing and equipping a secret army. There was also a question of what the Poles wanted to do with their secret army once it was fully developed. Certainly it would be employed against the Germans, but it took little imagination in London to see that it could also be used against Britain's Soviet ally.

British officials might feel conscience-stricken about "poor Poland, poor exiled Poles, poor Poles where-ever they may be," but that didn't preclude their need to keep on good terms with the Soviet Union. The high hopes that S.O.E. had in the summer of 1941 for cooperative subversive warfare with the U.S.S.R. had largely evaporated. Some joint propaganda work had been effected, and preparatory work was done for R.A.F. drops of N.K.V.D. agents and equipment into western Europe. But aside from the fact that Brig. Gen. George Hill was allowed to study partisan operations and apparently assisted in the preparation of the official Soviet handbook for partisan warfare, S.O.E.'s enterprise in Moscow accomplished little. The Soviets were already nervous about British delays and maneuvers, especially in the Balkans, and S.O.E. felt that further cooperation would be "full of dangers and at best would be very tricky." The troubles were not just political; they also arose out of a different view of how to wage resistance warfare. The Soviets were not interested in slow buildups or waiting around for invasion day. For them, the day had already come—the German army and the murder squads were already producing havoc in central Russia. The Soviets demanded immediate, all-out, and continual partisan attacks to weaken the enemy, no matter what the cost in German reprisals. Such a policy made sense in the East, not merely because of Stalinist ruthlessness, but because the struggle for survival was already mortal and the Germans, without any prompting from partisans, had already carried out far worse atrocities than they would ever perpetrate in western Europe.[33]

Despite being saddled with a policy of slow buildup, and quarantined from much activity in eastern Europe, America, and neutral territory, S.O.E. worked effectively in some nooks and crannies. Very successful selective demolitions were carried out in France and Norway, and in addition to explosive sabotage, P.W.E. and S.O.E. cooperated in encouraging work slowdowns and "undetectable" industrial sabotage, especially in France. The S.O.E. rumor mill also ground on, spreading bone-chilling tales throughout the war zone. As we have seen, however, some of these may have done as much harm as good to the victims of Nazi policy. In February 1942, a New York S.O. 1 rumor claimed that German economic troubles had become so severe that "a new law says no Jew under sixty may be deported to Poland." At a time when mass deportations to the gas chambers were in process, the circulation of such tales in the occupied territories certainly made it more difficult for Jews to see that their only possible chance of survival was to hide or fight.[34]

Though most of S.O.E.'s other gambles lacked such dreadful overtones, few of them produced a great effect and some were complete disasters. S.O.E.'s difficulties with the Belgian government in exile, for example, brought resistance activity in that country virtually to a standstill in early summer 1942. Although Churchill was still entranced by the idea of a Yugoslavian revolt under Mihajlović, and S.O.E. sent in as many as 50,000 gold sovereigns a month so Mihajlović could buy supplies—including guns from the Italian army—British activities did not so much inconvenience the Germans as exacerbate internal Yugoslav conflicts. Although the London government was unaware of it, Mihajlović was then collaborating with the Italians, while Tito was following Soviet guidelines and fighting the Germans regardless of the cost in reprisals. By recognizing Mihajlović as the supreme resistance leader and providing him with money and a feeble trickle of supply, the British alienated Tito, made relations with the Soviets more difficult, and stored up a reserve of political trouble for the future.[35]

But the ultimate S.O.E. catastrophe of 1942 took place in the Netherlands. In March 1942, the Abwehr penetrated the Dutch resistance movement and turned it. The Abwehr started by controlling an S.O.E. team in March, then successfully turned the next three missions sent in during May. Within the following nineteen months, Germany controlled the whole of what S.O.E. thought was its Dutch resistance organization. During that period, nearly 200 S.O.E. agent and material drops were made in the Netherlands, and all of them fell immediately into German hands. No one outside a small circle of German officials knew about this S.O.E. disaster at that time, but in its terrible way it was symbolic of the predicament in which S.O.E. found itself in 1942. As long as the British government continued to base its offensive policy on the three weapons of blockade, strategic bombing, and resistance, S.O.E. was nearly paralyzed. Forced to try to develop a resistance organization while dampening down risings, a perfect situation for German penetration had been created. Called upon to produce results, but not to cause political problems or act prematurely, S.O.E. had to take big chances and run a kind of subversive warfare self-promotion campaign that suggested it was doing great things but it could not provide details or hard data.

Although S.O.E. was careful to be discreet, it had become as eager for American support as any other British organization. Not only was it short of arms and aircraft, it required an active ally who could help open up full-scale subversive operations. Stephenson and various S.O.E. officials had worked assiduously prior to Pearl Harbor to turn Donovan's new C.O.I. into an American super-S.O.E. and S.I.S. Although the main spur that drove Donovan into secret intelligence was applied by the American services, British pressure and encouragement apparently played a much more important role in fueling his enthusiasm for special operations. Donovan was a war-horse, a man who loved action and the crunch of direct combat. His initial trips to Britain in 1940 and 1941 not only confirmed his belief in the reality and danger of a Nazi fifth column but impressed him, through suggestive evidence, with the wonders of Britain's subversive warfare system. As early as 21 October 1941, Donovan was forwarding to the president British reports that extolled commando raids and pointed to what might be accomplished by comparable American activity. That commando and S.O.E. operations were kept strictly separate in British organizational practice did not trouble Donovan or his British prompters. The major consideration for both Donovan and S.O.E. was to increase American belief in subversive warfare and to lay the groundwork for a large irregular combat organization.

Then, immediately following Pearl Harbor, Churchill, accompanied by a large staff, descended on Washington to coordinate strategy and organization and to further commit the United States to policies that coincided with Britain's situation and interests. Foremost among these was to maintain primary focus on Germany—the "Europe first" strategy—and to create a joint Anglo-American command structure, the Combined Chiefs of Staff (C.C.S.). American agreement to a combined staff would have important consequences in the United States since no American Joint Chiefs of Staff then existed. The creation of the Joint Chiefs of Staff, which became, under the president, the controlling center of the American war machine, necessitated additional organizational changes. Supportive joint committees and agencies were required to prepare proposals for the Joint Chiefs and to see that their policies, once established, were carried out. A new situation was thereby born at British initiative, which required adjustment or alteration of all Washington organizations related to national defense, including C.O.I.

However, the Anglo-American agreements of December 1941-January 1942 had other, even more profound effects on Donovan's organization. Churchill arrived in Washington shortly before Christmas with a series of memoranda setting forth his views on how the war should be fought in 1942 and 1943. While calling for a rebuilding of naval strength for the Pacific, his primary concern in 1942 was to tidy up the anti-U-boat war, accelerate air attacks on Germany, and clear the Germans from all of North Africa. With the ground thus prepared, American and British expeditionary forces would then be able to land on scattered shores of Europe in 1943 "with armies strong enough to enable the conquered populations to revolt." Here, beefed up with a preparatory North African campaign and the infusion of American forces, was the old British concept of subversion, air attack, and blockade in preparation for limited invasion and revolt which the British chiefs had established as their basic policy in the summer of 1940.[36]

Despite his eloquence, Churchill, and the British Chiefs of Staff who accompanied him, were unable to secure American agreement to all of this plan. The American generals and admirals were anxious to revenge Pearl Harbor and gain the offensive in the Pacific. They were further inclined toward a concentrated Anglo-American direct assault on the European continent as soon as possible. Overestimating British strength and underestimating the difficulties that would be encountered in creating a large modern American army, the military authorities of the United States hoped to bring the full strength of the country's manpower into a decisive battle against Nazi Germany in 1942 or 1943. In consequence, no firm decision on whether the Anglo-Americans would drive for North Africa or directly for the European continent in 1942–43 was made while Churchill was in Washington. But there was agreement on the need for offensive measures on land and sea to soften up the Germans and to help take some of the pressure off the Soviet Union, which had its back to the wall and was clamoring for a second front. Politically, and perhaps morally, Churchill and Roosevelt felt it inadvisable to fulfill the Soviet desire for a full-scale political agreement based on a formal recognition of Russia's June 1941 borders (thus conceding the Baltic states and eastern Poland to the U.S.S.R.), but they believed that other means had to be devised to reassure Stalin and strengthen the Soviet resolve to fight on. In actuality, the horrors perpetrated by the Nazis were doing more to accomplish those ends than anything the Anglo-Americans could do, but the two Western leaders concluded that increased aid to Russia and softening-up actions against the Germans in preparation for Anglo-American landings should be fundamental elements in their basic war plans.

Among the measures contained in the grand strategy agreed to on 31 December 1941, was a provision declaring that "subversive activity" and propaganda would be heavily employed to undermine and wear down Axis resistance. This passage authorized the British to make full use of their subversive warfare machinery, and, by inference, also opened the door to increased C.O.I. activity, in cooperation with Great Britain.

Donovan had been especially anxious to secure a green light for his subversive warfare ("S.O.E. type") plans ever since Pearl Harbor. The frustration of having to sit about shuffling papers while American forces—including MacArthur's in the Philippines—were engaged in brave and doomed struggles to buy time, was almost more than Donovan's gallant heart could bear. Propaganda and informational activities were no substitute for military action. On the day of Churchill's arrival, Donovan sent a plan to the president recommending the creation of an American "guerrilla corps . . . separate from the Army and Navy" imbued with a spirit and system analogous to that of the British commandos. Roosevelt directed the colonel to take the matter up with the British, and Donovan apparently found a warm reception for the idea in the prime minister's entourage. Four days before Churchill's party left Washington, the Bureau of the Budget authorized $1 million to C.O.I. for carrying out "special projects" on the Asian continent and "with the British."[37]

What Donovan had in mind, and what the president then encouraged, was the creation of an independent American raider force, whose primary function would be to penetrate enemy-occupied territories and give added heavy punching power to resistance forces. It was intended to function rather like a large commando additive to S.O.E.'s resistance support system. Donovan prepared the idea with great enthusiasm, drawing up plans, and asking for the assignment of military personnel to act as instructors in C.O.I. training schools and to serve as members of his raiding units. On 25 February 1942, with support from the British, he received the all-important formal authorization of the newly formed United States Joint Chiefs (J.C.S.) for C.O.I. "to organize and conduct secret subversive operations in hostile areas."[38]

Not everyone in C.O.I. was happy with what seemed to be an unnecessary dispersal of activities and resources. Donovan had to beat down the opposition even of Colonel Solborg, who had returned to Washington from his subversive warfare training in Britain convinced that all C.O.I. subversive and secret intelligence activities should be concentrated and put under his command. In consequence, Solborg was sacked as S.O. chief and sent on a mission to Portugal. The organizational dispersal continued with the immediate appointment of Colonel Goodfellow as the new head of S.O. (G) and David Bruce put in charge of Secret Intelligence S.I. (B) activities.[39]

While Donovan's subordinates could not block his assorted schemes, the British were able to adjust his raider–subversive warfare plan to their ends. During late January, in discussions with the Yugoslav minister in Washington, Donovan had hatched a scheme to form a brigade of some 200 "Yugoslav citizens resident here" which would be landed on the coast of Yugoslavia to give a "lifting" effect to the forces of Mihajlović. The British, who saw in his proposal an opportunity to tap the large American ethnic populations for agents in their S.O.E. and S.I.S. operations in the

Balkans and central Europe, warmly endorsed the idea. Under British prompting, the commando–raider plan came to be mixed up with an expanded effort to recruit in the United States a total of 2,000 Greeks, Yugoslavs, and various other groups of Balkan origin who would be paid by C.O.I. and initially trained under its authority prior to final training and subversive warfare employment by Britain. Although the plan was extremely convoluted, it received surprisingly warm support in Washington. By early March, the secretary of war had approved an initial allotment of 200 army officers and men to serve as instructors in C.O.I. training centers. G-2 also gave its endorsement to the plan for recruiting 2,000 American "ethnics" for British subversive warfare operations, subject to the condition that they would be employed under the authority of Anglo-American "theater or task force commanders."[40]

These subversive warfare and raider schemes enabled Donovan to start hooking C.O.I. into the organizational and operational structure of the J.C.S. But London, as well as many in C.O.I. itself, felt that the wide extension of Donovan's plans and enthusiasms had left the organization vulnerable to attack from rivals in Washington. The British were anxious to work closely with Donovan; C.O.I. was loyal to them, and unlike other American organizations (including the State Department), never seemed to question whether secret British intelligence and subversive organizations were as efficient as they claimed to be. The colonel had done yeoman service in January 1942, helping to secure B.S.C.'s exemption from the McKellar Act, which would have required registration of all British agents in the United States. The British were grateful. They wanted to make a go of the C.O.I. connection, and to seal the bargain they were ready to turn over to Donovan all of B.S.C.'s secret propaganda activities (S.O. 1) in New York.[41]

Nonetheless, indications that Donovan might be too weak a reed were so obvious in early 1942 that London could not ignore them. After a discussion in February with the C.O.I. representative in London, Hugh Dalton decided to send an S.O.E. man, Anthony Keswick, to the United States to scout out the colonel's position. The C.O.I. representative in London (Whitney), who was one of the main opponents of overwide dispersal of C.O.I. activities, had told Dalton that the colonel was soon likely to become exclusively an intelligence man, after "unwillingly" being forced to give up his other activities to the military and the Office of Facts and Figures. Dalton was worried that S.O.E. had put its "shirt" on Donovan, and he instructed Keswick to cut back B.S.C. activities in the United States and to explore other avenues that might lead S.O.E. to sources of American military supplies. When P.W.E. learned about the Keswick mission, it decided to send its own mission as well. Thus, Ritchie Calder and George VI's brother-in-law, David Bowes-Lyon, were dispatched to the United States in mid-March.[42]

The Washington Battle Over C.O.I.

Keswick and the P.W.E. delegation discovered that Donovan and C.O.I. were indeed in serious trouble by the spring of 1942. The colonel had managed to survive confused squabbles with the F.B.I. in December 1941 and January 1942 over poor intelligence coordination in New York and the perennial question of who controlled Western Hemisphere secret intelligence activity. After it became clear that Donovan was not trying to contest Hoover's Latin American monopoly, the Justice Department backed off—but not without leaving a few more black marks on the colonel's increasingly shady reputation as a bureaucratic imperialist. In February, Donovan lost another, and sharper, tussle with his old adversary Nelson Rockefeller. The Coordinator of Inter-American Affairs succeeded in thwarting Donovan's latest effort to secure complete control over the nation's overseas shortwave radio transmitters and though this defeat was not mortal, it suggested that the incorrigibly expansionist Donovan could be beaten.[43]

Indeed, with a number of C.O.I. opponents eager to strike, with Donovan and Sherwood at each other's throats, and with Congress unhappy about the size, cost, and disorder of government informational services, the stage was set in March for a full-scale effort to dismember C.O.I. The principal point at issue was a plan advanced by Budget Director Harold Smith, and White House staffer Samuel Rosenman, to consolidate all the government's foreign and domestic propaganda operations into a single Office of War Information. Predictably, this suggestion set off a carnival of plans and arguments, punctuated by protests to the president from both Donovan and Rockefeller, whose organizations stood to lose most if a comprehensive American informational service was established. All the regular performers participated as well, including Sumner Welles and Adolf Berle from the State Department and Attorney General Francis Biddle. Rockefeller stormed and raged and at one point threatened to resign if the proposed consolidation went through. Donovan seems to have stayed somewhat cooler, but he was careful to keep self-justifying memoranda moving to the White House and the J.C.S. during the spring.[44]

It was, all in all, a delightful bureaucratic battle, replete with intrigue and anger, and a president who allowed it to drag on endlessly by playing first the Sphinx and then Hamlet. Everything was rehashed, even the old allegation that C.O.I. was operating in Latin America, and though that charge had no serious foundation, it helped to keep the pot boiling. The main importance of the whole affair, however, was that it raised the possibility of a complete dismemberment of C.O.I. and dropped that issue into the lap of the J.C.S. Captain Francis C. Denebrink, who had been the navy's representative on the Board of Analysts in the pre–Pearl Harbor period, was charged by the chiefs with the task of studying Donovan's organization and making a recommendation on what should be done with it. His report, completed on 8 March, reflected the doubts and suspicions regarding all civilian wartime organizations (and C.O.I. in particular) that were rampant in the War and Navy departments. Denebrink concluded that C.O.I. should be abolished and its parts scattered; with R. and A. transferred to the J.C.S., the planned raider units, and perhaps F.I.S. as well, going to a regular branch of the military services; and the fate of the secret intelligence unit to be determined by the State Department in cooperation with a Joint Chiefs' committee. Furthermore, Denebrink concluded, Donovan's construction of a huge "war room" planned for Pennsylvania Avenue should be stopped, and the allotted funds given over to the J.C.S.[45]

Within a few days, the J.C.S. approved the basic proposals advanced by Denebrink and resolved to take up the matter of C.O.I.'s dismemberment in an "informal conference" with the president. In the second week of April, however, the secretary to the J.C.S., Gen. Walter Bedell Smith, began to have second thoughts. In light of Donovan's influence at the White House, Smith thought it might be possible to find an appropriate place for the colonel within the J.C.S. structure, and then all "the valuable parts of the C.O.I." could be "put under Chiefs of Staff control." When Donovan expressed sympathy for this idea, General Smith prepared a draft presidential order to rechristen C.O.I. the Office of Strategic Information and move it all, including F.I.S., under the authority of the J.C.S.[46]

A number of factors then combined to induce the Chiefs of Staff to reverse themselves and decide that they wanted to take over, and keep alive, the entire Donovan organization. From the C.O.I. side, the colonel welcomed this new control because he was nervous about the attacks being made by outside agencies and he was also eager to fit into the central war machinery as long as his organizations, and his freedom of action, were not destroyed. The J.C.S., for its part, recognized that Donovan's organization not only had influence in the offices of the secretaries of War and Navy as well as in the White House, but also that it had some "great talent" within its ranks. While many army and navy officers were so suspicious of Donovan and the organization that they only wished to capture it, others believed that it could perform valuable services for the military. One of the most important reasons why the Joint Chiefs seem to have decided to take the Donovan organization under their wing was the need to develop and control subversive warfare and raider activities. By mid-March, C.O.I. plans for aid to Mihajlović, a commando organization, and an "ethnic" raider force for the Balkans were all under consideration by the White House, the War Department, and various committees of the J.C.S. When General Smith made his proposal that C.O.I. should be taken over completely by the Joint Chiefs, he pointedly stressed that this would give them "over-all control" of these special service units.[47]

The chiefs accepted General Smith's advice and a draft proposal giving the J.C.S. control over C.O.I. was sent to the White House. Shortly thereafter, two more forward steps were authorized in the development of Donovan's subversive warfare projects. On 25 March, Henry Stimson gave in-principle approval to the commissioning of "aliens and foreign nationals" as officers in the U.S. Army, once they had passed through C.O.I. subversive warfare training that would prepare them to lead "ethnic" raider units. On the following day, a C.O.I. plan to send supplies to the Yugoslav resistance was also tentatively approved by the Joint Planning Staff (J.P.S.), and on 30 March Donovan was directed by the J.C.S. to cooperate with the British in its execution.[48]

The colonel's subversive warfare schemes were thus pulling his organization ever more deeply into the new war-making system of the United States, making it far less likely that C.O.I. would be totally destroyed. But the organization was not yet out of danger. The proposal to remove F.I.S. from Donovan's control so it could be placed in a new Office of War Information (O.W.I.) was still being hotly debated in the White House, and Donovan's most bitter opponents hoped that this amputation would lead to the complete dismemberment of C.O.I. Faced by a strong group of Donovan haters within the military, General Smith began to waver, and by May was leaning toward the idea that F.I.S. should be severed before C.O.I. was handed over to the J.C.S.[49]

Those within the military services who disliked Donovan, especially the new G-2, Gen. George Strong, were pushing for a complete end to C.O.I. in the spring of 1942. But with every day's passing, Donovan's various subversive warfare proposals were expanding and digging in to such a degree that by late spring a major campaign would have been necessary to remove them. Although hospitalized because of an automobile accident in early April, the colonel continued bombarding the White House and the J.C.S. with memoranda and suggestions supporting the continued life of his organization and extolling the wonders of propaganda and subversive attack. In mid-April, Assistant Secretary of War McCloy added his voice to those recommending strong American subversive warfare action in the Balkans. The British also did their part. C.O.I. men were enrolled in the new S.O.E. training school in Canada, S.O.E. specialists were provided to help develop subversive warfare weapons in America, and the British agreed in principle to set up joint operations with C.O.I. in the Balkans and the Middle East. By May, David Bowes-Lyon of P.W.E. was convinced that C.O.I. would survive in some form, "though with a distinctly more military bias."[50]

In the course of considering Donovan's various subversive warfare proposals in April, a large number of army and navy officers came to the conclusion that there was merit in the idea of leaving some aspects of guerrilla warfare operations in civilian hands. They wanted control of such operations, and insisted that guerrilla warfare be under the direction of the various theater commanders, but they were not happy about the prospect of assigning soldiers and sailors to guerrilla warfare duty. While various J.C.S. committees wrangled endlessly about how subversive and psychological warfare activities should be organized and controlled, there was overwhelming agreement that actual guerrilla operations should be carried out by civilians, not soldiers. Thus the Operations Division of the War Department; the army's G-2 and G-3 divisions; Gens. Joseph McNarney, Joseph Bull, and Dwight Eisenhower; Adm. Frederick Horne; the J.P.S.; and finally the J.C.S. itself all went on record by the end of April to the effect that the waging of guerrilla warfare should be left to civilians. Nothing could have done more to enhance the value of having C.O.I. placed under the J.C.S. umbrella than this across-the-board military resolve that civilians had an important subversive warfare role to play. Of course, the generals and admirals later would change their minds somewhat and authorize uniformed American officers to serve with resistance units. In the spring of 1942, however, they believed—as the British Chiefs of Staff did before them—that civilians should perform such services, and that Donovan's organization would be quite useful in this regard.[51]

With the military ready to place the bulk of C.O.I. under J.C.S. authority, a final organizational deal was quickly put together. Henry Stimson lay the first stone when he rejected the idea of giving Donovan an independent raider or guerrilla warfare command outside J.C.S. control. A second stone went into place in June, over Donovan's protests, when F.I.S. was indeed removed from C.O.I. and handed over to the newly established Office of War Information (O.W.I.) headed by newscaster Elmer

Davis. O.W.I. would henceforth control domestic and foreign information, including (white) propaganda operations outside Latin America. The remaining portions of C.O.I.—most importantly, R. and A., F.N.B., S.O., and S.I.—were passed to the Joint Chiefs and officially christened as the Office of Strategic Services (O.S.S.). On 13 June the president signed the two orders creating O.W.I. and O.S.S. respectively, and the deed was done.[52]

As we shall see in the next chapter, the creation of O.S.S. did not solve all of Donovan's organizing problems or give him unlimited authority to conduct operations. It also was just the beginning of the battle between Donovan and Davis over control of various propaganda and psychological warfare activities. But the executive order of 13 June did keep the intelligence and special operations units under the colonel's control and by giving this entity a name (O.S.S.), the order declared that it would have organizational integrity under the J.C.S. This was certainly as much as anyone could reasonably have hoped, considering the cannibalism rampant in Washington in the spring of 1942 and the vulnerability of the varied activities that the colonel had assembled under the name of C.O.I. The executive order of 13 June which called those activities (minus F.I.S.) the Office of Strategic Services merely froze into reality the various activities and branches that the colonel's busy mind had generated up to that moment. Donovan and the J.C.S. now had to hammer these into a coherent structure and make them an effective part of the American military system. But for us to be able to understand how this was done and why O.S.S. took the particular form that it did, a survey of what C.O.I. units had actually accomplished during the first six months following Pearl Harbor is necessary.

C.O.I. Branches and Their Accomplishments: 1942

Of all the C.O.I. branches, R. and A. probably fared most poorly in the period immediately after Pearl Harbor. From one of the two most important and active prewar C.O.I. branches, it became more like a civilian and professorial backwater in the first months of the war. The colonel's attention at that time had shifted primarily to military action abroad and bureaucratic civil war at home, and he had little time for informational research. The British, too, had no particular interest in R. and A. at this time, though some London officials believed that it had been created to offset the overly cautious and isolationist reports that Roosevelt had been receiving from other branches of the American government. Some useful connections between R. and A. and military intelligence were maintained after 7 December, but M.I.D. and O.N.I. actually cut the volume of classified material given to R. and A. because they claimed that tighter security was necessary.[53]

Partly offsetting these losses, however, were efforts made inside R. and A. to tighten the organization and systematize its operations. Although the Board of Analysts still radiated some of the atmosphere of a gentleman's club and leaned heavily on the colonel for guidance, it did manage to focus more attention on practical questions and took over some aspects of editorial supervision. A regular editorial committee was created in February 1942, which established basic regulations for the form and production of R. and A. reports—including decisions to use a consecutive numbering system and to mimeograph rather than print. It also enforced the basic rule that reports should be factual, with only limited inferences allowed. On occasion the Board of Analysts ordered revisions, and now and then rejected individual reports as "worthless."[54]

William Langer assumed more importance in the overall research program as the Board of Analysts lost importance, and Dr. Baxter was hobbled by illness and his duties at Williams College. In March, Langer received an assistant in the person of Carl Schorske, a central European specialist and former Harvard protégé of Langer's, who, having fallen victim to R. and A.'s penchant for unusual assignments, had been working on a subcommittee on equatorial Africa.[55]

The improved organization helped the branch improve the quality of its work and gave it clearer focus. Many reports were still produced on fringe matters, such as conditions in Greenland, and R. and A. continued to do Latin American research at a time when this produced more trouble between the embattled C.O.I. and its opponents in the F.B.I., the State Department, and Rockefeller's organization. But a strenuous effort was made to follow the colonel's direction to keep attention focused on "current and immediate problems for the assistance of strategists." The Map Division was very busy, as were the interview units in New York. Relevant reports were prepared on such matters as supply routes to the Soviet Union, German air losses, and the strength of the German Army. On some occasions, R. and A.'s estimates were closer to the mark than were comparable British studies. For example, its report on German air strength, prepared by the Economics Division in late March, was dead right in predicting an increase in production based on plant expansion and the use of foreign labor.[56]

But there were important errors, too. A report on Wehrmacht casualties, which Donovan presented to the president in early June, concluded that "further substantial losses" would compel Germany either to cut war production or reduce the size of her armed forces. Coming as it did at the very moment when Albert Speer's reorganization was dramatically raising German output and the overall size of the Wehrmacht was increasing, the R. and A.'s conclusion was dead wrong.[57]

On the whole, though, R. and A. avoided many such mistakes because it generally shied away from making overt predictions. The cautious men who still held the most important positions in the organization militated against boldness, and when they did make recommendations, the reports were usually too muddled to be taken seriously. On 9 December 1941, the Board of Analysts proposed that an Allied joint war council should be formed (a reasonable enough suggestion), but they went on to recommend that the war council should have a regional liaison group of Canadian, American, and Soviet representatives meeting in Alaska, of all remote places, at a time when the Soviet Union was not at war with Japan! One trembles to think what would have happened if the Board of Analysts had tried to act on another of its recommendations—this one decided on jointly with the colonel in February 1942—that a group be created within C.O.I. to take over the task of "out-thinking the Japanese."[58]

But as we have said, such aberrations were rare, and R. and A. research operations became much more efficient and somewhat more attuned to war needs in the six months that followed Pearl Harbor. Some solid foundations for future expansion were laid. Allen Evans went to London in May, the first R. and A. man to get an overseas assignment. Progress was also made in getting R. and A. studies into the hands of important policymakers in various departments rather than depending so heavily on Colonel Donovan's link to the president. Reports began to be sent to various sections of the War, Navy, and State departments as well as to other branches of government. Some of these were warmly received and avidly read, such as the Far Eastern reports that went to Stanley Hornbeck in the State Department. But since all the transmissions were made through ad hoc arrangements, in which personal contacts were used to "sell" R. and A.'s virtues, it is impossible to gain an overall picture of how important and influential this lateral transmission process actually was. One can see instances of close and effective cooperation, such as the work which the Mediterranean section did on North African coastal conditions in conjunction with M.I.D., but as late as the summer of 1943, most R. and A. leaders were depressed by how little there was to show for their labors. They still had not really grasped who their most promising and important customers would be. In March 1942, the army air corps inquired whether

R. and A. could form a team of analysts to do targeting research, but the Board of Analysts rejected its inquiry on the grounds that R. and A. had too much other work to do! At a time when C.O.I. was fighting for its life, such a rejection was, to say the least, imprudent. Considering that within another year a large proportion of the work performed by R. and A. in support of military operations was air targeting, the rejection of March 1942 indicates that R. and A. was still rather confused about where its real wartime significance lay.[59]

While R. and A. was struggling to find its proper place during the six months after Pearl Harbor, F.I.S. went forward on the assumption that virtually all international propaganda was within its preserve. Since F.I.S. was severed from the rest of Donovan's organization in June 1942, its activities have less direct significance for the C.O.I.-O.S.S. story than do those of the other branches, but some features deserve brief consideration. In the middle of the struggle for control of F.I.S., Donovan characterized his propaganda section as the "arrow of initial penetration" paving the way for subversive invasion. This image has been employed liberally by later Donovan enthusiasts who contend that the colonel always had a broad and coherent plan for psychological warfare. But even a cursory examination of F.I.S. operations in the early months of 1942 shows that the stinging archery image was not very appropriate. Most F.I.S. work consisted of routine informational labor: broadcasting F.D.R.'s speeches, preparing summaries of Allied and Axis broadcasts, and making plans for future propaganda operations. The propagandists were primarily concerned with practical problems, such as how to get American material circulated in neutral countries or how to discover an anti-Axis propaganda line for the Middle East that would not antagonize either Jews or Arabs. Despite the efforts of such militants as Edmund Taylor, the basic task of F.I.S. was to distribute cheerful platitudes that had a New Deal flavor. Sherwood said it best when he declared that "all U.S. information to the world should be considered as though it were a continuous speech by the President." The colonel himself reported to Roosevelt on 13 April (a month after he'd created the "arrow of penetration" image) that the planning group of the F.I.S. had decided to concentrate its propaganda on the twin themes of America's fighting "a people's war" and "a world-wide war of liberation." Claiming that "the destiny of America is not the destiny of a race or a class or of a military imperialism" but "the destiny of men [and women] as persons," the planning group intended to stress further that the United States had "vast stockpiles of food and raw materials" that it would use to bring joy to the human race as soon as victory was won. Commendable and self-flattering as such sentiments might be, they were hardly the stuff to serve as the first stage of a serious subversive penetration or assault.[60]

Sherwood's F.I.S. was a propaganda agency—no more and no less—and since C.O.I. had not been formed as part of a coherent plan, the removal of F.I.S. in June 1942 left behind few marks on the other branches forming the new O.S.S. It is true, however, that shortwave monitoring had been developed as a joint intelligence–F.I.S. function with large monitoring stations both on the east ("Bellmore") and the west ("Hollywood") coasts. When F.I.S. became part of the new O.W.I., Hollywood and Bellmore, supplemented by other "intercept" operations, were retained by Donovan and continued to receive and record foreign shortwave broadcasts until nearly the end of the war. This residue of what had once been a shared F.I.S. function gave Donovan and his new O.S.S. one crack through which to advance into the psychological warfare field. The O.S.S. also inherited a number of C.O.I. overseas agents who had initially gone abroad primarily to represent F.I.S. The original C.O.I. mission to London, for example, went for F.I.S. activities and only gradually took on intelligence reporting functions. Many of those first assigned to neutral capitals were also at first F.I.S. representatives, and although most transferred to O.W.I. when the split came, some, such as Bruce Hopper in Stockholm, went to O.S.S. A few others, including Gerald Mayer in the isolated post at Bern, continued to work for both O.W.I. and O.S.S. until the end of the European war.[61]

Such men, whether originally assigned to F.I.S. or not, helped develop and expand the Special Operations (or G) section and the Secret Intelligence (or B) section, in the months after Pearl Harbor. Aside from S.O.'s beginnings in North Africa and Asia, which will be discussed below, and the stationing of a few S.O. men in larger C.O.I. missions in London and Cairo, the section remained essentially a stateside operation in this period. There were, in fact, a total of only twenty-one people (including six technicians) abroad from all C.O.I. branches as late as May 1942. S.O.'s work was concentrated on setting up training establishments, securing personnel from the armed services, sending as many men as possible through British S.O.E. schools, and setting up a system for procuring special weapons—or "toys," as they were known in S.O.E. parlance. Colonel Goodfellow, who took over the S.O. work in the aftermath of the sharp break between colonels Solborg and Donovan, was anxious to get operational plans developed. But America was completely unprepared to carry out such operations and was thus wholly dependent on the British. In early 1942, a plan was outlined for American S.O. operations in France, but its author acknowledged that C.O.I. would have to depend on Britain for the supply of airlift, wireless communication, and the training of personnel. Since the Americans had virtually nothing of immediate value to exchange for all the assistance they desired from the British, most such early operational plans were stillborn.[62]

However, it was extremely difficult for Donovan and his aides to stand by as mere sympathetic onlookers in early 1942 while Anglo-American forces were meeting defeat on every battlefield. The colonel developed a scheme for a relief raid to the Philippines in which he himself hoped to participate. Details of what he had in mind are lacking, but it was to be coupled with an effort to invoke American sovereign rights in such a way that any Filipino who collaborated with the Japanese could be prosecuted for treason. Without American naval and air supremacy, however, Donovan's dream of a transpacific relief attack was not feasible—"mostly wind," in Henry Stimson's unkind phrase—and the colonel had to put it aside. Only one of the many operational projects developed by C.O.I.'s S.O. in this era had any measure of practical reality, and that was a plan to send "concentrated food and vitamins" to Mihajlović in Yugoslavia since the Allies had done so poorly in providing him with arms. But even this plan was not carried to completion, despite Roosevelt's support. Some material was apparently shipped from the United States to Cairo, but none of it ever reached Yugoslavia.[63]

C.O.I.'s S.I. branch was more fortunate than the S.O. section in a number of respects. Its operations were generally simpler and cheaper than those of S.O., and many of them could be "piggybacked" onto other American overseas activities. The majority of early S.I. postings abroad were to United States embassies and consulates in the neutral countries of Europe, Africa, and the Middle East and to the American diplomatic mission in Vichy France. A few intelligence missions using traveling scholars and businessmen were tried, and there was much consideration and experimentation with other ways to disguise agents, especially in places like Bern and Cairo, but placing S.I. men within State Department overseas missions continued to be the standard form of cover.[64]

The diplomatic cover arrangement, though simple and convenient, left a number of problems unresolved. Early C.O.I. administrative procedures were chaotic, and the files for the first months of 1942 are filled with complaints from all over the world that overseas representatives had not been paid in months. Part of the reason for such confusion rested within C.O.I. headquarters in Washington, but another part was probably due to the marginal abilities of many of those sent abroad in the early days. There was a special touch of genteel make-believe in early C.O.I. intelligence operations; it is difficult to imagine, for example, that any other intelligence system in 1942 would have sent an Ilia Tolstoy on an intelligence–S.O. mission to Tibet and allowed him to obtain his own kit from Abercrombie and Fitch![65]

Colonel Donovan's administrative right hand, Ned Buxton, labored valiantly to unsnarl the tangles and raise the quality of C.O.I.'s overseas representatives, but the efforts of C.O.I. alone could not smooth out all the serious difficulties. Some senior State Department officials such as Sumner Welles were cool toward C.O.I. in general and especially suspicious of the espionage rings that S.I. was operating under deep corporate cover in Saudi Arabia by June 1942 and wanted to extend to Liberia and China as well. Without State Department cooperation, S.I. expansion would have been impossible, so the section was forced to move with caution to make full use of its diplomatic connections. A special S.I. communications channel, the VICTOR channel, also was granted to the organization by the State Department. C.O.I. messages from overseas bearing the VICTOR code word were addressed to Howland Shaw at the State Department in Washington, and he then forwarded them to S.I. chief David Bruce.[66]

To increase the flow of S.I. information, a number of innovations were introduced and special projects employed in the first part of 1942. C.O.I. sent Treasury Department attachés openly to neutral capitals in Europe to collect commercial and economic data. In addition to the information secured from various British agencies, S.I. also made arrangements with the intelligence services of various governments-in-exile, especially those of Czechoslovakia and Poland, to secure information. Reports based on homeland agent sources were often highly accurate, but those touching on enemy plans or high politics tended toward wild speculation. The position of the exiled governments, like that of Britain itself, was still so shaky that their strategic appraisals were often highly colored by self-interest.[67]

Donovan had some good ideas for making use of available intelligence sources, including acquisition of confidential information from the Apostolic delegate, which seem to have worked well. He also conceived projects which, though reasonable, apparently were aborted due to practical or organizational snags. One such project involved using fishermen as contacts to build up an intelligence system in Greece. As we have seen, some of the colonel's ideas were doomed to failure simply because they were unrealistic. Immediately after Pearl Harbor, for example, Donovan conceived a plan to disguise S.I. men as State Department officials and secure Soviet approval for them to wander about in Siberia, the Caucasus, and Central Asia. The Soviet Union, which was highly suspicious of foreign travelers in the best of times, was not about to allow any such thing when the Germans were at Moscow's gates. The colonel also seems to have committed the cardinal sin of an intelligence chief in April 1942 when he unintentionally leaked information on Anglo-American operational intentions and Soviet strength to a Portuguese diplomat who passed it on to the Germans.[68]

Closer to home, S.I. men were more effective. They secured secret orders that had been issued to Spanish merchant captains, instructing them to sail for Argentina in the event that Spain entered the war on the side of the Axis. They also obtained twenty pages of reports that the Spanish ambassador in Washington had sent to Madrid in May. On another home-front, while Donovan did not succeed in his plan to reshape the Free French organization in North America so that it would more readily serve the interests of the Allies, C.O.I. did secure much information from Vichy French sources. Postwar accounts, however, have so relished alleged C.O.I. efforts to use a seductive lady named Cynthia to tempt officials of the Vichy embassy in Washington to reveal all that it is now difficult to measure exactly what happened. Some material seems to have been acquired at the Washington end of the Vichy communications system. But if Cynthia actually was used to open the way for an S.I. bag team to burgle the Vichy embassy and secure the French naval codes in the spring of 1942, as has been claimed repeatedly, the operation was both pointless and highly dangerous. The British Ultra team had been reading French naval messages since 1940; a C.O.I. break-in could have indicated to the French that their ciphers were insecure and led them to effect changes that would have closed off Ultra. Just such an escapade by O.S.S. occurred in Lisbon in 1943 and actually did threaten the American Magic operation for reading the Japanese codes. For C.O.I.'s reputation, then, it would be best to think that the popular 1942 sex and robbery tale about the Vichy embassy was in fact not true. This is especially so because in the spring of 1942, C.O.I. had acquired a source in Vichy itself that provided the Americans with high-level information. Over fifty diplomatic and military messages were turned over to C.O.I. between March and June 1942; after processing, this interesting material went right to the president.[69]

On balance, considering that a secret intelligence structure had to be developed virtually overnight, that C.O.I. was battling for its life, and that the country was faring badly in the war, S.I. did very well indeed in the first six months of 1942. By the end of that period, a network of S.I. representatives had been spread throughout most of the world and some special S.I. projects were working successfully. A flood of information was moving through S.I. channels by March and April 1942, which came from foreign intelligence sources and from direct reports via S.I.'s own representatives abroad. Reports on Germany were, quite naturally, especially numerous, and often of surprisingly high quality. For instance, by mid-February, C.O.I. had secured the full texts of two sermons in which Bishop Galen of Münster had denounced the Gestapo and its "euthanasia" operations.[70]

Faulty evaluations certainly occurred, and many of the reports from neutral capitals consisted of little more than idle gossip. Tidbits claiming that Hitler and the German generals were at each others' throats, or that there were deep splits within the Nazi Party, were common. Such rosy fantasies also kept the world press and British intelligence busy and should not be charged to the debit column of S.I. alone. The main flow of S.I. reports consisted of reasonably accurate reporting, and S.I. officials gradually learned how to pick out the best pieces and get them into the hands of the president and other high officials.[71]

C.O.I. in Asia and North Africa: 1942

May: Corregidor surrenders; Allies win the battle of the Coral Sea

To give another dimension to our appraisal of how well S.I. and S.O. developed, it will be useful to summarize briefly the activities of the two C.O.I. branches in the areas of the world in which they were most active—continental Asia and North Africa. C.O.I. gained its entry into the Pacific war zone through F.I.S. activities, and though these operations were welcomed in some areas, hospitality was sharply limited. General MacArthur wanted help with propaganda, but he developed his own intelligence and subversive warfare operations, first in the Philippines and then in Australia. By the time S.I. and S.O. were ready to offer him anything concrete, MacArthur had his own United States–Australian shadow warfare system already in existence.[72]

The British in India were at least as wary of C.O.I. as was MacArthur, and they did their best to keep all branches of the Donovan organization, including those concerned with propaganda, at arms' length. While making a few accommodating gestures, the British were afraid that an enthusiastic American anti-imperialist campaign might be as serious a threat to Britain's position in India as would the Japanese. London was forced to allow a few C.O.I. officials into Southeast Asia, but it did its best to control them and keep them away from the Indian nationalist movements.[73]

With the South Pacific and India out of the running, the only possible operational areas to consider were Burma, Korea, and China. Unfortunately for C.O.I., these areas were not very promising for special operations either. C.O.I.-type propaganda operations were difficult everywhere in Asia; one 1942 estimate concluded that there weren't a hundred shortwave receivers in "native" hands in either India or China.[74]

Despite the overwhelming obstacles in Asia (especially pronounced in the areas immediately around Japan) and Donovan's reluctance to deal with the Soviets there, S.O. and S.I. officials thought that Korea offered real possibilities. Korean refugee groups in the United States were carefully screened, and C.O.I. contact men concluded that Syngman Rhee was the best candidate around whom to build Korean resistance activities. But Brig. Gen. John Magruder (later head of O.S.S. intelligence services), who was in China as the leader of an American military mission prior to the arrival of Gen. Joseph "Vinegar Joe" Stilwell, reported to Washington that any effort to play the Korean card would cause difficulties for the Americans in China. Rather than offend Chiang Kai-shek, the State Department and various agencies of the J.C.S. joined forces to block attempts of "other governmental agencies"—meaning C.O.I.—to develop Korean sabotage and espionage activities. By June, both S.O. and S.I. were forced to back away from Rhee and file away their Korean subversive warfare plans for the time being.[75]

C.O.I. operations in Burma also were highly problematical. In early 1942, the Japanese were moving rapidly through Southeast Asia with the intention of seizing Burma and cutting the Allied land connection with China. The deeper the Japanese penetrated into Burma, the more nervous the British became about arming the native population for guerrilla warfare and the more obvious it became that no effective force stood in Japan's way. General Stilwell, as the new American commander in the China–Burma–India theater, made a valiant effort to hold north Burma, but his forces were beaten and scattered by the Japanese in the spring of 1942.[76]

By process of elimination, therefore, if S.O. and S.I. were going to get into the Pacific war, China was the only possible place to do it. Yet even in China prospects were none too good. The country was backward and exhausted from four years of war with Japan. By late spring 1942, the Japanese advance in Burma had cut off the last ground route into the country. Chiang Kai-shek was tough, dictatorial, and extremely suspicious of his allies. Having carried his share of the burden, Chiang was now ready to let Britain and the United States do most of the fighting against Japan while he husbanded his resources for a future all-out struggle with the Communists. American illusions about China and Chiang added to the difficulties. The United States wanted to believe that Chiang's Nationalist movement was democratic and that it had welded the Chinese people into an armed force eager to carry the war to the Japanese. This was, unfortunately, not the case. As the British had discovered to their sorrow, if an Allied organization were going to function in China, especially one concerned with intelligence or subversion, the Chinese would charge a high price and would make every effort to control such operations.[77]

Eager for action, and with no other prospect on the horizon, Donovan ignored the danger signs and threw his main Asian effort into China. He developed a full S.I.–S.O. plan for the country in January 1942; conferences were held, leaders for missions were chosen, and the recruitment and training of S.O. and S.I. team members was begun. Although General Stilwell was apparently less than enthusiastic about the plan, and General Magruder wired from Chunking that the establishment of an American guerrilla operation in China and any related effort to contact the Communists would "humiliate" Chiang, Donovan pushed on. Dr. Esson Gale, an elderly former official of the Chinese salt tax service who was designated by Donovan as S.I. chief for China, left in early February 1942 to set up a C.O.I. base in Chunking. But it became obvious that Stilwell would not accept the S.O. chief who Donovan wanted (Lt. Col. Morris De Pass), and C.O.I. had to try another man. The name of Carl Eifler (a former border patrol officer, then serving as an army major) came up in a discussion between Goodfellow and Stilwell, and the C.O.I. man jumped to the conclusion that Stilwell would approve an S.O. unit in China that was headed by Eifler. Donovan managed to wrestle Eifler away from his army station in Hawaii and brought him to Washington to head what became Detachment 101, the first S.O. combat unit formed by C.O.I.–O.S.S. When Detachment 101 had nearly completed its training and was about to depart for the Far East, however, more bad news arrived. Stilwell, from his post in China, flatly opposed the creation of an American guerrilla group there, whether it was led by Eifler or anyone else. The most that the general would concede was that if C.O.I. was determined to do some fighting, Detachment 101 might be set up in India in a effort to penetrate north Burma, the area that had the highest priority in Stilwell's plan to reopen land communication between India and China. Eifler, who was nothing if not resourceful (he thought it might be a good idea simply to purchase acts of sabotage from the Chinese), agreed with Donovan and Goodfellow that if he could not talk Stilwell into a China operation, then north Burma would have to be his operational area. So, in the waning days of C.O.I. the handful of men who made up Detachment 101 left for the Far East; by the time they arrived in India, C.O.I. had become O.S.S. and Eifler's force was the first O.S.S. combat unit ready to go into action.[78]

S.I.'s main China operation, though it had made a swifter start than its S.O. counterpart, also came to grief. Dr. Gale had planned to set up a network of old China hands in various regions of the country with the connivance of the Chinese authorities. But the Chunking government looked on Gale with great suspicion, as did the American ambassador, Clarence Gauss. Gale was a talker and socializer, a man who liked to make grandiose plans and show off his importance. As the leader of a secret organization he was, as Stanley Hornbeck of the State Department noted, "generally regarded as a minor disaster." Ambassador Gauss, who claimed to have known Gale for twenty-nine years, thought him so unreliable that he insisted on reading all his dispatches and withholding from him "the confidence of the Embassy." But Gale was blithely unaware of the suspicion and hostility that surrounded him and thought he was doing swimmingly. He reported to Washington that organizational headway had been made and that he had cleared up the ambassador's unfavorable attitude to C.O.I.[79]

In this situation, any progress that could be made in developing American secret intelligence in China would have to be made by others than Dr. Gale. One C.O.I. official named Alghan Lusey who was working on an F.I.S. assignment began to develop an association with one of Chiang's many intelligence and security organizations. The unit in question had the engaging name of the Bureau for Investigation and Statistics, and was run by a security policeman named Tai Li, whose toughness had earned him the nickname, "the Chinese Himmler." Although Lusey considered Tai Li's organization "utterly ruthless" and the "inner circle. . . a bunch of cutthroats," he did not think C.O.I. could turn its back on Tai Li. Considering the serious obstacles that stood in the way of attempting independent operations in face of the hostility of Chiang and men like Tai Li, Lusey suggested to Donovan that C.O.I. should attempt to come to an arrangement with the head of the Bureau for Investigation and Statistics.[80]

A modified version of this idea also came to another American representative in China during the spring of 1942. Comdr. Milton "Mary" Miles had been sent in March to head Naval Group China, with the main task of developing coastal intelligence and sources for the collection of weather information. As a man with long experience in China and with important friends in both the Navy Department and the Chiang government, Miles concluded that he could carry out his mission only if he worked as a junior partner with a powerful Chinese official. Miles and Lusey discussed the possibility of a double American deal with Tai Li, combining Naval Group China, C.O.I., and Tai Li's operations into one cooperative whole. In the course of late 1942 and early 1943, this plan evolved to shape O.S.S. and its intelligence organization in China. After a great deal of tugging and pulling, in April 1943 the Sino-American Cooperative Organization (S.A.C.O.) was organized, welding together the O.S.S. China operation (excluding Detachment 101, which escaped to India and Burma) with the operations of Commander Miles and Tai Li. Since neither Tai Li nor Miles was anxious to see O.S.S. develop and prosper, the S.A.C.O. agreement was a straitjacket that long restricted and constrained O.S.S. operations in the Far East.[81]

But this was only the overt side of S.I.'s early intelligence efforts in China. Beneath the surface, Donovan created another intelligence operation that was not made known to the Chinese and was not included in the Tai Li–Miles arrangement. It was formed in April 1942, when Donovan persuaded British insurance magnate C. V. Starr to let C.O.I. use his commercial and insurance connections in occupied China and Formosa to create a deep cover intelligence network. Although the State Department was nervous about the operation, Donovan went ahead and, with the cooperation of the U.S. Army, bypassed the diplomats in operating the communication system. Starr's people handled their own internal communication, then turned over their intelligence findings to Stilwell's headquarters for dispatch to the United States. Starr, who was residing in the United States at the time, provided these services to Donovan without charge as a patriotic service to the Allied cause. Later Starr became disgusted with what he considered Donovan's inefficiency and transferred his services to the British S.I.S. but the Starr–Donovan connection worked in China at least until the winter of 1943–44.[82]

The establishment of the Starr intelligence network, an operation so secret that it even escaped the attention of Chiang's security police (and of historians heretofore), was a major accomplishment for an intelligence organization barely six months old. We cannot evaluate the importance of information obtained through the Starr network since it went to Donovan alone, but the network's mere existence laid the basis for future S.I. expansion in Asia. If one considers all the obstacles and problems that stood in the way, the creation of Detachment 101 and the Starr–Donovan intelligence network only a few months after Pearl Harbor stands in the front ranks of C.O.I. achievement.

But it was in an area halfway around the world, in northwest Africa, that the C.O.I.'s activities were being watched most closely from Washington in the early months of 1942. As we have noted, the American government had been nervous about German activity and intentions in that region long before Pearl Harbor. The Murphy–Weygand agreement had been made, and twelve control agents, nicknamed Murphy's twelve apostles, had been stationed in the area during 1941 to check on German influence and gather general intelligence. In the months immediately prior to American entry into the war, Donovan had acquired authority to direct or coordinate the undercover aspects of this northwest African operation as part of his new secret intelligence system. But nothing had been done to implement this mandate prior to Pearl Harbor, and even immediately afterward the colonel's suggestions for greatly expanded intelligence and subversive warfare activities in the area fell on deaf ears.[83]

Then came Churchill's visit to Washington, with his emphasis on the importance of Allied operations in northwest Africa (code-named Gymnast). Although the American military was less than enthusiastic about what they saw as a wasteful diversion from the main task of limited landings on the European continent preparatory to a major invasion (code-named Bolero and Roundup), concern about conditions and possibilities in the northwest African region increased. The reports made by Murphy and his control officers were examined and reexamined more carefully, and C.O.I. began to send requests for specific intelligence to the control officers. C.O.I. recruited a World War I Marine hero and expert on the Middle East, Lt. Col. William Eddy, to take charge of northwest African undercover intelligence and subversive activities. After the necessary briefings and some discussion of possible operations to undertake in North Africa, Eddy was rushed off to his post in Tangier, arriving on 26 January 1942.[84]

All this might appear at first glance to be rather reasonable and effective, but as one goes beneath the surface it becomes obvious that American efforts in northwest Africa were plagued by confusion and inefficiency. The United States simply was not ready for war, and its military services—not to speak of ad hoc organizations like C.O.I.—seldom looked impressive when they moved into complex and sensitive areas such as North Africa. Some United States officials had rather bizarre notions about how to plan an operation in the region. One J.C.S. committee even thought it would be a good idea to take public opinion samplings there to determine whether the people wanted to be invaded by the Americans. There were also incidents of appalling clumsiness. Two of Murphy's control officers managed to acquire documents that described in detail the strength and deployment of the French air force in North Africa as of December 1941, and this material was immediately sent to the War Department for study. But in March 1942 it was discovered that the army planners had lost the documents and the whole intelligence job had to be done again![85]

The most serious trouble however, was caused by the lack of agreement among the various American authorities over what should be done in northwest Africa and with whom the United States should do it. Murphy was making cautious contacts with representatives of Vichy hard-liners, such as Adm. Jean-François Darlan, and also talking with pro-Allied leaders of the Vichy civil and military administration in northwest Africa. Donovan, who believed that a German occupation of Morocco and Algeria was imminent, wanted to develop resistance and stay-behind forces by working with the Moors in Spanish and French territory and at the same time encouraging an anti-Axis movement among pro-Allied Vichy officials. Encroaching on the Moorish question was surely the best way to alienate all French sentiment in North Africa, and Donovan ultimately chose to concentrate on working with sympathetic Frenchmen. However, he continued to have doubts about their reliability and never stopped toying with risky schemes for developing a Moorish stay-behind organization.[86]

Hovering above all other problems was the uncertainty within the Anglo-American supreme command regarding North Africa. The British, especially Churchill, continued to push for an invasion of French North Africa, while the Americans, led by General Marshall, refused to relinquish their dream of avoiding "side shows" to permit an assault on the European continent by late 1942 or early 1943. As the spring wore on, the Germans geared up for a renewed offensive in the east and simultaneously reinforced Rommel in northeast Africa, while the schizophrenia in the Allied command increased. While Britain trembled for the security of its position in Egypt, the Americans feared that if the western Allies did not do something drastic on the European continent, the Germans might inflict mortal injury on the Soviet Union.

In northwest Africa, the C.O.I. hawks, led by Colonel Eddy, believed that the Germans were likely to arrive in Morocco and Algeria any day, and they made resistance preparations accordingly. The control officers were driven on to act like full-scale intelligence agents and to forget about the niceties they had learned in "the Consular school of the [State] Department." Arrangements were made to smuggle in explosives, communications equipment, and weapons. Code and cipher systems were improved, and a C.O.I. shortwave radio system was gradually spread throughout Algeria, Tangier, and Morocco. In mid-March, the beaches were studied for suitable landing sites, and this information was sent on to C.O.I. Washington. With Eddy on the job in Tangier, Solborg in Lisbon, and the control officers tied together into a tight network for intelligence collection and sabotage operations, the C.O.I. was fairly well set—and very eager—for action.[87]

On 10 April Eddy gave the action signal. In a special emergency cable to Donovan, the C.O.I. chief in Tangier announced that "the French Command . . . anticipated" a German attack on French North Africa from Tunisia and possibly "simultaneously through Spanish Morocco." Eddy further reported that "the French were now determined to resist" and asked for immediate American assistance in the form of 28,000 land mines to strengthen their defenses. Two days later, he appealed for half a million dollars to help finance French resistance operations, and on 13 April he forwarded a request from his "French partners" that American heavy weapons be stored at some west African point, such as Liberia, so they could be transported by the French to Morocco or Tunisia "at H hour." The list of items for deposit in west Africa included 500 motorcycles, 150 artillery and antitank guns, 450 tanks, 150 additional vehicles, and ammunition for all the weapons.[88]

From the moment Eddy's first "special" message arrived in Washington, Donovan threw himself wholeheartedly into the task of securing everything requested for the "French High Command." He forwarded the cables to the J.C.S. and the J.I.C., while simultaneously praising Eddy's wide experience and good judgment. Donovan badgered his aides and Secretary Knox to get emergency supplies to Gibraltar so they could then be shipped to Eddy by means of a submarine or a Portuguese vessel. Members of the C.O.I. staff urged unlimited support for Eddy and for the French commander, Gen. Alphonse Juin, who they assumed had given the "call for action."[89]

Even such a cautious appreciation of the Eddy operation as that which Solborg sent to Donovan on 20 April did not succeed in cooling off C.O.I. enthusiasm. Solborg warned that the French "instigators" in North Africa were in fact two reserve lieutenant colonels who had good connections, to be sure, but who did not speak for General Juin. In Solborg's view, there was no prospect that active French generals would "commit themselves to us." While asking for "encouragement and support" for Eddy's "splendid endeavors," Solborg noted that a resistance buildup would take time and that money and small arms rather than heavy weapons should be sent. The C.O.I. man in Lisbon also implied that there was no sign of a German intention to attack northwest Africa immediately.[90]

But Donovan had no ear for such caution. Prior to J.I.C. consideration of the problem on 14 April, the colonel had strongly urged that Eddy's recommendations be followed ("he is not one to be easily duped"), and suggested that Pierre Laval's reappearance as head of the government in Vichy was a sign that there was substance to Eddy's dire forebodings. When the J.I.C. concluded that there was no evidence available indicating that a German invasion attempt was near at hand and that the Allies lacked the means to inhibit such an action in any case, Donovan was not mollified. On 20 April, the same day Solborg's cautious cable arrived, Donovan urged the American chiefs to have faith in Eddy and to authorize at least the shipment of money and land mines. But the chiefs leaned toward caution and relied more on the advice of their J.I.C. than on Donovan. C.O.I. was authorized to send some funds to Eddy for use in subversive operations, but the chiefs did not approve shipment of any war material.[91]

The careful stance of the Joint Chiefs reflected doubts about northwest Africa then held by most American generals. Marshall had succeeded in shelving invasion plans for the region for the time being, and all military eyes in Washington were fixed on the European continent. But the decision to give Eddy only very limited support also rested on a solid appraisal of the situation. There were no German preparations for an attack on northwest Africa in April, Eddy was not in contact with the highest levels of the French command there, and the so-called pro-Allied resistance was not yet prepared, nor particularly inclined, to act in support of Allied operations. Furthermore, the J.I.C. and the J.C.S. were quite right when they noted that the Allies did not have the wherewithal to stop the Germans if they chose to go in.

The J.I.C.'s suggestion that it might be a good idea to encourage French resistance so the Germans would have to fight to take northwest Africa rather than secure it peacefully seems rather crass, but the Americans were in no position to supply the large numbers of heavy weapons required to help the French make a serious stand. If the Germans decided to invade, as Rommel would show the British forty days later in Libya, they would have had the means to do so.

C.O.I. estimates of prospects in northwest Africa in April 1942 were wrong, and the Joint Chiefs were right to reject them. Eddy and Donovan had cried wolf, the chiefs had said no, and their appraisal had proven correct. It should have been a sharp rebuff for the young organization, but it did not temper Donovan's enthusiasms in the region one iota. Perhaps he perceived that Franklin Roosevelt was inclining toward a North African landing; in any event, the colonel kept right on pushing. As soon as Laval returned to office in Vichy, Donovan raised the possibility of making a deal with the fallen Darlan. When Eddy visited Washington in early June, he and Donovan continued to press the military authorities for massive assistance to those Vichy officials in north Africa who were inclined to the Allies. Solborg's prudent advice to Donovan was once again rejected, and Eddy went all out in his talks with army intelligence officers, claiming that C.O.I. had ceased all its activities with the Moors due to State Department insistence and was concentrating everything on the development of a strong French resistance organization in Algeria and Morocco. Eddy again asked for supplies, asserting that "we don't need to be timid about North Africa" and predicted that "if we sent an expeditionary force" to the area "there would be only a token resistance."[92]

On such a characteristically optimistic, and rather foolhardy, note the era of C.O.I. activities in northwest Africa came to an end. At this point Donovan's organization passed through its survival crisis and emerged as O.S.S. In assessing C.O.I.'s operational accomplishments, northwest Africa does not stand out as one of its brightest accomplishments. Eddy and Donovan had taken over the only extensive and relatively sophisticated overseas intelligence network that the United States possessed at the time of Pearl Harbor, but they had panicked in April, inaccurately estimating the situation and its possibilities, and their proposals were rejected by the J.C.S. Compared with the successful spadework that C.O.I. did against great odds in Asia or with David Bruce's achievement in putting together the foundations of a worldwide S.I. communications system, C.O.I. fared poorly indeed in northwest Africa. In the months that followed, however, when the new O.S.S. would try to flex its young muscles, northwest Africa would be the place where it would obtain the best opportunity to show what it could do. With Rommel over the border of Egypt and Gen. Erich von Manstein headed for the Caucasus, by July Franklin Roosevelt swung toward the view that the western powers could not wait until all preparations were made for an attack across the Channel. They had to strike quickly, and if northwest Africa was the only suitable target then that would have to be where the Americans would go. Once this was decided, the United States needed excellent intelligence, an effective sabotage organization, and all possible assistance that could be secured from sympathetic Frenchmen in the region.

Prior to June 1942, the efforts of Eddy and his C.O.I. champions in

Washington had done little to improve the image and prestige of Donovan's organization. But for the newly constituted O.S.S. the two most important tasks soon would be to chalk up a quick record of effective assistance to military operations in northwest Africa and to secure enough freedom of action from the Joint Chiefs to allow for a rapid expansion of O.S.S. psychological and subversive warfare. In the last half of 1942, the fate of O.S.S. would largely be decided in Algeria, Morocco, and Washington.

CHAPTER 4

O.S.S. and the Months of Frustration: July 1942-March 1943

Dear Mr. President:

... As you know, you have created an Office of Strategic Services (O.S.S.) under General Donovan and conferred upon it the function of conducting psychological warfare. You have also conferred upon Mr. Davis' Office of War Information (O.W.I.) the function of conducting foreign propaganda. Both of these functions are definitely weapons of war. These gentlemen ever since this was done have differed vigorously and at length as to the scope and jurisdiction of their respective duties. As the head of the War Department and thereby the civilian head of the administration of the Army, I am rather in the position of an innocent bystander in the case of an attempt by a procession of the Ancient and Honorable Order of Hibernians and a procession of Orangemen to pass each other on the same street. I only know that every Army commander hereafter conducting operations in a foreign theatre, if the present differences persist, will be subjected to great embarrassment and danger to his operations.

HENRY L. STIMSON TO F.D.R.
17 February 1943

THE presidential order of 11 July 1942 creating O.S.S. gave the units of the Donovan organization, exclusive of F.I.S., a new lease on life under the authority of the J.C.S. However, the order did not provide clear direction regarding what O.S.S. should do or how it should do it. The American military command, embodied in the J.C.S., was left with the task of determining the range of activities the Donovan organization would be allowed to perform and establishing the procedures to regulate that performance.

The J.C.S. took a full eight months to execute the task, and during that time, most O.S.S. operations were put on hold. An indication of the degree of paralysis that was forced on O.S.S. operations may be gained from the fact that it managed to spend only $25 million out of a $57 million budget during fiscal year 1942. That an emergency wartime organization under an aggressive expansionist such as William Donovan could not find ways to get rid of even half its allotted funds certainly suggests that it was not doing very well. Most of the troubles plaguing O.S.S. were produced by a host of bureaucratic enemies and competitors who wanted to keep the new organization out of their respective territories. O.S.S. was ensnared in a silken net of procedural rules, cloudy authority, and supervisory committees. Only gradually, after a severe crisis extending from late summer of 1942 to early winter of 1943, did the J.C.S. reach a consensus that produced for O.S.S. a distinct mandate and cleared it for action.[1]

To see why all this took so long, it is necessary to glance briefly over the position of the J.C.S., and the state of war, during the last half of 1942 and the first months of 1943. This was the period when the Allies won "turning point" victories on a number of fronts. In June 1942, the month of the birth of O.S.S., American air and naval forces destroyed a substantial portion of the Japanese carrier force at the Battle of Midway. Though nearly a year was to pass before American forces began to make rapid strides across the central Pacific, Midway eliminated the Japanese offensive threat and cut the length of the Pacific war by two or three years. In February 1943, the month before O.S.S. finally received an operational green light from the J.C.S., Field Marshal Friedrich Paulus surrendered the German Sixth Army to Soviet forces at Stalingrad, and three months later the remnants of the Afrika Korps capitulated to Anglo-American armies in Tunisia. These two defeats marked the end of German expansion; though the Wehrmacht still had great strength and a willingness to fight on, the initiative had definitely passed to the Allies.

Aside from the American ground units used in North Africa, the role of the United States in these victories was largely that of an air and naval power and a supplier of war material. Where air and naval forces were decisive, as in the Pacific, the United States took the lead. But in Europe, ground power was what talked and neither Britain nor the United States was ready for a standup struggle with the German Army in 1942. American strategy rested on a policy of mobilizing the full range of American resources (rather than just manpower) on what might be called a worldwide front. The productivity and technical sophistication of American industry and agriculture were at least as important to the cause of Allied victory as was the development of mighty armies, navies, and air forces. Yet the latter, too, were vital. Huge American naval and air forces were essential if the Allies were to have the punch to win in the Pacific and the Atlantic. Large American armies were necessary to combine with the British to form a western pincer against Germany and to join with the Marines and other Allied forces for an advance across the Pacific. Each element in this huge multifaceted mobilization was necessary, and the development of the separate parts had to be fitted into an overall military system that could win the war. Organization, planning, and coordination were thus indispensable, and it was up to the J.C.S. to fit the pieces together and bring them to bear upon the enemy in such a way that victory might be won as quickly and cheaply as possible.

Conceiving this big picture was relatively easy, but making the tough implementing decisions was not. The J.C.S. had to set the basic priorities on technical development and production of war material and arrange for the creation and training of large armed forces. Overly ambitious military leaders and bureaucrats had to be restrained and the hotheads controlled. Those tempted to seek quick confrontations, including General Marshall when he dreamed of attacking the European continent in 1942, had to be reined in, and American garrisons that stood in the way of the initial Japanese advance simply had to be written off, painful as this was to the military and political leaders. Above all, the J.C.S. had to avoid a direct ground confrontation with Germany until the supply battle had been won and America's forces were large enough and sufficiently seasoned to handle the Wehrmacht.

These generalizations seem simple and straightforward. But they depended for effect on a cold calculation that the U.S.S.R. could stand up against the full force of the German Army and the Luftwaffe in 1942 and gain time for a broad and deep American mobilization. In the words of a basic J.C.S. appraisal of 20 June 1942, American strategy rested on a belief that "the U.S.S.R. is capable of engaging fully the entire available striking force of the German Army and Air Force (i.e., 180–200 divisions [3 to 4 million men] and 2,500–3,500 first-line planes), imposing delay and heavy losses upon the attacker, although compelled to give ground." The

J.C.S. accepted that the Soviets would have to pay a heavy price, but concluded, according to the June 1942 appraisal, that after taking the Germans' heaviest blow they "would still be capable of carrying on the war" though possibly on a "greatly reduced scale."[2]

In actuality, the cost to the Soviet Union went far beyond anything imagined in the West. During the war, Anglo-American estimates of Soviet losses were pitched too low, and the exigencies of the later Cold War clouded the West's ability to see the facts. In four years of war, the U.S.S.R. lost some 18 to 20 million dead, including 7.5 million killed in battle. With roughly the same number of soldiers mobilized as in the United States, Russia had twenty-five killed in action for every American killed. Polish and Yugoslav losses were proportionately as large as those of the Russians, and the German–Austrian enemy also had 8–10 million killed in World War II, including 3.5 million battle dead.

A battle of annihilation was raging in the east in 1942 and, by keeping the raw and as yet poorly equipped American armies out of direct participation in that battle, the president and the J.C.S. surely saved the United States millions of casualties. Conversely, the Soviet Union and the people of the eastern occupied territories had to pay a frightful price to stop the Germans and gain the time to complete the wide-ranging American system of mobilization.

Even that was a very close call. The J.C.S. had to grant high priority to Lend-Lease aid to Russia and apply maximum Anglo-American air and naval pressure on Germany. Some operations, such as the invasion of northwest Africa in November 1942 (an action that will be discussed immediately below), were motivated in large part by a belief that some action was essential to take a portion of the load off the Soviet Union. From the Soviet point of view, these actions were trifling compared with the Russian sacrifice, but even such limited American measures laid extra burdens on the J.C.S. The chiefs had set their eyes on the main task of building up a mighty American force that would smother the Axis at the lowest cost in time and men; anything that deflected resources or attention from that task had to be put on the debit side of their ledger. Equipment that went to Russia meant so much less for American troops; raw materials and manpower used for the United States Navy and Air Forces were lost to army units. Diversions such as the one in northwest Africa cost men and material that might have been used in the final full-scale attack on the German-held continent.

The J.C.S. had to act like a miserly board of directors who try to deny small claims of clients and creditors so that resources can be concentrated on the big opportunity. It was an unpleasant business that put a premium on statistics, gross numbers, and the big battalions. Little room was left for clever innovation, ideology, or many of the martial virtues. Putting military bureaucrats in charge ensured clashes and problems for warriors like George Patton, who thought that the essence of the soldier's job was not to count people but to kill them.

At times the system also made the president nervous and petulant. The military structure was his creation, and he supported it, but the task was not always easy for the father of the New Deal. To head an organization run by military statisticians and business executives who did not care a jot about social reform or the creation of a brave new democratic world appealed to Franklin Roosevelt's head, but not to his heart. The president also had difficulty accepting the limitations that this orderly and systematic mobilization process imposed on his freedom to innovate and follow hunches.

But the system was an even heavier burden for the man who had been Franklin Roosevelt's war-games playmate in 1940 and 1941. William Donovan was a dreadful administrator who could be harnessed to bureaucratic routine only with great difficulty. Inspiration, bravery, impulsiveness, innovation, and surprise distinguished his personality as well as his view on how most things should get done. Donovan had grasped that the world and its ways of making war were rapidly changing, but it was not the prospect of winning by gross production that had caught his fancy. Rather, he was attuned to the possibilities offered by speed, deception, cleverness, and nerve. While the Joint Chiefs were counting on the birthrate and the factories of Dearborn, Michigan, Donovan had his eye on radio microphones and commandos. The chiefs presided over a military system that rested on order and predictability made possible by some of the changes associated with modern war. Donovan was convinced that the shortest and cheapest route to victory lay in exploiting the disorder and potential for surprise offered by new forms of struggle and strife. Without exaggerating the contrast, for certainly the J.C.S. valued innovation and surprise while Donovan appreciated the fundamental importance of gross production, the colonel and the chiefs had picked up different ends of the same stick. Since bureaucracy, organization, and committees were the basic medium through which the J.C.S. played its game, Donovan could not hope to win by performing solely on that turf. To gain a significant zone for its operations within the J.C.S. system, O.S.S. had to support its bureaucratic efforts with action in the field. To survive and prosper, Donovan and O.S.S. needed to demonstrate that they could assist military operations. In late 1942, the only place where they could hope to do that on a large scale was in North Africa.

Operation Torch: July–November 1942

21 June 1942: General Rommel takes Tobruk
Late June 1942: Rommel reaches El Alamein
23 October 1942: Montgomery attacks at El Alamein
8 November 1942: Operation Torch—Anglo-American landings in northwest Africa

As we have seen, even before becoming O.S.S., Donovan's organization had been very active in North Africa, and that activity had not been stopped by Eddy's mistaken alarm about a German invasion in April 1942. The C.O.I. control officers went on collecting intelligence, and Eddy continued to make sabotage preparations and carry on discussions with various pro-Allied French groups in the region. At the same time, Robert Murphy and the American diplomatic staff in Morocco, Algeria, and Tangier were talking with French civil and military officials who wanted to cooperate in an Allied endeavor against the Axis.

A confusing situation to be sure, complicated further in late June, shortly after O.S.S. was formed. Robert Solborg, Donovan's man in Lisbon, went to Casablanca and, with Murphy's blessing, talked with a group of officials who claimed that the senior officer of the whole French army, General Giraud, was prepared at the appropriate moment to put himself at the head of a French military force that would cooperate with an Allied invading army. Giraud, having recently escaped from a German prison camp, was in seclusion in Vichy France, but one of his former close subordinates, Gen. Charles-Emmanuel Mast, served as his spokesman in North Africa. After extended discussions, Solborg indicated to Mast that the United States would cooperate with the Giraud group and also gave a number of assurances that North Africa would be left in French hands after an Allied invasion.[3]

Solborg's North African mission chalked up a near record for action without authority or instructions. No one in O.S.S. had approved his trip to North Africa, no Allied invasion had been decided on when he went, and he had no authority to deal with the Mast–Giraud group. In fact, when he had been posted to Portugal in early 1942, Solborg was specifically instructed by Donovan to stay out of North Africa since the German Control Commission had concluded that Solborg was an American agent following his extensive survey in 1941. In consequence, when Solborg returned to Lisbon after meeting Mast in late June 1942, Donovan not only refused to follow up his North African leads but threw Solborg out of O.S.S. With his O.S.S. career having met a quick end, Solborg served in Lisbon solely as the United States Army's attaché. But the French in

North Africa were not told that Solborg and his pledges had been repudiated; in fact, Robert Murphy not only agreed with what Solborg had done, he continued to reassure the pro-Allied French conspirators that the United States was ready to form a partnership with them in the struggle against the Axis.[4]

The groundwork for future trouble was definitely laid by these suggestive talks and the rosy assurances given to the Mast–Giraud group. Problems and confusion also resulted from an Anglo–American agreement concerning control of special operations organizations in the North African region made in mid-June. When Donovan and Goodfellow then met with the S.O.E. chiefs to divide the world into O.S.S. and S.O.E. spheres of operational control, the British contended that they should control the North African area. To support their claim, they pointed to the strong S.O.E. organizations in neighboring Spain, Portugal, and Vichy France, as well as to the large S.O.E. communications center and arms dump in Gibraltar. But the O.S.S. leaders insisted that special operations in North Africa should be theirs, in part because the British were going to control nearly every other area in the world, but also because poor British relations with the Vichy authorities required that a potential Allied invasion into North Africa would have to be led predominantly by Americans. To break the deadlock, a compromise was developed whereby "general direction and control" went to O.S.S. with S.O.E. allowed to run missions into the area. The British M.I. 6 was not affected by the agreement at all. O.S.S. became the "predominant" Allied subversive warfare force in North Africa, but the Allied military authorities did not really grasp that S.O.E. had conceded North African primacy to O.S.S., so clear military directives on subversive control were never issued. Since Eddy and the regional M.I. 6 chief also loathed each other, there was precious little on-the-spot coordination between the British and the Americans.[5]

If North Africa had remained an operational backwater, these Anglo-American jurisdictional problems and the convoluted dealings with the French might have had only moderately serious consequences. But in late July 1942, a command decision was made to launch an Anglo-American fall 1942 landing in North Africa (Operation Torch) which was to take place with, or without, French cooperation. Many factors contributed to the making of the Torch decision, but it was not primarily the American military chiefs who wanted North African landings. The basic decision was made by Franklin Roosevelt, who partly yielded to Churchill's pressure, but whose dominant concern was to get American forces into action somewhere in 1942 so that pressure could be taken off the Soviet Union.[6]

The reluctant American military Chiefs of Staff and their more enthusiastic and experienced British colleagues therefore went to work in late July on the difficult task of planning Torch. Time was very short; only three and a half months were allowed for planning and preparation. Everyone agreed that to dampen the Anglophobe hostility of the Vichy authorities the operation should appear overwhelmingly American, but the United States troops were green, and their officers, including the commander of the operation, Dwight D. Eisenhower, had little or no combat experience. The logistics of Torch were extremely complicated, with one task force moving in from Great Britain while the second force sailed directly from the United States to the Mediterranean. These complex movements had to be kept secret from the Germans, a task somewhat at odds with the need to persuade the French authorities in North Africa not to resist the invasion. This need for secrecy, together with a desire to avoid political complications with the French, led the (C.C.S.) to completely exclude de Gaulle's Free French organization from the Torch planning. De Gaulle was let in on the secret only on the eve of the landings, a slight that later produced great difficulty for the English and the Americans in their dealings with the Free French but did not adversely affect the actual invasion, which took place in November 1942.[7]

The main Torch headache for the C.C.S. in the summer of 1942 was not de Gaulle but the weakness of the Allied invasion force. The 100,000-man Torch army would not be strong enough to achieve a striking success if the Germans were to concentrate substantial forces in the western Mediterranean and move them quickly against Eisenhower's expedition. If the Allies did not achieve complete surprise, they could face very rough going, and a whole series of cover and deception plans for the operation were therefore developed. At one time or another efforts were made to persuade the Germans that the Torch blow was aimed at the Portuguese Atlantic islands, northern France, Norway, Malta, Syria, and even Haiti. The British were initially anxious to keep attention away from Dakar, fearing that in light of the extreme anti-British sentiment generated in Vichy by the ill-fated Anglo-Free French attack there in 1940, a feint in that direction might stiffen the will to resist of the Vichy forces who would face the real blow (in Algeria and Morocco).[8]

But in the summer of 1942 stories circulated all through the Mediterranean that an Allied North African invasion was imminent, and in September an Allied courier carrying papers indicating the date and precise location of the landings was killed in a plane crash off the coast of Spain. Allied security had proved very leaky, and the Anglo-American command feared that their cover stories had been blown. Therefore, when Churchill learned from an Ultra intercept in early October that the Germans were massing U-boats off Dakar with the obvious intention of shielding what they thought was the intended point of Allied attack, he ordered the deception operations to be changed. In the last month before Torch, a Dakar invasion threat became the main deception target for the North African landings. Since the Germans had already convinced themselves that Dakar was the intended point of attack, this deception effort worked splendidly, and the landings in Morocco and Algeria achieved total surprise. Some O.S.S. champions have claimed that Donovan's organization was responsible for the success of the Dakar deception operation, but the chief credit should really go to Ultra and the innovative spirit of the British prime minister.[9]

The deception achievement was vital for the success of the operation, but it did not prove itself until the day of invasion. In the meantime, Eisenhower and his staff were tormented by the small size of their invading army. A reorganization that concentrated and strengthened the initial assault force was carried through in late August, but there were still fears that the Torch attacking units were not strong enough to carry their objectives. If the Germans struck quickly through southern France, Spain, and then across the Straits of Gibraltar, catching Eisenhower's forces in the rear, the Torch armies might be badly battered. Even if this threat did not materialize, the French in Morocco were likely to resist, and if they did, the invading force would be dangerously exposed while it tried to beat them down. A British military intelligence estimate of 31 August 1942 concluded that Vichy would order resistance to Torch and that the French Navy and the bulk of the army would "obey in the first instance." For the Allied invasion to succeed, the planners concluded, the Torch forces would have to go in hard and hope that an initial display of overwhelming force would convince the French to capitulate. But how the Allied commanders were to combine force with persuasion was not clear. The British naval commander, Adm. Sir Bertram Ramsay, plaintively asked the British chiefs in mid-October, "Do we appeal and then open fire?"[10]

Try as they might, the planners could not find a clear answer to that question. George Patton, who commanded the Western Task Force, was ready to forgo all efforts to dissuade the French from resistance. Waiting "until they shoot at us" was so alien to his nature that Patton considered preinvasion political maneuvering "tantamount to giving your opponent the draw in a gun fight." Patton was not in charge of overall planning, however, nor was he the supreme commander. In contrast to Patton, Eisenhower and the combined chiefs believed that political maneuvers, psychological warfare, and sabotage would have to be used to soften up the

French, and this meant that a heavy responsibility would fall on Robert Murphy and on Eddy's O.S.S. organization in North Africa.[11]

The activities of both Eddy and Murphy were mainly directed toward French officials and soldiers in North Africa who looked to General Mast, and ultimately General Giraud, as their leaders. These French patriots, led by a committee called the Five, wanted to assist any operation or movement that would give Frenchmen an opportunity to help recover the pride and confidence that they had lost during the humiliations of 1940. Their chief goal was the early liberation of France, but at least some of them were prepared to accept the necessity of an Allied invasion of North Africa as a step toward that end. They were, of course, in a highly vulnerable position, for cooperation with the Allies was treason in the eyes of Marshal Pétain and the Vichy authorities. After the ill-conceived and unsuccessful British attacks on Vichy forces at Oran and Dakar in 1940 and the subsequent poor Allied showing in the war culminating in the new offensive that took Rommel over the border into Egypt in June 1942, there were good reasons for Frenchmen to distrust the judgment and ability of the Allies. To protect their own positions and that of the French nation, the Five wanted Allied guarantees that Frenchmen would play leading roles in the invasion operation and that a French state would retain control of the administration in North Africa thereafter.

Quite obviously, Murphy, Eddy, and the joint military command were in no position to meet such French demands. The Allies were preparing to move a weak invasion force into North Africa immediately. Extended discussion with a shadowy French group that might prove to be unreliable was out of the question. The Allies wanted whatever help they could get in North Africa, but only on their terms. The assistance of willing Frenchmen would be welcome, but the planning, control, and timing of Torch had to remain completely in British and American hands.

For Murphy, and to a lesser degree for Eddy, the main job was to convince Eisenhower and his staff that they could get significant French support in North Africa, and at the same time persuade Frenchmen that they should cooperate without giving them all the details of Torch. Eddy and Murphy accomplished the first half of this mission by providing the Allied leaders with a rosier view of the Five's strength and willingness to aid an Allied invasion than the facts warranted. In a series of meetings with British and American officials in London and Washington, they painted a picture of a mighty resistance force in North Africa that needed only modest Allied support and encouragement to become the vanguard of invasion. Eddy had begun to sing this song in April, and he continued to do so all through the summer. Murphy exaggerated the power of the

Five in a number of reports during July and August, and on 16 September while in London he gave Eisenhower a glowing account of the strength and determination of the pro-American forces in Morocco and Algeria. Murphy's vision of massive support on the ground clearly had its effect on Eisenhower and his staff; the supreme commander's naval aide remarked in his diary that if everything Murphy anticipated "in the way of French cooperation" actually came to pass, "many of our worries will have been needless."[12]

However Murphy and Eddy had given the truth a generous stretch in order to encourage Eisenhower and his circle to feel so optimistic, and on the other side of their activities, the two American shadow warriors were also deceptively reassuring with the French. In conformity with Eisenhower's orders, they hinted to the Five that something big was in the wind, but the secret of the time and place of the Torch landings was only revealed to the French shortly before the Allied units hit the beaches.

Inevitably, the overly optimistic "facilitating" labor of Murphy and Eddy would later come under a cloud because the higher hopes they had aroused in both camps could not be realized. Some of the French and the Allied planners were left with a feeling that they had fallen victim to sharp practices. Viewed realistically, however, aside from a few instances of faulty judgment and self-delusion, Murphy and Eddy did what the situation called for. The Allies wanted to go into Morocco and Algeria but were hobbled by their sense of weakness. Many Frenchmen in North Africa wanted the Allies to come but were afraid that they would be so feeble and indecisive that the mission would fail. The Allies needed to be encouraged to act like lions and the French needed to be helped to believe in Allied power and ferocity. If that trick could be turned, Torch would surely succeed. For all their missteps and the fact that they too seem to have fallen victim to some of their own enthusiasm, Murphy and Eddy got this job done.

Their good work was supplemented by Allied efforts to influence the French through such customary psychological warfare devices as pamphlets and radio broadcasts. Eisenhower's deputy, Gen. Mark Clark, even suggested using skywriters to fill the air with messages proclaiming Allied goodwill. An additional Clark scheme—so wonderfully American—consisted of putting coupons in propaganda leaflets to Frenchmen, which could be surrendered to the Allies for cash prizes![13]

The final content of this propaganda blitz was determined by an Anglo-American team of P.W.E., O.W.I., and O.S.S. propaganda specialists. Despite a bit of Anglo-American sniping, the political strategy and the content of the propaganda produced no serious difficulties. There was trouble aplenty, however, over how to organize both political and propaganda activities. Eisenhower initially wanted to put the whole of subversive, propaganda, and political warfare into the hands of the British. But O.S.S. objections and the solid work turned in by Eddy's organization (contrasting markedly with the feeble efforts of S.O.E.), ultimately persuaded Eisenhower to increase the American role in all shadow warfare activities for Torch.[14]

Eddy was granted a special direct channel to Eisenhower's headquarters, and O.S.S. (black) and O.W.I. (white) propaganda people had their positions similarly enhanced in the course of the Torch planning. In Eisenhower's original scheme, they were to serve, along with the P.W.E., in a political warfare section under the direction of W.H.B. Mack, the Foreign Office man who warned of the German "termite" danger in 1941. But Mack's tenure as Torch political chief was short-lived because of the prevalent belief in the Anglo-American planning staff that all British influence should be muted to reassure the Vichy French. In addition, the O.S.S. chief in London, William Phillips, thought the arrangements gave O.W.I. supremacy over O.S.S. and vigorously protested to Washington. Donovan took up the cudgels in this battle, and after a brief flurry of what Gen. Alfred Gruenther called intramural difficulties, a new political–propaganda command structure for Torch was created in late October. Mack was pushed into the background, H. Freeman Matthews of the State Department was put in charge of political affairs, and a "neutral" American colonel, C. B. Hazeltine, was made chief of the Propaganda and Psychological Warfare Planning Section during the preinvasion and assault period. Peace was thereby established on the Allied Torch propaganda front, with O.S.S. propagandists settled in under Hazeltine in G-1 (Personnel), O.S.S.–S.I. men reporting to G-2 (Intelligence) and O.S.S. special operations people working under G-3 (Operations).[15]

In the meantime, Eddy had succeeded in fulfilling the intelligence assignment that the army had given to him. After journeying to London in mid-August to provide Eisenhower's staff with a general briefing on conditions in North Africa, he had returned to organize operations in Tangier. His network of control officers and subagents sent a large volume of intelligence reports to Eisenhower's headquarters and O.S.S. Washington in September and October. In addition to estimates of the political situation in French and Spanish North Africa, precise information was supplied on beach conditions, port traffic, and fortifications. Even a detailed account of the light arms held by the German Armistice Commission was transmitted to Eisenhower, and in mid-September Eddy sent C. V. Clopet, an experienced French hydrographer, to London to give the invasion commanders a complete picture of the conditions they would encounter in landing.[16]

Surely not all of Eddy's reports were accurate. A panicky message in early October claimed that 100,000 German and Italian troops were poised in Tunisia preparing for an invasion of Algeria. Eddy also committed a serious gaff by smuggling out the pilot of Port Lyautey without prior authorization from London or Washington. Eisenhower and Marshall were momentarily alarmed by the blunder, which they feared could indicate to the Germans one of the points where the Allies intended to land.[17]

Under the circumstances, however, these were minor blemishes. Eddy provided a large volume of detailed information which, when supplemented by attaché dispatches, Ultra decrypts, and M.I. 6 agent reports, gave Eisenhower's staff an unusually complete picture of operational conditions.[18]

Most other intelligence services sent Washington and London many more alarmist and erroneous reports of German strength and intentions than did Eddy and the O.S.S. representatives in Spain and Vichy France. Czech and Polish dispatches frequently reported massive—and imaginary—German buildups in the Mediterranean throughout the fall of 1942. But since Eddy's people were better placed on the spot and had excellent sources of information—including decrypts of German Armistice Commission messages slipped to them by French friends—they were able to avoid the worst errors and exaggerations. Understandably, the nervous Allied invasion command was grateful for the comprehensive and matter-of-fact reporting that characterized Eddy's team, and during the actual invasion the North African O.S.S. organization proved of additional great value by providing direct intelligence assistance. Eddy himself was stationed in Gibraltar to help coordinate intelligence during the landings, and two O.S.S. control officers were slipped out of Casablanca and Oran and went in with the invasion forces.[19]

In contrast to these solid intelligence achievements, Eddy's sabotage efforts registered very few successes. In late August, the North African O.S.S. chief asked Eisenhower's staff for instructions on sabotage targets, but General Gruenther and W.H.B. Mack replied that O.S.S. should stick to general preparations for the time being and that detailed guidelines would be provided later. In mid-September, plans were therefore made by Eddy and his S.O. men for a large number of sabotage operations, including attacks on power stations and the French Navy's oil reserve. But their arrangements for landing weapons and other sabotage supplies proved to be faulty, and this troubled O.S.S. itself and Eisenhower's staff.

No one seemed able to solve the problem, however, and the arms that were promised to Eddy's French "friends" never arrived in North Africa. Perhaps, as some have suggested, the lack of arms shipments from Gibraltar was caused by the jealous efforts of the S.O.E. to undermine the whole operation, but it seems more likely that the customary combination of errors and confusion that characterized all Anglo-American special operations projects in this period was the real villain.[20]

In late September, on orders from General Clark, detailed special operations (fifth column) objectives and priorities were laid out by Eisenhower's G-3, Gen. Lyman Lemnitzer. Since it was assumed that the French navy controlled the coastal areas and was determined to fight, Lemnitzer did not include immediate coastal defenses in his list of high-priority sabotage targets. S.O. operations were to be concentrated on presumably accessible targets, such as airdromes, while vital radio, power, and telephone stations were to be safeguarded for later Allied use. In the event of prolonged French opposition to the invasion, supplemental orders to S.O. units would be issued by the task force commanders. Here the matter remained until mid-October when Murphy, Eddy, and the task force commanders received their final S.O. instructions. These called for Eddy's men, and their French comrades, to cut the telephone connections to the French shore batteries and light flares to guide incoming Allied aircraft. Additionally, if possible, they were to seize and hold airfields and radio and telephone stations. Eddy replied on 23 October that he thought most of this could be done, although he could not guarantee the destruction of secret military radio stations or promise effective action regarding dock and port equipment.[21]

Eddy's optimism about conditions ashore was reinforced by General Clark's secret meeting with France's General Mast and some of his staff in North Africa on 22–23 October. Despite a good measure of the usual troubles that plague submarine and rubber raft operations, and some misunderstandings between Clark and the French, the American general returned from his adventure believing that the odds favored a successful landing. Eisenhower still anticipated some rough going, but he seems to have been reassured by Clark's report that the invasion force would receive substantial French assistance in Algeria and Morocco. On the eve of the landings, the deception plan also seemed to be working since the Germans were focused on Dakar; the great invasion convoy could therefore count on surprise when it would appear off the northwest African coast.[22]

The Germans and the Vichy French really were stunned when the North African landings began, but from the moment the Allied troops began to go ashore on 8 November, little else went according to plan. In the confusion of a night landing, troops were put in at the wrong points and often failed to receive adequate air and naval support. Many of the vessels used were not suitable for amphibious operations and, due to a poor system of cargo loading, units and equipment required for a rapid advance did not reach the beaches quickly enough. The Allied forces were initially unsure about whether they had come to talk or shoot, but the French navy had no doubts about its duty and fought back hard. The landing forces suffered casualties and were pinned to the beach at many points.

Pandemonium reigned among the Vichy authorities and also among the French "friends" of Eddy and Murphy. As we have noted, General Mast and his aides were told of the impending landings only a short time before they took place, and many of them were offended that the Allies had kept them in the dark for so long. The sabotage materials and weapons that had been so frequently promised did not arrive, and there was little time to work out new sabotage arrangements. A number of French officers whose cooperation was needed for the planned seizure of the airfields had been transferred, and these projects had to be abandoned. Through a series of mix-ups, Gen. Emile Béthouart, commander of the French division controlling Casablanca, was told of the invasion too late to make adequate arrangements for seizing senior French civil and military officials. In the Oran area, the Vichy French commander, Gen. Robert Boissau, who had no connections with the resistance, learned accidentally of the fifth column plans, and virtually all subversive operations in support of Patton's task force therefore had to be abandoned. At isolated points, especially in Algiers, some sabotage missions were carried out and General Juin was temporarily held prisoner by a small pro-Allied group that seized French military headquarters in a scene out of a poor nineteenth-century opera. In general, however, the subversive fifth column missions in support of the Allied forces failed completely.[23]

Confusion and uncertainty continued throughout the whole of 8 and 9 November, Eisenhower, code-named Jaywalker because of his Kansas birth, in the rather simpleminded code employed during the operation, could not get a clear picture of what was happening ashore. The ciphers used to communicate with Murphy and other Allied personnel in North Africa were found at the last moment to be suspect, and this seems to have crippled the elaborate communications network that had been created for the invasion. Furthermore, General Giraud, who had been brought out of France at the last minute, was less than enthusiastic about the invasion operation and insisted that he should be given the supreme command. Eisenhower and his chief of staff, Gen. Walter B. Smith (Indiana-born and therefore code-named Hoosier) spent endless hours trying to persuade "Kingpin" (General Giraud) to cooperate, but the most they could get was a shaky understanding whereby the French general agreed to go to North Africa with the Allied force as a kind of French associate.[24]

Even this scheme backfired because Admiral Darlan had unexpectedly made a trip to North Africa and was in Algiers at the time of the Allied landings. As the ranking French officer on the spot, he, rather than Giraud, held the key to an unobstructed Allied advance. Giraud quickly ceased to be "Kingpin," and the anti-Vichy "friends" of Murphy and Eddy were also pushed into the background. Darlan, after all, was the most prominent and notorious Vichy figure aside from Pétain and Laval, and he emerged as the man of the hour for the British and Americans. Despite his sinister reputation, the Allies had previously established some tentative contacts with the admiral; as recently as 17 October, the British Chiefs of Staff had declared that although they preferred to deal with Giraud, they felt "it would be wise" to keep Darlan "in play."[25]

The combined effect of Darlan's accidental presence in Algiers, the inability of the invasion force to strike quickly inland, and the failure to mobilize a pro-Allied fifth column put most of the strong cards in the admiral's hands. Eisenhower's fleet of troop transports and merchant vessels was floating off the coast, unable to land and highly vulnerable to attack as long as the Allies did not control the major North African ports. The troops who had gotten ashore were inching forward at some point, but they had not secured safe havens for the invasion fleet. Eisenhower believed he had little choice other than to deal with the French, and he sent Mark Clark to negotiate an arrangement whereby the Vichy forces would cease firing in exchange for Allied pledges that Darlan and the Vichy officials on the spot would retain a large measure of authority in Algeria and Morocco.

The resulting Clark–Darlan deal (10 November 1942) was bitterly criticized by many people in Britain and the United States. The liberal left denounced it as a sellout to Fascism, and ideologues in O.W.I. and O.S.S. were scathing in their attacks on this shabby exercise in realpolitik. In subsequent months (especially during the period of undiluted control by Vichy officials prior to Darlan's assassination on 24 December), Jews, Gaullists, and those who had been most active in helping the Allies prior to the invasion were harshly treated by the French authorities. Such conditions were grist for the mill of those who opposed the Clark–Darlan agreement, and many O.S.S. men who had been in North Africa prior to 9 November vigorously protested to the Anglo-American command that something had to be done to right the situation and protect the Allies' friends in North Africa. Very gradually, under Allied pressure, the French administration took on a more democratic, pro-Allied, and ultimately Gaullist, complexion. Paradoxically, just as gradually, the O.S.S. organization in North Africa became more politically conservative and, as we will see below, by late 1943 a number of its chiefs were distinctly anti-Gaullist.[26]

The political crusade to "free" North Africa, as well as the O.S.S. role in that operation, thus ended with a highly mixed record. Years later Eddy himself, while still relishing the adventure of it all, would bemoan the unpleasant political effect it had on North Africa and U.S. relations with de Gaulle. If one focuses on the North African events from the point of view of the effect they had on the fate and future of O.S.S., however, it is obvious that Torch was a major plus for Donovan's organization. The S.O. sabotage operations had not been successful, to be sure, but a fair-minded judge—and Eisenhower seems to have been one—recognized that the major reasons for that failure did not lie with O.S.S. The situation had been too complicated, the clock set too short, and the necessary weapons and sabotage supplies insufficient. On the other hand, in its propaganda work and especially as an intelligence gathering agency, O.S.S. had given important assistance to the Allied high command. The propaganda operations conducted by O.S.S., O.W.I., and P.W.E. never produced the walkover that some optimists had hoped for, but in the midst of a tricky operation, the British and American propagandists largely succeeded in maintaining and intensifying pro-Allied sentiment among the native population and the French. At the same time, Eddy had performed his intelligence tasks brilliantly. In the reappraisals after Torch, United States Army investigators found much to criticize about virtually every aspect of the invasion operation except intelligence. Combat units registered only a few minor complaints regarding faulty maps and the like, but there was near unanimous praise for the quality, abundance, and accuracy of the terrain and order of battle information that had been given to the troops. Not all of this achievement was due to O.S.S., certainly, but a substantial portion of it definitely was.[27]

These accomplishments brought real credit to the O.S.S. organization, and the experience of working in close cooperation with Eisenhower's Torch staff also went a long way toward proving that O.S.S. could be a useful partner to military commanders. A number of high-ranking army officers concluded that they could work easily with O.S.S.—a feeling that most of them did not have about O.W.I.—and this obviously worked to the advantage of Donovan's organization. As the first testing ground for American offensive warfare, Torch revealed a number of shortcomings and elements of amateurishness within the whole military machine, including O.S.S., which would have to be corrected. But in regard to whether or not Donovan's organization could render valuable assistance to American combined operations, the O.S.S. Torch team had provided a clear and very positive answer.

O.S.S. and S.O.E. in the Battles of London and Washington: July 1942–March 1943

22 December 1942: The basic O.S.S. charter approved by the Joint Chiefs of staff

11 March 1943: President Roosevelt reaffirms that O.W.I., not O.S.S., should control most overseas propaganda

The Torch achievement greatly strengthened O.S.S. for the organizational battles that developed during the fall and winter of 1942–1943. The placing of Donovan's organization—except for F.I.S.—under the Joint Chiefs had signaled to a number of personal and organizational rivals that it might be a good time to see whether a province or two could be detached from the colonel's empire. Some of the resulting skirmishes, such as those with the F.B.I. and the State Department over control of operations in Latin America and Hawaii, were settled quickly, and with J.C.S. support, O.S.S. dissuaded Adolf Berle from trying to reopen the question of relations between Donovan's organization and the State Department. In August and September 1942, O.S.S. and B.E.W. also worked out a highly successful cooperative agreement for pooling experts working on air force targeting and similar operations in London and Washington. Furthermore, Donovan's men soon grasped that adroit use of O.S.S.'s new status as an agency of the Joint Chiefs of Staff could help solve troublesome problems concerning such matters as supply, procurement, and travel priorities.[28]

However, in late 1942 and early 1943, O.S.S. witnessed much more bureaucratic war than peace, and the battles became so heated that it is easy to lose one's way among the details. The conflict and disorder arose primarily from the changed circumstances of the British and American governments. It is indicative of the general situation that at a time when O.S.S. was caught in the middle of fierce conflicts in Washington, S.O.E. was encountering very similar difficulties in London. Throughout the summer and early fall, while O.S.S. wrestled with O.W.I. in Washington, S.O.E. was squabbling with P.W.E. over control of British overseas propaganda. In early September, authority over all British propaganda aimed at enemy-occupied territory was finally given to P.W.E., and B.S.C. also gave the last of its propaganda operations to P.W.E. as well.

With the British and the Americans going over to the offensive, the actions of impulsive O.S.S. or S.O.E. buccaneers could not be allowed to disrupt operations. For Britain, as well as the United States, it was vital that the gigantic C.C.S. machine be allowed to roll on to victory. The Foreign and War offices in London made an extra effort to put S.O.E. under tight rein to prevent "silly" adventures. Certainly not every bizarre idea was rejected—the British Chiefs of Staff allowed S.O.E. to send special weapons overseas in July 1942 to be used in the event of an "outbreak of gas warfare"—but in spite of lapses and the continued presence in the subversive warfare organizations of a large number of young men who, in the words of an M.I. 6 veteran, "look a bit of a Stock Exchange-Movie-Foreign Office mixture," the controls were steadily tightened.[29]

Britain was more sensitive than the United States about the need to bring special operations into line with the government's postwar foreign policy, and S.O.E. in particular felt the long arm of control in this area. As early as October 1942, Anthony Eden was fuming about what he saw as S.O.E.'s willingness to "collaborate with parties of the Left," a tendency that the foreign secretary denounced as a "very dangerous doctrine." As long as S.O.E. could show that its work with leftists and revolutionaries was necessary to carry out operations essential to the war effort, the Foreign Office usually acquiesced, for London did not have crystal-clear priorities. In his mind Churchill was committed to the broad Anglo-American C.C.S. mobilization system, but in his heart he was devoted to defending imperialism, and his passions inclined him to a romantic enthusiasm for guerrilla warfare. Therefore, it was very difficult to keep the British war machine on a single track. On occasion, S.O.E. could find encouragement at Number 10 for some of its more surprising schemes because, as the prime minister's support for Tito would later show, Churchill was capable of putting military advantage and possible long-term political interests ahead of his revulsion to close cooperation with leftists.[30]

In general, however, the C.C.S. machine had taken possession of the center of Britain's war-making policy by mid-1942. Even the prime minister's emotional impulsiveness was given less room to express itself, though Lord Ismay could still regret Churchill's gift for acting "just like a child who has lost its temper." Tough mass-mobilization warfare is hard on imaginative and impulsive prime ministers and even harder on subversive warfare organizations. In March 1943—the same month O.S.S. finally obtained its clear operating instructions from the J.C.S.—the British military command put S.O.E. under closer military control. The British chiefs put an end to operational uncertainty by ordering that henceforth all S.O.E. operations be "related to our operational plans so that S.O.E. activities could contribute the maximum assistance to them." This was the language of the C.C.S. war machine, and as it was spoken in Britain so was it spoken in the United States.[31]

In America, where the biggest headache for the J.C.S. was not the president's temper but his love for innovation and improvisation, the years 1942–43 saw a substantial movement in the direction of military staff control. Roosevelt still gave policy its overall direction, and he managed to preserve many of the boards and bureaus that he found so useful in getting what he wanted in policy controversies. But the power and authority of the J.C.S. grew to such proportions that other organs of government, including the traditional departments as well as the various wartime agencies, found themselves outclassed. The J.C.S. not only controlled the men and the money but also had the responsibility of carrying the government's war plans directly to victory. Those who challenged the J.C.S. directly faced the argument that if the chiefs did not get their way, there would be a longer war, higher casualties, and a poorer chance of victory. Few politicians were tough enough, or sure enough of their ground, to do battle on such terms, and as the months of 1942–43 rolled by, even the president interfered less frequently in what had become J.C.S. business. The era of war games in the Oval Office was over; William Donovan and the others who had enjoyed easy access to the president in the free-wheeling days of early 1942 now found that months would pass without their being allowed to see him at all. Mr. Roosevelt focused more of his attention on long-term policy and only occasionally made sorties to set things right when he felt that the J.C.S. had gone astray. Day-to-day direction of the war was in the hands of the J.C.S., and every organ of American government was forced to adjust to that fact.

Obviously, once the Donovan organization passed under their control, the chiefs had to reshape it to better serve military needs. Such reorganization was inevitable since O.S.S. had not been created to implement military policy. It was overwhelmingly civilian both in personnel and outlook and like C.O.I. before it, was focused on Donovan and the White House, not on the supreme military command. Because it had not had a clearly defined position in the war-making structure, and William Donovan was its chief, it had emphasized inventiveness and improvisation. From June 1942 on, much of this had to change, for to the J.C.S. the battle alone was the payoff. It was the chiefs' duty, as well as their desire, to require all units under their control to follow orders, to keep their eyes fixed on the main military goals, and to fight and win what the J.C.S. thought were the decisive battles.

The task of reforming and refocusing O.S.S. to serve the J.C.S. was complicated by a number of considerations. Because O.S.S. depended heavily on presidential unvouchered funds, and because of Donovan's rather close relations with the president, there was an element of White House interest involved. Some aspects of O.S.S. operations also touched on high policy and politically sensitive issues. Secret intelligence and propaganda could not be dealt with summarily. Suspicion of governmental secret power and fear of manipulation by government propaganda was intense in the America of 1942–43, and in addition serious international complications could arise regarding both these matters if they were not treated deftly.

The military authorities in whose hands the fate of Donovan's organization rested also brought peculiar, and often negative, views to the task of refocusing O.S.S. Many of them were suspicious of all civilian organizations, and they had little patience with what seemed to them the confusing hodgepodge of O.S.S. They were, furthermore, apprehensive about Colonel Donovan's bureaucratic imperialism and his mercurial nature. Resentment against what the military services saw as encroachment on military and naval intelligence simmered on in O.N.I. and M.I.D., and there was also considerable skepticism about the preparations Donovan had made for special operations and commando activities. Some generals and admirals wanted simply to pillage O.S.S. by seizing its budget and valuable personnel and then discarding the residue. Others understood that whatever the difficulties, Donovan was right in his principle contention that unorthodox warfare was necessary. Men like General Marshall and Admiral Leahy were not altogether happy with Donovan and O.S.S., but they were as convinced of the reality of a dangerous Axis fifth column as were most other Americans, and it was their responsibility to organize the American response to irregular enemy warfare.[32] O.S.S. was therefore preserved, although reshaped, because the chiefs recognized that unorthodox warfare was important. But despite the positive view, negative feelings toward Donovan and his organization persisted and the interaction of these positive and negative attitudes ultimately determined the fate of O.S.S.

Regarding its budget, O.S.S. fared surprisingly well. The Bureau of the Budget was anxious to eliminate the overlap of activities that allegedly existed between O.S.S. and other organizations. In addition, as already indicated, there were those within the military hierarchy who were, in the words of an officer in the Operations Division, "very desirous of controlling" what they saw as the swollen budget of O.S.S. When push came to shove, however, the J.C.S. provided Donovan with strong support. O.S.S. was allowed interim three-month budget allotments until the full range and form of its activities could be determined. Whenever a basic three-month allotment proved insufficient, the J.C.S. approved the colonel's requests for more money, and Donovan won out during the final showdown with the Bureau of the Budget in August 1942. Military pirates were prevented from seizing the O.S.S. treasure, and Harold Smith and his Budget Bureau staff, failing in their attempt to trim back O.S.S. activities, were left to grumble that Donovan had "sold the President a bill of goods." [33]

The chiefs also moved expeditiously to provide O.S.S. with a general charter regularizing its existence as an instrument of the J.C.S. On 23 June, a directive designating O.S.S. as a J.C.S. supporting agency to perform "research, secret intelligence and subversive activities" was approved. On the same day, Donovan was made chairman of the newly reorganized Joint Psychological Warfare Committee (J.P.W.C.).

These two actions marked the end of the honeymoon between O.S.S. and J.C.S., however, and the military authorities went on to tackle the more sensitive questions of how to control the colonel and how to make certain that O.S.S. operations were integrated with military plans and operations. To achieve these ends, it was proposed that O.S.S. submit all projects to the J.P.W.C. or the (J.I.C.) for approval before they would even be considered by the Joint Planning Staff (J.P.S.) of J.C.S. The more this proposal was considered, the more opportunities arose for imposing additional restrictions on O.S.S., such as forbidding Donovan's organization from making agreements with foreign agencies without J.C.S. consent. Protracted discussions and the consequent revisions provided ample opportunity for old enemies of Donovan, such as the chief of G-2, General Strong, to try to confine O.S.S. within a maze of procedural requirements and military vetoes. O.S.S. succeeded in escaping some of the more diabolical torments conceived by General Strong and his associates, but the revised J.C.S. order of 14 August made all O.S.S. operations subject to control by theater commanders and required that O.S.S. plans pass through either the J.I.C. or the J.P.W.C. before they could be put before the J.C.S. or its planning board (J.P.S.). [34]

Since O.S.S. did not have a clear mandate to perform any specific activities, nearly every proposal it put before the J.I.C. and J.P.W.C. was shredded. The army members of these committees, like most top army officers, were now uncertain about what should be done regarding guerrilla warfare. Some wanted it to be carried out by soldiers under military command, whereas others believed that such activities would be in violation of the laws of war and should be left to civilians. Whichever approach O.S.S. took—whether asking for allotments of soldiers to be trained as guerrillas or for permission to train foreign civilians for the task—it ran into trouble. During July 1942 Donovan managed to secure a few additional military officers to act as instructors, but he could get no further with his grandiose plans for a large guerrilla army. Then in early August the colonel was shrewd enough to combine his efforts to get authorization for his guerrilla warfare organization with a request that the J.C.S. formally approve the agreement that he had negotiated with the British S.O.E. in June to divide the world into American and British spheres of subversive warfare activity. The J.C.S. was obviously reluctant to give up any American operational territory or to scotch a deal made with America's closest ally. On 18 August, after two weeks of wrangling, the J.C.S. issued a paper authorizing some O.S.S. guerrilla warfare functions (J.C.S. 83) and approved the O.S.S. subversive warfare agreement with S.O.E. a week later.[35]

Donovan immediately made plans to train dozens of forty-man "troops" of guerrilla warriors drawn from American ethnics and foreign nationals. He even created a Strategic Service Command within O.S.S. to direct and train this guerrilla army. But whereas the J.C.S. order of 18 August had given O.S.S. clear authority to prepare guerrilla forces, it had not clarified whether these men were to be soldiers or civilians. So Donovan was halfway back to square one, still begging for training personnel and unable to get approval to develop the militarized commando-type units so dear to his heart.[36]

On 10 September 1942, General Strong dropped another shoe, insisting that neither the J.I.C. nor the J.P.W.C. should approve any additional requests for the use of army or navy personnel in O.S.S. operations because O.S.S. had not been declared a military organization. The chief of G-2, who had a seat on both committees, had been sniping at every O.S.S. request for personnel and operational approval submitted during the previous two months. The general seems to have believed that he had a holy mission to control O.S.S. and stop its incursions into areas that he believed should be the preserve of G-2 and other sections of the army. The personnel allotment issue provided him with an excellent weapon because Secretary of War Stimson had recently ruled that to avoid dispersal of manpower, no more army personnel should be authorized for duty with civilian organizations. Donovan gamely tried to work his way ahead, submitting one request after another for military personnel for his training schools, but though he managed to obtain a few men here and there, Strong had blocked him yet again.[37]

Months of haggling and spools of bureaucratic red tape brought the O.S.S. to a near standstill by the early fall. The J.I.C. consistently blocked Donovan's proposals for new intelligence operations; the colonel could not get personnel for his guerrilla-commando units; the J.P.W.C. endlessly debated the true meaning of the phrase *psychological warfare*. Then in September the prospects for O.S.S. began to brighten. Eddy's pre-Torch activities were flourishing, and some generals believed that O.S.S. might deliver them from the tight spot in which they found themselves regarding North Africa. The idea of militarizing O.S.S., which General Strong had proposed as another means of restraining Donovan's organization, now began to receive sympathetic consideration from a number of staff officers who thought it might help to break the logjam. Donovan indicated that he favored the militarization of O.S.S., and in mid-October General Marshall suggested that at least O.S.S. supervisorial personnel should be commissioned in the army or navy.[38]

Building on this basis, the new secretary of the Joint Chiefs, Brig. Gen. John R. Deane (who took over the post when Gen. W. Bedell Smith became Eisenhower's chief of staff for Torch) launched an effort on 22 October to get O.S.S. the clear mandate to operate that had so long eluded Donovan. Deane, who was on friendly terms with Donovan, told General Marshall that he was "sold on O.S.S." and urged that Donovan's organization be at least partially militarized and receive "a clear definition" of its functions so it could render "maximum benefit" to the military. Significantly, this plea, which rested on Deane's contention that O.S.S. had rendered "extremely valuable services" to the military, came just two and a half weeks before the Torch forces hit the beaches and represented the peak of military goodwill that Eddy's North African efforts netted for Donovan's organization.[39]

General Marshall, who seems to have been under considerable pressure from such influential O.S.S. officials as James G. Rogers, an old friend of Stimson's, immediately acted on Deane's suggestion and called for the J.P.W.C. to prepare a study that would "clearly define the functions of the several branches of the Office of Strategic Services." This request produced another round of J.P.W.C. haggling over the definition of psychological warfare and further efforts by General Strong to limit and control O.S.S. intelligence and related activities. Donovan sensed, however, that the mood of the military high command was tipping more favorably toward O.S.S., and instead of acquiescing in the delaying chatter, he counterattacked by boldly contending that every O.S.S. activity was worthwhile and therefore should be approved by the J.P.W.C. and the chiefs. More talk and maneuver followed during early November, and in consequence two recommendations were sent up the chain of command to the J.C.S.: a majority recommendation shaped by General Strong to reduce O.S.S. to a nonentity, and a minority recommendation, drafted by the O.S.S. representative of the J.P.W.C., calling for the chiefs to confirm all existing O.S.S. programs and broaden its authority to carry out intelligence operations.[40]

By early December 1942, a month after Torch, the J.C.S. finally faced the clear question of whether O.S.S. was to be or not to be. However, military Chiefs of Staff committees have no more desire for confrontation and tough decisions than do other committees. As Winston Churchill remarked to Harold Macmillan in November 1943, if you take a group of extremely brave military men, call them a staff committee, and "put them at a table together," what you then get is "the sum of their fears." True to this maxim, the J.C.S. decided that instead of meeting the O.S.S. issue head-on, it would try to find a lateral escape route. General Marshall's deputy, Gen. Joseph McNarney, developed a face-saving plan whereby O.S.S. would formally renounce all intelligence activities that overlapped with those of O.N.I. and M.I.D., after which the J.C.S. would militarize the organization and give Donovan authority to plan and carry out projects for "military psychological warfare." As part of this mandate for psychological warfare, O.S.S. would retain virtually all its old functions—research, secret intelligence, counterintelligence, and subversive warfare—and its main existing subsections, including S.O., S.I., and R. and A., would also remain intact. Thus, only the description of its function—as an agent of psychological, not subversive, warfare—would be changed by the McNarney plan. O.N.I. and M.I.D. would be granted the official monopoly of military and naval intelligence that they had wanted, and Donovan would secure a sufficiently broad and loosely defined zone of activity to keep his organization, and his busy brain, fully engaged.[41]

During the discussion of the McNarney plan, a few reservations were registered by the chiefs. Admiral King was rather doubtful and called for someone to explain to him what "the expression psychological warfare means." Those advocating compromise wished to keep open this central point, so in reply General Marshall cited several "specific instances, such as the fall of France and various enemy undercover operations," thereby suggesting that psychological warfare should be taken to mean subversive warfare and fifth column activities. Admiral King continued to grumble about the lack of clarity but ultimately went along with the McNarney plan, and the chiefs met the initial objections of a number of civilian organizations such as B.E.W. and Rockefeller's organization, by making minor revisions in the basic proposal. With that done, the J.C.S. formally approved the McNarney Plan (J.C.S. 155/2/D) on 22 December 1942. The existing O.S.S. was thereby turned into the military's psychological warfare agency, and by this act, both Donovan and the Joint Chiefs believed that they had produced a very clever compromise.

The colonel concluded that he had finally found the gate open and immediately requested G-1 to provide his organization with large numbers of military personnel. The request was sympathetically received by the army, and on 9 January 1943 the Deputy Joint Chiefs of Staff approved a general procedure for supplying O.S.S. with military manpower. By February 1943, Donovan actually began to receive the officers he had long coveted for training his guerrilla and commando groups, and other amenities that had long eluded O.S.S., such as the right to use the Army Postal Service (A.P.O.), soon followed. In mid-February, O.S.S. and M.I.D. even reached agreement on a system for exchanging some intelligence information.[42]

However, in dodging one confrontation over O.S.S. by putting Donovan's group in charge of military psychological warfare, the J.C.S. had stirred up a hornet's nest. At the center of that nest was O.W.I., which harbored such bitter feelings toward O.S.S. dating from the days of C.O.I. that, as one British P.W.E. report noted, there was "no relationship" at all "between O.S.S. and O.W.I. in Washington." The trouble between the two organizations had increased, as British observers saw it, because O.W.I. personnel were more overtly pro–New Deal, more "left wing, . . . anti-British," and liberal "than the sort of men one meets in O.S.S."[43]

Whatever the relative importance of an angry past and present ideological differences, O.W.I. was seriously threatened by the J.C.S. grant to Donovan of exclusive authority over military psychological warfare. Elmer Davis, the O.W.I. chief, could not ignore the challenge, and probably goaded on by Robert Sherwood (who hated Donovan), he immediately counterattacked. Even before the chiefs had formally approved their directive, Davis declared that it clashed with the duties that the president had given to his organization and warned that he would fight against any diminution of his authority. When the J.C.S. went ahead and issued the order, most other organizations played along with the chiefs' decision and appointed representatives to the new psychological warfare committees formed by O.S.S. But Davis would have none of it and repeated to the chiefs and O.S.S. that rather than yield, he would carry the struggle on to the White House.[44]

O.W.I. soon so livened up the controversy with backstairs intrigue and stories planted in the press that the J.C.S. decided that O.S.S. had to be strengthened. General Deane recommended, with concurrence by the chiefs, that Donovan be promoted two grades to the rank of major general to help him overawe his opponents, but the president was not taken with the idea, and Donovan was made only a brigadier general with an assurance that an "early" promotion to major general would be kept "in view." Franklin Roosevelt had not been pleased by the expansionist foray that Donovan and the chiefs had made into the realm of psychological or "non-boom-boom" warfare. Government propaganda was a sensitive domestic issue, and Congress was unhappy about the duplication of government informational services and their inflated budgets. Many Republicans were convinced that the chief executive's control of a large information and propaganda machine boded ill for them, and the general public was highly nervous about anything that looked like military control of news distribution or the press. Under prompting from the Bureau of the Budget, Roosevelt decided to support O.W.I. Preparations were made for issuing a new executive order confirming O.W.I.'s monopoly of government informational activities, with minor reservations for Rockefeller's Latin American activities and a possible role for Donovan's black propaganda. To add to the difficulties that such a new executive order might bring down on the chiefs and O.S.S., a chance meeting between General Strong and the president in early February 1943 threatened to reopen the question of shaving off a number of O.S.S. activities and assigning the remainder to the War Department.[45]

After a moment of panic during which General Marshall leaned toward the idea of truncating O.S.S. and then transferring it from the J.C.S. to the War Department, cooler military heads prevailed. Whatever their doubts about O.S.S., the chiefs were even more terrified by the prospect of having to deal exclusively with O.W.I. on matters of propaganda and psychological warfare. The generals and admirals saw Davis's organization as an irresponsible band of civilian enthusiasts who could cause considerable trouble for the military high command. A meeting of the Joint Chiefs on 23 February resounded with talk of the "valuable results" that O.S.S. had produced whereas O.W.I. men were characterized as merely "a nuisance to the theater commanders." Even General Strong, probably the greatest O.S.S. hater of all, had no use for the O.W.I. Months earlier he had even suggested to Donovan that an O.S.S. propaganda school be given the delectable jargon title of "Personnel Relations School" in order to deceive O.W.I. and thus prevent it from expanding further into the field of military propaganda.[46]

The chiefs therefore dealt with the threat posed by the impending triumph of O.W.I. by the well-tested method of in-group compromise. On 24 February, Adm. William Leahy met with General Eisenhower's brother Milton, a high O.W.I. official, and quickly struck a deal. O.W.I. would stay out of Latin America, leave black propaganda to O.S.S., and coordinate its propaganda programs with the military authorities. In return O.S.S. was to give up its implied claim to control over all psychological warfare, restricting itself to the military aspects of the task as the official psychological warfare agency of the J.C.S.[47]

Donovan struggled against this fate, cooking up schemes for a new independent psychological warfare organization under someone such as White House aide Jonathan Daniels and pleading with the president not to further circumscribe O.S.S. authority. By this time, however, Donovan's spell over the White House had been broken. He had not seen the president for months, nor was he able to talk with Roosevelt at this time. His letter contending that any diminution of his psychological warfare plans would "disrupt our usefulness" arrived at the White House but apparently had no effect on the course of events. On 11 March, a new presidential executive order was issued confirming O.W.I.'s propaganda supremacy and leaving O.S.S., shorn of its grandiose psychological warfare pretensions, under the authority of the J.C.S.[48]

A recent C.I.A. account of these bureaucratic wrangles has suggested that they were part of a dark intrigue to inflict serious injury on O.S.S. Such a view seriously misstates the case. It was the J.C.S. that tried for an expansionist solution to its problems with O.S.S. by moving the latter organization further into the area of psychological warfare. The O.W.I. quite rightly defended itself and managed to triumph. In retrospect, it seems perfectly obvious that wartime necessity and the responsibilities of the J.C.S. required that O.S.S. be circumscribed and regulated in 1942–43. No government trying to win a world war by means of a complex system of economic and manpower mobilization could have permitted uncontrolled and impulsive activities like those of C.O.I. and O.S.S. to continue. O.S.S. was allowed to retain its control of black propaganda and of R. and A., S.O., and S.I. activity. It was fitted into the war-making machine instead of being destroyed or splintered. Under the circumstances, this was surprisingly enlightened treatment and was the most that anyone could reasonably have hoped for.[49]

THE SHADOW WARRIORS

Inside O.S.S., and the British Connections:
July 1942–March 1943

Though the scope of O.S.S. control of psychological warfare was limited by the presidential order of 11 March, the J.C.S. stuck to its word and allowed Donovan's organization to control those activities that remained within the military sphere. At the end of December 1942, the War Department disbanded its psychological warfare branch, and though open (white) activities passed to O.W.I., O.S.S. picked up men and equipment for its black operations. Some squabbles with O.W.I. occurred after 11 March 1943, and relations were strained between the two organizations at home and abroad. But the J.C.S. gave O.S.S. strong support and tried to break down "the Chinese wall" that separated O.S.S. from Davis's organization.[50]

Throughout the rest of the war, O.S.S. was able to throw the authorized mantle of military psychological warfare over its intelligence, counterintelligence, and guerrilla warfare activities, which was a major factor in fending off serious assaults on the organization by unfriendly military critics like General Strong. From March 1943 on, for example, O.S.S. regularly supplied the White House Map Room with S.I. and R. and A. reports because it contended that these contained information useful in determining the direction of the nation's psychological warfare policy. One can imagine the opposition that such a formal O.S.S. intelligence link to the Map Room would have brought forth from O.N.I. and M.I.D. if Donovan's organization had not been able to justify its actions as military psychological warfare.[51]

The O.W.I. triumph of 11 March also may have saved O.S.S. from considerable controversy and self-delusion. The few propaganda plans that O.S.S. managed to prepare before its psychological warfare monopoly was lost again do not seem to have been very impressive, and one cannot honestly say that its psychological warfare planning group, which brought together men as different as the conservative James G. Rogers and the left-liberal Harry Dexter White, offered much promise of providing the United States with a coherent and effective psychological warfare program.[52]

O.S.S. rightly complained that the new mandate restricted its efforts to develop programs rapidly that would exploit the surprises of war. Many O.S.S. plans had to pass through three levels of approval before the organization could act on them, and in most parts of the world O.S.S. had to function under the control of theater commanders.[53]

Yet the partial militarization of O.S.S. helped to open avenues that had previously been blocked to it, and backing from the J.C.S. allowed it to solve a number of its internal organizational problems. The J.C.S. allowed O.S.S. to continue many assorted intelligence activities, including its interview units in New York. The J.C.S. naturally balked at some of Donovan's more peculiar schemes, including his proposal to invite the public to send O.S.S. Washington any snapshots that might have possible military value. Since the plan would have entailed extensive correspondence with everyone who responded to the proposed radio appeal to determine whether such photographs as that of Aunt Mabel at the pyramids would be useful to the army, it was merciful that the chiefs said no to this idea. The J.C.S. also acted reasonably in circumscribing much O.S.S. field photographic activity, which overlapped the photographic work of the Army Signal Corps.[54]

The J.C.S. helped O.S.S. maintain its dominant position on the Interdepartmental Committee for the Acquisition of Foreign Periodicals (I.D.C.) without having to shoulder all the work and expense of this valuable operation. After months of involved negotiation, O.S.S. primacy on the I.D.C. was assured and a procedure for the arbitration of outstanding disputes by the Bureau of the Budget developed. Not everyone was thereby made completely happy. The great Chinese scholar, John K. Fairbank, who had been sent to China by O.S.S. in 1942, thought that the best solution would have been to merge O.S.S. collecting operations with the propaganda work of O.W.I. Such notions were not only impractical but also bordered on heresy, and Fairbank concluded that it would be best for him to leave O.S.S. and work solely as a document collector for the I.D.C.[55]

The loss of one scholar, even one as eminent as Professor Fairbank, was a small price for O.S.S. to pay for achieving organizational tranquility on the I.D.C. J.C.S. muscle facilitated this achievement, and the same can be said for the ease with which O.S.S. overcame the purchasing and jurisdictional problems associated with producing new weapons and equipment for subversive warfare. Government agencies responsible for procurement and development resisted independent O.S.S. weapons development, and Donovan's people also had trouble persuading private contractors to supply O.S.S. with armaments. A lawyer for the Federal Cartridge Corporation sought information from Donovan in July 1942 so that he could advise his client whether to fill an O.S.S. order for 4 million battery cups and primers. After doing some research on O.S.S. and discovering that the executive order of 11 July 1942 declared that its job was "to collect and assemble information," the lawyer could not understand how it had become "a purchaser of cups and primers."[56]

In matters like this, and in holding rival developmental agencies at bay, the J.C.S. provided valuable assistance by giving O.S.S. military respectability. An army colonel, Garland Williams, took control of O.S.S. supply and procurement and immediately made reforms. Comic interludes still occurred, including delightful exchanges between Colonel Williams and W. B. Billinghurst, the weapons designer loaned to O.S.S. by S.O.E. Billinghurst wished to make the sheath of O.S.S. fighting knife as dull in color as possible to camouflage it, but Williams had other ideas. He wanted a brightly colored sheath because the fighting knife was meant "to have a moral [sic, morale?] effect" on O.S.S. and therefore had to be made "as attractive as possible" to "impress the person receiving it." At the time, the colonel thought that morale (if not morality) was the most important consideration, and as time went on and life in O.S.S. became dirtier, the camouflage matter would take care of itself. Billinghurst did not press his side of the case further because, as he told the colonel, he believed that "the use of fists is a more natural thing for an American than is the use of a knife" and that O.S.S. should put its major effort into the production of a "knuckleduster." But when the first knuckleduster came off the production line, Colonel Williams was disappointed because it appeared "entirely too humane." So O.S.S. subversive weapons designers had to continue their work on brass knuckles until they produced a model capable of such a "crushing effect" that it brought joy to the hearts of both Billinghurst and Colonel Williams.[57]

The J.C.S. could not help resolve such detailed disagreements about subversive warfare "toys," but the chiefs did arrange for O.S.S. to draw support from Vannevar Bush's Office of Scientific and Research Development. Through the help of this major government think tank, and the assistance provided by S.O.E. and the O.S.S. Advisory Research Panel (which featured such scientists as George Kistiakowsky among its members), Donovan's organization developed the sophisticated weapons and sabotage materials needed to wage subversive warfare.[58]

By a series of arrangements concluded with the British in the course of 1942 and early 1943, the overseas operational position of O.S.S. was also fairly well delineated. In June 1942, at the same time that the executive order creating O.S.S. was issued, Donovan, Goodfellow, and Colonel Williams were in London negotiating a general understanding with the leaders of S.O.E. and other British organizations. The Americans wanted better liaison with British intelligence agencies and were also anxious to come to an agreement with S.O.E. about O.S.S.–S.O.E. field liaison, joint weapons development, financial cooperation, a division of areas of influence— Donovan's organization wanted to operate independently in some zones— and prospects for joining the British on S.O.E. drops into France and the

Balkans. Assisted by Colonel Williams, Goodfellow negotiated a general agreement with S.O.E. in mid-June 1942. Though complicated, cooperation on matters of finance, training, and equipment was worked out with minimal difficulty. The British also granted the Americans a secondary "S.O.E. role" in Cairo and Stockholm and in France, Norway, and the low countries, potential areas of Allied invasion. The British also promised that America's subversive warfare role would be increased in the invasion area once the landing plans were set and the American role on the continent determined.[59]

Because the Foreign Office had "practically reduced to nothing" S.O.E. operations in Portugal, the British found it easy to go half and half with the Americans on the Iberian peninsula as well as in Switzerland and much of Southeast Asia. But S.O.E. insisted that it alone should control other spots that were sensitive for London, including India, the S.O.E. liaison with Soviet Russia, and all of east and west Africa. If prior agreement with Britain were secured, O.S.S. special operations missions might be allowed to operate in India and sub-Saharan Africa, but only under an S.O.E. comptroller.

In the final agreement, O.S.S. was allowed only slim wedges of the world for independent operations—Finland, China, the Atlantic islands, the southwest Pacific, and northwest Africa. The British conceded American primacy in northwest Africa only with great reluctance, and as we have seen, S.O.E.'s caution in shipping arms to Eddy's people during the Torch operations caused serious difficulties for O.S.S. subversive operations there. Since General McArthur never allowed O.S.S. to maintain an independent force within his theater, British recognition of an O.S.S. primacy in that region amounted to nothing. The O.S.S. monopoly on special operational activity in Finland and the Atlantic islands also came a cropper because neither area was the center of significant subversive activity during World War II. So all O.S.S. received was the top position in China, where S.O.E. efforts had already failed, and in northwest Africa, where Britain controlled most of the arms and supply flow. Even in these two areas, S.O.E. had the same right to try to operate as a junior partner as O.S.S.–S.O.E. theoretically had in S.O.E. areas.[60]

This box score might suggest that S.O.E. took its cousin from "48 Land" (as the United States was known to S.I.S.), but in reality Goodfellow secured about all that hard bargaining could achieve. At the time of the agreement, O.S.S. had little beyond potential in the realm of weapons production and manpower, and there was no real S.O. organization of any size. As late as October 1942, S.O. had only designated eight overseas operational locations (three in Asia, two in the Near East, two in Africa, and London). Of these, Eddy's operation and that of Detachment 101 in Burma were the only ones really functioning. On the other hand, although S.O.E. needed money and supplies and tended to exaggerate the extent of its activities—there was only one S.O.E. liaison officer in Yugoslavia until late 1942—a large S.O.E. organization actually existed. In light of these circumstances, the June 1942 S.O.E.–O.S.S. subversive warfare partition of the world was reasonably fair, though it provided Donovan's S.O. men with scanty room for operation.[61]

While Goodfellow was coming to terms with S.O.E., Donovan spent mid-June explaining his operations to the British Chiefs of Staff and attempting to establish channels through which to secure more intelligence from London. Exchange with the intelligence services of the Polish, Czech, Norwegian, and Dutch governments in exile were regularized, and talks were initiated with other exile governments. In addition to the rather vague assurances that he could get some S.I.S. and Foreign Office intelligence, Donovan persuaded the Ministry of Economic Warfare to give his people access to a large portion of the intelligence material in its possession. The result was a substantial increase in the quantity of economic and S.O.E. agent intelligence received by O.S.S., but most of the sensitive British material that Donovan managed to see still came to him from Stephenson in New York.[62]

Donovan also had a very hard time getting high-level intelligence from the American military authorities in 1942. Since M.I.D. was reluctant to enter into a full interchange with O.S.S., Donovan's organization was unable to see much from its most secret sources, Ultra and Magic. In the summer of 1942, O.S.S. officials denied that they had set up a "black chamber" to surmount this barrier, but there are indications that they had made a beginning in cryptography. Their efforts were cut short by a September 1942 directive ordering Donovan's people "not to engage in any work of this nature," and all O.S.S. code cracking ceased.[63]

In the fall of 1942, O.S.S. did manage to improve the technical level of its own encoding system by purchasing complex machines of the Enigma type from the Hagelin Company of Stockholm. But the ban on code cracking remained, and a J.I.C. order of 23 October 1942 excluded O.S.S. from direct access to information that the Allies had secured by decoding enemy messages.[64]

O.S.S. finally secured a limited intelligence interchange agreement with General Strong's M.I.D. in February 1943, but it still had little access to Magic and Ultra. Donovan's people were only allowed to see, in paraphrased form, those portions of such material that M.I.D. saw fit to give them. Even the information that the army acquired from P.O.W. interrogations was paraphrased to "exclude all indication of [the] mechanics of interrogation and technical and combat data" before it was handed on to O.S.S.[65]

Then in early spring 1943, after the position of O.S.S. had been clarified by the new executive order and the subsequent actions of the J.C.S., Donovan made a significant breakthrough into important areas of British and American secret intelligence. In the new organizational setup, O.S.S. had received definite authority to carry on counterintelligence activities, and in the course of March Donovan built on that basis to establish a close working arrangement with British counterintelligence (M.I. 5 and M.I. 6). Large military offensive operations were in the offing, yet M.I. 5–M.I. 6 found themselves strapped for men, materials, and money to cope with the enormous counterespionage problems that such operations entailed. The British therefore made an unprecedented offer. O.S.S. could get full access to the M.I. 5–M.I. 6 counterintelligence archives, including the records on security suspects and enemy agents, if Donovan's organization would make available the men and materials necessary for a complete counterintelligence partnership. The O.S.S. chief quickly accepted the proposal, at last securing regular access to some decoded material. As part of the deal, M.I. 5–M.I. 6 authorized O.S.S. counterintelligence "to study and summarize British decodes of any [Axis] intelligence message," which meant that Donovan's people were allowed to read the raw decrypts of German Abwehr traffic.[66]

Donovan then assaulted another barrier that the O.N.I. and M.I.D. had put in the way of O.S.S. access to intelligence information. Pleading jurisdictional primacy and decrying the evils of duplication, General Strong and Adm. Harold C. Train had succeeded for months in preventing the Director of Censorship from providing O.S.S. with secret information discovered in the course of censoring activity. Once Donovan had the M.I. 5–M.I. 6 deal and the Abwehr decrypts in his pocket, however, he made short work of the censorship problem. In mid-April, General Deane asked the J.C.S. to drop the censorship ban, arguing that O.S.S. was "more apt" to gain valuable intelligence material from this source than was "either the ONI or the MIS." On 27 April, the chiefs agreed, and from that date O.S.S. was allowed to receive all the raw censorship material that it desired.[67]

Many shifts in the structure of Donovan's organization were produced by O.S.S.–S.O.E. arrangements (June 1942), the changes made to the O.S.S. mandate by the J.C.S. (December 1942–March 1943), and the new opportunities for O.S.S. intelligence and counterintelligence activities that resulted from its restriction to military psychological warfare (March

1943). Throughout the various reorganizations, which need not be chronicled in detail, an inner circle consisting of Donovan's old friends and business associates, including Atherton Richards, James Murphy, Otto Doering, Ned Buxton, and William Vanderbilt, kept control over the administrative machinery of O.S.S. Some specialists, such as the paymaster, W. L. Rehm, and the director of research and development, Stanley Lovell, also held onto their positions through thick and thin. By early 1943, however, many changes of personnel had occurred and all of O.S.S. had become more bureaucratic, with extra layers of administration inserted at nearly every level.

The operations sections were also thoroughly reorganized. David Bruce left Washington in late 1942 to head the O.S.S. London office, and a new post of deputy director of O.S.S. intelligence services was created. To fill it, Donovan chose Brig. Gen. John Magruder, who had had trouble with George Marshall over Magruder's 1941–42 mission to China. Magruder was declared surplus by G-2, and Donovan jumped at the chance to get him. By early 1943, O.S.S. Deputy Director for Intelligence John Magruder was presiding over three subsections: S.I., led by Whitney Shepardson; R. and A., under William Langer; and F.N.B., headed by Dewitt Poole. A second deputy director's position for psychological warfare was kept vacant, but the subchiefs for that section—Lt. Col. Ellery Huntington of S.O. and Frederick Oechsner of Morale (black propaganda) Operations (M.O.)—were in place by early 1943. (Both were replaced in 1944; Lt. Col. Carl O. Hoffmann became S.O. chief, and Col. K. D. Mann headed M.O.)[68]

The increase in bureaucracy and the long-awaited authorization for action brought a vast influx of personnel to O.S.S. To test recruits and train new people, screening procedures had to be developed. Out of this came the various O.S.S. suitability tests and the first large-scale use of the assessment method of situational testing (now so popular with corporations) in the United States.

These changes affected every branch of Donovan's organization, but the impact varied from one branch to another. For R. and A., the two most basic developments were William Langer's assumption of branch direction from Dr. Baxter and the simultaneous subordination of the branch to General Magruder's overall control. Also, many R. and A. projects were refocused and the relations between R. and A. and other organizations changed. Since much of R. and A.'s work was still being done for O.S.S. rather than for other branches of the government (in the last three months of 1942, over two-thirds of R. and A.'s approved projects were for O.S.S. customers), good relations with S.I. and S.O. were important. Some information was secured from S.I. in return for the R. and A. studies done for that branch, but there were serious doubts in R. and A. about the sophistication and accuracy of much S.I. reporting. To strengthen its own position and expand the pool of researchers from which it would draw, R. and A. began to subcontract some projects, especially to scholars at the University of California at Berkeley and Stanford University. Even so, the branch was unable to meet all the special requests made to it for studies and had to severely curtail the amount of topographical work it did for S.O.[69]

Like other branches of O.S.S., R. and A. was anxious to establish good relations with the military. Much of this concern focused on such practical matters as setting appropriate security classifications for the studies produced by the branch, for once R. and A. came under the authority of the J.C.S., its reports and memoranda suddenly became matters of military security. During 1942 and 1943, a barrage of stamps signifying "confidential" and "secret" turned what had previously been scholarship into a series of national secrets. R. and A. was anxious that such marks of military importance should not lead the War Department or the J.C.S. to interfere with research methods or project scheduling. In the end a balance was struck whereby R. and A. did limited work for M.I.D. and O.N.I. and received some intelligence from them. The three units (R. and A., O.N.I., M.I.D.) also joined forces to produce the Joint Army and Navy Intelligence Studies (J.A.N.I.S.), which focused on specific matters of strategic importance.[70]

The agreements that O.S.S. had reached with B.E.W. in the fall of 1942 facilitated a close relationship between it and R. and A., especially regarding the selection of bombing targets. In addition to the Washington B.E.W.–R. and A. operation, a larger joint section was developed in London's Berkeley Square to assist the targeting work of the Eighth Air Force. This was a major factor in the establishment of a large R. and A. "outpost" in London in the course of late 1942 and early 1943, but this outpost also assisted other branches of O.S.S. stationed in the United Kingdom and secured political and military information for R. and A. headquarters in Washington. While aid to the American military and O.S.S. authorities in the European theater was the primary duty of R. and A. London at this time, Langer insisted that the outpost serve the needs of O.S.S. Washington as well. To accomplish this, good relations for the exchange of information with the British were essential. R. and A. provided British offices with a large number of regular R. and A. studies and on occasion carried out special research projects requested by the British. Not everything R. and A. produced was highly prized by His Majesty's officials, but a number of people in London thought Langer's organization did valuable work. One reason why P.W.E. sought to maintain a liaison with O.S.S. was because John Wheeler Bennett thought R. and A. "produced interesting reports."[71]

The range and form of R. and A. reports changed somewhat during the early era of J.C.S. control. Whereas some "trend memoranda" were produced to deal rapidly with important matters still in flux, the primary concern was to tighten up the procedures for initiating and approving regular projects. Headway was made in this area, but since the top O.S.S. leaders could demand any study that struck their fancy, it was difficult to make the system work smoothly. William Donovan could, and did, insist in October 1942 that R. and A. make a study of "The Rat Population," and in the same month Stanley Lovell (O.S.S. research and development chief) ordered R. and A. to examine "Japanese Peculiarities." Since researchers had to be pulled off regular projects to investigate such whimsies, it is not surprising that R. and A.'s efficiency campaign was not totally successful. But sufficient progress occurred to earn the branch a reputation for quick and accurate research work. In consequence, more outside customers sought its services, and by the second quarter of 1943, half the projects on which Langer's people were working were intended for other government organizations than R. and A.[72]

Like R. and A., the S.O. and S.I. branches were seriously affected by O.S.S. squabbles with the military authorities and O.W.I. in late 1942 and early 1943. Both branches found their training and supply programs restricted by the endless bickering and the failure to secure general approval for operational projects. Broadly speaking, S.I. was in a stronger position than S.O. because it already had a large number of agents placed in United States diplomatic missions abroad, and following a few minor administrative adjustments, these people continued to report to Washington through the State Department and later through special O.S.S. channels. Both S.I. and S.O. faced the same difficulties in expanding their operations, for until a general O.S.S. mandate to act was secured, they could only move forward when a specific possibility showed itself in some overseas theater. To understand what was happening to these two branches at the time, it is therefore necessary to take a rapid Cook's tour of the world, starting where O.S.S. was strongest, in the North African theater.[73]

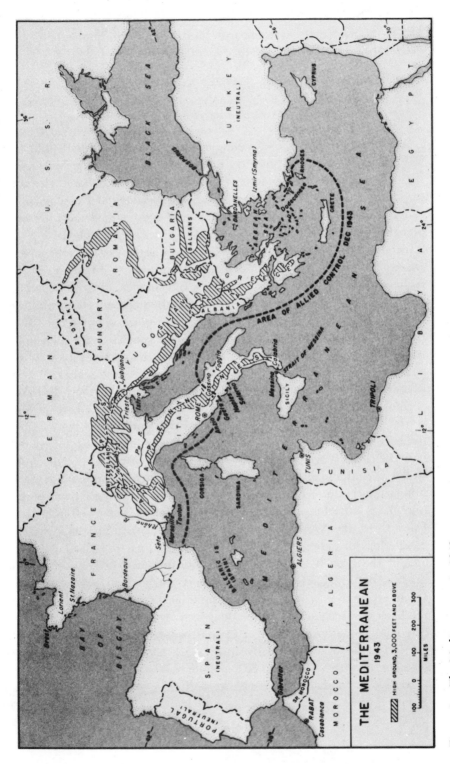

Figure 1. The Mediterranean in 1943

O.S.S. in the North African and Mediterranean Theaters: November 1942–March 1943

January 1943: British Eighth Army conquers Tripoli
January 1943: Winston Churchill and Franklin Roosevelt confer at Casablanca
March 1943: British and American forces enter Tunisia in force

After the completion of Torch, Eddy's organization found itself in an anomalous position. Technically, Eddy headed a five-man S.O. mission that operated out of Eisenhower's headquarters (Allied Force Headquarters, or A.F.H.Q.) under the cover name Experimental Detachment G-3 Provisional alongside an S.O.E. detachment code-named the Interservice Signals Unit-6. At this time, however, O.S.S. no longer enjoyed a regular S.I. connection with North African G-2, for Eisenhower's intelligence unit was composed solely of British and American military intelligence people, including M.I. 6 men under the name Interservice Liaison Detachment (I.S.L.D.). The British, with a large staff and equipment dumps in neighboring Gibraltar, were eager to develop a subversive warfare operation in northwest Africa. They immediately set up a special forces mission near Algiers code-named Massingham and a special forces sea base at Bône near Cape de Garde—or Villa la Vie—to facilitate the seaborne infiltration of M.I. 6 and S.O.E. operatives into Tunisia and southern Europe.[74]

The speed and efficiency with which the British established subversive warfare operations in North Africa left Eddy and his small staff far behind. O.S.S. had money but lacked equipment (even O.S.S. Washington had been told it would have to wait four to five months to get just six walky-talkies) and had no clear mandate for action from the American military authorities. Eddy's initial concern was to protect from persecution those Frenchmen who had assisted him in the pre-Torch period. From there, the North African O.S.S. detachment turned its attention to countering an anticipated German effort to turn the Arab population against the French and American authorities. In late November, Eddy made an informal agreement with Robert Murphy to keep the pre-Torch agent networks in place for counterintelligence purposes and to serve as the basis of subsequent S.I. operations in southern Europe. But no American military authority issued a formal order to this effect, and in late December Donovan was unable to persuade the J.C.S. to approve an immediate shipment of S.I. and S.O. people to North Africa.[75]

So as the Torch forces slowly worked their way eastward to engage Rommel, there was little for Eddy and his O.S.S. cohorts to do. The retreating Afrika Korps was heavily reinforced when it reached Tunisia, and when battle began there in earnest in early 1943, O.S.S. still was not able to give Eisenhower much help. O.S.S. men participated in psychological warfare planning, but little combat propaganda work was actually done, and there was even less special operations activity.[76]

The O.S.S.'s desire to play a bigger intelligence role was blocked by a number of factors. Initially, the North African theater had no J.I.C. When one was established in early 1943, Eisenhower still preferred oral rather than written briefing from G-2. He did not put great faith in studies prepared far from the scene of battle, and until the Kasserine Pass disaster of February 1943—when the Germans caught the green Americans napping and gave them a sharp knock—he was content to let his British G-2, Brigadier Erich Mockler-Ferryman, who depended heavily on Ultra, handle the job in his own way. But in the aftermath of Kasserine, it was decided at Eisenhower's headquarters (A.F.H.Q.) that G-2 had misread the sources and had probably depended excessively on Ultra. Consequently, Mockler-Ferryman was removed and another Britisher, Brig. K. W. D. Strong (not to be confused with Maj. Gen. George Strong, the American G-2 in Washington) was made Eisenhower's G-2. At the same time, the intelligence system of A.F.H.Q. was reorganized to increase the range and variety of the information it obtained. A major result of reorganization was increased air reconnaissance and P.O.W. interrogation, but greater agent work and much-needed technical and background reports were also demanded. The I.S.L.D. stepped in to provide the bulk of this material, but by the spring of 1943 S.I. and R. and A. also found a larger market for their wares.[77]

In the meantime, the general O.S.S. plan for North Africa had been working its way through the maze of J.C.S. committees in Washington since early November. The army authorities in the American capital were sympathetic to expanded O.S.S. operations in the North African theater (especially in light of Eddy's achievements in the pre-Torch period), and they were also anxious not to fall behind the British. Both Gens. Albert Wedemeyer and George Strong wanted to avoid joint Anglo-American subversive operations because they felt "it would be embarrassing" if the British were involved in operations from the "American base of operations" in Algeria. For once, even the army supply people raised no serious objections, and General Marshall urged Eisenhower to give O.S.S. needs special consideration. Yet when the time actually came to establish the shipping priorities, O.S.S. received little consideration, and in early 1943 a special survey mission under Colonel Huntington had to be sent to Eisenhower's headquarters to study the situation. Once in North Africa, Huntington realized that creating independent S.I. and S.O. operations would be impossible. The British setup was too large and too well established, and Eisenhower was too strongly committed to the principle of mixed Anglo-American staffs. Therefore, although S.I. intelligence collection operations were to be kept separate from those of I.S.L.D., Huntington agreed that most of the information obtained should be pooled and that S.O. would work with S.O.E. under the direction of a joint policy committee. Similarly, O.S.S. black propaganda (M.O.) units would continue to operate in conjunction with O.W.I. and P.W.E. on the Psychological Warfare Board (P.W.B.) established at Eisenhower's headquarters. All this was arranged and agreed to by the Joint Chiefs in the course of February, and O.S.S. operations in northwest Africa, Italy, and the Iberian peninsula were thereby given a blueprint for action under Eisenhower's authority.[78]

This authorization of O.S.S. activities in the western Mediterranean came too late to affect the Tunisian campaign, which ended with the capitulation of the remainder of the Afrika Korps in early May. But the new O.S.S. setup strongly influenced O.S.S. activities in Italy. It was obvious that once the North African campaign ended, the British and the Americans would want to make some move against the Axis powers in the Mediterranean area. In the early spring of 1943, Donovan was already planning political maneuvers for southern Europe and wondering how he could gather up the "thousands" of refugees strewn about "the basin of the Mediterranean" to form subversive assault groups for attacks on the continent.[79]

A great deal of Anglo-American effort went into developing psychological warfare plans intended to show the Italian people that the Allies, not the Germans, were their friends. While carefully avoiding "any incitement to social revolution in Italy" because the Allies wished no trouble with the Vatican or the Italian monarchy, the P.W.E. plans called for all-out attacks on Italian morale and on the Italian people's faith in their leaders and their German ally. Following Torch, the Germans had occupied Vichy France and had moved strong forces into Italy to facilitate reinforcement of the Afrika Korps. The Anglo-American psychological warriors consequently hoped to create in Italy resentment about this de-facto occupation by its expansive German ally. British P.W.B. planners thought it would be all to the good if the psychological warfare campaign resulted in enough Italo-German trouble to force the Nazis to occupy the peninsula in force, for a large number of German forces would then be tied down. The psychological campaign was not intended to liberate Italy but to force the Germans to hold back as many troops as possible from the battles raging in North Africa and the Soviet Union.[80]

In conjunction with many other American and British organizations, O.S.S. played a part in developing the Italian psychological warfare campaign. Even Nelson Rockefeller insisted on being consulted because of the need to build up Western Hemisphere support for operations against Italy. But no matter how effective this battle of words turned out to be, Eisenhower soon needed heavier weapons for use against the Italians. Plans for an invasion of Sicily had begun in December 1942, and while British and American psychological warriors vied to suggest the best ploys for weakening Italian resistance, the operational planners hammered into shape their preparations for Husky (their code name for the invasion of Sicily) between January and March 1943. By 1 March, Eisenhower had asked Washington for guidance on the final form of the preinvasion psychological assault on the Italians, and the military planners had begun preparing for special operations in Sicily. A top S.O.E. executive, Lieutenant Colonel Keswick (the man who had checked up on C.O.I. in early 1942), was charged with preparing S.O.E.–O.S.S. activities for Husky, and on February 25, Eddy passed to O.S.S. Washington an urgent request from Eisenhower's A.F.H.Q. to send over eighty Italian-speaking S.O. men (including thirty radio operators) as quickly as possible.[81]

The Husky preparations raised the possibility that O.S.S. finally might be allowed to show what Donovan's organization could do in a broad range of operations. But before examining in the next chapter what O.S.S. actually accomplished in the Sicilian and Italian campaigns, it is first necessary to move on through the Mediterranean to Cairo and the remainder of Africa to see how the other outposts of S.I. and S.O. had fared during the period of organizational difficulty that marked the first nine months of O.S.S.

By October 1942, although Donovan had not yet established a liaison base in Cairo and had no S.O. agents stationed in the eastern Mediterranean or the Middle East, a substantial number of S.I. agents were in the region. S.I. stations were established in Iraq, Iran, and Transjordan, and a fairly substantial operation was functioning in Turkey. Of course, this string of agents did not always function smoothly; Donovan repeatedly had to chastise his chief Turkish agent—appropriately code-named Runner—for preparing hurried and inaccurate reports.[82]

Still, the Middle East was a tricky area in which to operate, and the young O.S.S. had done well in establishing such an extensive network so quickly. An enormous S.O.E.–S.I.S. center in Cairo radiated its influence throughout the whole zone, and the British gave little encouragement to an O.S.S. presence there. The British Political Intelligence Centre Cairo was not about to step aside for the Americans. With a great deal of money to spend, and an extensive string of agents and Italian collaborators, the British could easily hold their own.[83]

For resistance support activities, the British also seemed to be well positioned. A force of four B–24 Liberators was stationed in Cairo to provide supplies and equipment to resistance forces in the Balkans, and after a slow beginning, the British achieved a startling success in late November when a group of communist and noncommunist Greek guerrillas led by British Liaison Officers (B.L.O.) destroyed the vital Gorgopotamos railroad viaduct. As a result, S.O.E. Cairo and the London government decided to allow B.L.O.s to remain in Greece, and the fall of 1942 saw a great expansion of Greek resistance, with direction, support, and leadership provided by the British.[84]

Despite these achievements in Greece, British attention was chiefly focused on Yugoslavia. In the fall of 1941, Mihajlović had been proclaimed the hero of the anti-Axis resistance by London and the Yugoslav government in exile, and a year later, the British government gave his movement official recognition. S.O.E. had poor field communications in the Balkans, but gradually a few on-the-spot reports, plus refugee tales and evidence from the Soviets, suggested that a Tito–Mihajlović civil war was raging in Yugoslavia and that Mihajlović was actively collaborating with the Italian occupation forces. By October–November 1942, both the R. and A. and F.N.B. branches of O.S.S. had concluded that Mihajlović was in fact working with the Axis. British authorities were nervous about the whole Yugoslav situation in the closing days of 1942, but it was only when the first low-level intercepts of Abwehr messages from the Balkans began to reach Cairo in January 1943 that S.O.E. decided an effort had to be made to put enough observers into Yugoslavia to check on the situation.[85]

Consequently, for all its outward appearance of organizational strength, late 1942 and early 1943 was a very trying time for S.O.E. Cairo. As a top S.O.E. official B. Sweet Escott later remarked, even S.O.E. had concluded that presiding over a civil war in Yugoslavia "did not seem to be quite what Mr. Churchill meant" when he had told Dalton in 1940 "to set Europe ablaze." S.O.E. Cairo was still torn by internal troubles, and until Montgomery's decisive victory over Rommel at El Alamein in early November, British political prestige in the Middle East was very low. An unusual degree of restraint thus prevailed among British subversive warriors in Cairo. S.O.E. and S.I.S. stood aloof from such schemes as sending a Soviet mission to Tito and effecting joint operations with the N.K.V.D. in

Ankara. They were equally cool toward Donovan's plan to establish a large O.S.S. mission in Cairo for launching extensive operations into the Balkans.[86]

Donovan longed to find additional zones of action for himself and his men, and he was not troubled by the complexities of the Balkan situation or the British difficulties there. The imprint of his "successful" mission to the area in 1941 was still upon him, and he believed that America in general, and O.S.S. in particular, could succeed in Balkan and Middle Eastern areas where the "imperialistic" British were doomed to fail. Aside from establishing a base in Cairo, Donovan hoped to send a large body of O.S.S. men into Lebanon. Armed with masses of equipment and a quarter of a million dollars, the proposed Lebanon group would use the American colleges in the region as bases for wide-ranging propaganda and subversive warfare operations against Axis agents and sympathizers in the Middle East.[87]

Naturally, the British strongly resisted both the establishment of an independent O.S.S. base in Cairo and the projected operations from Lebanon into an area that London considered its special preserve. However, Donovan had the president's warm support for the Lebanon scheme because Roosevelt was apparently deeply worried by the threat posed to the Middle East by the German penetration into the Caucasus from the north and Rommel's pre–El Alamein pressure on Egypt. In October, the president instructed Sumner Welles to tell the British "frankly" that to aid the Allied cause the "considerable" United States "influence and prestige" in the Middle East should be thrown behind the Lebanon plan.[88]

Still London stalled, agreeing only to a small O.S.S. survey mission. Then the victory at El Alamein in early November strengthened the British, and they became even more resistant to Donovan's proposals. Stiff British opposition combined with the administrative and supply difficulties that O.S.S. encountered with the J.C.S. and the American theater commander in the Middle East to slow Donovan's Cairo and Lebanon plans to a crawl. Most of the Lebanon scheme was quietly shelved, and by February 1943 Donovan had managed to secure only the in-principle agreement of the J.C.S. and the American theater commander, Gen. Lewis Brereton, to the establishment of an O.S.S. base in Cairo. The British continued to fight the proposal tooth and nail, however, and Donovan seems to have been deeply hurt by their attitude. Within a few months, when he was able to speak with the full weight of the American J.C.S. and General Eisenhower behind him, he would pay the British back in kind and force them to give him a large share of the action in the Balkan war. But in the spring of 1943 his time had not yet come, and for a while yet O.S.S.

remained a weak, marginal force in the eastern Mediterranean.[89]

Donovan's relations with the British in sub-Saharan Africa were much more harmonious during this period. London had the largest direct political and economic stake in the region and controlled extensive colonial centers for S.O.E. and S.I.S. activity. The Americans had one excellent operating base in their semicolonial foothold in Liberia, where a team of five S.I. men was already operating in October 1942. At that time, O.S.S. also had three S.I. and seven S.O. men in British colonies, plus one man in the Congo, two in Angola, and three operating in French colonial territories. Nearly all these agents were attached to American diplomatic missions, including a seven-man S.O. team in Nigeria, but it seems likely that an S.I. man concentrating on the area extending from Gambia to Khartoum was attached to Pan American Airways.[90]

Since there was little serious ground action against the Axis in sub-Saharan Africa, O.S.S. and the British shadow warfare organizations there were able to concentrate on intelligence and counterintelligence. Much effort was expended on controlling alleged Axis agents and providing as much intelligence security as possible for the vital Allied shipping that passed around the Cape to Egypt and India. Initially, free from the tight military restrictions that existed in active combat theaters, Donovan's people and the British buccaneers in sub-Saharan Africa had more freedom to indulge their adventuresome spirits. Consequently, the State Department was rather busy in the fall of 1942 trying to prevent O.S.S. escapades because Donovan and his subordinates never thought of "diplomatic repercussions" when they worked up such projects as stealing Axis ships in Portuguese African ports. By late 1942, the United States military was forced to act; O.S.S. Africa gradually passed under the control of an American theater commander, Gen. S. W. Fitzgerald, and the most exuberant days of O.S.S. adventure in Africa were over.[91]

O.S.S. in the European Theater of Operations:
June 1942–March 1943

August 1942: The Dieppe raid
January 1943: The German Sixth Army surrenders at Stalingrad

The O.S.S. men stationed in Europe in late 1942 had not had many days of operational opportunity. London was the first O.S.S. overseas post, and by October 1942, five S.I. men were already stationed there, and three S.O. and two S.I. men intended for Ireland were still waiting to go in. But most of the work of the London station consisted of liaison with British agencies.[92]

It was a poor time for S.O. operations. S.O.E. had organized a number of strikingly successful sabotage actions in Norway, but reprisals had been heavy. Although sabotage and underground organizations in France continued to develop, the Combined Operations attack on Dieppe failed, and the operation of separate S.O.E. and Free French resistance and intelligence networks was causing organizational confusion and political tension. At that time, through infiltration and other subversive operations, the Abwehr controlled some of the resistance units in France and the whole S.O.E.–Dutch resistance organization. Relations were also strained between S.O.E. and the security organizations of the Belgian government in exile. S.O.E. was still toying with dramatic means of increasing the agent flow to the continent, including the use of N.K.V.D. agents, but the really powerful offices of the British government (the Foreign Office, the Chiefs of Staff, and Number 10) sharply limited the scope of such enterprises. In September, formal coordination machinery connecting S.O.E. and O.S.S.–S.O. was established in London, and the American military authorities also gave vague assurances that they would "coordinate" the "services" of O.S.S. with their military plans.[93]

But S.O. London actually had very little to coordinate in late 1942 and even less opportunity to carry out subversive operations in continental Europe. It was the U.S. government's turn to flirt with Vichy in hope of easing a landing on the continent. Washington was extremely suspicious of de Gaulle, so much so that on 8 October 1942, John Franklin Carter, who frequently mirrored the more paranoid tendencies of the Oval Office, gleefully reported to Roosevelt that he believed that he had uncovered a plot between de Gaulle and John L. Lewis (Roosevelt's bête noire in the United Mine Workers) to seize control of the U.S. government![94]

In such an atmosphere, S.O. cooperation with de Gaulle's resistance organization was extremely difficult. As long as O.S.S. representative Nicol Smith remained at Vichy, it was at least possible to study resistance operations firsthand and make cautious contacts with pro-Allied circles in France, but when the Germans occupied the whole country after Torch, even this tenuous connection was severed. All that O.S.S. representatives in London could do was to keep trying to move their plans for continental S.O. operations through American and British committees and hope that the gradual buildup of O.S.S. manpower and the increasing pressure to get back on the continent in force would ultimately work in their favor.[95]

O.S.S.–S.I. London had somewhat more to show for its efforts during 1942 and early 1943. David Bruce actually managed to arrange full coordination and exchange of information between the various American intelligence services stationed in Britain. S.I. London was therefore far ahead of any other O.S.S. outpost or even the home office in this regard. Shepardson, Phillips, and Bruce also established close relations with some British intelligence organizations and with the intelligence services of most of the governments in exile. Some valuable spinoffs resulted, including an arrangement approved by the J.I.C. in September 1942 to establish a special O.S.S. station in Buenos Aires for securing information from Belgian and Dutch residents there.

Inevitably, some of the information received from Allied sources was flawed, and neither S.I. nor the regular officials in Washington were as yet sufficiently experienced to sort out the bad items from the good. In October 1942, for example, the Czechs told S.I. that the chief of staff of the German Army, Gen. Franz Halder, had been replaced by a General Tretzler. In fact, Halder's replacement was Gen. Kurt Zeitzler, but S.I. duly sent information about the appointment of the imaginary General Tretzler to Washington, and Tretzler had a long and illustrious tour of duty in American records, ultimately reaching the War Department's Operations Division and even the office of the president. On the other hand, the Czechs also provided S.I. with extremely detailed and valuable information on German railroad traffic, but it appears that in 1942 the American authorities were not always able to sift such wheat from the chaff.[96]

Due to circumstances over which S.I. London and Washington had little control, O.S.S.'s hope of monopolizing the flow of valuable information from Polish intelligence was lost during this period. The Polish government in exile was anxious to build up its credit with the political powers in Washington and decided to supplement its exchanges with O.S.S. by making direct deals with other American agencies. In December 1942 and January 1943, the Poles came to understandings with the Carter organization and Army G-2 to provide them with high-level intelligence on German military operations. From the moment this information began to arrive in the offices of Carter and General Strong in January and February 1943, O.S.S. had lost its monopoly and became merely one of a number of channels through which Polish intelligence information reached Washington.[97]

Such developments were frustrating for S.I. London, and there were other disappointments. In August 1942, O.S.S. London warmly seconded a British proposal that combined British, O.S.S., and Free French (Jedburgh) missions be organized and parachuted into France. This plan—which called for dropping uniformed men behind enemy lines to assist French Resistance forces and was thus parent of the Jedburgh and Sussex schemes used in 1944—was considered by various American army and J.C.S. committees between August and October 1942, and if it had managed to stay alive until early 1943 when O.S.S. received its general mandate to act, it would most likely have been approved. But Allied reluctance to cooperate closely with de Gaulle's organization and Eisenhower's nervousness about dropping men in uniform on intelligence and sabotage missions gave General Strong an opportunity at the time of Torch to persuade the War Department that the whole tripartite Jedburgh idea was dangerously "leaky." Consequently, the first Jedburgh plan was killed by the War Department in early November, and the aspirations of O.S.S. London were again thwarted.[98]

At the end of March 1943, two major barriers still stood in the way of all S.I. London's operational plans: His Majesty's government refused to approve the use of the United Kingdom as a base for independent S.I. secret intelligence operations, and American European theater commander Gen. Jacob Devers had not approved the basic S.I. program for the European Theater of Operations. Until these obstacles were overcome— and nine more months would pass before substantial headway was made—S.I. London simply had to keep crawling along while giving maximum support to those in the S.I. toeholds on the continent.[99]

S.I. operatives in the four centers—Stockholm, Madrid, Lisbon, and Bern—located in neutral countries faced different local situations. The Stockholm operation, which in October 1942 was composed of three S.I. representatives, had reasonably friendly relations with its British intelligence cousins, no jurisdictional troubles with the military, and few run-ins with the State Department. Tightly controlled from Washington by Calvin Hoover of the S.I. Scandinavian desk, S.I. Stockholm unobtrusively went about its business and established a creditable record for acquiring useful intelligence.[100]

The situation was more complicated in Spain and Portugal. British shadow warfare organizations were strongly represented in both areas, and once plans for Torch were under way, the Iberian peninsula was an object of constant concern for British and American generals. It was vital for Allied Mediterranean operations that Spain and Portugal remain neutral, but since rightist regimes were in control in both countries and German forces were pressed against Spain's Pyrrenean border in the post-Torch period, Iberian neutrality appeared extremely shaky. It was thus chiefly to make certain that Allied subversive warfare organizations worked to preserve and strengthen this neutrality that O.S.S. Iberian operations were finally put under Eisenhower's control in February 1943.

At the time of Torch, S.I. had at least eight representatives in Spain,

Portugal, and the Canary Islands, all charged with the job of monitoring Spanish and Portuguese neutrality and maintaining a check on German influence. O.S.S. work on the peninsula was complicated by the number of United States agencies concerned with the Iberian question. The State Department and O.W.I. were represented there, B.E.W. fought to assure neutrality through economic leverage, and even Rockefeller's organization managed to work its way into the business by contending that what was done in Spain could have ramifications in Latin America.[101]

Throughout October and November, a subcommittee of the J.P.W.C. wrestled with the problem of establishing guidelines for psychological warfare in Spain. Its conclusions were, however, more negative than positive. All parties agreed that it would be unwise when dealing with Spain and Portugal to be specific about military plans because the Allies might wish to seize the Azores and that it would be best not to touch on such delicate issues as Basque separatism or imperialism. When the meetings ended, the B.E.W. was still confused about what it should allow to be sold to Portugal, and there was little agreement on what the propaganda directed at the Iberian population should stress aside from emphasizing that the Allies were bound to win the war. Wallace Harrison of Rockefeller's office thought it would be nice if "nonpropaganda films, such as Snow White" were shown in Spain, and Donovan pointed to the desirability of secretly subsidizing United Press to get more American stories into Spanish newspapers. But there was too much confusion and uncertainty among the American officials and agencies concerned with psychological warfare for the creation of a tight or coherent policy. Therefore, the subcommittee agreed to wash its hands of most of the problem and to keep quiet about "O.S.S. special operations and activities in Spain."[102]

This decision had serious consequences because it allowed O.S.S. to envelop its own activities and those of other American agencies in Spain and Portugal in a cloud of obscurity. In July 1942, O.S.S. had started to move some of its operatives under deeper cover, and with ample money and the latitude given it by the J.P.W.C.'s decision, Donovan's organization was able to pursue a wide range of activities that caused concern among State Department officials. Spain was a Fascist country that had close links with Nazi Germany and Mussolini's Italy as well as with the Allies. Numerous Republican opponents of the Franco regime, both within and without Spain, were looking for Allied groups that would assist them in their efforts to get rid of the Franco government. O.S.S. was therefore in an awkward position, made more delicate by the inexperience of its own personnel and the personality of Carlton Hayes, the American ambassador in Spain. Hayes, an authority on modern European history, was one of the few academic historians entering American government service in the Second World War who managed to serve in an agency other than O.S.S. He was assertive, rather excitable, and determined to fulfill to the letter his State Department instructions to keep Spain neutral at all costs.[103]

Trouble between O.S.S. Spain and Ambassador Hayes developed almost immediately. As early as August 1942, the ambassador complained to the State Department that "a great deal of the so-called 'information'" being sent to Washington by O.S.S. men in Spain was "little more than hearsay." In late 1942, the ambassador and Donovan managed to smooth out some O.S.S. personnel problems, but Hayes soon recommended that the whole O.S.S. organization in Spain be placed under the authority of the embassy's military attaché. When Washington failed to act on this suggestion, the volume and tempo of Hayes's complaints about O.S.S. increased. By the early spring of 1943, the ambassador had given up hope of trying to work with the American subversive warfare organization and, while collecting evidence to support his distaste for O.S.S., was biding his time until the right moment arose for an all-out attack on Donovan's organization.[104]

Compared with this time bomb ticking under O.S.S. operations in Spain and Portugal, the organization that Donovan's men created in Switzerland was a model of efficiency and security. Two O.S.S. agents were already in Bern by October 1942, but it was the arrival of Allen Dulles in November 1942 that turned S.I. Switzerland into the most important and active continental intelligence post of the Donovan organization. Dulles had extensive business and government connections. His older brother, John Foster, was acting as Thomas Dewey's chief foreign policy advisor in the Republican shadow cabinet, and Allen Dulles himself had served as an American diplomatic representative in Switzerland during World War I. The younger Dulles had left his private business to join the Donovan organization in C.O.I. days and had performed S.I. supervisorial duties in New York for a year.

After being picked to lead the Bern mission, Dulles headed for Switzerland in early November and crossed from Spain into Vichy France on 8 November, the day the Torch invasion began. Barely avoiding internment in France, Dulles dashed for the Swiss frontier. After some bureaucratic delay, he was cleared for entry into Switzerland on 9 November by a Vichy official who remarked, "You see our resistance is only symbolical."[105]

Whether or not Vichy resistance on 8–9 November 1942 was indeed symbolical depended on one's point of view—Dwight Eisenhower was rather inclined to the negative—but the incident at the Swiss border did foreshadow the role that Dulles would play in Bern. For nearly twenty-two months, he was sealed off in Switzerland, unable to leave his post until the Allied invasion armies advancing from Normandy reached the Swiss border in September 1944. During that time, Dulles was forced to depend on his own resources as he functioned in surroundings cramped by the reality of Nazi power and a confusion of political loyalties. While hammering together an organization out of whatever American resources and personnel he could find, Dulles immediately started reporting to Washington on conditions within Germany and Axis-occupied territories. He also began searching for individuals and groups whose service with Hitler was only "symbolical" and whose reservations might allow room for American psychological attack or political maneuver.

From his arrival in Bern, Dulles's dispatches touched on many of the fundamental issues facing Allied wartime policy. True to O.S.S. practice, Dulles sent off numerous undigested reports from sources of varying reliability, but he frequently added extensive comments of his own, and occasionally his assessment of a special problem was comprehensive. Since he had been sent to Bern at a time when Donovan thought that psychological warfare would be the password for broadening the scope of O.S.S. activities, Dulles keyed most of his evaluations to matters relating to American propaganda. Such papers inevitably touched on aspects of high policy, and it was here that Dulles had his greatest impact, initially by helping to shape the political appraisals of O.S.S. Washington and then, as his reports received wider circulation in late 1943 and early 1944, by affecting to some degree official opinion in the State Department and elsewhere.

Dulles made contact with people who claimed to speak for a German resistance movement as early as January 1943. He was initially cautious, but since he was not limited by such tight controls on handling approaches from enemy nationals as were his S.O.E. colleagues in Switzerland, his door was open a bit wider. Because of his contacts in France, O.S.S. representative in Bern was also in a position to provide Washington with regular reports on the resistance movement there. At the time of his dash across France in early November, Dulles opined that no matter how much Washington disliked de Gaulle, "the fact remains that Gaullism and the Cross Lorraine have been effective symbols for underground resistance." While advising Anglo-American authorities not to attempt to "destroy these symbols," Dulles also noted that there were conservative, military, and anticommunist groups in France whose resistance tendencies, if encouraged, might serve as a counterweight to de Gaulle. Such dispatches may well have helped fuel the frantic but ultimately futile attempt of American officials in Washington and North Africa (including some in

O.S.S.) to undercut the difficult de Gaulle by boosting Giraud as the "real" leader of the new France.[106]

In light of Dulles's subsequent importance as postwar European O.S.S. chief and later still as director of the C.I.A., great interest is generated by his early reports on the best line for American policy to take regarding Germany, Italy, and the Soviet Union. In contrast to the views he came to hold by late 1943, Dulles was not initially opposed to the unconditional surrender policy that President Roosevelt abruptly announced to the world in the course of his Casablanca meeting with Churchill in January 1943. Although the O.S.S. representative in Bern felt that unconditional surrender should not be mandatory in dealing with the Axis satellites, he maintained that despite Goebbel's rantings, unconditional surrender was an "absolutely sound psychological warfare" position when applied to Germany. Dulles declared on 31 January 1943 that as Axis strength weakened, the realization that the "prolongation of [the] struggle" would not "lead to [a] negotiated armistice" should in the long run "break down the will to resistance." The Bern representative acknowledged, however, that this effect would only be relized if the populations of the Axis countries were given some hope for the future.[107] While recognizing as he transmitted dispatches chronicling the deportation of Jews to extermination camps that Germany was perpetrating unspeakable atrocities, Dulles rarely gave way to the feeling that the German and Italian people should merely be left to reap the whirlwind. He granted that there was little prospect of a popular uprising even in Italy and predicted in February 1943 that most likely there would be an attempt engineered from within the Fascist Party to oust Mussolini "by the group Ciano, Umberto, Grandi, Badoglio, Caballero."[108]

Since with the exception of Cavallero (as his name is actually spelled), all those listed would play important roles in the coup that brought down the Duce five months later, Dulles's estimate was remarkably accurate. But even if no popular uprising could be anticipated in Axis countries, Dulles still thought that it was important for the British and the Americans to continue propagandizing both to try to tip German and Italian public opinion toward the Allies and to encourage those who wanted to overthrow Mussolini or Hitler to take bold action. As early as December 1942, Dulles registered his belief that "the chief reason for any hesitation on the part of anti-Nazi and anti-Fascist elements in both occupied and unoccupied Europe to give us their undivided support is due to their fear of communism." On 1 February 1943, he claimed that if the United States was not sufficiently willing to overlook past sins, "a series of internal revolutions" that "would turn communist" or perhaps lead to "a peri-

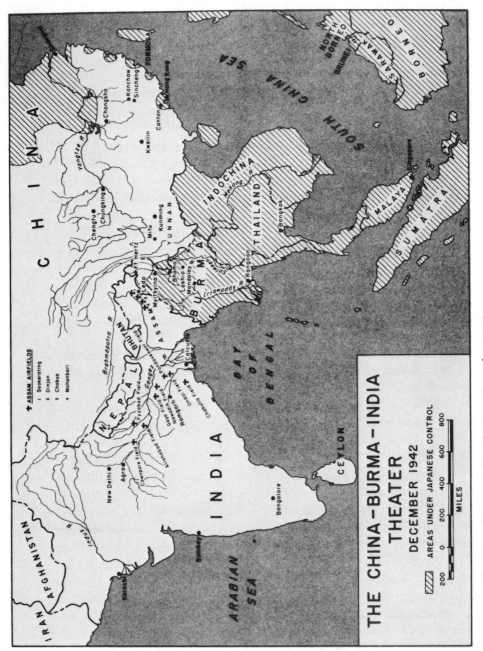

Figure 2. The China–Burma–India Theater, December 1942

od of Communism" might follow the collapse of Fascism. To fill out the details of this bleak picture, Dulles reported to Washington on 10 February that he had learned indirectly from a Russian source that the Soviet Union believed that time was on its side and that with Poland soon to be within its grasp and France supposedly leaning toward the communist orbit, Stalin would be able to work his will in Europe at war's end.[109]

Since the Germans had nearly succeeded in cracking the code used by Dulles and had completely deciphered at least one of his messages in this period, these reports probably made interesting reading in Berlin as well as Washington. Yet the importance of the dispatches goes beyond their revealing the anticommunist suspicion of the Soviet Union that would characterize Dulles's subsequent public career. More significant was his insistence at this early date that the United States assume a strong stand in dealing with Soviet Russia. At the time, the Soviet Union was carrying nearly the full weight of the Allied war against Germany, the western Allies had not even reached the continent, and the British and American governments were especially anxious to soothe Stalin with promises of a second front and postwar cooperation. O.S.S. was still an undeveloped aspect of an Anglo-American military organization that had not yet proven itself. But since O.S.S. Washington did not call Dulles to account for his anti-Soviet views in late 1942 and early 1943, it was virtually inevitable that as O.S.S. became more powerful and influential, Dulles's hard line would have an increasing influence within and without Donovan's organization.[110]

O.S.S. in Asia: June 1942–March 1943

June 1942: The Battle of Midway
August 1942: American forces land in the Solomon Islands

The pleas of O.S.S. anticommunists such as Allen Dulles to contain the Soviet Union in the later stages of the war did not cover the full range of political tendencies within O.S.S. Another major current evident in late 1942 and early 1943 pointed in a very different direction. Especially in Asia, O.S.S. men from Donovan down to the lowliest enlisted man tended to have a strong anti-imperialist streak, oblivious of the fact that their own labors were developing "something strongly akin to imperial responsibility" for the United States. Donovan's men vied with O.W.I. representatives to see who could pour the most scorn on the undemocratic principles of their British, French, and Dutch allies in Southeast Asia. Furthermore, because O.S.S. found it so difficult to secure a clear field in which to implement its subversive operations in Asia, it was prepared to look anywhere and to accept aid from virtually anyone in order to take some action. As a result, by war's end O.S.S. had parted company with its European colleagues in several areas of Asia and was joining hands with various native, anti-imperialist groups, some of which were communist. By the early spring of 1943, the anti-imperialist and prorevolutionary inclinations of O.S.S. already were clearly manifest in Asia.[111]

On paper, O.S.S. Asia looked stronger than it actually was in 1942. In the fall of that year, Donovan's organization boasted that it had four S.O. and three S.I. operations in the Far East. Of the four S.O. units, however, only one, Detachment 101, was actually operating. In October 1942, Colonel Eifler established a base camp in Assam in northeast India, 400 miles from a planned operational area in northern Burma. A few 101 probes went overland into Burma in late 1942 with discouraging results, and it was immediately decided to switch to parachute landings. On 26 January 1943, the first O.S.S. men were dropped into northern Burma, and ten more went in soon after. By March, Eifler's men were spreading out over the north, and the first landings had taken place in central Burma.

To expand their efforts, the handful of Americans in Detachment 101 relied heavily on Europeans who had lived in Burma, but the basis of the whole operation was close cooperation between American O.S.S. men and Kachin tribesmen. The Kachins provided 101 with the contacts, jungle skills, and much of the killing power that turned northern Burma into a hell for the Japanese occupation forces. Without detracting from the courage or the achievement of the American O.S.S. men in the partnership, it must be said that without the Kachins there would have been little S.O. activity in Asia in 1942–43. Eifler and his men were successful because they united with a strong native group that had deep grievances against the Japanese. It was the good fortune of 101 that such effective anti-Japanese warriors as the Kachins were available in an area where the American theater commander, General Stilwell, wanted subversive warfare operations to be carried out by O.S.S.[112]

Detachment 101 showed that when all the necessary elements converged, even a small subversive warfare force could produce striking results. But Burma was the only place in Asia where everything came together in the early phase of O.S.S. Donovan and his colleagues tried to form a Free Thai Army to serve in Thailand as the nucleus of an operation similar to that of 101, but the preparations soon became ensnarled in State Department red tape, factional struggles among the Thais, and the unwillingness of the Nationalist Chinese to have Free Thais operating from Chinese bases. Further north, O.S.S. managed to send a two-man S.O. unit into Tibet in the fall of 1942, but the mission—which consisted of Ilia Tolstoy and Brooke Dolan, two professional adventurers turned O.S.S. men—was little more than a prank. Tolstoy and Dolan, whose O.S.S. cover names were Mud and Slug, were supposedly sent to identify possible sabotage locations in the event that Tibet was occupied by the Japanese. There was actually no Japanese threat to Tibet, then or later. "Mud and Slug" just had a good romp, while alerting Lhasa to the existence of an armed America and causing the British and Chinese to suspect that the United States had political ambitions in the region.[113]

The British in India were already on their guard with Americans, especially enthusiasts from organizations like O.W.I. and O.S.S. When William Phillips left his post as O.S.S. chief in London during November 1942 to become President Roosevelt's special representative in India, Donovan tried to make use of this connection to expand the operational zone open to O.S.S. But the British commander, General Wavell, who was already having difficulty coping with the rivalries and confusion produced by the presence of three British shadow warfare organizations in his domain (S.O.E., S.I.S, and P.W.E.) was not enthusiastic about having O.S.S. arrive in force. Wavell passed Phillips off to the viceroy, and the viceroy handed him on to the secretary of state for India, who turned over the whole question of creating a large O.S.S. unit in India to the British Chiefs of Staff. The chiefs, who were more than a match for Donovan, concluded that they would permit O.S.S. liaison officers in India if the Americans would arrange comparable S.O.E. liaison in MacArthur's South Pacific theater. This proposal was a piece of brilliant gamesmanship, for although it seemed fair, O.S.S. was in no position to secure access to MacArthur's domain for itself or S.O.E.[114]

Drawing heavily on both Australian and U.S. Army resources (and employing a few key British shadow warfare personnel), MacArthur had assembled an Allied Intelligence Bureau, a guerrilla warfare unit and comprehensive intelligence system that ranged from distant coast watchers to the centralized coordination organization operating in his headquarters. Repeatedly, Donovan tried to get O.S.S. into the South Pacific to work alongside, or in tandem, with MacArthur's Allied Intelligence Bureau. In July 1942, MacArthur rejected O.S.S. requests, forwarded by the J.C.S., that Donovan be allowed to run subversive or psychological warfare operations in his theater. When in January 1943, Donovan sent a personal emissary, Joseph Hayden of the Board of Analysts, to meet with the general, the result was the same. Hayden had been a colleague of MacArthur during the 1930s, and the general was cordial in his dealings with the

O.S.S. man. But MacArthur's obsessive fear of any interference from Washington reinforced by the suspicions of his staff, produced another rejection of O.S.S. operations in the South Pacific.[115]

Thwarted in the Pacific and in India, O.S.S. turned once more to China. Donovan had the highly secret Starr network operating under deep cover in that country and was determined to push further, despite warnings from British officials that Nationalist China was highly suspicious of foreign intelligence services and would not "allow foreigners to play with her guerrillas." O.S.S. Washington developed a plan (code-named Dragon) for running an extensive intelligence operation in occupied China in cooperation with the Chiang government, using business operations as a cover. Chinese and American agents were supposed to bribe Japanese officials and their Chinese collaborators to secure information on the Japanese military setup in China, Formosa, and the Japanese home islands. Dragon was rather farfetched and had little chance of securing the approval it needed from the J.C.S., General Stilwell, and Chiang Kai-shek, among others. Presented to the J.C.S. in mid-July, the plan was placed on hold during the late summer to give Donovan's Pacific emissary, Dr. Hayden, an opportunity to sell it to Stilwell and the Chinese. Hayden left Washington in mid-August, but the vicissitudes of wartime travel delayed his journey. In the meantime, Donovan made another abrupt shift, and when Hayden arrived in Chunking he found a cable instructing him to shelve Dragon because another plan for O.S.S. China to operate "entirely under direction [of the] proper Chinese official" was in the works.[116]

The word *proper* was singularly inappropriate in this context because the official in question was Tai Li and the plan under consideration was the cooperative agreement known as the Friendship Plan that Captain Miles and Alghan Lusey of the C.O.I. had worked out with "the Chinese Himmler." The Miles–Lusey–Tai Li plan recommended that the two countries pool all their intelligence equipment and personnel in China to create a joint Chinese–American intelligence operation. The two chiefs of the operation—Miles and Tai Li—could each veto projects deemed objectionable.

However one viewed the Friendship Plan, it provided Chiang with the perfect means for strangling American secret intelligence operations in China. But Lusey, who had brought the scheme to Washington in September 1942, succeeded in convincing Donovan that in view of Chinese suspicions, the only way that O.S.S. would ever be able to function in the area was to become a junior partner to Captain Miles in the Friendship Plan. Donovan, desperately eager to carry out large O.S.S. activities somewhere—the J.C.S. had not yet issued their general go-ahead order—

jumped at the apparent opportunity. In early November 1942, Hayden therefore was ordered to find out whether General Stilwell would support the Friendship proposal.[117]

Joseph Hayden was not a Chinese specialist, but he was also no fool. Having carefully prepared for his mission and possessed of a large number of Chinese contacts in Chunking, he was able to judge the lay of the land. Wherever he looked, the prospects for American military activity in China looked dim in late 1942. Stilwell was determined to take offensive action in the theater, but his chief of staff, Gen. Thomas G. Hearn, frankly told Hayden on 1 November that the Nationalists were "not doing any aggressive fighting" and that the best that could be hoped for was containment of a substantial number of Japanese troops in China. To compound the difficulties and the doubtful prospects for O.S.S. China, Gens. Claire Chennault and Joseph Stilwell were at each others' throats, and Chennault had complained to Donovan about the alleged overcaution of Stilwell. The War Department learned of this incident, and its resulting displeasure did nothing to smooth relations between Chennault and Stilwell or to increase the latter's confidence in O.S.S.[118]

For all these reasons, Joseph Hayden's talk with Stilwell on 8 November 1942 was not very encouraging. The general had doubts about Miles, the Chinese, the Friendship Plan, and O.S.S., but most of all he was inclined to feel that the Friendship proposal was not worth the airfreight that would be necessary to support it. Stilwell was mainly interested in getting an American ground force and combat equipment into China to spark a Chinese offensive into northern Burma. Doubtful competitors for tonnage over the Himalayas (the hump), such as the Friendship Plan, did not kindle his enthusiasm. Stilwell reluctantly agreed on 8 November that if the Chinese bought the plan he would not oppose it, and Hayden told Donovan that under the circumstances this was probably the best that could be done.

Hayden nevertheless predicted future trouble between Miles and Stilwell, and he suspected, rightly, that Miles's primary concern was not the waging of subversive warfare but the buildup of a U.S. Navy intelligence empire in China focusing on the collection of weather information for the American fleet. As the O.S.S. representative saw the situation, Miles nonetheless had subversive warfare prospects in China sewn up, and O.S.S. could either accept his offer and be cut into a portion of the action or reject it and stand little chance of developing any operational base there. In December 1942, at the same time that the J.C.S. gave O.S.S. its approval for action, Donovan took the gamble on the Friendship Plan and went along with Miles. The O.S.S. director appointed Miles head of O.S.S. China and raised no objection to the terms of the S.A.C.O. (Sino-American Co-operative) Agreement that went into effect in April 1943.[119]

The S.A.C.O. Agreement, which formalized the Friendship Plan, was, however, a snare that the wily Tai Li had used to bind Miles, O.S.S., and the American government, hand and foot. The document set forth a solemn agreement between the president of the United States and Tai Li(!), whereby America promised to execute all its secret intelligence and subversive warfare operations in China through the Friendship Plan. The United States was to provide the equipment, pay the bills, and accept a Tai Li veto over all operations and all intelligence communication with Washington. When Hayden finally saw the paper setting forth the formal S.A.C.O. terms in April 1943, he was horrified and denounced the proposal as "thoroughly bad." But by then it was too late. Miles had come to Washington, lined up the support of the navy brass, and with William Donovan as his partner, had maneuvered the S.A.C.O. Agreement through the bureaucracy and secured the approval of Franklin Roosevelt.[120]

By becoming Miles's auxillary in the S.A.C.O. Agreement, Donovan had led O.S.S. China into a cul-de-sac. American army leaders did not trust the intelligence from S.A.C.O. and were reluctant to carry out exchanges with the Chinese because they believed that Tai Li was primarily interested in getting his hands on American Magic and British Ultra decrypts. Tai Li was not excited by the prospect of ambitious intelligence or guerrilla operations against the Japanese, and Miles was in no bigger hurry than Tai Li.[121]

So the picture that circumstances painted of O.S.S. China as a partner of Captain Miles and Tai Li was a still life. Donovan managed to get a few of his men into the S.A.C.O. organization, which was fittingly headquartered in a place called Happy Valley, but no discernible action occurred. O.S.S. still had Starr's extra secret intelligence operation, since its existence had not been revealed to the Chinese. But aside from that, in early 1943, O.S.S. China had virtually nothing else actually functioning.

William Donovan could not be easily stymied, however, and even before the S.A.C.O. agreement was signed, his men were beginning to explore the possibility of working in China on the political left as well as on the right. On 11 February 1943, William Kimbel of O.S.S. discussed the situation in communist north China with State Department officials. O.S.S. was anxious to discover the extent of communist operations in the north, to determine "what we should plan for in psychological warfare in those areas." The Kimbel–State Department talks were only a first probe, and State did not approve O.S.S. suggestion that Robert Service be sent north on an exploratory mission. But it was clear that Donovan was not willing to roll over and let O.S.S. China be stillborn. If the rightist Chiang regime would not clear a way for him, he was prepared to turn left. At a time when even the British military attaché in Chunking reported to London that Mao's forces were "not communists at all in the true sense of the word" and that "independents would be a better word for them," the blandishments of the Chiang government were not enough to keep Donovan away if he thought Mao offered brighter prospects for putting O.S.S. into the field against the Japanese.[122]

In the early spring of 1943, the O.S.S. director was prepared to try S.A.C.O., grit his teeth, and bide his time. Because of the agreements that O.S.S. had made with O.W.I. and the J.C.S. in late 1942 and early 1943, Donovan's organization would soon secure a huge influx of military personnel and equipment. Donovan's main task during the summer and fall of 1943 and on into 1944 was thus to build up O.S.S. and gradually work it into action at every point where opportunity offered. Once the American theater commanders recognized its value sufficiently to allow him onto the battlefield, Donovan would be able to sweep past obstacles like S.A.C.O. and let loose upon the enemy the full force of an American shadow warfare machine. When that moment came, no ideological reservations would stand in his way. Subversive warfare action was what Donovan craved, and from March 1943 onward, he went forward as if, after many disappointments and false starts, he had finally found the road that would lead to his goal.

CHAPTER 5

On the Way:
March 1943-June 1944

> Bill [Donovan] longed for a field command
> (as Teddy Roosevelt had also yearned in his
> older years). As this was impossible, he flung
> himself into O.S.S. liked a caged lion.
>
> JAMES GRAFTON ROGERS

O.S.S. Washington: March 1943–June 1944

WITH O.S.S. and O.W.I. responsibilities at last delineated and a clear mandate issued by the J.C.S., Donovan's organization found that spring 1943 indeed marked the beginning of a golden era. Relatively harmonious working relations soon evolved with Elmer Davis of O.W.I., and associations with most other bureaucratic neighbors were also cordial.[1]

British observers noted that the reputation of O.S.S. rose quickly with the American military during 1943. Baron Richard Coleridge of the British Joint Staff Mission, who thought Donovan was "a good chap," believed that O.S.S director's relations with the J.C.S. had improved, and Sir Harold Redman concluded that O.S.S. was "in the ascendancy" by mid-September. The army and the J.C.S. showed a greater willingness to deal with the practical problems facing Donovan and were no longer as easily panicked by special O.S.S. projects. In September–October 1943, the J.C.S. routinely revised the basic O.S.S. character at Donovan's request to make it more suitable for use as the organization's field manual. The revision, which consisted mainly of striking out the phrase *psychological warfare* and substituting *strategic services* instead, passed through the J.C.S. machinery without crisis or controversy. Specific issues that earlier would have been troublesome, such as coordinating O.S.S. weapons development with that of the military and guaranteeing that O.S.S. cipher security meet military standards, were handled easily in this new era of good feeling. When the War and Navy departments turned to matters that directly concerned O.S.S., such as the formation of a committee on military government, Donovan's organization was included as a matter of course.[2]

By late October 1943, the organization's standing with the military was so good that the new head of the J.C.S. secretariat, Capt. Forrest Royal (General Deane had gone to Moscow to head the American Military Mission there) recommended that Donovan be raised to the rank of major general. With this quickly accomplished, Major General Donovan and his organization took another step toward military respectability, and in the spring of 1944, General McNarney told Mr. Clarence Cannon of the House of Representatives that although the military authorities did not foresee much expansion of O.S.S., it had "made very substantial contributions to the war effort."[3]

Still, overabundance of exaggeration and self-adulation persisted in Donovan's organization even in 1943. Both the plans that O.S.S. prepared for the J.C.S. and the new O.S.S. field manual contained considerable pretentious blather and double-talk. Dyed-in-the-wool opponents of O.S.S. in the military also had not disappeared. Until he left G-2 in February 1944, General Strong made the life of O.S.S as unpleasant as possible, and Admiral King, with the concurrence of other navy men associated with the J.C.S., tended to be unsympathetic to O.S.S. Furthermore, there was a general uneasiness about whether a "quasimilitary" organization was really a suitable instrument for preparing men for battle, even when it was called subversive warfare rather than front-line combat. As a last resort, when things became too tranquil, Assistant Secretary of State Berle and the F.B.I. could be counted on to stir up some trouble by suggesting that O.S.S. had made incursions into the Western Hemisphere.[4]

Indeed, although they kept out of Latin America, Donovan's legions had not lost all their adventuresome zip. In June 1943, the B.S.C. complained that an O.S.S. team had told Canadian officials that North Africa must not be left to the French and that "eventually" the United States would have to "take these territories in hand." As a B.S.C. official reported to London, such remarks had made a "very poor impression" on the Canadians, who were rather sensitive about all things French and unnerved by their proximity to this expansive colossus. Such gaffes aside, O.S.S. tendency to leak sensitive diplomatic information to other government agencies deeply worried the State Department. The failure of O.S.S. to keep its varied activities under tight supervision also caused concern. In early 1944, State learned that because Donovan had issued no instructions to the contrary, a diplomat in Baghdad had been sending reports on Iraqi shipping to O.S.S. every month since early 1942. When the man in Baghdad asked if he should continue sending reports, the State Department hurriedly told him no, but the incident did make officials wonder what all those O.S.S. people stationed in remote corners of the world since the early C.O.I. days actually had been doing during the subsequent two years of war. In May 1943, General Strong discovered that one of them in Mozambique was planning to kidnap and assault what O.S.S. had determined were Axis agents. The fact that O.S.S. man had undertaken this activity because he was "very greatly influenced by MUGGERIDGE [Malcolm Muggeridge], the British intelligence officer . . . with whom he is collaborating" did not save him from the wrath of General Strong, who quickly forced O.S.S. to give up the use of mugging as an instrument of war.[5]

Emphasizing such misdemeanors would distort the facts and cause us to overlook the great change that had taken place in O.S.S. Donovan's organization was no longer notorious for its buffoonery, and its mistakes were no worse than those of most other American organizations. The U.S. Army was perfectly capable of committing astonishing breaches of security, including the mismailing of a group of top secret D Day invasion documents to a private residence in a German-American district of Chicago in March 1944. The J.C.S. also stubbed its toe on occasion, and in April 1943 one of its committees was forced to admit that the chiefs' intelligence coordination structure, built around the J.I.C., had never functioned effectively and needed an overhaul.[6]

The position of O.S.S. in early 1944 was a model of contentment and tranquility compared with that of the British shadow warfare organizations. Reform had not solved Britain's problems, and S.O.E., P.W.E., and S.I.S. continued their interminable tag wrestling. In December 1943, the German penetration of the S.O.E. network in the Netherlands became known to London officials, and the bitterness of the conflicts intensified. The R.A.F., which always had been reluctant to divert aircraft from the bomber offensive to support S.O.E. operations, now learned that a number of its aircraft had been lost over the Netherlands because of the German entrapment of S.O.E. Again, S.O.E. was forced to fight for its very existence, and by late January 1944, Lord Selborne's organization had been placed under even tighter control.[7]

When measured against this free-for-all, O.S.S. procedures seemed exemplary. Col. C. R. Peck, a liaison officer assigned to Donovan's headquarters by the J.C.S., worked out most of the difficulties that arose between O.S.S and the armed services. By the end of May 1943, the O.S.S. no longer was required to secure J.C.S. approval of its operational plans in individual countries; once the chiefs had accepted a general O.S.S. plan for a given theater of operations, Donovan's headquarters had only to work out the details with the appropriate theater commander.[8]

Having finally found the appropriate strips of red tape, O.S.S was able to develop an efficient system for the acquisition of army and navy personnel by late 1943. Donovan's organization was given a quota of military and naval manpower and then allowed to draw against this quota to meet its needs. The initial army quota totaled 4,323 personnel for the second quarter of 1943; and the marine and navy quota, 586. Donovan immediately petitioned for an increase, and the army granted him 1,300 more personnel in September 1943. The organization's maximum allotment of army personnel was raised again in 1944 to 7,571. To smooth out the system and give O.S.S. access to the specialists it needed for its activities, procedures were also established for granting draft deferments and direct commissions to civilians in O.S.S.[9]

Although numerous civilians were still employed by O.S.S., military personnel came to predominate by late 1943. The militarization of Donovan's organization increased its prestige and influence in wartime Washington, but the heavy military recruiting had its most profound effect overseas. In June 1943, O.S.S. had only 560 personnel stationed in military theaters abroad, 260 of whom were civilians. By the end of October 1943, the total number of military personnel in Donovan's organization had jumped to 6,000, and 5,200 of these were already overseas. The overseas movement of O.S.S. men and women in uniform continued during the spring and early summer of 1944, culminating in large transports made shortly before and after D Day (6 June 1944). The number of O.S.S. personnel overseas peaked at approximately 6,000, with another 1,200 military personnel and 2,000 to 3,000 civilians remaining in the United States. Numerous intertheater transfers of O.S.S. military personnel occurred after that date, but the basic personnel pattern of the organization—primarily military and stationed overwhelmingly overseas—definitely had been established by early 1944.[10] It is this aspect of O.S.S. development in 1943 and early 1944 rather than the increase in size that is most noteworthy, for by comparison, S.O.E. was still much larger. In the spring of 1945, the British organization employed 11,000 military and 2,500 civilian and auxiliary personnel for resistance warfare alone, whereas Donovan's organization dealt with black propaganda, intelligence, and counterintelligence as well. The overwhelming military coloration and the heavy deployment overseas of O.S.S. personnel were what revolutionized the organization and changed its whole impact on the war.[11]

Customary measures of bureaucratic success such as budget size did not accurately reveal the changed position of O.S.S. In May 1943, when President Roosevelt was given a choice between drastically increasing the O.S.S. budget (and altering its structure) or upping it by a mere $10 million to around $35 million, he took the cautious alternative, noting, "I think that from 35 to 40 M. [illion] is enough." In the spring of 1944, the O.S.S. budget was not doubled, as Donovan wanted, but it was given a solid increase to a total of $58 million. These increases did not begin to reflect the changes that had occurred in the organization, however, for O.S.S. overseas personnel had increased 1,000 percent in just five months. Only the close partnership with the military had made that development possible, and O.S.S therefore had to prove that the support given to it by the J.C.S. was justified.[12]

The O.S.S. Branches

Responsibility for meeting the military's needs fell initially on Donovan's top administrative officials, especially Ned Buxton, Charles Cheston, and Atherton Richards. However, most of the practical labor involved in actually developing activities useful to the military and putting them into operation was handled by the separate divisions and branches. The tasks facing S.O. were probably the most direct and obvious. It had to provide the military with men trained to carry out sabotage operations and guerrilla warfare in enemy-occupied territory. Complicated though these skills were, S.O. Washington had basically three straightforward jobs: finding men brave enough for S.O. duty, getting them adequately trained, and shipping them to locations where the army would allow them to operate. S.O. Washington also had to do its best to realize Donovan's plans for commando-type operational groups. The dream of having his own commando force had been surging in the general's breast ever since late 1941. A separate Operational Group (O.G.) section under Col. Ellery Huntington was established in June 1943, but bureaucratic battles and personnel problems prevented its accomplishing much until the fall. At that time, the army gave up on its hope of creating special crack "ethnic" battalions, such as the so-called "Greek Battalion" (the 122nd Infantry Battalion—Separate) and turned over most of these men to O.S.S. S.O. and the new O.G. section thereupon redoubled their efforts to create combat operational groups, and in late 1943, the first of these shock troops for raiding and resistance support went into action along the Italian coast.[13]

Another O.S.S. branch that served the military directly was Morale Operations (M.O.). This unit, which became increasingly busy during 1943 and 1944, used rumors, pamphlets, and black radio broadcasts to undermine Axis morale. Since the American M.O. men worked closely with both their British counterparts and the theater commanders, few important policy decisions fell directly to M.O. Washington. But overseas, and especially in London, M.O. was very active in late 1943 and in 1944, and this activity has confused the public mind and clouded many issues then and since.

In light of the numerous postwar allegations of wartime capitalist conspiracies, it is rather disturbing to discover that in 1943 Allied black propaganda spread the story that Henry Ford and the director of the British Motor Company were collaborating with Nazi industrialists. The black propaganda people hoped that these rumors would cause dissension in Nazi ranks, but all that they seemed to have accomplished was postwar controversy. Similarly, the rumor circulated in March 1944, that Dresden would not be bombed because the Allies planned to make it their postwar headquarters after Berlin had "been bombed off the map," did nothing to weaken Axis will to resist but may have caused German civilians to concentrate in that Saxon city, thereby increasing the unnecessary slaughter produced by the raids of 1945.[14]

Even in terms of wartime policy, M.O. frequently was going one way, when the official Anglo-American position was going another. While Washington and London were proclaiming that they would play no favorites and that unconditional surrender was their only policy in early 1944, Allied black propaganda was spreading the tale that the Allies were assembling a "white" list of good Germans who would be rewarded in the postwar period for their assistance to the Allied cause. Nor was this the only occasion on which M.O. and P.W.E. were out of synchronization with Allied policy. In May 1944, when Allen Dulles was trying to coax the German generals into overt resistance to Hitler, the black propagandists released a rumor that the Nazis were already preparing another "June 30 purge" (referring to the blood purge of the S.A. in 1934) and would immediately liquidate anyone who stepped out of line, including "those generals who have been criticizing the Party."[15]

What M.O. and its British associates hoped to accomplish by such rumors is hard to imagine, but what does seem clear is that by 1943, information contained in intelligence reports being sent to Washington sometimes bore a striking resemblance to earlier black rumors. Two years after P.W.E. circulated stories alleging that masked Jewish doctors were being used on the Eastern Front because the Germans had suffered such heavy casualties, O.S.S. Lisbon reported that following the heavy air raids on Berlin "medical aid organizations are accepting Jewish nurses and doctors" for service in bombed-out cities. Both the original rumor and the Lisbon O.S.S. report were false; Jews were actually being worked to death and exterminated in gas chambers during this period. But it seems likely that by late 1943 both the Nazis and the Allies had released so much propaganda that the line between truth and falsehood, rumor and intelligence frequently had become too blurred even for the Allied intelligence men to see their way clearly. Disquieting as such considerations may seem to us today, they did not trouble unduly either M.O. officials or American military commanders during the way. Their eyes were focused on breaking the enemy front, and whatever might contribute to that end, whether bombing or black propaganda, was welcome to them as long as it did not interfere with front-line combat operations. Military Commanders were sensitive to the use of black propaganda only if it kept the Allied intelligence systems from functioning effectively. Since such military intelligence activities as air reconnaisance, code cracking, and P.O.W. interrogation were little affected by the use of rumors, they did not have to confront the problem directly. It was O.S.S.–S.I., charged with the duty of running agents and collecting secret intelligence, that had to cope with the task of sorting the true from the false, artifice from actuality. Probably the most significant achievement of O.S.S. Washington in 1943 and 1944 was that its intelligence estimates were reasonably close to reality, thereby convincing the J.C.S. that the various branches of General Magruder's Intelligence Services Division were actually doing their job.[16]

Magruder had under his direct control S.I., R. and A., F.N.B. and Counterintelligence (X-2). In addition, the I.D.C., which operated under O.S.S. auspices, was supervised by Magruder's office. Though it has never received much attention, the I.D.C. brought an enormous number of foreign publications to Washington. In August 1943 alone, I.D.C. circulated over 150,000 issues of printed and microfilm publications to seventeen government agencies. F.N.B. also acquired a large amount of information for government use by drawing on its numerous contacts in "ethnic" America. In contrast to I.D.C., F.N.B. did some evaluation of the information it acquired and circulated it not only to offices in Washington but to British and American missions abroad.[17]

But the heart of Magruder's intelligence empire lay in the three large intelligence branches: X-2, S.I., and R. and A. Of the three, S-2 was still being formed throughout most of 1943 and the early months of 1944. The vast quantity of materials on counterintelligence provided by the British needed to be absorbed and a worldwide undercover network of counterintelligence agents established. So pressing was this need that many immediate counterintelligence operations were assigned not to X-2 but to S.I., which continued to perform counterintelligence functions in many areas of the world until the end of the war. The operational theaters naturally received top priority because as soon as a general found himself in charge of a recently liberated rear area, he immediately required assistance from X-2 and the army's Counterintelligence Corp (C.I.C.) to maintain security.

Consequently, the main function initially performed by X-2 Washington was to feed the operational theaters, and only in late 1944 did it have enough counterintelligence information on hand to offer much help to the military and civilian authorities in the American capital.

Since S.I. was older and better established, its Washington headquarters was more quickly able to channel all information from abroad to important customers. Donovan's private courier service to the Oval Office may have been temporarily interrupted in 1943 (there is a long gap in the files), but items thought to be of special significance were still sent directly to the J.C.S. S.I. also exchanged considerable information with O.N.I. and M.I.D., as well as with the intelligence services of the British and exile governments. In addition, a regular flow of S.I. material went to the White House Map Room for use in psychological warfare planning, and to various civilian agencies, especially the State Department.[18]

British intelligence men and political observers thought highly of the S.I. leaders, especially David Bruce and General Magruder. A number of M.I. 6 and N.I.D. officials believed that S.I. was far ahead of them on Far Eastern matters. In July 1943, an N.I.D. official remarked that British "Far East intelligence from C's organization [M.I. 6] has now dwindled to a trickle from a few Chinese coolies." Consequently, the British intelligence establishment was prepared to cooperate with Washington on Far Eastern intelligence in order to draw on O.S.S. intelligence assets in Asia. S.O.E. had learned about the Starr operation in China and thus were more prepared to take S.I. seriously. After his first meeting with Magruder, the new M.I. 6 man assigned to collect Asian intelligence in the United States characterized the general as "an able, intelligent man with far greater knowledge of China than any equivalent officer possesses in our organization."[19]

Not every aspect of S.I. received such high marks from British observers. The same M.I. 6 man who praised Magruder thought S.I. intelligence training mediocre and concluded that the "average results of their average agent will therefore be inferior to ours." He predicted that the S.I. would "produce a very considerable quantity of medium grain information" drawn from an "enormous network" operated "without regard for expense." Looking over the broad sweep of S.I. reports, this evaluation seems accurate. It must be noted in defense of S.I. and the efforts of General Magruder, however, that the organization was not given direct access to American Magic or British Ultra decrypts, and without these "golden eggs," S.I. material inevitably seemed at best "medium grain."[20]

S.I. was a new organization working a terrain where operations were notoriously difficult and failures frequently ludicrous. However much General Magruder and his aides tried to avoid them, comic incidents were inevitable. In November 1943, for instance, the former baseball player Moe Berg tried to meet S.I. training test requirements by securing surreptitious entry into a defense plant through the use of a counterfeit letter on White House stationery. He bluffed his way into the Glenn Martin aircraft factory, but unfortunately for Berg and for S.I., he was then apprehended, and a dreadful hue and cry was raised by Washington bureaucrats who feared that such novice secret agents might penetrate their inner sanctuaries. As Henry Morgenthau remarked with the eye of a prophet twenty-five years before Watergate, if O.S.S. would "go to that length" to get Moe Berg into an aircraft plant, "what will people on the National Republican Committee do?"[21]

Yet the J.C.S. stood staunchly behind Magruder during such crises, refusing to let critics use them as pretexts to interfere with S.I.'s overseas operations. Even Adolf Berle was told flatly in December 1943 that he might as well stop complaining about S.I. connections with foreign secret services because the J.C.S. insisted that O.S.S. continue to obtain information through such channels. Where the chiefs failed Magruder was in refusing to allow him to go ahead with a plan for a joint American intelligence agency that would have pulled together the various disparate intelligence organizations. Magruder contended that too much manpower and money was being expended by O.S.S., M.I.D., and O.N.I. to get mediocre results and that a joint coordinating agency with authority over the various independent intelligence services should be established to consolidate and evaluate material for the J.C.S. In Magruder's proposal, which was made to the chiefs in July 1943, the R. and A. branch, reinforced by military and naval intelligence men, would have become the core of the evaluative process, serving a function analogous to the C.I.A.'s later Board of Estimates. However, the Joint Chiefs simply ignored the Magruder plan; no joint agency was created, and the various independent American intelligence services continued to go their separate ways.[22]

Their efficiency was certainly reduced thereby, but R. and A. was probably the biggest loser. As Magruder told the chiefs, the mandate given to R. and A. by the J.C.S. was diffuse and confusing. Langer's branch was still trapped in the pit into which it had fallen in 1941 when the Board of Analysts failed. It was a research organization, barred from critical evaluation and uncertain for whom it was to do research. Morale in the branch inevitably suffered, and during the summer and fall of 1943, William Langer received a number of protests from section chiefs and staff members who wanted basic changes. Many of the men and women in the branch felt that their talents and time were being wasted on make-work projects. They wanted R. and A. at least to take over all evaluation for S.I. if it were not to provide evaluation for a centralized J.C.S. intelligence agency. Despite the urgings of Richard Hartshorne and other R. and A. leaders, however, even this expansion of the branch's responsibility did not occur. William Langer seems to have been reluctant to confront Magruder and Donovan on the issue directly, and he also did not take the lead in finding important consumers for R. and A. work. The responsibility for searching out government officials interested in R. and A.'s services and then organizing research projects that would be useful to them fell primarily to the division and section chiefs.[23]

Since many R. and A. men were rather scornful of S.I. evaluation work and repelled by what they saw as the exaggerated secrecy of their O.S.S. intelligence cousins, relations between the two branches were often strained. R. and A. personnel delighted in uncovering S.I. gaffes, and Langer's files bulged with exposés of S.I.'s pretentious claims and comic blunders. By early 1944, however, a relatively harmonious working arrangement had developed between R. and A. and S.I. Washington, which though never cordial, was at least free from incessant bickering.[24]

R. and A. gradually developed reasonably efficient internal operating procedures, and the size of the branch stabilized at 950 to 1,000 employees in 1944. But Langer's people continued to suffer from a sense of being second-class citizens. R. and A. and its F.N.B. neighbors were usually the last to find out what was going on in O.S.S. and invariably received small allocations of money and personnel.[25]

As O.S.S. grew more militarized, the essentially civilian character of R. and A. became more obvious. Even when R. and A. men were taken into the military service, which happened to many who stayed in Washington and nearly all who went overseas, the outlook of Langer's branch was quintessentially that of civilian scholarship. As the R. and A. chief in Sicily explained to a meeting of intelligence officers at Palermo in January 1944, even though R. and A. was an organization using "specially trained military personnel," they were really "military in name only," since few "had even [had] basic military training." Because most of the R. and A. people loosely togged out in military attire were academics, it was sometimes difficult to keep them focused on assigned projects. They had a tendency to wander off to examine whatever interested them, and only tight supervision could keep their thirst for knowledge within approved limits. Even William Langer undertook a special private assignment for the State Department in July 1943, preparing a study of American policy toward Vichy France (later published as *Our Vichy Gamble*). Langer took on this task partly because, like most of his subordinates, he simply could not pass up a chance to see all the secret information in the government files.[26]

The key to R. and A.'s successes lay primarily in this very scholarly enthusiasm, for its foundation lay in its ability to obtain useful information from routine documents and published materials. Even though many reports were prepared by R. and A. researchers on their own initiative and copies of some finished reports ended up in the wastepaper baskets of outside agencies, R. and A.'s work enjoyed a general reputation for technical excellence. R. and A. also produced a large number of special studies for outside agencies; in April 1944 alone, the Map Division turned out twenty-one maps for the J.C.S., thirteen of which were classified top secret.[27]

Sometimes these special projects placed very heavy demands on the R. and A. staff. In September 1943, Harold Deutsch was only allowed nine working days to complete a study of foreign workers in Germany that had been requested by M.O. On occasion, too, R. and A. walked a thin line in determining whether requests fell within the O.S.S. mandate to do research only on matters of foreign, not domestic, intelligence. To establish its worth, R. and A. had to produce as much significant work and to satisfy as many important customers as possible. Rules therefore had to be bent and some corners cut. Even though occasional projects had very ominous overtones, such as a special S.O. request in November 1943 for targeting studies on the water systems of Far Eastern cities, if R. and A. was to prove its mettle, doubts had to be suppressed and the warriors shown that Langer's branch could deliver the goods.[28]

Thus, just as Donovan had tried to convince the military of the usefulness of O.S.S. in general so Langer attempted to sell R. and A. to the rest of O.S.S., to the military, and to wartime civilian agencies. Unlike Donovan, Langer had developed a clear sense of which customers were most important. In the early summer of 1943, R. and A. outposts overseas were instructed to balance work for local agencies and reporting to Washington. Although conceding that "service to the theater commander on the spot" was an important function for overseas R. and A., the chief of R. and A.'s Far Eastern Section stressed to his people in India that the needs of R. and A. Washington had to be met as well. Similar instructions were issued to other R. and A. outposts chiefs, and when events pointed to an overwhelming Allied victory, both Langer and his top assistants further shifted the emphasis. Studies on occupation policies and postwar administrative problems began to loom large in R. and A. work by the fall of 1943, and a special Civil Affairs Section of R. and A. under Hajo Holborn was created to work closely with the appropriate departments of the War and State departments. If Langer had had his way, R. and A. London would have focused almost completely on occupation policies as early as January 1944, but under pressure from Donovan, service to the local American military and O.S.S. agencies in Europe continued to receive a high priority.[29]

Langer was the first branch leader in O.S.S. determined to make his unit useful after the war as well as during it, and the branch gave attention to broad postwar policy issues at an early date. In March and April 1944, R. and A. began serious study of Britain's long-term political policies, on the assumption that in the postwar period the interests of the United States and those of Britain would divide on some crucial matters. R. and A. still assumed that Britain was America's closest ally, but times were changing. Whereas British power had peaked, America's strength was steadily increasing. It was only natural that attention in Washington tended to move past Britain and focused increasingly on the other rising colossus, Soviet Russia.[30]

O.S.S. and Conservative Political Warfare

Although many R. and A. studies in 1943 and early 1944 examined the power potential and probable policies of the Soviet Union, most of this work was descriptive with neither overtly ideological nor highly emotional overtones. Other branches and groups in O.S.S. were, however, not so reticent. Some extremely conservative people held positions of importance in F.N.B., some sections of S.I., and on various O.S.S. boards and committees. In addition, elements of both psychological warfare and strategic intelligence were still part of the O.S.S. mission, which inevitably raised questions about where the United States should stand in regard to various ideologies of the Right and the Left.[31]

Franklin Roosevelt was reluctant to get into a full-scale ideological conflict with anyone, preferring to stick to homilies while counting on personal diplomacy and American power to smooth the way in the postwar period. But as Allied victory neared, bringing with it the prospect of an East–West occupation of Europe and Asia, it became more difficult to hold ideological warfare at arm's length. Pressing questions on the United States' attitude toward Soviet Russian and the course Allied occupation authorities should follow in conquered territories needed answers. As a group of intelligence officers acknowledged at a meeting in Palermo in February 1944, the biggest problem facing an effective counterintelligence program in Sicily was that "there is no definition of what exactly constitutes a Fascist, and what ideas and precepts are classified under Fascism." With no clear conception of the enemy's ideology, eradicating it was indeed difficult. Since many people were equally confused about the Soviet Union, it was just as hard for them to decide what stand the United States should take in regard to postwar Russia.[32]

But a handful of conservative ideologues within O.S.S. did not have the latter problem. Men like James Grafton Rogers, Dewitt Poole (the chief of F.N.B.), and John Wiley had no doubt that the Soviet Union intended to capitalize on its military triumphs over the Nazis to establish dictatorial communist control of much of Europe and Asia. When Moscow began to make extensive propaganda use of captured German officers like Field Marshal Paulus following the surrender of the German Sixth Army at Stalingrad, these O.S.S. men showed signs of increased nervousness. Then in late July 1943, the Soviets announced the creation of a Free Germany Committee (*Freies Deutschland*), featuring a captured German general, Walther von Seydlitz, among its members, and Poole, Wiley, Rogers and the other O.S.S. rightists fell into a near panic. They saw the creation of *Freies Deutschland* not as merely a Soviet psychological warfare weapon to undermine the Nazis, but as the first overt step in a long-range Soviet plan to weaken Germany in preparation for a communist takeover in central Europe. In numerous memoranda circulated to the State and War departments, the White House, the J.C.S., and even the British, O.S.S.

conservative hard-liners insisted that the time had come for the West to develop a tough political line toward the Soviet Union, allowing the British and the Americans to slug it out with the Russians in psychological warfare.[33]

Although De Witt Poole was a leading participant in the conservative frenzy over *Freies Deutschland,* not all F.N.B. memoranda reflected hard-line conservative views. Similarly, many S.I. reports dispatched from neutral outposts did not indicate excessive worry about Soviet intentions. But there were still signs of nervousness. In March and April 1943, S.I. reports from Bern, Lisbon, and the Vatican claimed that a new Nazi–Soviet deal was in the making. By October, S.I. London and Bern decided that these reports were incorrect, but in the meantime Bern had been caught up in the storm over *Freies Deutschland.* In mid-September, Dulles asserted that the formation of *Freies Deutschland* indicated that "while we and [the] British have been devoting ourselves to [the] military sphere with [the] slogan unconditional surrender as [the] sole political program, [the] Russians have been active and effective in [the] political sphere vis-a-vis Germany." To have suggested that it was the British and the Americans rather than the Soviets who had been active in the military sphere up to September 1943 was preposterous, but Dulles repeatedly emphasized the threat that he believed *Freies Deutschland* represented to the "maintenance of western democracy in central Europe." He even forwarded a report to Washington asserting that a deal had been struck in Germany between the Gestapo and representatives of the German Communist Party (K.P.D.).[34]

During the fall and winter of 1943–44, the fear and loathing of *Freies Deutschland* receded at most S.I. outposts and even became somewhat less impassioned among the Washington O.S.S. conservatives. But Allen Dulles continued to send O.S.S. headquarters reports delineating the various aspects of what he saw as the Soviet challenge. Some of these dispatches merely called upon American psychological warriors to checkmate the rising tide of Soviet influence occasioned by Red Army victories. Others criticized the policy of unconditional surrender, urging American authorities to modify it sufficiently to permit negotiations with Axis satellites (presumably Rumania, Bulgaria, and Hungary) and to hold out some hope to the German people. After the fall of Mussolini (late July) and the beginning of the Anglo-American occupation of Sicily and south Italy (September 1943), Dulles became uneasy about the Allied tendency to hold rigidly to the principle of unconditional surrender and then, after an Axis capitulation or an Allied advance, to support men like Darlan or Pietro Badoglio, who were "generally considered reactionary." Dulles felt that the "Russians have been subtler" both in the way they applied unconditional surrender (emphasizing that punishment would only fall upon the guilty) and in the policies they pursued in occupied territories.[35]

Even though the O.S.S. representative in Bern questioned the close Anglo-American identification with rightists, he was much more worried about what he saw as Western laxity in building up barriers against communism. While granting that the extreme left faced much opposition in occupied France, Dulles warned Washington in December 1943 that Soviet prestige in France was "immense" and that communism was "gaining in strength." Regarding Germany, Dulles contended that the West should encourage the moderate socialists and the Catholic center to help create a counterbalance to what he saw as the rise of the communists and *Freies Deutschland*. Here was the American Cold War position already laid out in 1943, for Dulles argued that only this course would make it possible to avoid "political chaos in postwar Germany, which would facilitate the establishment of a Communist state."[36]

In early 1944, Dulles was directly contacted by members of the German resistance group associated with Ludwig Beck and Carl Goerdeler whose aim was to overthrow Hitler and make a deal with Britain and America. He apparently did not encourage the anti-Soviet hopes of these men, but he did keep his door conveniently open to them and to emissaries from the Axis satellites. He also sent a barrage of reports to Washington claiming that the Germans (like all Europeans) were leaning ever more strongly toward the Soviet Union because they feared that some dark intention lay behind the West's reluctance to openly declare its policy toward postwar Germany.[37]

Dulles's dickerings with conservative German resistance circles and his warning to Washington that Germans needed an incentive to prevent their turning East—which was surely incorrect—were not merely part of an anticommunist or anti-Soviet conspiracy. His primary concern was to persuade the United States government to pursue a more energetic program of political and psychological warfare. Dulles believed that this program could be best effected by making an arrangement with "good Germans" who would overthrow Hitler or at least contribute to the more rapid disintegration of Nazi power.

Yet the Bern O.S.S. representative was genuinely alarmed by the strength that Communists were likely to have in postwar Europe and by the aura of power and future glory that encircled the Soviet Union in the post-Stalingrad era. Since he was the most prolific and influential S.I. political reporter in Europe, his views had a special weight with O.S.S. leaders and perhaps also with those in the J.C.S. and the State Department who were conservatively inclined. For a while, the Bern dispatches also encouraged O.S.S. rightists like Poole, Rogers, and Wiley, who were still warning that United States policies could "bring the war successfully to an unsuccessful conclusion." [38]

This extremely conservative and anti-Soviet group in O.S.S. Washington ultimately concluded that it could not get its way because, to the J.C.S., "victory in the field" was all that mattered. Rogers resigned from O.S.S. in early 1944, denouncing as politically unsound the policy of unconditional surrender and the failure of the United States to stand up to the Russians. Poole slipped into the background in the course of 1944 and in the spring of 1945 gave up the directorship of F.N.B. to become a special adviser to Donovan. John Wiley remained on the O.S.S. advisory board and like Poole continued to urge a more overtly political and anticommunist course, but he was careful to avoid direct confrontation over basic policy. As early as September 1943, Wiley had turned from direct assaults on Roosevelt's cautious approach to oblique recommendations such as one suggesting that although unconditional surrender should remain the official American policy, O.S.S. black propaganda might suggest that the United States was only out to get the Nazis and would follow a benevolent policy toward "good Germans." [39]

Donovan's All-Out Attack on the Axis: March 1943–June 1944

The dire forebodings and political warnings of the conservatives constituted a genuine, if limited, feature of O.S.S. that may have increased the worries of American policymakers about the Red Menace. But to overemphasize this or any other feature of Donovan's organization would allow the main point to slip out of focus. The men and women of O.S.S. were overwhelmingly idealistic, believed in what they were doing, and were confident in their ability to do it. O.S.S. was not an organization of doubters or nay-sayers but something more akin to a cross between a Rotary Club and Moral Rearmament. Even O.S.S. academics—those notorious sceptics—had a full measure of enthusiasm. As the great French literary scholar Julien O'Brien confided in a letter to a Columbia colleague just before he left for London to work for S.I., "I am inwardly very proud and very pleased at the prospect of being sent overseas." [40]

From Donovan down, the tone of O.S.S. was not dread of communism or anything else but confidence in the ability of Americans to get things done. The general believed that inspired amateurs could do anything, and he was always rushing about trying to prove it. Most of those in the organization directly touched by Donovan's influence were captivated by his rare blend of confidence and enthusiasm. Men as calm and clear-eyed as journalist Wallace Deuel were so entranced that they were ready to follow him through thick and thin. In September 1943, Deuel saw Donovan after he had returned to Washington from observing the landings in Italy, and noted approvingly that the general had "an expression on his face as ecstatic as that of a 10 year old Irish kid who's just sneaked in a circus under the tent."[41]

Surely Donovan was rash—Deuel told his parents that he planned to work for Donovan for a long time "assuming he stays on and isn't killed"—and a number of his assistants felt that his very enthusiasm might "unconsciously upset" some of the organization's most promising enterprises. He was likely to go too far, often antagonizing people by pushing many another organization "into doing its job." Because he made frequent and prolonged inspection trips overseas that kept him out of Washington for months, O.S.S. lacked sustained, evenhanded direction. When in his office, Donovan was likely to approve the first bright and exciting project laid before him.[42]

It was extremely difficult for the O.S.S. director to stand aloof from an enterprise that seemed to have promise, no matter how long the odds. In October–November 1943, former C.O.I.–O.W.I. official Theodore Morde, who had gone to work for the *Reader's Digest*, visited Ankara, apparently without authorization from anyone in the U.S. government. In Turkey, Morde discussed the possibility of negotiating a settlement between Germany and the West with the German ambassador, Franz von Papen. A more foolhardy escapade than Morde's would be difficult to imagine, combining as it did a violation of the principle of unconditional surrender, a clear instance of negotiating behind the back of the Soviet Union, and the use of von Papen, one of the slipperiest Germans in modern history. All Washington officials but one wished to disavow Morde without qualification. The exception was of course William Donovan, who was even prepared to try his hand with the likes of Morde and von Papen to see if anything beneficial to the Allies might develop. Consequently, the White House and the State Department had to slap Donovan down hard, ordering him to drop the Morde affair. Yet rebuffs of this kind, which happened repeatedly, apparently did not trouble the General at all. Blocked at one point, he merely moved along the line like a nimble halfback until he found some other point that appeared to be an opening.[43]

It was this limitless enthusiasm that made Donovan, and O.S.S. in general, so attractive to many people. Perhaps he was "somewhat miscast" for "derring-do," being rather too unsteady and impulsive. Perhaps too, as Edmund Taylor ultimately suspected, he was too much of a seeker, "a modern Cortez who . . . never quite found his Mexico." Yet while on the trail he was so exciting and interesting that it is little wonder that lively spirits were attracted to him. Even the president could not stay at arm's length for long, and in the fall of 1943, the records indicate that Franklin Roosevelt opened his door more frequently to the general than he had done the year before.[44]

Donovan's nimble mind could be a pleasure to savor even when it meandered off the track. After listening to the general expound on whether the English or the Soviets best embodied the Elizabethan spirit in 1944, an M.I. 6 man was compelled to remark that "I rather think the General, bless him, has got this Elizabethan surge a bit on the mind." But the Englishman still summed up his impressions of Donovan by noting in his diary, "what an attractive, agreeable and shrewd character Big B. [Bill Donovan] is. I enjoyed this talk with him, and the whole atmosphere of the man, a great deal."[45]

Even though Donovan possessed all these qualities, had he not possessed a fighting heart, O.S.S. would have made little headway in 1943–44. The U.S. military command realized in this period that the really serious American battles were only just beginning. The Soviets had suffered enormous casualties—even O.S.S. estimated their losses as at least 7.5 million military dead and permanently wounded by the spring of 1944—and the Red Army had also wreaked heavy damage on the Germans. Yet after the two-and-a-half year slugging match on the Eastern front both Russia and Germany were still on their feet, and the J.C.S. estimated that there were more men in the German armed forces in October 1943 than there had been the previous spring.[46]

When the British and American armies met large German ground forces head-on in Italy and later in France, they were up against a tough, hardened, and experienced foe. The German people appeared ready to fight to the end, and the Western armies could anticipate little except bitter resistance. To win the crucial battles, Western military leaders would have to strike the Wehrmacht anywhere it would be hit effectively. In February 1944, the J.I.C. bulletin for the Mediterranean theater concluded that the German Army had concentrated roughly 60 percent of its strength in the east, 17 percent in France, 7 percent in Scandinavia, and 8 percent each in Italy and the Balkans. It stood to reason, therefore, that the Anglo-American forces should try to deliver their main blow to the large enemy forces in France as soon as possible and at the same time pin down and cripple as many of the enemy as they could in other regions of western Europe.[47]

To achieve this end, O.S.S. skills—secret intelligence, black propaganda, sabotage, and partisan warfare—might all play a useful role. But fighters were needed most. After the plans and preparations had been completed, the job of an army is still to kill, and when the time for killing comes, real warriors are at a premium. O.S.S. had a chance to accelerate its development in 1943–44 because the organization overcame its bureaucratic troubles and was given a green light at the very moment when the serious battle began. But it was chiefly successful because, in George Marshall's words, Donovan was "a fearless and aggressive character" determined to achieve victory for his country, his organization, and for the cause of subversive warfare that he had come to espouse.[48]

The Iberian Crisis: February–November 1943

To go into action, Donovan had to quiet the doubters and remove the remaining obstacles to effective action in overseas theaters and at O.S.S. outposts in neutral countries. In the spring and fall of 1943, the most serious obstacle lay in Spain, where a crisis developed that threatened to put a crimp in O.S.S. operations everywhere. The patience of the long-suffering United States ambassador, Carlton Hayes, finally snapped in the spring of 1943. Hayes, rather touchy and anxious to maintain Franco's neutrality, was outraged by what he considered the irresponsible antics of the O.S.S men in Spain. In a series of dispatches, Hayes and his consuls complained about alleged O.S.S. blunders and urged Washington either to put Donovan's men under the authority of the military attaché in Madrid or withdraw them from Spain. Hayes's protests, one of which extended to twelve pages, cited many O.S.S. indiscretions. There were tales of prodigality and profligate behavior, replete with black market money deals and entrepreneurial adventures with nylon stockings. The ambassador also contended that O.S.S. Spain had shaky code security, was producing little useful information, and through its activities with opposition elements such as the Republicans and the Basque separatists, was endangering the United States policy of keeping Franco happy and neutral. By making use of questionable Spanish subagents and by "notoriously uneducated, indiscreet, and intemperate" behavior, O.S.S. men in Spain were, as Hayes saw it, threatening America's political position in the Iberian peninsula.[49]

O.S.S. leaders in Washington initially tried to tiptoe past the crisis, declaring that they were preparing to send a new and better mission chief to Madrid. The military authorities also moved cautiously on the matter, indicating that they did not want O.S.S. placed under the authority of the military attaché. When Eisenhower was asked whether or not he wished to retain overall operational supervision of O.S.S. Spain, he replied that he did, and most of the J.C.S. staff concluded that O.S.S. personnel selection was the big problem and that some arrangement for pooling intelligence in Spain and posting new O.S.S. men to Madrid would quiet Hayes.[50]

The ambassador was not put off by half-measures however, and continued to demand that Washington take strong action. Consequently, the J.C.S. decided that a serious investigation was necessary and as a first step called on Donovan to answer Hayes's charges. In a twenty-five-page memorandum, the O.S.S. director denied a number of Hayes's specific accusations, quibbled with some of his data, and argued vigorously that O.S.S. should continue to function in Spain, independent of the military attaché. In the course of his defense, however, Donovan made two important admissions.

First, he conceded that O.S.S. was dealing with the Basques, which he justified on the grounds that an S.O. stay-behind resistance force had to be built up in the event of a German invasion. Since the chances of such an invasion in April 1943 (several months after the dramatic defeat at Stalingrad) bordered on zero, this statement inevitably raised a few eyebrows. A second admission made by Donovan in his memorandum to the chiefs was even more damning. At the very beginning of his paper, the general wrote "let me state frankly that Spain has been our greatest difficulty." With such an honest but nonetheless definite acknowledgment that O.S.S. Madrid was in trouble, the J.C.S. had to look more deeply into the matter.[51]

An extended discussion of the Spanish situation took place in a J.C.S. meeting of 9 April 1943. Donovan, who was invited to appear before the chiefs, again granted that Spain was "a big problem" and that since O.S.S. had been compelled to start American secret activities virtually from scratch, many of the men involved in overseas operations were "virtually amateurs." Admiral Leahy took the opportunity to regale the group with tales of his own troubles with C.O.I.–O.S.S. when he served as ambassador in Vichy (1941–42), which made Donovan and O.S.S. look poor indeed. However, General Marshall and Admiral King immediately jumped to Donovan's defense, for they were inclined to believe that the Spanish issue was a clash between the caution of the State Department and the more daring attitude of O.S.S. Marshall noted that "some of our ambassadors cannot take things 'on the chin'" and urged strongly that except for one O.S.S. representative, Donovan's people should be removed from American diplomatic missions and "run the show from down the street." Admiral King strongly seconded Marshall's views, and the chiefs ultimately concluded that no further investigation was necessary. The State Department was told that the difficulty would be solved by reducing the number of O.S.S. men in the embassy, while leaving control in the hands of the newly appointed O.S.S. mission chief, Gregory Thomas.[52]

Had Donovan been blessed with a sliver of luck, the matter would have ended there, but his subordinates chose this moment to commit two major fumbles. An O.S.S. shipment of pistols was sent to Spain in mid-June, "plainly manifested as such" and addressed to, of all people, Ambassador Hayes. The Ambassador was outraged, ordered the shipment "returned to the senders," and lodged another stiff protest in Washington. This misdeed was bound to cause Donovan trouble, but it was soon overshadowed by the second, and bigger, bungle.[53]

At some point in June, O.S.S. Portugal used an undercover agent in the Japanese embassay to purloin documents from the code room. Shortly thereafter, both Italian and Japanese officials concluded (from what source is not now clear) that something was seriously amiss. On 24 June, Tokyo received an alert from its Rome mission stating that "an American espionage agency in Lisbon" had penetrated the Japanese Embassy and among other things was "getting Japanese code books." Pandemonium followed the receipt of this message. Japanese authorities in Tokyo and Lisbon, afraid that their ciphers had been compromised, instituted immediate special security measures and began a comprehensive investigation. American and British military intelligence officials, who were actually reading the coded Japanese Lisbon–Tokyo Magic traffic, were as alarmed as the Japanese, for if Tokyo doubted the security of their diplomatic cipher (known to the British and American officials as J.M.A.), it might change codes. J.M.A. was a principle Japanese diplomatic cipher whose elimination would have seriously diminished the amount of Japanese coded material that could be read by Magic. To make matters worse, the British and American decoders were using J.M.A. as a lever to open up the complex Japanese military ciphers, and in June 1943 they believed they were on the verge of a decisive breakthrough.[54]

When Washington learned that O.S.S Lisbon caper threatened the Magic intercepts, alarm was universal, and General Strong, nearly berserk, denounced the "ill-advised and amateurish" activities of Donovan's men. In Strong's excited opinion, the Lisbon affair, augmented by the bungles in Spain, showed that O.S.S. was "a menace to the security of the nation." Therefore, a new, more comprehensive investigation of O.S.S. operations on the Iberian peninsula began immediately, and O.S.S. leaders again rolled out their well-worn defenses. Donovan wisely tried to stall, hoping that Japanese nervousness over cipher security would quiet down without the abandonment of J.M.A.[55]

By late summer, the Japanese had indeed calmed down, and once British and American cryptographers were sure that Magic had not been blinded by the Lisbon mess, everyone relaxed and took a more reasoned view of the situation. The J.C.S. appointed a special investigator, Col. C. J. Gridley, to study Iberian O.S.S. operations. The colonel was sympathetic to Donovan's organization and was capable of standing up to Ambassador Hayes and State Department officialdom. By September, Gridley had worked out a new setup for O.S.S. Spain and Portugal, which was accepted by Donovan and Hayes in a November "treaty." The American intelligence agencies in Spain and Portugal (M.I.S., O.N.I., and O.S.S.) were instructed to pool their information in the two countries. In addition, O.S.S. Spain was thoroughly reorganized and its operations sharply limited. All S.O. and M.O. activities in Spain ceased, and S.I. was restricted to operations approved by the ambassador and the attachés. Hayes was also given a special veto on all O.S.S. appointments in Spain as well as the right to read all incoming and outgoing O.S.S. messages.[56]

This arrangement put O.S.S. Spain in a more dependent and auxiliary position than Donovan wanted. But the restrictions imposed on O.S.S. Spain did not mark the demise of the organization in the Iberian peninsula. O.S.S. people in the region did have a penchant for risky enterprises, but they were not alone in this. It is instructive to remember that S.O.E. had had trouble in the area since 1941 and in July 1943 again fell into difficulties with the Foreign Office because of its Spanish adventures.[57]

Furthermore, O.S.S. snapped back quickly from its initial failure in Spain. The reforms instituted after the O.S.S. Lisbon fiasco trimmed the adventuresome independence of O.S.S., thereby making it a more effective instrument of the U.S. military. In late 1943 and early 1944, S.I. Madrid collaborated with the Free French Penetration Mission (F.P.M.) to create a huge intelligence network of several hundred agents operating in occupied France. By the summer of 1944, this Medusa project seems to have been the most extensive secret intelligence operation in Europe run by an American agency. O.S.S. Spain was rapidly expanded (receiving ten additional staff in January 1944 alone) to service Medusa. A large and effective organization was developed for smuggling Medusa messages across the Franco–Spanish frontier. Pouch communication from Spain brought London and Algiers a vast quantity of highly valuable information on the German military in France both before and after D Day.[58]

When defending his Spanish operations before the J.C.S. in April 1943, Donovan had conceded that his organization had made mistakes but had added that he was guided by the principle that "when we stumble we try to fall forward." In the Iberian area he did just that. By late 1943, O.S.S. Spain had changed from a minus to a huge plus in his campaign to prove to the J.C.S. that his organization could be a real assistance to the army and navy of the United States.[59]

O.S.S. European Reporting from Other Neutral Countries

The other O.S.S. stations in neutral European countries also produced significant results, though perhaps their activities were of less direct value to combat operations, and were certainly less traumatic, than those in Spain. S.I. Stockholm ran extensive intelligence strings into German-occupied Norway and Denmark and also into Finland and Germany itself. The operations were often intricate, and apparently some of them were expensive; the allotment of special funds to O.S.S. Stockholm for one six-month period ran to a quarter of a million dollars. Nevertheless, a large quantity of technical and scientific information on the German war effort was secured via Stockholm. Furthermore, this O.S.S. base was apparently the first to devote serious attention to gathering secret information on the Soviet Union, a risky enterprise. O.S.S. Stockholm also became involved in a harebrained scheme to dispatch an O.S.S. man named Abraham S. Hewitt into Germany itself in late 1943. Since the journey was to have been arranged by a most dubious travel agent, Felix Kersten (Himmler's Finnish masseur) and the reception committee was to include the head of the intelligence section of the S.D., Walter Schellenberg (and perhaps Heinrich Himmler himself), it was fortunate that Donovan scotched the mission, assuming, as he told the White House, that the president did not want Americans "in Germany on such a basis."[60]

O.S.S. Bern, under Allen Dulles, was another highly active post that produced a wide range of valuable information despite its worries about Soviet intentions. Dulles appears to have been the most cautious of the O.S.S. outpost chiefs stationed in neutral countries, for there are no indications in the available records that he authorized any foolhardy forays at this time. He was, however, accustomed to giving his subordinates much latitude, usually sizing up a possible intelligence contact only once before turning over the actual operation to one of his subordinates. Since some of those who worked for Dulles (especially Guido von Schultze Gaevernitz) had numerous European contacts and were inclined to be bold, this system secured much information in the short run. But later it would also offer temptations for political adventure when Germany began to disintegrate.[61]

In 1943–44, Dulles's natural caution kept matters well under control. Although he did not pass over all unorthodox sources of information—he held long consultations with Carl Jung to secure insight into psychological warfare techniques for use in Germany—the O.S.S. representative in Bern was not inclined to take chances. He was a conservative lawyer, prudent businessman, and staunch Republican. To counter those who have portrayed him as an O.S.S.–C.I.A. ideological prophet and superspy, it is instructive to look at the handful of messages he received from his brother John Foster during this period to get a sense of his background. John Foster's letters are chilly, formal documents having nothing to do with espionage, ideological issues, or national policy. All John Foster was concerned about in 1943–44 was getting Allen back to New York as soon as possible to pull his oar in the family law firm.[62]

It is also useful to remember that even though Allen Dulles's reports carried a measure of extra weight in Washington because of his earlier career in the foreign service and his close connections with the top O.S.S. leadership, American officialdom was not hanging on his every word. Some important people seem not even to known that he was serving as the O.S.S. man in Bern. In January 1944, after Dulles had been reporting from his Swiss post for fourteen months, Gen. John Hilldring, the chief of the Civil Affairs Division of the War Department, asked the State Department if it could perhaps enlighten him on "the present whereabouts of Mr. Allen W. Dulles."[63]

Though he was not the wonder worker of later myth, Dulles was a solid and highly effective outpost chief. Extensive order-of-battle information went to Washington from Bern in 1943–44. Technical information on the Wehrmacht was also dispatched, including reports on German aircraft defenses, submarine production, and developmental work on the V–1 flying bomb and the V–2 rockets. Once again, caution is in order regarding the significance of the V–1 and V–2 material uncovered by Dulles's office, for even though it was important, similar information was obtained from other sources. No single source discovered Hitler's secret weapons; by collecting various pieces, the Allies put together a quite accurate jigsaw picture of the V–1 and V–2, but as late as winter 1944, they were still uncertain of the aiming mechanism used on Hitler's rocket weapon.[64]

A number of the early reports on Germany's ability to conduct gas and bacteriological warfare came from Bern. Since the Germans ultimately did not use either of these weapons, one might contend that Dulles and his staff alarmed Washington unnecessarily. Indeed, the J.C.S. staff expended much energy investigating the questions raised by Dulles's reports. However, it was the O.S.S. representative's job to provide Washington with information on any matter of possible military value. It was not up to him to decide whether Hitler, fearing mass retaliation, would ultimately draw back from use of either of these nightmare weapons.[65]

In the opinion of O.S.S. Washington, some of the reports sent from Bern pegged German armament production too high and also tended to overestimate the damage inflicted by Allied air raids. On occasion, Dulles's prognosis of Hitler's intentions went astray; for instance, on the very eve of the massive and disastrous attack on Kursk that sealed the fate of the German Army in the East, he predicted that the Führer would not attempt any "large-scale offensive against Russia."[66]

Yet in information gathering, Dulles's drawbacks were offset by his far more substantial accomplishments; in securing the services of a German Foreign Office official named Fritz Kolbe (cover-named George Wood), he scored the most significant Allied secret agent triumph of the war. From August 1943 to mid-1944, Kolbe made a series of trips to Switzerland, bringing with him hundreds of microfilm copies of secret German Foreign Office documents. Since much of this material (O.S.S. code-named the Kolbe documents the Kappa or Boston series) concerned Germany's cooperation with its allies and satellites, it contained information of great military and political value, and as even Kim Philby acknowledged, it was very useful in filling out Ultra decrypts.[67]

On one occasion in April 1944, when reporting to Washington on the breadth and depth of the Kolbe documents, Dulles remarked that they showed "a picture" of Germany's "imminent doom and final downfall." This observation was immediately challenged by members of the American army staff in Washington, with one colonel noting that it "would be extremely unwise . . . from a military point of view" to assume that Germany was finished. With the issue put thus, Dulles quickly backed off, emphasizing that he had not meant that Germany would disintegrate forthwith. Such incidents illustrate the difficulty of Dulles's task in providing Washington with a picture of German morale that would be both accurate and reliable throughout the shifting conditions of combat. Dulles's estimates of the mood in Germany went up and down, as indeed did German morale. In the aftermath of the Hamburg raids in October 1943, for instance, the O.S.S. representative declared that with two more such cataclysms Germany might crack (after the war, Albert Speer said the same thing). By and large, however, he accurately grasped that, the war and the Nazi regime being what they were, these "stubbornly obedient people" no longer had morale "as we normally use the term," but "tired, discouraged, disillusioned, bewildered" merely trudged on because they could "see no alternative other than to continue their struggle."[68]

Dulles did not always gauge successfully what Hitler, his Nazi Party lieutenants, and the German army leaders were actually doing. Some of his reports on the Führer's methods of planning and conducting military operations were indeed accurate, but he also fell victim to the same tales of Hitler's madness and of the Prussian officers' efforts to make him a figurehead that had beguiled the British since the first days of the war. Despite such errors, Dulles's overall reporting on Germany was judicious, providing O.S.S. Washington with its most complete picture of conditions in the Third Reich.[69]

Reports on Italy from O.S.S. Bern were not as comprehensive and multifaceted as those on Germany. Many order-of-battle reports on the German and Italian Fascist forces in Italy were sent to Washington, and Dulles tried to gauge German intentions in the peninsula following the coup that toppled Mussolini. His early dispatches greatly overestimated the number of Wehrmacht units on the spot, and he was rather slow in reporting the speed of the German buildup in late July and early August. More significantly, he consistently misjudged Hitler's intentions, and in one dispatch after another asserted that German forces would not enter central and southern Italy in force when in fact they were already en route.[70]

On the political aspects of the Italian situation, the O.S.S. Bern representative was much more successful. He accurately charted the circumstances leading to the Duce's fall, and, following the coup, emphasized the risks of becoming too intimate with the reactionary forces associated with the monarchy.[71]

O.S.S. Bern rendered especially valuable services regarding the Italian and French resistance. Dulles did not exercise operational control over French resistance forces, which were under the supervision of the Free French in London and Algiers in conjunction with the S.O.E.–S.O. special operations headquarters in London. Overall Allied direction of Italian resistance operations was conducted by A.F.H.Q., first in Algiers and later in Caserta, but poor communications between the south and the occupied north led to Dulles's office playing an important role in arranging contacts between the Allies and Italian resistance leaders in October–November 1943 and in supervising some subsequent operations. Money and supplies passed directly from O.S.S. Bern to the resistance forces in France and north Italy, but Dulles had control over little useful war equipment, and the Vichy French, Fascist Italian, and Swiss border control was so tight during 1943 and the first half of 1944 that such traffic was of moderate significance.[72]

Important information on the German military establishment in both France and Italy reached Bern through resistance circles, but it lacked the breadth and the value of the information obtained via Spain. Tight border control was a serious obstacle, and relaying detailed information on from Bern—which was closed off except for radio–telephone communication until September 1944—was much more difficult than from Madrid. Furthermore, Bern was not as near to the vital Atlantic and Mediterranean landing sites as were the Spanish observation posts and it was difficult to secure information on those areas until military operations moved closer to the Swiss frontiers.

Whatever his problems with supply and intelligence, Dulles gave enthusiastic moral and monetary support to resistance forces in both France and Italy. While concerned about communist underground elements in both areas, he was not an alarmist, and the struggles and sacrifices of the resistance movements clearly struck a responsive cord in him. Allen Dulles did his very best to convince Washington that they were brave, responsible, and deserving of Allied support.[73]

Overall, one may conclude that O.S.S. Bern, as well as the other O.S.S. outposts in neutral European countries, rendered highly useful service in 1943–44. Their political reporting probably had little impact on high-level policy decisions in Washington, and it is highly debatable whether their work on psychological warfare had any significant influence on the course of the war. But in assisting resistance movements and even more in operating intelligence networks, they produced tangible benefits for the American military. Since Donovan was staking his case on proving to the J.C.S. that O.S.S. could provide real assistance, O.S.S. missions in Stockholm, Madrid, and Bern were major assets in the general's 1943–44 campaign.

O.S.S. Mediterranean

May 1943: Afrika Korps surrenders in Tunisia
July–August 1943: Anglo-American invasion of Sicily (Husky)
September 1943: Landing at Salerno
June 1944: Rome falls

Assessing O.S.S. performance in the operational theaters is more complicated than a similar assessment of the neutral posts because the rush and confusion of battle made it difficult for peripheral organizations to leave clear marks. The scene of the greatest O.S.S. military action in 1943 and the first half of 1944 lay in the North African Theater of Operations (N.A.T.O.), but many obstacles stood in the way of O.S.S. attempts to play a truly significant role there. Following Torch, Eddy's S.O. organization had failed to find an arena for effective operations during the North African campaign, and when the veteran Eighth Army arrived in Tunisia, British influence inevitably increased. M.I. 6 had already obtained the inside track on much intelligence activity, and British authorities could draw heavily on the huge special operations resources of Gibraltar and the Middle East headquarters at Cairo. S.O.E. alone had as many men in the western Mediterranean by the end of 1943 as did O.S.S., and if portions of British intelligence and P.W.E. were added to the S.O.E. totals, the number of British secret warriors far exceeded that of the Americans. Furthermore, although O.S.S. possessed a small group of supply vessels (including one captured French submarine, the *Casablanca*,) for delivering men and material to occupied territories, the British delivery system was much larger and the R.A.F. initially controlled the only four aircraft assigned to covert operations in N.A.T.O. by Allied headquarters. British authorities held tightly to their aircraft monopoly—weak as it was—and used it to control O.S.S. operations by requiring that all S.I. and S.O. requests for airlift be approved by the appropriate section of S.O.E. or M.I. 6.[74]

Moaning about the situation, Donovan appealed to the J.C.S. for American aircraft to support O.S.S. activities in N.A.T.O. but no United States special operations machines actually appeared in the theater until early 1944. The O.S.S. men in North Africa had no alternative but to be as productive as possible in a game rigged against them. Donovan's men played an important part in the P.W.B. (over some O.W.I. protests) and a small R. and A. unit went to work on political reporting and map production. S.I. and X-2 did intelligence and counterintelligence work in North Africa, tracking Axis influence and gathering information of military value. S.I. collected sufficient useful intelligence from its limited forays into occupied France, its December 1942 submarine mission into Corsica, and its Spanish and North African sources to earn an August 1943 commendation from Eisenhower's leading American intelligence officer, Gen. L. W. Rooks. Throughout most of the summer of 1943, however, S.I., like the other branches of O.S.S., was hampered by the airlift shortage and by difficulty in establishing a secure place in Eisenhower's system. Ike's G-2 was still British (Gen. Kenneth Strong) and British organizations, such as the experienced M.I. 6., quite naturally tended to find most favor at A.F.H.Q.[75]

Then in August 1943, O.S.S. benefited from a reorganization in Algiers that was intended to regulate activities that did not fit neatly into the military organizational system. S.O.E. and M.I. 6 were not affected by these changes, retaining the designations I.S.S.U.-6 and I.L.S.U., but every other irregular warfare group was designated a Headquarters Company, or Regiment, Provisional. The P.W.B. became the 2679th Headquarters Company (Prov.), the American contingent in Allied Military Government was designated the 2675th Regiment (Prov.), and all O.S.S. in the western Mediterranean was combined in the 2677th Headquarters Company (Prov.)." In the course of the reorganization, Eddy was transferred to field S.O. operations, and command of the 2677th Headquarters Company was given to Col. Edward Glavin, with a series of other colonels and lieutenant colonels serving on his staff.

Grumbling about bureaucratizing and the inanities of "the colonels" began almost immediately, but the reorganization that created the 2677th Headquarters Company greatly expanded O.S.S. activity in N.A.T.O. Henceforth, Donovan's organization had some coherence, could concentrate its strength, and was able to exert more influence on the military leadership.[76]

Using the 2677th Headquarters Company as an organizational foundation and the networks left over from Torch days for additional assistance, S.I. and X-2 expanded their activities in Africa. By a special arrangement with X-2, S.I. controlled all counterintelligence in sub-Saharan Africa and worked with the British to police enemy agents and prevent the smuggling of critical raw materials to the Axis.[77]

The sub-Saharan operations of O.S.S. functioned smoothly, but strains developed in North Africa. Glavin and much of the S.I. leadership in Algiers were strongly opposed to de Gaulle, and as the French administration in Algeria and Morocco became increasingly Gaullist, trouble resulted. But S.I. needed French assistance in North Africa, and the French wanted O.S.S. assistance for their activities in metropolitan France, so the tense Franco–O.S.S. marriage of convenience continued, and O.S.S. North African intelligence and counterintelligence operations were not seriously impeded.[78]

No comparable disputes troubled O.S.S. support of Allied operations in Italian territory, but there were other problems. Neither O.S.S. nor S.O.E. had established close connections with significant Italian resistance organizations by the summer of 1943. The Italian opposition had only begun to cohere in the spring of that year, and the first cautious contacts between

S.O.E. and groups in Italy such as Count Carlo Sforza's Partito d'Azione took place in April. The British and the Americans were so short of links with the Italian resistance that S.O.E., relying on its Moscow contacts, made arrangements to have N.K.V.D. operatives dropped into Italy to further Allied contacts there. The organizational obstacles proved too formidable, however, and at the time of the invasion of Sicily in July 1943 (Operation Husky), neither the British nor the American subversive warfare organizations were in a position to provide much assistance.[79]

Once again, British military intelligence held the inside track in providing order-of-battle intelligence to the invasion commanders, but British organizations were not much ahead of the Americans in counterintelligence and special operations. M.I. 6 had "practically no information on Husky suspects" as late as April 1943, and S.O.E. was forced to admit in May that it had no Italian- or "Sicilian"-speaking personnel available aside from four Italian-speaking Slovenes it had located in Cairo. Since S.O.E. had been operating in Italian colonial areas for nearly three years, such lack of foresight may seem astounding, but this was just one in a rather remarkable series of deficiencies that plagued the Husky preparations. So many breaches of security had occurred by mid-June that a special intelligence summary was issued chronicling the worst indiscretions. Whoever left the complete plans for Husky in his uniform jacket when sending it to the cleaners seems to have won the palm, for the laundryman put it to use, and pages of the Husky plan soon turned up in North Africa with laundry lists written on the back![80]

In such a setting, S.O.E. and O.S.S. failures were not very noticeable. A last-minute effort to recruit Italian-Americans for special operations was begun too late, so it was the U.S. Navy's special operations personnel, or "Beach Jumpers," rather than either S.O.E. or O.S.S. personnel, who preceded the invading army on 10 July. But Italian-American O.S.S. special operations men began to arrive in the theater in force soon after and were used in follow-up operations. A few O.S.S. men also joined with O.W.I. and P.W.E. to manage the Husky propaganda campaign, and the chief of the P.W.B. for the invasion was an O.S.S. man. O.W.I. and the British P.W.E. did most of the propaganda work, however, which was probably just as well for O.S.S., since bitter Anglo-American controversies raged over what line should be followed. The Americans were inclined to be soft, wishing to hold out hope to the Sicilians to weaken resistance, whereas the more realistic British wanted to avoid making inflated promises. Inevitably, a middle road was found, but considerable Anglo-American hard feeling remained.[81]

Once the Allies were firmly established in Sicily, O.S.S. had little direct part to play except in counterintelligence activities and the establishment of offices for S.I. and R. and A. No documentary evidence now available substantiates recent insinuations that O.S.S. personnel played a major role in the revival of the Mafia on the island. Military government records show no sign of large Mafia activity until early September, two months after the landing, and there are indications that when the Mafia did begin to raise its head in some areas, sharp action by the Allied authorities, including arrests and the selective arming of the poorer farmers, forced it to submerge again. Complaints of a more serious Mafia revival first arose in late October, and there were allegations that Allied personnel of Sicilian origin were assisting the Syndicate. But a report by military intelligence on 29 October 1943 singled out Allied civil affairs officers and not O.S.S. men as the culprits, and with the island in the hands of regular army authorities and most O.S.S. personnel either remaining in Algiers or moving forward onto the mainland with the combat units, strong O.S.S. connections with the Mafia resurgence seems improbable. Allied policies may have made a Mafia comeback easier—the Allies released all P.O.W.s of Sicilian origin within eight days of the start of the campaign—and individual Italian-Americans may have helped establish this permissible policy, but it seems unlikely that O.S.S. was pro-Mafia.[82]

In any event, such political considerations were then distinctly secondary to British and American commanders, who sought to overrun the island quickly and open a route to the mainland. With both British and American forces fighting well, this objective was soon attained, and as civil affairs officers pursued their assorted tasks, from controlling the Mafia to retrieving Lord Lilford's collection of stuffed birds for the British Museum, the military commanders prepared for the invasion of mainland Italy. Mussolini had fallen victim to a coup in the course of the Sicilian battle, and the Badoglio government which followed tried to snuggle closer to the Allies without bringing down the wrath of the Germans. British and American commanders were divided in their attitude toward Badoglio and a possible Italian campaign. The Americans were reluctant to mount a massive attack that might drain off forces from the main invasion of France, but the British were more inclined to probe what Churchill called the soft underbelly of Europe. Not until the first week of September did the Allies reach the mainland as the British Eighth Army crossed the Strait of Messina and a predominantly American Fifth Army invasion took place at Salerno, south of Naples. The landings were timed to coincide with the surrender of the Italian government, an arrangement that had been secretly prepared weeks before. The situation remained extremely unclear however, with respect to both German intentions and

the practical benefits that the Allies might secure from Italian cooperation. As the appropriately tortured psychological warfare jargon of an Allied black propaganda directive of 10 September described it, the "picture we should give following the surrender of Italy is somewhat obscure
until events clarify."[83]

Within a few days, Hitler provided the necessary clarity. The Wehrmacht grabbed every scrap of Italian territory it could and fought a vigorous defensive campaign. The Allies soon realized that, contrary to Fifteenth Army Group intelligence predictions, the Germans would not settle
for mere "delaying actions in southern and central Italy," and a brutal
slugging match followed. As Robert Murphy, then Eisenhower's political
adviser, declared, the "military stakes were too high" for either side to
show much "regard for the civilian population" or "afford much human
kindness." Allied artillery and air power were pitted against strong German defensive positions, and death and destruction rained down on the
civilians and infantrymen, who bore the brunt of the fighting.[84]

At the time of the Salerno landings, O.S.S. and S.O.E. were ordered to
use all their resistance connections to produce "an immediate hampering
of the movement of German troops to the beachhead area." Special operations preparations had been so poor, however, and conditions so confusing that neither S.O.E. nor O.S.S. was able to provide significant assistance
to the invasion. A survey of the Italian government and armed forces
made soon after the landings by the British general F. N. Mason-Macfarlane indicated that O.S.S. and S.O.E. might nonetheless have a more
promising future in Italy. Mason-Macfarlane concluded that there was
little hope of using the existing Italian Army as an Allied fighting force,
and the Italian political and military leadership also appeared nearly use-
less. In Mason-Macfarlane's words, the king was "pathetic, very old, and
rather gaga." The British general therefore advised the Allies to use the
available Italian resources for subversive warfare, and "we should go flat
out on S.O.E. and P.W.E."[85]

As a result, northern Italian resistance was left pretty much on its own,
with only limited assistance provided by the Allied command and S.O.E.
and O.S.S. representatives in Switzerland. In southern and central Italy,
however, S.O.E. and O.S.S. attempted to develop Italian resistance and
O.S.S.–Italian O.G. units to support Fifth and Eighth Army operations.
Responsibility for coordinating all resistance operations was given to Gen.
C. S. Sugden of G-3, and arrangements were made to tap the intelligence
sources of the Italian government as well as those of the resistance.[86]

Donovan also tried to engage in some higher-level maneuvers. An Italian
torpedo expert was located by O.S.S., removed from Nazi-occupied terri-

tory, and brought to the United States. The O.S.S. chief further delivered a secret communication from Badoglio to President Roosevelt in January 1944, and in May O.S.S. slipped a special Badoglio representative (Professor Guido Pazzi-Rossi) into Washington, where he was hidden at the Statler Hotel. These capers were apparently intended to establish direct American connections with the Italians through O.S.S., which would undercut British influence in Italy. However, the president and the State Department were much more cautious than Donovan. The torpedo expert was allowed to remain in the United States, but Pazzi-Rossi was sent back to Italy without seeing any top American officials, and Roosevelt gave no direct encouragement to Badoglio.[87]

The landings in Italy raised a number of other issues for O.S.S. that could not be sidestepped so easily. Among them was the question of Sardinia and Corsica. American and British leaders had met in Quebec shortly before the Salerno invasion, and the Combined Chiefs of Staff had considered what should be done about Corsica and Sardinia. General Marshall suggested that Sardinia could provide an opportunity to "give the O.S.S. a run" and would allow Donovan to "use his stuff." The C.C.S. concurred with Marshall's suggestion, and in late August Eisenhower was directed to let loose O.S.S. and S.O.E. personnel against Corsica and Sardinia. No action was taken until after the Salerno landing, however, when an O.S.S. mission under Lt. Col. Serge Obolensky went into Sardinia, and an S.O.E.–Free French mission led by Maj. Colonna d' Istria (with six O.S.S. men attached) landed in Corsica.[88]

The O.S.S. mission in Sardinia suffered a few casualties amid the confusion of the German withdrawal, but no general uprising occurred, and no large Allied forces were landed. As Ike's deputy chief of staff exclaimed, the Sardinia operation was rather "like comic opera," with Gen. Teddy Roosevelt, Jr., and a handful of men arriving to take over the island in the name of the Allies. The conquest of Corsica was more difficult, for French shock troops (Battalion de Choc) had to carry out a full-scale invasion. S.O.E. resistance support activities failed to provide substantial assistance to the invading forces because once the attack began, many resistance fighters seized the opportunity to settle scores with Vichy officials instead of performing their assigned invasion-support tasks. A number of observers therefore concluded that the resistance would behave similarly on D Day, inclining Eisenhower's command to doubt the value of resistance activity prior to the Normandy invasion. In Corsica itself, however, the invasion ended well for the French despite the resistance difficulties. The Battalion de Choc rapidly took control of the island, and by November, Sardinia and Corsica were serving as Allied special force bases for operations against Italian and French coastal areas.[89]

In Italy, special operations moved ahead much more slowly. The Allies were up against twenty-one tough German divisions that fought doggedly, and in the north, the Nazis had put Mussolini in charge of a new Fascist regime that nominally controlled northern Italy but mainly served the Germans. In late 1943 and early 1944, the Allied struggle against the Germans and Mussolini's Fascist republic became harsher and more costly. Gradually S.O.E. and O.S.S. had to adjust to the realities of a long, slow campaign and began establishing special operations bases in southern Italy, improving their organizational structures, and cooperating more closely with the Fifteenth Army Group, which took over the supervision of the battle once the British Eighth and the American Fifth armies joined forces at Salerno. By November 1943, Colonel Eddy had departed both the Mediterranean and O.S.S., leaving S.O. operations in Italy under the direct control of the 2677th Headquarters Company and Colonel Glavin. In the same month, a line of demarcation was drawn between La Spezia and Ravenna for overall control of resistance activities with the Fifteenth Army Group in charge south of the line and Eisenhower's own staff (A.F.H.Q.) exercising general control to the north. Between September 1943 and June 1944, when Rome fell, O.S.S sent many missions into central and northern Italy in conjunction with S.O.E., M.I. 6, and other British organizations. In addition to intelligence and regular S.O. resistance support missions, O.S.S. and the British used commando-type operational groups for raids on the northern coast and the offshore islands. For the first time, large numbers of O.S.S. men went into action in Europe and henceforth, O.S.S. men were suffering and dying in Europe. On occasion whole missions were lost, including a force of fifteen near La Spezia in March 1944.[90]

The quieter and less martial aspects of O.S.S. were greatly expanded during late 1943 and the first months of 1944. A.F.H.Q. and the Fifteenth Army Group were developed as regular channels for reporting to G-2, and as valuable reports began to come in from behind-the-lines missions, S.I. prestige rose. X-2 was also active, joining with both the British and the U.S. Army's counterintelligence corps to control German and Italian Fascist agents and carry out covert observation of Italian political developments. R. and A. provided political and economic reports, did target work for the air force, and assisted both civil affairs officers and P.O.W. interrogators. M. O. worked with other groups on the P.W.B. board to develop a massive campaign to undermine the morale of the Axis troops in the peninsula while building up support for the Allied cause among Italian civilians.[91] O.S.S. also assisted Allied P.O.W.s escaping from northern Italy and gave support for the intelligence task forces attached to the British and American armies ("S" forces). O.S.S. and British special units therefore provided genuine assistance to the Allied cause. By June 1944, it was estimated that 15,000 partisans were already armed in Italy, and the speed with which O.S.S. developed the means to help encourage the growth of the resistance movement was highly impressive.[92]

Despite these achievements, O.S.S. could not get completely out from under a great cloud that hung over all the special operations activities of the Italian campaign. That the Allied war in Italy moved slowly and at great cost was a heavy burden for all the Allied forces to bear. But all this effort was expended to pin down twenty-one German divisions, whereas Yugoslavian and Greek special operations, augmented by the fear of an invasion, had been able to contain nearly the same number of Axis forces in the Balkans without using any regular Allied invasion forces. To better understand this situation, we should survey developments in the Balkans and the Middle East to see how they influenced Allied operations in Italy.[93]

The efforts made by O.S.S. in 1942 and early 1943 to enter the Middle East theater in strength had little result. A few O.S.S. men were stationed in Cairo and Istanbul, but no large inflow of American personnel occurred. The much-heralded O.S.S. survey mission that went out in late 1942 returned in March 1943 to report that it would be best just to support the Arabs and perhaps quiet Jewish opposition to such a policy by establishing a Jewish colony in Libya.[94]

O.S.S. leaders in Washington held onto their grandiose dreams about the region. But the J.C.S. took over two and a half months merely to approve an O.S.S. request that military personnel already alloted to the organization be used for intelligence work in Turkey, and the British still opposed any strong O.S.S. move into the eastern Mediterranean area.[95]

S.O.E. and the other British special units were heavily represented in Greece and Yugoslavia by the spring of 1943, with 150 men in Greece alone and operations beginning in Albania as well. Legions of British political and military support personnel for Balkan operations were stationed in Cairo, and eighteen heavy R.A.F. aircraft were available to provide support for special activities, compared with four such aircraft in the western Mediterranean.[96]

The British were not thereby united on every issue, for deep divisions existed, especially between S.O.E. and the Foreign Office. But Britain's leaders were agreed that it would be best to keep the Americans out of the area for as long as possible and that the spring of 1943 was an especially bad time to let them in. London's honeymoon with Mihajlović was coming to an end. A long British policy struggle culminated in an April 1943 decision to send S.O.E. missions to Tito while simultaneously trying to persuade Mihajlović to end his collaboration with the Axis. Mihajlović was to be urged to engage in general resistance warfare against the Germans, whatever the cost in reprisals, with British supplies as a reward if he fought, and a denial of supplies and perhaps increased aid to Tito if he did not. It was a chancy enterprise that gradually tipped the British toward Tito, but London believed that it was the only card left to play.[97]

Having settled their policy as best they could, the British agreed to allow some O.S.S. missions into the Balkans. Donovan's men were permitted into Yugoslavia under direct S.O.E. supervision, and while it encouraged O.S.S. to try its luck immediately in Bulgaria and Rumania where the British had no missions at the time, S.O.E. also hinted that O.S.S. would later be allowed into Greece and Albania. Donovan seized the opportunity, and O.S.S. men joined British personnel on their missions to Tito and Mihajlović in August and entered Greece in September. Although early S.O.E.–O.S.S. field relations seem to have been harmonious throughout the Balkans, O.S.S. officials were highly critical of British political activities in southeast Europe. Britain's "imperialist" policies in Albania and Greece were condemned in O.S.S. reports to the president in October, and when London swung its support to Tito's communist movement in Yugoslavia, some O.S.S. men denounced this policy as well. Praise of Mihajlović and doubt about the efficacy of the Communists in Yugoslavia filled O.S.S. reports and, surprisingly, General Strong, O.S.S.'s old nemesis in G-2, took the same line.[98]

But the British were not deflected from their aggressive special operations policy in the Balkans by American scolding, especially when in September 1943 the Italian armistice offered the prospect of increased Allied subversive activity in the area. British air support for special operations was stepped up, and S.O.E. Middle East (with its cover name changed from M.O. 4 to Force 133) was more effectively integrated into the military planning of Gen. Henry ("Jumbo") Wilson's Middle East command. Nineteen S.O.E. missions were in Yugoslavia by mid-October 1943, with 140 special operations personnel (including 2 O.S.S. men) split between Mihajlović and Tito. In Greece, S.O.E. had 53 missions, comprising 201 men (again including 2 O.S.S. members), whereas 8 missions with 24 men, none of whom were American, were deployed in Albania. S.O.E. estimated that in these three countries S.O.E.–O.S.S. missions had armed a quarter of a million resistance fighters, 75 percent of whom were Tito's partisans.[99]

As of October 1943, the major obstacle to expanding the Balkan resistance force still further was not a shortage of partisans or of S.O.E.–O.S.S. personnel but the difficulty of getting in supplies, especially to Tito. On 11 October, the British Middle East Commander, General Wilson met with Eisenhower to discuss moving the supply base for Yugoslav S.O.E. operations from Cairo to southern Italy, which was closer to the Dalmatian coast. Eisenhower was receptive but when told of Yugoslavia's political complexities decided that he "did not want to be encumbered with political relations with the Yugoslav Government" and refused to put the supply base under his command. Therefore, an Advance Force 133 base was established in the heel of Italy under the command of General Wilson in Cairo instead of Eisenhower's A.F.H.Q. in Algiers. In the immediate neighborhood of the new Advance Force 133 base in the Bari–Brindisi area were the other S.O.E. and O.S.S. organizations that served under Eisenhower's command and directed special operations aimed at central and northern Italy. Relations between Advance Force 133 and its S.O.E.–O.S.S. neighbors appear to have been reasonably friendly, although the anomalous situation of two special operations working side by side while actually serving two different theater commanders caused some friction, and the inflow of S.O.E. people from Cairo meant that S.O.E. strength in Italy greatly exceeded that of O.S.S.[100]

The move of Advance Force 133 to southern Italy was a step toward integrating British and American special operations that might have ended the era of uncoordinated activities and intense O.S.S.–S.O.E. rivalry. Before peaceful cooperation could be established, however, controversy over subversive operations erupted anew in the Mediterranean theater in the fall of 1943. At issue was a scheme by Donovan with grave political features. Citing the August 1943 agreement between Churchill and Roosevelt at Quebec that Allied subversive operations in the Balkans should be intensified, Donovan proposed that Germany's Balkan satellites—Bulgaria, Rumania, and Hungary—be encouraged to desert the Axis. By exploiting communist fears of the conservative Balkan leaders, he contended, the satellite governments could be enticed into changing sides. In making his recommendation, Donovan declared that O.S.S. had available two high-level specialists on the region: Col. C. C. Jadwin (whom O.S.S. had borrowed from G-2) and a former Bulgarian banker in the American service, Col. Angel Nissimov Kouyoumdjisky.

Donovan proposed to focus subversive political pressure on Bulgaria, for not only did Jadwin and Kouyoumdjisky have contacts there but though that country had aided the Germans and declared war on Britain and America, it never had formally gone to war with the Soviet Union. The O.S.S. director therefore hoped that the Bulgarians might be tempted to make peace with London and Washington and then would move completely into the Allied camp by crawling back along the narrow bridge of formal diplomatic relations that still connected Moscow and Sofia.

Donovan's Balkan scheme was not just another example of psychological warfare but a plan for an American political offensive in the region. As the general informed the J.C.S. on 20 August 1943, he wanted to induce the Balkan states to use their forces to isolate German units in the area and assist in "the establishment of relatively stable non-Communist but not anti-Russian governments in the Balkans." How this could be done when the leading political circles there were violently anti-Soviet Donovan did not explain, nor did he make clear how the Americans were going to offset British influence in the region or the overwhelming power of the Red Army, which was already approaching the Rumanian frontier. As the Joint Strategic Survey Committee examining the proposal observed, it was "difficult to understand how activities of the character proposed by O.S.S can be carried out without involving the U.S. in commitments of some sort." But on 7 September 1943, the J.C.S. approved Donovan's proposal, and while instructing O.S.S. to inform the British and Soviets "of what we are doing," specified that O.S.S. "should not consult with the Soviets on the political phase of the proposed operations."[101]

Donovan thereupon organized a three-man Jadwin Mission made up of Jadwin, Kouyoumdjisky, and Maj. Murray Gurfein (formerly district attorney under Governor Thomas Dewey in New York) and sent it to Istanbul to contact the Bulgarians. The general tried to cover his flanks by securing State Department approval for the Jadwin Mission and also made two unusual efforts to reassure the Soviets. He primed General Deane, the new American Military Mission chief in Moscow, to suggest during the Moscow Foreign Ministers' Conference in late October that O.S.S. ought to carry out extensive subversive warfare operations in the Balkans. When Eden and Molotov were taken aback by this suggestion, Donovan flew to Moscow in December and told Molotov directly that he wanted to try to work Bulgaria out of the war. Ambassador Averell Harriman, who was present at the Donovan–Molotav talk, reported that the Soviet foreign minister raised no direct objections to the proposal, but it must be emphasized that Donovan of course did not tell Molotov that the object of the enterprise was the creation of "non-Communist governments" in the Balkans.[102]

While pursuing a deceptive course with the Soviets, Donovan was even less open with the British. During October–November 1943, the general was especially bitter about British political activities because he believed that they were obstacles to O.S.S. Balkan operations. He was chaffing to upstage London and had pointedly refused to cut S.O.E. or M.I. 6 into the Hungarian contacts that O.S.S. had recently developed in Istanbul. Donovan also failed to inform the British of the Jadwin Mission, and when Cairo got wind of it in late December, British officials were outraged. Condemning the operation as a politically dangerous violation of existing S.O.E.–O.S.S. agreements, S.O.E. leaders in Cairo demanded that the contact be broken off. By this time, however, Jadwin and Kouyoumdjisky had actually managed to lure a Bulgarian representative to Istanbul, so after some Anglo-American consultation and a formal notification to the Soviets, a series of Allied discussions with the Bulgarians took place in Istanbul between January and March 1944. Although Jadwin and his associates worked hard to produce an agreement, and the Allies carried out some Balkan air raids to help bring the Bulgarians "to their senses" (as Molotov had suggested), the talks ultimately broke down. The Soviets were reserved because time was on their side, while the British, still fuming over the "deception" practiced by O.S.S., resented having to play a supporting role in a region that they had traditionally considered their preserve. Success would only have been possible if the Bulgarians could have been made to face up to the reality of postwar Soviet power and had drawn on American support to secure the best deal they could from Moscow. But Sofia was unwilling or unable to make this leap, the Jadwin talks sputtered out, and Donovan's grand design for subversive political warfare in the Balkans failed.[103]

In addition to intensifying Soviet suspicions of Anglo-American activities in southeast Europe, the Jadwin affair also reinforced London's determination to control tightly any O.S.S. operations in the Balkans. In the fall of 1943, London had stepped up its attempts to benefit from its support of resistance operations. While going all-out in Greece to tip the balance toward resistance forces favoring the conservative monarchists and away from the Communists, the British had paradoxically also moved closer to Tito and away from Mihajlović in Yugoslavia. This move reflected in part the general Anglo-American policy of supporting those groups actually fighting the Germans, but it was also an effort to retain some British influence with what had become the strongest force in Yugoslavia. A high-level British mission under Fitzroy Maclean (a Foreign Office man commissioned as a brigadier) went in to Tito in September, and when Donovan made a move to play political broker among the various Yugoslav factions during October, he was bruskly rebuffed by Churchill. The following month, at the Teheran Conference, Roosevelt went along with a joint British–Soviet statement that made no mention of Mihajlović, while declaring that the Allies would provide extensive aid to Tito. Donovan still clung to the hope that a compromise between Mihajlović and Tito was possible, but O.S.S. men who went into Yugoslavia as part of the British missions to Tito were convinced that the partisans were the only significant fighting force in the country. In fact, reports from Linn Farish, the top O.S.S. man assigned to the partisans, helped tip the American president toward accepting the pro-Tito resolution at Teheran.[104]

To round out their effort to tidy up Balkan operations and keep Donovan and O.S.S. in harness, the British used the change of Mediterranean command in January 1944 to place firm controls on the whole S.O.E.–O.S.S. structure. When on 8 January, Eisenhower left A.F.H.Q. for England to take charge of the Allied invasion of western Europe, British Middle East Commander General Wilson was made commander of a new combined Mediterranean Theater of Operations. Since the Combined Chiefs had previously given Eisenhower "responsibility for the conduct of guerrilla and subversive action" in the western Mediterranean, and Wilson combined Eisenhower's powers with his own in the Middle East, control over every S.O.E. and O.S.S. operation in the Mediterranean basin passed to him in January 1944. To implement his authority, Wilson decided to leave operational control for Greece, Turkey, and the upper Balkans in Cairo, direct Yugoslav and Italian operations from southern Italy, and allow Algiers to oversee activities in southern France.[105]

Donovan objected to two features of Wilson's reorganization: he did not want S.I. operations to be merged with those of British secret intelligence, and he objected to placing O.S.S. personnel in Yugoslavia under Maclean, whom he did not like, and accused of being merely a political agent for the Foreign Office. Some members of the American military hierarchy were highly suspicious of British intentions in the Balkans; Eisenhower's naval aide, Harry L. Butcher, even noted in his diary in January 1944 that Wilson was "interested primarily in the politics of the Balkans and his thoughts of the war go primarily to subversive activity." For the J.C.S., however, the need to keep O.S.S. intelligence operations completely independent, with a clear channel of communication direct to Washington, was paramount.[106]

In a meeting with British military and civil authorities in Algiers on 17 January, Donovan staunchly resisted British pressure, and despite Foreign Office insistence that O.S.S. be brought to heel, General Wilson, his political adviser Harold Macmillan, and S.O.E. felt it best to yield. Because the

J.C.S. and the State Department took a strong stand and Churchill made a last-minute decision to keep Maclean exclusively as his own man, in March 1944 the Americans were finally allowed to send an independent mission to Tito (much to Maclean's disgust) and S.I. independence in the Mediterranean was grudgingly accepted by the British.[107]

Anglo-American differences on Yugoslavia were not yet over, for a conservative faction in O.S.S. continued to hanker after a deal with Mihajlović long after the British pulled their missions out of his area in February 1944. O.S.S. Washington urged that a "pure" intelligence mission, accompanied by a group to assist downed Allied fliers, be sent to Mihajlović. After securing the approval of the State Department and the president, such a mission was actually readied in April despite bitter opposition from the British. Only a last-minute appeal by Churchill to President Roosevelt stopped the mission from actually going in.[108]

Even this incident did not extinguish the torch that O.S.S. carried for Mihajlović, which might lead us to conclude that O.S.S. had a preference for conservative, or even reactionary, movements. Later C.I.A. activity may seem to support this conclusion, but care should be exercised here. Having overcome their earlier doubts, O.S.S. Washington and the J.C.S. placed a high value on the partisans' fighting ability in 1944, and they made strenuous efforts to get supplies to Tito and to keep as many O.S.S. missions as possible in partisan territory. In the Balkan caldron, no simple explanation of the motives and actions of any group sufficed.[109]

For both O.S.S. and S.O.E. in southeast Europe, ideology, military expediency, and organizational interest all came into play. As the outside organization in Greece, where Churchill and the Foreign Office strongly supported the conservatives and the king, S.O.E. was forced to press hard to gain any assistance for the left-wing E.A.M., which was doing most of the fighting against the Germans. With British influence in Greece directed to the political right and away from the most effective guerrilla force in the country, O.S.S. naturally leaned to the left and was perhaps even more sympathetic to E.A.M. than was S.O.E. In Yugoslavia (and to some degree in Albania) where all agencies of the British government were united in support of a partisan group that was simultaneously leftist and militarily effective, O.S.S. dragged its feet, and even as it supported Tito, continued to pine for Mihajlović.[110]

Obviously, in light of these varied positions, to contend that O.S.S. was inherently rightist or leftist in the Balkans is to go wide of the point. O.S.S. was primarily inclined to follow the J.C.S. principle of military necessity and support the big battalions. Donovan's people, like the U.S. government in general, were also affected by American domestic ethnic politics, and the majority of Greek-Americans were antiroyalist and leaned somewhat to the left while Yugoslav opinion in the United States tended to be sympathetic to Mihajlović and violently anticommunist. O.S.S. leaders were further eager to make a name for their organization by getting out from under the shadow of the British and showing what they could do on their own. Thus, they inevitably sought to diverge from the main thrust of British political and subversive warfare, whatever it might be. This latter attitude probably contributed most to the principal tensions within the Anglo-American subversive system in the Mediterranean theater.

Wilson managed to keep on top of the situation because in 1944 he put together a comprehensive and balanced system that turned Mediterranean special operations into the largest and most efficient Allied shadow warfare organization in the world. An important side effect of this development was that O.S.S. there became the pioneer unit of Donovan's effort to fuse a broad range of his organization's activities onto Allied military operations. O.S.S. Mediterranean blazed the trail that Donovan's other groups would try to follow in late 1944 and 1945.

Following the move of Advance Force 133 to Italy in November 1943 and Wilson's appointment as supreme commander in January 1944, Mediterranean shadow warfare consolidation advanced very rapidly. In February 1944, a special operations planning section was established in G-3 under the American major general Benjamin F. Caffey. This unit pooled the operational proposals of the various intelligence and special operations organizations, making sure that they coincided with military operations. In April 1944, a British major general, W. A. Stawell, who had long headed special operations in the Middle Eastern theater, was designated commander of special operations Mediterranean and ordered by Wilson to establish his headquarters in southern Italy.[111]

From its headquarters in the Bari–Brindisi area and its auxiliary centers near Cairo and Algiers, Stawell's special operations organization supplied all authorized S.O.E. and O.S.S.–S.O.E. missions. Although it had no role in directing intelligence operations (all of which had overriding priority), Stawell's command furnished air and sea lift for M.I. 6 and O.S.S.–S.I. missions, as well as for "A" force, the Allied air crew and P.O.W. rescue organization. In addition to these support services, Stawell's unit also controlled "Z" force, which was responsible for the special training given to the Yugoslav partisans in southern Italy, and Forces "133," "266," and "399," which handled the supplies sent into the Balkans. Immediately following the Allied landings in Italy, a group of O.S.S. men had pioneered trans-Adriatic seaborne shipment of supplies to the partisans, but by early 1944 this activity had been regularized and made part of the overall special operations support system.[112]

The main special operations centers in southeast Italy were chiefly supply bases where such related activites as parachute training were carried on. With its extensive packing facilities, the Bari base complex could handle 2,000 tons of Adriatic seaborn shipments monthly, plus 850 tons of air lift as early as February 1944. Although actual delivery depended on weather conditions, especially for air drops, Special Projects Operations Center (S.P.O.C.) Mediterranean succeeded in sending large quantities of supplies to resistance forces. In January 1944, for example, S.P.O.C. Mediterranean airlifted one and a half times as many supplies to Greece, Yugoslavia, and Albania as were airlifted to all of northwest Europe in the same month (192 tons compared with 127 tons). In addition, S.P.O.C. Mediterranean supplied 18.5 tons to Greece and 2,892 tons to Yugoslavia by sea at a time when no seaborne supplies went to the resistance in northwest Europe at all. In subsequent months, the supply pattern in the Mediterranean shifted somewhat as large deliveries to the Italian resistance began and Algiers concentrated on providing aid to southern France prior to D Day. With better weather in the spring and early summer, successful air drops increased in all theaters, but the relatively high ratio of resistance supply delivery of the Mediterranean theater compared with other areas held firm until the weeks immediately preceding the Overlord landing in Normandy in June 1944.[113]

Of course, some resistance groups in the Mediterranean area thought that the Allies were not doing enough to help them. The Allied organizations most closely associated with the resistance also tended to feel that they were being short changed, especially by the Allied air forces, which were reluctant to divert aircraft from regular bombing operations. With some justification, a few Americans believed that the British used the shortage of air lift as just another excuse to inhibit the entry of American units into areas that London considered sensitive. O.S.S. was long denied the right to send its O.G.s into Greece on the grounds that there was not enough lift to maintain them. But it must be recognized that such units did require many supplies, and the lift capability was in fact severely limited. Resistance groups were more anxious to receive supplies than they were to see the arrival of Allied advisory officers or even O.G.s. As one British liaison officer remarked in the early spring of 1944, if the Allies sent the Yugoslav partisans any more "bodies" (agents and liaison officers) before large quantities of supplies arrived, "the bodies would be eaten." In March 1944, thirty-eight heavy aircraft (Halifaxes and Liberators) were stationed in Italy for special operational activities, ten more "heavies" were reserved for flights over the Alps to Poland, and four squadrons of lighter aircraft were available on a part-time basis. A few additional aircraft were scattered from Cairo to Algiers. With this force, plus the seaborne lift that gave substantial assistance to Tito and some aid to southern France, Stawell and his staff had to service all of Italy, southern France, and the Balkans, an area made up of 200,000 to 300,000 square miles of enemy-held territory.[114]

Given the scale of the problem and the limited equipment and delivery means available, S.P.O.C. Mediterranean carried out an impressive range of actions in the first six months of 1944. In addition to landing and maintaining hundreds of S.O.E.–S.O. and M.I. 6 missions in the Balkans, Italy, and southern France, numerous other unorthodox operations were carried out. A large number of aircrew rescue missions, including the O.S.S. mission in Serbia called "Alum" were kept in the field for long periods. Special attacks were launched on Germany's vital chrome supplies by resistance groups in Greece and Yugoslavia under the direction of the S.P.O.C. Repeated efforts were made by both S.O.E. and O.S.S. to encourage resistance activities in Hungary and Bulgaria by sending in special operations missions. Although some useful intelligence seems to have been secured, S.O.E. casualties were especially high and results of popular resistance were meager in both Bulgaria and Hungary. The raiding operations along the Adriatic coasts of Yugoslavia and Italy and along Italy's western shore also incurred heavy losses. A substantial force of O.S.S.–O.G.s, plus three commando units and elements of the British Special Raiding Regiment, were concentrated in southern Italy for reconnaissance raids, resistance support operations, and protection for the Adriatic "ferry service" to Tito. Some of the operations undertaken by these units had elements of action-for-action's-sake, but they helped secure coastal observation posts, and through the use of heavier weapons, provided the lightly armed resistance movements with a morale-raising increase of punching power.[115]

For both the intelligence and special operations teams that went into enemy territory, moments of glory were rare. It was a tough, dirty business, with high risks, grave uncertainties, and few clear indications of large-scale success. Resistance units had to be organized, equipped, trained, and taken on missions. Intelligence useful to A.F.H.Q. had to be gathered from friend and foe alike. Supply drops had to be arranged, money and material distributed, and a continuous effort made to quell factional and political strife. One of the few light spots in this business was the opportunity to let one's imagination run riot when the time came to code-name the actual missions. Thus, in May 1944 S.O.E. ended up with a Fungus mission in Istria, and an O.S.S. mission in Slovenia in the same period was called Cuckold. But special operations duty was primarily full of sickness, danger, and boredom, interspersed with bursts of action to raise the score in the S.P.O.C. "gamebook." The "gamebook" recorded the number of Axis troops that resistance forces claimed to have killed in the Mediterranean area. Month by month, the "gamebook" chronicled the growth of resistance power, until by March 1944 A.F.H.Q. calculated (probably with some exaggeration) that each month the resistance was killing approximately 4,700 Axis personnel, including "about 2,100 Huns."[116]

As the date for the main cross-channel invasion of France (Overlord) neared, resistance activity in the Mediterranean was keyed to assisting the invasion plans of Eisenhower's Supreme Headquarters Allied Expeditionary Force (S.H.A.E.F.). Operations were organized throughout the area to obscure Allied intentions, destroy transportation networks, and pin down German forces so that reinforcement of the Nazi defences in Normandy would be limited. Although this meant that resistance members actually were working to retain their Nazi tormentors in their territory during the spring of 1944, S.P.O.C. diversionary operations to assist Overlord were loyally carried out by resistance groups from northern Italy to eastern Greece.[117]

However, the major assistance rendered by A.F.H.Q. special operations to Overlord was the intelligence and resistance support sent into southern France. Even before Overlord preparations began in earnest in April 1944, A.F.H.Q. had been very active there. In addition to the extensive Free French intelligence links run from Algiers and the various S.I.S. and O.S.S.–S.I. networks spread out from Spain and North Africa, resistance support operations had long been run from North Africa by the French authorities and A.F.H.Q. All these activities came under closer A.F.H.Q. control in April, and a series of additional special intelligence missions were sent in during the last sixty days before D Day. On the basis of plans developed by S.H.A.E.F., operations were prepared in southern France for sabotage of the main railroad and highway routes to inhibit the flow of German reinforcements to Normandy immediately following D Day. Large quantities of weapons and sabotage supplies were sent in by the special Operations Sea Borne Force and the nineteen special operations aircraft then stationed at Algiers. Two special uniformed Jedburgh resistance support teams were landed in southern France on D Day minus one, and another Jedburgh team went in on D Day. In the course of the summer of 1944, eleven additional Jedburgh teams, plus four French speaking O.S.S. O.G.s, were fed into the resistance battle from Algiers.[118]

Not all of the S.P.O.C. plans and operations in support of Overlord were successful. Intelligence was difficult to coordinate, lines were sometimes crossed, and important information was overlooked. Planning and operational confusion was especially hard to avoid because even as S.P.O.C. was being used to support the Normandy landings, A.F.H.Q. was already planning its own full-scale invasion of southern France (Operation Anvil), which the Combined Chiefs of Staff had scheduled for late summer. Given the circumstances, S.P.O.C. did a highly effective job; much intelligence information was secured for A.F.H.Q. and S.H.A.E.F., and German movement from southern France to the Normandy beachhead was seriously disrupted.[119]

On one issue, however, A.F.H.Q. contributed to the unleashing of a bitter controversy. Eisenhower originally had intended to try to "dampen down" mass popular uprisings on D Day to help avoid massive German reprisals. However, A.F.H.Q., led by Wilson and Harold Macmillan, contended that a mass uprising was inevitable and that it would be better "to direct" rather than vainly try to suppress it. Wilson and Macmillan also feared that Britain's "future relations with France" could be seriously damaged if the French "got the impression that we were too proud or too correct to take the Resistance Groups seriously." Under pressure from the French and A.F.H.Q., Eisenhower softened his stand, apparently in part because Wilson spoke of sending in some French commando-type forces to stiffen large-scale Maquis operations.[120]

When the priorities for air lift were tallied just before D Day, only nineteen aircraft were available, an insufficient lift for intelligence missions, sabotage operations, and the scale of supplies required for heavily armed units to support the Maquis. Therefore, the heavy support groups did not go in and S.H.A.E.F. and A.F.H.Q. merely hoped that when the general rising occurred, some means would be found to sustain it. An A.F.H.Q. plan of May 1944 declared: "It is the policy of SOE/SO to develop specifically Maquis regions to the utmost with the object of creating a major diversion in the enemy's rear. After Overlord D-Day, Balkan conditions are expected to develop in S.E. France, with whole areas entirely free of the enemy."[121] Events proved, however, that southern France was not Yugoslavia. The Germans were too strong, much of the terrain was not suitable for guerrilla warfare, and without heavy weapons, the Maquis was decimated when it attempted to stage a stand-up fight.

A clear line therefore connected A.F.H.Q.'s faulty Overlord planning and the tragedy of the Vendôme in late July when, following the post–D Day uprising, the Germans lured the Maquis into the open and gave it a severe mauling. But the nub of the issue was not, as some have implied, that A.F.H.Q. was attempting to take advantage of the resistance or trying to have it exterminated to ease the task of postwar occupation. On the contrary, because Wilson and Macmillan feared the political consequences of discouraging an uprising they could not prevent, they actually encouraged a large-scale action by the Maquis. When Churchill's enthusiasm for a diversion in southeastern France (which will be discussed below) at the time of D Day was added to A.F.H.Q.'s long experience with resistance in "Balkan Conditions" it was easy for Wilson and his staff to stumble into the pattern of wishful thinking that led to the Vendôme. This policy was neither farsighted nor politically courageous but neither was it based on contempt for the French or malice toward the Maquis.

Tragedies like that of the Vendôme were possible in any area where A.F.H.Q. supported shadow warfare operations because no matter what efforts were made in Bari or Algiers, the range of resistance and intelligence activities far exceeded the supply, lift, and support resources available. The rivalry between the various Allied organizations involved compounded the difficulties. S.O.E. and M.I. 6 were suspicious of each other, and the prime minister, as well as the War and Foreign offices, were on guard against both of them. The various branches of O.S.S. scrambled for relative advantage, while the State Department, the J.C.S., O.W.I., and the War Department kept anxious eyes on them all. The special organizations of Britain and the United States were linked together for various activities, but the British were highly sensitive to American incursions (especially in the Balkans), and the Americans deeply resented British dominance and what they saw as Britain's political manipulations.[122]

These difficulties, compounded by the troubles within the various resistance movements and exile governments, make sharp criticism of A.F.H.Q.'s shadow warfare arrangements inappropriate. The far-flung and relatively efficient system that existed in the Mediterranean theater by mid-1944 was a substantial achievement. Much of the credit must go to Wilson, Stawell, and their staffs, but it should also be stressed that O.S.S. played a major part in the range and success of these special operations.

The Mediterranean theater gave the Anglo-American forces and shadow warfare organizations the experience and toughness they needed. Here was where the British and American combat units, and their commanders, became hardened veterans, knowledgeable in the methods of modern warfare and able to meet the Wehrmacht on even terms. It was here, too, that Donovan was finally able to put his organization into operation on a large scale and show what an American shadow warfare system could accomplish.

O.S.S. and the European Theater of Operations: March 1943–June 1944

July 1943: The Red Army wins the battle of Kursk
March 1944: The first 800-plane American raid on Berlin; the Red Army reaches the Rumanian frontier

The Mediterranean theater was the great school and showcase for O.S.S., but Axis and Ally alike considered that area little more than a military sideshow. The decisive Anglo-American action of the European war was destined to come on the Atlantic coast of France, and in 1943–44 Western military commanders were absorbed in the preparations for Operation Overlord. Within O.S.S., responsibility for western European operations fell largely on the London office, which was under the direction of David Bruce. Prior to D Day, 6 June 1944, this office carried on a wide range of planning activities, exercised a loose supervision over the Dublin, Stockholm, and Bern outposts and carried out general R. and A., S.I., M.O., and X-2 functions. O.S.S. London was dependent on the British and exile government organizations for most of its information, yet it pioneered such O.S.S. activities as the development of close intelligence ties with continental labor groups. As the war progressed, however, O.S.S. London's intelligence reports to Washington were overshadowed in scope and quantity by those from Bern and Stockholm.[123]

R. and A. London carried on the combination of political and economic research common to all R. and A. operations. In addition, it was especially important because it did target work for the Eighth Air Force and provided instruction to the army civil affairs officers who were supposed to be in charge once the British and American armies actually reached France. Although prevented from engaging in P.O.W. interrogation until after D Day by the long arm of G-2's General Strong, R. and A. London managed to come to terms with two other plagues that often had tormented Langer's band of scholars. Unusually harmonious working relationships were developed by London R. and A. with both O.S.S.–S.I. and O.W.I. Since all American organizations in London believed that they were not adequately supported from Washington, they sought to cooperate more with each other, and R. and A. took advantage of this situation to work its way into joint enterprises (including a number of military intelligence targeting teams) that would have been impossible in the American capital.[124]

Despite such quiet achievements, O.S.S. London went through a long period of general paralysis before it received authorization from the J.C.S. to carry out a complete spectrum of shadow warfare activities. The general O.S.S. plan for Europe was forwarded to the American commander in London in early July 1943, but General Devers (who served as theater commander until Eisenhower moved up from A.F.H.Q. in February 1944) wanted the British to supervise a number of O.S.S. activities and also sought to have O.S.S. contacts with the exile governments controlled by an American army officer. Donovan objected violently to both proposals. An acrimonious controversy followed, bringing nearly all O.S.S. London activities, including the preparations for Anglo–American–French intelligence missions in support of D Day and O.S.S.'s plans to operate in northern Norway, to a standstill.[125]

The British government quickly stepped in to take advantage of this American civil war. British obstacles were put in the way of O.S.S. Norwegian plans, and London asserted a general right to supervise virtually all O.S.S. intelligence and special operations in western Europe. The latter move actually played into Donovan's hands, however, because in October 1943 the O.S.S. director used it to convince the Joint Chiefs that General Dever's proposals would have the effect of placing O.S.S. intelligence under British control. Always sensitive to the need for the United States to have absolute authority over its own intelligence activities, the J.C.S. ordered Devers to establish O.S.S. intelligence autonomy in Europe regarding both the exiled governments and the British. His Majesty's government protested against this decision for four months but in the end was forced to yield.[126]

Joint Chiefs' approval of the O.S.S. European plan in October 1943 at last made possible establishment of a Norwegian operation, and the Westfield Mission in Stockholm immediately began to feed supplies and equipment over the border into northern Norway. Simultaneously, a large build up of O.S.S. personnel for the whole European Theater of Operations (E.T.O.) took place, and S.I. and S.O. went to work on various projects to assist the D Day invasion. Devers was still wary of antagonizing the British, and S.I. had to move cautiously, but the planning work was on its way.[127]

That O.S.S. London provided any assistance to D Day was a creditable accomplishment in light of the political and policy conflicts that had to be surmounted. No sooner had the difficulty over securing J.C.S. approval for its theater plan been overcome than O.S.S. was embroiled in another controversy that sprawled from February 1944 to the very eve of D Day. While in North Africa recuperating from a bout with the flu during January–February 1944, Winston Churchill became enthralled with the idea of building up large diversionary resistance operations in southeast France. Guerrilla warfare had always had a strong appeal for the old romantic, and the prospect of providing substantial British aid to a project that would assist Overlord and bring London a great harvest of French gratitude entranced him. Without informing the American government or the new S.H.A.E.F. commander Dwight Eisenhower, Churchill established an organizational committee to increase aid to the French resistance and to funnel that aid to the Maquis regions of southeast France.[128]

The Americans also had been asked by de Gaulle to step up assistance to the French resistance, and though some officials, including Assistant Secretary of War John J. McCloy, were highly sympathetic, Washington was not much interested in the matter until late February when word arrived that Churchill was launching off on his own. An inquiry then demonstrated that the Americans had not heretofore taken French resistance aid very seriously and that none of the people supposedly in charge of the problem—from Donovan to Eisenhower—had much idea of what was actually going on. Once alerted to the issue, however, Eisenhower began to tidy up his resistance arrangements, which prevented Churchill from diverting special operations assistance from the Normandy area to southeast France.[129]

American officials, especially those in O.S.S., also quickly grasped that there could be serious political trouble if the French gained the impression that only Britain was concerned about aiding the resistance. When Washington learned in April that de Gaulle had in fact stated that assistance to France was coming exclusively from Britain, the State Department sprang into action and urged the Joint Chiefs to do something to improve America's resistance-support image. Though emphasizing that they were "of course" not asking the military to act simply to gain political advantage, State Department officials from Secretary Hull to H. Freeman Matthews contended "that our British friends have consistently done their best to monopolize the credit for what is being done," and State wanted to combat "this sort of thing." To meet the State Department request, the J.C.S. surveyed its overseas commanders in March and April to determine the extent of existing aid. The results, which were consolidated and sent to the president on 10 May 1944, were indeed devastating. Between February and April the Americans had flown from England and North Africa a total of 253 supply missions and delivered 220 tons to the French, while in the same period the British had flown 1,586 missions and put in 1,230 tons of supplies. Thus, British support had been at least five times that of the Americans. If the British had tried to "monopolize the credit" for aid to the French resistance, they had also done most of the work.[130]

As a result of the Anglo-American controversies over special aid to southeast France and the role of the two countries in general resistance support, the U.S. government was forced temporarily to shelve its doubts about de Gaulle and offer more assistance in the final month prior to D Day. The American organization that most benefited from this last-minute conversion to the virtues of resistance support was, of course, O.S.S. Requests for additional O.S.S. personnel for Europe immediately received Ike's blessing, and the military authorities were now more willing to help O.S.S. overcome obstacles to its invasion-support preparations.[131]

Certainly not all difficulties fell away immediately. The generals could not completely overcome their professional distaste for irregular warfare. Some were troubled by legal doubts, and others feared for any American military personnel who were caught by the Germans. The air force chiefs (especially Ike's British deputy commander, Air Marshall A. W. Tedder) were reluctant to divert aircraft to S.O.E.–S.O., and additional lift for pre–D Day special operations was only secured very late. Ike and his staff also had their doubts about the effectiveness of the resistance. The difficulties over Torch had left a shadow that was deepened by the subsequent uneven performance in Corsica. Not until 8 April, two months before the invasion, did an entry on the importance of having an "effective fifth column" appear in the diary of Ike's naval aide, Harry Butcher, and in late April Butcher was still wondering whether "we are hoping for too much" from the resistance, which he thought might turn out to "be more like the attitude of the French in North Africa."[132]

Some developments gave credence to Butcher's doubts. The centralized Free French resistance network had been attacked and severely mauled by the Gestapo in June 1943, and that same summer a number of S.O.E.'s French circuits were penetrated. Despite enormous effort, S.O.E. had failed to develop significant resistance movements in Germany or Austria, and the French Provisional government was opposed to S.O.E. action in Germany that might put French laborers or P.O.W.s there at risk.

French public opinion had been so angered by the civilian casualties caused by Allied air raids that British and American propagandists launched a May 1944 campaign to convince the French that "immediately after an RAF night attack" on a French military target, the Luftwaffe bombed neighboring residential areas "to incite anti-British feeling."

Some French industrialists were even insisting that they receive promises of postwar Allied compensation before they would agree to let the resistance sabotage their plants rather than have the R.A.F. bomb them. These poor omens inclined a number of British and American officials other than Butcher to wonder if there were anything to the resistance talk except idle boasting.[133]

The rivalries between the various Anglo-American and French groups engaged in resistance support activities also boded ill for a full-scale, integrated resistance operation on D Day. Two resistance networks (R.F. and F.) and dozens of different intelligence rings operated inside France. The British and Americans eyed each other suspiciously, the Free French had doubts about both of them, and the various resistance-support organizations of each country also sharply disagreed.

In March and April 1944 all this absurdity peaked when an acrid controversy erupted between S.O.E. on one hand and P.W.E., M.O.I., and the British Broadcasting Corporation (B.B.C.) on the other over S.O.E.'s request that it be allotted radio time in the immediate pre–D Day period to give final instructions and the order to rise to the resistance armies. Although S.O.E. only had requested eight minutes of B.B.C. time on each of four days, Lord Selborne complained to the prime minister on 22 March that M.O.I. and the B.B.C. directors were "unable to promise me any allocation of . . . broadcasting time during the D Day period at all." As late as 4 April, M.O.I. informed Selbourne that it still did not want B.B.C. used to relay S.O.E.'s call for a resistance uprising because it believed that it would be "grossly improper that the prestige of the B.B.C. should be sullied in this manner." So bitter and ludicrous was the whole affair that even Churchill washed his hands of it. Only after extensive negotiations were Selborne and Bracken able to reach a last-minute compromise allowing the famous B.B.C. bong to sound and the "standby" code words to go out on 1 June, with the "action" messages following on 5 June 1944.[134]

In face of such inanities, the Anglo-American intelligence and covert operations staffs preparing for D Day showed great steadiness and devotion in the period immediately prior to Overlord. The O.S.S. share of this work, though smaller than that of either the Free French or the British, was nonetheless substantial. In the realm of intelligence activity, S.I. used its established sources (especially the Bern circuits and the joint O.S.S.–Free French Medusa operations from Spain) and also participated in the tripartite (British–French–American) Sussex and Proust operations developed for the Normandy invasion. Sussex and Proust teams were special intelligence units made up of French military personnel recruited by

O.S.S. and M.I. 6 to go in shortly before or after D Day to provide detailed information on the strength, deployment, and movement of German military forces. To make the system effective, a complex system of "pathfinder" agents had to be sent in first to lay the groundwork for military intelligence collection. Special arrangements were also necessary for the receipt of information, including the stationing of O.S.S.–S.I. and M.I. 6 intelligence officers with the Allied armies to relay Sussex and Proust reports to fighting units.[135]

The entire organization had to be put together between October 1943, when O.S.S. finally received J.C.S. approval to operate in the European theater, and May 1944, when the first agents were parachuted in. Despite harassment from both the British and some S.I. leaders in London, O.S.S. Sussex and Proust preparations were completed on time. The 115 agents recruited by O.S.S. were either in training or trained by D Day and, according to plan, approximately one-third were already in France at that time. A heavy flow of Sussex and Proust reports was reaching London by mid-July, in good time to assist the Allied armies in their Normandy battles and the open country operations that were soon to follow.[136]

Certainly not all, or even a major portion, of the intelligence gathered for the battles in France came from Sussex or other O.S.S. sources. Donovan himself once estimated that 80 percent of Overlord field intelligence was secured by the Free French rather than the British or Americans. It is also undeniable that all the espionage and intelligence organizations, including the French, failed to locate and use effectively available pieces of vital information. For instance, a professor of geology at the Sorbonne secretly sent London a complete record of French tidal conditions and beach gradients, which should have been of great value to the invading force. But the documents were lost within the intelligence bureaucracy and played no part in D-Day planning. Such mistakes do not, however, alter the general point that Allied intelligence in general, and O.S.S.–S.I. in particular, were highly successful in rapidly mounting an intelligence support system for the invasion.[137]

In addition to these S.I. preparations for D Day, O.S.S.–M.O. did its usual work trying to strengthen pro-Allied sentiment among the French and undercutting German morale. More directly pertinent to the invasion was the pre–D Day activity of the O.S.S.–S.O. Despite its best efforts, S.O. was even more obviously a junior partner than either S.I. or M.O. Both the Free French and the exile governments of other occupied countries had long cooperated with S.O.E., and as we have seen above, Britain provided the bulk of resistance support supplies and airlift up through D Day. Although S.O.E. would later claim that O.S.S. was kept in a secondary role due to a lack of trained personnel, a combination of British eagerness to keep the Americans subordinate and a reluctance on the part of the American military leaders to give O.S.S.–S.O. authority or adequate support was the chief cause of the difficulty.[138]

Given its late start, O.S.S.–S.O. made rapid strides. It went under the authority of S.H.A.E.F. in November 1943, and a joint S.O.E.–S.O. Special Projects Operations Room began to function on 14 May 1944. Once the D-Day landing occurred, the Operations Room directed overall resistance operations by serving as a communications link between the various resistance groups and the special force teams attached to the Allied armies. It was hoped, and largely realized, that this system would allow resistance operations to serve the immediate needs of the invading armies.[139]

The resistance was told that 417 specific railroad cuts in France and Belgium, concentrated on four major lines, were to have top D-Day priority, with other rail, highway, and telecommunication objectives placed second. In addition to large quantities of light weapons, 174 bazookas and 1,460 antitank mines already had been dropped by D Day, to facilitate these attacks, and a variety of Allied support units were ready to give direction and greater punch to the resistance effort. Seventeen operational teams, including two from O.S.S., were designated as support for the large resistance movement formed by Polish workers in northern France. Six British S.A.S. commando-type reconnaisance units plus two O.S.S. O.G.s were also ready for use before, or just after, D Day, with additional S.A.S. and O.G. units held in reserve to be thrown in during the battle. Jedburgh teams made up of a radio operator, one French officer, and either a British or an American officer, were to provide general direction of resistance operations and make certain that high-priority targets were actually hit. Seventy-three Jedburgh teams (approximately one-third O.S.S.) were in training or ready to go in from England by D Day, with fifteen more in Algeria and ten additional teams standing by for possible use in Belgium and the Netherlands.[140]

After revelations of British preponderance in resistance support rocked Washington in April and May, O.S.S. activity in all aspects of D-Day subversive operations increased markedly in the last month or two before Overlord. By the time de Gaulle's Gen. Marie-Pierre Koenig was formally installed as commander of the French Forces of the Interior on 2 June (in time for the start of the operational phase of the D-Day resistance campaign), O.S.S. had become a respectable participant in the great invasion enterprise.[141]

Halfway through 1944, O.S.S. was at last getting an opportunity in the

European and Mediterranean theaters to demonstrate that it could give significant aid to military operations. In the post–D Day period, when Allied armies closed in on Nazi Germany, Donovan's cadres would have one final opportunity in Europe to follow General Marshall's earlier suggestion and really "show their stuff."

O.S.S. Asia: March 1943–June 1944

November 1943: U.S. Marines take Tarawa
December 1943: Stilwell starts his Burma offensive
June 1944: Marines take Saipan; first B–29 raid on the Japanese home islands

The European theater was only half of America's Second World War, and, to gain a clear picture of how O.S.S. evolved, it is necessary to make a rapid survey of Donovan's organization in Asia during the middle phase of the conflict. In contrast to Europe, most O.S.S. efforts in Asia continued to meet with frustration throughout 1943 and the first half of 1944. The attempt to create serious resistance movements against the Japanese by building on exile groups within the United States had made little progress. Syngman Rhee's Free Korean movement was anathema to the State Department, and consequently, Donovan's men were compelled to keep it at arm's length. The Free Thai Army found more favor with the diplomats and was pushed vigorously by O.S.S., but with deep political divisions among the Thais and the Nationalist Chinese government showing extreme coolness to the Thai advance party in Chunking, the enterprise barely had moved off point zero by the middle of 1944.[142]

O.S.S. efforts to find some action in the South Pacific during this period also failed. An operational plan for the whole Pacific region and a specific one for the South Pacific were routinely shot down by Adm. Chester Nimitz, Gen. Douglas MacArthur, and the J.C.S. in June and July 1943. Despite the high hopes raised in O.S.S. headquarters by a MacArthur invitation to Donovan to visit the area in the spring of 1944, the meeting between the two old warriors did not gain O.S.S. operational access to the theater. Donovan's subsequent attempt to coax Admiral Nimitz into conceding a role to O.S.S. also had meager results. Aside from authorizing the visit of an O.S.S. expert on special weapons to his command area and requesting Donovan's help in securing twenty trained underwater demolition experts, Nimitz joined MacArthur in refusing to allow O.S.S. into the Pacific.[143]

Such rejection was difficult for Donovan, but there was perhaps some consolation in the fact that he was not alone in failing to get his organization into the Pacific sanctuary. O.W.I. was similarly frustrated by MacArthur's rejection of its propaganda programs, and Sherwood was highly irritated by MacArthur's arrogance. Even British intelligence organizations were formally barred by MacArthur's command from operating in the area, and consequently, some rather remarkable tales circulated in London about events there. So severe was the information blackout that M.I. 6 was forced to fall back on one of its oldest methods for discreetly securing information from "troubled" areas. In November 1943, the editor of the *London Times*, Barrington Ward, agreed to let M.I. 6 use the *Times* correspondent in Australia, Ian Morrison, as an unpaid observer to keep an eye on MacArthur and his doings. Henceforth, from this and whatever other sources the British could work in Australia, London acquired a somewhat better picture of southwest Pacific developments. But in an atmosphere of inter-Allied secrecy and cloak-and-dagger espionage, considerable distrust remained.[144]

Donovan's inability to operate in the southwest Pacific could not even be rectified by this kind of traditional espionage—spying on one's own army is even worse than spying on an ally's—and probably more in sorrow than in anger, the general was forced to accept defeat in his 1944 campaign to play a part in the Pacific theater. As in the first phase of the conflict, O.S.S. could only work on the mainland in Asia, and Detachment 101 in Burma still led the way. As late as fall 1943, Eifler's group consisted of only twenty-five Americans, but along with the Kachins, it was carrying on a bruising guerrilla war against the Japanese in northern Burma. As their successes mounted and the day approached for launching General Stilwell's long-prepared campaign to reopen the Burma Road into China, the importance of Detachment 101's actions loomed larger. During the last half of 1943, however, all O.S.S. activities in India and Southeast Asia, including Detachment 101, were caught in the middle of a British–American ping-pong game for control of Asian covert operations.[145]

Beginning in March 1943, the British and American Chiefs of Staff exchanged volleys on the form of supervision required for O.S.S. in India, Burma, Thailand, and Indochina. The most delicate areas for the British were obviously India and Burma; for the Americans, control of their own intelligence activities, authority over Detachment 101, and a desire not to appear "imperialist" were paramount. When in March the Americans asked Britain to approve the expansion of O.S.S. in India, London replied that in exchange Britain wanted a supervisorial right over all O.S.S. operations on the subcontinent, including O.S.S.

intelligence and Detachment 101. Donovan protested this proposal in a memorandum to the American Chiefs. He argued that the British should not control S.I. anywhere and stressed that in the original O.S.S.–S.O.E. agreements of June 1942, Burma had been designated a shared resistance-support area. In his usual pithy way, the United States theater commander, General Stilwell, told the Joint Chiefs that he had a low opinion of S.O.E., a high opinion of Detachment 101, and declared that he would rather have O.S.S. withdrawn from India altogether than share control of it with the British. On 14 May 1943, the United States Deputy Chiefs of Staff followed these recommendations, deciding that Detachment 101 should stay under Stilwell and that the British should be granted no control over American intelligence.[146]

Britain hung very tough, although it was militarily weak in the area and needed American military support and assistance from some O.S.S. special services, such as Japanese language specialists. On 5 May 1943, London demanded that all reports produced by O.S.S. in India (even those of R. and A.) be shown to British officials before their dispatch to Washington. At the end of May, replying to the American chiefs' rejection of complete British control of O.S.S. operations in India, the British Chiefs proposed the establishment of an Anglo-American J.I.C. in India, with a mixed intelligence staff from the two countries. The American Chiefs of Staff immediately queried Stilwell on this proposal, and while awaiting his reply put a freeze on the transport of all O.S.S., O.W.I., and related personnel destined for India and Southeast Asia. On 6 June, Stilwell replied that he found all the British suggestions "objectionable" because he believed that Britain tended "to make intelligence fit policy" and that by pooling intelligence with the British "all information would cease to be unbiased and impartial." The American commander also worried that the Chinese would protest an Anglo-American merger by putting a freeze on all information from Chinese sources.[147]

Caught between the British obsession to dominate their allies in India and Stilwell's belief that to have a chance to operate effectively in China he had to keep free of Britain, the J.C.S. hammered out a compromise in which "liaison" rather than pooling would be used to link up Anglo-American intelligence on the subcontinent. Stilwell was somewhat less than enthusiastic about the idea, characterizing it as analogous to "piling Ossa on Pelion" when "Delhi is already full of Ossas sitting on committees." But if it would break the deadlock, he declared it would be "acceptable if the War Department wants it."[148]

Donovan was ready to agree to any arrangement that would give him some measure of autonomy. He had prepared grandiose plans for continental operations in Asia and had managed to get a new O.S.S. chief to Delhi before the J.C.S. instituted its temporary freeze on new personnel. In early August, he negotiated a revised agreement for S.O. operations in Southeast Asia with S.O.E. that allowed both organizations to go into all areas from Burma to Sumatra, with S.O.E. supervising missions out of India and Australia; and O.S.S., those out of China. The implementation of this agreement was left hanging fire, however, until the bigger question of general British supervision of O.S.S. operations and American intelligence in India was settled.[149]

In early August, the British responded with yet another scheme that would have given Britain a veto over all operations from India and provided for an "exchange of personnel" between the intelligence staffs of the two countries. Stilwell predictably registered his opposition to both ideas and the J.C.S. concluded that it should put forth a further compromise. At the Quebec conference in 1943, Roosevelt had just agreed to Churchill's suggestion that an independent Southeast Asian Command (S.E.A.C.) be established under the command of Adm. Lord Louis Mountbatten with Stilwell serving as his deputy in charge of the American China-Burma–India Theater (C.B.I.). Although the jurisdictional line between S.E.A.C. and C.B.I. was at best hazy, in Southeast Asia, Mountbatten would henceforth be acting as supreme *Allied* commander and would have formal authority over all British and American forces in the theater. This development seems to have calmed most of London's worry about American anti-imperialist indiscretions in India. It also made it easier for the J.C.S. to present a compromise to Stilwell, once it was definitely established that the American general would have command in China, which he desired. In early September 1943, the deal was made. Stilwell received absolute control over Detachment 101, the intelligence services of both Britain and the United States kept their operational integrity in China and India, and while Mountbatten controlled all special operations from Indian territory Stilwell did the same from China.[150]

This Anglo-American agreement and the establishment of the new S.E.A.C. theater seemed to open prospects for O.S.S. activity in Asia, and Donovan quickly prepared to visit the area to give his organization a boost. But successful O.S.S. operations in Asia turned on more than Anglo-American cooperation. The heart of mainland Asia still lay in China, and even with the S.A.C.O. agreement, O.S.S. had not managed to produce much action in that country during 1943. Planning had been done, and many intimations had come from Tai Li that great developments were imminent. But nothing of importance ever seemed to happen. As most knowledgeable British and American observers agreed, the core of the trouble was that the weak Nationalist government was preparing as best it could for a future struggle with Mao Tse-Tung and was therefore "loath to expend its remaining strength against the Japanese." Yet while leaving the bulk of the serious fighting against Japan to the Americans, Chiang was not willing to give his Allies a free operational hand in China. Face had to be preserved as much as possible, and independent foreign enterprises, especially those in the intelligence area, had to be controlled to preserve the domestic image of the regime and disguise its military weakness. Donovan still had his super secret intelligence net operated by C. V. Starr, but even here trouble was brewing. British M.I. 6 had learned all about the Starr operation in September, and by late 1943 an M.I. 6 official in Washington was trying to turn some of Starr's people, encouraging them to work for Britain rather than the United States.[151]

By late summer 1943, after S.A.C.O. had produced nothing but six months of evasion and delay, Donovan was bombarded by requests from his subordinates that he do something to get O.S.S. China moving. In October, the situation produced threats of resignation even from key Far Eastern specialists in O.S.S. Washington, and the harassed O.S.S. chief of S.E.A.C.–C.B.I., Col. Richard Heppner, urged that yet another reorganization of O.S.S. intelligence in China be attempted. Therefore, in late 1943 Donovan journeyed to Asia to help launch the new O.S.S. operations in S.E.A.C. and to try once more to break the S.A.C.O. logjam. Before leaving Washington, the general prudently secured President Roosevelt's prior approval for the establishment of facilities "independent of the Chinese . . . [and] independence of operations." Following a brief courtesy call on Mountbatten, Donovan traveled to Chunking in early December. Confronting Tai Li and Commodore Miles directly, Donovan demanded that the American side of S.A.C.O. be divided into two equal sections, one for O.S.S. and the other for Miles' Naval Group China. Brushing aside the reservations of both Tai Li and the commodore, the O.S.S. director used his presidential sanction to get what he wanted and warned Tai Li that nothing—not even Tai Li's purported Gestapo methods—would stop him from putting O.S.S. intelligence agents into the field.[152]

Donovan's threats sounded so impressive that Commodore Miles and his naval patrons in Washington were forced to give in, and O.S.S. secured control of a separate section of S.A.C.O. Col. John Coughlin was appointed the new chief of O.S.S. in C.B.I., and vast plans were developed by

O.S.S. offices in Chunking and Washington. Numerous O.S.S. personnel and masses of intelligence and special operations equipment were soon shipped to India for "hump" flights into China. R. and A. Washington began to do the preparatory studies for S.O. and S.I. Chunking operations, and both the British and the Americans once again started toying with the possibility of using the American position in Nationalist China as a starting point for intelligence forays into the communist north.[153]

While in China, Donovan agreed to provide General Chennault's American Fourteenth Airforce with R. and A. target analysis people. In January 1944, the practical arrangements were completed for a large R. and A. operation in Fourteenth Air Force headquarters at Kunming, and by March, O.S.S. men were producing highly useful targeting information for Chennault and his staff. To back up his new and varied intelligence operations, Donovan arranged with M.I. 6 to begin another highly secret intelligence network in Japanese-occupied China completely independent of the Chinese government. This M.I. 6 scheme was called the Clam project because the principle agent, Konrad Hsu (who had been located by M.I. 6 in New York), had a passion for steamed clams. Using various business and family connections in China and a Canadian communications network to throw both the Japanese and Tai Li off the scent, M.I. 6 used S.I. money and support to run the Hsu Clam intelligence ring in occupied China from March 1944 to the end of the war, and perhaps beyond.[154]

Although all this cloak-and-dagger activity sounds impressive, and valuable work was done by O.S.S. for the Fourteenth Air Force even in the first months of 1944, Donovan's establishment of an "independent" O.S.S. contingent within S.A.C.O. did not really break into the open. China was too complicated, too full of intrigue and nuance, for anything to happen that simply. As the men of R. and A. Chunking gradually discovered, it was one thing to force Tai Li to say he would cooperate and something else to get him actually to do so. R. and A. was supposed to run a cooperative research and analysis office in Chunking in conjunction with a team of Chinese researchers provided by Tai Li. When the R. and A. men arrived in early January 1944, they found an office containing a handful of Japanese publications and a group of young Chinese who were introduced as their research colleagues. The R. and A. men settled into their new office, and whiled away the hours sparring with Chinese officials about how much O.S.S. would pay to secure material from Tai Li that was worth studying. Meanwhile, the Chinese "researchers" in the office spent their time "reading the local English and Chinese newspapers, novels and other things" while "some read English out loud to improve their command of that foreign tongue." Gradually, the R. and A. men began to realize that no real research material was ever going to come from Tai Li and that if nothing were changed they would be lost for all eternity in a room in Chunking filled with letter writing, chess playing, "loud talking, chanting, and occasional bursts of song or whistling." By the end of April, Washington was again bombarded with pitiful messages from O.S.S. China urging that someone in a position of authority do something that would allow the O.S.S. men assembled in Chunking to perform a bit of actual war work.[155]

If Donovan's trip to China, and the shake-up he carried out there, had little lasting effect aside from the establishment of the new O.S.S. unit with the Fourteenth Air Force, the impact of the general's visit to S.E.A.C. headquarters was also not as great as appearances seemed to suggest. After leaving Chunking, Donovan had a number of long conferences with Lord Mountbatten and came away with the impression that the S.E.A.C. commander would create a large special operations force that would include substantial O.S.S. elements. A new O.S.S. command structure for the theater was immediately established with Colonel Heppner in charge, Donovan's old newspaper colleague Ed Taylor as his temporary deputy, and Col. Robert Hall directing R. and A. activity (which Mountbatten appeared to value highly). As was customary in O.S.S. when opportunity appeared to knock, Heppner immediately developed a broad spectrum of rather vague operational plans, and by the end of December O.S.S.-S.E.A.C. thought it was off and running.[156]

But beneath his charming veneer, Lord Mountbatten was less than entranced with either General Donovan or his organization. The new Southeast Asia commander reported to London in November 1943 that O.S.S. activities remained "a mystery" to him. When he learned of Donovan's impending visit, he remarked warily, like the good sailor he was, that the prospects were for "heavy water ahead." Mountbatten's primary task in Southeast Asia was to use the limited resources available to him to help Britain recover some of the prestige and influence it had lost during the debacle of 1941–42. The resources of Britain's ally would be welcome to Mountbatten in his pursuit of that goal, but any independent political action by the Americans would not. Lord Mountbatten expected the Chinese to attempt "to muscle us out of most of S.E.A.C." and thought that "O.S.S. and O.W.I. seem likely to adopt a neutral attitude and to expect us to show appreciation if they refrain from being hostile." The new S.E.A.C. commander was therefore determined to place all irregular warfare units in the theater, especially those of the Americans, under his direct supervision. He fulfilled the terms of the deal made by the C.C.S.

allowing direct O.S.S. intelligence reporting to Washington, but the M.O. work done by Donovan's organization was put under tight S.E.A.C. control, and all S.O. activities were concentrated in a newly created P Division that was firmly directed by Capt. G. A. Garnon Williams of the Royal Navy.[157]

This closely controlled British command structure allayed Mountbatten's fears of O.S.S. potential for mischief. The size and extent of the bureaucratic maze at Mountbatten's new headquarters would keep the O.S.S. chiefs harmlessly occupied for a considerable period. Since S.I. and S.O. already were sniping at each other in the Asian theaters and O.S.S.– S.E.A.C. also had strained relations with some of the American diplomats in the area, protracted squabbling was inevitable. In this atmosphere, actual operations against the enemy were limited, for as a British observer noted at the time, "how seldom one hears the word 'Japan' while such problems are afoot." Mountbatten's command did not move to its permanent headquarters in Ceylon until May 1944, and as late as the summer of that year, O.S.S. officials in Delhi and Ceylon were reporting to Washington less about what they were doing than what they intended to do once S.E.A.C. was actually in operation.[158]

So despite Donovan's visit and all the subsequent reorganizing and paper shuffling, little had changed for O.S.S. in Southeast Asia. After nearly two years of O.S.S. presence in the region, Detachment 101 was the only unit doing any fighting. Despite a few organizational changes, 101 remained largely unaffected by the bureaucracy in Delhi and Ceylon. During Donovan's visit, Colonel Eifler stepped down as 101 commander (apparently for medical reasons) and was replaced by another old 101 hand, Col. William Peers. The new 101 commander quickly set to work developing operational plans with General Stilwell, who was about to launch a new Burma campaign. When Stilwell's February attack began, Detachment 101 and the Kachins were immediately engaged in a vast guerrilla war. By June 1944, this bloody battle was reaching its climax as Stilwell and 101 gained control of the territory necessary for building a connecting link to the Burma Road, which would once again give China a land connection with the outside world.[159]

Showing great bravery, Detachment 101 had produced solid successes in the period up to June 1944. Across the Himalayas, the O.S.S. team working with the Fourteenth Air Force could also point to some real accomplishments during it first six months of activity. But these two operations were exceptional. Shortage of personnel and material contributed to the general failure, and the tendency of all the higher authorities in Washington to put Europe first played a part as well. But the most important factor was the Asian political riddle, for throughout the whole region more was required than the mere approval of an American theater commander for O.S.S. to go into action.

In the Mediterranean, O.S.S. could work through Ike's headquarters to prove itself useful and then continue to expand, with marked adjustments, when Wilson took over. In western Europe, O.S.S. had posts in both neutral countries and in England that could be enlarged once an American general became the supreme Allied commander. But in China, Stilwell was fighting so desperately to establish his own position that he could do little for anyone else, and in India no one really looked with sympathy on the idea of a strong, independent, American subversive warfare organization.

Therefore, as America entered the final fourteen months of the Second World War, there were really two O.S.S. organizations. Each of them was in a special situation, and each faced a distinct challenge. For the larger O.S.S. Europe, the primary task was to exploit the operational opportunities it now possessed to show what an integrated shadow warfare organization could actually accomplish and thereby help lay the foundations for O.S.S.'s postwar life. O.S.S. Asia, on the other hand, needed to cut through the political knots and produce shadow warfare operations on a sufficiently broad front to avoid having the war end on a downbeat for Donovan's organization. In late 1944 and on through 1945, although both groups strove mightily and seemed to come within a hair's breadth of success, the main prizes would ultimately elude them.

CHAPTER 6

Victory and Failure:
June 1944-September 1945

Question as to relative value of Office of
Strategic Services to Theater Commander
has arisen before House Appropriations
Committee in connection with their
consideration of O.S.S. budget estimate for
fiscal year 1946.
Your views requested urgently.

JOINT CHIEFS OF STAFF TO EISENHOWER,
MCNARNEY, WEDEMEYER, AND SULTAN
22 May 1945

The European War: June 1944–May 1945

The climactic year of the European war opened with a series of dramatic Allied victories. In Italy, following the fall of Rome on 4 June, the
Fifteenth Army Group drove the Germans out of central Italy and after
heavy fighting captured Florence in late August. Simultaneously, on the
Overlord invasion front, after spending six weeks widening the Normandy
beachhead, Eisenhower's armies broke through the German defenses in
late July and began to fan out across northern France. With an additional
mid-August Anglo-American landing in the south (Operation Anvil), the
German position in the west became untenable. By late September, the
Allies had cleared all French territory except the mountainous east central

region around the Vosges, and Eisenhower's forces had entered Belgium and at isolated points had crossed the German frontier. Meanwhile, in the east, the Red Army had launched a massive assault of its own that by the fall had knocked Bulgaria and Rumania out of the war and placed Soviet forces in central Poland and across the border into East Prussia.

As fall turned to winter, the extended supply lines, mountainous terrain, and poor weather gradually slowed the advance of all three Allied armies. The Red Army faced stiffening resistance in western Poland while in the south and west, the British and Americans were caught in battles of attrition around Bologna in Italy and along the western German border. During the last months of 1944 and the first part of 1945 the Allies suffered delay, heavy casualties, and frustration. Each of the three Allied powers was also caught in at least one embarrassment.

For the Americans, the reversal was purely military. Hitler's December offensive in the Bulge caught the United States command napping, and a great deal of effort that produced heavy losses was required to set things right by mid-January 1945. Britain took its own military bloodying in October 1944 when the British Parachute Army was badly mauled by strong German forces at Arnhem in Holland. On the other side of Europe, Britain also had to endure a great political trauma in the fall of 1944, for its attempt to prop up the royalist government in liberated Greece was met by strong opposition from the communist-led E.A.M. guerrilla army. Bitter fighting between Gen. Sir Ronald Scobie's forces and the Greek guerrillas ensued, and Britain appeared to be as much conquerer as liberator. Finally, a sordid episode in Poland during the fall of 1944 reflected badly on the Soviets. When Warsaw rose, Soviet armies were positioned immediately east of the city, but they did not budge during the two-month battle between the Polish Home Army and the German occupation forces. The Red Army only advanced after the Germans had suppressed the uprising. To virtually all observers, letting the Nazis crush the Poles before taking over the country was a blatant example of Stalin's crudest power politics.

The period of Allied military frustration ended in January–February 1945 with a renewed Soviet offensive in the east and an Anglo-American advance toward the Rhine. Once the American Ninth Army crossed the Rhine at Remagen in early March and additional crossings were made soon after by other American and British formations, the German defenses in the west began to crumble. The Fifteenth Army Group in Italy was unable to break through the German defenses until mid-April, but by then the British and American armies under Eisenhower in the west, and the Soviet forces in the east, had sliced deep into Germany, with American units already on the Elbe by 12 April.

Until the last moment, the Allied governments still feared that the Nazis would carry out some final atrocity against Allied captives or try to make a last-ditch stand in an Alpine redoubt. But with Hitler's suicide at the end of April, the pin holding together the pieces of the Third Reich was removed, and the Nazi system fell apart, leaving the German military chiefs, Gen. Alfred Jodl and Field Marshal Wilhelm Keitel, to surrender to the Allies on 8–9 May 1945.

O.S.S. European Reporting in the Summer of 1944

The operational units of O.S.S. obviously played a part in the Allied victory, and we will concern ourselves with their activities shortly. But through its reporting function, Donovan's organization also sought to influence policy decisions in Washington, and we will examine this aspect of O.S.S. European activities first. The range and the impact of O.S.S. reports on Europe rose and fell in three stages paralleling the battle phases. During the summer and early fall of 1944, O.S.S. dispatches primarily were concerned with immediate military and political issues, but winter 1944–45 saw European O.S.S. turning more of its attention to long-term questions of American policy and the place O.S.S. hoped to occupy in the postwar government. From the spring of 1945 until the demise of O.S.S. in September, the European activities of Donovan's organization were played out in an atmosphere of ever-greater discouragement and gloom.

The 1944 phase of rapid military advance found O.S.S. in a comparatively strong position. Its relations with other agencies were generally harmonious and its budget and manpower position intact. The O.S.S. director was nonetheless unable to work his organization directly into the mainstream of policy formulation. In June 1944, Donovan asked the J.C.S. for guidelines on the primary interest of the United States in Europe, suggesting that America should try to be a stabilizing influence between Russia and Britain. But the military authorities refused to reply. The generals still wanted to dodge foreign policy controversies and furthermore did not wish to make any statement suggesting that wartime agencies like O.S.S. would continue into the postwar period. Consequently, O.S.S.'s main hope of influencing U.S. policy toward Europe lay in the old game of distributing its reports to all and sundry.[1]

O.S.S. reports on Europe and the Mediterranean area ranged over subjects as diverse as living conditions in Naples and Arab discontent in Algiers, but most reports examined conditions in France and Germany. The reports on France focused on two major issues: the possibility of a communist drive for power and concern over the undemocratic character of de Gaulle's Provisional government. The majority of O.S.S. reports on France in the summer of 1944 tended to deemphasize the communist danger. Allen Dulles was nervous about the French Communists in the early fall of 1944, but even he concluded by the end of November that they had "overplayed" their hand and were weaker than they had been during the summer.[2]

Regarding de Gaulle, O.S.S. representatives, including Dulles, sent in many dispatches pointing to chinks in the French general's armor. In June, Donovan even suggested that de Gaulle not be recognized as head of the government but be given a military command under Eisenhower— a suggestion that struck the State Department's H. Freeman Matthews "as a pure pipe dream." However, not all O.S.S. opposed de Gaulle (although such tendencies surely existed), and Donovan did not always pander to President Roosevelt's deep dislike of the French general. There were O.S.S. men in R. and A. and other branches who strongly supported de Gaulle, and the comprehensive report on the French resistance prepared by O.S.S. in mid-July (and just classified by C.I.A.) expressed confidence in de Gaulle's commitment to democracy and observed that the best way to weaken the Communists was to recognize de Gaulle's Provisional government. O.S.S. sent this report to the president, and on at least one other occasion, Donovan urged Roosevelt to try to find some common ground with the French general.[3]

In contrast to its French reporting, the flow of O.S.S. intelligence on Germany in the summer and early fall of 1944 naturally leaned heavily toward such military matters as order-of-battle information, V–1s and V–2s, and the effects of allied air raids. On German military issues, as for the majority of other issues, the single most important O.S.S. station was Bern, where Dulles had at his disposal the documents obtained from Fritz Kolbe. The Kolbe reports contained highly useful information regarding German knowledge of the accuracy and effect of their V–2 attacks on London. To prevent the Germans from refining their aiming apparatus, the Allies were anxious to keep Berlin in the dark regarding the effect of the V–2 campaign, and the Kolbe material was highly esteemed by the J.C.S. and the British. Without forgetting that the Allies also gained relevant information on this matter from other high-level sources such as Ultra, it is clear that O.S.S. dispatches played a significant role in combatting the rockets and flying bombs.[4]

A broad range of less specifically military O.S.S. reports on Germany also reached Washington during the summer of 1944. Many of these concerned German morale and the relative position of Hitler and the generals, while from Kolbe Dulles was able to secure data regarding Japan and the German satellites. On occasion, the accuracy of statements contained in some of these O.S.S. reports was challenged by other intelligence organizations, but Donovan's people unquestionably uncovered German intelligence pearls in this period.[5]

Because of his connections with the German resistance, Dulles was in a good position to report on the 20 July attempt to assassinate Hitler. Prior to the actual bomb attempt, Dulles and other O.S.S. officials had sent Washington generally cautious reports regarding German opposition. Dulles had urged Washington to offer hope of considerate treatment to those who tried to overthrow the Nazis but had warned that the Goerdeler–Beck circle was staunchly anti-Communist and anti-Russian. The Bern representative, like most American and Soviet observers, was skeptical about all German resistance movements. After holding secret talks with resistance spokesman Adam von Trott zu Solz during June, American officials in Stockholm were so suspicious and so confused that they thought von Trott was "possibly a Nazi propagandist."[6]

Whether Dulles provided the German resistance with a clear picture of Anglo-American policy prior to the attempt on Hitler's life has long been a matter of controversy and conjecture. The O.S.S. reports now available suggest that he did not give overt encouragement to the anticommunist inclinations of the Beck circle but may have gone further than official American policy by hinting to the plotters that they could anticipate a friendly reception in Washington if their assassination effort succeeded. Dulles asked Washington for permission to give such overt assurances, and when the response was silence, kept asking again and again. When this fact is combined with the postwar claims of resistance survivors that they had received hints from Dulles of a favorable Western attitude, the scales indeed seem to tip in that direction.[7]

But it should be added that toward contacts in Bern from Germany's satellites (for which more detailed information is currently available), Dulles definitely took a hard line. Although in dealing with purported agents of the Axis satellites he was not subject to the same tight controls as the American military attachés, Dulles had no patience with the tendency of Hungarian and other emissaries to conclude "that because their table manners are better than those of their neighbors" they deserved special treatment. In mid-July, the O.S.S. representative in Bern suggested that the best way to deal with these "past masters in [the] tactics of passive resistance and quiet obstructionism" would be to "knock these ideas out of their heads and bring them down to the cold realities of the military necessities of the situation."[8]

After 20 July, when the bomb placed by Count von Stauffenberg went off in the Wolfsschanze, O.S.S. observers seem to have lost a measure of their clear vision. On 26 July, William Langer's brother Walter sent Donovan a five-page report claiming that the whole assassination attempt was a fake staged to elicit German popular sympathy for the Führer. Dulles was not that far off base, but many of his reports immediately following the attempt were unclear as to what the plotters had actually done and were even more confused about the prospect for additional coups. In an effort to explain what had happened and what was likely to follow, Dulles fell back on his anticommunist convictions. In a series of July and August reports, he warned that with the failure of the "western oriented" Beck–Goerdeler–Stauffenberg resistance effort, Germans opposed to the Nazis would turn eastward and look to *Freies Deutschland* for succor. Then in mid-August, Dulles was told by a resistance survivor that at the time of the bomb attempt, Stauffenberg had already given up on the West and was prepared to deal with the Soviet Union. The claim that Stauffenberg had shifted the resistance in a more pro-Soviet direction (which appears actually to have been false) compelled Dulles to do some immediate backing and filling. However, the conclusion that he ultimately drew from Stauffenberg's supposed eastward lean was to redouble his effort to persuade Washington to launch a new propaganda campaign to woo the Germans away from communism and the Soviet Union.[9]

O.S.S.'s Lost Opportunities in Washington. Fall/Winter: 1944–45

September 1944: Stimson–Morgenthau battles over occupation policy for Germany

Many of Dulles's reports on the 20 July plot did not reach Washington prior to December 1944. Therefore, before jumping to the conclusion that these or any other O.S.S. reports set U.S. policy on a particular (and especially anti-Soviet) course, we should note that important developments altered the position and influence of O.S.S. in Washington during this, the

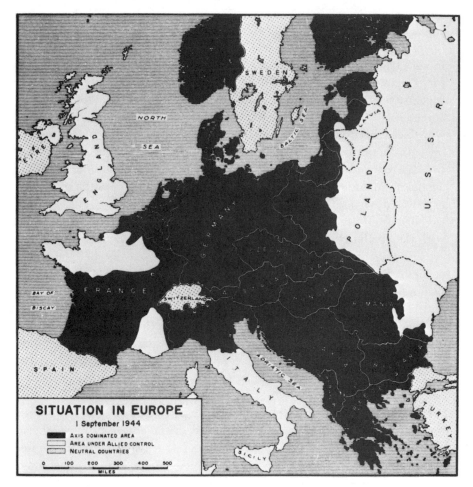

Figure 3.   The Situation in Europe, 1 September 1944

second phase, in the mature life of Donovan's organization. When in late July and early August, the Allied advance from Normandy showed promise of producing a complete German collapse, a victory fever gripped much of official Washington. One consequence was a desire to prepare for the postwar period by gradually abolishing many emergency wartime organizations. Regular bureaucrats, congressmen, and tax lobbyists were agreed that the sooner such reductions were made the better, and F.D.R., who faced his fourth presidential election in November 1944, was not unsympathetic to this thinking. As a result, O.S.S. found itself forced to prepare reduced personnel and budget estimates, and like other wartime agencies—including S.O.E. in Britain—had to face the question of whether it would have a postwar existence.[10]

Unlike such organizations as O.W.I., which simply fainted when faced with the challenge, O.S.S. fought for its right to life. Concern about the organization of American long-term intelligence already had begun to occupy officials within and without O.S.S. in early fall 1944. In October, Donovan brought forth a general recommendation (upon which R. and A. had lavished much attention) for the establishment of a postwar central intelligence agency that would report directly to the president. The long and checkered career of this proposal will receive additional consideration in chapter 9, but a brief survey is necessary here since some aspects of the matter bear on the impact made by O.S.S. European reporting in the fall of 1944.[11]

Donovan's plan for a central intelligence agency was bitterly opposed by army and navy intelligence officers, and in the course of November a series of skirmishes in the J.C.S. committees left it badly battered. Representatives of most regular civilian agencies except the F.B.I. showed themselves more sympathetic to the general idea of a central intelligence agency than did the military, but no one outside O.S.S. was prepared to accept Donovan's plan *in toto*. Many officials in the State Department were worried that an independent central intelligence agency would encroach upon the traditional prerogatives of the department. The president, though suspicious of some of the irregular activities of O.S.S., was definitely inclined toward a greater consolidation of intelligence than had existed before World War II. Yet even Roosevelt appears not to have been ready to go as far as Donovan. Then, in January and February 1945, while the O.S.S. director was in Europe (in part seeking information on intelligence centralization from the British), Donovan's plan was leaked to the press, presumably by the American military. Anti-administration newspapers, led by the *Chicago Tribune* and the *Washington Times*

Herald, had a field day with Donovan's plans for what they characterized as a "super spy system" and an American "Gestapo Agency." [12]

In March 1945, the military opponents of Donovan's scheme seized their chance, and by citing the adverse climate created by the press campaign, succeeded in delaying consideration of the proposal. Donovan quite understandably felt he had been fouled because the plan never again received a full airing. The shelving of Donovan's proposal was highly significant to the long-term development of intelligence systems in the United States, but Donovan's 1944–45 campaign to create a postwar central intelligence organization also had an important effect on the focus and influence of O.S.S. itself. To advance his postwar plans, the O.S.S. director was anxious to be as intimate as possible with the State Department in the fall of 1944. The diplomats, highly suspicious of every rival and sensitive about O.S.S. criticisms of their activities, also felt that Donovan was often much too reckless. Yet when compared with some other irregular secret wartime organizations, such as that of John Franklin Carter, O.S.S. seemed a paragon of virtue. [13]

Carter had managed to intertwine some of his projects with those of other intelligence organizations, including O.S.S.'s. One of his major projects, developing biographies of 10,000 top Nazis, was done in cooperation with Donovan's people. It contained some useful work (as well as such serious omissions as the name of Adolf Eichmann) but was tainted by Carter's obsessive desire to get information out of Hitler's old crony, Ernst "Putzi" Hanfstaengl. The Carter group was handing out $5,000 per month in 1944 for the care and feeding of "Mr. Sedgwick," in the distant hope that Putzi would provide useful data on the Nazis and improve American psychological warfare. Initially enthusiastic, F.D.R. (who had known Putzi at Harvard) turned cautious on the Hanfstaengl project in early 1944 and later in the year funds for Mr. Sedgwick were cut off and he was handed over to the British. [14]

Despite its peripheral role in the Putzi affair, to a number of State Department officials O.S.S. seemed a sober alternative to the likes of Carter. O.S.S. counterintelligence (X-2) sent many reports to branches of the State Department during this period, and although a number of them appear to have been little more than rumor mongering, sections of the department such as the Foreign Activity Correlations Division, were eager to get them, and on occasion profusely thanked X-2. R. and A. also continued to supply State with numerous reports, and along with F.N.B., courted State Department officials, attempting to get them to declare that O.S.S. reporting was vital to the department. R. and A. was the most successful O.S.S. branch in securing State Department endorsements, and Langer's people made additional strides in working their way into German occupation planning.[15]

Although we will consider R. and A.'s special survival efforts in greater detail in chapter 8, notice should be taken of the shift Langer had made by the fall of 1944 in his branch's activities from immediate support for military operations to projects that would help R. and A. continue in the postwar era. By late January 1945, he declared in a special R. and A. directive that "the obligation of the present leadership of the Branch, of the Divisions and the Outpost, is to establish objectives that look forward to a long-range future, rather than to be satisfied with only plans for immediate and terminating objectives." Given this outlook, R. and A. reports in late 1944 and 1945 cannot be considered merely as instances of wartime activity. R. and A.'s overriding concern was survival, which inevitably added shadings to its reporting and above all to the marketing of its reports.[16]

Edward Stettinius, who served as acting secretary of state during the frequent illnesses of Cordell Hull in the latter half of 1944 and was then made secretary when Hull resigned in December, had a high regard for Donovan and O.S.S. Stettinius welcomed assistance from the general's organization and was extremely generous in return. In October 1944, when Langer and Donovan asked for a State Department letter of endorsement to strengthen their position with the Bureau of the Budget, Stettinius not only agreed but allowed O.S.S. to write the letter and merely signed it![17]

With such a friend, O.S.S. was able to slip some of its reports into various phases of the State Department paper flow in the fall of 1944 despite the suspicions of department traditionalists. Political issues were coming to the fore, and even though the State Department and Edward Stettinius were hardly towers of strength, the era in which international political questions could be deferred, or handed over to the J.C.S. to be settled on the basis of military necessity, was definitely coming to an end. Here, then, was an opportunity to increase O.S.S.'s immediate importance and assure its claim to a significant postwar role. If Donovan had been a steady, hard-boiled organization chief, O.S.S. might well have cut a wide swath in American policy during fall 1944. In fact, though enthusiastic and hard-driving, Donovan was far from steady. A British Foreign Office characterization prepared in the early summer of 1945 stressed that he was "more of a fighter than an administrator, with an Irishman's wit and mercurial temperament." The ethnic reference was surely gratuitous, but the emphasis on a fighting heart, shaky administrative skills, and a mercurial temperament was correct. Donovan was too eager for combat, had too much restless energy, and was too changeable in his moods and interests to remain in Washington for months at a time doing the dreary job of gradually nudging his organization along to increase its influence and establish its position on strong foundations. Having spent a few days or weeks in Washington looking over his organization, swapping ideas with the heads of other departments, and chatting with the president, the general was off again, touring O.S.S. installations from Europe to Asia and getting as close as possible to actual combat.[18]

These overseas tours were not merely pleasure jaunts. Donovan undoubtedly used his influence on many occasions to expand the range of O.S.S. overseas activities. S.I. intelligence in Europe, for instance, depended heavily on close cooperation with other Allied intelligence services, and Donovan's personal appearances certainly helped give his organization more influence there. Nonetheless, this peripatetic life meant that Ned Buxton, Charles Cheston, and their associates were left to mind the store at least half the time in 1944 and 1945. The administrative machinery of O.S.S. was firmly established by this time, and routine relations with other agencies and with the J.C.S. functioned smoothly. But Donovan's deputies lacked the influence and authority necessary to mount a strong drive to increase the role of O.S.S. in American councils.[19]

The overall impact of O.S.S. fluctuated with the prospects for Donovan's postwar intelligence plan, the favor of the president, the effect of individual reports, and the advantages sometimes garnered from connections with the old boys' network. But from the fall of 1944 the president was failing, and in January 1945 Donovan's intelligence plan was badly wounded. O.S.S. influence was not rising, no basic reform was possible, and the organization continued to make an impact only through side roads and byways.

This situation makes it impossible to judge accurately the broad imprint of O.S.S. reporting on American policy formation in the winter of 1944–45. In addition, the irregular procedures used by O.S.S. left a number of loose ends in late 1944 that led to unpleasant skirmishes with other agencies, and allowed O.S.S. to be stung in the intelligence game. Since O.S.S. could not categorically reject any action that might score a success, adventurers always had room to operate, and these activities often brought down the wrath of the State Department and other agencies. When Donovan quietly slipped de Gaulle's intelligence chief André Wavrin (better known by his alias Colonel Passy) into the United States in December 1944, both the F.B.I. and the State Department objected, and F.D.R. himself finally ordered him to leave. State also categorically refused to join with O.S.S. in its efforts to secretly arrange the publication of the diaries of Mussolini's foreign minister (and son-in-law) Count Galeazzo Ciano.[20]

Proposals that Donovan's own people came to characterize as ridiculous were sometimes sent to the State Department and then bounced back to O.S.S. Unseemly quarrels occurred over allegations by O.S.S.–X-2 and British Security that State Department missions had been penetrated by Axis agents. One such messy affair in Mozambique prompted the American consul to remark that he felt it unfair for the counterintelligence people to pick on him, making accusations against his Portuguese clerk when the British consulate general employed "a Polish Jew and well known pimp."[21]

These adventures in unpleasant controversy and ethnic slurs did little for the O.S.S. image, but the loose ways of Donovan's organization also created security problems. On at least one occasion, O.S.S. was badly taken. In October and November 1944, Donovan's organization recruited an Italian civilian named Virgillo Scattolini, who supposedly had high-level connections at the Vatican. The man actually had no important Vatican contacts and therefore sold O.S.S. a series of sham reports. One group of Scattolini creations, labeled the "Black" series, discussed supposed Vatican doings. Many of these were widely circulated, and dozens went to the president between November 1944 and April 1945. Since along with masses of fabricated gossip about Vatican internal politics, the "Black" reports contained some anticommunist comments, there is a remote possibility that they exerted a tangential influence on American policy decisions.[22]

More significantly, the "Black" reports indicate that O.S.S. security was dangerously porous. These were very clumsy forgeries. Yet to the ultimate embarrassment of U.S. intelligence officials, they were accepted as genuine and through O.S.S. channels reached the highest levels of the American government. Initially, the State Department was as badly fooled by Scattolini as was O.S.S. Assistant Secretary of State James Dunn reported to O.S.S. on 13 February 1945 that he appreciated the reports and "looked forward to receiving them." O.S.S. officials pointed proudly to the Scattolini operation—it was even featured in a recommendation that Colonel Glavin be decorated—and when in the course of 1945 Scattolini went too far in creative nonsense, thereby arousing State Department suspicions, Donovan blamed the failure on a subagent.[23]

Since Scattolini's crude handiwork moved along so well, it is surely not impossible that other fabricated, or planted, information worked its way into Washington's policy decisions through the multitude of varied and irregular channels that O.S.S. was forced to use to bring its material to the attention of American officials. Until the O.S.S. files are finally opened

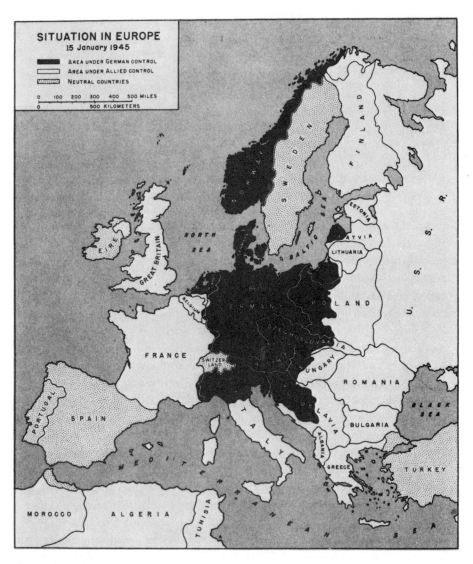

Figure 4. The Situation in Europe, 15 January 1945

completely and we are able to see the raw sources of the information used in S.I. and X-2 reports, doubt must hover over every consideration of O.S.S.'s impact on American policy for Europe as well as other areas.

O.S.S. European Political Reporting and Propaganda Activity: Winter 1944–Spring 1945

December 1944: The Battle of the Bulge; British–E.A.M. clash in Greece
February 1945: Yalta Conference
April 1945: Death of Franklin Roosevelt

Among the basic issues facing U.S. policymakers in the winter of 1944, the state of German morale and the possibility of a Nazi collapse were among the most important. O.S.S. representatives in Europe sent many reports to Washington tracing the gradual decline of Axis morale. These reports were generally cautious; O.S.S. observers were initially less inclined to see an imminent German collapse than were some optimists in Washington. In spite of his anticommunist warnings, Dulles had become more wary of dickering with Germans on the issues of resistance and surrender, and it appears that the British consul in Zurich was the only British or American representative who may have been encouraging German hopes for a separate peace in the winter of 1944–45.[24]

As always, the covert propaganda staffs of the British and O.S.S.–M.O. were pouring forth a flood of rumors, many of which were so complex and double-edged that they made the task of judging what was going on in Axis countries extremely difficult. In mid-August, Rumor Directive 115 instructed the purveyors of black propaganda to spread the tale that the Nazis were trying to use atrocities to provoke the British and the Americans into *retaining* the policy of unconditional surrender so that the German people would continue to feel that there was no alternative but to fight on. What anyone in O.S.S. or P.W.E. hoped to accomplish by spinning such contrived wheels within wheels is difficult to imagine. But the black propagandists had by this time moved off into a special world of their own. It was the Chief of London M.O. Fred Oechsner who had the idea of preparing a psychological study of Hitler to guide his covert propaganda operations. The resulting work by Walter Langer, which was known in O.S.S. as the "spiced-up" version and cost the organization $2,500 in Langer's fees, was heralded after the war as an Allied intelligence project prepared to predict the course Hitler would follow as he approached his end. In fact, it was just another of M.O.'s wild schemes, using juicy tidbits from the Führer's life to addle the brains of the population of central Europe.[25]

American intelligence gatherers and analysts had many more practical concerns. What top British and American officials wanted to know in the winter of 1944 was whether Germany was about to collapse. A combined R. and A. and M.I.D. study in August had concluded that German resistance would "not continue beyond 1 December 1944." But since this paper was in part based on the claim "that by the end of 1944 the size of the German army will be substantially decreased," many in the military were unimpressed. When one officer in the Operations Division came across the statement about the declining size of the German Army, he noted in the margin "marvelous my dear Watson." As German resistance stiffened in October, prophets in R. and A. and M.I.D. became more cautious and by early November reached a second profound conclusion, deciding that unless the Allies made "a major breakthrough," German resistance was likely to continue until spring. Even this was too optimistic for Franklin Roosevelt, who had cautioned Budget Director Harold Smith in late August that the Bureau of the Budget should not move too quickly on demobilization plans because the president felt it "quite likely that at least six months would be required before the end of the European war" and that Germany might even hold out for another year.[26]

Unable to get much guidance from O.S.S. and other intelligence groups on when the European war would end, American policymakers turned their attention to the equally worrisome question of *how* it would end. The general consensus of R. and A. and M.I.D. studies was that any German government was "unlikely to surrender" and that hostilities would peter out in an atmosphere dominated by last stands and final atrocities. There was much apprehension among the British and American leaders, as well as the governments in exile, that P.O.W.s and foreign workers in German hands might be butchered. There was also a strong belief in Anglo-American circles that the Nazis would establish defensive redoubts in the Alps and that when these were overcome the Nazi Party would go underground.

Few O.S.S. reports from Europe seem to have touched on the question of final massacre, but from September on, many dispatches, especially from Bern, predicted that redoubts would be established and that the Nazi Party was preparing to submerge itself and survive. When in October 1944 the Nazi leaders learned of Henry Morgenthau's plan to "pasturize" Germany by destroying her industry, and Goebbels used the Morgenthau plan to flay the German people with the threat that they would be decimated by minions of the American Treasury Department, Dulles contended that the Nazis would in consequence surely fight to the end and then go underground. Although many Bern dispatches declared that the Morgenthau plan was a disaster for Anglo-American psychological warfare, O.S.S. was never loath to find a customer for its products, and from January 1945 on, Dulles's reports on Germany—even those contending that Britain and America should entice German sentiment away from the Russians—were regularly sent to Henry Morgenthau. The secretary of the treasury was neither cowed nor overly impressed. Once when the president sent him an O.S.S. memorandum setting forth the importance of German farm implement production for the European economy, Morgenthau merely replied to the White House, "So what?" On another level, the theme constantly reiterated in O.S.S. dispatches of the danger of a Nazi underground was grist for Morgenthau's mill, and he may have used it to strengthen his demand that extreme putative measures were required in Germany during Allied occupation.[27]

The president was also much exercised by this threat, and in September 1944, Donovan used Dulles's dispatches on the underground danger as the basis for a plan (sent to the White House on 2 September) that put counterintelligence in the center of O.S.S. operational plans for Germany. Donovan proposed to mount a massive clandestine campaign against the anticipated Nazi underground, a plan that, parenthetically, would provide full-time O.S.S. employment in central Europe for a long time to come. Since the proposal rested on Donovan's knowledge of Roosevelt's "concern that Nazism should not survive this war by going underground," it gained the support of men like Morgenthau and was rapidly approved by the J.C.S. Although certain groups in O.S.S. were not enthralled with the idea, desiring to stake the organization's case more on the Asian war and the postwar need for a worldwide intelligence and counterintelligence service, Donovan continued to push his anti-Nazi underground program vigorously. Only in the spring of 1945, when it became obvious to even the truest believers that the German population was sinking into apathy and that no serious Nazi underground was developing, did the general finally give up and go on to other matters.[28]

While it took some time to show that Donovan had picked up the wrong end of the stick in his enthusiasm for combatting a putative Nazi underground, a serious error made by Allen Dulles regarding the German Ardennes offensive, later known as the Battle of the Bulge, revealed itself more rapidly. In November and early December, Hitler had brushed aside the objections of some of his generals and had concentrated a large panzer force opposite the American First Army in the Ardennes in an offensive gamble to split the British and American armies. When the German blow fell in late December, it achieved complete surprise and initially made substantial headway.

German success in the Bulge resulted primarily from the failure of Anglo-American combat intelligence (perhaps spoiled by overdependence on Ultra) to detect signs of the German buildup. As we will see below, if the American First Army had made use of O.S.S. tactical resistance units for intelligence purposes as other American units under S.H.A.E.F. did, the Germans might have been more effectively thwarted. As it was, the First Army was caught unaware and suffered unnecessarily heavy casualties.

Even though they had been insufficiently vigilant in this instance, the American army commanders had realized since November that the campaign against the Wehrmacht was no longer a romp. Slow and bloody plodding characterized the drive toward the Rhine in early winter 1944, and even the resistance forces in what remained of German-occupied France were told to bide their time because the Nazis were strong enough to cope easily with a general uprising. All the old weapons that had been earlier employed to help wear down a tough and stubborn enemy had to be put to use once more. A black rumor campaign to encourage strikes among German railroad workers was tried, even at this impossibly late date, and another major effort was mounted to get as many children and parents as possible to ride the Reichsbahn to increase congestion on the lines and make work easier for the Allied air forces.[29]

But Allen Dulles failed to grasp that Allied forces were encountering stubborn resistance, and he sent Washington a number of reports in late November that, though sometimes tentative, declared that Germany was on the edge of disintegration. Then in early December, Dulles supplemented these dispatches with a group of cables declaring that Hitler was so ill and emotionally unstable that the "main authority in Germany" had passed to Himmler, Goebbels, and Bormann. On the very day when Hitler sprang his surprise in the Bulge, Dulles was still reporting that German resistance was nearing its end and that the Führer's position had deteriorated so badly that "Himmler proposes to keep him in the upper background as a sort of von Hindenburg." This whopping intelligence error would have been an embarrassment even if no one of importance in Washington had read these reports, but their effects may have gone farther. In the winter of 1944, O.S.S. Washington was hailing Dulles as its top overseas representative, and the full texts of the reports were sent to many agencies in the American capital, including the War Department, the J.C.S., the State Department, and the office of the president. Margin marking on the War Department copies of two of the cables shows that at least there someone was reading them. O.S.S. was so proud of its Bern reporter that copies of his 6 and 16 December messages describing the supposed chaos in Germany and the de facto fall of Hitler were sent to the Soviet government as items of especially great importance.[30]

It would be absurd to contend on the basis of the scanty evidence that Dulles's reporting contributed directly to the surprise achieved by the Germans in the Bulge. But he was definitely looking in the wrong direction, and his reports may have helped diffuse the hard-boiled skepticism needed by top American officials to deal with someone as tough and crafty as Hitler. Dulles had swallowed Hitler's cover stories for the Bulge offensive, and despite his subsequent attempts to explain away his error, this incident could hardly have helped his reputation, or that of O.S.S., within the inner circle of the American government.[31]

Events in eastern Europe and the Balkans also tended to push O.S.S. to the periphery of American policymaking during the fall and winter of 1944. The main international political issue agitating Washington at this time was the fate of Poland, now passing under Soviet occupation. O.S.S. had given some support to the Polish resistance since 1942, but it had done so only through British channels. In July 1944 and again in September, Donovan put forth plans for direct O.S.S. operations in Poland, but before these could be considered, the Warsaw uprising cut short any prospect of an independent American operation. Consequently, during one of the most dramatic resistance actions of the war, O.S.S. was on the sidelines and was not involved in the anguished Anglo-American policy struggles over Poland. For the long-term image of the Donovan organization, this may have been just as well, for the Polish resistance question was a tough, and ultimately tragic, business.[32]

While O.S.S. stood aside during the Polish crisis, it was squarely in the middle of the political difficulties that erupted in the Balkans during late 1944 and early 1945. In fact, from Churchill's point of view, O.S.S. itself was a major cause of the trouble. Allied military policy still emphasized that the primary objective was to tie down the maximum Axis forces in the area so that the main German armies could be smashed in northern Europe. But this consideration and concern about German atrocities in the region, slipped a notch as the politics of resistance took center stage. Britain's effort to restore the Greek monarchy sharpened opposition from the leftist resistance movement (E.A.M.–E.L.A.S.), and the British landings in Greece in October were followed by a full-scale clash between the British and E.A.M.–E.L.A.S. in December. The U.S. government stood aloof from the British operation, clucking disapprovingly about British imperialism and hence driving London to distraction. Self-conscious about their activities and angered by the tone of moral superiority adopted by their ally, British officials were seeking a scapegoat long before General Scobie's forces came to blows with E.A.M.–E.L.A.S. in December. From late August, Foreign Office officials in Cairo complained bitterly not only about O.S.S. Greek-Americans "who are hostile to us and no doubt cause trouble" but also about Donovan's alleged statement that he would not use his organization "as a tool of British imperialism."[33]

Many Greek-Americans did work for O.S.S. and, along with Donovan, most tended to worry less about a communist threat in Greece than about the risks the British were running in trying to foist the Greek king on an unwilling population. B.S.C. officials in New York tried to convince London that there really was no O.S.S. intrigue; American governmental and public opinion was overwhelmingly opposed to British policy in Greece, and Donovan's men were merely giving voice to the prevailing American view. Some British officials grudgingly conceded that O.S.S. "misdeeds" were the result of "crusading enthusiasm" rather than a diabolical political plan, but Churchill, frustrated and angered by American press critics (especially Drew Pearson) was determined to take his revenge. On 24 August, he sent to S.H.A.E.F. a letter for Donovan, who was touring the continent, warning him that "very formidable trouble" was brewing over O.S.S. activities in the Middle Eastern theater and that if the matter was not set right by the general, Churchill was going straight to the president. The letter arrived at S.H.A.E.F. too late to catch the O.S.S. chief, who had just departed from Europe. The only satisfaction the prime minister received was a note from Gen. Bedell Smith stating that he too was "worried" by Donovan's "predilection for political intrigue" and had learned that it was best to keep "a firm hand on him."[34]

In late September, Churchill poured out his criticisms of O.S.S. to Roosevelt at the second Quebec conference, but the president, who was at least as doubtful as Donovan about British support of royalist pretensions in Greece, gave the prime minister little comfort. O.S.S.–S.I., R. and A., and X-2 missions remained in Greece (along with an O.G. unit that Donovan had finally managed to get in), where they cooperated reasonably well with British forces, assisting in the evacuation of British prisoners from E.A.M.–E.L.A.S. territory during the fighting and even providing General Scobie's forces with intelligence information. As late as January 1945, however, London was still agitated by what it alleged were (and what in fact seem to have been) O.S.S. leaks to the press of information that showed British operations in Greece in the worst possible light. The whole O.S.S.–Greek affair went a long way toward dissipating the goodwill that Donovan had earlier built up in London.[35]

O.S.S. also had trouble with the British over Yugoslavia, but here the

ideological sensitivities were reversed. After abandoning the collaborationist Mihajlović in late 1943, the British were anxious to provide as
much aid as possible to the partisans, thereby increasing British political
influence with Tito so that a mixed partisan–royalist government might
be established after the war. Churchill was particularly eager to establish
an effective partnership with Tito and to that end made the famous 50/
50 zone of influence agreement with Stalin in the fall of 1944.[36]

But the Americans did not have such distinct or impassioned concerns
in Yugoslavia. United States officials in the Mediterranean tended to look
askance at British and Soviet jockeying for position in Yugoslavia, especially since these two governments were frequently using Lend-Lease
supplies in their effort to curry Tito's favor. The head of the O.S.S. mission to Tito was impressed by partisan military capability and organization but in July 1944 urged the Big Powers to take the lead in ending the
conflict between partisan forces and those of Mihajlović.[37]

In August 1944, an O.W.I. (not O.S.S.) representative in Cairo, Reuben
Markham, mounted a blistering attack on Anglo-American aid to the
communist Tito, which reverberated all the way to the offices of the
J.C.S. In late August, O.S.S. strengthened its mission to Tito, but within a
fortnight Churchill was appealing to President Roosevelt to control the
"strong Mihajlović lobby" he claimed was being run by Donovan and
O.S.S. Two days later, the prime minister protested even more vigorously
when he discovered that O.S.S. had sent an intelligence mission in to Mihajlović forces. The president yielded, admitting that he had made an
error in authorizing the S.I. mission, and ordered Donovan to withdraw
his men. Although the president was firm enough on this point to override
O.S.S., it is obvious that he was far less pro-Tito and anti-Mihajlović than
the prime minister. When Donovan sent Roosevelt stamps that had been
gathered in Mihajlović's territory by O.S.S. missions (which should not
have been there), the president's reaction was merely to note that he was
"delighted" to get these additions to his collection.[38]

O.S.S. was thus permitted to act with less than deliberate speed in pulling its intelligence mission out of Mihajlović's area, which created more
political trouble. The head of the mission, Robert McDowell, was a conservative anti-Titoist who apparently encouraged Mihajlović to believe
that Britain and America would ultimately assist him in his struggle with
the communists. During his stay with Mihajlović, McDowell also consented
to contacts from German agents who presented proposals for a separate
peace between the Nazis and the Anglo-American forces. It took considerable work by O.S.S. to calm Soviet suspicion of these activities, and an
even greater effort was required to keep McDowell from unleashing a

general policy controversy over aid to the partisans when he finally came out of Yugoslavia in November 1944.[39]

By this time, the British were so committed to their pro-Tito policy and so fearful of the possible political consequences of Mihajlović's remaining in the country that in mid-November Harold Macmillan, on instructions from the Foreign Office, secretly asked the American diplomatic representative at Caserta to have O.S.S. slip Mihajlović out of Yugoslavia. The Americans decided to reject this proposal as too hot for anyone to handle, but they continued to try to find a compromise solution to the Yugoslav civil strife. O.S.S. played a role in the designation of the Ban of Croatia (Ivan Šubašić) as premier of the Yugoslav government in exile in an attempt to reconcile the various Yugoslav groups at home and abroad. Bernard Yarrow, the O.S.S. liaison man with the governments in exile in London, enjoyed good relations with most of the principles there, including young King Paul and Šubašić. Yarrow sent O.S.S. Washington copious reports on every twist and turn in London–Yugoslav politics, including the minutes of secret meetings that King Paul and Šubašić held with the British.[40]

But Britain and America soon learned that their activities were largely beside the point. Tito had put together a military machine that could stand up to the Germans, and he was not going to be deterred by the likes of Šubašić or Mihajlović. Furthermore, he quickly made it clear to S.O.E. and O.S.S. that he would not tolerate Anglo-American infringement on Yugoslav sovereignty or his authority. In September 1944, he forbade O.S.S.–S.O.E. liaison with partisan units below the level of army corp headquarters, and despite complaints from London and Washington and a threat to withhold supplies, he made this order stick. By the end of the year, O.S.S. representatives reported that Tito was firmly in the saddle, and though he desired recognition by the Western Allies, was unlikely to relax his control over the country, or change his program, to get it. O.S.S. and British intelligence drew the obvious conclusion, and as the war against the Germans moved into northern Yugoslavia, their representatives in the country spent more time filing reports about the partisans than they did studying the retreating Germans.[41]

While Tito was extending his communist system over Yugoslavia, Moscow was establishing its own regimes in every area conquered by the Red Army from Estonia to Bulgaria. East–West uneasiness resulted, especially over the fate of Poland, and many European O.S.S. reports to Washington, as well as R. and A. reports prepared in the American capital, focused on the new authoritarian governments being established in eastern Europe. However, the tone of the reports was far from hysterical, and a number of them contended that some of the movement to the Left in Bulgaria and Rumania was caused by popular demand rather than Soviet pressure. Signs of nervousness about a possible rise of communism all over Europe appeared in a number of memoranda, but most O.S.S. papers dealing with eastern Europe centered on matters that had little to do with East–West relations, such as Nazi threats to Jews in Hungary and the efforts of British and American counterintelligence organizations to track down German agents in the area.[42]

Central eastern Europe was, however, too complex and unstable in the winter of 1944–45 to make life easy for intelligence people. Both S.I. and F.N.B. were concerned about the future actions of the Czech government, especially after Eduard Beneš, head of the government in exile, told Yarrow in October that although he was not inclining toward communism, he was absolutely determined to expel Germans from the Sudetenland and at all costs to get along with the Soviets to avoid ever again being "faced by another Munich." On the other hand, some anti-Nazi emigrés in R. and A., including Franz Neumann, had started wondering aloud whether a hard line toward Germany, including loss of her eastern lands to Poland and Czechoslovakia, was desirable since it would "make the revival of democracy if not impossible, at least extremely difficult."[43]

In late 1944, O.S.S. authorities were also having trouble securing Soviet approval for the entrance of O.S.S. teams into the Balkan states, now under Red Army control. Donovan ultimately managed to secure Russian authorization for the operation of some O.S.S. units in southeast European countries, but these experiences heightened his suspicions of Soviet intentions. By late October 1944, the O.S.S. director was urging Harriman to press Moscow to soften its repressive policies in Rumania, and a few indications from early 1945 suggest that O.S.S. intelligence planning in Turkey had already begun to turn away from Berlin and was focusing on Moscow.[44]

However, it is much too easy to say that O.S.S. and its chief were merely incipient Cold Warriors. Both S.O.E. and O.S.S. were anxious to increase liaison with Soviet agencies, and despite some rather well-publicized German overtures to the Soviets in October, O.S.S. did not believe that there was any danger of a Nazi–Soviet separate peace in the winter of 1944–45. A special R. and A. study commissioned by Langer in January 1945 concluded that although the Soviets were expansionist, they also were inclined to solution by partition and would accept some compromises and blendings of political and economic systems.[45]

The atmosphere in which O.S.S. had to operate in the transitional winter of 1944–45 was well characterized by a remark made to a group of

Anglo-American military leaders in mid-January 1945 by that gifted expert on East–West relations, Joseph Stalin. Commenting on his Western allies' need for a diversionary Soviet offensive during the last stage of the German Bulge offensive, Stalin said: "We have no treaty but we are comrades. It is proper and also sound selfish policy that we should help each other in times of difficulty. It would be foolish for me to stand aside and let the Germans annihilate you; they would only turn back on me when you were disposed of. Similarly it is to your interest to do everything possible to keep the Germans from annihilating me."[46]

Reporting in the Third and Final Phase in O.S.S.'s European Life: Spring–Summer 1945

May: Defeat of Germany—V.E. Day
August: Defeat of Japan—V.J. Day

Stalin's statement described precisely the general situation in winter 1944–45, when the Germans still had some strength and options. However, it no longer held true in the spring and summer of 1945, as German power withered away and East and West were left to face each other in central Europe. American attention was divided, with Japan replacing Germany as the chief object of military concern and questions of European combat gradually yielding to those of occupation. The death of President Roosevelt in mid-April put an additional pale of uncertainty over American policies and prospects.

The end of European hostilities inevitably produced changes in O.S.S. Many of its combat personnel were transferred to Asia, and the loss of F.D.R. ended the close connection that Donovan had enjoyed with the White House, boding ill for the future of the general's organization. The flow of O.S.S. dispatches from Europe continued, and Donovan managed to deliver some of them to the offices of the new president, Harry Truman, and Secretary of State, James F. Byrnes (who took office in June 1945) but neither had close associations with Donovan, liked freewheeling skull sessions such as those enjoyed by Roosevelt, or were sympathetic to either intelligence organizations or irregular contacts with the White House.[47]

O.S.S. reports on Europe piled up in Truman's files, but there is no indication that they exerted any influence on his thinking about the last stage of the European war or about postwar policies. Donovan's plan for a postwar intelligence system had been upset in February by the controversy over press leaks and the charge that he was preparing to create an American Gestapo. Then, just as the O.S.S. director had begun to push it gently forward again, he was stopped short by the death of Franklin Roosevelt. Neither the new president nor the military authorities were prepared to take the lead in postwar intelligence reform. Virtually all public discussion of the issue ceased, and as war in the European theater ended, only the Bureau of the Budget, long suspicious of Donovan's sprawling and unorthodox kingdom, was quietly pursuing the question of what should be done with the multitude of wartime intelligence organizations. Donovan, as if unable to face the bad omens in Washington, spent ever more time and energy on worldwide inspection trips, and a cloud of uncertainty and then of impending ruin formed over his organization.

O.S.S. also stumbled on a number of sensitive matters in the last weeks of European hostilities. The rumor manufacturers circulated tales on the great strength of *Freies Deutschland* and claimed that the Allies did not intend to punish the top Nazis as war criminals. It is simply impossible to imagine what motivated these rumor campaigns, but others, such as one accusing the Nazi bigwigs of extensive last-minute corruption, were intended to "counteract any tendency for a Party 'legend' to emerge," by inventing further indiscretions to accompany the "utterly sordid nature of the Party's end." This fabricated excess—when Nazi wickedness needed no embellishment—ultimately boomeranged, allowing Nazi apologists to contend later that the evidence for all Nazi misdeeds was merely Allied "propaganda."[48]

Confusion, uncertainty, and numerous myths were also left behind by the last-minute efforts of O.S.S. to elicit local German surrenders. These attempts were made in northern Germany, Austria, and elsewhere, but the most famous and important was Operation Sunrise, the endeavor of Dulles's O.S.S. Bern team to arrange with S.S. Obergruppenführer Karl Wolff the surrender of the German forces in northern Italy. Operation Sunrise ultimately secured the capitulation of German Army Group C a few days before the general German surrender, thereby saving lives and property. It also raised hopes in German circles that the Americans were interested in a pre- or postsurrender deal with those Germans who were ready to cooperate with Britain and America in the creation of a new noncommunist European system. The Soviets, however, jumped to the conclusion that the surrender operation was an attempt to arrange a separate peace at the last minute, and when the Soviets were refused permission to participate in the talks with Wolff on their own terms, Molotov and Stalin bitterly castigated the U.S. government.[49]

Although surely the Soviet reaction was partly a product of Stalin's notorious paranoia, as well as his desire to appear tough and overpowering, O.S.S. errors and some diplomatic fumbles in Washington also contributed to the difficulties. In addition, the Soviets may have been especially indignant because the same O.S.S. with which they had been dealing regularly in Moscow and London, and for whom they had smoothed the way in the Balkans, now refused to cut them into the Sunrise surrender operation. In any event, the Soviets retaliated for Sunrise by being less cooperative on a whole range of matters, including the O.S.S.–N.K.V.D. exchange system, and Soviet heavy-handedness on the Sunrise affair left a residue of hurt feelings in Washington. (See chapter 7.)[50]

Yet even though Sunrise made the atmosphere chillier, the issues that produced the greatest Soviet–American tension in Europe during the spring and summer of 1945 were Poland and Yugoslavia. In both areas, O.S.S. played little part in the rising American willingness to stand up to what Washington saw as Moscow's undemocratic and threatening behavior in eastern Europe. O.S.S. dispatches from Europe did chart undemocratic Soviet activities in eastern Europe. But most dispatches sought to be balanced, not alarmist, and the overall tone of O.S.S. reports was no more hawkish than that of the daily run of American press coverage. O.S.S. reports on Poland were largely derivative, although Donovan was obviously jolted when he learned in February 1945 that "a surprising" number of army officers of the intelligence services of the government in exile intended to return "home" to Soviet-occupied Poland. As for Yugoslavia, Operation Sunrise allowed Anglo-American forces to go into Trieste at the last minute, and a confrontation with Tito resulted. O.S.S., like many other Western Allied organizations, felt Tito's wrath, and its missions were required to leave the country in May 1945. But their is no indication in the available records that O.S.S. was either the object of any special harassment by the Yugoslavs or played any significant role in the decision of Churchill and Truman to stand firm against Tito's pressure on Trieste.[51]

Regarding conditions in the Soviet Union itself and the dynamics of Soviet policy, O.S.S. reports were thus generally restrained and evenhanded in the months before V.E. Day. There are hints that the shift of O.S.S. intelligence attention toward Moscow was accelerating, which was neither surprising nor heinous, for as Stalin himself had said, the East–West "comradeship" rested merely on the self-interest of the two parties. Given the dramatic developments of the last stages of the war, the first East–West bumps and bruises in Europe, and the mood of overstrained excitement that gripped Allied peoples everywhere, it was to the credit of O.S.S. that it did not fall prey to wild anti-Soviet hysteria. In January

1945, when appraising the factors that might lead to a third world war, R. and A. deemphasized the likelihood of direct Soviet–American trouble, focusing instead on the possibility of a Soviet–British clash in Europe that might then draw in the United States.[52]

Just as European hostilities ended, however, a tendency toward realpolitik became manifest in O.S.S. In early May, a paper on the "Problems and Objectives of United States Policy," prepared by Donovan's organization for the Joint Strategic Survey Committee, was circulated to all high Washington civil and military offices and to the president. This paper, while contending that the United States should demonstrate a "readiness to understand and consider" Soviet interests and "anticipate potential problems by developing solutions and compromises well in advance," asserted that the only way peace could be secured was for the United States to create a power bloc to "serve as a counterweight to Russia." In addition to increased hemispheric defense and expanded Pacific bases to offset Russia's emergence "as a far more formidable power in Asia," a "West-European-American sphere" needed to be created to cope with Russia's great power and her determination to hold on to all of eastern Europe. The O.S.S. planners believed that "for 10 to 15 years" the Soviet Union desired to "avoid another major war" but that the only way for the West to guarantee even this short interval of peace was to work out a German settlement acceptable to both sides and then engage in polite but tough bargaining with the Soviet Union to secure a balance of power.[53]

Coming as it did after a long period in which consideration of power blocs or postwar trouble with the U.S.S.R. were forbidden topics in Washington, this advocacy of a tough policy based on raw power and East–West spheres of control indicates that in the summer of 1945 the O.S.S. leadership was beginning to march to a different drummer than most Americans. This paper circulated through Washington two months prior to the successful test of the atomic bomb in New Mexico and three months before the end of the war in the Pacific theater. At that time, most of the country's officials and the overwhelming majority of its people had their attention focused solely on ending the war as quickly as possible and getting on with the banquet of peace and prosperity that had been promised for the postwar period. The top O.S.S. leadership, on the other hand, was turning its strategic mind (to use John Kenneth Galbraith's phrase) toward the next non-American, authoritarian political force in the world and was hoping to redirect the newly created American military–economic machine in that direction. In the view of Donovan and his top aides, that was what a strategic intelligence service should do, and they were apparently not prepared to wait and see how things developed in the postwar world or deterred in their strategic planning by the obvious desire of the American people for peace, quiet, and a respite from war and international political crises.

This difference of outlook between the O.S.S. leaders and the rest of the country on the general course of American policy for the immediate postwar era was what probably doomed Donovan's organization. The general was trying to sell the need for a large permanent intelligence system to a country whose leaders and people had had enough of war and political dangers and of the kinds of organizations created to cope with them. The more Donovan and his aides pointed to a possible Soviet threat and other dangers in the world as reasons for a permanent United States military and intelligence establishment, the less anyone wanted to hear what they had to say. As we will see below, O.S.S. plans for a postwar intelligence system were not so much contested in the summer of 1945 as they were merely endured until hostilities ended and the president could arrange to get these troublesome people out of town.[54]

Therefore, although Donovan made a few attempts to bring his views on postwar Europe and the importance of strategic intelligence to Truman's attention, the main flow of O.S.S. reports on Europe exerted little or no discernible influence on American policy during the last phase of O.S.S. Since Allen Dulles's cautious attempt to repeat the Sunrise success by helping to arrange a Japanese surrender failed, O.S.S. Europe could not claim to have helped end the war in the Pacific theater. Even though O.S.S. performed important services both in the prosecution of Nazi war criminals and in the de-Nazification efforts, these activities were hardly intelligence operations and in any event were accepted by most Americans as so self-evidently necessary that they brought no special kudos to Donovan's organization.[55]

The young Truman administration was not yet interested in long-term strategic planning. The new president was trying to keep on top of hundreds of domestic and foreign problems via an operational system that he found shockingly disorganized and inefficient. Isolated tidbits of information sent to him through what he considered improper channels were not part of the solution, in Truman's view, but were part of the problem. As he told the Budget Bureau director two weeks after becoming president, one of his primary goals was to change the system that left piles of unsolicited reports cluttering up his desk.[56]

Still, a few limited O.S.S. carry-overs may have influenced European policy formation in the postwar period. R. and A. reports on Europe produced in 1945 frequently were retained as reference works by various departments and then later utilized when Washington roused itself for a more active role in European affairs. A number of secret mid-1945 intelligence contacts made by O.S.S. in Sweden, Germany, Poland, and perhaps with the young Israeli intelligence service, were not taken up immediately by the Washington authorities, but they may have been utilized later.[57]

Yet even if we take account of these carry-overs, and a few other thin threads extending from O.S.S. into the future, we must still conclude that Donovan's organization did not mold broad American policy for Europe in 1945. From its first day to its last, O.S.S. was not the central agency for long-term strategic policy formation that Donovan had first advocated. Its impact on American policy for Europe was irregular, tangential, and after the first weeks of 1945, of declining importance. O.S.S. left its main mark not as a "strategic service," but in its functions as an operational agency, assisting American military forces in the field. Therefore, to complete our picture of O.S.S. in Europe, we must turn our attention to O.S.S. activities in the service of S.H.A.E.F. and A.F.H.Q.

O.S.S. and the Battles in Europe: June 1944–May 1945

July–August 1944: Breakout from Normandy
December 1944–January 1945: The Battle of the Bulge
March 1945: American forces cross the Rhine at Remagen

The great popular uprising that erupted across the face of Europe in June 1944 profoundly affected the Anglo-American view of resistance warfare. The waves of sabotage and guerrilla attacks upon the Nazi occupation forces in the wake of D Day and the fall of Rome caught the imagination of the British and American public and its leaders. The picture of brave men and women, assisted by S.O.E. and O.S.S., directly confronting the powerful and vicious Nazis sent a shiver of exultation through the Allied world. Even to such British and American champions of resistance as Donovan and Lord Selborne, the scale and force of the great popular explosion, moving out from its French epicenter in waves that stretched as far as Scandinavia and Yugoslavia, was "bigger than anything . . . anticipated."[58]

The Allied commanders, Generals Wilson and Eisenhower, were also deeply impressed by the display of resistance power. Resistance units had faithfully followed the orders of the Allied command and had succeeded in crippling German reinforcement in Normandy. Most military observers agreed that sabotage, when coupled with air attack, had delayed German military movement by approximately forty-eight hours. Some crucial formations—including the Second Panzer Division, which attempted to move up from southern France—were stalled for even longer and ultimately had to leave behind much of their heavy equipment. The British and American generals also recognized that the Nazi effort to cope with popular attacks required use of forces for counterinsurgency which the Germans would otherwise have moved into Normandy.[59]

The intelligence aspect of resistance labors had produced further gratifying results for the Allied command. Especially in France, the system whereby Sussex tactical intelligence was fed to the Special Force Officers assigned to Allied armies had functioned very smoothly and gave the combat units a rich supply of information on the strength and movement of German forces. S.H.A.E.F. expressed its gratitude in a series of informal commendations to the resistance and to S.O.E. and O.S.S. support organizations. A senior member of Eisenhower's G-2 staff described the Sussex information as "very helpful," and noted that its accuracy was "gratifyingly high" compared with regular M.I. 6 reports. An S.H.A.E.F. message of 19 August praised the "substantial contribution" the resistance had made to the Anglo-American advance, and Eisenhower himself conceded that underground warfare in France "had been far more effective" than skeptics had believed possible.[60]

Consequently, the Allied commanders immediately took a number of steps to further increase the operational value of resistance activities. Eisenhower requested additional O.S.S. personnel from Washington and poured in heavier resistance support groups, including S.A.S. and O.S.S.–O.G. formations. Both A.F.H.Q. and S.H.A.E.F. further arranged for resistance actions to coincide more closely with overall Allied battle strategy. S.H.A.E.F. also tried to smooth the way for the resistance by agreeing to turn a blind eye to resistance reprisals against the Wehrmacht that fell outside the rules of war while insisting that the German High Command recognize the French Forces of the Interior (F.F.I.) as a legitimate combat force covered by the Geneva Convention.[61]

The most significant innovation, however, was a determined effort by S.H.A.E.F. to harness the sabotage and intelligence activities of the resistance to Allied tactical operations. The major move in this direction was made during July in Brittany when Gen. George Patton's army, breaking out of the Normandy bridgehead, swung southeast into an area swarming with resistance forces and O.S.S., S.O.E., and S.A.S. units. An agreement was quickly improvised whereby resistance groups fed tactical intelligence to the Special Force Officers of the advancing Allied armies and, on specific orders, performed acts of sabotage immediately ahead of Patton's lead units. In addition, Wehrmacht forces bypassed by Patton's rapid advance were frequently encircled and forced to capitulate by resistance groups strengthened by S.A.S. and O.G. formations. These arrangements accelerated Patton's progress and helped him retain maximum punch in his strike force.[62]

S.H.A.E.F. immediately saw that tremendous tactical sabotage and intelligence benefits could be derived from resistance and extended this arrangement to all the advancing Allied armies on the Western Front. Some O.S.S. purists objected to having the main focus of their activities shifted from strategic to tactical operations, and David Bruce, O.S.S. chief of the European theater, protested against the untidy organizational situation created by intermixing S.O. and S.I. functions. But Eisenhower was the supreme authority over O.S.S. in western Europe, and he got his way. In any case, Bruce soon discovered that by shifting the center of S.I. activities from Britain to the continent, he could elude the controls that the London government had used to restrict his operations.[63]

By September 1944, every large Allied formation in western Europe included a unit to coordinate tactical operations with the resistance, and virtually all the S.O. and S.I. activities of O.S.S. in the battle area had been fitted into this structure. A month later, under prompting from S.H.A.E.F., the same system was extended to the Allied forces in Italy. Special force tactical units made up of S.O.E. and O.S.S. personnel were assigned to both Fifteenth Army Group and Fifth Army headquarters. The Eighth Army in Italy, which already had an O.S.S. contingent, was also offered an S.O.E. resistance liaison unit, but for reasons that are not readily apparent from the available records, it was refused. Nonetheless, by September–October, the tactical orientation of special operations was dominant in Italy, and Allied missions with the resistance were told that any O.S.S. or British agent in enemy territory "executing tactical missions . . . must be given precedence."

The importance of the general move of O.S.S.–S.I. and –S.O. operations in the European and Mediterranean theaters to a tactical and immediate battle-support orientation cannot be overemphasized. Not only did it shift much O.S.S. activity away from the long-term strategic intelligence functions that Donovan had originally envisioned for his organization—and would attempt to revive in the last stage of the war—but it was also a culminating step in the general's campaign to protect his organization by making it useful to the military. When we examine the evaluations of O.S.S. made at the end of hostilities by such military leaders as Eisenhower, it was the tactical intelligence and resistance support activity of the organization that was signaled out for praise. O.S.S. helped sell the High

Command on the tactical value of resistance activity, and once its value was demonstrated, O.S.S. rose in the generals' estimation.[64]

During the summer and fall of 1944, the Allied High Command greatly increased the supply allotments to the resistance forces in the battle zone and also upped the number of aircraft serving the needs of special forces. The French underground was naturally the major beneficiary of this increase. Between D Day and early September 1944, Britain and America flew in over 7,000 tons of arms and ammunition and 100 Jeeps to the French resistance. In part trying to offset the political capital that London had gained from its earlier resistance support, Donovan arranged a spectacular daylight delivery of over 300 planeloads of supplies to central France on Bastille Day 1944. In addition to arms and supplies, 74 Jedburgh teams, 1,574 S.A.S. personnel, and 18 O.S.S.-O.G. teams were sent in to strengthen French underground and secret intelligence activities during the three-month period following Overlord.[65]

A portion of the supply flow was dispatched in support of the Allied invasion of southern France (Operation Anvil), which occurred in mid-August. Over 260 tons of supplies and 175 agents were dropped into southern France in the first two weeks of August, and liaison between the resistance and Gen. Alexander Patch's Seventh Army functioned very smoothly. General de Gaulle and the Free French still had grounds for complaint, however, because General Wilson, who exercised overall supervision of the Anvil operation, had encouraged the French to believe that a large French paratroop force would be sent into the Massif Central, even though the A.F.H.Q. staff already had decided against such an operation. Following several instances of pre–D Day deception by the Allies in dealing with the F.F.I. and the mid-July German slaughter of the Marquis on the Vercors plateau, the failure to deliver the promised paratroop operation gave de Gaulle reason to suspect Anglo-American forthrightness.[66]

Yet the British and Americans did put nearly 300 of their own personnel behind enemy lines in support of Anvil, including 20 Jedburgh teams and 5 O.S.S. O.G.s. The resistance provided saturation intelligence coverage in the preinvasion period. The Medusa network operating via Spain was especially important, and during the actual landing, members of the resistance were used as intelligence line crossers in unusually large numbers. The O.S.S. detachment attached to the American forty-fifth Division employed more than 100 such young French resistance intelligence operatives during Anvil. In a postinvasion appraisal of intelligence collection, A.F.H.Q. G–2 singled out the work of O.S.S–S.I. for lavish praise. Noting that the Allied command had been provided with a "phenomenally accurate" picture of enemy activities, Col. H. B. Hitchens of G–2 estimated that 50 percent of the information came from O.S.S., 30 percent from the Free French, and only 20 percent from British circuits. The colonel emphasized that this O.S.S. achievement provided "a signal example of what can be done by an agency of this kind" when it works "in closest cooperation" with an operational headquarters.[67]

S.O.E.–S.O. guerrilla support operations for Anvil were equally successful. Four days after the landings, an A.F.H.Q. operational appraisal declared that "the intensification of all types of sabotage and guerrilla action seems to have led the Germans to a state of utter confusion." German troops were fleeing in all directions, and by 9 September the Special Force Headquarters Weekly Review stated that so much of the Wehrmacht in southern France had been killed, captured, or encircled that "guerrilla operations have virtually come to a standstill."[68]

General Patch's Seventh Army raced north to hook up with Eisenhower's main force, which was itself galloping eastward toward Germany and northward into Belgium. With the exception of the liberation of Paris, where resistance forces played a leading role, Eisenhower's advance across northern France in August and September was too rapid for the French underground to provide much direct assistance. When the eastern drive slowed to a crawl in late September, the remaining German-occupied territory in France was so small, and the Wehrmacht units so strong, that little resistance activity was possible. In November, when the Free French requested permission to establish an intelligence network in German-occupied east and central France, S.H.A.E.F. refused because the Allies already had *two* intelligence networks there. The resistance had done all it could do; from this point on, conventional army ground power had to open the door from France into Germany.[69]

Further north, however, resistance units continued to directly support Allied ground operations in the fall and winter of 1944–45. From the pre–D Day period on, the Belgian resistance carried out extensive intelligence and sabotage actions to assist the Allied campaign. Belgian resistance activities, strengthened by Allied supplies and Jedburgh teams, accelerated as Allied forces swung north. Soon after British units crossed the Belgian frontier on 1 September, a general uprising occurred that assisted Montgomery in wresting control of much of the country from the Germans by mid-September. In late September, the Allied command chose not to worry unduly about the pockets in eastern Belgian territory still in German hands and also decided that the Belgian resistance would not be employed in efforts to infiltrate Germany. The Belgian resistance was therefore demobilized amid government nervousness about weapons and disorder and complaints from resistance members that their work and sacrifice had not been sufficiently appreciated.[70]

As the British edged across the Belgian–Dutch frontier in the second week of September, they entered the realm of the most ill-fated resistance movement in western Europe. The Netherlands resistance performed intelligence services for the Allies throughout the war, and the Dutch people made heroic public stands against Nazi repression and persecution. But the German infiltration of the S.O.E. networks in 1942–43 cast a long shadow. Not until mid-August 1944 did the Allies again parachute in resistance organizers (two agents on 13 August), and the first large supply drop and Jedburgh mission went in during mid-September. A few days later, an S.A.S. team and four more Jedburgh groups were dropped to strengthen resistance support for the Arnhem operation. Dutch underground people provided such valuable tactical intelligence at Arnhem that the Allied command was "delighted with them." But the battle was lost and the Dutch population forced to endure another dreadful winter of German occupation, made especially hideous by shortages of food and fuel and mass deportations to Germany.[71]

During the long winter, the Dutch resistance performed extensive sabotage, but its equipment was pathetically weak—an Allied estimate made late in September concluded that only 200 resisters were armed in the whole country. Morale inevitably suffered, the S.D. again succeeded in infiltrating the organization (fortunately only on a small scale), and there was serious political strife and internal dissension. The Allied special operations authorities became so alarmed at one point that all Allied liaison officers were ordered to break contact with resistance people in Holland. In December 1944, S.O.E. resorted to an extreme countermeasure to help its resistance associates and had the R.A.F. bomb an S.D. detention building in the center of Rotterdam. This time S.O.E. and the R.A.F. were lucky. Eleven imprisoned resistance members escaped, and since the neighboring Catholic school demolished by the raid was empty, there were no civilian casualties. When S.O.E.–R.A.F. later tried the same trick in Copenhagen, both the prison and surrounding civilian structures were fully occupied, and the large number of civilian casualties that resulted has left a permanent cloud over this kind of operation.[72]

A nucleus of Dutch underground units endured through the terrible winter of 1944–45, and with the aid of S.O.E. Special Force Officers—for in Holland the direct contribution of O.S.S. was marginal—assisted Allied forces during the spring 1945 offensive that finally drove the Nazis out of the low countries. This action by the Dutch resistance was the final achievement of the combined S.O.E.–O.S.S. special force organization to effect tactical cooperation between the armies of S.H.A.E.F. and the resistance forces of western Europe.[73] S.O.E. and O.S.S. made one additional effort to support S.H.A.E.F. by trying to develop underground assistance for the advance of Eisenhower's armies. Since Donovan believed that in entering the enemy homeland the "center of gravity must be forward," S.O.E. and O.S.S. each mounted its own operation against the Reich, but they were required to coordinate their activities under the direction of S.H.A.E.F. No matter how one looked at the situation, prospects for developing an effective tactical support movement in Germany were not bright. The Nazi security forces remained very strong, and the population was still caught in the fatalistic lockstep that made any form of popular action extremely difficult. The Allied advance had slowed to a crawl along the western German border in October and at a time when talk of the postwar repression proposed by Morgenthau filled the air, German civilians had little reason to believe that it was in their interest to take personal risks to help Eisenhower's armies move forward.[74]

The Allies nonetheless roughed out a wide range of subversive warfare and resistance schemes to be used in Germany. There was a plan for covert abduction of V–2 technicians, another for subverting the Cologne police force, and a more extensive project for utilizing foreign workers to gather intelligence and carry out sabotage. O.S.S. began training S.O. and S.I. teams for German missions, and both Donovan's organization and the French intelligence service received agent reports from a few isolated spots inside the Reich. Given Donovan's longing for a struggle with the putative Nazi underground, many O.S.S. officials (including the present C.I.A. director, William J. Casey) busied themselves preparing for the showdown that they thought would occur once the occupation period began.[75]

The obstacles in the way of S.O.E. or O.S.S. activities in direct support of Allied military operations in Germany were, however, simply too formidable. The Allied High Command absolutely forbade use of Allied military prisoners within Germany for subversive or intelligence purposes because of its overriding fear of German reprisal. The Allied governments, especially that of France, were opposed to any operation that might put foreign workers inside Germany at risk. When the British and the Americans tried a small test drop of incendiary weapons, named Braddock II, to foreign workers in September 1944, the action brought a stiff French protest. Gradually, in cooperation with the French, cautious O.S.S. and S.O.E. plans to make some use of foreign workers for subversive warfare purposes were developed. But the French did not agree to a renewed experiment with Braddock II until the end of February 1945, and before it could be carried out, the Anglo-American forces had crossed the Rhine, and a wide open offensive battle was spreading over Germany. Suddenly the pressing question was not what foreign workers and Allied P.O.W.s could do for the Allied armies, but what the Allied authorities needed to do to help protect these groups from possible last-minute massacres. Hurried studies were undertaken to see if S.O.E. and O.S.S. could send in emergency rescue and protection missions, but British and American subversive warfare organizations came up short. Between S.O.E. and O.S.S. only thirty-two wireless operators and a like number of liaison officers were ready to go in, and S.H.A.E.F. was forced to depend on Special Allied Airborne Reconnaissance Forces to do the job, supplemented by a small S.O.E.–O.S.S. increment.[76]

Therefore, despite much postwar comment to the contrary, neither S.O.E. nor O.S.S. pierced the Reich sufficiently to truly benefit the Allied armies. To measure the accuracy of this statement one needs only to study the 29 January 1945 S.H.A.E.F. directive to O.S.S. and S.O.E. listing in order of priority the shadow warfare activities that the Allied command wanted performed inside Germany. The first and most important item was the task of "encouraging groups of German servicemen to desert or mutiny." Second on S.H.A.E.F.'s priority list was given to "organizing groups of workers to take strike actions." Sabotage of German rail traffic into the Ruhr came next, followed in descending order of importance by other acts of assorted sabotage, cautious organization of foreign workers, and intelligence collection. No mention was made in the directive of deep intelligence penetration nor of emergency measures in preparation for a war with a Nazi underground. But the directive did state categorically that S.H.A.E.F. wanted O.S.S. and S.O.E. to take no long gambles; they were admonished "NOT [to] arm dissident German elements save in exceptional circumstances with the express permission of this Headquarters." S.H.A.E.F. had clearly decided to play it safe with subversive warfare in Germany and gave S.O.E. and O.S.S. tasks that were virtually impossible to fulfill. In the final three months of that war, with runaway German soldiers hanging from telephone poles everywhere, no mutinies, strikes, or Ruhr railroad sabotage could be produced by S.O.E., O.S.S., or any other subversive warfare organization trying to work inside Germany. Consequently, the final O.S.S.–S.O.E. activities in support of Eisenhower's armies fizzled, but this fact should not detract from the impressive record of achievement that special force tactical operations had rolled up in western Europe in the post–D Day period.[77]

The O.S.S.–S.O.E. tactical operations on the Italian Front were rather more fortunate, continuing to accelerate in power and importance right up to the moment of final victory. In the early stages of the campaign, to be sure, Italian resistance leaders, as well as the O.S.S. and S.O.E. personnel who worked with them, complained that Italy was left near the rear of the queue. During the three-month supply buildup prior to Overlord that was intended to help tie down German forces, even the Greek resistance was scheduled to receive nearly as many supplies as were the Italians. Whereas in mid-summer, the French were being given over 2,000 tons of supplies per month, only 216 tons of supplies were dropped to the Italian resistance between mid-July and mid-Av ;ust. Despite this small support, the Italian underground carried out extensive sabotage and intelligence operations, especially when, after the fall of Rome, it momentarily appeared that the German hold on the peninsula might soon be broken. The number of S.O.E. and O.S.S. missions in north Italy was sharply increased and by the fall of 1944 was roughly equal to those in other areas of the Mediterranean theater. The September decision of Fifth Army and Fifteenth Army Group to follow the lead of S.H.A.E.F. and integrate resistance activity into tactical operational planning further enhanced the status of the resistance and its S.O.E. and O.S.S. associates. In the same month, the American Army Air Corp substantially augmented the number of aircraft allotted to resistance support activities, and the Italian underground was a major beneficiary of this increase.[78]

But then in November 1944, just when it appeared that the Italians would cease to be the orphans of the resistance, another sharp reverse came. The Allied offensive ran out of steam and was unable to penetrate as far as the Po Valley. The winter weather in northern Italy was atrocious, and supply flights into the Alpine region were extremely hazardous. The clear-moon periods essential for effective aerial supply had virtually ceased by November, and the Italian resistance, which had come out into the open to assist what it had been told was a victory offensive, was now trapped without cover or adequate supply. The Allied command might describe this as an unpleasant turn in the fortune of war rather than the result of "indifference or bloody-mindedness," but that was small consolation to the Italians, who were being slaughtered by the Nazi and Italian Fascist security forces. Lacking supplies and safe havens, the resistance was unable to follow the advice broadcast by Field Marshal Alexander that it was time for a hiatus from resistance activity. Much resistance blood was spilled that winter, and much bitter ink has poured forth from the pens of resistance champions in the years that followed.[79]

The winter of 1944–45 was so trying and confused for the Italian underground that everyone had difficulty finding his way. An S.O.E. man dropped in north of Genoa in late November discovered that he had landed in an O.S.S. mission run by an Italian, while the neighboring resistance unit was a left-wing Italian force led by a British army captain who had escaped from a war camp. Despite such muddle, and the resentment at what appeared from the field as Allied indifference, the nucleus of the underground movement held on and continued to inflict damage on the enemy throughout the winter.[80]

Later in the winter, increased supply drops from the American Sixty-fourth Troop Carrier Group, which began flying out of Tuscany, did much to improve the morale, as well as the armament, of the resistance. Once again a buildup of underground strength occurred, and for the first time, the Italians received substantial supply lifts and resistance support missions. By mid-February, there were twenty-six S.O.E. missions in northeast Italy alone, and large numbers of S.O.E. and O.S.S. teams in Lombardy and the northwest. When Field Marshal Alexander's major offensive began on 9 April 1945, the underground army was larger and better armed than it had been the previous summer. During the month of April 1945, there were thirty-six O.S.S.–S.O. missions in northern Italy plus ten O.G. units, and the Allies put in nearly a thousand tons of supplies. O.S.S. sources accounted for roughly half this tonnage, which was split three to one in favor of arms and ammunition over "nonwarlike" combat supplies. Italians might complain with justice that even so they never caught up with the rate of supply flow to other areas. Tito obtained over three times as many supplies during the war as did the Italian resistance, and in April 1945 the Yugoslavs still received more than the Italians (1,147 to 998 tons) even though much of the fighting had ended in Yugoslavia and some East–West tensions were already manifest there.[81]

Italian complaints were surely justified, but the Italian resistance nevertheless had adequate means to do its job in spring 1945. As Alexander's offensive began to gain momentum, a general rising took place, and the Wehrmacht and Nazi–Italian Fascist security forces found themselves attacked from all sides. In addition to the direct assault of the Fifth and Eighth armies supported by the R.A.F. and the Army Air Corps, the Axis rear areas were assailed by S.A.S. troops, O.S.S.–O.G. missions, commando units, S.O.E. and O.S.S. teams, and the full weight of the Italian resistance formations. There were even some attacks by groups of Russians who had been brought to Italy by the Germans to serve as auxiliary troops and had then gone over to the Italian resistance, and on 15 April, a Special Operations Situation Report declared that near Montecelli, three barges had been blown up by "Sabotage Group German Deserters." The resistance took control of the major cities of northern Italy, including Genoa and Milan, prior to the arrival of the Allied armies, and the campaign ended in a fiesta of triumphant military cooperation between the resistance and the British and American armies.[82]

The final stage of the Italian campaign was the most dramatic European demonstration of what O.S.S.–S.O.E.-assisted resistance units could accomplish in tactical support of the Allied armies. A postwar Anglo-American military appraisal concluded that in April alone, the resistance in northern Italy liberated 125 cities and towns, killed 3,000 Germans, and accepted the surrender of 81,000 more. Even if one questions the precision of such calculations, which, given the nature of resistance warfare, can at best be approximations, there is little doubt that in the final advance, the Italian underground functioned as an effective "fourth arm" along with the air, sea, and land forces of the Allies.[83]

One might object that this triumph was offset by the failure of Field Marshal Alexander's command to make effective tactical use of the resistance potential in neighboring Austria. Yet even though it is true that Alexander was given military responsibility for resistance activity in Austria, and a handful of supplies were sent in during late 1944, A.F.H.Q. decided by January 1945 that "indigenous resistance in Austria was negligible" and the winter weather made the landing of subversive support missions too risky. Alexander concluded that an Austrian resistance would not be operational soon enough, so he ignored it as a possible tactical support force. A.F.H.Q. authorities maintained loose contact with dissident Austrians through Bern and Caserta solely because they might prove helpful in dealing with such potential problems as Nazi underground activity in the occupation period. So the resistance "failure" in Austria, like that in Germany, does not disprove the general rule that when an Anglo-American military command in Europe agreed to close tactical liaison with a broad popular resistance force linked to O.S.S.–S.O.E., the Allies reaped huge military benefits.[84]

Furthermore, there is a hint in the available records that the reverse may also have been true and that refusal to affect tactical resistance liaison could have dire consequences. In December 1944, every Allied army under S.H.A.E.F. and A.F.H.Q. except one had a special force unit coordinating with the resistance. Only the American First Army refused to have such a unit, which was therefore withdrawn and assigned to Twelfth Army Group. During the many later postmortems on the failure of First Army intelligence, which allowed Hitler's offensive to achieve complete surprise in the Bulge, no notice seems to have been taken of this fact. Perhaps the First Army was just unlucky, but it seems at least possible that if members of the resistance in eastern Belgium had been kept on the job and tightly coordinated with First Army, Hitler would have found it much more difficult to perpetrate his coup in the Bulge in December 1944.[85]

Given the obvious tactical importance of O.S.S. intelligence operations from Italy to the Netherlands (and perhaps as a negative factor in the Bulge as well), the question of how S.I. operated in a combat theater needs to be considered. S.I. and S.I.S. field missions—both line crossers and air drop missions—nearly always had top priority, and the basic system was for S.I. reports to go to O.S.S. theater headquarters (in the Mediterranean the 2677th was designated a Regiment rather than a Company in 1944), from which they were funneled to the various army formations. An S.I. unit to handle line crossers and distribute reports was attached to Fifth Army as early as September 1943, and the weekly total of raw S.I. reports containing German military intelligence distributed by the 2677th was already 89 in December 1943. By December 1944, the number of such items seems to have risen to at least 50 per day. In addition, S.O. missions in northern Italy sent back an enormous volume of military intelligence—over 2,000 reports on the Axis military reached the 2677th headquarters between December 1944 and February 1945.[86]

It is more difficult to judge how much of O.S.S. intelligence gathered from other sources actually came to be utilized in tactical military operations. We know that O.S.S. had 44 agents in the Iberian peninsula, the Azores, and Madeira in the summer of 1944 and that O.S.S. received nearly 8,000 cable and pouch reports from that area. The S.I. staff of 7 in Portugal had 300 subsources, and O.S.S. Istanbul gathered much information from such Balkan and Middle Eastern sources as the Jewish Refugee Agency. In the same period (summer 1944), O.S.S. Switzerland had agents working into northern Italy and the Balkans, plus 14 strings totaling 100 agents operating in France and another 40 agents working against Germany itself. On at least some matters Dulles sent copies of his Washington dispatches to O.S.S. headquarters at S.H.A.E.F. and A.F.H.Q. But how much, if any, of this information—except for the Medusa material at the time of Anvil—actually got down to tactical combat units in time for them to make effective use of it still remains a mystery. Much of the same uncertainty hovers over the impact of major O.S.S. background studies such as the huge thirteen-volume opus it prepared on the geography of northwest Normandy in July 1944 because most final intelligence briefing papers, including the intelligence notes developed by G-2 S.H.A.E.F. and A.F.H.Q., contain few references to the original source of specific information.[87]

It is certainly safe to assume that the bulk of the target analysis work done by R. and A. for tactical air forces had immediate battle application, as did the target interrogations of German prisoners carried out in Italy by R. and A. for the Army Air Corps. But measuring the combat effect of this last task turns out to be very difficult, for P.O.W. interrogation consisted of picking up tiny pieces of fragmentary information. It was, as one of the interrogators, Lt. Frederick Burkhardt, reported to Corey Ford in November 1944, rather analogous to the method used by Mae West's maid to acquire a fur coat, for according to the old tale, "Mae West and her maid . . . both wore 1,000 dollar fur coats [but] Mae got hers by finding a man with a thousand dollars while the maid got hers by finding a thousand men with one dollar." When looking back from a distance of thirty-five years, one cannot judge Burkhardt's labors as fairly as the maid's because we cannot determine how many pieces of fur the R. and A. interrogators actually found, much less establish how many of them helped make valuable coats.[88]

Yet one must not dismiss as unimportant any intelligence activity merely because its tactical impact is not immediately apparent. O.S.S. men were amateurs at the game of tactical intelligence—of the 373 Americans trained in the Mediterranean theater combat intelligence course, only 14 were O.S.S. men—and they had to move their material along in any way they could. Sometimes an item of information traveled a circuitous route before it made a mark. For example, a February 1945 O.S.S. intelligence bulletin prepared in Nice, France contained information on German and Italian security forces along the Franco-Italian border. The report went to A.F.H.Q., where an alert O.S.S. man routed it to Headquarters Number 1 Special Force (S.O.E.), which then passed it on to a very grateful Detachment 10 which was working with resistance units on the Italian side of the same border.[89]

However much one leans to the positive side, though, it seems unlikely that the bulk of those in the large O.S.S. rear-area staffs in Europe made substantial contributions to tactical operations. Many of those people saw themselves as strategic intelligence analysts and believed, understandably but incorrectly, that their work was the most important task that O.S.S. performed. The cold fact is that the American military in general, and O.S.S. in particular, had too many rear-area personnel. The headquarters staff of Twelfth Army group under S.H.A.E.F. numbered 14,000 in February 1945—as large as a combat division—and as the chief commissioner of the Allied Control Commission in Italy, Adm. Ellery W. Stone, remarked in the same month, there were eleven major and enumerable minor agencies reporting on Italian conditions. Decrying the duplication and lack of coordination, Admiral Stone concluded that if anyone "read all the reports issued, he would have a most confused idea of what is happening in this country."[90]

In late 1944 and early 1945, O.S.S. transferred personnel to the Pacific, but its reductions were proportionately smaller than those of S.O.E. The Mediterranean allotment of army personnel for O.S.S. actually rose between January and October 1944 from 1,398 to 2,100 officers and enlisted personnel. October 1944 also saw O.S.S. Mediterranean slightly exceed the number of S.O.E. personnel in the field (386 to 383), but the O.S.S. total included S.I. and O.G. missions, whereas S.O.E. was only supplying resistance support. Therefore, it seems that even in the period of the highest combat commitment of O.S.S., no more than one in six personnel in an operational theater like the Mediterranean were actually in combat. If we add in the O.S.S. staffs in London, Washington, and elsewhere, the combat percentage of the whole organization was very much lower.[91]

But Donovan's organization was not above using pretentious blather to make itself look more important and combative than it was; in February 1945 an O.S.S. official unblushingly described the plan to transfer an R. and A. unit into Allied-occupied Germany as "the spearhead of the R. and A. penetration" of the Reich. O.S.S. waded into the rear-area intrigues and organizational fights with boundless gusto. As one R. and A. man dryly remarked twenty-five years later while describing wartime O.S.S. factional struggles in London, "for brazen ambition and skillful jockeying of personalities give me a good research organization any time."[92]

One hopes that amid all the bureaucratic wrangling, the assorted rear-area units of O.S.S. actually produced practical benefits for the combat forces. The covert propaganda activities of M.O. employed a great many people and produced an enormous amount of propaganda—Bern O.S.S.–O.W.I. alone distributed more than 6 million leaflets and underground newspapers to Axis-held areas during the war. The O.S.S. counterintelligence service (X-2) also kept large staffs busy pursuing possible enemy agents and filing reports on security conditions in the European theater.[93]

Perhaps the propaganda work strengthened the resistance, weakened the general will of the Wehrmacht, or persuaded individual enemy soldiers to lay down their arms, but the indirect and imprecise nature of propaganda warfare makes it impossible to say. Similarly, when one reads Donovan's glowing reports to presidents Roosevelt and Truman on wartime X-2 activities in Europe or the accounts of some of X-2's anti-S.D. work in postwar Germany, the old fifth column passions seem to ride again, and we might conclude that here was a powerful instrument of war. Yet we now know that Axis secret intelligence operations were in fact quite feeble in the last phase of hostilities, posing little threat to Allied military forces, and when we examine actual X-2 field reporting, we find that O.S.S. counterintelligence was mainly concerned not with sabotage or espionage but with general political conditions and the activities of assorted dissidents in Allied-occupied territory. The way in which the men of X-2, and their army counterintelligence colleagues, sometimes conducted themselves when offered potentially valuable internal security information also fails to inspire great confidence. In January 1945, an intelligence "T" force made a quick sweep through newly liberated Strasbourg, and one of its most valuable discoveries was a comprehensive membership list of the whole Nazi Party in Baden, complete with an evaluation by the Nazi Party (N.S.D.A.P.) Personnel Office indicating the party loyalty of each member. When the "T" force tried to give the list to the counterintelligence authorities at S.H.A.E.F., however, the Counter-Intelligence Corps was not interested, and the N.S.D.A.P. list was ultimately filed away in the Civil Affairs Office. That the counterintelligence people found this kind of information valueless on the eve of the full Allied dash into Germany suggests that they may have been seriously out of step with the situation and with the perspective of the top British and American commanders. For if there was one civil affairs issue that did concern the generals it was the possible threat posed by armed civilians during the initial phase of occupation in *every* area.[94]

This apprehension caused formidable problems for those O.S.S. political analysts who had concluded that even left-wing factions in the resistance posed no danger to the Allied armies moving into France and Italy. Maj. H. Stuart Hughes finally convinced General Patch's staff that Communists would not try to seize power at the moment of liberation, but it took much work in southern France in conjunction with advance units of the U.S. Army, and a series of on-the-spot reports, to turn the trick. In Italy, nothing could soothe the fears of the A.F.H.Q. staff once the British ran into trouble with E.A.M.–E.L.A.S. in Greece. A staff officer of Number One Special Force declared in January 1945 that there was "no doubt that those who control Communist bands [in Italy] are preparing to seize power by force when the Germans are expelled by the Allies." The American G-3 representative at A.F.H.Q., Gen. Lyman Lemnitzer (later chairman of the J.C.S. and commander of NATO forces), was somewhat more restrained, but nonetheless warned in the same month "that the introduction of surplus arms into Northwest Italy at this time will constitute a serious threat to our efforts to maintain law and order in that area upon occupation thereof by our forces." Consequently, A.F.H.Q. decided to control the flow of arms to the Italian partisans during the last phase of the campaign so that the resistance could maintain morale and a moderate punching power but would not emerge from the conflict as a powerful armed force. Special care was taken to restrict the quantity of weapons sent to northwest Italy, where left-wing elements were strong and border troubles between France and Italy threatened to produce armed clashes. A similar policy was followed in northeast Italy, for there the Italian resistance and Tito's partisans already were circling each other warily, due to the burning question of which country would control Trieste and the province of Venezia Guilia in the postwar period.[95]

In restricting the flow of weapons to the Italian resistance, the British and American military leaders were consciously sacrificing a tactical advantage to an obsession for law and order. Such politically tainted decisions had been extremely rare during the full fury of the campaign, but as V.E. Day neared, they became more common, and in the occupation era, order and internal security were in high fashion. O.S.S. and S.O.E. personnel who previously had been honored because of their close collaboration with the fighting underground found that some military government officers now regarded them with suspicion as the consorts of revolutionaries and troublemakers. Every manifestation of irregular warfare, even efforts to recruit French or Dutch personnel for subversive warfare operations in the Pacific colonies, were watched with varying degrees of coolness or suspicion.[96]

But the generals' last-minute concern for order and sobriety must not blind us to the fact that S.O. and S.I. men and women, working closely with the resistance and producing tangible tactical services for the armies, were the ones who convinced Patton, Eisenhower, and Alexander that O.S.S. was worth its salt. In the broadest sense, most of the other activities of O.S.S. in Europe rode on the coattails of tactical S.O. and S.I. during the battle period. Even in the areas that were not penetrated by Anglo-American forces, such as Scandinavia and Yugoslavia, it was the indirect military effects of O.S.S. resistance-support activities that chiefly interested S.H.A.E.F. and A.F.H.Q. Every German formation that could be held in these areas meant one less unit facing the armies of the major Allies. Although O.S.S. remained a junior partner to S.O.E. and S.I.S. in Scandinavia and the southern Balkans—that is, in Denmark, Norway, Yugoslavia, Greece, and Albania—it was the only American organization doing its part to keep the German units there out of the way of Eisenhower and Wilson. S.H.A.E.F. was both inaccurate and unfair in failing to appreciate that German forces were pinned down in Denmark largely by the scale of the bloody underground warfare waged there, while the large Wehrmacht units in Norway owed their presence less to the Norwegian resistance—largely paralyzed by German reprisals—than to Hitler's mad fear of a new invasion. Its failure to grasp the horrendous price paid by the Yugoslav population throughout the war to withhold what was seen as a mere handful of German divisions from the main Eastern and Western fronts was even less just.[97]

Battle command is a harsh business, however, and S.H.A.E.F. and A.F.H.Q. were only being true to their trade when they insisted that O.S.S. resistance support and intelligence activities had to pay their way even in eastern European zones likely to be occupied by the Red Army. The Western Allied commanders allowed S.O.E. and O.S.S. to experiment with resistance movements in such difficult areas as Austria and Bulgaria, but if they failed to prosper, the support was eliminated. Along with some concern to block shipments to Germany of such vital materials as chrome, the overriding objective during the final phase of the Allied offensive was still to hold German units in the periphery. Every resistance support operation was judged primarily on that basis, and if it failed to deliver or threatened to cause serious difficulties with the Soviet military command—as in Czechoslovakia—the British and American generals did not hesitate to cut it back, even though they realized that such action might have adverse postwar political repercussions.[98]

In pursuit of valuable order-of-battle intelligence, the British and American commanders were prepared to take bigger risks in eastern Europe. S.H.A.E.F. and A.F.H.Q. approved O.S.S. intelligence exchanges with the N.K.V.D. and also authorized X-2 counterintelligence cooperation with the Soviet authorities in occupied Bulgaria and Rumania. At the same time, they either acquiesced to, or quietly encouraged, O.S.S. and British intelligence reporting on the military operations of the Yugoslav partisans. But there were distinct limits to O.S.S. freedom of action even in the realm of intelligence collection, for the Western Allied command consistently refused to authorize large-scale S.I. operations in Hungary because O.S.S. could not overcome Soviet opposition to such activities.[99]

Furthermore, every O.S.S. action in southeast Europe during the last phase of the war was piggybacked on an operation directly beneficial to the Army Air Corps. In addition to the targeting information sent back by S.I. missions stationed in the Axis-occupied Balkans, O.S.S. had four teams of weather observers for the air force in Yugoslavia as early as June 1944. O.S.S. also provided air rescue services in Yugoslavia and Albania during the summer, and crew rescue was the main justification Donovan used to rush O.S.S. teams into Rumania and Bulgaria during the brief August 1944 interval when these countries were abandoned by the Axis and had not yet been fully occupied by the Red Army. This was a physically dangerous and politically hazardous enterprise that caused trouble with the Soviets, but in the eyes of the army, air crew rescue was worth it. By 3 September, over 1,000 United States air crew members who had been held prisoner in the two countries were back in American hands, and on 14 September Army Air Corps Chief of Staff General Arnold extended his "sincere thanks" to Donovan and O.S.S. for the "tremendous boost to morale of AAF personnel in the Mediterranean" provided by the "release of these crews."[100]

The dramatic August 1944 O.S.S. air rescue operations in Rumania and Bulgaria marked the outer geographical limit—and perhaps the extreme limit in political risk as well—of Donovan's attempt to meet the direct needs of the American military commanders in Europe. Of course, we may question whether these activities, as well as some of those with the French and Italian resistance, were worth the political perils. But the military authorities certainly thought they were justified and at the end of hostilities praised O.S.S. for the military support services it had provided. In a late May 1945 cable to the J.C.S., General McNarney of A.F.H.Q. lauded the "outstanding job" performed by Donovan's organization in the Mediterranean, and Eisenhower declared that the value of O.S.S. in E.T.O. "has been so great that there should be no thought of its elimination."[101]

In Europe, Donovan won his gamble to prove to the American generals that O.S.S. could deliver. But what of the Pacific, where naval war made ground commanders less significant, and the political and economic miseries of half the world's population could not help but intrude on the thinking of America's political and military leaders?

O.S.S. in Asia: June 1944–August 1945

October 1944: MacArthur lands in the Philippines; General Stilwell is replaced by General Wedemeyer in China
April 1945: Okinawa taken by United States Tenth Army
August 1945: Atomic bombs dropped; Russia declares war on Japan; V. J. Day

The Allies won in Asia in 1944–45 because of a methodical American advance northward through the Pacific. The drive along the "outer line," which took the United States's naval, marine, and air forces through the Solomon, Gilbert, and Marshall island chains in 1943–44, culminated in the conquest of Saipan and Guam, keys to the Marianas, in June and July

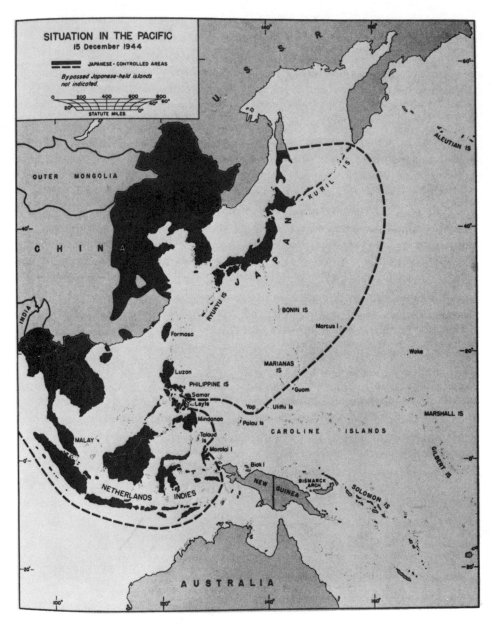

Figure 5.   The Situation in the Pacific, 15 December 1944

of 1944. Three months later, the American central Pacific island-hopping machine linked up with MacArthur's forces, which had driven straight up along the "inner line" from New Guinea and the Dutch East Indies. The Japanese occupation forces in the Philippines were overwhelmed, and in the last great surface engagement of the war, the Japanese Imperial Navy was given its death blow in the battle of Leyte Gulf. The way was rapidly cleared for the final island-hopping advance on the Japanese home islands. B–29 raids on Japan began in June, and from November on, with Superfortresses operating from advance air strips on Saipan, Japanese cities were systematically consumed by the heaviest conventional bombing of the war. In February and March of 1945, the marines took Iwo Jima, the first crucial point on the way north, and between April and June, the United States tenth Army conquered Okinawa, the gateway to Japan.

The cost of the Iwo and Okinawa operations to the United States was horrific—65,000 Americans dead and wounded, over a third of the total American battle casualties in the Pacific War. (Less than 20 percent of America's one million World War II losses occurred in the Pacific. The vast majority took place in Europe between June 1944 and May 1945.) Assuming that Iwo and Okinawa were merely an overture to the bloodbath that would be required to overwhelm Japan itself, the United States command concentrated its forces, laid its plans, and carried out massive conventional air raids on the home islands in July 1945. Then, shortly after the atomic bomb was successfully tested in New Mexico, President Truman and his advisers decided—in one of the most far-reaching decisions of the war—literally to burn Japan into submission by dropping the atomic bomb, first on Hiroshima (6 August) and then on Nagasaki (9 August). Between these bombings, the Soviet Union declared war on Japan and the Red Army poured over the border into Japanese-occupied Manchuria and Korea. With all hope gone, the cities devastated, and the mushroom clouds rising, the Emperor chose "to endure the unendurable" and ordered the Japanese government to surrender to the Allies.

The Pacific war thus ended with an overwhelming display of American military power. The relentless drive of 1944–45 showed that the American military had the means and determination to win by the most direct application of military force. Side routes, maneuver, and negotiation were all eschewed as the United States blasted its way to victory, following the simple principle that the shortest way between two military points is a straight line. The import of that strategy was for Japan total defeat, for posterity the reality of American conventional and atomic power, and for those who fought for the Allies in Asia the realization that unless they had been aboard the American transpacific express, they had played only a marginal part in the allied victory in Asia. The long struggles in Burma and China and the last-minute operations in the Dutch East Indies, Malaya, and Indochina were incidental. They tied down some Japanese forces (although once the United States gained total air, surface, and submarine superiority, Japan could not move many troops out of Southeast Asia in any case) and perhaps contributed to Tokyo's conclusion that all was lost. But they were not what produced the crushing American victory of August 1945.

It was difficult for Chinese officials to accept that after eight years of war with Japan, they actually had played little part in the decisive drive to victory. This was also true of the British, who had hoped to restore their prestige in Southeast Asia, and for the American troops who had fought and suffered in the "forgotten" campaigns of C.B.I. But no one found this pill more bitter to swallow than William Donovan, who had longed for a final opportunity to show what O.S.S. could do in the Second World War and to establish "a pattern for [the] postwar" world.[102]

The O.S.S. director had striven valiantly to get aboard the island-hopping special. He had courted MacArthur and Nimitz, developed special plans to assist naval and amphibious operations, and tried to place O.S.S. people on the P.W.B. in Australia. But he was blocked at nearly every turn. A few intelligence missions were carried out in Java and Sumatra on the fringe of MacArthur's advance by O.S.S.–S.E.A.C. in 1944, and thirteen S.O. men seem to have been quietly given to MacArthur for use in the Philippines near the end of the year. In the spring of 1945, the O.S.S. chief in China, Col. John Coughlin, hoped to work O.S.S. men into MacArthur's preserve by allowing them to remain with the Twentieth Air Force, which was preparing to move from India to the Pacific. Through the efforts of Joseph Hayden, some tenuous connections were maintained between MacArthur's staff and R. and A. throughout 1944–45. But all attempts to get regular O.S.S., S.I., and S.O. units into the Pacific theater were ultimately prevented by Nimitz and MacArthur.[103]

The Pacific army commander felt that his authority and ego were best protected by avoiding Washington agencies such as O.S.S. and using the special operations machinery that he had developed in cooperation with the Australians. MacArthur was even willing to close his eyes to the fact that some of the "Australians" were actually British. Twenty percent of the personnel of Special Operations Australia (S.O.A.) in May 1945 were British S.O.E. men, and the inflow of British personnel seems to have increased in the summer of 1945. But these people were not directly connected to London or Washington, and that was what mattered to MacArthur. When in May 1945 he was asked by the J.C.S. for his estimate of

Donovan's organization, MacArthur replied, much to the joy of O.S.S. haters, "I know little of its methods, have no control of its agencies, and consequently have no plans for its future employment."[104]

Although it may not seem possible, O.S.S. apparently was held in even lower esteem by Admiral Nimitz. In keen competition with the army and very protective of his own forces, the admiral gave Donovan two quick points in the debit column because he was an army officer and because his O.G.–S.O. activities threatened to compete with those of the Marine Corps. Furthermore, the O.S.S. director was never in a position to give Nimitz the kind of information that he most required: hard data on the position and movement of Japanese naval units. Donovan's charm seems not to have melted the admiral's reserve on the few occasions when the O.S.S. director attempted to present his case, and as early as June 1944 British observers concluded that although Nimitz was "keen" on special intelligence missions, he thought "little" of O.S.S.[105]

Neither were the two navy representatives on the J.C.S., Admirals Leahy and King, passionate admirers of O.S.S. and when stiffened into hostility by the machinations of navy men like Commodore Miles in China, they refused to press Nimitz to open the Pacific door for Donovan. Even when the war in Europe drew to a close, and O.S.S. was able to transfer experienced personnel to Asia, the admirals resisted the few navy voices that suggested Donovan's units be put to work in the Pacific. Through much of 1944, O.S.S. Washington worked on a plan for special operations into the Kuriles to gather direct intelligence on Japanese defenses. The plan, called Operation Dart, kicked around various departments and committees in Washington for five months and was supported by General Arnold, the Air Corps chief of staff. But neither the admirals on the J.C.S. nor General Marshall spoke in its favor, and it was killed by Admiral Nimitz in April 1945. The O.S.S. plan for a more ambitious penetration of Formosa (Operation Triangle), although developed in great detail, was dispatched even more quickly. Put up to the Joint Chiefs in late March 1945, Triangle was rejected by the J.C.S. in the second week of April on the ground that Formosa already had been bypassed and was not worth a special operation.[106]

The O.S.S. proposal for S.I.–S.O. operations in Korea drew a somewhat more favorable response, even though the proposal did not envision dazzling opportunities for success. Korean refugee groups in the United States were divided into warring cliques, and though O.S.S. was inclined toward factions led by Syngman Rhee and Kilsoo Hann, the State Department was wary of suggesting official American recognition of any group. The army was dubious about basing a large guerrilla operation on Koreans from the United States because of its unhappy experience with other "eth-nic" units, and General Wedemeyer in China was afraid that any attempt to make use of Koreans would cause trouble with the Chiang government. O.S.S. was forced to admit that recruiting personnel was a serious problem for large-scale operations and hinted that Koreans might be recruited in Siberia (at a time when the U.S.S.R. was not at war with Japan!) or from the Korean population of occupied northern China, which, in the O.S.S. view, consisted of people engaged in "smuggling, dope peddling, and the operation of gambling dens, opium dens, and brothels." [107]

These prospects did not entrance the State Department, but by April 1945, American diplomats were more anxious to get something going in Korea. State Department officials observed that action by the Koreans might "encourage other peoples of Asia who have been conquered by the Japanese to increase their resistance." Furthermore, reports had reached Washington (apparently from O.S.S.) that the Russians had "trained and equipped a considerable number of Koreans in Siberia," and the State Department advised the J.C.S. on 23 April that "it would be most unfortunate if the only trained group of Koreans available to assist the Military Government of Korea after liberation should be those with Communist indoctrination." In the summer of 1945, O.S.S. rapidly developed a plan for a series of penetrations of Korea (the Napko Project), yet this effort failed, too. Wedemeyer approved, and so did MacArthur; even Admiral Nimitz agreed to furnish a submarine for the mission, though he did "not favor the project at this time." Since these messages were dated 11–12 August 1945, after the *second* atomic bomb had been dropped on Japan and less than a week prior to Tokyo's surrender, it was too late for O.S.S. combat operations in the Pacific theater. [108]

At war's end, the only small O.S.S. unit actually functioning under the authority of Nimitz or MacArthur was an M.O. group beaming black propaganda broadcasts at Japan. Even this rather routine activity had been slow in developing. M.O. did not begin its Japanese black radio training program until July 1944, and Donovan secured endorsements for the project from former ambassador Joseph Grew and O.W.I.'s Elmer Davis before Admiral Nimitz approved it in March 1945. Finally in late April, M.O. began black medium band broadcasts from Saipan, and so to this limited extent, O.S.S. did play a minor part in America's final move against Japan. [109]

Even if these broadcasts weakened the confidence of individual Japanese, none of the available evidence suggests that they played a part in the ultimate decision of the Tokyo government to surrender. Nor was O.S.S. markedly successful in its general intelligence work on Japanese intentions or in its attempts to make effective use of contacts with Japanese intermediaries. S.I. did not acquire much high-level information on Japan, and the few cautious negotiation probes made by low-level Japanese contacts in Lisbon and Bern during June and July 1945 came to nothing. Dulles was absolutely right when he decided that the approach made in Bern was "a trial balloon without much authority or backing" and that O.S.S. should treat it as so "full of dynamite" that "the slightest misstep might have serious consequences."[110]

From only one source did O.S.S. get a large volume of material on the inner workings of the Japanese government, and that source was not Japanese. In fact, it was not a real intelligence source at all. The dozen or so O.S.S. "Vessel" memoranda that reached the State Department and the White House between January and April 1945 were produced by the Italian documents manufacturer Scattolini, who rose to new heights by faking reports on imaginary Vatican contacts with the Japanese in Rome and Tokyo. Scattolini kept busy creating and embroidering the tale that the Japanese believed they could hold out forever in the Pacific war because they were certain that the Soviet government would not turn against them. The Italian forger even threw in an imaginary conversation between the Japanese ambassador in Rome and Myron Taylor, earlier President Roosevelt's emissary to the Vatican, as well as another between the Apostolic delegate in Washington and "a very important White House spokesman."[111]

Considering that fables regarding U.S. government personnel invited exposure by O.S.S. counterintelligence, Scattolini's "Vessel" fabrications were surprisingly successful. Other agencies of the American government quickly realized that there was something wrong with Scattolini's Japanese game. When one of the "Vessel" reports asserting that Russia was Japan's ace in the hole was forwarded by the White House to President Roosevelt at Yalta (February 1945), Army G-2 immediately sent along a rebuttal declaring that it was "outright propaganda" that was "probably deliberately planted" on O.S.S. by the Japanese. In early March, the State Department informed Donovan that it too was suspicious of "Vessel" information, and in reply, the O.S.S. director declared that his people had their doubts and were investigating the documentary trade that was flourishing around the Vatican. But doubt did not prevent Donovan from sending a final "Vessel" dispatch on supposed Vatican mediation efforts to the State Department and the White House on 11 April 1945, the day before the president died.[112]

Apparently, this was the last "Vessel" report to reach the higher echelons of the American government, although O.S.S. may have continued to purchase Scattolini's material for use within O.S.S. itself. Any serious adverse effects on American foreign policy from the "Vessel" reports seems to have been avoided, but the affair hardly brought credit to O.S.S. methods or gave Donovan's organization a claim to having assisted the final onslaught against Japan. Harry Truman's suspicion of unsolicited reports and secret political maneuver guaranteed that O.S.S. would not be allowed to produce another "Vessel"–White House connection. When in August 1945, just after Japan surrendered, the O.S.S. director sent Truman a petition from a Mr. Ku, who claimed to head the "provisional government of Korea," the president slapped Donovan down hard. "I would appreciate your instructing your agents," Truman wrote to the O.S.S. director on 25 August, "as to the impropriety of their acting as a channel for the transmission to me of messages from representatives of self-styled governments which are not recognized by the Government of the United States." The day of freewheeling political secret warfare was obviously over, and Donovan was forced to abandon the field, having failed to score significant triumphs during the direct drive upon Japan or in the initial occupation period.[113]

In C.B.I., Donovan's organization was much more active and managed to hang on longer. As the R. and A. chief for China wrote to Langer after a talk with Donovan in January 1945, the general believed that China was "to be the last stand for O.S.S. during the war." The R. and A. man predicted that there would inevitably be "bigger and better schemes" reflecting the "official attitude . . . that it is going to be a great show." This optimistic tendency was so pronounced within the higher echelons of O.S.S. that when a new intelligence chief was sent to China in April 1945, he immediately reported to Donovan that the China theater offered O.S.S. "a greater opportunity than any other theater at any period in the course of the war."[114]

Inevitably, O.S.S. China was reorganized once again to take advantage of the potential that Donovan and his aides thought was slumbering there. In late 1944, the O.S.S. director secured President Roosevelt's authorization for O.S.S. to go beyond its activities in S.A.C.O., its work with the Fourteenth Air Force, and its deep cover missions (Starr and Clam) to establish a fully autonomous operation under the new American theater commander, General Wedemeyer. Since Wedemeyer had won his spurs serving in the Operations Division under Gen. George Marshall, he had some reservations about Donovan but was fully committed to the system of theater command authority favored by the War Department and the J.C.S. When Donovan visited China in January 1945, he found that Wedemeyer wanted to clean up the whole confused jumble of ad hoc intelligence arrangements and private armies that had grown up under Stilwell. Apparently, both Donovan and Wedemeyer told the Chinese Nationalist government and Commodore Miles that the era of do-nothing organizations and interminable liaison must end. In March 1945, Wedemeyer demanded of the J.S.C. absolute authority as theater commander, and though Miles and the Navy Department fought a stiff rear-guard action, Wedemeyer's arguments prevailed, and O.S.S., S.A.C.O., and Naval Group China were put directly under him.[115]

Not all O.S.S. China's troubles were solved thereby. American policy put Nationalist China in the foreground—"Americans as a whole have apparently sold out to the Kuomintang" in the words of the China R. and A. chief—and Chiang's people were strong enough on occasion to make life difficult for O.S.S. But as Donovan's staff knew all too well, the regime was so weak and so obsessed by its fears of the Communists and all foreigners that it was unable to act as an effective ally against the Japanese.

O.S.S. also stumbled badly in its attempts to work with the Chinese Communists, and on this occasion it did not fall forward. The United States military sent a small survey party into the communist stronghold of Yenan in July 1944, and in October Donovan warned the president that he expected S.O.E. to attempt to operate in the same area soon. O.S.S. general plans for China in the years 1944–45 laid great emphasis on how effectively the Communists were combatting the Japanese, especially when compared with the hesitant and inefficient activities of the Chunking government. In an "unofficial and private" memorandum sent to R. and A. in January 1945, John Davies declared that in ignoring the Communists and giving exclusive support to Chiang, the United States was playing Moscow's game: Mao would be dependent solely on the Soviets for the support necessary to challenge the Nationalists at war's end.[116]

In this atmosphere, an O.S.S. leadership hungry for areas where easy shadow warfare gains might be made inevitably went into northern China. The U.S. Army sent a second group to Yenan in late December 1944 (the Dixie Mission) which, with the grudging assent of the Nationalist government and the new American Ambassador to China, Patrick Hurley, was to explore the possibility of tripartite (American–Nationalist–Communist) military attacks on the Japanese. At the last minute, a senior O.S.S. man, Col. Willis Bird, was added to the Dixie Mission. Wedemeyer's chief of staff, Gen. Robert McClure, later claimed that he allowed Bird to go because with Wedemeyer temporarily absent from Chunking and having heard that Donovan was on his way to the Nationalist Chinese capital, McClure had to do something "to forestall a proposal by General Donovan . . . that he and his party be permitted to go" to Yenan. Indeed, prior to Donovan's arrival in C.B.I., O.S.S. China had made plans for northern China, and Charles Fahs, Joseph Spencer, and a handful of other O.S.S. officials "dreamed up" a Yenan mission scheme while "sitting in Delhi waiting for the [Donovan] show to arrive."[117]

But even though the broad Fahs–Spencer proposal for northern China gained Donovan's support, it never had a chance, because Colonel Bird's activities with the Dixie Mission destroyed any possibility of American subversive warfare operations in northern China. Bird agreed "tentatively" to cooperate with the Communists in northern China, including the establishment of an S.O. training school, O.S.S. equipment for 25,000 communist guerrillas, and provision of "at least 100,000 Woolworth one shot pistols for the People's militia." When word of these activities reached Chunking, the Chinese Nationalists and Ambassador Hurley exploded. Wedemeyer was forced to provide the J.C.S. with a long report on what had transpired, and he declared that although he did not believe that "these unauthorized loose discussions" were the primary cause of the "breakdown" of American efforts to get the Communists and Nationalists to cooperate, he apologized profusely that "my people became involved in such a delicate situation."[118]

Restricted to Nationalist-held territory in the aftermath of the Dixie Mission disaster, O.S.S. China did a creditable job during the last seven months of the campaign. Large R. and A. units were active both with the Fourteenth Air Force and in Chunking; 45 people had been assigned to R. and A. Chunking by July 1945. The overall authorized O.S.S. allotment for Wedemeyer's theater rose to 2,000, and by late May that figure was "being approached rapidly." The 400 O.S.S. instructors used to train Chinese guerrilla units were the first really experienced American combat troops in China, and a British observer noted that they were "wonderfully effective" in working with the Chinese. By late May, 20 trained Chinese commando and intelligence units, with O.S.S. advisers, were ready to go into action in support of Allied operations.[119]

Yet even a clear chain of command and far more material and manpower than O.S.S. China had dreamed of possessing in Stilwell's day were not enough to allow Donovan's people to cut a wide swath. The earlier arrangements that the O.S.S. director had made for his organization in China continued to create problems. Tai Li eyed O.S.S. suspiciously, and O.S.S. refused to vouch for the accuracy of Tai Li's intelligence reports. Paradoxically, every other authority in China, from the American Embassy to the Communists, was wary of Donovan's outfit because O.S.S. long had been associated with the "notorious General Tai Li of the Chinese

Gestapo." To make matters worse, a marine general assigned to O.S.S. set a new record in adverse public relations during an October 1944 banquet in Chunking. Having drunk to excess, the general put on a spectacle before Tai Li and other S.A.C.O. officials, loudly accusing China of "God Damn obstructionism," asking Tai Li about Chiang Kai-shek's "new woman," time and again called the Chinese "Chinamen," and demanded that Tai Li bring on the "Sing Song girls." This catastrophe resulted in a barrage of cables to Washington, apologies to the Chinese, the recall of the marine general, and an embarrassed report from Donovan to the White House. But nothing could undo the fact that the incident gave the shrewd Tai Li an excellent tool with which to pick away at the position and image of O.S.S. China.[120]

The affair of the marine general indicates in an extreme form O.S.S.'s personnel problem in China. In this complex political and cultural setting, getting large personnel allotments was simply not enough. Unless the people sent to China had the requisite language skills and cultural sensitivity, the possibilities for effective action were sharply circumscribed. Even the optimistic O.S.S. intelligence chief in China, Col. John Whitaker, was forced to admit in April 1945 that the organization's output was bound to be rather "superficial," since "our S.I. officers can speak neither Japanese nor Chinese."[121]

In the last phase of the China campaign, Donovan's people made a good try with what they had. M.O. black propaganda operations spread out over Japanese-occupied China, hewing a middle line that they hoped would not unduly antagonize either the Nationalist authorities or the Communists. Chinese guerrilla units, trained and frequently led by O.S.S., cooperated closely with the regular combat formations in the Chinese–American summer 1945 offensive that attempted to open a way through southern China to the sea. But this operation had lost its military significance even before it was launched in July 1945 because the main American naval squadrons were already far to the north, girding for the final attack upon Japan. Before the Chinese or O.S.S. reached the coast, the atomic bombs had been dropped, Japan had surrendered, and as the official American historian subsequently remarked, time had "run out" on the China theater.[122]

Immediately following the end of hostilities, O.S.S. teams were dropped into northern China to collect intelligence and to assist in the recovery of American P.O.W.s, including Gen. Jonathan Wainwright. These well-publicized operations—President Truman was notified that two of the O.S.S. men dropped into Manchuria were from Missouri!—helped to create an impression of O.S.S. presence in continental Asia at war's end.

When O.S.S. teams fanned out across Manchuria and other regions of northern China in August and September 1945, they had numerous encounters with Chinese communist and Soviet units. A number of these contacts were not friendly—Donovan reported to the president in mid-September that his O.S.S. men and other Americans were "very unpopular with the Soviets" in Mukden—and the most notorious incident, the killing of O.S.S. man John Birch by a Chinese communist patrol, has fueled the fires of American anticommunism for a generation.[123]

But neither these last-minute activities, nor the fact that some O.S.S. assets in China became the nucleus of the American postwar intelligence apparatus on the Asian continent, alters the conclusion that O.S.S. China did not produce the dramatic triumphs that Donovan and his aides had desired. O.S.S. operations fell just a little short in unraveling the China tangle; it was partly undone by August 1945, but the war ended before Donovan's warriors could demonstrate that the trick was being turned. Even if they had succeeded in time, their shadow warfare triumphs still would have been played out in a secondary area, which was only marginally important when compared with what American air, naval, amphibious, and atomic power had done against Japan.[124]

What had happened to O.S.S. China during the last phase of the war occurred again, with some variations, to Donovan's organization in Southeast Asia. This was the first area in which C.O.I.–O.S.S. had put a combat unit into action (Detachment 101) and one of the last in which it succeeded in sending into the field a broad range of shadow warfare activities. In this region, U.S. policy had its least friendly brush with European imperialism (the French in Indochina) and here, Anglo-American relations were most strained.

As early as November 1944, O.S.S. found itself involved in controversies with the French Provisional government about S.O.E. and O.S.S. recruitment of French officers for use in Indochina. At the same time, S.H.A.E.F. was asked by the Dutch to give high priority to its recruitment of Dutch marines for use in the East Indies. But these matters were initially little more than irritants to the Americans. What Washington saw as the major issue was a British effort to use Mountbatten and S.E.A.C. to recover Britain's imperial position in Southeast Asia. Donovan claimed in an October 1944 report to the president that there was "little doubt" that the British, Dutch, and French authorities had made a secret deal to restore their Southeast Asian imperial sway and that they intended to use "American resources" to this end, while "foreclosing the Americans from any voice in policy matters."[125]

Donovan was incorrect in accusing London of masterminding a secret plot to reestablish colonialism in Asia, but the British were anxious to restore their influence there. While seeking to maintain good relations between London and Washington and taking care not to challenge overtly American primacy in China, Britain was determined to push hard in Southeast Asia despite its relative loss of worldwide power and influence. In July 1945, an S.I.S. official suggested to London that it might be wise to soft-pedal trouble with the United States for the time being because when the Soviets ultimately entered the Pacific war "America would then be more likely to cooperate with us" and an Anglo-American deal would be possible. But London was in no mood to yield in Asia, and Brendan Bracken's reply to S.I.S. could have characterized the whole British position: "our policy is to give up nothing."[126]

At S.E.A.C. headquarters in Ceylon, Mountbatten was more subtle but equally determined. Not only did he wish to reinstate Britain's colonial position in the region, as he informed the Foreign Office in September 1944, he believed that since a French government had been reestablished in Paris "it will become increasingly difficult to exclude the French from Southeast Asia and the longer we delay in according them reasonable military participation, the greater the danger of introducing political complications." Since in Mountbatten's view "the Americans seem to have no constructive ideas on the subject except that they want to exclude us" it was vital that London push past the "American obstruction" and take the lead in harnessing French resources for the war against the Japanese in Southeast Asia. Like Churchill, Mountbatten saw that a weakened Britain would need to cultivate the western European countries both at home and in Asia, but a formal secret deal between Mountbatten and the French was not made in S.E.A.C. anymore than such an arrangement had been made—or was necessary—in London. The S.E.A.C. commander merely understood that because they had common colonial interests in Asia, European states had to be pulled together.[127]

Given the military situation, time was required to place significant force behind the aspirations of the British government and Lord Mountbatten. In April 1945, with the European war in its final stage, S.O.E. put 1,147 tons of supplies into Yugoslavia, 506 tons into Scandinavia, and a total of 276 tons into all of Southeast Asia. Most of these supplies (239 tons) went to Burma, and 75 S.O.E. personnel were put into Burma in April as well. With the end of the European war, the British were free to transfer more of their resources to Asia, and S.O.E. activity there increased. Sixty-four tons went in during the first week of July, and S.O.E. was still dropping over 50 tons per week in the last fortnight of the war. The Southeast Asian S.O.E. contingent numbered 2,000 military personnel by June and remained above 2,000 after Japan's surrender. In addition, S.O.E. headquarters in Delhi was authorized a huge civilian personnel allotment, ranging between 7,500 and 8,200 people, which suggests that London used the Southeast Asian S.O.E. contingent as a catchall organization for those who would do the work of reestablishing British authority in the area.[128]

In Southeast Asia, relations between O.S.S. and S.O.E. were generally harmonious in the field, as they were in other combat areas. Even in Burma and Malaya, the territories most sensitive to the British, few O.S.S.-S.O.E. scrapes occurred because Britain's units concentrated in the southern half of these two countries while the Americans worked mainly in the north. Like S.O.E., O.S.S. rapidly built up its strength in the region. In fact, the American buildup began first and kept pace with that of the British even after the end of the European war. Donovan's people had missions in, or courier routes established for, all the Southeast Asian countries by April 1945, and the number of O.S.S. wireless sets operating had risen from 5 to 134 between February 1944 and March 1945. But there was great uncertainty regarding what policy all this activity should serve aside from Donovan's desire to make a big splash for his organization and show the efficacy of shadow warfare.[129]

As early as April 1945, the head of R. and A.'s Far East Division Charles Fahs, complained to Donovan that "in general in the Far East but particularly in Burma, India, and Kandy, there seems to be no clear line established, either in the Theater or by Washington, as to relations with the British." President Roosevelt was leery of assisting European colonial activities, and in April 1945 the State Department urged O.S.S. to be careful that its work not be "associated" in Burmese minds with that of the British. Yet American diplomats were also nervous about O.S.S. "overenthusiasm" and the "personal views" of some of its members. Furthermore, the American military deputy commander under S.E.A.C., Gen. Daniel Sultan, was anxious to end autonomy of the organization and bring its functions completely inside the regular army and navy chains of command once it had done its work in Burma.[130]

Opinions within O.S.S. on what policy the organization should be pursuing in Southeast Asia also changed markedly in the course of 1944–45. From the spring of 1944 to that of 1945, though some of Donovan's people in S.E.A.C. were already seriously upset by the prospect of aligning with European imperialism, most O.S.S. attention was focused on trying to secure enough elbow room to operate under S.E.A.C. and in giving all possible assistance to Detachment 101. Until March 1945, Detachment 101 was engaged in supporting operations to clear the Japanese from northern Burma, thereby putting the whole of the Burma Road and its surrounding countryside in Allied hands. During this campaign, which was led first by General Stilwell and then General Sultan, Detachment 101 and the Kachins provided extraordinarily valuable intelligence and guerrilla support, especially in the battle for the vital Myitkyina airstrip and in the final drive against the Japanese stronghold of Lashio. The regular army commanders in charge of the offensive, including Stilwell, were generous in their praise of Detachment 101, which at the start of the campaign consisted of no more than 300 to 400 Americans.[131]

When in April 1945 Burma operations moved out of Kachin territory and into the Shan states in the central part of the country, it was more difficult for Detachment 101 to score dramatic triumphs. The central Burma campaign finally ended victoriously in June 1945, and administration of the area was turned over to the British in July. But by that time, the focus of O.S.S. attention in S.E.A.C. had moved elsewhere. Donovan's people were operating in Malaya, but they began there very late, were always in the British shadow, and never achieved dramatic results. O.S.S. operations in Thailand, however, were somewhat more significant.[132]

When occupied by the Japanese in 1941–42, Thailand had declared war on Britain and had seized a slice of Burma but had not gone to war with the United States. Having blown hot and cold on plans for a Thai legion ever since 1942, O.S.S. decided in late 1944 (without informing the British) to send a regular covert mission into the country to gather intelligence and see if effective political warfare contacts could be made with Thai officials. Thai authorities took the O.S.S. men into a kind of protective custody, shielding them from the Japanese police and allowing them to gather intelligence. Increasingly worried by the advance of the Allies and apprehensive that Japan would tighten its grip on Thailand in the course of the final showdown in Asia, the Bangkok government attempted to use the O.S.S. channel to make a deal with Washington. In February 1945, one of the "captured" O.S.S. men was slipped out of the country to act as courier for a secret Thai plan to increase O.S.S. covert activity and bring in an American division to assist the Bangkok government in changing sides. The J.C.S. was cool toward the proposal, believing Thailand to be unimportant in the final attack on Japan and not worth the commitment of a regular American formation.[133]

Then, in the second week of March, Japanese occupation forces in neighboring Indochina moved against the French collaborationist administration of the colony, arresting French officials, disarming the French army and police units, and seizing direct control of the administration of the territory. This action alarmed the Thais, who feared that a similar fate awaited them. It also alarmed the State Department, which wished to avoid political complications, and O.S.S., which wanted nothing to interfere with its covert action projects. The military still opposed use of regular American forces but went along with the State Department request for increased O.S.S. activity in Thailand. This decision pleased a number of political activists within O.S.S.–S.E.A.C. who had long advocated a more distinctly "pro-American" political program in Southeast Asia. As early as August 1944, the R. and A. chief of O.S.S.–S.E.A.C., Cora DuBois, stressed to Washington that the area was "the largest unexploited colonial region of the Far East" and that "the U.S. position in the next Pacific war will be greatly influenced by the present effectiveness of O.S.S. in this theatre." In June 1945, an unidentified O.S.S. intelligence officer in S.E.A.C. recommended that O.S.S. people "shift the emphasis" of their "intelligence activities in Thailand" so that assistance to British forces received "lowest priority" while primacy be given to information of value to combat units in the Pacific and in China and "political or economic intelligence" that reflected the "increasing State Department interest in Thailand, particularly with regard to post-war developments in that country."[134]

Yet Washington did not decide to go all out in Thailand, while London was determined to push hard. In April 1945, S.E.A.C. swept aside Thai protests and notified Bangkok that it was concentrating S.O.E. clandestine operations in the Kengtung region that Thailand had seized from Burma. Following V.J. Day, after helping to rescue Allied P.O.W.s, Donovan's people were forced to stand aside helplessly as Thai government officials fraternized openly and happily with the defeated Japanese and the British moved in to force a peace treaty on Thailand that returned Kengtung to Burma and gave Mountbatten a measure of control over the Thai armed forces.[135]

In Indochina as in Thailand, there was some awakening of American political assertiveness and hence a willingness to compete with the British during the last phase of the war. The nub of the issue in Indochina was whether or not the French Provisional government should be allowed to play a part in organizing S.E.A.C. operations into Indochina. As we have seen, Mountbatten favored French participation, and at the second Quebec conference in September 1944, the British tried to persuade American officials that this course was wisest. The issue could not be so simply resolved, however.

When the Japanese occupied Indochina in late 1941, the Vichy French administration of the colony had been forced to cooperate and thereby became a kind of quisling Japanese governmental machine. But the Allied victory in France in June 1944 destroyed Vichy, put de Gaulle's Provisional government into power in Paris by August, and left the Vichy administration in Indochina in political limbo. As the Allies moved closer to the Gaullist Provisional government, tension rose among the French in Indochina, with a handful of Vichy hard-liners condemning de Gaulle and trying to stick with the Japanese, and the vast majority of French men and women in the colony slipping into some form of pro-Allied and anti-Japanese opposition. Inevitably this situation weakened the usefulness of the French administration to the Japanese and prompted them to take over complete control of the colony in March 1945.[136]

In addition to the troubles caused by the emergence of a Gaullist challenge in Indochina, Anglo-American policy was complicated by the attitude of Franklin Roosevelt. The president neither liked nor trusted de Gaulle and had such a general distaste for formal colonialism that he was reluctant to recognize French sovereignty in Indochina or to assist the French in restoring their position there. In the summer and early fall of 1944, the president was under considerable pressure from Donovan and the British to authorize S.O.E. and O.S.S. use of their French resistance friends in Indochina, but Roosevelt declined to do so, disturbed by neither French complaints nor British pressure. In October 1944, he told both the J.C.S. and the State Department that "American approval must not be given to any French Mission being accredited to S.E.A.C. and that this Government has made no final decision on the future of Indo China." When in December 1944, the French and British renewed their requests that French officers be assigned to S.E.A.C. and that they be allowed to participate in Indochinese operations, the president once again rebuffed them. On 1 January 1945, Roosevelt notified the State Department that as had already been made "very clear to Mr. Churchill," the president did "not want to get mixed up in any Indochina decision," which he felt was "a matter for post-war." Roosevelt added that, "by the same token, I do not want to get mixed up in any military effort toward the liberation of Indochina from the Japanese."[137]

This might seem to have settled the matter, since the United States appeared to have a definite, if extremely short-range, policy on Indochina. Postwar observers have frequently pointed to Roosevelt's coolness on the French position in Indochina as proof that in 1945 other options were available beside the one that ultimately led down the road to the debacle in Vietnam. But the documentary record currently available shows that even President Roosevelt could not stick firmly to his own policy of noninvolvement in Indochina.

In January 1945, the French launched yet another effort to wriggle into Allied Indochina operations, requesting permission to establish a liaison officer in the Philippines to supply the U.S. Navy with weather information originating from agents in Indochina. They also pressed General Wedemeyer for permission to establish a French mission in Chunking to work with the Americans on special operations and intelligence activities. The J.C.S quickly disposed of the French attempt to use weather reports to get into the headquarters of Nimitz or MacArthur, but China was a more difficult problem. Although Wedemeyer was cool toward the establishment of any more liaison missions and did not want a French officer assigned to his headquarters, he was getting useful intelligence from French sources in Indochina and was also under heavy pressure from O.S.S. to use China as a base for infiltration into Southeast Asia. In early February 1945, General Marshall took up the China–Indochina matter with the president and thereafter, the J.C.S. once more informed General Sultan "that he should not authorize the use of O.S.S. personnel under Mountbatten in Indo-China." But on 9 February, Wedemeyer was informed by Gen. John E. Hull that

> The President indicated that he had no objections to your carrying out intelligence and subversive operations in Indo-China. He indicated that he was in favor of anything that was against the Japs provided that we do not align ourselves with the French. The President has not changed his attitude concerning dealing with the French authorities in such a way as to give French interests in the Far East official recognition. . . . You say they [the French] are providing valuable intelligence. . . . Pending receipt of instructions to stop it, I certainly would continue such intelligence activities as you feel necessary to carry on and maintain such contacts with the French as are necessary for this purpose. . . . It was not the Joint Chiefs of Staff desire, in my opinion, to limit you in the use of O.S.S. personnel in French Indo-China.[138]

This message hardly provided Wedemeyer with a straight or well-defined path through the thicket of Indochinese colonial politics and special operations. But Roosevelt's authorizing shadow warfare operations into Indochina from the American-controlled Chinese theater while prohibiting them from British-controlled S.E.A.C. indicates that his hard-line Indochina policy was beginning to shift under the pressure of military events. Then in March 1945, the Japanese clamped down in Indochina, and by seizing control of the whole administration, drove numerous French officials, especially military officers, into outright resistance. The government in Paris desperately sought to aid these resisters, and both Washington and London were bombarded with requests for assistance. Admiral Leahy thought it would help French *amour propre* if a French officer was at least permitted to talk with Wedemeyer, and even though the American commander in China was still not enthusiastic about having a French liaison officer on his staff, the president approved the assignment of Gen. Roger Blaizot to Chunking on 13 March. Four days later, the American J.P.S. was toying with the idea of letting Wedemeyer increase aid to Indochina, including the dispatch of the 500-man Corps Léger d'Intervention because such "'token' operations" might lure the French away from S.E.A.C. and prevent Mountbatten from making a large-scale move into Indochina. In fact, a few O.S.S. missions did go in from China to render assistance to the French in the course of March.[139]

By early April, an Anglo-American confrontation was shaping up over Indochinese policy. Chennault had secured definite evidence that the British were sending covert operational supply missions into Indochina without notifying the China theater as required by agreements between Washington and London, and on 30 March 1945, General Marshall fired off a stiff protest to the British warning that "we are riding for a fall out there" if this practice did not stop. Mountbatten quickly agreed to inform Wedemeyer of supply missions into Indochina and conceded to him a veto on activities that clashed with his operations from China. But then on 11 April, Churchill tried to push the issue further, and in a message to the president, called for a joint message confirming the Mountbatten–Wedemeyer agreement because in the prime minister's view it was "essential not only that we support the French by all the means in our power, but also that we should associate them with our operations into *their* country" [italics added]. Emphasizing that "it would look very bad in history if we failed to support isolated French forces in their resistance to the Japanese," Churchill tried to use the French–Japanese clashes to persuade Roosevelt to reverse policy and consent to the inclusion of the French "in our councils as regards Indo-China."[140]

It is difficult to estimate how Roosevelt might have replied to this message. In early April 1945, O.S.S. was still banned from operating into Indochina from S.E.A.C. but was allowed to do so from China. President Roosevelt had not formally changed his policy of refusing to endorse French claims in Indochina, but he had approved the assignment of a French liaison officer to Wedemeyer. The American military remained firmly committed to the view that with American forces closing in on Japan for the kill, regular Allied units should not be diverted for operations in Indochina. Yet relations with the French government were also a factor. It was difficult to ignore appeals from Paris—despite black thoughts about de Gaulle—when French forces were fighting and dying in clashes with the Japanese, especially since the French officials calling for Allied aid were the same people with whom the Anglo-Americans had cooperated in the 1942–44 covert resistance aid campaigns in metropolitan France.[141]

In any event, the issues raised by Churchill were not immediately confronted because Franklin Roosevelt died the day after the prime minister's message was received. The reply prepared by the American military authorities (and apparently dispatched on 13 April), while declaring that Wedemeyer would "give to the French resistance groups such assistance as is practicable without prejudice to his present or future operations," merely confirmed the limited notification agreement made between Wedemeyer and Mountbatten and dodged the broader questions.[142]

A problem avoided does not necessarily disappear, however, and Indochina continued to cause trouble between the British and the Americans. In late April and on into May, Mountbatten claimed that he was authorized to operate in Indochina—although no British liaison officers had yet been sent in—because he had secured Chiang Kai-shek's verbal agreement to such activities in November 1943. The British S.E.A.C. commander was offended that the Americans were skeptical about the existence of this "gentleman's agreement" with Chiang, and he was not mollified by General Marshall's view that the best thing to do was "drop further argument about the verbal agreement." Wedemeyer was also irritated by the Indochina situation because he felt that Mountbatten was running off on his own and was still not providing adequate information on S.E.A.C. shadow warfare support missions. The Mountbatten–Wedemeyer clash became so bitter that on 30 May 1945, Wedemeyer requested the War Department to suspend shipment of all Lend-Lease supplies destined for British "clandestine organizations in SEAC" until the conflict was settled![143]

At this point, however, the new American president, Harry Truman, intervened to produce a definite shift in American policy. Truman was obviously not enamored of Roosevelt's notion of placing prewar Asian colonies under trusteeships, had no particular hostility toward de Gaulle and no special feelings about Indochina. In an early June meeting with the French ambassador, Truman agreed to withdraw all American political objections to assistance for French military activities in Indochina and directed the War and Navy departments henceforth to plan military operations there solely "on their military merits." The president did inform Ambassador Hurley that he intended "at some appropriate time to ask that the French Government give some positive indication of its intentions in regard to the establishment of civil liberties and increasing measures of self-government in Indochina." This qualification amounted to little more than window dressing, however, for Truman had decided to let the Anglo-American military assist the French in recovering their position in the colony. Wedemeyer was ordered by Marshall to drop his complaints about Mountbatten's activities, employ whatever forces in Indochina appeared to offer the best prospect of causing "maximum damage to the Japs," and to allow no other principle than that of military necessity to govern his actions in Southeast Asia.[144]

Consequently, the last sixty days of the Asian war saw a substantial inflow of O.S.S., S.O.E., and French shadow warfare personnel into Indochina from both the American China command and the British-dominated S.E.A.C. area. Some useful intelligence was undoubtedly collected, and covert French and Indochinese resistance groups (including the Viet Minh) were assisted, but prior to the end of hostilities no Allied clandestine force had succeeded in inflicting serious losses on the Japanese in Indochina. Since no large-scale Allied forces appeared in Indochina during the first month after the formal Japanese capitulation, additional O.S.S. and S.O.E. missions went in to assist in the liberation of Allied P.O.W.s after V.J. Day. During this interregnum, the Japanese retained control of the colony's administration, while various native groups ranging from Ho Chi Minh's Communists to the Annamite confederation of Bao Dai (who had collaborated with the Japanese) made moves to establish an independent native government for Indochina. Some cursory talks took place between the Annamites and French officials, but the latter were not forthcoming, the anti-French mood of all the native movements gradually hardened, and there was a "general sale or gift of arms by the Japanese to the Annamites." O.S.S. men moved among the French and British missions and also contacted various Indochinese groups, including the Communists. Predictably, O.S.S. people tended to be sympathetic to the nationalist and anticolonial desires of the population. Since they constituted the only means by which the Indochinese could hope to create a counterweight to the British and French colonial authorities, they were warmly received. Although on occasion it was indicated that the Indochinese were "not politically mature" or were "being misled by Japanese agents-provacateurs and Communist elements," a large number of pro-Annamite dispatches were sent to Washington by O.S.S. On at least one occasion, Annamite (not communist) spokesmen even requested via O.S.S. that the United States make Indochina an American protectorate.[145]

But Washington had no sympathy for native Indochinese movements, and did not object, in late September, when a British S.E.A.C. task force (Gremlin), under Air Chief Marshal W. G. Cheshire moved into Indochina, crushed the Annamite forces, which Cheshire considered "rebels," disarmed the Japanese Army, and reestablished a French colonial administration. O.S.S. personnel were compelled to stand aside during this operation (the O.S.S. chief in Indochina was mistakenly killed by an Indochinese group during the struggle) and were evacuated soon after the main fighting ended in late September.[146]

Since O.S.S. had made contact with Ho Chi Minh during August and September of 1945 and for the most part had been treated warmly by the Annamites, a postwar myth soon arose (growing to major dimensions at the time of the Vietnam War) that through O.S.S., America had been given an opportunity to turn the fluid Indochina situation in a positive direction but had muffed it. In fact, the immediate postwar O.S.S. political contacts with Indochinese movements were minor and the lost opportunity consequently an illusion. O.S.S. was in Indochina in some force only because in June 1945 President Truman had reversed Franklin Roosevelt's policy and had decided to support the French. If Truman had maintained Roosevelt's cautious policy, the host of O.S.S. people scurrying about making contacts with the natives in August and September 1945 would not have been in Indochina at all. They were there because the issue had already been settled; Washington had decided to keep out of the way and let Mountbatten and the British hoist the French back into the saddle in Saigon.

O.S.S. operations in Indochina, as in every other area of continental Asia, constituted secondary supportive actions in military backwaters. The American government had resolved not to fight a major continental Asian conflict in the Second World War but to triumph through naval, amphibious, and air operations in the Pacific. Its armed might was not used directly during hostilities to shape postwar political events in the sensitive zones of northern China, Korea, the British colonies of Southeast Asia, or French Indochina. This decision gave Donovan an opportunity to show some of his "stuff" in Asia but only because Washington had previously concluded that these areas were not on the main path to victory over the Japanese and that politics did not justify the diversion of large Allied forces.

Therefore, no matter how fast William Donovan ran or how hard his people struggled to overcome the obstacles created by political conflicts and the shortages of supplies, O.S.S. could in no way score a dramatic triumph in Asia. It could not lay solid foundations for postwar American influence because it did not have the physical strength to do so; weak as they were, even the British and the nationalist Chinese had more ground forces on the Asian continent at the end of the war than the Americans. Although hostilities in the Pacific finished with a rush, O.S.S. Asia could not end the war in the blaze of glory that Donovan desired. On V.J. Day, all eyes were fixed not on shadow warfare but on Japan, the U.S.S. *Missouri,* and the B–29s with their atomic bombs. In August and September of 1945, the men of O.S.S. Asia, like all the others who had played a supporting role on the fringe, were forced to pack their gear and head for home. By the time most of them reached the United States, President Truman had signed the order dissolving O.S.S., and by the end of September 1945, Donovan's organization was no more.

But if Donovan's organization was disbanded at war's end, how did the United States acquire a centralized shadow warfare system out of the Second World War, and what were the threads leading from O.S.S. to the C.I.A.? The chronological record of 1940–45 that we have just presented lays the basis for answering these questions. To do so effectively, however, we must now move away from the dynamic elements that determined the form and evolution of O.S.S. itself and concentrate on those features that helped to keep the O.S.S. legacy alive after the dissolution order of September 1945. Foremost among these features were, of course, the overt efforts of Donovan and his colleagues, spread over the years 1943–47, to encourage the creation of a postwar intelligence organization. In addition, the R. and A. Branch of O.S.S. pioneered efforts to link up the strategic intelligence needs of wartime with those of the postwar period. More fundamental even than these features was the success of Donovan's organization in transcending some of the problems of ideology. To become an integral element in the regular American governmental system, shadow warfare had to be able to cope with changing ideological antagonisms. By examining the wartime relations between O.S.S. and the Soviet N.K.V.D., we will be able to see how Donovan and his aides demonstrated that an American shadow warfare organization could go beyond traditional ideological hostilities to pursue what it saw as its own, and the nation's, interests.

CHAPTER 7

O.S.S. and Ideology:
The N.K.V.D. Connection

I want to express my appreciation for the
spirit of friendly cooperation you have
shown us. We have tried to reciprocate. I
think the degree of success we have had so
far in our joint enterprises shows what Allies
may do together.

WILLIAM J. DONOVAN TO
GENERAL P. M. FITIN
Chief External Intelligence Division,
N.K.V.D.
10 October 1944

DURING the four decades that have passed since the creation of Donovan's organization, many observers have claimed that ideology played a major role in determining O.S.S. policies and actions. But those who have made such assertions have disagreed sharply on just which ideology dominated the organization and what the effects of the alleged ideological taint actually were.

Conservative and cautious United States ambassadors such as Carlton Hayes in Spain and Lincoln MacVeagh in Greece thought during the war and immediately after that O.S.S. was "slanted toward the left" and was indulgent of communism. Both Winston Churchill and Chiang Kai-shek believed that some O.S.S. activities in their countries aided Communists.

During the great postwar Red Scare, rightists contended that since O.S.S. included veterans of the Spanish Civil War Abraham Lincoln Brigade in its ranks, and employed prominent Marxists, including Herbert Marcuse, Noel Field, Maurice Halperin, and Paul Sweezy, Moscow at times must have been calling the tune.[1]

Whereas these critics felt that O.S.S. had too many left-wing drive-wheels, others believed that it was too cautious and politically conservative. Such liberal activists as Peter Tomkins contended that the administrative "colonels" to whom Donovan turned over much of the day-to-day control of O.S.S. in 1943 tipped the organization sharply to the right. Both S.O.E. and the partisans held that O.S.S. was unsympathetic to the left in Yugoslavia, and a number of resistance leaders of varying political persuasions in France, Italy, and other countries thought this was true of their areas as well. During the 1970s, some new left revisionists, such as Gabriel Kolko, revived and extended the argument, suggesting that O.S.S. was perhaps the tip of the capitalist lance that America sought to hurl at the Soviet Union.

Somewhere in between the right and the left critics of O.S.S. came a third highly influential group that has asserted that Donovan's organization was, despite some blemishes, the embodiment of an American liberal ideology, characterized by humanitarianism, optimism, and generosity. Although this is rather a tall order for an instrument of war to fill, writers such as R. Harris Smith and David Schoenbrunn have persuaded portions of the public that, in contrast to the manipulative activities of the British and the brutality of the Soviets, American subversive warfare and central intelligence during World War II worked for the cause of morality. Allegedly, O.S.S. was animated by moral passion and eschewed the cold, repressive methods later associated with the C.I.A.

The information set forth in the preceding chapters should suggest that all three of these ideological pictures of O.S.S. might best be regarded with considerable skepticism. Certainly U.S. policy and public opinion were then more optimistic and self-confident than they are today, and these sentiments were manifest in O.S.S. as they were in most other American wartime organizations. Furthermore, the United States's official World War II policy was a model of simplicity: win the war quickly and create a world of peace, freedom, and abundance secured by the continuation of the wartime alliance of the United States, the United Kingdom, Soviet Union, and Nationalist China (with France thrown in as an also-ran). Leaving aside as best we can the question of whether or not such a policy was realistic—or a policy at all in the customary sense of the word—a number of seldom mentioned undertones in the prevailing

American attitude definitely colored policy. Among these was a suspicion of all authoritarian systems, including that of the Soviet Union and the colonial administration of Great Britain. There was also concern about whether Nationalist China could actually sustain itself in the postwar world and whether the United States would be able to keep the Soviet Union and Britain from clashing in Europe and Asia. All these worries were rather wide of the mark, for Britain was much weaker than Americans thought, Chiang's China was weaker yet, formal imperialism was doomed, and only the United States and the Soviet Union would emerge from the war as superpowers. Yet suspicion of Britain and the desire to prop up China and pummel imperialism were attitudes sincerely—if often quietly—held by most Americans, and they were inevitably manifest in O.S.S. as well. That assorted "anti" tendencies were also present in the American spirit, ranging from anticommunism to anti-Semitism, should surprise no one, nor should it be a shocking revelation that elements of this negativism existed in an organization as large and as heterogeneous as O.S.S.

The documentary evidence currently available shows that all these fears and concerns expressed themselves inside O.S.S. but that the organization as a whole did not deviate significantly from the "ideological" mainstream of American wartime policy. The conservative faction, led by John Rogers, John Wiley, and Dewitt Poole, tried and failed to push Washington into overtly anti-Soviet power politics in late 1943. Such liberals as H. Stuart Hughes had somewhat better luck reassuring Washington and the generals about leftists in the resistance and the need to recognize that French public opinion would not allow de Gaulle to be pushed aside. However, the British and the American commanders still did everything they could to emasculate the resistance as quickly as possible, and Franklin Roosevelt and his close advisers never overcame their deep antipathy toward what they saw as de Gaulle's authoritarian tendencies.

In Southeast Asia and northern China, O.S.S. field detachments may seem in retrospect to have overstepped the bounds in supporting communist and antiwestern resistance movements. But at the time, both the American military commanders and many Washington officials looked on this activity with sympathy for reasons that had nothing to do with *leftist ideology* as we now use that term. The White House, the State Department, and Generals Stilwell and Wedemeyer were all anti-imperialist; that is, opposed in principle to European possession of Asian territory as formal colonies. Strange as it may seem, they did not extend their thinking much beyond revulsion at the injustice and degradation seemingly associated with the British raj. They were sure that such systems of government should end, but what ought to take their place and how the United States, as the world's greatest capitalist power, should deal with such areas once imperialism ceased, seems not to have troubled them. They simply believed colonialism wrong and furthermore thought the colonial powers—Britain, France, and the Netherlands—and Nationalist China too weak in Asia to do much of the real fighting against Japan. They did become nervous when O.S.S. cavorted with Chinese Communists and a resistance movement in Indochina that was as anti-French as it was anti-Japanese. But, the senior American authorities were also uneasy and embarrassed that "democratic America" was allied with exploitive yet impotent imperialists in Asia. What they—and O.S.S.—ultimately would have done had they been required over a long period to balance off their fear of strong radicals against their dislike of feeble imperialists is an intriguing question, but one that is impossible to answer. The atomic bomb settled the military aspect of the problem, and the American High Command was then free to withdraw from most of the Asian mainland with suitable moralizing about the evils of colonialism. The main political question was finally clarified after much difficulty when in the late 1940s the U.S. government proclaimed a policy of ending overt imperialism while trying to stabilize Asia on the basis of continued economic and political domination by the West.

As a peripheral organization whose political warfare mission put it partly out of step with the big battalion mentality of the J.C.S., O.S.S. inevitably had pushed America's vague wartime policies to the limit. Like S.O.E., O.S.S. also had discovered that to produce change in an enemy-occupied territory, one had to depend on people who desired change, which necessarily meant that Donovan's organization would lean more frequently toward the political left than toward the conservative right. As so frequently happened, the practical experience of O.S.S. was very similar to that of S.O.E. (even though some O.S.S. men were reluctant to be too closely associated with any agency of imperial Britain) for both organizations had to show the military High Command that subversive warfare produced results. Inevitably, emphasis fell on an experimental, or pragmatic, approach, which if Charles Peirce and William James are correct may itself be a philosophy, but actually meant that customary political and ideological values would not be allowed to stand in the way of any promising shadow warfare project.

To see what this tendency toward pragmatism could lead to, it is instructive to examine the relations between S.O.E. and O.S.S. on the one hand and the subversive warfare organizations of the Soviet Union on the other. Only by exploring how organizations such as S.O.E. (whose godfather was the Tory Winston Churchill) and O.S.S. (which was led by the conservative Irish-American Catholic William Donovan) could end up as partners with the Soviet N.K.V.D. will we really be able to grasp the limited impact of ideology in Anglo-American shadow warfare.

Until Hitler's attack on Russia in June 1941 tossed Britain and the Soviet Union into each other's arms, S.O.E. officials had never dreamed of cooperating directly with the N.K.V.D. In fact, S.O.E. had developed plans to sabotage Russia on the grounds that although the Soviet Union and the United Kingdom were not at war with each other, anyone who had a nonaggression pact with Germany and was supplying Hitler with war material could hardly be a friend of Great Britain. Even after the Nazi attack on Russia, S.O.E. continued to develop plans to blow up such vital Russian economic prizes as the Caucasus oil industry, which had to be kept out of German hands in the event Soviet resistance crumbled. But taking a cue from Churchill's declaration that "anyone who marches against Hitler is our friend" and realizing that Britain was so desperately weak and vulnerable that it could not be choosy, Dalton and the S.O.E. chiefs immediately decided to add one of their men to the Cripps mission sent to Moscow in June to explore the possibility of subversive warfare cooperation with the Russians. Sir Stafford Cripps himself initially hoped that this would not have to be arranged by a regular British official through normal channels but "through some Slav, possibly, Czech, tough." This proved impossible, however, and S.O.E. sent an army sapper, Col. Robert Guiness, to explore the Moscow ground in June, and in August, Col. (later Brigadier) George A. Hill went to the Russian capital to head an S.O.E. team that was given the cover name of the SAM Mission. Shortly thereafter, an N.K.V.D. colonel, I. Chichayev, whose cover assignment was that of Soviet counsellor to the Allied governments in exile, was designated N.K.V.D. liaison man in London.[2]

Some hard bargaining was necessary to make even this exchange possible. S.O.E. and N.K.V.D. promised not to mount subversive missions in each other's territory. The British further agreed to help the Russians with some covert operations drops into western Europe, and in return for this assistance, the N.K.V.D. pledged that it would undertake no independent subversive activities in the Middle East. Both sides acknowledged that joint missions might be useful but decided to postpone them for the time being.

While trying desperately to build up a solid defense against the Wehrmacht after Hitler's forces had shredded the Russian formations on the western border, the Soviets were in no position to undertake ambitious subversive warfare projects beyond their own frontiers in the fall of 1941.

The British, although possessed of somewhat greater freedom in their covert actions, reacted with their usual caution regarding the Communists.

Furthermore, British subversive warfare people had little room to maneuver because the Soviet authorities were as much on their guard with S.O.E. as they were with other foreign organizations. In July, a member of the British military mission complained to London that "none of us here can move a yard without being followed," and when the Germans threatened Moscow, Hill was moved to Kuibyshev with the diplomatic corps. Col. A.P. Ossipov, the N.K.V.D. subversive warfare official assigned to work with Hill, seems to have been cooperative enough. Ossipov did not even take serious offense at the fact that Hill had been an anticommunist operative in Russia during the First World War or that his S.O.E. staff included a man who was violently anti-Russian and anti-Soviet. Ossipov admired Hill's "professionalism," so personalities and past records were not the main stumbling block. Nothing much happened, though, because neither side was willing in the late fall of 1941 to take what appeared to be the huge risks necessary to make subversive warfare cooperation truly productive.[3]

When in late 1941 and on into 1942 the position of both Britain and the Soviet Union changed for the better—the former by America's entry into the war and the latter by this and by the Red Army's defensive triumph before Moscow—N.K.V.D. and the British shadow warfare groups tried again. P.W.E. arranged for some propaganda coordination with Soviet authorities, and British intelligence officials began to provide the U.S.S.R. with military intelligence information. Yet even at this time the London government remained cautious about the quality and quantity of the intelligence information handed over to the Russians. Official commentators now suggest that it was "low-grade cypher stuff," and it is indeed likely that little or no high-grade Ultra-derived information was given to the Soviet Union. But an air of mystery hangs over the whole matter because of British official reticence. All statements about Anglo-Soviet intelligence relations made by a government that developed Ultra yet continues to claim that on 22 June 1941 it ceased *all* deciphering of Soviet codes for the duration of the war are difficult to take seriously.[4]

In regard to S.O.E.'s dealings with the Russians from early 1942 on, we are on somewhat firmer documentary ground. Despite a brief spat over Soviet protests against S.O.E. support of Mihajlović, Hill was given a larger role in assisting N.K.V.D. covert operations. He was taken behind German lines to study Soviet partisan tactics in February and March of 1942, and later claimed that after returning to Moscow, he actually helped Ossipov prepare the official Soviet handbook on guerrilla warfare! In the late summer of 1942, Hill journeyed to Istanbul and Cairo to explore the possibilities of launching S.O.E.–N.K.V.D. missions from those locations. He then flew on to London, bringing with him the first N.K.V.D. agent S.O.E. was to drop in a western European country (Belgium). While in London, Hill conferred with Colonel Chichayev, the N.K.V.D. man, trying to facilitate the infiltration of more N.K.V.D. agents into western Europe. As a result of Soviet requests and Hill's labors, Russian agents were henceforth taken to Britain by sea, and with the blessing of the chief of S.I.S. ("C"), S.O.E. arranged the western European N.K.V.D. agent drops.[5]

How many N.K.V.D. men were actually put into western Europe by the British is unclear (an S.O.E. document of January 1945 speaks of "a small number . . . mostly in 1943") and the present East–West political climate makes the clarification of details unlikely. However, available documents hint that Hill helped to arrange for N.K.V.D. drops into Germany and the Balkans and that he also exchanged subversive warfare equipment ("gadgets") and Balkan intelligence information with the N.K.V.D. The brigadier himself was not altogether happy with his role— remarking in his diary when making arrangements for the first N.K.V.D. agent drop, "oh dear, I'm not at all pleased about this." S.O.E. headquarters in London and Cairo were similarly uneasy, and after much deliberation in 1943 finally vetoed plans for joint N.K.V.D.–S.O.E. operations from Turkey.[6]

Whatever their doubts, British officials had pioneered the opening of East–West shadow warfare cooperation during the years 1941–43. In that era, C.O.I.–O.S.S. concerned itself only indirectly with Soviet affairs and made no attempt to initiate direct coordination with the Russian secret services. R. and A. of course studied Soviet conditions, and some S.I. reports on the U.S.S.R. reached Washington. However, after the demise of his first wild post–Pearl Harbor scheme of sending C.O.I. agents wandering through Russia under State Department cover, Donovan was cautious about dealing with Soviet officials in Washington. That he agreed to accept information on alleged Axis subversives from the American Communist party without informing the F.B.I. that he was doing so suggests that he believed it was possible to deal with "Reds" but was not yet ready to take chances with the Soviet government. The S.O.E.–O.S.S. treaty of June 1942, which divided the world into zones, declared that since O.S.S. "had no intention, for the present at least, of dealing with Russia, there was no need to work out any arrangements for collaboration for this area."[7]

In mid-summer 1943, however, when O.S.S. was flexing its muscles following the receipt of an organizational green light from the J.C.S., the question of liaison with the U.S.S.R. began to take on new significance. Apparently, R. and A. was the first O.S.S. group to suggest that one of Donovan's men should be stationed in Moscow. The O.S.S. representative on the I.D.C. then began to push this proposal, and in early November, Donovan secured the president's approval for a plan to send Stanley Weinberg openly to Moscow to collect printed material of value to R. and A. On one level, this was merely one more example of the effort made by various British, Canadian, and American organizations to increase the flow of Soviet press material reaching the West. It is also possible, however, that a casual conversation between Brigadier Hill and an O.S.S. official during a stopover in London in October 1943 had whetted Donovan's appetite for a bigger deal with the Russians.[8]

In any event, the head of the American Military Mission in Moscow, General Deane, who was a personal friend of Donovan, also had a chat with Brigadier Hill in the late fall of 1943. From this conversation, Deane concluded that large-scale O.S.S. coordination with the Russians would be worthwhile only if O.S.S. appeared highly professional and if the Soviets agreed to such activities as the use of their agents in China on Donovan's behalf. General Deane cautioned Washington that no O.S.S. activity in Russia should be attempted without first making thorough preparation with the Soviet authorities. Donovan consequently decided to meet with General Deane and Ambassador Harriman at the Cairo Conference in late November to discuss the whole matter. In the course of the conference, Deane and Harriman apparently suggested that the O.S.S. director fly to Moscow and personally present his case to Soviet officials. Following a short sojourn in China, the peripatetic O.S.S. chief followed this advice and arrived in Moscow in late December.

Donovan went to Russia with the intention not only of closing some kind of deal that would put O.S.S. in Moscow but also of obtaining a Soviet endorsement for his plan to entice Bulgaria out of the war by secret discussions with dissident elements in that country's governing circles. On Christmas Day 1943, Donovan and Harriman met with Foreign Minister Vyacheslav Molotov and found the Soviet official in a generous mood appropriate to the season. Of course, Donovan did not tell Molotov that he intended to dangle the possibility of forming an anti-German, but noncommunist government in front of the Bulgarians to encourage them to change sides. So when the Russian foreign minister heard that the O.S.S. director proposed to use subversive pressure to get the Bulgarians to desert the Axis, he gave the project his blessing and recommended that the United States and Britain also bomb the Bulgarians to help bring "them to their senses." Even though Stalin was away from Moscow at the time, a situation which usually prevented Soviet officials from agreeing to anything expeditiously, Molotov was apparently ready to look on Donovan with great favor, and in Harriman's words, "showed considerable interest in Bill and everything he said."

The second proposal that the O.S.S. director laid before Molotov was a plan for O.S.S. and a "comparable Soviet organization" to undertake large-scale intelligence coordination facilitated by an exchange of missions between Moscow and Washington. The available evidence suggests strongly that Donovan proposed this exchange without prior approval by the J.C.S. or the president. But of course Molotov had no way of knowing that Donovan was actually winging it, and the Soviet foreign minister warmly welcomed the idea and promised quickly to arrange a meeting between Donovan and the representatives of the "comparable Soviet organization."⁹

With a speed that General Deane had not seen equaled during his two months in Moscow, Molotov immediately acted on his promise. Two days after Christmas, Donovan and Harriman, with the State Department's Charles Bohlen acting as interpreter, were taken to N.K.V.D. headquarters to meet with Colonel Ossipov (who was already dealing with Brigadier Hill) and Maj. Gen. P. M. Fitin, the head of the Soviet external intelligence service. The atmosphere was as warm and friendly as one could hope to find in a secret police headquarters, even though General Fitin insinuated at one point that Donovan might have some ulterior motive for coming to Moscow and the personal appearance of Colonel Ossipov was so ominous that General Deane thought that the Soviet official could pass as "the boon companion of Boris Karloff."

Donovan opened the meeting with a survey of O.S.S. activities and went on to recommend O.S.S.–N.K.V.D. cooperation and an exchange of missions between the Soviet and American capitals. When General Fitin asked what "specific lines of cooperation General Donovan had in mind," the O.S.S. director cited three: the exchange of intelligence information, the coordination of agent operations in enemy countries to prevent Allied "agents working at cross purposes," and a swap of plans for "physical subversion" (i.e., sabotage) projects in Axis territory. General Fitin greeted Donovan's exposition with the statement that he and the N.K.V.D. "heartily welcomed" the O.S.S. director's proposals and "wished to express their thanks" for the American initiative.

The tone of the meeting was one of calm "professionalism," with no mention of any ideology—communist, democratic, or fascist. Donovan "emphasized that he was not attempting to make their decision for them" but merely inviting the N.K.V.D. to cooperate "if the Soviet Government considered it in the national interest to do so." The N.K.V.D. chiefs reciprocated in kind, accepting Donovan as an equal in the spy masters game. The group chatted amiably about coordination problems that agents might face in the field and the difficulties involved in developing subversive warfare equipment. In the course of the discussion, Colonel Ossipov, as the head of the N.K.V.D.'s subversive warfare section, "appeared particularly interested in the possibilities of plastic explosives." General Fitin, on the other hand, was more concerned about agent infiltration problems and wondered whether American facilities might be used to send N.K.V.D. agents into France and western Germany. Donovan gave Fitin's question an encouraging reply, noting that agent infiltration assistance was "entirely possible" and O.S.S. "would be glad to help in any way it could."

Donovan later claimed that he told the Soviets that the exchange deal was conditional on J.C.S. approval, but there is no such statement in the surviving record of the meeting—presumably made by Charles Bohlen— nor does it appear that Donovan raised the question of Soviet–American cooperation on intelligence matters for Japan, as he subsequently implied that he had. It was the Russians who declared that full implementation of the exchange deal would require approval "by higher organizations of the Soviet Government" (that is, Joseph Stalin), but Donovan nonetheless had good reason to feel that he would get what he wanted, for Fitin also stated that a number of matters "could be considered as decided." The N.K.V.D. general agreed to the immediate establishment of an O.S.S. mission in Moscow headed by Col. John Haskell as Donovan recommended, and also declared that "the exchange of certain information could begin right away."

The O.S.S. director must have come away from the meeting echoing Fitin's sentiments that now it "would be possible to work out a very fruitful and firm cooperation" and that "their relations would grow stronger." Within a few days, Donovan was informed via General Deane that the "higher organizations of the Soviet Government" had assented to the exchange and already had designated the N.K.V.D.'s Col. A. G. Grauer to lead a seven-man mission to Washington. On the eve of his departure from Moscow on 6 January, following a delay occasioned by squabbles over air transport, Donovan sent a cable to O.S.S. Washington announcing his triumph, stating that he also had agreed to an "exchange of special devices and equipment," and ordering the development of a full O.S.S. mission for Moscow as a matter of highest priority.[10]

This message, augmented by Deane's report on the deal to the J.C.S.

emphasizing the N.K.V.D.'s "enthusiastic desire to cooperate," immediately put the O.S.S. Washington staff and the J.P.S. planners to work. The O.S.S. preparations for a Moscow mission reveal a number of interesting considerations, including the high hopes, ultimately frustrated, of securing valuable information on Japan from the N.K.V.D. It is also clear that the O.S.S. staff attached the highest importance to the proposed mission and among its ten members listed two colonels and William Langer's top administrative assistant, Ensign Carl Schorske. The O.S.S. planning showed throughout a readiness for tough, hard bargaining. As Charles Fahs wrote to Langer on 15 January, "we must pay for materials we get from the U.S.S.R. with comparable materials from the U.S." Fahs was sure that everything had to be done on "a trading basis" and though the United States should not "give more than we receive," it was important to convince the Soviets that the Americans were serious and not just "snooping for information on communism in the Far East or Soviet policy there." As usual, there were some unintentionally humorous moments, such as Richard Hartshorne's 20 January suggestion that the N.K.V.D.—the secret police of the world's most devotedly atheistic government—might provide the United States with valuable information on "the role of the Church and the Vatican" in Europe. By and large, however, the O.S.S. planning was cool, calm, devoid of ideological considerations, and, though keyed to a larger mission than General Deane thought feasible, very well done.[11]

The J.C.S.'s consideration of the O.S.S.–N.K.V.D. mission exchange plan also began in a thoroughly businesslike way. On 3 February, a three-man subcommittee of the J.P.S. was chosen to study the plan and prepare recommendations. After checking with the State Department and receiving a departmental concurrence from Bohlen, the J.P.S. subcommittee concluded on 10 February that "the military advantages which may be derived from such reciprocal exchange of O.S.S. [and N.K.V.D.] missions appear to outweigh the disadvantages." Therefore, the J.P.S. recommended J.C.S. approval.

But on the same day (10 February 1944), J. Edgar Hoover dispatched to the White House by special messenger a "personal and confidential" memorandum to presidential aide Harry Hopkins denouncing the plan in the strongest possible terms, claiming that although O.S.S. had not yet secured the approval of the J.C.S. for the proposal, he had learned of it "from a confidential but reliable source [G-2?]." The F.B.I. chief asserted that the plan was "a highly dangerous and most undesirable procedure" for it would "establish in the United States a unit of the Russian Secret Service which has admittedly for its purpose the penetration into the official secrets of various government agencies." He further declared that the British government had refused close cooperation with N.K.V.D. in the United Kingdom because "the fundamental purpose of its operations there was to surreptitiously obtain the official secrets of the British government."

Since at that very moment His Majesty's government was contentedly carrying out liaison with the N.K.V.D.'s Col. I. Chichayev, who had been established in London in much the same way that Colonel Grauer was to be established in Washington, that portion of Hoover's accusation was not correct. He was also not altogether accurate in claiming that O.S.S. had failed to secure the approval of the J.C.S., for though Donovan seems not to have given the chiefs prior warning, the plan had been under consideration by the J.C.S. staff for ten days at the time of the F.B.I. chief's letter to the White House. Yet there is no question that Hoover's letter, bristling with phrases like *potential danger* and *highly dangerous*, had the desired effect on the White House.[12]

On 11 February, Hopkins penned a note to Roosevelt's secretary urging that the Hoover letter not be destroyed but be shown to the president "at once." As soon as Roosevelt saw it, he did exactly what Hopkins thought he would do: he sent it on to Admiral Leahy with instructions to "take this up with the Joint Chiefs of Staff." By 15 February, the Hoover letter was already worrying the J.C.S. staff, and O.S.S. officials were beginning to show concern as well. Haskell cabled General Deane to make no further move on the mission exchange until the situation cleared, and other O.S.S. officers tried to convince the secretary of the J.C.S. that "Mr. Hoover's apprehension was unfounded and that the proposed Russian mission to this country would be controlled."[13]

But the F.B.I. director could not be blocked that easily. On 15 February, five days after writing to Hopkins, Hoover sent a denunciation of the O.S.S.–N.K.V.D. exchange to his immediate superior, Attorney General Frances Biddle, which was at least as damning as the one that had gone directly to the White House. Hoover declared that the N.K.V.D. had already "been engaged in attempting to obtain highly confidential information concerning War Department secrets" and that establishing an official N.K.V.D. mission within the United States would "be a serious threat to the internal security of the country." Adding that he failed to see "any real purpose or justification for the establishment of such an agency here," Hoover stated flatly, and incorrectly, that "the British have no such arrangement with the N.K.V.D." Francis Biddle immediately sent a copy of the letter to the president, stressing in an accompanying note that

"Hoover considers this a serious threat to the internal security of the country," and suggesting that Roosevelt "give further consideration to the arrangement before it is consummated."[14]

Not to be completely overshadowed by the F.B.I., another old opponent of O.S.S. also joined in the attack. On 16 February, during an introductory J.P.S. discussion of the proposed exchange, the army representative, General Roberts, informed the other planners that G-2 did "not favor the plan proposed by the O.S.S.." The J.P.S. refused to be stampeded by G-2 or the F.B.I., however, and decided to defer its decision until it had heard from O.S.S.[15]

On the following day, O.S.S. hurled the unfortunate Colonel Haskell into the breach. Haskell had accompanied Donovan to Moscow, and was the chief-designate of the O.S.S. exchange mission, but he had not been present during Donovan's talks with either Molotov or the N.K.V.D. chiefs. In support of the plan, he advanced the obvious argument to the J.P.S. that the United States had heretofore secured little information from Soviet sources and that O.S.S. hoped to fill the gap, especially in regard to Balkan and Japanese data. He also contended that Deane and Harriman had recommended that a reciprocal mission be proposed as the best way to obtain Soviet approval for intelligence exchange. Colonel Haskell added that the exchange might make possible O.S.S.–Soviet-combined operations "in areas such as Yugoslavia" and he also made the rather surprising suggestion that the exchanges would provide O.S.S. black propaganda specialists with an opportunity to study the "effective propaganda technique" that the Russians were using against Nazi Germany. If he was referring to such activities as those of *Freies Deutschland,* this notion could hardly have been reassuring to the military.

Two errors made by Haskell in answering J.P.S. questions may have further discouraged the authorities. Responding to a query from Col. C.V. Gridley, who was trying to explore the possibility of attaching the N.K.V.D. men to the Soviet military attaché's office just as the B.S.C. was coordinated with the British Joint Staff Mission, Haskell said that "to his knowledge" only O.S.S. had liaison with B.S.C. Actually, the F.B.I. was also working closely with Stephenson's group. Even more serious was Haskell's incorrect answer to a question from Adm. Bernard Bieri regarding the situation in Britain, for the O.S.S. colonel replied that "it was his belief that the U.S.S.R. does not have a similar [i.e., N.K.V.D.] mission in London."[16]

These fumbles are mentioned not to be critical of Colonel Haskell—who certainly had enough to deal with under difficult circumstances—but to show that the J.P.S. was not given an artificially rosy picture of the exchange plan. Haskell ended by making it sound more unprecedented than it actually was. With Hoover's letter in hand and Haskell's incriminating answers, it would have been reasonable for the J.P.S. to have concluded that setting up an N.K.V.D. mission in Washington would be a security threat. But the J.P.S. did nothing of the kind. Noting that they hoped that the proposed N.K.V.D. group could be associated with the Soviet military or naval attaché, the J.P.S. confirmed the conclusion that their subcommittee had reached before the arrival of the Hoover letter and recommended that the J.C.S. authorize the N.K.V.D.–O.S.S. mission exchange.[17]

The J.C.S. usually followed the advice of its planning staff, but the N.K.V.D.–O.S.S. exchange had by now become far from routine. On 18 February, Biddle sent yet another memo regarding it to Roosevelt as if trying to jog his memory and make him pay heed to Hoover's warnings. Once again, Roosevelt turned to the J.C.S., and in a classic one-line display of buck passing, on 19 February asked Admiral Leahy: "What do we do next? F.D.R."[18]

With rumors flying that the president was inclined to kill the plan, Admiral Leahy's staff did the only thing it could do. The matter was put on top of the agenda for the next J.C.S. meeting on 22 February, and arrangements were made for General Donovan to be in the waiting room to answer the chiefs' questions. J.C.S. members were provided with copies of the J.P.S. recommendation, Hoover's letters to Hopkins, and the letter to Biddle that had gone to the president. As Gen. Kenneth Royall noted, it was better to make all the necessary arrangements to go ahead with the discussion, because even if the president made it clear in advance that he opposed the mission, the J.C.S. would still be able to "disapprove the paper."[19]

This maneuvering sounds less like the J.C.S.'s acting as the president's board of military advisers (as envisioned in the formal arrangements made in 1942) than the president subtly using the J.C.S. to get what he wanted without having to openly assume responsibility for his actions. But if that was what was supposed to happen, the J.C.S., like the J.P.S., did not completely follow the game plan.

During the meeting of 22 February, Donovan was permitted to present his side of the case. He reiterated to the chiefs much of what had been said previously about the deficiencies of existing intelligence coordination with the Russians and added that along with exchanging available material on Germany and Japan, he hoped to gain new information by cooperating with the Soviets in sending both O.S.S. and N.K.V.D. intelligence missions into Germany and Austria. The O.S.S. director brushed aside

Hoover's claims that the presence of an official N.K.V.D. mission would pose a new threat to American security. The N.K.V.D., he said quite reasonably, "is already here and has been for many years." If anything, Donovan contended, having "a definite mission" would actually benefit American security control because such a group could then "be checked." He also suggested to the chiefs, in the only documentary indication we have that his N.K.V.D. plans might have been double-edged, that the cooperation would allow O.S.S. to "observe their methods" and "would give us an opportunity to see how successfully we can expect to work with the Soviet[s] in the future."

After making these statements, Donovan left the meeting, and the chiefs began to debate among themselves whether to approve the mission exchange. As frequently occurred when O.S.S. matters were being discussed, the navy members, Admirals King and Leahy, were the most critical. Leahy led the opposition, citing Hoover's and Biddle's letters and declaring "that General Donovan's idea did not appeal" to him. General Marshall, however, thought the F.B.I. could well be alarmist and emphasized that he and the other chiefs might "be denying ourselves possible information from the Soviet[s] if we fail to exchange missions." As usual, General McNarney echoed Marshall, and General Arnold of the Army Air corps, who was always Donovan's strongest champion on the J.C.S., said "that if the O.S.S. can get anything from the Soviets he would approve such a mission." Faced with the army's inclination to favor the exchange idea, King and Leahy wavered. Finally Leahy suggested that since the chiefs were not ready to reject the idea out of hand but that approval would be unwise in light of Hoover's letter, perhaps he should discuss the matter privately with the president. His colleagues agreed, and the matter was put on hold to give Leahy an opportunity to take it up with Roosevelt.[20]

Apparently, the president felt this was an extremely sensitive issue because three weeks were allowed to pass, during which O.S.S. leaders planned and fidgeted, before he reached a decision. On 15 March, the J.C.S. was given the word that Roosevelt had finally rejected the exchange plan. Faced with a clear presidential veto, both O.S.S. and the chiefs yielded without demur. The only voices immediately raised to challenge Roosevelt's decision came, surprisingly enough, from Americans in Moscow. On 17–18 March, General Deane and Ambassador Harriman sent a series of cables to Washington criticizing the president's action and asking him to reconsider. Ambassador Harriman's message of 18 March was the stiffest protest, and one of the most impassioned dispatches he ever transmitted during his years in Moscow. After reviewing the history of the exchange project, the ambassador referred to it "as the first tangible evidence of the spirit of cooperation voiced at the conferences in Moscow and Teheran." He also noted that the Soviets already had begun to provide useful information to O.S.S. via General Deane and observed that "we have here penetrated for the first time one intelligence branch of the Soviet Government and I am certain this will be the opening wedge to far greater intimacy in other branches, if pursued." Noting that rejection of the exchange at this point might endanger other United States activities such as the stationing of air forces in the U.S.S.R., Harriman continued, "I cannot express too strongly my conviction that our relations with the Soviet Government in other directions will be adversely affected if we now close the door on this branch of the Soviet Government after they have shown cooperative spirit and good faith." To drive home his view that a rejection of the N.K.V.D.–O.S.S. exchange plan would forfeit a possible turning point in East–West relations, Harriman concluded his message by stating to the president that "this matter is of such importance . . . that with your permission I am prepared to return to Washington at once in order to discuss it with you and the Joint Chiefs of Staff."[21]

Coming as it did from a man who was a power in the Democratic Party and would soon be renowned for tough, realistic bargaining with the Russians—in his recently published memoirs, this message was heavily edited to conform more closely with that image—one might have expected the dispatch of 18 March to create quite a stir. But having once made up his mind, Franklin Roosevelt was unwilling to allow the explosive issue to be opened up again, and Harriman's message was handed over to the J.C.S. staff for reply. With G-2 eager to provide any help it could to keep O.S.S. pinned on the ground and Admiral Leahy determined to avoid giving Harriman the slightest encouragement in his opposition or his desire to return for consultation, the matter was quickly disposed of. During a cursory discussion on 28 March, the J.C.S. decided not to question the president's decision, and Admirals King and Leahy used the occasion to remark that in the future "some action should be taken to prevent O.S.S. from committing the United States Government without prior approval." After the meeting, Leahy prepared a cable to Harriman declaring that the N.K.V.D.–O.S.S. exchange had only been "deferred because of timing" due to "the domestic political situation."

This last phrase was quite likely the most delicate characterization of the conservative J. Edgar Hoover's political clout ever devised. The president apparently appreciated its artistry, for the message was dispatched to Moscow over Roosevelt's signature on 30 March. The O.S.S.–N.K.V.D. exchange system had been "deferred" forever; a post hoc protest by Secretary of State Hull was easily brushed aside in early April, and O.S.S. was never able to revive the scheme that both Donovan and Harriman thought had a chance of improving East–West relations.[22]

Quite clearly, the N.K.V.D.–O.S.S. exchange plan fell victim not to the government's anticommunist ideological conviction but to old-fashioned domestic political expediency. "Conservative" Admiral Leahy and J. Edgar Hoover, united with the "liberal" Francis Biddle, Harry Hopkins, and Franklin Roosevelt to defeat it, while the group that had supported the proposal, featuring Generals Donovan, Marshall, McNarney, Deane, and Arnold, together with Ambassador Harriman, lacked any distinct ideological coloration at all. Not even the most determined red baiter could characterize the latter group as a collection of "Com-symps" or the former as the darlings of the Birch Society. Hoover was probably animated by an equal mixture of hostility to O.S.S. and dread of the N.K.V.D., but Hopkins, Biddle, and Roosevelt surely acted as they did because they feared that Hoover would let the conservative press loose on the administration if they went through with the deal. The "domestic political situation" that stopped the president from approving the exchange was not distrust of the Soviet secret police but apprehension about what Hoover and his conservative friends might do. That may make the presidential decision partially ideological but if so, the ideology was less a fear of communists than of anticommunists.

While losing this dramatic encounter, however, Donovan and his pragmatic associates also won a quiet but significant victory of their own. In the course of Donovan's meeting with Fitin and Ossipov on 27 December 1943, it had been agreed that intelligence exchange would begin immediately, using General Deane's military mission as a post drop. At least as early as late February 1944, Donovan sent information to Fitin by this route, and the Soviets were reciprocating by the second week of March at the latest. When on 8 April Deane informed Fitin and Ossipov that there had been a "postponement" in the formal exchange of missions, the N.K.V.D. men were "disappointed" but were quick to declare that they were anxious to continue swapping intelligence through Deane's office. On 21 April, O.S.S. officials formally notified the J.C.S. that this information exchange was functioning, but the American military commanders— including Admiral Leahy—imposed no restrictions or limitations on its operation.[23]

Among the earliest items of information that O.S.S. sent to the N.K.V.D. was material on an anti-Soviet Abwehr ring that Donovan's X-2 had cracked in Turkey. The Soviets responded with gratitude both to this and to the supplementary information that O.S.S. provided on the case and in return warned O.S.S. to drop its plan to employ a Russian national in Switzerland named Sokdline because the N.K.V.D. had also tried him and found him unreliable.[24]

This American counterintelligence initiative was apparently what first kindled real N.K.V.D. enthusiasm for informational exchange, and counterintelligence would continue to interest the Russians long after they had cooled on other aspects of the O.S.S.–N.K.V.D. connection. Yet it seems to have been the Soviets who were the first to hand over an important regular intelligence report regarding the Axis. During his visit to Moscow, Donovan had told the Russians that he was keen on getting information on Bulgaria because of his plans to entice her away from the Axis. By 11 March, General Deane had in his hands a twenty-eight page N.K.V.D. memorandum on Bulgarian conditions covering everything from her strategic raw material situation to the number of Axis vessels in the Black Sea. Deane was so impressed by this "very complete and detailed intelligence report" that he arranged for its immediate delivery to Cairo and Washington by an officer "with special priority for air travel." Although R. and A. was not entranced with the N.K.V.D.'s Bulgarian report, it does seem to have persuaded O.S.S. Washington that the channel offered really valuable intelligence exchange opportunities. On 11 April, Colonel Haskell sent Deane a long dispatch setting out the four main categories of information sought by O.S.S.—sabotage methods, Far East matters, Balkan issues, and "questions relating to Finland, Spain, Germany"—plus sixty-four specific queries ranging from the German attitude regarding unconditional surrender to "the volume of oil produced by coal liquefaction in Karafuto." To secure answers to these questions on 11 April Haskell shipped Dean 27 S.I. reports and 32 R. and A. reports to be offered in exchange. Ten days later, Colonel Buxton sent an additional 13 S.I. reports, followed in May by 126 more O.S.S. reports, 41 of which had been produced by R. and A.[25]

General Deane's routing notes indicate that the vast majority of these items—if not all of them—were immediately handed over to the N.K.V.D. After what appeared to have been a slowdown of document shipments from O.S.S. in the summer and fall of 1944, another flurry occurred in December 1944 and January 1945. Included among this group were forty-six more R. and A. reports and at least two of the special dispatches on German conditions, prepared by Allen Dulles, that gravely underestimated German strength and Hitler's position on the eve of the Battle of the Bulge.[26]

In exchange, the Russians appear not to have provided as many reports—on this, however, the archival record is not crystal-clear—but some of them were of high quality. A one-page summary of industrial bombing targets in eastern Germany and western Poland, which Fitin gave to Deane on 27 September, was so detailed—a chemical plant at Nakel near Bromberg was sited as "1,200 meters from the station along the highway" to Posnan—that it must have been compiled mainly from ground agent reports. On a number of occasions, Donovan sent special thanks for such items through General Deane, and at least once (in regard to an August report on Axis economic conditions) asked additional questions of the Russians. The O.S.S.–N.K.V.D. exchange system permitted the Americans to acquire large quantities of Soviet publications as well. Many of these were technical items that previously had not been available in the West. The flow of published data was deemed so important in Washington in late 1944 that an R. and A. specialist on Soviet industry, Thomas P. Whitney, was added to the embassy staff to handle it.[27]

The O.S.S.–N.K.V.D. channel also may have facilitated other Soviet–American exchanges. It seems plausible to conclude that the sudden decision of the Red Navy to exchange naval intelligence on Japan with the United States in February 1944 owed something to the fact that the N.K.V.D–O.S.S. connection began operation in that month. It is even possible that members of the American military mission in Moscow gained greater freedom of movement because of this connection. Certainly, prior to February and March of 1944 the Soviets rarely allowed American military officers to see such sensitive units as the Polish Third Division, armed and trained by the Russians, which Gen. W. E. Crisp was allowed to examine thoroughly in late March.

It may be stretching the point to give the O.S.S.–N.K.V.D. connection much of the credit for the greater Soviet willingness, manifest in the spring of 1944, to consider favorably Soviet–American air force planning for future operations against Japan. But the timing is interesting, and considering Donovan's close relations with General Arnold, so is the fact that the O.S.S. chief was attempting to use his influence to smooth relations between the American Army Air Corps and the Red Air Force in southeast Europe as late as January 1945. Certainly it is not impossible that Harriman's claim in March 1944 that successful O.S.S.–N.K.V.D. coordination might lead to "greater intimacy" with "other branches" of the Soviet government was for a time actually realized.[28]

In any event, N.K.V.D.–O.S.S. cooperation provided more than an exchange of documents. Some attempts were made to coordinate black propaganda, and during the first meeting between Donovan and the N.K.V.D., the possibility of swapping subversive warfare gadgets was discussed. The Soviets raised that issue again in mid-April, and later that month O.S.S. assured the J.C.S. that arrangements had been made to clear all such exchanges with War Department technical experts. Apparently, the J.C.S. put some restrictions on this activity in May, but when in November 1944 Fitin asked for a sample of the microfilm camera used by O.S.S. field agents, Donovan agreed to send him one, and General Deane raised no objection. It seems probable that in addition to the microfilm camera, samples of other O.S.S. gadgets also went to the Soviets, but current restrictions on access to O.S.S. records makes a firm statement impossible. The main reason for the uncertainty is that from the available records we know that exchange between N.K.V.D. and O.S.S. was not restricted to Moscow, but the C.I.A. has not allowed anyone to see the records that would show what was traded at other points.[29]

From July 1944 on, Donovan was eager to increase the range of liaison activities and the number of contact locations. In July, he suggested to Fitin that contact be established in London, Stockholm, and Bari, Italy. During September, he recommended that Yugoslavia, Greece, Rumania, Bulgaria, Hungary, Austria, and Czechoslovakia also be made exchange points as quickly as possible. Fitin sidestepped or stalled on most of these suggestions—he once drily remarked that there was no N.K.V.D. representative in Stockholm—but on 2 August, he agreed to establish contact in London. Col. I. Chichayev, who was already working as the contact with S.O.E. there, was designated the N.K.V.D. London liaison man with O.S.S., and on 29 August Donovan told Fitin that O.S.S. London was already in touch with Chichayev "and satisfactory arrangements have been worked out." In light of this statement and supplementary evidence indicating that the London channel operated for at least eight months (until April 1945), we can assume that significant O.S.S.–N.K.V.D. material moved along this route. But again, until the C.I.A. opens the records, the details of what was traded will remain a mystery. Since the British government still has not even publicly admitted that it dealt with N.K.V.D. in London during the Second World War, we may have a long time to wait.[30]

But we will not have to wait to discover when and where the N.K.V.D.–O.S.S. connection ran into trouble. The major source of difficulty was, quite naturally, in the Balkans. The first moment of friction occurred in the spring of 1944 when S.O.E. and O.S.S. failed to invite N.K.V.D. to join them in subversive operations in Rumania. After some complaints, N.K.V.D. backed off, but then Molotov went on the attack, accusing Churchill of hatching dark Balkan plots. Since British policy in the area was more assertive than that of the United States and O.S.S. had by then closer relations with N.K.V.D. than did the S.O.E., it was only natural that the Soviet foreign minister would aim his heavy guns at the British.[31]

But when the big blowup came in the fall, it was not with S.O.E. but O.S.S. and was initiated not by overt intrigue or underground operations but by the issue of air crew rescue. As early as May 1944, the American Army Air Corps asked O.S.S. to develop plans for saving the large number of its crews held prisoner in Rumania and Bulgaria. By August, although the Anglo-American special operations setup for these two countries was still in a rather confused state and the C.C.S. had ordered that not even air rescue teams were to be sent in without its prior consent, A.F.H.Q. and O.S.S. had developed an emergency procedure for finding and saving the captured air crews. At the very end of August, when the Bulgarian and Rumanian governments deserted the Axis and before the Soviets entered the countries in force, O.S.S. air rescue teams were rushed in. They did their relief work quickly and effectively, thereby earning the gratitude of the Army Air Corps. But when the air crews came out, some special force personnel—both O.S.S. and S.O.E.—remained to perform intelligence functions.[32]

From the documentary evidence now available, it appears that the O.S.S. and S.O.E. men who remained were only collecting intelligence from the Rumanians and the Bulgarians and picking up whatever had been left behind by the retreating Wehrmacht. But quite understandably the field commanders of the advance Red Army units looked on these activities with great suspicion, and on 25 September, the Soviet High Command ordered all O.S.S. and S.O.E. personnel out of Bulgaria. To avoid a major incident, they did as they were told, crossing the border into Turkey, while cables of inquiry and protest passed thick and fast between Caserta, Washington, and Moscow. Before the cumbersome C.C.S. machinery could be geared up to produce a formal complaint to the Russians, Donovan stepped in and used the Deane–Fitin connection to resolve the difficulty. On 27 September, Fitin responded to Donovan's request for assistance by informing General Deane that he had made arrangements with the Red Army to allow O.S.S. and S.O.E. back into Bulgaria. But the price was high, and it kept rising.[33]

The initial condition that Fitin imposed for the return of O.S.S. to Bulgaria was that Donovan provide the N.K.V.D. with a list of all O.S.S. personnel who would be in Bulgaria and in every other area occupied by the Red Army. Donovan agreed, and in September and October, the N.K.V.D. was given the names of all O.S.S. men in Bulgaria, Rumania, and Yugoslavia, and of those already in, or planning to enter, Czechoslovakia. To further regularize the position of O.S.S. units in areas held by the Soviets, it was agreed in mid-November that such formations would be attached to the American sections of the Allied Control Commissions. In addition, O.S.S. was compelled to operate "in cooperation with the corresponding Soviet organizations (i.e., N.K.V.D.) in Soviet-occupied territory," and though "not necessarily divulging the actual motive of the work" they were doing would nevertheless operate "on the basis of general directives given to them from time to time by General Deane and General Fitin." On the basis of a suggestion made by General Deane, the radio communication linkup through which these general directives were sent from Moscow to O.S.S. and N.K.V.D. in central and southeast Europe was to be operated exclusively by the Soviet authorities.[34]

Given the extreme Soviet sensitivity about anyone—especially a foreign intelligence service—observing what they were doing in their newly occupied territories, the fact that O.S.S. was able to remain, and help some of their S.O.E. cousins to stay on as well, was a remarkable accomplishment. General Fitin felt, quite rightly, that he had done O.S.S. a big favor in securing Soviet agreement to the arrangement. In light of Stalin's paranoia, Fitin had indeed gone beyond the call of inter-Allied comradeship and may well have put a dangerous mark on his own record. The O.S.S. teams, especially in Rumania, collected large quantities of material left by the Germans and were able to do extensive bomb damage analysis. A generous percentage of the documents collected were shared with the Russians, with 1,500 pages going from Donovan to Fitin in one shipment on 30 October. The O.S.S. counterintelligence team in Rumania led by Lt. Comdr. Frank Wisner (who later was to play a highly important role in the early C.I.A.) also "succeeded in establishing very valuable X-2 contacts with the Russians," and in December 1944, Donovan provided the N.K.V.D. with information on an anti-Soviet plot being hatched by Rumanian military officers.[35]

Yet on balance, once the Allied fliers had been rescued, retention of the O.S.S. teams in eastern Europe produced little positive benefit for either O.S.S. or East–West relations. Whatever significant information O.S.S. acquired from the region was obtained by direct cooperation with the Soviet authorities, and O.S.S. talk about "secret work" and "cover" was absurd. And so are postwar tales suggesting that O.S.S. successfully laid a basis for a Cold War anti-Soviet underground or secret intelligence service in the area during this period. With the N.K.V.D. holding the name of every O.S.S. man stationed in the region, an anti-Soviet resident of Rumania, Bulgaria, or any other eastern European country who was imprudent enough to make contact with one of Donovan's people would almost certainly have come to the attention of the Soviet secret police. Indeed, if the

O.S.S. presence effected subversive movements in eastern Europe at all, it was more likely by serving as an unintentional vehicle for N.K.V.D. entrapment of dissidents rather than as a significant aid to those opposed to Soviet domination.

The best that O.S.S. men could do was to stand back and watch as the Russians suppressed dissent, eliminated noncommunist political parties, and seized American- and British-owned oil equipment in Rumania. The O.S.S. dispatches to Washington that recounted these developments, although they added little if anything to what was available from State Department and press sources, may have helped to deepen U.S. government suspicion of Russian intentions. Certainly Donovan concluded, despite his appreciative messages to Fitin, that the Soviet Union was up to some devilment. In December 1944 the O.S.S. director would not permit R. and A. reports to go to the N.K.V.D. on areas of Germany other than those intended to be part of the Soviet zone. As early as 29 September 1944, when Donovan reported to the president that Fitin had granted permission for O.S.S. to return to Bulgaria, he added that the original expulsion order, when combined with Tito's directive restricting O.S.S. movements in Yugoslavia, "show that the Russians intend to dominate this area and . . . propose going up to the Adriatic."[36]

Most other Washington authorities were not then prepared to go that far, but they had become more nervous about the Soviets and less willing to allow O.S.S. a free hand in such politically sensitive regions. On 2 October 1944, the J.C.S. issued a new, rather murky directive authorizing O.S.S. to continue contact with the N.K.V.D. but ordering that henceforth "any agreements with the Russians" would be "subject to confirmation with [sic] the Joint Chiefs of Staff." Yet even this restriction, and Donovan's sharpened suspicions of the Soviets, did not end the O.S.S.–N.K.V.D. hookup. From December 1944 until at least February 1945, Donovan's organization sent the N.K.V.D. extensive material on Germany through General Deane. Fitin and his colleagues also rendered assistance to O.S.S., especially in trying to locate survivors of an ill-fated S.I. mission that had gone into Czechoslavakia and lost many of its personnel to the Gestapo.[37]

During January and February of 1945, S.O.E. and O.S.S. were trying to hang onto their central European connections with N.K.V.D. But it seems likely on the basis of the Moscow connection, which is the only one we can currently study, that the East–West intelligence linkup was noticeably less active at that time than it had been six months earlier. Then, in early April, when East–West relations deteriorated even further because of the controversy over Dulles's Sunrise surrender project in northern Italy, O.S.S. was made to feel the force of Soviet displeasure. O.S.S. requests for a liaison arrangement in Paris and permission for Donovan to visit Bucharest and Sofia were politely, but firmly, rejected by the N.K.V.D. Fitin also pleaded a heavy work load in declining to meet with Donovan when the O.S.S. chief visited the continent in mid-April. More significantly, Colonel Chichayev was recalled, and Fitin informed General Deane that "for the time being" O.S.S.–N.K.V.D. contact would no longer be possible in London. N.K.V.D. was careful not to burn all its bridges and sent effusive condolences on the death of President Roosevelt to both Deane and Donovan on 13 April. Donovan not only expressed his appreciation for this gesture but made his own effort to keep the line of communication open and as free as possible from unnecessary suspicion. Much to the amusement of Harriman and Deane, in late May the O.S.S. director asked them to inform Fitin that there was no truth to Drew Pearson's allegation that he was "planning an attack on Russia."[38]

The broad sweep of the N.K.V.D.–O.S.S. relationship, revealed by the communications made through General Deane's office, suggests that in late 1944 and on into 1945, Donovan and his organization were perhaps a half step ahead of the rest of the U.S. government in the development of a policy of suspicious reserve toward Soviet Russia. But one incident indicates that in pursuit of what he saw as a significant intelligence opportunity, Donovan was prepared to take a much larger leap in that direction. In November 1944, O.S.S. Stockholm was offered an opportunity to buy from Finnish sources numerous Soviet military documents, as well as the key to the decoding method that the Finns had used to decipher them. Donovan, Buxton, and a former O.S.S. chief in Stockholm informed the State Department of this offer in mid-November. After some deliberation, Secretary of State Stettinius decided that such a transaction "would be inadvisable and improper." The State Department officers who informed Donovan of Stettinius's decision thought that it had been accepted by the director of O.S.S. and that the deal was dead. But Donovan did not abandon the project. In early December, O.S.S. Stockholm purchased 1,500 pages of Soviet material and the code keys from Finnish representatives and also learned that "certain codes of the State Department had been tampered with" by the Finns or the Germans.[39]

On 11 December, Donovan reported to Roosevelt that he had purchased one military and three diplomatic codes and had turned them over to the State and War departments, but he apparently did not tell the president that these were Soviet codes. Although Donovan's memorandum to Roosevelt claimed that this was the only disclosure he was making of "these facts," State Department officials had the whole story within four days. When the department's adviser on political relations, James Dunn, asked O.S.S. why it had gone ahead in spite of Stettinius's objections, he was told by Colonel Buxton that "General Donovan felt that it was of such importance that he was willing to take the entire responsibility for dealing with this matter." Buxton added that "if there was any question as to the responsibility for undertaking this action, they, O.S.S., would stand entirely responsible for whatever was done."[40]

The usually timorous Edward Stettinius refused to back off on this occasion however. Two days before Christmas 1944 he went directly to the president and protested Donovan's code purchase. According to the secretary of state's own notes, Roosevelt told him "to see that the Russians were informed on this matter at once" and to report back to the White House "exactly what has been done." A state department–presidential order was immediately issued to O.S.S. that the codes and the documentary material be immediately given to the Soviet government. Consequently, on 5 January 1945, Colonel Buxton penned an artful message to General Deane. He declared that O.S.S. had secured "from enemy sources" 1,500 sheets of material "purporting to contain the key to certain Russian codes both military and N.K.V.D." Buxton claimed that Donovan, as "a loyal ally," had acquired the material "as soon as he found it was procurable" because he "felt that the documentary proof would be of more assistance to our ally than would a mere statement that we were reliably informed that such codes existed in enemy hands." Buxton continued this fairy tale with a hint that Donovan had made the purchase with the approval of Secretary Stettinius and the president, and concluded, twenty-five days after Donovan had told the president that he had turned the documents over to both the War and State departments, by stating that "we have made no study of this material."[41]

Deane, who apparently was not told of the affair's shady background, informed General Fitin on 9 January that O.S.S. urgently wanted the N.K.V.D. to have someone in Washington collect "some papers" that were "of immediate importance" to the Russian government. Before Fitin could work out a solution to the pickup problem, O.S.S. Washington acted. By 15 February, the codes and the documentary materials had been turned over to the then Soviet ambassador (and now foreign minister) Andrei Gromyko.[42]

To those who have lived through thirty-five years of Cold War cloak-and-dagger adventure, the most surprising feature of this curious episode is probably the United States government's decision to send the codes back, for this virtually guaranteed that the Russians would change their ciphers. In our Ian Fleming world, this appears to be an act of great power madness akin to giving an opponent the scientific formula for an important secret weapon. But on second thought, it is easy to see that given the circumstances of early 1945, the code purchase itself had been an extremely risky undertaking. Finland had just capitulated to the Soviets after fighting as an ally of Nazi Germany for three and a half years. Anyone with a modicum of political experience should have seen that for the American government to buy the codes of one of its major allies from the Finns was to expose Washington to the threat of maximum political blackmail by Helsinki and Berlin. On the eve of Yalta, with the termination of both European and Pacific combat hanging in the balance and the problems of the postwar period stretching nearly to infinity, Franklin Roosevelt, the J.C.S., and the State Department were staking their whole policy on maintaining the best possible relations with the Russians. Whatever the lessons learned later in the Cold War, it was obviously not in the interest of the United States to permit such a *cause célèbre* to threaten the Grand Alliance at that moment. In this context then, it was not the decision to return the codes that was naive; that was merely an effort to make the best of a bad job. The really irresponsible gamble had been taken by Donovan when he purchased the codes in the first place.

Even this, possibly the greatest folly committed by O.S.S. during the war, does not mean that beginning in December 1944 Donovan's organization was irrevocably committed to a full-scale ideological shadow war against communism and the Soviet Union. There were indeed signs that in the spring of 1945 O.S.S. was literally shifting its attention from Nazi Germany to Soviet Russia. On 16 April, the Reseda intercept station that had been homing in on Nazi in-clear radio propaganda began to work on comparable Soviet broadcasts. The O.S.S.–N.K.V.D. communications channel also hints at this shift. In mid-May, among the regular, though thinner, run of O.S.S. items sent to General Deane for transmission to the Soviets was one for American Military Mission chief's own use. It was a copy of the special fifteen-page O.S.S. paper on the "Problems and Objectives of United States Policy" completed on 2 April that had recommended that while the United States ought to seek accommodation with the Soviet Union, it should also build up a strong political-military position in western Europe, the Western Hemisphere, and the central Pacific in the event that Russia failed to cooperate.[43]

This revelation may be sufficient to convince some Cold War enthusiasts that for O.S.S. and its associates the anticommunist die was cast by the spring of 1945. But if so, not all those then involved yet realized it. When in late May the chief of R. and A.'s Soviet Affairs Division asked General Deane why the Soviet military budget for 1945–46 was pegged so high in light of the probable end of hostilities, the general gave a number of possible explanations. The only explanation not offered by General Deane was the possibility that the U.S.S.R. might be intending to use its military forces for political intimidation or to expand Soviet territory.[44]

Such considerations may still not be enough to give pause to those determined to see O.S.S. as the advance cadre of Cold War ideologues, for though General Deane was the crucial man in the O.S.S.–N.K.V.D. connection, it was also O.S.S. man Geroid Robinson who had asked him the leading question on the Soviet budget. However, when we examine the O.S.S.–N.K.V.D. traffic passing through Moscow in July and August of 1945 following the end of hostilities in Europe and even stretching beyond the Pacific conflict, the picture of an anti-Soviet O.S.S. monolith evaporates. On 11 July 1945, Donovan telegraphed Deane requesting that he notify General Fitin that O.S.S. had in its "custody" the radio communications system for a Nazi intelligence network in the Balkans directed against the Russians and asking the N.K.V.D. to share in the elimination of the ring. The network in question had been developed by S.S. Strumbannführer Wilhelm Hoettl, deputy chief of the S.D.'s foreign intelligence section (Amt 6E) and had first been offered to O.S.S. by Hoettl as trade bait even before the Nazi surrender. On 3 June, O.S.S. seized the communication center of the ring in Steyrling and tested the radio setup to see whether Hoettl actually had agents functioning in the Balkans. Two S.D. agents, Kurt Auner in Rumania and Paul Neunteuffel in Hungary, responded to the test call signals sent out by O.S.S. from Steyrling. Having satisfied himself that Hoettl actually had an anti-Soviet Balkan network, and having concluded that his "ulterior motive in turning over [the] network to [the] U.S. was [the] hope that it be used against Russia and thus embroil the two nations with resultant German gain," Donovan decided to cut the N.K.V.D. into the process of liquidating the chain.[45]

In his message to General Deane on 11 July, Donovan accurately described the situation. He reported that O.S.S. had "ascertained [the] range of [the] network and [the] truth of Hoettl's claims concerning [the] presence of agents in the Balkans" and had concluded that in turning over the network to O.S.S., Hoettl "was evidently motivated by [a] desire to stir [up] trouble between [the] Russians and ourselves." To thwart the S.D. man's designs, Donovan asked Deane to make the information available to Fitin, to inform him that O.S.S. had "placed this matter" in the hands of Allen Dulles (then O.S.S. chief for Germany) and to "discuss with the Soviet Union means of eliminating Hoettl's entire organization." After a brief delay apparently occasioned by communications difficulties, Col. M. W. Pettigrew, temporarily serving as acting head of the American Military Mission during a brief absence of General Deane, sent Fitin a slightly paraphrased version of Donovan's message. Three days later, General Deane, back on duty in Moscow, reported to Washington that he had just had a conference with Fitin who he found, not surprisingly, "genuinely interested" in the O.S.S. report on Hoettl. But Fitin, who had become more cautious as East–West relations cooled, indicated that to give practical form to his "genuine desire" to develop "definite plans for collaboration" in wiping out Hoettl's ring, he desired additional information. Specifically, Fitin wanted to know if any documents had been captured with Hoettl, how the Americans knew the ring was aimed against the Russians, whether the United States had uncovered any other anti-Soviet espionage operations, and finally what plans Dulles had for eliminating the network. Donovan seems to have thought these questions reasonable and on 30 July told Deane to tell the N.K.V.D. general that Fitin could make arrangements for as many N.K.V.D. representatives as he wished to meet with Allen Dulles and one or two other O.S.S. men in Berlin. At that time, the captured material would be presented to the Soviets, and the two secret services could then decide how to wipe out Hoettl's operation.[46]

Although on 31 July O.S.S. had shown its desire to cooperate on counterintelligence matters by giving Fitin the home address in the Soviet zone of a German soldier who O.S.S. thought had knowledge of top secret Nazi statistical material, Fitin was still extremely wary about making a move on the Hoettl affair. On 1 August, the N.K.V.D. general notified Deane that "for the preliminary orientation of our men who will be designated to meet Mr. Allen Dulles," he required copies of the materials "seized at Hoettl's headquarters containing information about work against the U.S.S.R." and any "testimony of Hoettl's" related to such activity. He added that prior to a meeting with Dulles, "it would be desirable" for the Soviets to receive the names of those captured with Hoettl and full information on any other Nazi intelligence men who had worked against the Soviets and were currently in American hands. Considering that Donovan had freely invited the N.K.V.D. to participate in closing down Hoettl's intelligence string, these preconditions for a meeting with Dulles seem a bit thick.[47]

Apparently, the whole situation was by now making the American War Department uneasy, and on the same day (1 August) G-2 S.H.A.E.F. was asked for a full explanation of the situation surrounding the Hoettl matter. On 3 August, Eisenhower's G-2, Gen. Edwin Sibert, who had cooperated with O.S.S. on the counterintelligence operation from the beginning, sent Washington a detailed report. Noting that O.S.S. and S.H.A.E.F. had considered it "too dangerous to continue to operate the network without notice to the Russians," Sibert stressed that to guarantee that the ring was completely wiped out, they had concluded that "Russian cooperation" was necessary. Even before the arrival of this message, however, G-2 Washington had decided that "we must go through with the meeting" between Dulles and the N.K.V.D. because "it would be an expression of bad faith to withdraw now." The army intelligence people thought that Donovan had gone too far in trying to cooperate with the Russians, however. G-2 believed that a joint Soviet–American counterintelligence investigation would probably hurt United States security in southeast Europe because it might inadvertently peel back the cover from O.S.S.'s "own network in the Balkans." [48]

George Marshall was disturbed by another aspect of the affair, since he felt that Donovan had shown poor judgment in not first checking with the War Department and the J.C.S. before making his initial approach to Fitin. Donovan sought to defend his action on the ground that he saw the Hoettl case as "an operational matter of a temporary nature" rather than one of basic policy. Marshall was obviously not impressed by this explanation, and the O.S.S. director seems to have been instructed to clean up the case as quickly and neatly as possible. On 30 August, he sent a dispatch asking Deane to inform Fitin that a meeting between Dulles and N.K.V.D. representatives was essential before any other joint action on Hoettl could be undertaken. The O.S.S. chief declared that he was still prepared to go ahead with a joint meeting and hoped that Fitin would also "find it desirable to do so." But if the Soviets insisted on preconditions, then O.S.S. would "be obliged" to go it alone and would "liquidate the existing chain." [49]

There ended the East–West consideration of the Hoettl matter, and this was also the last message to pass through the O.S.S.–N.K.V.D. exchange center in Moscow. Three weeks later, Harry S. Truman signed the order abolishing O.S.S., and by 1 October Donovan's organization was a thing of the past. Looking back over the broad sweep of material that was exchanged between O.S.S. and the N.K.V.D., especially in light of the Hoettl case, it is possible to draw some measured conclusions about the role of leftist and antileftist ideology in O.S.S. policy. No Anglo-American organizational leader who acted as Donovan did regarding Hoettl in July 1945 can simply be written off as a pioneer Cold Warrior or anticommunist ideologue. Yet it is also true that in dealing with such issues as that of the Soviet codes, Donovan hardly revealed himself as a man ideologically inclined to be helpful to Soviet Russia.

What an analysis of the O.S.S.–N.K.V.D. connection suggests most clearly is that Donovan was always ready to act like an intelligence "professional" and to work shoulder to shoulder with those he saw as his counterparts in other countries. He was also inclined to move boldly, even recklessly, in grasping what he felt to be the big chance. In setting up the connection with the N.K.V.D. in purchasing the Soviet codes, and finally in his handling of the Hoettl affair, Donovan plunged in where most intelligence men would have been reluctant to act. This impetuosity resulted partly from the general's temperament and partly from the recognition that proof of O.S.S.'s value to the military was essential if the organization was to be kept alive. As hostilities drew to a close, the tactical functions of O.S.S., which had been so praised by the military, also withered and died. If any group analogous to O.S.S. was to survive into the postwar world, Donovan had little choice but to return to his old theme of importance of strategic intelligence. Since the Soviet Union was the only power about which Washington had any serious "strategic" worry in 1945, Donovan's salesmanship had to focus on that country.

Whether engaging in activities that would strengthen the position of the United States vis-à-vis the U.S.S.R. (as with the codes) or in working hand in hand with the Russians (as in the Hoettl affair), Donovan wanted to prove that a "strategic" intelligence organization would be valuable in postwar America. Therefore, from beginning to end, it was apparently opportunism rather than pro- or anticommunist fanaticism, that exerted the strongest influence on the policy of O.S.S. toward Russia in the years 1944 and 1945.

CHAPTER 8

The Research and Analysis [R. and A.] Branch of O.S.S. and Strategic Intelligence

Yesterday I produced the first, and I hope the largest, of the series of bi-weekly reports that stretches ahead of me like a dusty road.

CHANDLER MORSE (R. AND A. LONDON) TO
WILLIAM LANGER
17 April 1944

BOOKS on American secret agencies invariably contain a few passages of praise for the scholars who systematize and analyze intelligence materials. The education, intelligence, and devotion of these researchers is ritually held up like a trophy to demonstrate to the public that intelligence organizations are staffed by respectable people of high quality. But with that done, and a handful of remarks made about the vital importance of research reports, writers on intelligence hurriedly return to their familiar clandestine world of beached rubber boats and trenchcoats in doorways.

But the research and analysis functions really are the heart of intelligence agencies. As the C.I.A.'s David Phillips recently remarked, the major tool of the intelligence trade is the 3 by 5 index card, not the gun or the knife, for only through the organization and study of individual pieces of information does an agency learn anything worth knowing. This was especially true in the case of C.O.I.–O.S.S. because the Research and Analysis Branch was established prior to those for secret intelligence or covert operations, and the initial value of Donovan's organization lay far more in studying intelligence information than in originating it. William Langer's staff was the first to demonstrate what scholarship could accomplish for an intelligence agency. R. and A.'s adaptation of the techniques of academic study to the requirements of shadow warfare and the sale of this product to American leaders was a vital element in the development of a regular, central, intelligence system in the United States.

As we have seen, Donovan's initial vision of a scholarly organization that would arrange information so that a Board of Analysts could use it to make policy suggestions to the president never got off the ground. R. and A. was not fitted into the structure of American decisionmaking during World War II, and the analysis function (in the sense of producing overt recommendations on policy) was nearly always muted. Langer's branch owed its success to an effective marketing program and the development of a research report system that produced information of interest to many government officials in a form that they found useful. How Langer and his staff adjusted academic scholarship and publication methods to the requirements of the government is, therefore, a matter of some significance.

Most of the people who initially made up the Research and Analysis Branch were academics who came from Ivy League schools. Harvard and Yale contributed the largest number of recruits, many of whom (such as the young Stuart Hughes and Sherman Kent) were gentlemen scholars from the oldest and most influential circles in the country. This emphasis on the eastern academic establishment accurately reflected the condition of American higher learning in the humanities and the social sciences in the late 1930s. At that time, northeastern academia dominated American higher education, and young scholars of humble background (outside the sciences) could only make a mark by having the Ivy League stamp placed upon them. The initial R. and A. staff included a large number of those not born to the purple (including William Langer himself) and even some children of recent central European immigrants. But nearly everyone in early R. and A. from Arthur Schlesinger to Carl Schorske had received a generous measure of Ivy League education stressing modern scientific research techniques and a belief that elitist higher education harmonized with the interests of the social and political groups who ran the country.

When R. and A. was created, a large group of historians and geographers moved for the first time directly from the campus to join with the economists (who were more familiar in Washington) to form a government service agency. Furthermore, R. and A. was an unusually pure academic ghetto, despite its handful of journalists and former diplomats. For unlike the British system, where academics were spread throughout a number of secret services, Langer's organization had a virtual monopoly of the scholars working in American intelligence during the Second World War. Because of the Ivy League coloration, R. and A. personnel were attuned to the way of thinking of top American officials, for at that time the Foreign Service was staffed with people from the "best" circles who had also been educated in northeastern colleges and universities. Even the president, and a general like George Patton, could read French rather well, and General Stilwell was able to invert a classical epigram in a cable to the War Department, confident that his meaning would be understood. God was still rather firmly seated in heaven, and the system of "acquaintanceship and association," which a cruder time would relabel the *old boys' network*, was functioning.[1]

Building on government officials' respect for polite learning and scholarship, Langer's people experimented until they found a format that effectively encompassed intelligence research. As the R. and A. chief declared to William Donovan near the end of the war, "the staff . . . trained itself in the requirements of strategic intelligence and . . . worked out new methods to meet these requirements." The first important achievement was to establish a report system resting on the general faith in a method that, as Private Arthur Schlesinger remarked to a group of R. and A. researchers in London in June 1945, was known as "thoroughly objective and neutral" research. This attitude grew out of the belief that the social sciences were directly analogous to the physical sciences and (as Ranke expressed it) that historians were capable of grasping the past as it really was (*wie es eigentlich gewesen ist*). This view seems rather naive today, given relativist doubts about social and historical truth, but the 1940s was the heyday in America of the scientific approach to history, and educated people, whether in academia or the State Department, did not blanch when presented with "definitive" studies purportedly based on scientific, social, or historical research. Beyond a wide use of sources, avoidance of the first person singular, and an absence of overt political partisanship, little was necessary for a work to pass as scientific scholarship. In Arthur Schlesinger's 1945 view, "there should be no personal pronouns, no wisecracks, no slang or clichés, and care should be taken about the use of color words such as 'reactionary,' 'progressive,' 'left or right.'"[2]

This anonymous, unemotional tone was used throughout R. and A. reports because it corresponded to the views on science and objectivity held by both Langer's people and officials in other government agencies. For field reports, nothing more than this flat, two-dimensional presentation was required, since the author's acts of judgment were buried in the selection and arrangement of the materials, and no overt conclusion or recommendation was called for. Preparation of formal R. and A. Branch reports was a more complex matter, however. These reports, which included at least a summary and general conclusion, required somewhat more overt evaluation and usually embodied the work of more than one researcher. Consequently, machinery had to be established for supervising and approving work in progress. By 1943–44, every planned R. and A. project had to have a proposal statement prepared setting forth the subject, the name of the project leader, the probable customers, and the time and resources required to do the job. After a project was approved by the Section and Division chiefs, it went before the Projects Committee (long chaired by Richard Hartshorne) where it was sometimes amended before being authorized. Once completed, the report passed back through the same process of Section, Division, and Projects committee approval and was frequently revised and heavily edited before being mimeographed.[3]

This system deviated noticeably from the research practices then followed by most scholars in the humanities and social sciences. Requiring prior authorization by administrative superiors was the most obvious difference, but use of a "team approach" in which groups of researchers worked on a single project was also virtually unknown among historians and geographers at that time. A great deal of training and supervision were necessary to fit the more individualistic scholars to the team mold, but this approach was an essential element in the R. and A. system. Many of the special attributes, limitations, and methods of particular disciplines had to be sacrificed to the need for integrated research reports. As Langer declared in 1945, R. and A. broke "the artificial barriers separating one approach from another" to produce a strategic intelligence research method. This accomplishment not only made R. and A. more influential but helped pave the way for the area studies and interdisciplinary projects so popular at American universities in the postwar era.[4]

While training researchers to play by team rules, R. and A. also tried to teach government officials to "formulate the kind of questions to which intelligible answers can be expected." Thus, Langer's people were blending governmental and academic methods and interests in many ways. This was only possible because through much of the life of R. and A. the team mentality was not disturbed by the need to put overt policy recommendations into reports. In 1944 and 1945, the establishment of an Executive Committee and a special Director's Committee to prepare papers on such topics as how the United States should deal with Britain in the postwar period did lead R. and A. to make some more direct policy recommendations. As the war drew to a close and political policy questions superseded the demands of military necessity, pressure also rose to include policy suggestions in other R. and A. memoranda. "The Guide to Preparation of Political Reports" prepared by R. and A. in May 1944 merely had declared that "a rigid distinction is to be drawn between political intelligence reports and policy recommendations," but by November of that year the head of the Projects Committee concluded that if R. and A. continued to eschew policy recommendations, it would be relegated "to the position of a relatively irresponsible academic organization, more or less on a par with the Foreign Policy Association—save for its greater access to classified intelligence." The war ended before R. and A. could start developing many full-scale policy proposals, but the more highly charged political atmosphere of the last stage of hostilities led to some animated clashes over the content and conclusions of individual reports, including a July 1945 tussle over the German Socialist Party (S.P.D.) that pitted Herbert Marcuse, Carl Schorske, and Sherman Kent against Richard Hartshorne and the Projects Committee.[5]

Because the wartime focus on military necessity remained (albeit uneasily) until the end of O.S.S., this kind of R. and A. civil war was kept to a minimum and the system of "objective and neutral" strategic study was allowed to mature. Certainly, peace and tranquility did not reign undisturbed, for academics can usually find some way to make roads divide. As J. A. Morrison observed in 1945, R. and A. went through a period of *Sturm und Drang* in 1943, "when the 'regionalists' and 'functionalists' were eating largely of the apple of discord and there was much confusion in Zion."[6]

Such scholarly clashes failed to distrupt R. and A.'s evolution toward intelligence team work, in part because of peculiarities in William Langer's system of rule. The R. and A. chief possessed an imposing manner but was actually very deferential toward higher authority and had serious trouble acting like a boss who could easily hire and fire. Langer's problem with authority was made acute by his superior, for he mainly had to serve William Donovan. The general's peripatetic enthusiasms and cavalier attitude toward administration did not make life easy for any of his branch chiefs. But Langer was greatly impressed with Donovan and on occasion gave expression to his feeling even in official correspondence. In a July 1944 dispatch to Chandler Morse, the R. and A. chief revealed that he was in the highest spirits because Donovan had "on two occasions" actually "sat down for an hour and a half with our so-called Chief's Committee. . . . "I am genuinely sorry that he is leaving again in the near future," Langer told Morse, because "you know from your own experience how stimulating he is."[7]

The special pull that Donovan exerted on Langer helped make the R. and A. chief move his organization further in the direction of combat-support activities during the middle war period. R. and A.'s strategic intelligence team system was beginning to jell in 1942–43 at the very time when Donovan's longing for combat and his need to impress the J.C.S. led him to give battle activities overriding priority. Although Langer later tried to console himself with the thought that the general never really "lost his interest in R. and A.," to others associated with the branch Donovan emerged as "a character left over from the days of the condottieri." To keep in touch with this very special superior, Langer reluctantly had to allow R. and A. to move toward the battle zone and somewhat away from pure "strategic intelligence." The R. and A. outposts that had been established in London and Chunking during 1941 and 1942 had remained remote from the scene of combat, and except for the emphasis on map and targeting work done in London, the activities of these missions differed little from those performed by R. and A. Washington. But in 1943, an R. and A. buildup occurred close behind the front in the Mediterranean theater, and Rudy Winnacker, who initially "ran almost a one man show" there, convinced Donovan that R. and A. "could be really effective in connection with operations . . . very close to the front." Consequently, Langer allowed R. and A. activity to spread into many more battle-related activities, including tactical air force targeting, briefing of S.I. and S.O. combat missions, and some P.O.W. interrogation and document collection immediately behind the advancing armies. Donovan kept insisting that R. and A. move up with the forward echelon in every theater, and by the end of 1944 in Burma, an R. and A. man (Cap. Charles Cox) had become the combat intelligence officer of Detachment 101.[8]

The battle-related activities of R. and A. certainly enhanced its reputation with some army officers and the "action" sections of O.S.S. abroad, such as S.I. Donovan also was more inclined to meet the needs of Langer's people because of the branch's overseas activity. In May 1944, when the general learned that securing army approval for the transfer of nineteen R. and A. men to the European theater would be difficult, he told David Bruce to hide or "bury" the R. and A. request within the quotas reserved for S.O. and S.I. As everyone within R. and A. realized, the branch benefited further from its overseas and combat-related operations because these activities brought much information to Washington useful in preparing strategic intelligence reports.[9]

But there was nonetheless a general uneasiness in the branch about the dispersal of R. and A. activities so that scholarly energies could be channeled into immediate combat support. Many researchers were so uncomfortable working in "tainted" political climates that the R. and A. chief in China had to advise Langer that it would be best not to send anyone "too sensitive or idealistic" to Chunking. R. and A. outpost chiefs, as well as Langer's people in Washington, realized that no matter what they did "as a non-combatant branch," R. and A. was somewhat out of step with the rest of Donovan's organization. In November 1944, Stuart Hughes decried the "concerted attack on the R. and A. Branch" in the Mediterranean theater, which he thought had been "begun by the General [Donovan] himself, epitomized by his own phrase of 'getting belly to belly with the enemy.'" In Hughes's opinion, "this romantic point of view on R. and A. work has done us nearly irreparable harm."[10]

Langer shared Hughes's preference for keeping R. and A. a purely strategic intelligence research organization, but he was simply unable to challenge William Donovan directly. Therefore, to hold the main focus of the branch on strategic intelligence teamwork, Langer developed a complex and unusual leadership system. This highly structured branch was organized around a series of divisions that changed from time to time but by March 1944 had shaken down into two main regional divisions (Europe–Africa and Far East), with specialized divisions for such matters as Civil Affairs, Current Intelligence, Economics, and Maps. A number of divisions were subdivided into sections, and in 1944 prominent scholars, including Louis Franck (western Europe), Walter Dorn (central Europe), and Ralph Bunche (Africa), were serving as section leaders. Langer used tough academic administrators like Sherman Kent, Charles Fahs, and Arthur Robinson to control the branch's main divisions, with Carl Schorske and William Applebaum serving as special administrative assistants. Prominent scholarly names were also featured among the outpost chiefs, with Chandler Morse in London, Robert Hall in China–India, and Stuart Hughes in the Mediterranean during 1944. Administrative talent and executive image played an important role in Langer's choice of outpost chiefs. The R. and A. chief wanted a "tall, attractive-looking and energetic" man (Lt. Edward Rhetts) as R. and A. chief for S.E.A.C. rather than Cora DuBois, even though the latter had "much greater . . . professional competence," mainly because Rhetts had more "executive experience." Even Langer's old colleagues, such as Crane Brinton, were passed over for key posts when the R. and A. chief thought that they would come up short as administrators. Such preference for administrative prowess is certainly not unknown in academia, for only outsiders believe that the grove surrounds an ivory tower, but the role that Langer played within this administrative machine was peculiar. The branch chief assumed a position analogous to that of chairman of a board of directors, only rarely undertaking such unpleasant tasks as directly firing an outpost chief. Even when he did shoulder the full burden of administrative responsibility, he was inclined to be extremely polite while doing his best to paint his own behavior in a favorable light with such declarations as "I tried my darndest to help you."[11]

Langer's "soft" leadership method did not mean that he was an absentee landlord or mere figurehead. His division chiefs and special assistants were given clear direction regarding what he wanted, and on most occasions he gave them adequate backing. He also established a procedure whereby regular fortnightly activity and progress reports were required of all divisions, sections, and outposts. Langer himself produced a huge volume of correspondence with his subordinates. Regular letters of three, four, or five single-spaced typed pages were sent by the branch chief to R. and A. men stationed abroad. Furthermore, he was careful to keep his finger on the pulse of the whole organization. Every report from an overseas R. and A. post, though it might be addressed to a specific division, passed over Langer's desk, and his comments and replies show that he actually read them.[12]

To keep abreast of all the organization's activities, Langer encouraged every R. and A. person overseas to "write back even when there is nothing of world-shaking importance to communicate." Much of the resulting correspondence had a chummy tone, and outpost chief Robert Hall in China, who had an established academic reputation, was an army colonel, and had known Langer for years, could ask the R. and A. chief for a "good old Bill to Bob" letter to help straighten out a disagreement. But the niceties of academic status were also maintained, and the salutations on letters between Langer and Maj. Stuart Hughes (an outstanding former student who Langer liked and admired) remained "Dear Stuart" and "Dear Mr. Langer," throughout the war years. Langer was a master of the system of leadership through reports and correspondence, and before dispatch, even letters to the outpost chiefs from officials as highly esteemed as Franz Neumann had to have the R. and A. chief's prior approval.[13]

Through the massive exchange of correspondence, Langer exerted a direct, if rather fatherly, control over every aspect of the organization. The reports and letters primarily were intended to insure that every person in R. and A. abided by the basic principles of Langer's system. There were three cardinal principles. First, the "objective and neutral" report preparation procedure, including full regard for the team method and close supervisorial control, had to be followed by all R. and A. personnel whether they were in the Library of Congress or Istanbul. Second, the production of strategic intelligence reports in Washington had to be accepted as the *raison d'être* of R. and A., and every dispersal of R. and A. personnel that cut into the production of these reports was to be avoided. Third, all R. and A. people, even those immediately subordinate to O.S.S. or army commanders in the field, had to recognize that they were primarily Langer's people and their chief duty was to R. and A. Washington.

Controversies that rattled R. and A. Washington's relations with two important overseas outposts in 1944 will serve to illustrate how well Langer used the silken glove and how determined he was to tolerate no deviation from his basic principles. In January 1944, Harold Deutsch was sent on a liaison mission to London, and to help focus his work, Carl Schorske provided him with a four-page memorandum on "Outpost Home Office Relations," setting forth the chief shortcomings of R. and A. London. The major issue, as Schorske saw it, was that the London outpost was topsy-turvy and that "the inadequacy of the London leadership," had prevented creation of a "unified program." Liaison with British and American organizations, bomb targeting work, and the like, had in Schorske's view spread the organization too far and too thin. R. and A. London had lost sight of cardinal principle number two, and its political reporting to Washington had fallen behind the service it provided to the U.S. Army, various Allied agencies, and the O.S.S. organization in the European theater. This was unacceptable, as Schorske reminded Deutsch, because "the attitude of the political sections in Washington . . . is that men sent overseas are men lost to the work of R. and A.," and if anything was to be recovered from this loss, home reporting had to have top priority.[14]

A copy of the Schorske memorandum "drifted by devious but inevitable ways" into the office of Crane Brinton in London, and on 22 January Brinton penned an artful, if rather offended, reply to Langer. As head of R. and A. London's political reports section, Brinton was on the spot; as a senior Harvard colleague of William Langer (during a time when Carl Schorske was a student there), he had a sense of being ill used. Brinton summarized all the difficulties that he, as well as R. and A. London's pioneer, Allan Evans, had encountered in trying to get Langer's organization established in the British capital. To secure information, it was necessary to have something to trade, which inevitably took time and effort.

London's abundance of agencies and committees, including what Brinton called "the 57 varieties of M.[ilitary] I.[ntelligence,]" made it no simple matter to acquire anything worth dispatching to Washington. Brinton gently tried to suggest to Langer that "the relatively *parvenue* character of our own agency in the intelligence field" made it extremely difficult to satisfy Donovan's demand that all O.S.S. branches show positive results in helping the military and at the same time meet Langer's insistence that service to Washington should have undisputed top priority. Brinton was prepared to admit mistakes, but while granting that R. and A. London's work was "scattered," insisted that the group had followed Langer's first cardinal principle, and did "make up a real team."[15]

Langer hurriedly sent Brinton a "word by way of apology," declaring that although he shared some of Schorske's views, he "decidedly disagree[d] with others." Stressing that since the Schorske memorandum was a "purely domestic internal document" rather than a formal dispatch to the outpost, it had not passed through the normal tight controls, Langer declared that "we have not yet reached the stage of back-stairs procedures," and in any event "all the boys have done a grand job and I am very happy to take this opportunity to say so." Nevertheless, within a month Brinton and Evans were passed over, and Chandler Morse was sent from Washington to London to take charge of the R. and A. outpost and bring "order, organization and purpose into the work of the boys at Brook Street."[16]

The second incident occurred in May 1944, when in response to Langer's order that one of the top R. and A. researchers, Lt. John Sawyer, be sent back to Washington, Mediterranean Outpost Chief Maj. Stuart Hughes protested to R. and A. Washington and also raised the matter with his immediate O.S.S. superior in Algiers, Colonel Glavin. Glavin sided with Hughes and requested that Donovan override Langer, and the general followed Glavin's lead and asked the R. and A. chief to allow Sawyer to stay where he was. Langer yielded to Donovan, but at the same time sent a blistering letter to Hughes declaring that he was "decidedly displeased by the way this whole matter was handled." Hughes had violated cardinal principle number three, failing to put his obligation to R. and A. Washington above all others. "We decide here who shall go into the field," Langer told Hughes, "and we must reserve the right to recall men if in our judgment they are badly needed here or elsewhere." The R. and A. chief stressed that "what bothers me most about this whole episode is that you should have been inclined to stake your judgment against ours," because "your responsibility is primarily to me and when you are instructed to return a member of the staff here, I think you are fully justified in raising objections to me but not in raising strong protests which end with the whole matter being taken out of our hands."[17]

A month later, Langer had calmed down and in another long letter on the Sawyer affair indicated to Hughes that he was prepared to let the matter drop. The major had been attentive to Langer throughout, conceding his ultimate authority, but had not groveled. Still, Langer had the last word, for while burying the hatchet and noting that he found Hughes's reports "distinctly interesting and valuable," he casually observed that Lieutenant Applebaum, who had been doing "a marvelous job" as "a sort of efficiency expert" in R. and A. Washington and elsewhere, would soon be calling in Algiers. Langer indicated that this should cause Hughes no alarm, for the Algiers–Italy outpost seemed to be in "very good condition." Still, he thought it "an excellent idea to have somebody of Bill [Applebaum]'s type" look over the R. and A. Mediterranean operation for "a month or six weeks"![18]

In any event, all went well, for Hughes and Applebaum got on famously, and the lieutenant duly reported to Langer that Hughes's operation was, as advertised, in "very good condition." But both the Hughes–Langer clash over Sawyer and the affair of the Schorske memorandum (and a number of complaints about R. and A. research talent's being wasted) reveal a good deal about William Langer's system and shed an interesting light on the long-term evolution of R. and A. Obviously, in one way or another, Langer was determined to have his way, and the three cardinal principles of scientific scholarship, strategic intelligence primacy, and the supremacy of R. and A. Washington were going to be upheld. But Langer's use of the soft and indirect approach also had other important effects. Apparently, some of his people had a dreadful time determining what he wanted, for the records are studded with letters from R. and A. people asking him to clarify his meaning or complaining that he had not been completely candid with them. This uncertainty was an unavoidable side effect of the R. and A. chief's desire to shun confrontation and hard-line administrative techniques. It further meant that in R. and A., one had to pick up hints and signs to get along. Langer's domain was a highly refined in-group, bound together not only by a common academic background and the development of a new method of strategic intelligence research but also by the system of incessant correspondence and authoritative innuendo. Inevitably, R. and A. became something of a thing apart, especially at a time when the rest of O.S.S., and indeed the whole of American society, thought in terms of brisk military orders and lucid chains of command. By binding his people together around basic principles and indirect forms of communication, Langer gave them the cohesiveness to withstand conflicts with outside American and Allied agencies or with other branches of O.S.S. When in 1945 the final showdown threatened to dissolve Donovan's O.S.S. empire, Langer's way also made it easier for R. and A. to conclude that it was truly unique and therefore had a right to try to arrange for its own postwar afterlife.[19]

Long before the end of O.S.S., the cohesiveness and sense of mission in Langer's branch had helped to give R. and A. its well-deserved reputation for efficiency and productivity. Although the total number of R. and A. personnel never exceeded 1,000 (982 seems to have been the top figure, with approximately one third overseas), Langer's staff produced an enormous amount of work. Numerous special trend and current intelligence reports were prepared both in Washington and in the field. Such reports were in part intended to assist policymakers within and without O.S.S. who needed information on immediately pressing problems, but they also served as source materials for the formal R. and A. studies and maps prepared in Washington. These formal studies ranged in length from a few to hundreds of pages and covered subjects from "The Debate on British Foreign Policy in the House of Commons on 28–29 September 1944" (R and A 2654) to "Manpower Shortage and the German Collapse in 1918" (R and A 2232). The R. and A. Map Division provided the S.I. and S.O. branches of O.S.S., as well as various military offices, with special detailed maps for combat missions and also produced larger survey maps for the use of policymakers. As early as March 1944, the R. and A. London outpost had assembled a research library of 15,000 reports and documents, and in a single fifteen-month period in the middle phase of the organization's history (January 1943 through March 1944) 700 formal R. and A. reports were completed. Overall, as Langer informed Donovan in August 1945 in his final appraisal of R. and A. achievements, the branch produced in excess of 3,000 formal "research studies" and 3,000 original maps.[20]

Throughout its history, the leaders and staff of the branch showed a willingness to experiment and innovate. Although R. and A. personnel did not go on intelligence missions, never slipping ashore in rubber boats or making parachute drops, some were included in the O.S.S. teams that went into the recently occupied Balkan capitals in the fall of 1944, and on occasion (such as the fighting in Greece during the winter of 1944) R. and A. people came under fire. But most of R. and A.'s inventiveness was focused on such matters as new methods of target analysis and the identification of untapped sources of research information. In the last two years of the war, Langer's people gathered much current information on conditions abroad through a regular program of questioning returning American civil and military officials. The R. and A. man in Istanbul, Dean Woodruff, sharply increased the value of information secured from travelers arriving in Turkey from the Balkans by simply using detailed maps of the area during interview sessions. By moving researchers about from one project to another and refusing to restrict personnel to the analysis of specific geographical zones or academic specialties, useful data was acquired from unlikely places. By mid-May 1945, nine R. and A. specialists were working in Europe collecting and analyzing data on Japan that turned up in neutral countries or had been found in the files of Tokyo's German ally.[21]

R. and A. benefited from its close ties with American universities and professional associations. The recruiting of regular staff was made easy through the use of the regular academic channels that linked R. and A. members together with their faculty colleagues and former students. Although Langer was unable to realize his early hope that R. and A. become the clearing house for the relations of all American intelligence agencies with universities, the high scholarly stature of those in R. and A. guaranteed that the branch would have a special relationship with the academic community. As early as the fall of 1942 (beginning apparently with Stanford and the University of California at Berkeley), a number of R. and A. research projects, or portions thereof, were subcontracted directly to university departments and individual civilian scholars. By the end of the war, the top leaders of R. and A. (including Sherman Kent, Charles Fahs, Geroid Robinson, and Preston James) concluded that a permanent system had to be developed to facilitate the consultation activities of university specialists who could assist government intelligence agencies doing "research on foreign areas." This conclusion was undoubtedly the genesis of the close structural tie between American universities and intelligence agencies that, though it has not received as much publicity as the now famous academic–military research linkup, nonetheless permanently affected the independence and tone of much academic activity. But it would be a distortion to suggest that the bridges that R. and A. helped build between the universities and American intelligence agencies originated in a shady plot. In the general effort to secure victory over the Axis that prevailed in America during World War II, nearly everyone rejoiced to see all civilian institutions serve the military cause, and there was little feeling that it might be better to keep some distance between temples of free inquiry and the darker aspects of modern war. In our era of concern about connections between academia and government agencies, it is important to remember that academic officials were so oblivious to such notions during the Second World War that hallowed institutions, including Cal Tech, not only did research for the military but actually *manufactured* rockets for the army.[22]

In this atmosphere, R. and A. officials were free to employ their considerable talent for wheeling and dealing to benefit their organization as well as the war effort. Langer and his staff were gifted expansionists, managing to work their way into many distant corners, and once on the ground, manifesting genuine staying power. By September 1944, thirty-one R. and A. personnel were already in Paris and forty-four were still in the Mediterranean theater a month after V.E. Day. Until February 1945, Langer managed to hold onto a special R. and A. office to study North American affairs, and an unobstrusive little R. and A. office in Honolulu hung on until August 1945. On occasion, R. and A.'s broad interests and appetites compelled it to shoulder some unwanted burdens, including the time-consuming task of preparing the history of O.S.S. so dear to the heart of William Donovan, but Langer's people were generally better at getting what they wanted than what they didn't. In the course of the war, R. and A. even broke through the State Department's reluctance to grant access to its cable traffic, and in the last phase of hostilities Langer's people were routinely shown all items of interest except those that involved "disclosure of Departmental policy." When regular bureaucratic means failed to get R. and A. officials what they desired, they were sufficiently adept at political maneuver to attain it frequently from the flank. After a long hassle over G-2's refusal to allow R. and A. to participate directly in P.O.W. interrogation in the S.H.A.E.F. theater (although it was authorized to do so in the Mediterranean), Sherman Kent concluded in August 1944 that there was "no sense going further" by direct assault. After considering a number of possible ways to get to the object by other means, Kent decided that "the most profitable line to follow" would be "to so indoctrinate some G-2 interrogators that they will be able to do a good job for us."[23]

Officials this proficient at fitting means to ends substantially aided R. and A. in wielding an influence out of proportion to its small size and low budget. But a bigger factor in the effect of Langer's branch was the flow of its reports to other branches of O.S.S. and to various agencies of the American and Allied governments. We can uncover copies of R. and A. reports in virtually every corner of the mountain of Allied World War II files. From the White House to the British intelligence staff, from Henry Morgenthau's domain to the files of S.I.S. officials, R. and A. reports and maps found a place in the holdings of Anglo-American executive officials and their staffs. Most of these reports, tucked away in file drawers, bear no comment or other marking to indicate how those who received them felt about the work of Langer's people. On occasion, we run across a remark suggesting that an official doubted whether a particular report had any special merit, and somewhat more frequently there are signs that R. and A.'s products were held in high esteem. In May 1943, the British Military Intelligence staff informed another British agency that "O.S.S. surveys are of direct interest to us," and in June 1944, the B.S.C. lodged a stiff protest when Langer temporarily cut off the flow of R. and A. reports to Stephenson's group. In May 1945, Samuel Rosenman, one of the few Roosevelt White House advisors who stayed close to President Truman, indicated that he found an O.S.S. report on the Soviet attitude on war crimes "most interesting," while two months earlier, in a silent tribute to the excellence of R. and A.'s studies of Germany, Henry Morgenthau began to pass them on to Harry Dexter White to help him build a case for following a tough occupation policy following the demise of the Third Reich.[24]

Although such scattered comments certainly provide no precise basis for measuring the overall impact of R. and A., it is important to note that Langer and his associates were keen to avoid adverse comments on their handiwork. Rigid controls were used to avoid outside distribution of branch working papers or materials that the Projects Committee had declared unsatisfactory. "The European Political Report," edited in London during 1944–45 by the "leftist" Paul Sweezy, was an especially sensitive issue. R. and A. officials leaned on Sweezy to make him eliminate the "definite political bias" found in early issues of the report, and Donovan told Chandler Morse that Sweezy should take great care in the use of words like *politics* and *report* in order not to excite the jurisdictional worries of the State Department. The final versions of Sweezy's commentaries appear in retrospect to be pretty tame stuff, characterized less by its "leftist" bias than by a tendency to hang onto old fantasies regarding the stupidity of the Nazi leadership and the mighty power of the Prussian officer corps.[25]

Some great castles recently have been erected on the shallow foundations provided by the existence of a particular R. and A. report or the discovery of a copy in a State Department or J.C.S. file. Extreme caution should be used in regard to such matters, for the records of the psychological warfare office of the White House Map Room—one of the few places from which comprehensive data is currently available—shows rather surprising facts regarding the reception of R. and A. material. Of the forty-nine R. and A. reports sent to the Map Room in 1944–45, nine were placed in the regular files, fourteen were put in a cabinet or closet, the fate of eight more is not indicated, and the single biggest group, totaling eighteen, was "destroyed by burning" immediately after receipt. Since reports sent to the Map Room were supposed to be used in the formulation of psychological warfare policy, it is difficult to understand why R. and A. sent some of the reports it did and equally unclear why they were handled the way they were upon arrival. Retained in the active files along with such reports as one on "The Greek Political Crisis" were reports on the "Organization of European Waterways" and the "First Two Months of the New Guatemalan Government." Among those destroyed were a detailed study of South Germany (burned in December 1944, when that region already had been scheduled as the American zone of occupation), in addition to reports on native nationalism in North Africa, "The French Intelligence Service," "The Government of the New Philippines," and the "Crisis in the Mexican Sinarquista Movement." How psychological warriors could find Guatemala more significant than Mexico or the organization of European waterways more important and relevant than hard data on the area of planned American penetration is simply impossible to imagine.[26]

Therefore, the mere presence of a particular R. and A. report in any agency's files proves very little about the value of Langer's branch, for if the practices of the Map Room are any guide, the decisions to retain or destroy a particular report might as well have been made by drawing straws. However, the sheer volume of R. and A. materials sent out demonstrates that many officials beyond the confines of Langer's branch valued the researchers' achievements. In the year 1944 alone, a million requests were received for R. and A. maps, and between January and July 1945, 9,026 pieces of R. and A. work (including multiple copies of individual items) went to the State Department. One-third of R. and A. working time was devoted to "basic research" and "self-initiated projects" even at the end of 1944, but during its four-year life span, R. and A. gradually evolved into a service agency for other organizations and departments. So many special high-priority report requests were received that the branch had to set limits regarding how much short-schedule work could be accomplished. Little by little R. and A. learned to deal with the emergency demands of William Donovan and also was able to meet other high-priority needs such as those of Averell Harriman on the Russian food situation; a mysterious "Mr. X," who petitioned Sherman Kent for a study of "aspects of the political and social situation in France and Spain" in mid-1943; and Pan American Airways, which was authorized to receive "a number" of secret and confidential documents from Langer in March 1942.[27]

Langer's people seem to have safely steered their way through the most dangerous political waters produced by controversial requests for assistance. The Justice Department and the F.B.I. received some R. and A. information on possible Nazi links with right-wing "subversives" in the United States. This work did not take Langer and his staff too far over the line that barred them from working on domestic matters and probably helped quiet F.B.I. suspicion of R. and A., whose research on Latin America touched on an area that the F.B.I. director and the State Department regarded as their own special joint preserve. R. and A. also survived with its reputation intact from the heated 1944–45 battle over German occupation policy. R. and A. did have to provide the basic research for Hugh Wilson's farfetched scheme to break up the Reich by encouraging individual Germans to launch separatist movements in the postwar period. But at an "enjoyable luncheon" with Henry Morgenthau and his staff, Langer smoothed the way for the utilization of R. and A. reports by the Treasury Department, and the War Department also employed some R. and A. materials as ammunition in its campaign to convince Morgenthau that his "pasteurization" program was folly. As befitted a specialist in German history facing a policy controversy over Germany, Langer managed to emerge from the "pasteurization" conflict in something of the style of an honest broker.[28]

This consequence was all the more surprising because the Civil Affairs Division of the War Department and those divisions of the State Department most concerned with occupation policy were among the best regular customers of R. and A. work. From July 1943 on, R. and A. agreed to provide Gen. John H. Hilldring of the Civil Affairs Division with most of the basic research he required in establishing policies and precedures for all territories occupied by American forces. The demands of various non-O.S.S. agencies for R. and A. work certainly rose and fell, but overall, the Civil Affairs Division and the State Department, along with various J.I.C. committees, were the best customers for the reports provided by Langer's branch. Therefore, especially in such matters as occupation activities, R. and A. played an important, if backstage, role in shaping American policy simply by supplying a great volume of information and establishing special liaison arrangements with certain non-O.S.S. agencies. In May 1944, the Projects Committee appointed a number of key individuals to act as R. and A. liaison men with the branch's main customers. These included five R. and A. men to work with J.C.S. committees, among them Carl Schorske and Everett Gleason; two with the State Department; and two with the War Department, one of whom was Hajo Holborn, who directed occupation policy research.[29]

These arrangements helped give consumers of R. and A. products the feeling that their needs were being met. Langer's people were also willing to go an extra mile to avoid trouble and please important people. In August 1944, O.S.S. created a new security classification called "Control," which was intended to denote material "unsuitable for release to non-American agencies," thereby easing the risks inherent in producing research reports on matters that would be offensive to America's allies. On occasion, R. and A. men were also ready to alter the form of their presentations, if not the basic content, to produce a stronger impact. In May 1945, Edwin Martin, one of the branch's top Far Eastern economic analysts, recommended after a talk with Donovan that a report on Chinese inflation be rewritten in "a more scholarly" way since it would then "impress General Wedemeyer more effectively."[30]

The inordinate lengths to which R. and A. went to please its customers helped to make Langer's branch seem to be a friend to everyone and a mortal enemy to no one. Momentary scrapes between R. and A. and other branches of O.S.S. certainly occurred, but Langer's people did extensive and valuable work for every segment of Donovan's empire. Langer's branch was intended to be a service agency, and it unquestionably provided more work and more information to every single O.S.S. unit, from M.O. to S.I., than it ever received in return. R. and A. people often felt like stepchildren, ill used and unappreciated, but no non–R. and A. official of O.S.S. could long carry a serious grudge against Langer's branch since it was inexpensive and always gave more than it received.[31]

An organization practicing charity is appreciated even within an intelligence community, but probably more so by outside organizations. R. and A.—despite its fundamental desire to emphasize strategic intelligence—provided various forms of assistance to an amazing range of non-O.S.S. customers. Every committee of the J.C.S. and nearly every division of the War Department (as well as some sections of the Navy Department) received aid from R. and A. The civilian departments of the government, led by State, as well as most of the temporary wartime boards and committees (especially the B.E.W.) also benefited from the work of Langer's people. Every theater command overseas drew on R. and A. information, as did nearly all United States diplomatic missions. Many British organizations acquired R. and A. materials, and even the N.K.V.D. was among the beneficiaries of R. and A.'s largesse.[32]

Certainly, some officials in the research sections of American and British intelligence were suspicious of the competition that R. and A. might provide, and many State Department officials greeted the rise of another research and reporting agency with less than good humor. But simply because of its openhanded generosity, R. and A. inevitably made more friends than enemies. By the end of the war, thousands of American civilian and military officials had grown accustomed to using the kind of "objective and neutral" research reports produced by Langer's people.

It cannot be emphasized too strongly that the wide-ranging distribution of R. and A.'s products and the indirect way the branch's reports came to bear on policy formation helped to give R. and A. a positive image. Customers who found the reports useful tended to favor continuation of the organization after the war, while those who did not benefit from R. and A. research were likely to be indifferent rather than hostile. The very fact that it is now so hard to determine how R. and A. work directly shaped American policies shows how difficult it would then have been for anyone to be a determined enemy of R. and A. because no one could blame Langer's branch for a lost policy battle or accuse it of having crossed jurisdictional lines to become much of a direct challenge to the authority of an existing department. R. and A. was so respectable and respectful, so conscientious and helpful, that it inevitably acquired the aura of virtue.

Not that the record of R. and A. was completely devoid of blemishes. Despite the elaborate system for approving and expediting report preparation, it was discovered in November 1944 that more than sixty "current" projects had been dragging on for over six months. Some of the completed reports were also not above criticism. A special report on the forthcoming British election forwarded to Langer in early July 1945 concluded not only that the Torys would win but that they would defeat labor by seventy seats. When, three weeks later, Labor scored the most overwhelming victory in the history of modern British elections, some egg was left on the face of R. and A.[33]

Furthermore, although R. and A. was much more restrained than other branches of O.S.S., at times one of Langer's people looked precipitate. In January 1942, Maurice Halperin of the Latin American Division even called for full-scale covert "intervention" in Mexico at a time when he himself saw little evidence of great Axis influence there.[34]

Also, although R. and A. had a much better record on the employment of women and ethnic minorities than other branches of O.S.S. or of the government in general, it was not flawless in this regard. R. and A. utilized a great number of women researchers, perhaps as many as 25 percent of the total research force, but with very few exceptions they were limited to low-level positions. Langer had no compunction about frankly declaring in a letter to O.S.S.–S.E.A.C. that one of the reasons he did not want to make Cora Dubois R. and A. outpost chief there was his belief "that a man could function better than a woman as [an outpost] chief of R. and A." Langer's eagerness to impress those in authority, especially General Donovan and his military entourage, undoubtedly contributed to

R. and A.'s tendency to have women walk behind and to the left. But other factors, including simple racism, were involved in the way the branch treated some ethnic minorities.[35]

Refugee and immigrant scholars of European extraction generally received a warm and respectful welcome in Langer's branch. German scholars were valued highly not only because of the obvious fact that their homeland was the object of much of R. and A.'s labor but also because the German tradition of "scientific" scholarship in the social sciences and humanities fitted neatly into the R. and A. system of "thoroughly objective and neutral" reporting. R. and A. was not teaming with temporary foreign residents, as some accounts have suggested; most of those born abroad took out citizenship papers, and by March 1945 the branch employed only forty-seven aliens, of whom eleven Germans constituted the single biggest national group. Nonetheless, by 1943, there was a large and influential German refugee contingent in R. and A. featuring, among others, Hajo Holborn, Franz Neumann, and Otto Kirchheimer. Many of these people were distinctly leftist in their political predilections, and nearly all had been classified as non-Aryan by the Nazis, although few were practicing Jews. Certainly in the elitist atmosphere that had prevailed in prewar Ivy League academia, they would have been considered Jews, and few of them could have hoped for entry into the club of prestigious American university life. But in R. and A., they were respected, and such men as Neumann and Holborn (the latter having already been taken aboard at Yale), enjoyed a status of special esteem and honor. This phenomenon constituted a real breakthrough in extending the social base of American academia (in the social sciences and the humanities) and would contribute to the further broadening of the social groups represented in American higher educational faculties during the postwar university boom.[36]

Those of Asian extraction in R. and A., even if they were American citizens, did not fare so well. Partly because of suspicions that through the S.A.C.O. connection the Chinese government was using devious methods to exploit its relationship with O.S.S. to secure American secrets, the Far East Division of R. and A. had a policy forbidding "contacts" between its members "and persons of Chinese race." But the suspicion and hostility regarding Chinese went beyond mere security consciousness. As an official of the R. and A. Far East Division reported to Langer in January 1945, "we have been extremely reluctant to employ American citizens of Chinese origin with full security privileges, and at present have only one." When the same official learned that the Map Division employed "with full security clearance a Chinese with Chinese citizenship," he declared that "off hand we would consider [such action] quite questionable" and asked that before any division of R. and A. granted full security rights to "anyone of Chinese race," an opinion "be secured from the Far East Division."[37]

If such treatment was given to American citizens whose ancestors came from a country that was allied with the United States, it is not surprising that Japanese-Americans had a difficult time. Although Langer's branch made use of many nisei researchers both overseas and in Washington and also recruited nisei for service with other O.S.S. branches, the lot of the nisei was not easy. They were not promoted rapidly in R. and A., were unable to receive full security clearances, and in Washington were forced to work in a special, screened off area in the Library of Congress. Many nisei deeply resented this situation, and in July 1945, one of them, Hatsumi Yamada, addressed a stiff letter of protest to the chief of the Far East Division. Noting that he had volunteered for the U.S. Army and then had been transferred to O.S.S. without his consent, Yamada cited the slights and shabby treatment to which nisei in R. and A. were subjected and requested either "an outright discharge" or that he be allowed to go back to regular army service so that he could "be free from the O.S.S. where discrimination is practiced." The security office remained obdurate regarding Yamada's appeal, but R. and A. officials were anxious to make changes, partly because they feared that Yamada's complaints might reach the press and partly because when forced to confront the issue squarely they opposed the continuance of such discrimination. Late July and August 1945 saw lively exchanges between O.S.S. Security and the R. and A. administrative office, with the latter contending that consideration of the nisei "as a group apart immediately means discrimination of the worst type" and that "one of the things we are fighting in this war is to end discrimination against groups of people because of race, color or creed." But R. and A.'s conscience awoke too late to win the battle for antidiscrimination and what Yamada politely called the very "unpleasant atmosphere" in the special Library of Congress section remained until V.J. Day.[38]

When we pass beyond the realm of human relations and equal opportunity to examine areas in which R. and A. had a demonstrable impact on American policy formation, Langer's branch also fails to pass without some black marks. As one would suspect, from the fall of 1944 on, R. and A.'s work on the Soviet Union found an increasingly warm reception in the State Department. Geroid Robinson's Soviet specialists did extensive special work for the department's use in Washington and also assisted the American Embassy in Moscow. So highly did the embassy rate R. and A.

studies that in late November 1944 George Kennan not only requested that more be sent but also asked Charles Bohlen "to emphasize to Dr. Robinson that his work is very useful to us." An incident involving Acting Secretary of State Edward Stettinius that occurred in the same period is rather unnerving just because it reveals the extent to which the State Department depended on R. and A. material. On 22 November, Stettinius conferred with Soviet Ambassador Gromyko, and afterward received a note from Charles Bohlen urging him to be cautious on such topics as the Baltic states and Red Army–Communist Party relations in his talks with Soviet officials. To underscore his point, Bohlen appended R. and A. study 2521, "The Relative Positions of the Communist Party and the Red Army under the Soviet Regime." In reply, the obedient Stettinius reported that Gromyko had not brought up these issues in their recent talk but promised "I shall study this matter [i.e., the R. and A. report] with care" before holding another conversation with the Russians. That unknown to its creators an R. and A. report was being used like Phybate notes to prepare an inadequately informed acting secretary for test matches with the Soviets is hardly reassuring about the impact of R. and A. work on American policy.[39]

This is true especially because at least one group of R. and A. reports that attracted high-level State Department interest contained a very serious error. R. and A. reports prepared in the summer and fall of 1944 on Soviet wartime losses tended to conclude that the Soviets were capable of very rapid postwar recovery even without outside aid because Langer's researchers severely underestimated Soviet wartime population loss. In October 1944, one of these studies (R. and A. 2060), which based its prediction of a speedy recovery on an estimated total Soviet net population loss during the war period of 3.4 million when the true figure ranged between 15 and 20 million, moved through the higher reaches of the State Department. After careful study, the department's F. F. Lincoln declared that though the view that Russia would attain full reconstruction within three years "may be overly optimistic," the report's basic conclusion that the U.S.S.R. could get back on its feet quickly without foreign aid "appears sound." Bohlen was somewhat more doubtful, believing that the study pitched the loss figure too low and disregarded various intangibles in the recovery process. But in his memorandum to Assistant Secretary of State Dean Acheson, Bohlen stated that the R. and A. study's conclusion was solid enough to serve "as a corrective to certain exaggerated opinions as to the degree of Soviet dependency on economic assistance from abroad in the postwar period as a possible means of political pressure."[40]

Recent studies have indicated that when in 1945 the United States backed off (or as some contend, reneged) on Harriman's offer of a recovery loan to the Soviet Union, the East–West chill turned colder. The fact that an erroneous R. and A. conclusion helped convince State Department officials that Russian policy toward the West could not be seriously affected by a loan (since it would quickly recover in any case) means that the R. and A. impact in this case was negative. Furthermore, R. and A. did not conclude from Bohlen's remarks on this study that its estimate of Soviet casualties was too low and continued to base its summaries of Soviet power on the minuscule loss figure. If Adam Ulam is right that American postwar policy was long hamstrung by Washington's overestimate of Soviet strength and a failure to understand how seriously the Soviet Union had been hurt during the war, the impression that these erroneous R. and A. studies made on State Department officials may have been part of the problem.[41]

Nor was this the only R. and A. error that had serious policy consequences. In the fall of 1943, R. and A. joined with two other research groups (the Foreign Economic Administration and the Committee of Operations Analysts) to study the Japanese steel industry. The resulting report, which was used to plan some of the strategy for bombing Japan, failed to recognize that Japanese steel plants were annually producing 5 million tons under capacity because of a shortage of raw materials. Consequently, much of the bombing effort to reduce Japan's output by striking at steel plants failed because 5 million tons of plant capacity had to be destroyed before any loss of production began to occur.[42]

Therefore, we must be cautious in concluding that Langer's people were wonder workers merely because there was little overt criticism of R. and A. at the time. R. and A. was, despite its various achievements and failures, a political organization like any other. What was vital for it to maintain and expand its position was merely a general reputation for efficiency and productivity. By late summer 1944, that reputation had clearly been achieved, for when the Bureau of the Budget surveyed R. and A.'s customers, it concluded that the "almost unanimous" opinion was "that the work which the Branch had done had been excellent and valuable." That was what Langer needed most in the battle for R. and A.'s postwar survival, and with the Bureau of the Budget on his side, he mounted a fall 1944 effort to get an R. and A.–type unit into the permanent structure of the American government.[43]

Langer had been keeping his eye directed on the far horizon for a long time prior to the fall of 1944. From at least the summer of 1943 onward, R. and A. outposts had been instructed to keep long-range strategic intelligence in the forefront of their thinking. Research projects, such as one on the French Provisional government carried out in North Africa in April 1944, clearly had as their object the development of a body of information useful in analyzing the postwar behavior of various governments. In January 1944, in a letter to David Bruce in London, Langer went so far as to say that "we expect a shift of major emphasis" from "studies for military plans to those for post-hostilities, primarily military government and civil affairs." The postwar potential of civil affairs work was also one of the factors that led Langer in August 1944 to launch his more overt and concerted attempt to establish R. and A. on a long-term basis. Chandler Morse in London had made substantial headway in convincing Gen. Cornelius Wickersham and his army planners engaged in preparing for the occupation of Germany that R. and A. would be of great value to the American contingent of the Allied Control Council. Members of Wickersham's staff believed that it would be beneficial to play along with O.S.S. because in their opinion it would "continue to operate after the cessation of organized resistance, because of its favored governmental position and the Congressional appropriations which sustain it." This forecast turned out to be poor, but it established a climate in the fall of 1944 that allowed Langer and Morse to push R. and A. into the preparations for the occupation of Germany. On 17 August 1944, Langer went so far as to tell Lieutenant Applebaum that the whole future of R. and A. in Europe "will hinge on whether or not the tie-up with Wickersham and the ACC [Allied Control Commission] can be affected."[44]

On the same day that he alerted Applebaum to the vital importance of German occupation planning for the future of R. and A. in Europe, Langer told Morse how "immensely pleased" he was regarding the progress with Wickersham and also brought the London R. and A. chief up to date on the broad range of efforts he was making to strengthen the branch's position during the transition from war to peace. At this moment (August 1944), when the British and American armies were in full gallop across France and a belief in imminent victory was sweeping Washington, Langer believed it essential to move fast. He told Morse that "we feel that we are at a turning point here in Washington" and that action on a broad front was required. The R. and A. branch chief was working with Gen. Stanley Embrick of the Joint Strategic Survey Committee, trying to secure "an adequate mandate to get into [general] post-hostilities work" for the military. Langer was also "plugging along" with the State Department, hoping eventually to entice the diplomats into making a formal request for R. and A. services instead of merely using branch reports since this would help give R. and A. a claim on a permanent place in foreign policy formulation. The biggest success that Langer's general campaign had scored to date, however, had come with the Bureau of the Budget. Not only had the budget people concluded that R. and A.'s customers were satisfied with its output, but some budget officials had also indicated to Langer "that the R. and A. had a real future in the post-war intelligence setup and that the role we would play would depend on how efficient and tight we could make the organization." [45]

This assessment seems to have encouraged Langer to redouble his efforts to make R. and A. as "efficient and tight" as possible and inclined him to seize every opportunity to show that the branch could have postwar utility. While continuing to urge his staff to do everything in its power to maximize R. and A.'s role in the occupation plan for Germany, he used Hajo Holborn, who had no Japanese expertise but enjoyed a very high standing with the army's Civil Affairs Division, to open the door for the branch's participation in the preparations for Japanese occupation. In a 22 September 1944 letter to W. L. Ream of the O.S.S. administrative unit, Langer set forth a number of factors that Ream might use in justifying a long-term R. and A. budget. Together with German and Japanese occupation work, the branch chief contended that "as tension mounts in South America," the importance of the Latin American Division would increase, and additional personnel would be required. [46]

In December 1944, Langer thought he had scored a big double breakthrough in his campaign to assure R. and A.'s long-range existence. When Donovan and the R. and A. chief persuaded Acting Secretary of State Stettinius to sign a letter to the Bureau of the Budget declaring that the department placed a high value on R. and A. work, Langer concluded that a large portion of the battle had been won. He acknowledged that it would still be necessary to do some "pushing on" with State Department officials, but he believed that there was no longer any "fundamental obstacle" to developing "very close working relationships" with the department. Langer held that a formal R. and A. agreement with State was within his grasp, and as he told Chandler Morse, "we have an open road ahead of us." [47]

The R. and A. chief was equally optimistic about the prospects for the branch offered by the plan that Donovan had "batted up" for a postwar central intelligence agency. R. and A. did "a good deal of work" on the preparation of the plan, and though Langer suspected that Donovan would have to yield on his insistence that the agency be directly responsible to the president rather than a Three Department (War–Navy–State) Board, he was generally highly confident. He thought, erroneously, that the plan "went over first-rate at the White House and with the Bureau of the Budget" and did not believe, despite some foot dragging, that the

State Department "is hostile to the scheme." He predicted to Chandler Morse on 9 December that "the larger part of it will go through, and some sort of an integrated intelligence agency will emerge."[48]

In the resulting mood of tough confidence, Langer produced an exuberant new directive for the R. and A. outposts in Europe. Though somewhat toned down in its ultimate form, the directive jettisoned service to "the armed forces in the present emergency" as the primary activity of R. and A. The draft of the 29 January directive declared that the "fundamental premise" had been "radically changed": "In view of the arrangement sealed with the State Department, and in view of the progress of plans for a permanent intelligence organization in which R. and A. would be incorporated, it is the obligation of the present leadership of the Branch, of the Divisions and of the Outposts, to establish objectives that look forward to a long-range future, rather than to be satisfied with only plans for immediate and terminating objectives." The finished form of the directive cut out the references to the State Department deal and the supposed progress of Donovan's postwar intelligence plan, but the admonition to focus on projects with a long-range future remained in place.[49]

On into spring 1945, and even following the derailing of Donovan's intelligence plan by press leaks and the death of Franklin Roosevelt, R. and A. officials kept emphasizing to their subordinates that the main function of the branch was the collection of "strategic intelligence" related to "the protection of United States [long-term] interests and security." Gradually, however, the uncertainties of the situation and the dark clouds gathering over Donovan's organization and his postwar plans undercut Langer's confidence and forced him to follow a softer, and less direct, approach to the goal of preserving R. and A.[50]

State Department officials had countered O.S.S. by simply stalling on such efforts as one to get the department to depend on R. and A. as its main source of maps because some State Department officials recognized that this effort was part of "the natural human desire of OSS to seek self-perpetuation." In May, the R. and A. outpost chief in Paris, Lt. John Sawyer, pleaded for some clarification of the branch's postwar position because time did not seem to be on Langer's side. Other American government agencies in Paris were going onto a permanent footing, and "a group in G-2" was "hostile to the continuance of an independent OSS." Even more serious, French agencies were beginning to take a closer look at British and American clandestine services and "French officials and private citizens have begun to inquire, either by direct question or implication, what American agency we represent." Sawyer emphasized that although he realized that "this is simply part of a larger OSS question," the fact remained that "the effectiveness of our work and the morale of the staff will suffer if some definition is not reached."[51]

Langer turned to Donovan with his troubles, declaring that although both he and the O.S.S. director had long held that R. and A. should have an important role to play in peacemaking and as a postwar intelligence research group, "little, if any, progress has been made" in that direction. In fact, Langer now realized the postwar intelligence plan was stymied and the "antagonism and inter-agency jealousy" it had spawned was so intense that "the rivalry which developed between OSS and MIS" during the war threatened "to become generalized and extended to a number of other agencies." Furthermore, the R. and A. branch chief had learned from General Magruder that despite the arrangements made in the fall of 1944, it was "most unlikely that the State Department will ever be willing to recognize the right of OSS personnel to do . . . overt study and analysis." Pointing further to the kind of problems faced by Sawyer in Paris and the undeniable reality that vital R. and A. people were becoming nervous over the uncertainty and were beginning to look for other harbors, Langer urged Donovan to do what he could to end R. and A.'s "role of Cinderella."[52]

At this point, however, there was little that the harried Donovan could do beyond approving R. and A.'s own efforts to go into such postwar activities as that of war crimes prosecution with "the purpose of strengthening its basic program" rather than continuing simply to be of service to other government agencies. R. and A. people went on with their research duties and were busy "planning out activities" even after V.J. Day. But Langer was not able to pull off any dramatic last-minute life-saving coup, and many old R. and A. hands lost heart. From China, Joseph Spencer wrote to Washington on 26 September, "this letter is a swan song for JES [Joseph E. Spencer] and perhaps one of the last to be written if fate overwhelms R. and A."[53]

Though rather confusing in its course, however, fate did not simply crush R. and A. The terms of the order abolishing O.S.S. that President Truman signed on 20 September 1945 (Executive Order 9621) treated R. and A. differently from the other main branches of O.S.S. All the other major segments of Donovan's kingdom were to be immediately handed over to the War Department for reshuffling or dissolution as the secretary of war thought best. But R. and A., retitled the Interim Research Intelligence Service (I.R.I.S.) was assigned to the State Department and remained there until the end of 1945, by which time it was assumed that the postwar plans for the State Department and a peacetime intelligence organization would be sufficiently clarified to determine the final address of R. and A. Consequently, although a few overseas sections of the branch temporarily passed under War Department authority, most of the R. and A. people who did not return to civilian life immediately spent three months working in the State Department under I.R.I.S., followed by an additional two years in State in a unit called the Office of Research Intelligence (O.R.I.). During much of this period, old R. and A. researchers, from Stuart Hughes to Otto Kircheimer and Sherman Kent, often found themselves even more on the periphery than they had been in the heyday of O.S.S.–R. and A., for hard-line State Department officials viewed them with extreme suspicion. Nonetheless, the R. and A. nucleus survived and in 1947–48, although many of its veteran staff had by that time drifted off to various civilian academic pursuits, it became the first distinct building block in the new C.I.A.[54]

The postwar course followed by individual R. and A. veterans varied greatly, chiefly because of age and circumstance. Most mature, established scholars who had taken leave from their universities to serve in R. and A. merely returned to the academic fold in 1945. Many younger men and women who had not found a firm rung on the academic ladder before the war, as well as most refugee scholars, remained temporarily in the various R. and A. successor organizations until they could find suitable teaching positions. Some of those who had moved into R. and A. in 1941–42 from low-level teaching jobs and subsequently began to raise families felt it was impossible to adjust to poorly paid academic positions and therefore continued in intelligence research work alongside a few people who had become entranced by the intelligence game. With the directorship of the various State Department and C.I.A. intelligence research units from 1945 to the mid-1960s being held by either William Langer or Sherman Kent (with a brief tenure by Colonel Eddy of Torch fame), it was not difficult for a competent R. and A. veteran to stay on and prosper.

Many of the links between the R. and A. people who returned to academia and those who stayed in intelligence research units were not severed. Old friendships and four years of common experience remained. It is difficult to think of another circumstance in which nearly 1,000 academic researchers in the humanities and social sciences worked side by side for three to four years and thus had such an opportunity to gauge the competence and performance of their colleagues. Many of those who returned to the campus were by then enthusiastic advocates of the system of team work and "objective and neutral" research that had been developed by R. and A. Programs in policy studies, interdisciplinary programs, and strategic studies blossomed in the late 1940s and early 1950s on the hundreds of campuses revitalized by the inflow of students and money made possible by the G.I. Bill and expanded government support for higher education. Some of the able graduates produced by these programs, and by those of the traditional disciplines, were sent along the road to C.I.A. headquarters at Langley, just as some professors who were R. and A. veterans continued to serve as advisers and consultants to their wartime colleagues who remained in the intelligence community.

It was perfectly natural that the R. and A. alumni evolved into an American academic elite, roughly analogous to the group that Fritz Ringer identified as "academic Mandarins" in interwar Germany. They were able, highly skilled, and had special ties that bound them together. That the links continued in the postwar period betokens no dark purpose, for all academic activity runs on various forms of fraternal connection (there is no female equivalent in the English language). To the majority of R. and A. veterans, the old branch ties and the links with (and service to) those who had continued on in Langer's footsteps seemed perfectly natural. Only during the Vietnam crisis were many of the bonds severed, amid much anguish and soul-searching.

It was in the Vietnam era, too, that the public became more aware of the range of American intelligence activities and more attuned to the world of plot and counterplot. Fear of conspiracy has since become so intense that there are those who see the links between wartime and postwar intelligence, as well as the connections between intelligence agencies and other aspects of American society, as elements in a common plan of intrigue and deceit. Therefore, it must be strongly emphasized that the various postwar activities of R. and A. veterans, as well as the evolution of the R. and A. system into the research and analysis unit of the C.I.A., did not occur through conspiracy or deception. In fact, as we have seen, it did not even owe much to William Langer's early 1945 campaign to establish the branch on firm postwar foundations, for the debacle over Donovan's postwar intelligence plan and the inability of Langer to get a firm deal with the State Department squelched the branch's sortie into high politics.

R. and A. gained immortality simply because it was not very threatening to regular agencies and because it had developed a new system of intelligence research that provided useful assistance to government leaders. Furthermore, and most important, R. and A. survived in one form or another because it brought to intelligence activity academics of such quality that once government leaders became accustomed to their services, they were unwilling to forgo them. The ability of R. and A. scholars enabled this kind of intelligence unit to live on, for they were willing to study many of the tough problems and on occasion had flashes of unusual insight.

On 18 August 1945, nine days after the atomic bomb was dropped on Nagasaki, R. and A. man Gregory Bateson in S.E.A.C. addressed a four-page memorandum to William Donovan on the "influence of [the] Atomic Bomb on Indirect Methods of Warfare." Bateson observed that the "general principle upon which these bombs operate are already known to a large number of physicists" and therefore "no high degree of security in regard to the atomic bomb can be expected" because "all the major powers are likely to have this sort [of weapon] within the next ten years." What the bomb had done was to change the balance of warfare so that the advantage lay clearly with attack rather than defense. Since in Bateson's view America and England would be reluctant to use preventive war as a means of protecting their vital interests, other (and presumably more aggressive) powers would become ever more dangerous threats to peace once they acquired the bomb. In the meantime such powers—surely the Soviet Union was not far from Bateson's thoughts—would turn "to 'peaceful' rather than 'warlike' methods of international pressure" and would "not resort to open aggression until they have thoroughly softened us up by propaganda, subversion, sabotage, diplomatic and economic pressure."

In August 1945, Bateson thought that atomic bombs would simultaneously revolutionize warfare and international relations. Conventional standing armies and navies had immediately lost much of their former importance, while the significance of air forces and atomic production facilities had sharply increased. But the "'peaceful' methods of war" such as "guerrilla tactics, white and black propaganda, subversion, social and ethnic manipulation, [and] diplomatic pressure" were hidden factors whose value had risen just as acutely, for as Bateson stressed, "all of these are immune to atomic attack." The fifth column scare seemed to ride again in this vision, and Bateson showed the usual O.S.S. tendency to go overboard on the power of shadow warfare. The great anthropologist was certainly onto some of the significant truths of the postwar period, however, when, in ending his paper, he urged Donovan and his aides to try to bring the realities of the atomic revolution to the attention of America's leaders, for shadow warfare would have increased importance in the postwar period.[55]

With people in its ranks capable of looking such harsh realities in the face and producing such clear predictions, it was inevitable that an R. and A.–type unit would find a place in the postwar government structure. "Langer's way" lived on because it built the bridge over which such academic skills could pass on to be of permanent service to American intelligence.

CHAPTER 9

Conclusion: O.S.S. in Pursuit of Eternal Life

Like a faithful if somewhat jaded lover, I
am continuing the Paris/Washington letter
despite the fact that the last letter I received
from you was dated 20 August.

WARREN BAUM TO O.S.S. WASHINGTON
8 October 1945

THE FIGHT to survive waged by Langer's R. and A. Branch during the last year of the war was the most determined and successful of O.S.S. attempts to achieve permanence, but a desire for immortality had floated about Donovan's organization from its earliest days. As Edmund Taylor observed long after the war, "in the back of his mind" Donovan had "always had the long-range goal of founding a permanent U.S. intelligence and political warfare service." Many O.S.S. leaders understood and shared Donovan's desire to use wartime circumstances to lay the basis for a permanent change in America's intelligence organization and the scale of its intelligence activities. The O.S.S. man charged with reorganizing O.S.S. intelligence and counterintelligence networks in North Africa, Leland Rounds, reported frankly in October 1943 that he was "setting up an organization which will be able to function for a long period after the war." In January 1944, Hugh Wilson of the O.S.S. Planning Group declared proudly that in its intelligence efforts, O.S.S. had established "the beginnings of something" that would be "of overwhelming importance" to "the future" of the American government.[1]

Throughout the history of O.S.S., Donovan and his staff showed an enthusiastic desire to expand the range of the organization's activities. This passion to move into new forms of endeavor gained much force from a sincere inclination to assist the American war effort. But there was also an interest in getting on as much ground as possible and marking up a record of achievement that would stand the cause of "strategic service" in good stead during the postwar period.

Donovan's enthusiasm for irregular warfare and intelligence centralization was definitely the driving force behind the tendency to promote the continuation of such activity during the postwar era. Like other devotees of the novel—such as "Little Bill" Stephenson, who predicted in February 1943 that the future belonged to the "younger and abler" S.O.S. rather than the "old and rather obsolete" S.I.S.—Donovan believed it vital to the security of the United States that a clandestine warfare system be made a permanent part of the American government machinery. A large number of Donovan's staff also had acquired such an enthusiasm for shadow warfare activity during the course of the war that they became evangelists for the cause of intelligence activity. The great game was so fascinating, as Allen Dulles remarked to Robert Murphy in 1951, that "once one gets a taste for it, it's hard to drop." Most O.S.S. leaders never revised the misguided vision of an all-powerful Nazi fifth column that had motivated much of their early enthusiasm for clandestine warfare. Throughout the war they saw themselves as sentinels standing in the front line against the most dangerous manifestation of the Nazi menace, and when O.S.S. began to function successfully in intelligence and resistance-support operations, they believed that they had discovered how to cope with all present and future subversive threats to the United States.[2]

For people who saw the preservation of O.S.S. as a matter of principle and urgent necessity, Donovan's 1944–45 battle for survival took on aspects of a crusade. O.S.S. and C.I.A. spokesmen have presented it as a religious parable, with Donovan as the far-seeing prophet, the military authorities and the Bureau of the Budget as a blind and hostile mob, a naive Harry Truman as Pontius Pilate, and an execution (Executive Order 9621) followed by redemption and resurrection through the creation of the C.I.A. in 1947.[3]

Such a vision of the events of 1944–45, that may be a trifle blasphemous, also oversimplifies to excess, ignores the mood of the time, and fails to point to the shortcomings of Donovan's campaign to preserve something analagous to O.S.S. Although there was enthusiasm in the United

States for a brave new world (complete with the Four Freedoms and ar-rangements to insure peace), and, as victory neared, some optimistic fore-casts about an "American century," the deeper and broader tendency in American life and government was to view the war as a special emergen-cy that had to be overcome so that the country could return to its "nor-mal" ways of peace and plenty. This feeling was obviously not realistic; the 1930s had hardly been an era of abundance, and the dream of effec-tive isolation had been badly compromised even prior to 1939. But the vision was nonetheless sincerely held by a majority of the population. Most Americans expected to be paid back for the hardships of the war by acquiring the benefits of a bigger and better version of the good old days. The Administration found it prudent not to challenge this attitude undu-ly, because the population was thereby more willing to make great short-term sacrifices to produce the huge wartime economic and military ma-chine. But there was a tacit understanding that once the war was over, wartime government regulations would disappear quickly, the budget would be slashed, and the size of the armed forces would be sharply re-duced. Nor were many regular government officials in either civilian de-partments or the armed forces overly upset by the prospect of postwar reductions. They tended to look with pleasure on the prospect of ridding themselves of the assorted special agencies, dollar-a-year men, draftees, and reserve officers, thereby returning to the clear-line administration and leisurely ways that made up their version of prewar nostalgia.

Donovan and his O.S.S. associates made a serious tactical error in not recognizing the overwhelming strength of this mood in 1944–45. The O.S.S. director believed that by pointing to the innovations that had been produced since 1939 he could get a permanent clandestine service estab-lished simply by selling the president and the civil and military leaders on the idea during the last stages of the war. Thus, he assumed the onus of trying to persuade the American leaders, and ultimately the people, to abandon their main hope and accept that the war had made such funda-mental changes that the old America was gone forever. Perhaps if he had argued that by creating a huge clandestine service the American govern-ment could have a security shield without large standing forces, Donovan would have appealed to the desire to avoid the great responsibilities and costs of superpower status. But the O.S.S. director chose to base his case on the need to include a centralized clandestine service in a huge postwar American defense and security system. In so doing, he probably made it inevitable that O.S.S. would be destroyed and time would pass before public and government opinion swung around to accepting some of the unpleasant implications of America's role as a superpower.

The peculiar self-righteousness and missionary approach that Donovan employed also contributed greatly to the short-run defeat of his proposal for a permanent subversive warfare organization. The O.S.S. director tried to get his way on this matter, as on most others, by a mixture of new ideas and personal charm. His style endeared him to many—an S.I.S. official remarking shortly after the war that "he is such a dear old thing . . . a brave and shrewd and lovable person for all the blarney"—but this was not the stuff that impressed many bureaucrats or those with a sense of precise organization. Such men as Henry Stimson managed to keep "impatience" with the "eccentricities" of Donovan and his organization under control until the end of the war, but long before 1945 some of the O.S.S. director's most intimate early associates had given up on him, including Francis Miller, Calvin Hoover, James G. Rogers, and Bruce Hopper. Erratic in the extreme, Donovan had little ability to work through administrative channels. The only chance of immediate success his postwar plans ever possessed lay in a tough, long-term, and consistent program for dealing with other departments and agencies. O.S.S. desperately needed allies and partners, but the director shunned the swaps, or bargains, that might have made possible the build up of a coalition to support some form of regular centralized intelligence and subversive warfare system. As David Scott, Under Secretary of State in the Foreign Office, noted as early as mid-1942, Donovan was not only "no organizer," he was "a child in political matters." In his mad rush, he never even stopped long enough to mend fences, and so by the time the war ended, even though O.S.S. had scattered individual admirers through a number of agencies, there were also many who nursed real or imagined slights and grievances. Furthermore, despite some presidential favor, O.S.S. lacked a firm bureaucratic foundation even in the wartime system. As a J.C.S. dependent, O.S.S. never had its own regular spokesman or lobbyist with Congress. The organization's budget was arranged by informal deals between the president, the J.C.S., and the Bureau of the Budget. If a question about Donovan's organization rose on the Hill, it was not an O.S.S. official who went there to present Donovan's case but a colonel or brigadier general from the J.C.S. staff who tried to keep Congress pacified. The individual members of the Joint Chiefs could look to their respective departments (War and Navy) for organizational clout, but O.S.S. lay in such a limbo that it could not even make direct contact with many of the channels of regular government.[4]

Self-evidently, for an organization led by William Donovan and situated like O.S.S. to have carried through so radical a change during the war as the establishment of a permanent central intelligence and subversive warfare system would have taken something close to a secular miracle. In tracing the course of Donovan's campaign for a postwar intelligence program, the specifics that led to the immediate defeat of his efforts and the consequent demise of O.S.S. are therefore of only moderate importance because the broad trend of events pointed so overwhelmingly in that direction. The real significance of Donovan's attempt to save his creation is that it forced many government agencies to confront the issue of establishing a permanent central intelligence agency at a very early date. The O.S.S. initiatives served to rally central intelligence advocates, and the struggles over Donovan's proposals became forums allowing O.S.S. people to advance their views and officials in other agencies to move in the direction of some kind of central intelligence system. In the course of the wartime discussions (as well as in subsequent works by O.S.S.–C.I.A. champions), a number of fables were also created that helped to legitimize and enoble Donovan's central intelligence legacy.

O.S.S. made its first overt attempt to promote a permanent central intelligence agency in the early fall of 1943. At that time, Donovan was especially anxious to impress the military authorities because of the ongoing controversy over the O.S.S. position in Spain as well as the reluctance of American military and British authorities to grant S.I. the right to operate independently in the E.T.O. (see above, p. 218 and p. 248). It was also a period when some officials in the War Department were brooding on the possibility of including O.S.S. within a general merger of O.N.I. and M.I.D. During July and August of 1943, General Magruder put forward his proposal that some intelligence unification occur immediately, and soon after, Donovan declared to General Deane that he intended "to lay the foundation for permanent American intelligence activity on the continent" as soon as American forces entered Europe in force. In early August, the O.S.S. director also called upon Colonel Eddy in the Mediterranean theater to prepare a general statement on the value of O.S.S. When Eddy failed to put the major emphasis on "a long-term program of establishing an independent American secret service which should be maintained in time of peace as well as war," Donovan took up the question of a permanent American central intelligence service with Eisenhower's chief of staff, Gen. Walter Bedell Smith. While viewing the landings at Salerno on 9 September, Donovan raised the postwar intelligence question with Smith, and apparently succeeded in eliciting from him a request that O.S.S. put its postwar intelligence proposal on paper.[5]

The resulting postwar intelligence plan, which Donovan sent to General Smith on 17 September 1943, contained a number of very interesting features. The O.S.S. director called for the creation of a central intelligence and subversive warfare organization as "an integral part of our military establishment," but this "Fourth Arm" of "the fighting services" was to be headed not by a soldier but by a civilian appointed by the president. The 17 September 1943 Donovan memorandum specifically rejected placing the proposed central intelligence agency "directly under the control of the President and responsible to him alone" because such an arrangement "would run the danger" of producing "distracting political consequences both for the Presidential incumbent and for Strategic Services." Instead, the fourth arm, which was to include all the 1943 O.S.S. activities—R. and A., S.I., S.O., and M.O.—would serve under the authority of the J.C.S., and its civilian director would be a full and equal member of the J.C.S. To help reduce military opposition to the proposal, especially from O.N.I. and M.I.D., Donovan specifically declared that the fourth arm would not undertake "combat or operational intelligence." Nonetheless, the A.F.H.Q. analysis of the plan made on Smith's orders by Lt. Col. James O. Curtis stated that the proposal was hopelessly tainted by its civilian features, for "in the last analysis the object of all intelligence is to further the missions of the armed forces."[6]

The September 1943 Donovan central intelligence proposal was a peculiar and somewhat contradictory hybrid. Having abandoned his earlier total dependence on presidential favor that had carried C.O.I. through the first phase of its existence, Donovan attempted to build up a case for a postwar strategic services agency that would meet the needs of the J.C.S. But to avoid trouble with M.I.D. and O.N.I., he had been forced to stress the civilian aspects of such an organization and avoid combat or operational intelligence. By so doing, he made his proposal vulnerable to the kind of criticism of all things civilian made by Colonel Curtis, and in the process disavowed any interest in the tactical intelligence activities that, ironically, would be the O.S.S. services that combat commanders like Eisenhower found most valuable in the course of 1944 and 1945.

Since the September 1943 proposal for postwar intelligence was quietly buried following the negative evaluation made by Colonel Curtis, Donovan was able to start with a fairly clean slate when he mounted his second offensive for a permanent central intelligence agency in the fall of 1944. The O.S.S. director still had not figured out how to create a fourth arm that would avoid stirring up the jealousy of the military intelligence sections, and there also seemed no way to capitalize directly on the recent O.S.S. tactical intelligence and resistance support achievements in the European and Mediterranean theaters.

But a number of developments in the fall of 1944 suggested that better prospects might be emerging for a more distinctly civilian postwar intelligence system. The victory fever raging through Washington in the wake of Eisenhower's rapid advance across northern France raised the possibility that hostilities in Europe would soon end and the military's stranglehold on American foreign policy might be relaxed. O.S.S. already had made headway in arranging a place for itself in the German occupation program as well as the expected postwar pursuit of a Nazi underground. Postwar problems were taking on greater significance, and even though the threat of a general American demobilization posed an immediate threat to O.S.S., the need for new intelligence to meet the situation that would be created by V.E. and V.J. days seemed to offer opportunities.[7]

As so frequently happened in the course of World War II, developments in Washington were being paralleled by those in London. Nervousness about postwar dangers was rising among British officials, and as early as the last day of August 1944, a British general from the military intelligence service sounded out John Franklin Carter on how the United States intended to prepare for the "next war," in which the West would face "Russia as the opponent." In the course of the fall, the Foreign Office showed itself more willing to consider the possibility of preserving S.O.E. because of the need for a postwar organization to carry out what Anthony Eden once referred to as "unacknowledgeable activities."[8]

In Washington, the State Department was the first American agency to put forth postwar intelligence proposals. On 21 August 1944, an unidentified State Department official reported to a department colleague that Acting Secretary of State Stettinius had declared that "he was dreaming ahead of some coordination between FBI, State, Army and Navy into a world intelligence plan, perhaps way in the future," and that a memorandum on this subject "should go to the President and the Secretary [of State, i.e., Hull] authorizing someone to do something about it." This set off a round of State Department postwar intelligence planning that produced various discussions and draft proposals during September and early October. By mid-October, a plan calling for the State Department to play the central role in the coordination of postwar intelligence was before the J.I.C.[9]

The State Department attempt to take the lead on the long-term intelligence question forced O.S.S. officials to move rapidly on their own postwar preparations. In mid-September, a paper was prepared setting forth ways to justify O.S.S. operations so that the organization could improve its budget position and to assist "the conversion of the agency from a war to a peacetime basis." The memorandum contended that the best case could be made for O.S.S. by a three-point presentation drawing favorable "analogies" with the intelligence services of other countries, evaluating "striking examples of OSS operations where the pay-off can be presumed to be very high," and "citation of a large number of typical OSS operations with more limited cost and value data." The R. and A. branch and members of Donovan's staff were quickly put to work drawing up a new plan for a postwar agency, a summary draft of which first went to the White House on 24 October with the full proposal following on 18 November.[10]

The Donovan plan for postwar centralized intelligence that was put forward in fall 1944 bore little resemblance to the proposal keyed to the J.C.S. that the O.S.S. director had made a year earlier. Donovan decided in October and November of 1944 that central intelligence should be "returned to the supervision of the President," with creation of an agency directly under the chief executive's control. The 1944 "central intelligence service" envisioned by Donovan was to contain the by then customary O.S.S. activities—those of S.O., S.I., X-2, M.O., and R. and A.—but there was no mention of direct support to the armed services and no reference to the tactical resistance aid and intelligence activities that O.S.S. was at that moment performing so well. The new central intelligence service would focus on long-term strategic intelligence and information touching on the "national security, policies and interest of the United States." Furthermore, the new service and its supervisorial advisory board would coordinate "the functions of *all* [italics added] intelligence agencies of the Government" and would have the exclusive right to do the "final evaluation, synthesis and dissemination within the Government" of reports on American policies "with respect to national planning security in peace and war and the advancement of broad national policy."[11]

Since this paper challenged the position of every agency dealing with information gathering and foreign policy and had been sent to the White House without prior arrangement with other agencies or departments, it was guaranteed to produce an all-out attack on O.S.S. As a move in the game to preserve an O.S.S.-type organization under Donovan's direction, it was therefore an unmitigated disaster. But as a goad to force the pace of the consideration of long-term intelligence, it functioned admirably, for to smite the O.S.S. upstarts, every agency of the regular government was compelled to clarify its position and confront more directly the shortcomings of the prevailing intelligence system.

The military authorities who dominated the J.I.C. machinery, which logically was the locus for consideration of Donovan's proposal, were able to get in some pretty hard licks against the O.S.S. director and the cause of highly centralized intelligence in the course of November and December 1944. One military report curtly dismissed Donovan's ideas as "unsound and dangerous," and the military members of the J.I.C. study committee concluded by mid-December that although a measure of intelligence coordination was desirable, no central intelligence agency of any kind should be established. Some of Donovan's old civilian rivals, including John Franklin Carter, landed a few additional jabs. In an October memorandum to the president, Carter suggested that Donovan's central intelligence service be created as a dummy to fool the British (who he claimed with some justice had penetrated O.S.S.) while another more secret unit be established to carry on serious undercover activities. In early January 1945, Carter recommended that only O.S.S. personnel be permitted to deal with Allied intelligence services, so that once O.S.S. was abolished—as Carter assumed it would be—America's wartime associates would have no direct paths into the regular intelligence units of the American government.[12]

Although some officials in the regular civilian departments of government, such as Francis Russell of State, were anxious to check Donovan's "determined effort to centralize in a permanent agency to be attached to the Executive Offices the overall foreign intelligence operations of the Government," most civilians were willing to go further in Donovan's direction than were the military. The civilian members of the J.I.C. study committee (O.S.S., State, and Foreign Economic Administration representatives) decided in December that a regular central agency to collect and consolidate foreign intelligence information should be established, but to get this support the O.S.S. representative was forced to agree that the proposed agency be responsible to a three-secretary-board (War, Navy, and State) rather than directly to the president. On 22 December 1944, after an extremely long and detailed discussion of the situation, the full J.I.C. concluded that the military men and the civilians were so hopelessly divided that separate reports representing the views of the respective groups would have to be forwarded to the J.C.S.[13]

Donovan did not remain passive while the J.I.C.–J.C.S. machinery moved along its regular track. In early November, he challenged Carter's criticism of his plan, declaring that the British had not penetrated O.S.S., and accused Carter of still being in the "horse and buggy" stage of intelligence thinking. The O.S.S. director also did his best to secure testimonials and corroborating information for his plans, acquiring a two-page letter of praise from B.S.C.'s William Stephenson in mid-November 1944 and a mass of information on Britain's intelligence organization that Constantine Fitzgibbon secured for Donovan from the director of Military Intelligence during January 1945. In a progress report that the O.S.S. director sent to President Roosevelt in late December 1944, Donovan intimated, as had his representative on the J.I.C. study committee, that to gain approval for his overall plan, he would be willing to have the proposed central intelligence service made responsible to a three-secretary-board rather than the president if Roosevelt felt that to be desirable. But having managed to stay in Washington for two months, Donovan left the United States for another around the world tour shortly after Christmas 1944. He had still not made any serious attempt to line up support for his proposals from other agencies, and none of the leaders of the major executive departments or the White House had yet indicated clearly where they stood on the matter. McCloy had "brought up" the postwar intelligence proposal in a discussion with Henry Stimson on 13 December, but the secretary of war chose not to take a leading role in dealing with the question. In a memorandum to the president on 15 December, Stettinius had indicated a willingness "to discuss with General Donovan the future status of his organization and the means by which his work might be most effectively coordinated with ours," but he had also emphasized that "an inter-departmental board" in which State had the dominant role should supervise any postwar intelligence service.[14]

The president, as usual, was cautious in showing his hand. In mid-November, during a discussion with Budget Director Harold Smith, Roosevelt stated that some "trimming off" of informational agencies, such as Rockefeller's Coordinator of Inter-American Affairs Office, was needed. He also indicated that he had learned to take the declarations of intelligence agencies with considerable reserve, for though Latin America was supposed to be the preserve of the F.B.I., the State Department, and Rockefeller's group, the president believed "that Army intelligence and Navy intelligence were probably in South America" and Donovan's organization was "probably there, too," even though "he had indicated that OSS was to stay out." On 17 January 1945, Roosevelt finally gave Stettinius the green light to discuss the intelligence situation with Donovan, Stimson, and Forrestal. The president stated to the secretary of state that "at the end of the war there simply must be a consolidation of Foreign Intelligence between State and War and Navy" but then continued (in a phrase conveniently omitted from the recent C.I.A. history of O.S.S.), "I think it should be limited to military and related subjects. This should not take in the commercial angle in the first place, though the organization should have the benefit of a commercial summary every month." Franklin Roosevelt's World War II experience had convinced him that military intelligence consolidation was necessary—at that very moment another Pearl Harbor inquiry was in the works—but he seems not to have been entranced by Donovan's plan for rigid centralization. The emphasis in the president's note to Stettinius on cooperation between the State, War, and

Navy departments, and also on "military and related subjects" and omission of the kind of "commercial" and related information that had lain at the heart of Donovan's original C.O.I., suggests strongly that the O.S.S. director had failed to convince Franklin Roosevelt of the wisdom of his grandiose postwar central intelligence scheme.[15]

Consequently, when the J.C.S. documents on the plan were slipped to hostile newspapers in early February 1945 and a press campaign denouncing Donovan's proposed "super Gestapo Agency" spread out over the country, the White House made no effort to intervene on the O.S.S. director's behalf. The British Embassy in Washington may have been right that there was "considerable heartburning in Administration circles" over the press revelations, but it was the scandal itself that most concerned Roosevelt's supporters. British speculation that Congress might have been favorably inclined toward the plan if there had been no adverse newspaper publicity because American lawmakers were "quite interested in protecting Americans against the wily British and Russians" was merely a *bon mot*.[16] From the moment the press campaign broke loose, no one in the administration or Congress lifted a finger to help the O.S.S. director. It was immediately obvious that Donovan had been waging his campaign alone, and at this point the general's failure to make alliances and line up organizational support for his enterprise had its most deadly effect.

When he returned to Washington in mid-February, Donovan (in the words of Lord Halifax) still had "no intention of seeing his creation die with the war," but the general had become a lonely penitent. He appealed to the J.C.S. for an investigation of the press leaks and urged that consideration of the central intelligence proposal be carried forward despite the furor in the newspapers. But all Donovan received in return was an assurance that an investigation was underway—the culprit was never identified, though gossip at the time pointed the finger at G-2—together with the conclusions of General Marshall and Admiral Leahy that in light of the newspaper ruckus, the whole postwar intelligence matter should be shelved for the time being.[17]

With Donovan wandering alone in the wilderness, some of his opponents took the occasion to get in extra licks of their own. John Franklin Carter came up with an alternate plan for postwar intelligence centralization that proposed placing most clandestine, secret intelligence, and coordination functions within the State Department. The military was not much taken with this idea; G-2's Gen. Clayton Bissell observed that Carter showed "a complete lack of awareness of the scope of military and naval intelligence." But in the view of Bissell and his colleagues, Carter (in contrast to the dreadful director of O.S.S.) at least "correctly" recognized that intelligence was "inherently a departmental matter." Faced with the various proposals to centralize intelligence functions, Admiral King observed to Secretary Forrestal at the end of March that such plans as those of Carter and Donovan "sounded logical" but "had elements of danger." The admiral "pointed out that over a long period of time such an agency might acquire power beyond anything which had been intended for it," and he doubted "whether such an agency could be considered consistent with our ideas of government."[18]

Such seemingly edifying thoughts, when expressed by a chief of naval operations who was very anxious to protect navy authority, were self-seeking as well as extremely threatening to Donovan's proposal. The same may be said of the recommendation by the Budget Director Harold Smith that the president do nothing on the various central intelligence proposals until the bureau had an opportunity to carry out "a comprehensive study." This admonition sounds reasonable in light of the "tug-of-war going on between some of the agencies" concerned with intelligence, but Smith was pushing his own group forward as the natural arbiter of the various claims, and thus he too had become a major participant in the game of deciding what postwar arrangements should cover the ground currently occupied by the numerous intelligence and subversive control agencies.[19]

All the various bureaus and departments interested in intelligence matters were now armed in their own defense, and O.S.S. attempts to advance the central intelligence plan or work more deeply into such postwar operations as the occupation of Germany and Japan ran into stiffer resistance. Donovan understood that for him it was now the Oval Office or nothing, and he poured out his troubles to the president. On 6 March 1945, he even sent Roosevelt a copy of the draconian British Official Secrets Act that he hoped the White House might "be interested in considering as a model" for coping with such matters as "the recent instances in which official classified material has been made public." Since in the previous month O.S.S. man Frank Bielaski had played a major role in breaking open the "Amerasia" case in which John Service and others were accused of purloining O.S.S and State Department documents, Donovan had a number of reasons to be concerned about security enforcement. At this particular moment, in contrast to many instances in the past, no one was pointing a finger at O.S.S. as an active center of inspired leaks in Washington, so Donovan could safely champion the cause of tight security. The O.S.S. director was also aware that it was in the interest of his postwar intelligence plan to show what O.S.S. had accomplished in regard to antisubversive operations so far and to point to possible new threats that were looming abroad. A long report setting forth the ways in which British–O.S.S. cooperation had helped in the prosecution of Nazi spies and saboteurs was sent to the White House in late February, along with a dispatch suggesting that the Soviet occupation authorities in Poland might be preparing to take over and make use of a substantial number of the intelligence people of the Polish government.[20]

Such moves were merely pin pricks, for unless Donovan could force the regular departments of government to act quickly on the central intelligence issue, resistance would continue to harden. The O.S.S. director tried to get things moving once again via the White House, and in early April he secured presidential approval for a series of letters to the various departments soliciting their opinion of the postwar intelligence plan. The queries were sent out on 5–6 April and one of the first replies, that of Secretary of the Treasury Morgenthau, came back on 12 April. Morgenthau stated that the plan was "not sufficiently clear" for him to express "a firm opinion," but he confessed that he was "skeptical as to the necessity or propriety of establishing such an agency." The secretary of the treasury found most objectionable the idea of making a huge intelligence machine depend directly on the president, whose "burdens" were "now monumental" and should not be increased "if we can avoid it." This was probably more prophetic than Morgenthau realized, for on that same day, even as Biddle, Stettinius, and Forrestal were discussing how to reply to Donovan's question about the central intelligence plan, word reached Washington that Franklin Roosevelt had died at Warm Springs, Georgia.[21]

The loss of President Roosevelt was a shock to the whole nation because no other chief executive had ever so dominated a long pivotal era in American life. For William Donovan, the president's death removed the last hope of success for his pied piper effort to establish his own central intelligence agency. By 1945, Donovan's association with Franklin Roosevelt had become much less intimate than in the early years, and the president had grown skeptical about the general and the activities of his organization. But Roosevelt had a soft spot in his heart for this brilliant and impulsive man and would most likely have let him have a good run at his goal, even though his ideas and methods virtually guaranteed that he would not gain the prize. As it was, with all departments of government united against him, no support in Congress, and a new president in the White House, all was lost.

After waiting for the new president to get his bearings, Donovan gently raised the question of his postwar intelligence plans in two memoranda to the White House in early May 1945. When this overture received no encouragement, the general did not follow up the matter, and as was his custom when the political situation looked grim, buried himself in internal O.S.S. business and worldwide inspection trips. It was just as well, for the secretaries of War, State, Navy, and the Attorney General had closed ranks against him and recommended that no overall intelligence change be made during the war. Francis Biddle, who was certainly not an unbiased witness, since his F.B.I. had a large stake in the ultimate resolution of the intelligence issue, also informed Truman that in his opinion President Roosevelt "was never particularly enthusiastic" about the "rather complicated over-all intelligence" plan that Donovan had put forward.[22]

During April, May, and June, the new president indicated in his talks with Budget Director Harold Smith that his inclinations were basically different from those of people like William Donovan. Truman did not like haphazard access to the Oval Office or any kind of secret government organization. He was adamant in his opposition to unsolicited reports, and he was highly suspicious of every organization involved in secret or anti-subversive operations, including the F.B.I., Carter's organization, and O.S.S. Champions of O.S.S. (and then the C.I.A.) would later be offended that Truman gave expression to his hostility to secret organizations in the spring of 1945 by saying that he was opposed to the establishment of a "Gestapo" in the United States. O.S.S.–C.I.A. advocates have taken this to mean that the new president had been brainwashed by the February 1945 press campaign to oppose what was then characterized as Donovan's "Gestapo plan" into believing that the proposal called for a domestic secret police force. Such simple causality misstates the case. No top American governmental official in 1945 had a clear idea how the Nazi S.S. and police apparatus was actually structured or which units were concerned with domestic surveillance and which were employed for intelligence and subversive operations abroad. They therefore used terms like *storm-troopers* and *Gestapo* to denote any Nazi secret police or intelligence organization. The words were surely censorial, but aside from condemning government use of secret and terrorist force, they were without precise meaning.[23]

Harry Truman was the embodiment of the American people's longing to get back to the good old days as soon as possible, and as the vast majority of his fellow countrymen would have done, when he came to choose which wartime agencies would be abolished first, those involved in secret and undercover operations were near the top of the list. Since the Bureau of the Budget was obviously inclined to favor sharp decreases in government activities, and Harold Smith was suspicious of all American secret organizations from F.B.I. to O.S.S., Truman was inclined to leave the matter in the hands of the bureau. Smith claimed that his staff had developed some expertise in intelligence organizational matters in the course of trying to keep on top of the budget requests of secret organizations, so the new president had reason to believe that the Bureau of the Budget could lead the way toward a sane and modest solution to the general intelligence question. Therefore, throughout the spring and summer of 1945, Truman shunted all suggestions regarding central intelligence to his most trusted staff members, Fred Vinson and Samuel Rosenman, and directed them to clear all such material with Harold Smith.[24]

The spring and summer of 1945, during which the Bureau of the Budget monopolized the central intelligence field while William Donovan and Harry Truman ran in different directions pursuing their respective duties, saw no improvement in the position of O.S.S. or its director's plans for postwar intelligence. Liberals around Henry Wallace were nervous about what they alleged was "the speed with which Colonel [sic] Donovan's outfit is growing reactionary," and Wallace himself felt that there were "many dangerous implications" in Donovan's postwar intelligence plan. In mid-May, the conservative opposition press launched another salvo from the other direction, accusing O.S.S. of various dark pretensions and announcing that General MacArthur and Admiral Nimitz thought so little of O.S.S. that they had refused to have Donovan's organization in their theaters of operation. The House Military Appropriations Committee, which was then discussing the budget, immediately took an interest in the matter, and Congressman John Taber threatened to accept the press accusations as valid unless the J.C.S. did something to refute them. Members of the J.C.S. scurried about trying to figure out what to do, and in part because Assistant Secretary of War McCloy insisted that "a fair appraisal of the great value of OSS" be made, cables were ultimately sent to all theater commanders asking them to forward an estimate of O.S.S. work and the projected need for O.S.S. activities in their respective theaters. When the results came in, General Sultan in S.E.A.C., joined by MacArthur and Nimitz, indicated that O.S.S. had little or no future value, but Wedemeyer, Eisenhower, and General McNarney (A.F.H.Q.) gave Donovan's organization high marks and foresaw some further need for its services. Although Admiral Leahy still refused to give O.S.S. his endorsement, and the J.C.S. staff continued to waffle about which course to follow, all the theater commanders' replies were sent up to the Hill. Congressman Cannon and others were still inclined to "liquidate the thing [O.S.S.] immediately," but they were also highly impressed by Eisenhower's statement that O.S.S. had been very beneficial in tactical-support activities, and therefore under gentle prompting from the J.C.S., the committee did not include a provision specifically abolishing O.S.S. in the 1946 budget but did sharply slash the funds allotted to it. Donovan's organization was allowed to last until the end of hostilities, but no powerful group in either the legislative or executive branches showed any eagerness to have it continue beyond the war.[25]

From May to August of 1945, while Langer and other O.S.S. officials pleaded for support, and personnel left the organization in droves, Donovan and his aides did virtually nothing to either defend the position of O.S.S. or promote a postwar intelligence agency aside from sending another handful of self-congratulatory reports on O.S.S. wartime activities to the White House. Therefore, organizations unsympathetic or hostile to Donovan merely had to wait until attrition and the end of the war destroyed whatever remained of the O.S.S. director's political position. General Marshall did not make a move until 24 August 1945, nine days after V.J. Day, when under prompting from Budget officials concerned to wind up the activities of wartime agencies, he asked the J.C.S. staff to take up the matter of postwar intelligence again. Four days later, Marshall requested the J.C.S. to immediately pull all military personnel out of Donovan's organization and to order a substantial reduction in the civilian staff and remaining budget allotment of O.S.S. The debates then were repeated in the J.C.S. and its committees, with General Arnold and a few others anxious to preserve O.S.S. "assets" and the majority of military intelligence personnel contending that though some coordination was feasible, no new central agency should be created for the postwar period. By the second week of September, a J.P.S. subcommittee, by a razor-thin vote, brought forth a recommendation that O.S.S. be abolished by 31 December 1945 and that its "assets" be divided between the War and State departments.[26]

Donovan tried to meet this military onslaught by a quixotic last-minute defense. On 25 August 1945, he wrote the Bureau of the Budget, declaring that since O.S.S. was on a liquidation budget and Donovan himself planned to return to civilian life in early 1946, it was essential that provision be made to save O.S.S. "assets" and "know-how" by immediately establishing the postwar central intelligence agency that the O.S.S. director desired. But Donovan did not then go on to challenge his military opponents directly, make an overt appeal to the White House, or mount a last-ditch effort to find allies in the State Department. Instead, he quietly prepared a massive public relations campaign to release stories that would glorify O.S.S. achievements and promote the cause of a postwar intelligence agency. Professional journalists on Donovan's staff, especially Wallace Deuel, were outraged that Donovan and the assorted "Wall Street corporation lawyers, aspirin salesmen, advertising executives and teachers in boys' private prep schools" whom he had selected to organize his publicity operation, chose to leak carefully edited accounts of O.S.S. work to select magazines rather than hold an open press conference. The War Department public relations officer, Gen. Alexander Surles, refused to have anything to do with the operation, and Deuel ultimately resigned in disgust from "Uncle William's" organization to become a "relatively honest newspaper man again." But those with a sturdier commitment to the central intelligence cause continued on their way, and well before the end of August 1945, Allen Dulles had leaked a long story on the Operation Sunrise negotiations to end the war in Italy to the *Saturday Evening Post*.[27]

By 10 September, even the British Embassy was aware that O.S.S. had "taken the wraps off some of its activities in a bid to rally support behind Donovan's plans for a permanent centralized United States Secret Service." But by then it was already too late, for the fate of O.S.S. was not sealed in the press or affected by the series of memoranda that Donovan had by now sent to President Truman on the dangers posed by foreign intelligence services. The basic issue was decided within the inner recesses of the White House in the first week of September. During a 5 September meeting between the president and Harold Smith, the Budget Director declared that his bureau was "making a comprehensive study of intelligence," and Truman made it clear that he wanted the various secret agencies trimmed to the bone. Shortly thereafter, the president's Committee on Agency Liquidation, made up of Samuel Rosenman, Harold Smith, John Snyder, and George Allen decided "to dispose of OSS by a transfer of its research staff to State and its clandestine activities and administrative facilities to the War Department." By 10 September, the Bureau of the Budget had drafted a dissolution order stating that O.S.S. "assets" would be split between the State and War departments, but no specific date was given for its abolition. Three days later, President Truman indicated that he approved the dissolution plan and that he intended to carry it through "even if Donovan did not like it."[28]

The O.S.S. director had learned indirectly of the impending order to split up what was left of O.S.S., and he most certainly was not pleased. Bureau of the Budget officials claimed on 13 September that "the General blew up a great storm" when he got the news, and Harold Smith reported to Truman that the O.S.S. director "was storming about our proposal to divide his intelligence service." Donovan immediately sent a short memorandum to the president on 13 September urging "that in the national interest, and in your own interest as the Chief Executive" the O.S.S. "assets" should not be "severed and transferred to separate agencies" but should be kept together "as a complete whole." On the same day, the O.S.S. director stepped up his public relations campaign. A general order was issued to present and former O.S.S. personnel authorizing verbal disclosure to "family and friends" of virtually all the organization's activities and establishing a procedure whereby O.S.S. people could secure from Donovan's office permission to publish accounts of their exploits. On 14 September the United States Information Service began to issue a series of press releases on O.S.S. achievements that emphasized the work that had been performed in support of resistance movements. Foreign Office officials in London sniffed that it was "indeed ironic that a 'secret service' should have to mount a publicity campaign on its own behalf," and the British Embassy in Washington dismissed the press campaign as O.S.S. "blowing its trumpet," but overnight American newspapers and magazines were full of accounts of O.S.S. exploits.[29]

Disturbed by O.S.S.'s publicity campaign and the imminence of its dissolution, some J.C.S. officials tried to rouse themselves at the last minute to delay the final breakup of O.S.S. until the end of the year. But having made up his mind, Harry Truman was not deterred by J.C.S. committees, Donovan's protests, or the O.S.S. publicity effort. On 17 September, the State Department had indicated that it would be willing to take on the R. and A. Branch of O.S.S. and would serve as the leader in working out a long-term solution to the central intelligence problem. On 19 September, the final form of the dissolution order declaring that O.S.S. would be peremptorily abolished and its parts scattered within twelve days was prepared by the White House staff and the attorney general. On the afternoon of 20 September, the dissolution order was laid before the president by Harold Smith, and without hesitation or discussion, Truman quickly "glanced over the documents and signed the order."[30]

With that, the formal end came for America's first central intelligence agency. Though O.S.S. had been born of high hopes and initially bore some of the attributes of a militant goddess of liberty, it had died, as Heine had remarked when musing on the last squalid days of the Frankfurt Assembly in 1849 "like a prostitute in a saloon." The abrupt and cold manner in which O.S.S. was abolished added to the general feeling of many of Donovan's people that they had been ill used and insufficiently appreciated. O.S.S. never had had an opportunity to pursue its original goal of serving as a long-term strategic service organization, and most of the military support operations that Donovan's people had conducted occurred very late in the war. V.E. and V.J. days came before O.S.S., hemmed in by jealous and suspicious rivals (and requiring time to learn its trade), got into full stride and showed what it could do. Donovan and his top aides wanted a second chance, and the crass dismissal order of 20 September 1945—"our demise," as an R. and A. man called it—added a note of bitterness and a desire for vindication to this basic craving.[31]

The feeling that Donovan's ideas should have another opportunity obviously played a significant role in the flow of events that extended from the abolition order of 20 September 1945 to the creation of C.I.A. in July 1947. This attitude was given some chance for expression within the government structure because of the retention of nucleur ex-O.S.S. units in the State and War departments. The two surviving O.S.S. cadres were both very small. The R. and A. unit in State dropped in size to only 500 people as it passed through its various changes from R. and A. to I.R.I.S., to O.R.I. in the years 1945–47. The size of the Strategic Services Unit (S.S.U.) in the War Department is more difficult to gauge, but even though its initial budget allotment was five or six times that of R. and A.– I.R.I.S.–O.R.I., it is unlikely that it ever exceeded 750 people. In late October 1945, Whitney Shepardson, who had remained temporarily with S.S.U., complained to Francis Miller that they were so short of printing and copying facilities that "the next thing you know we will be using those mid-Victorian copy books with wet clothes so beloved by the old ladies of Threadneedle Street."[32]

Yet even in this setting of shortage and bureaucratic poverty, the nucleur O.S.S. units performed services that fitted them into the postwar operational system. A number of diplomats spoke up in favor of retaining S.S.U. secret intelligence units in Southeast Asia from the early fall of 1945, and the War Department supported this view. S.S.U.–S.I. activities also continued in China and occupied Germany, where a number of O.S.S.–S.S.U. officials, including Allen Dulles and Richard Helms, helped make the transition to peacetime intelligence operations. At some crucial points during the immediate postwar changes, former O.S.S. people who had remained in S.S.U. arranged acts of passage. In October 1945, Colonel Goodfellow, who had long been active on behalf of Korean resistance forces during the war, was the official in charge of the American operation that moved Syngman Rhee into Korea. The S.S.U. unit also placed on the record an account of O.S.S. activities to help offset the negative impressions left by the sudden demise of Donovan's organization. In July 1946, S.S.U. overcame M.I.D. objections and secured J.C.S. approval for the preparation of an official history of O.S.S. This volume, which drew on earlier O.S.S. history projects begun during the war by Wallace Deuel and Langer's branch, was completed in September 1946. Long before it was made available to the general public in the mid-1970s, it played a subtle role inside the government, providing O.S.S. advocates with a basic handbook to support their claims to past accomplishments and their right to seize new shadow warfare opportunities.[33]

Although somewhat fettered by State Department obstructionism, Langer's veterans in I.R.I.S.–O.R.I. also helped to keep the Donovan legacy alive. The form of their reporting work continued unchanged, and with the State Department unwilling to integrate the unit completely into the department and some I.R.I.S.–O.R.I. people longing to belong once again to an integrated central intelligence service, the small core of former R. and A. people remained separate and distinct. Like their colleagues in S.S.U., these I.R.I.S.–O.R.I. people maintained close ties with their old O.S.S. colleagues in other offices of government and in civilian life. From the earliest postwar period, these connections were used to secure useful research information or to check on sources. The importance of these links was so obvious and so potentially useful to the directors of I.R.I.S.–O.R.I. that between December 1945 and February 1946, one of their highest priority projects was the preparation of a keysort biographical filing system of all American former intelligence personnel.[34]

The cause of central intelligence was also advanced between 1945 and 1947 by events that transpired in the early postwar era. When the dissolution order was issued (20 September 1945), President Truman had declared that some form of "comprehensive foreign intelligence program" should be developed under the leadership of Secretary of State Byrnes. From late 1945 until the act establishing the C.I.A. was passed by Congress in July 1947, a struggle over centralizing intelligence occurred in Washington, and a kaleidoscope of changing intelligence coordination systems passed in and out of existence. Since, as a Foreign Office official again emphasized, "the Americans make no secret of their 'secret' activities," much of this conflict was waged quite openly, with traditionalists in the State Department and the military intelligence services grimly holding onto their prerogatives and Truman persisting in his hostility to the creation of a "Gestapo." The argument turned steadily in favor of those who supported an O.S.S.-type central intelligence organization, primarily because during 1946–47—despite opposition from people like Henry Wallace—the rising Cold War pressures forced traditionalists, especially those in military intelligence, to recognize that something should be done quickly to increase the worldwide flow of intelligence information and to centralize its evaluation. The reorganization of the armed forces, leading to the creation of a new, unified Department of Defense in 1947, also helped open the door for the establishment of C.I.A., as did the feeling that since the Soviets did not play fair, provision had to be made for carrying out dirty tricks.[35]

While these basic changes were pointing ever more directly toward the creation of the C.I.A., the O.S.S. legacy continued to assist the centralized intelligence cause. The very existence of the O.R.I. and S.S.U. units meant that the building blocks for a new and unified intelligence organization were at hand. Furthermore, in his initial order to War Department officials concerning S.S.U., John J. McCloy had made it clear that the unit was not to be broken up or merely preserved as a museum piece but maintained "as a going operation." Although officially outside the government following 20 September 1945, Donovan was also unwilling to stand aside and let his creation evaporate. In early October 1945, he made a private arrangement with William Stephenson to carry on one of their joint super secret intelligence networks in China, and in the same month he sent a memorandum to President Truman predicting that unless radical subversive warfare countermeasures were quickly utilized in Scandinavia, the Russians would keep on pushing and "you will find the same pattern developed there as now exists in Bulgaria." Three months later, the former O.S.S. director was urging Samuel Rosenman to push on with the centralization of intelligence and "to take a personal interest" in the creation of a new O.S.S.-type organization.[36]

Since much of the policy battle over a new intelligence organization was fought out publicly, Donovan and his colleagues were able to make full use of the well-established methods of lobbying politics and media pressure. In October 1945, Donovan suggested helping the cause by the creation of a "quiet organization" of former O.S.S. men. The purpose of the group, as Ned Buxton informed James Rogers, would be "to keep the idea and functioning of Central Intelligence" alive "any way we can find to do so." The suggestion of a "committee of 100" analogous to the 1940 "aid to Britain" group was quickly expanded, and the resulting Veterans of Strategic Service (V.V.S.) organization had 1,300 members as early as 1948. The formal pressure group activities of the V.V.S. were supplemented by enthusiastic central intelligence promotional work by individual former O.S.S. men and women. Allen Dulles was especially busy speaking to such important groups as the faculty of the Air War College at Maxwell Field on the significance of building on the wartime O.S.S. experiences to meet the "national requirements for intelligence." Dulles was anxious to counter any adverse press criticism of O.S.S. wartime activities, yet at the same time, both he and General Lemnitzer welcomed the use of such unorthodox promotional devices as "True Comics" to spread the word of the accomplishments of Donovan's organization.[37]

There were also links between those O.S.S. men who had stayed on in S.S.U. and the publicity activities of Donovan people who had left government service. On 10 December 1945, General Magruder informed David Bruce that advantage should be taken of the congressional investigation of the attack on Pearl Harbor to have "the *Times* and the *Herald Tribune* comment editorially to the effect that the Pearl Harbor investigation points up again the need of a C.I.A." Bruce turned to Allen Dulles for assistance, and on 13 December Dulles replied that he would see what he could do "to help get some useful editorial comment from the *Times* and the *Tribune*." It is not possible to tell whether this particular initiative by Dulles had any special effect, because both newspapers were at that moment pointing to a wide range of conclusions that might be drawn from the Pearl Harbor investigation, and in any event, this was but one item in an energetic campaign that Dulles was waging to provide material for Republican members of the investigatory committee.[38]

Under the laws and customs of the country, O.S.S. veterans had the right to carry out public relations endeavors in favor of central intelligence, and even attempts to promote favorable press comment by those inside the government were not uncommon in Washington. What was unusual was the passion with which former members of Donovan's organization pursued the cause of getting some form of their wartime organization into the regular United States government. No one in the War Shipping Board or the Office of Censorship ever dreamed of creating a veterans' organization to promote and make permanent the organization in which they had done their wartime service. One of the most important features of Donovan's role as a leader was his ability to imbue his associates with such enthusiasm for his ideas and causes that many of them took on the attributes of evangelists. Where else could one find someone as zealous as the Donovan champion who in July 1946 suggested to Allen Dulles that they spread the story that because George Washington employed some irregular means of warfare, the Father of the Country had been a pioneer in the use of O.S.S.-type operations.[39]

This crusading zeal obviously helped provide some of the drive necessary to push the C.I.A. bill on to passage in July 1947, but that event did not end the promotional efforts of O.S.S. veterans. The V.V.S. continued to prosper, Dulles and his associates went on giving speeches linking O.S.S. enterprises to the creation and maintenance of the C.I.A., and Donovan used every possible opportunity to press his views on such important people as Secretary of the Navy Forrestal and Dwight Eisenhower. Dulles still mined his O.S.S. experiences for material to aid the political causes that he favored. In late 1950, during the Korean War, he considered for the first time writing a book about Operation Sunrise because "in view of our present position vis-à-vis Russia" it would be a means of getting into print the insulting messages that Stalin had sent to President Roosevelt during the effort to prompt a German surrender in Italy. The intensification of Cold War conflict in the early 1950s strengthened the connections between the C.I.A. and the O.S.S. central intelligence lobby, and in November 1950, because of the Korean War emergency, the V.V.S. brought up to date "its confidential file on the special skills of its members" to better meet the recruitment needs of the C.I.A. and other intelligence agencies. In 1951, Donovan provided the names of suitable O.S.S. veterans to the then C.I.A. Deputy Director Allen Dulles, and when in early 1953 President Eisenhower selected Dulles as director of the C.I.A., the appointment was much praised by former members of Donovan's organization. During Dulles's tenure as C.I.A. director, many of the links between the agency and the central intelligence enthusiasts among the veterans of O.S.S. seem to have been tightened. A former O.S.S. man, John Wiley, came forward in February 1958 to offer his services in turning the Council of Islamic Affairs into a front group for C.I.A. anti-Soviet activities in the Middle East, and at least two O.S.S. veterans were members of the Princeton Associates, which served the agency as a kind of gentlemanly board of advisers. In a speech to the V.S.S. delivered shortly after his retirement from the agency, Dulles provided the ultimate testimonial to the O.S.S.–C.I.A. connection. While referring to the First and Second World Wars as "two fratricidal wars [that] weaken[ed] the West" and laying heavy stress on the evils of communism, Dulles described O.S.S. as the "backbone of the C.I.A." and praised the V.S.S. for having "kept up tradition," while serving as "a built-in reserve in case of emergency."[40]

Certainly, it would be a mistake to portray the relations between O.S.S. veterans and the C.I.A. as uniformly harmonious. In 1946, at the beginning of the Cold War era, some extreme political conservatives from O.S.S. such as DeWitt Poole called for harsh measures against the Soviets and denounced the "young Jew boys" in the State Department who still wanted to punish the Germans. There was also a small cadre of old O.S.S. war-horses led by Stanley Lovell who were ready to do anything to anybody; so much so that as late as 1963, Lovell proclaimed publicly that "once war is declared, to reason is treason." But a few O.S.S. veterans such as Francis Miller were thoroughly disillusioned with "quixotic Donovanesque" activities, concluding in January 1946 that the O.S.S. director "was completely incapable of laying foundations for the future, and what he did lay were mostly in sand." As R. Harris Smith has emphasized, there was also a large group of O.S.S. veterans for whom liberal and democratic causes were of the utmost importance. Few such people were included in the ranks of those who strove to create a Central Intelligence Agency and fewer still participated in the agency's Cold War offensive operations.[41]

Furthermore, even among the intelligence professionals, there were distinct limits to what could be done in the name of the old-time comradeship. One of the points inherent in the campaign to create a real central intelligence agency was the importance of putting an end to the kind of haphazard and irregular distribution of intelligence reports that had characterized O.S.S. Everyone gradually came to agree with the position taken by Gen. Lucius Clay in 1945 when he declared, "I do not want any intelligence, no matter how good, unless it is produced by a staff under my control." This attitude also meant that even though O.S.S. enthusiasts had achieved many of their successes by publicity campaigns and once it was created, the C.I.A. tried to have books sympathetic to O.S.S. produced by making arrangements with Cornelius Ryan and others, limits had to be set to promotional activities. Allen Dulles, who had himself been so active on the publicity trail, in 1955 first denied a request from Donovan that O.S.S. veteran Peter Tompkins be aided in his book research by being given access to O.S.S. files. Ten years later, when Tompkins tried again and had Dulles intercede for him it was Richard Helms who informed his old World War II colleague that the agency had decided that it would "not open the records and that we are not going to permit individual access to any documentation."[42]

In this sense, the very drive for the institutionalization of intelligence long sought by O.S.S. activists vitiated the innovativeness and unusual associations that had given Donovan's organization so much of its strength and dynamism. Yet the knitting together of diverse groups and individuals from different classes, ethnic groups, political outlooks, and professional groups had been done so well that by the 1950s and 1960s it was unnecessary to give it much reinforcement. For example, when the war had ended, William Stephenson created a South American trading company in part "to do something for some of the talented fellows in the mission (B.S.C.) here," and he had taken on veterans of O.S.S. as well as those from the British secret service. Less international cohesions of former intelligence activists occurred in countless law firms, newspapers, academic departments, and industrial enterprises throughout the United States. To an unusual degree, this created a network of communication that helped bridge some of the widest gaps in American society and could be called upon in cases of need long after the war ended. For example, when in December 1964 former British intelligence man Hugh Trevor Roper had the temerity to attack the Warren Commission report in the Sunday *Times*, Commission member Allen Dulles turned for advice on what to do to former C.I.A. and O.S.S. man Frank Wisner. Wisner in turn contacted ex-O.S.S. man and former Kennedy adviser Arthur Schlesinger, who recommended that since Bernard Levin had just published a piece attacking Trevor Roper, it would therefore not be necessary for Schlesinger himself to produce a rebuttal. But it is difficult to imagine that any other American World War II agency created a system of intimate contact between people as diverse as Schlesinger, Wisner, and Dulles that was capable of such rapid and smooth communication twenty years after the end of the war.[43]

The network of close personal connections established in O.S.S. and frequently maintained in the postwar world illustrates one of the most significant features of the long-range influence of Donovan's organization on subsequent American development. It seems obvious that O.S.S. was more influential in its impact on people's ideas and imagination than in its practical wartime achievements. The simple fact that O.S.S. was the first American attempt to create something approximating a central intelligence agency itself has had a very important effect on opinion. O.S.S. had to serve as the prototype for subsequent intelligence centralization efforts in the United States, and the peculiarities in Donovan's organization inevitably left marks on the American system of government. The eclectic tendencies of the O.S.S. chief created confusion about what properly belonged in a central intelligence agency, and some of this confusion carried over into the postwar era. Donovan's enthusiasm and missionary zeal, which touched so many of his subordinates, also convinced a large number of Americans who would be influential in the postwar period that his kaleidoscopic ideas were right and proper and that some kind of permanent central intelligence system was necessary. These people had pioneered a wide range of activities, from undercover espionage to armed support for foreign subversive organizations, which were new to Americans. Among their various innovations were such measures as close contact with the Thai government, the training and leadership of Nationalist Chinese guerrilla units, and intimate cooperation with moderate European trade unions. These innovations were to be pushed to extremes by the C.I.A. after the war. Since the initial steps into such activities were taken by O.S.S. with great moral fervor and were considered by many O.S.S. veterans (and much of the public) to have been completely legitimate in time of war, it was much easier in the postwar period for C.I.A. merely to move on to excess.

Another significant aspect of the Donovan intelligence inheritance lay in the area of quasi-secrecy. The enthusiastic and expansive Donovan always had some of the qualities of a promoter. He had close ties to major newspapers, surrounded himself with press men, and placed newspaper executives in crucial positions within C.O.I.–O.S.S. C.O.I. was itself at least as much a propaganda as an intelligence organization. Therefore, C.O.I.–O.S.S. was never secret in the way that the Soviet N.K.V.D.–K.G.B., the German Abwehr–S.D., or even the British S.I.S., were secret. Not only were Donovan's units established by publicly announced executive orders, their programs and internal organization were an open book to the J.C.S., and few of their operations remained secret from American and Allied officials overseas. Gossip about the organization abounded in Washington and frequently appeared in newspapers even during the wartime period. To cap the public and publicity aspects of O.S.S., during the fall of 1945 Donovan resorted to open press warfare to defend the organization and gain support for his postwar intelligence plans.

The British, and presumably other governments, found this a most peculiar way to conduct secret affairs, but Donovan's publicity campaigns strengthened his hand in the short run and helped establish a long-term quasi-secret style for American intelligence organizations. The innovative Donovan could not operate effectively through normal channels, and to make any mark he had to be as inventive in Washington as he was in the field. By bringing his case directly to the attention of the top military authorities and the White House, he most likely prevented his organizations and the cause of central intelligence from being crushed early on by O.N.I. and M.I.D. Later in the war, it was only because Donovan launched a long, hard, and semipublic campaign within the American government in favor of the proposition that the United States should not be dependent on any foreign power for its raw intelligence—not even Britain—that S.I. emerged as an autonomous operation. It seems highly likely that without someone as assertive and publicity-conscious as Donovan in the crucial position of "American intelligence director," the larger and more experienced British intelligence and covert organizations would simply have coopted American shadow warfare operations in the course of World War II.

Therefore, William Donovan played a crucial role in the process whereby World War II laid the foundations for a large-scale independent American intelligence system. But since O.S.S. and then the C.I.A. were only made possible by publicity and extensive governmental and public debate on the merits of shadow warfare operations and central intelligence, they could in no way be truly secret, with sensitive operations buried in obscure recesses of innocent-looking government departments. Carter's operation had been really hidden, so well hidden, in fact, that the public never knew that it existed, and therefore it could be abolished without raising a ripple of protest from anyone. O.S.S. was quite different, for it had made "secret" operations and central intelligence public property, which gave it a claim on extended influence and also helped to create the peculiar situation whereby for forty years American "secret" organizations and activities have been among the most widely known political phenomena in the world.

The long-term evolution of an American intelligence system also owed a great deal to the main propositions that Donovan and his supporters put forth in their publicity campaign to increase the worthiness of O.S.S. and help establish a postwar central intelligence organization. The fundamental tenet of the 1945–47 campaign was that Donovan had produced a basic plan for strategic intelligence early in the war, had developed C.O.I.–O.S.S. as the implementing instrument of that vision, and that the subsequent achievements of those organizations demonstrated the validity of Donovan's plan with such force that a comparable postwar organization should be established. In fact, aside from championing every form of unorthodox warfare that came to mind, there was little that was constant about Donovan's views on strategic services, central intelligence, or anything else. Initially, he advocated the establishment of a propaganda and information coordinating agency (C.O.I.), then quickly moved on and added a range of other activities extending from secret intelligence to commando operations. He then lost control of open (white) propaganda, and subsequently, not a word was said by Donovan or his many champions to the effect that such propaganda should be included in a postwar intelligence agency. During the main part of the war, Donovan was possessed by a hunger for combat and found his best market in battle-related activities. His plan for strategic services therefore shifted to emphasize operational groups, resistance-support operations, secret intelligence, and black propaganda, while R. and A.–type strategic intelligence research slipped into a secondary position. In this era (1943 and early 1944), when the O.S.S. director advanced his ideas for a postwar central intelligence agency, they were, in conformity with his organization's practice at that moment, keyed to service to the military and subordination to the J.C.S. However, as hostilities drew to a close, it became increasingly obvious that when the army and navy were cut back, there would be little future for

O.S.S. services if they were based chiefly on military-support operations. Furthermore, the rising reality of American postwar power and the likelihood that the next era would generate many new "strategic" issues seemed to offer better opportunities for an autonomous agency—directly under the president—that would stress the collection and coordination of strategic information. All the promotional efforts made by Donovan and his associates between 1945 and the creation of the C.I.A. were therefore keyed to the strategic information aspect of central intelligence. But the former O.S.S. director and his friends also worked assiduously to create the impression that his latest postwar intelligence plan merely continued the kind of activity that O.S.S. had carried on from its inception. In fact, O.S.S. had not operated directly under the supervision of the president since early 1942, had done limited strategic intelligence work during the war, and had made its mark as a handmaiden of tactical military operations.[44]

Therefore, it is fair to conclude that one of the oddest features of the postwar American intelligence system—namely, subordinating C.I.A. directly to the president and thereby making disavowal of unfortunate actions extremely difficult—arose from Donovan's last-minute vision rather than from O.S.S. wartime practice. Two other noteworthy anomalies in Donovan's proposal (which were taken over by the C.I.A.)—the inclusion of covert operations under central intelligence and the separation of cryptography (in N.S.A.) from the rest of secret intelligence activities—did, however, parallel the peculiar operational position that Donovan's organization had occupied during World War II. Thirty-five years of institutional experience, and the repetition of the tale of direct O.S.S.–C.I.A. continuity, have made the queer presidentially directed central intelligence system made up of covert operations, espionage, and research (but not cryptography) seem normal to Americans. But it is actually a very odd arrangement that owes more to the promotional abilities of Donovan and his friends than to any historical precedent or the laws of nature.

The vision and viewpoint of Donovan and his associates also played a significant role in another important aspect of American postwar policy. From the first days of World War II, Donovan had been captivated by the power and potential of subversive warfare. His own worries about the German fifth column, intensified and amplified by his British friends, produced an awesome mental picture of Nazi subversive prowess that never left Donovan's thoughts. His mistaken belief that the Nazis were particularly adept at intelligence and subversive operations led him to overestimate the importance of shadow warfare and underestimate the significance of conventional weapons and economic factors in the Second

World War. This tendency remained in Donovan's thinking and the mythology of O.S.S. throughout the conflict, but it had few serious adverse effects at the time because the J.C.S. kept O.S.S. activities harnessed to a strategy of mass mobilization and the use of the big battalions. When at war's end the enormous American conventional weapons force was demobilized, however, the belief that shadow warfare could serve in lieu of regular forces took on more significance. The people of the United States were wary of atomic war, unwilling to pay for a huge standing army, but desirous of reaping the benefits of being the world's greatest power. Since the Soviet Union was the only other power in the world of any consequence and the Russians made generous use of shadow warfare methods, it was easy to put clandestine and political warfare techniques into the foreground. And throughout the early stage of postwar policy evolution, the Donovan group was always at hand, claiming that it had great expertise in shadow warfare and pointing to what it asserted was a glorious record of covert operational triumph during World War II. What Donovan's people did not indicate—and probably did not fully grasp—was that whatever achievements they had made between 1942 and 1945 had been conditioned by the fact that they were merely serving as auxiliaries to an allied conventional military and economic mobilization that constituted the greatest concentration of armed might the world had ever seen.

Whether myth or not, the O.S.S. claim to independent shadow warfare prowess strengthened Washington's belief that it could retain superpower status cheaply and helped lead the United States into making its central intelligence agency into something that it hoped could produce shadow warfare magic. Even though this was done with a minimum of malice and with more self-deception than cynicism, the results were serious. The U.S. government increasingly attempted to fill the gap between its two main power instruments—atomic weapons and economic muscle—with the devices of shadow warfare. As the position of American economic and atomic supremacy was challenged by other countries and the population of the United States continued to avoid as much of the cost of standing armies as possible, dependence on covert operations and deception sharply increased.

The effort to prop up America's position by heavy reliance on shadow warfare rested on sand, however, because there was no basis to believe that such operations could win much on their own. Great power shadow warfare had only played a significant role as a supplementary instrument of military operations in World War II, and both the story that Hitler won great battles by means of a fifth column and the tale that O.S.S. went it alone were fables.

As early as 1961, a high C.I.A. official grasped what was wrong, observing during a postmortem on the Bay of Pigs that large-scale Agency operations had inevitably gone sour "because the system kept calling on us for more and more even when it should have been obvious that secret shenanigans couldn't do what armies are supposed to do."[45] The ambitious shadow warfare enterprises undertaken in the subsequent twenty years—epitomized by the debacles in Vietnam—have pointed to the same conclusion.

From O.S.S. to the present, shadow warfare has shown that it is no substitute for basic military and economic strength. Donovan's legions assisted the American armed forces in World War II, and the C.I.A. later helped fill in some of the chinks in the awesome postwar armor of the United States. But as the era of East–West superpower dominance draws to a close and the world evolves into a new complex multipower configuration, it behooves Americans to put aside romance and mind the two most important facts of the O.S.S. story: despite the best efforts of Donovan and his successors, no shadow warrior ever found a magic wand and the great power game was always too demanding to allow "secret shenanigans" to do "what armies are supposed to do."

List of Abbreviations

A.F.H.Q.	Allied Force Headquarters (Mediterranean)
B.E.W.	Board of Economic Warfare (American)
B.L.O.	British Liaison Officer
B.S.C.	British Security Coordinator
"C"	The Director of the British Secret Intelligence Service (S.I.S.)
C.B.I.	The China–Burma–India Theater of Operations
C.C.S.	The Combined Chiefs of Staff (British-American)
C.I.C.	Counterintelligence Corps (American)
C.O.I.	Coordinator of Information
D Day	Allied Landing In Normandy, June 6 1944
D.N.I.	Director of Naval Intelligence (British)
D Section	Early Covert Operations section in British S.I.S.
E.A.M. and E.L.A.S.	Military and political units of leftist Greek resistance
E.T.O.	European Theater of Operations
F.F.I.	French Forces of the Interior (i.e., Gaullist resistance)
F.I.S.	Foreign Information Service (a section of C.O.I.)
F.N.B.	Foreign Nationalities Branch of C.O.I. and O.S.S.
F.O.	Foreign Office (British)
F.P.M.	Free French Penetration Mission
G-1	Personnel Division (American Army)
G-2	Intelligence Division (American Army)
G-3	Operations Division (American Army)
I.D.C.	Interdepartmental Committee for the Acquisition of Foreign Periodicals (American)
I.R.I.S.	Interim Research Intelligence Service (first postwar form of O.S.S.'s R. and A. Branch)
I.S.L.D.	Inter-Service Liaison Detachment (cover name for the British S.I.S. in the Mediterranean theater)
I.S.S.U.-6	Inter-Service Signals Units-6 (cover name for the British S.O.E. in the Mediterranean theater)
J.C.S.	Joint Chiefs of Staff
J.I.C.	Joint Intelligence Committee (both Britain and the United States had a J.I.C.)

List of Abbreviations

J.M.A.	Japanese Military Attaché Code
J.P.S.	Joint Planning Staff (American)
J.P.W.C.	Joint Psychological Warfare Committee (American)
M.I.D.	Military Intelligence Division (American)
M.I.S.	Military Intelligence Service (American)
M.I. 5	Military Intelligence Section 5 (British counterintelligence section on British territory)
M.I. 6	Military Intelligence Section 6 (the same as S.I.S., the British secret intelligence service; also operated as a counterintelligence service in non-British territory)
M.O.	Morale Operations (black propaganda section of O.S.S.)
M.O.I.	Ministry of Information (British)
N.A.T.O.	North African Theater of Operations (American, 1942–44)
NATO	North Atlantic Treaty Organization, post–World War II
N.I.D.	Naval Intelligence Division (British)
N.K.V.D.	Soviet Security Service (Domestic Security Police, Foreign Secret Intelligence, clandestine operations)
N.S.A.	National Security Authority (American, postwar)
N.S.D.A.P.	The Nazi Party
O.G.	Operations Group (commando-type unit in O.S.S.)
O.N.I.	Office of Naval Intelligence (American)
O.R.I.	Office of Research Intelligence (postwar version of O.S.S. R. and A. Branch)
O.S.S.	Office of Strategic Services
O.W.I.	Office of War Information (American)
P.W.E.	Political Warfare Executive (British)
R. and A.	Research and Analysis Branch (of O.S.S.)
R.A.F.	Royal Air Force (British)
S.A.C.O.	Sino-American Cooperative Organization
S.A.S.	Special Air Service (British commandos)
S.D.	Nazi Security and Intelligence Service
S.E.A.C.	Southeast Asian Command (Mountbatten)
S.H.A.E.F.	Supreme Headquarters Allied Expeditionary Force (i.e., command of D Day and post–D Day continental operations)
S.I.	Secret Intelligence Branch of O.S.S.
S.I.S.	Secret Intelligence Service (another designation for British M.I. 6)
S.O.E.	Special Operations Executive (British clandestine operations organization)
S.O. 1	Special Operations #1 (the black propaganda section of British S.O.E.)
S.O. 2	Special Operations #2 (the clandestine operations section of British S.O.E.)
S.P.D.	German Socialist Party
S.P.O.C.	Special Projects Operations Center (Mediterranean theater)
S.S.U.	Special Services Unit (the clandestine operations and secret intelligence unit from O.S.S. in the postwar War Department)
V–1	German flying bomb
V–2	German rocket bomb
V.S.S.	Veterans of Strategic Service
X-2	Counterintelligence (American)

Guide to Frequently Cited Sources

AFHQ—RG (Record Group 331). Suitland, Maryland: Federal Record Center.

Barker—Barker, Elisabeth. *British Policy in South-East Europe in the Second World War.* London; 1976.

Butcher Diary—Harry C. Butcher Diary. DDE Papers. 1916–1952. Dwight D. Eisenhower Library, Abilene, Kansas.

CAB 65—CAB 65: War Cabinet Minutes. London: Public Record Office.

CAB 69—CAB 69: War Cabinet Defense Committee. London: Public Record Office.

CAB 79—CAB 79: Chiefs of Staff (COS) Minutes. London: Public Record Office.

CAB 80—CAB 80: Chiefs of Staff (COS) Memoranda. London: Public Record Office.

CAB 122—CAB 122. Joint Staff Mission, London: Public Record Office.

Cadogan—Diary of Sir Alexander Cadogan. Winston S. Churchill Library, Cambridge University.

Dalton Papers—Hugh Dalton Papers. British Library of Political and Economic Science, London School of Economics.

Diplomatic Branch—RG 59. Diplomatic Branch. Washington, D.C.: National Archives.

Dulles—Allen W. Dulles Papers. Princeton University.

Eisenhower—Pre-Presidential Papers, DDE Papers, 1916–1952. Dwight D. Eisenhower Library, Abilene, Kansas.

Eisenhower Papers—Chandler, Alfred D., Jr., and Stephen E. Ambrose, eds. *The Papers of Dwight David Eisenhower: The War Years.* 5 vols. Baltimore and London. 1970.

FO 371—FO 371: Major Diplomatic Files. London: Public Record Office.

FO 898—FO 898: Political Warfare Executive. London: Public Record Office.

FO 954—FO 954: Lord Avon's Papers. London: Public Record Office.

FRUS—*Foreign Relations of the United States.* Washington, D.C.

Goodfellow—Millard Goodfellow Papers. Hoover Institution, Stanford University.

Harold Smith—Harold Smith Papers. Franklin D. Roosevelt Library, Hyde Park, New York.

Hayden—Joseph R. Hayden Papers. Bentley Library, University of Michigan.

Hinsley—Hinsley, F. H., et al. *British Intelligence in the Second World War.* New York: 1979 and 1981. Vols. I and II.

Hoover—Hoover, Calvin. *Memoirs of Capitalism, Communism, Nazism.* Durham, North Carolina: 1965.

Hornbeck—Stanley Hornbeck Papers. Hoover Institution, Stanford University.

Horne—Horne, Allistair. *To Lose a Battle.* Boston: 1969.

Hyde—Hyde, H. Montgomery. *Room 3603.* New York: 1962.

Langer—Langer, William L. *In and Out of the Ivory Tower.* New York: 1977.

Lee—Leutze, James, ed. *The London Journal of General Raymond E. Lee: 1940–1941.* Boston: 1971.

Loewenheim—Loewenheim, Francis L., Harold D. Langley, and Manfred Jonas, eds. *Roosevelt and Churchill. Their Secret Wartime Correspondence.* New York, 1975.

Guide to Frequently Cited Sources

Map Room—Map Room Files. Franklin D. Roosevelt Library, Hyde Park, New York.
Marshall—Marshall Papers. George C. Marshall Library, Lexington, Virginia.
Morgenthau—Henry Morgenthau, Jr., Diary. Franklin D. Roosevelt Library, Hyde Park, New York.
OF—Official File. Presidential Files. Franklin D. Roosevelt Library, Hyde Park, New York.
PREM 4—PREM 4. Confidential Papers. London: Public Record Office.
PSF—President's Secretary's File. Franklin D. Roosevelt Library, Hyde Park, New York.
RG 165—RG 165. ABC Files. Modern Military Branch. Washington, D.C.: National Archives.
RG 218—RG 218: Joint Chiefs of Staff and Combined Chiefs of Staff Files. Modern Military Branch. Washington, D.C.: National Archives.
RG 218 Leahy—Admiral Leahy's Files. Modern Military Branch. Washington, D.C.: National Archives.
RG 218 Postwar—Joint Chiefs of Staff Files (as distinct from wartime general chronological series). Modern Military Branch. Washington, D.C.: National Archives.
RG 226—Research and Analysis Branch of O.S.S. Collection. Modern Military Branch. Washington, D.C.: National Archives.
RG 334—RG 334. Military Mission to Moscow Files. Modern Military Branch. Washington, D.C.: National Archives.
SHAEF—Selected Records of S.H.A.E.F. Dwight D. Eisenhower Library, Abilene, Kansas.
Smith and Agarossi—Smith, Bradley F., and Elena Agarossi. *Operation Sunrise*. New York: 1979.
Spears—Spears, Sir Edward. *Assignment to Catastrophe*. New York: 1955. Vol. II.
Stettinius—Edward Stettinius Papers. University of Virginia.
Stimson Diary—Diary of Henry L. Stimson. Yale University.
Sweet-Escott—Sweet-Escott, Bickham. *Baker Street Irregular*. London: 1965.
Taylor—Taylor, Edmund. *Awakening From History*. Boston: 1969.
Troy—Troy, Thomas. *Donovan and C.I.A.* Washington, D.C.: C.I.A., 1981.
Truman—Papers of Harry S. Truman. Harry S. Truman Library, Independence, Missouri.
War Report—Roosevelt, Kermit, ed. *War Report of the OSS*. New York: 1976.
Wilkinson—Gerald H. Wilkinson Papers. Winston S. Churchill Library, Cambridge.
WO 106—WO 106: Directorate of Military Operations and Intelligence. London: Public Record Office.
WO 193—WO 193, Directorate of Military Operations. London: Public Record Office.
WO 204—WO 204: AFHQ Records. London: Public Record Office.
WO 208—WO 208; Directorate of Military Intelligence. London: Public Record Office.
WO 219—WO 219: S.H.A.E.F. London: Public Record Office.

Notes

Prologue

1. This account and all quotes in the prologue come from a combat patrol report, Korcula, 20 April 1944, *WO 204*/1970. See also *AFHQ*, Force 266 Sitrep File, Roll 37A.

2. Kermit Roosevelt, ed, *The War Report of the OSS* and *The Overseas Targets* (New York: 1976 and 1977); Thomas F. Troy, *Donovan and C.I.A.* (Central Intelligence Agency: 1981); Corey Ford, *Donovan of O.S.S.* (Boston: 1976). Richard Dunlop's *Donovan: America's Master Spy* (Chicago: 1982) rests on more ambitious archival work but remains in the tradition of unlimited eulogy. Anthony Cave Brown's *The Last Hero* (New York: 1983) appeared as *The Shadow Warriors* was in press, and it was therefore impossible to make extensive use of that volume in this study. Brown and I use some of the same material, though drawn from different sources, to reach very different conclusions about the meaning, activity, and importance of O.S.S.

Chapter 1

1. The most moving account of the campaign is still *Horne*.

2. Louis de Jong, *The German Fifth Column in the Second World War* (Chicago: 1956), pp. 69–77.

3. *Hinsley*, I, pp. 163–164.

4. Siegfried Westphal, *The German Army in the West* (London: 1951), p. 86.

5. B. H. Liddell Hart, *The German Generals Talk* (New York: 1948), p. 124.

6. *Horne*, pp. 289, 306, 329.

7. Ulrich Liss, *Westfront 1939–1940* (Neckargemünd: 1959), pp. 188 and 256; *Horne*, pp. 317, 381, 394; B. H. Liddell Hard, ed., *The Rommel Papers* (New York: 1953), p. 20

8. B. H. Liddell Hart, ed., *The Rommel Papers*, p. 25; Henri H. Giraud, "The Causes of the Defeat—Military Causes." (Mimeographed Copy, Hoover Institution); Marc Bloch, *Strange Defeat* (London: 1949), p. 47.

9. William L. Shirer, *Berlin Diary* (New York: 1941), p. 365.

10. *Taylor*, p. 271; *Horne*, pp. 381–383, 567, 579; Marc Bloch, *Strange Defeat*, p. 25; William L. Shirer, *The Collapse of the Third Republic* (London: 1970), p. 882; Gen. Andre Beaufre, *1940. The Fall of France* (London: 1965), p. 212; *Spears*, II, p. 176.

11. Robert O. Paxton, *Vichy France: Old Guard and New Order* (New York: 1972), p. 21; William L. Shirer, *The Collapse of the Third Republic*, p. 807.

12. *Horne*, pp. 443 and 453; William L. Shirer, *The Collapse of the Third Republic*, pp.

Notes

1062–1068; Marc Bloch, *Strange Defeat*, pp. 50–51; Jacques Benoist-Mechin, *Sixty Days That Shook the West*, p. 301.

13. *Spears*, II, p. 101.

14. Louis de Jong, *The German Fifth Column in the Second World War*, pp. 1–5.

15. *Spears*, II, pp. 43–45.

16. Louis de Jong, *The German Fifth Column in the Second World War*, especially pp. 91–94, 202–206, and 241–242; William L. Shirer, *Berlin Diary*, pp. 379–380 and 434–442.

17. Louis de Jong, *The German Fifth Column in the Second World War*, pp. 76–77 and p. 91; William L. Shirer, *The Collapse of the Third Republic*, p. 744.

18. Ulrich Liss, *Westfront 1939–1940*, p. 188; Winston S. Churchill, *Blood, Sweat and Tears* (New York: 1941), pp. 279–80; Henri H. Giraud, *The Causes of the Defeat*, p. 15.

19. Jacques Benoist-Mechin, *Sixty Days That Shook the West*, p. 259.

20. William L. Shirer, *Berlin Diary*, p. 385.

21. *Horne*, p. 579; David Dilks, ed., *The Diaries of Sir Alexander Cadogan 1938–1945* (London: 1971), p. 308.

22. Jacques Benoist-Mechin, *Sixty Days That Shook the West*, pp. 209 and 224.

23. Louis de Jong, *The German Fifth Column in the Second World War*, pp. 95–99 and 207–213; Hinsley, I, p. 167. For the turning of agents, see J. C. Masterman, *The Double Cross System in the War of 1939–1945* (New Haven: 1972).

24. Statement by F. M. Sheldon, 24 July 1941, *FO 898/114*. See also the chapter "Grand Time" in *Sweet-Escott*, pp. 17–39.

25. *Hinsley*, I, pp. 275–276; Martin Green, *Children of the Sun* (New York: 1976), pp. 250–251 and pp. 320–325; Lord Gladwyn, *Memoirs* (New York: 1972), p. 106.

26. *Spears*, II, p. 133.

27. Lord Gladwyn, *Memoirs*, pp. 101–105; Diary, 16 May 1940, *Dalton Papers*.

28. *Hinsley*, I, p. 234 and pp. 246–248.

29. 21 June 1940, *Cadogan*. The work of David A. Stafford is basic to any discussion of British policy in this period. See especially "Britain Looks at Europe 1940," *Canadian Journal of History* 10, no. 2 (August 1975), and *Britain and the European Resistance 1940–1945* (London: 1980), Chapters 1 and 2.

30. Diary, 1 July 1940 and memorandum Cadogan to Dalton, 2 July 1940, *Dalton Papers;* David A. Stafford, "The Detonator Concept: British Strategy, SOE and European Resistance After the Fall of France," *Journal of Contemporary History* 10, no. 2 (April 1975) 197–202. Note that Dalton was not always as tough as he seemed. He thought Clement Atlee, probably the most soft-spoken man in British politics, would make a good shadow warfare czar. Hugh Dalton, *The Fateful Years* (London: 1957), II, p. 367.

31. Hugh Dalton, *The Fateful Years*, II, p. 368. The recently published diaries of Sir Bruce Lockhart provide an interesting chronicle of early British shadow warfare troubles, Kenneth Young, ed., *The Diaries of Sir Robert Bruce Lockhart 1939–1965* (London: 1980), II passim.

32. The Hitler quote comes from *Horne*, p. 231.

33. William L. Langer and S. Everett Gleason, *The Challenge to Isolation 1937–1940* (New York: 1952), pp. 449, 469, 474–476, and 505; Robert A. Divine, *The Reluctant Belligerent*, 2nd ed. (New York: 1979), p. 92.

34. William L. Shirer, *The Collapse of the Third Republic*, p. 780; Louis de Jong, *The German Fifth Column in the Second World War*, pp. 105–106; *Hyde*, p. 72. The persistence of fifth column language is interesting. When in May 1959 Allen Dulles praised William Donovan, one of the points that he emphasized was the latter's July 1949 warning regarding the dangers of "the Communist Fifth Column." Donovan File, Box 81, *Dulles*.

35. *Hyde*, pp. 69–70. Aside from the 1937 acquisition of information on the Norden bombsight, recent research suggests few German intelligence successes in the United States. David Kahn, *Hitler's Spies* (New York: 1978), pp. 329–331. See also Ladislas Farago, *The Game of Foxes* (New York: 1971).

36. Don Whitehead, *The FBI Story* (New York: 1956), pp. 181–230; Stanley E. Hilton, *Hitler's Secret War in South America 1939–1945* (Baton Rouge: 1981), passim. David Kahn concluded after an exhaustive study that "the enormous efforts of Germany's Latin American spies had, in general, gone for naught." David Kahn, *Hitler's Spies*, p. 327.

37. The Reynaud quote in the previous paragraph comes from Jacques Benoist-Mechin, *Sixty Days That Shook the West*, p. 333. David L. Porter, *The Seventy-Sixth Congress and*

World War II 1939–1940 (Columbia, Missouri: 1979), p. 127.

38. Elliott Roosevelt, ed., *F.D.R.: His Personal Letters 1928–1945* (New York: 1950), IV, p. 1026; David L. Porter, *The Seventy-Sixth Congress and World War II 1939–1940*, p. 134.

39. Henry Stimson was inclined to accept all Ambassador Bullitt's fifth column tales at face value, and the president was obviously troubled by fifth column worries, see 31 July, 1 August, and 26 September 1940, Vol. 30, Roll 6, *Stimson Diary*.

40. Harold L. Ickes, *The Secret Diary* (New York: 1954), III, p. 215; 16 July 1940, Vol. 30, Roll 6, *Stimson Diary*.

41. David King was providing M.I.D. with information in the 1920s, as was Gero von Schulze Gaevernitz in early 1940. David King to Col. B. Smith, 6 March 1951, Personnel Data File, King Papers, Hoover Institution; and Brig. Gen. Barnwell R. Legge Statement, 22 October 1945, Correspondence Folder, Gerno von Schulze Gaevernitz Papers, Hoover Institution.

42. *Lee*, p. xvii and pp. 3–21.

43. David E. Kostoff, *Joseph P. Kennedy. A Life and Times* (Englewood Cliffs, New Jersey: 1974), pp. 239–274; Dispatches from 18 July 1940 on, 740.00118 EW 1939, *Diplomatic Branch*.

44. "History of the Military Intelligence Division," United States Department of the Army, 1959–61, Chapter 31, p. 8 (Microfilm Copy, Hoover Institution); 26 June 1943, File 1/3, *Wilkinson*; *Hyde*, pp. 52–59.

45. Martin Green, *Children of the Sun*, p. 320; 4 April 1941, Memorandum II, 7/3, *Dalton Papers*; *Hyde*, passim. Although Hyde's book is somewhat expansive it remains within hailing distance of the documentary evidence, while William Stevenson's *A Man Called Intrepid* (New York: 1976) should be approached with extreme caution, as even Hyde's latest book indicates (H. Montgomery Hyde, *Secret Intelligence Agency*, London: 1982, foreword).

46. Harold Ickes, *The Secret Diary*, 24 December 1939, III, p. 93.

47. E. Roosevelt, ed., *F.D.R.: His Personal Letters*, IV, pp. 975–976. O.S.S. veterans tend to exaggerate the closeness of the Roosevelt-Donovan connection, but British shadow warfare writers such as Hyde and Stevenson go overboard on this matter.

48. The point on the Irish Free State comes from *Lee*, p. 187. *Taylor* has particularly good characterizations of Donovan such as that on p. 348.

49. *Taylor*, p. 319; William L. Langer and S. Everett Gleason, *The Challenge of Isolation 1937–1940*, p. 715; *Lee*, p. 163; George Baer, *Test Case* (Stanford, California: 1976), pp. 186 and 329; Corey Ford, *Donovan of O.S.S.* (Boston: 1976), passim. The reference to Roosevelt's interest in the Catholic Church comes from Robert Murphy, *Diplomat Among Warriors* (Garden City, New York: 1965), pp. 68–69.

50. Edgar A. Mowrer, *Triumph and Turmoil* (New York: 1968), pp. 314–317 (Mowrer was still clinging firmly to Nazi fifth column stories in 1968, see pp. 314–315); Ronald Tree, *When the Moon Was High, Memoirs of Peace and War 1897–1942* (London: 1975), pp. 126–127; *Lee*, p. 21. For an instance of officials adding to Donovan's mission, see Col. H. K. Rutherford to Stettinius, 13 July 1940, D-Miscellaneous File, Box 119, *Stettinius*.

51. For the exaggeration, see *Hyde*, pp. 36–40. 5 and 12 August 1940, Vol. 31, Roll 6, *Stimson Diary*.

52. Lord Lothian to F. O., 10 and 16 July 1940, *FO 371/24237/A3542*; Secretary Hull to the embassies, 11 July 1940, 740.001 EW 1939, 4570A *Diplomatic Branch*; Kennedy to State (2 cables), 740.0011 EW 1939, *Diplomatic Branch*. Hyde is incorrect when he says Kennedy was not notified, *Hyde*, p. 37.

53. *Lee*, p. 26; Donald McLachlan, *Room 39* (New York: 1968), p. 226; Ronald Tree, *When the Moon Was High*, pp. 126–127; Lord Lothian to F. O. 8 August 1940, *FO 371/24237/A3542*; Sir Arthur Salter to the prime minister, 17 August 1940, *FO 371/24237/A3542*.

54. John G. Winant, *Letter from Grosvenor Square* (Boston: 1947), p. 50; *Lee*, pp. 27–28; Statement by General Emmons, August 1940, U.S. Military Mission to U.K. File, Delos C. Emmons Papers, Hoover Institution.

55. Hyde claims that the fifth column material was provided by B.S.C., but obviously Mowrer secured much of it in London. *Hyde*, p. 41.

56. Frantisek Moravec, *Master of Spies* (London: 1975), pp. 161–168. The first chapters

Notes

of *Hinsley*, I, show the extreme British security concern over Ultra in this period, which made it impossible for Donovan to have been cut in during the summer of 1940.

57. 2 August 1940 diary, *Dalton Papers*.

58. Sir Arthur Salter to the Prime Minister, 17 August 1940, *FO 371/24237/A3542*; Lord Lothian to F. O., 8 August 1940, *FO 371/24237/A3542*; J. R. M. Butler, *Lord Lothian (Philip Kerr) 1882-1940* (London: 1960), p. 297; 6 August 1940, Vol. 31, 12 August 1940, Vol. 31, Roll 6, *Stimson Diary*; Mark Lincoln Chadwin, *The Hawks of World War II* (Chapel Hill: 1968), p. 93.

59. On General Strong, 4 February 1944, *Wilkinson*, and 20 August 1940 listing, COS (40) 273, *CAB 80*. 23/24 October 1940, Vol. 31, Roll 6, *Stimson Diary*; W. S. Culbertson to Secretary Hull, 2 December 1940, Culbertson Papers, 1940 File, Box 20, Library of Congress.

60. Col. William J. Donovan and Edgar Mowrer, "Fifth Column Lessons for America" (Washington: 1940); Jong, Louis de, *The German Fifth Column in the Second World War*, pp. 136–137; 16 September 1940, Vol. 31, Roll 6, *Stimson Diary*.

61. 2 December 1940, Vol. 32, Roll 6, *Stimson Diary*; Lord Lothian to Butler, 9 November 1940, *FO 371/24263/A4750*. On this trip Churchill was definitely anxious to see Donovan, two notes prior to mid-December 1940, and a note of a Donovan–Churchill luncheon after his arrival, *FO 371/24263/4925* and *FO 371/24263/5194*.

62. Lord Lothian to F.O., 1, 4, and 5 December 1940, *FO 371/24263/4925*; State Department to Lisbon, 30 November 1940, 740.00118 EW 1939/20A, *Diplomatic Branch*.

63. 2 December 1940, Vol. 32, Roll 6, *Stimson Diary*; Hyde, pp. 43–45; Discussion of Donovan by F.O. officials, 28 November 1940, *FO 371/24251/A4965*; British reception and Donovan talk with F.O. officials, 18/19 December 1940, *FO 371/24263/5194*.

64. Donald McLachlan, *Room 39*, p. 348; *Hinsley*, I, p. 238.

65. Diary, 10 December 1940, Dalton to Sir Campbell Stuart 16 August 1940, note on John MacCaffrey 30 November 1940, Dalton talk with Sikorski 23 December 1940, 18/1, and II 7/3, *Dalton Papers*; Lord Gladwyn, *Memoirs*, p. 107.

66. 3 December 1940, Diary, *Dalton Papers*; 21 August 1940 mtg., COS (40), *CAB 80*.

67. Diary, 20 December 1940, *Dalton Papers*; 14 January 1941, *Cadogan*; Discussion of SOE operations, March–December 1941, *WO 193/603*; *Sweet-Escott*, p. 61.

68. *Hinsley*, I, p. 154.

69. *Hinsley*, I, pp. 259–260 and 347–360; J. R. M., *Grand Strategy* (London: 1957), II, p. 459; *Barker*, pp. 86–93; Jozef Garlinski, *Poland, SOE and the Allies* (London: 1969), p. 47.

70. On secret information for Donovan, see Secretary of State for Air to Lord Halifax, 7 December 1940 and Duff Cooper's 10 December comment, *FO 371/24263/5059*; 18 January 1941 F.O. note on Hull's "touchy" attitude, *FO 371/26194/A183*; Chargé in France to State, 9 December 1940, *FRUS 1940*, II, p. 417.

71. Six Donovan to Knox messages ranging from 17 January to 14 March 1941, as well as six more messages from U.S. Balkan and Middle East missions ranging from 23 January to 21 February 1941, all concerned with Donovan's trip, are in 740.0011 EW 1939, *Diplomatic Branch*.

72. British Embassy in Athens to Sofia and F.O. comments, 18 January 1941, *FO 371/26194/A183*; John O. Iatrides, ed., *Ambassador MacVeagh Reports: Greece 1933-1947* (Princeton, New Jersey: 1980), p. 484; American legation in Baghdad to Near East Division, 21 February 1941, 740.00118 EW 1939/230, *Diplomatic Branch*.

73. MacVeagh to Department of State, 3 February 1941, 740.00118 EW 1939/153 and Donovan to Knox, 20 February 1941, 740.0011EW 1939/8560. Regarding Donovan and Iberia, the most important British sources are in *PREM 4/25/5* and F.O. discussion, 27 February 1941, *FO 371/26924/C2118*. On British sensitivity regarding Spain, 2 March 1941, Diary, *Dalton Papers*. The most important American sources on Donovan and Iberia in 1941 are in Ambassador in Spain to State, 28 February 1941, *FRUS 1941*, II, pp. 881–883; and Donovan to Knox, 11 March 1941, 740.0011 EW 1939/8950, *Diplomatic Branch*. See also Sir Samuel Hoare, *Ambassador on Special Mission* (London: 1946), p. 110.

74. War Cabinet discussion on Greece, 24 February 1941, *CAB 65/21* W.M. (41) 20th Confidential Annex; Donovan to Knox, 20 February 1941, 740.0011EW 1939/8560, *Diplomatic Branch* (For his retention of this view see Donovan to Maddocks, 3 February 1943, ABC 381, Mediterranean Area, [12–3–42], Sec. 1, *RG 165*); Ambassador Lane to State, 28

January 1941, 740.00118 EW 1939/79, *Diplomatic Branch*; American Mission in Bucharest to State, 29 January 1941, 740.00118 EW 1939/95½, *Diplomatic Branch*.

75. Ambassador Earle to State, 740.00118 EW 1939/183, *Diplomatic Branch*.

76. Ambassador MacVeagh to State, 3 February 1941, 740.00118 EW 1939/153, *Diplomatic Branch*; Ambassador Hoare to F.O., 27 February 1941, *PREM 4/25/5*; *Hyde*, p. 45; Ambassador Lane to State, 1 February 1941, 740.00118 EW 1939/152, *Diplomatic Branch*; David A. Stafford, *Britain and the European Resistance*, pp. 53–54; David A. Stafford, "SOE and British Involvement in the Belgrade Coup d' État of March 1941," *Slavic Review* 36, no. 3 (September 1977), 339–419; *Barker*, pp. 91–95; Ilija Jukić *The Fall of Yugoslavia* (New York: 1974), pp. 59–62; Mark C. Wheeler, *Britain and the War for Yugoslavia 1940–1943* (Boulder, Colorado: 1980), Chapters 1 and 2.

77. War Cabinet minutes, 24 February 1941, W.M. (41) 20th Confidential Annex, *CAB 65/21*; Ilija Jukić, *The Fall of Yugoslavia*, p. 57.

78. Churchill's interest in Donovan and British officials' desire to be gracious and appreciative to him show up repeatedly in the February–March 1941 material in *PREM 4/125/5*. See also Piers Dixon, *Double Diploma* (London: 1968), p. 62; and Ambassador MacMurray to State, 27 February 1941, *FRUS 1941*, Vol. 3, p. 826. Eden even poured out his gratitude regarding Donovan to Harry Hopkins, who was visiting Britain, Hopkins to State, 7 and 8 February 1941, 740.0011EW 1939/8145 2/5 and 3/5, *Diplomatic Branch*. Maj. Gen. Sir John Kennedy, *The Business of War* (London: 1957), pp. 87–88; Churchill to Roosevelt, 10 March 1941, *Loewenheim*, p. 133.

79. F.O. comments, January 1941, *FO 371/29722/R600* and March 1941 *PREM 4/25/5*. 11 March 1941, Diary, *Dalton Papers*.

80. Donovan to Knox, 11 March 1941, 740.0011EW 1939/8944, *Diplomatic Branch*.

Chapter 2

1. Donovan Correspondence File, Box 5, Archibald MacLeish Papers, Library of Congress; 16 and 20 March 1941, Vols. 32 and 33, Roll 6, *Stimson Diary*.

2. Dulles speech, World War II File, Box 17, *Dulles*; Mark Lincoln Chadwin, *The Hawks of World War II*, passim; Fight for Freedom Collection, Hoover Institution; Correspondence May 1941 File, Box 1, *Hayden*.

3. 13 March 1941 memorandum by Mr. Mack, *FO 371/28378/Z1924*. In spring 1941, Donovan warned Hopkins of the German threat to North Africa. See Robert E. Sherwood, *Roosevelt and Hopkins* (New York: 1948), p. 283.

4. *Hinsley*, I, pp. 312–314.

5. 12/13 February, 15 and 17 April 1941, Vol. 33, Roll 6, *Stimson Diary*.

6. *Harold Smith*, Box 13.

7. Personal Data File, David W. King Papers, Hoover Institution; Murphy to State, 14 January 1941, 740.0011EW 1939/7444, *Diplomatic Branch*; Robert Murphy, *Diplomat Among Warriors*, pp. 66–90.

8. On the background of the Solborg mission, 11 and 23 January 1941, Childs and Miles memos, 740.00118 EW 1949/82 and 319, *Diplomatic Branch*. Six Solborg reports in March (8, 13, 18, 20, 28) as well as one of 5 May are in the files. They apparently have been overlooked by scholars because they are unsigned and keyed with the heading "referring to the Department's 29 January telegram," which was the notification to diplomatic missions of Solborg's trip. 740.0011EW 1939, *Diplomatic Branch*.

9. The de Gaulle reference is in a 3 February 1941 French statement, *FO 892/66* Public Record Office, London. The McCloy–Stimson exchange, 17 and 21 May 1941, Roll 103, Stimson Papers, Yale University. For the whole question, see Arthur Layton Funk's excellent volume, *The Politics of Torch* (Lawrence, Kansas: 1974).

10. Solborg reports were urgently requested by Washington 7 May 1941, and then he was ordered to return to Washington 25 July 1941, 740.00118 EW 1939/259 and 426, *Diplomatic Branch*; Murphy to State, 1 September 1941 informs Washington of the German protest, 740.00118EW 1939/575, *Diplomatic Branch*. David Kahn seems to be right when

Notes

he says it was the deciphering of the State Department code used by Murphy in mid-August (not the State Department codes used by Solberg when he was in North Africa) that tipped off the Germans; David Kahn, *The Codebreakers* (New York: 1967), p. 498.

11. 21 and 28 March 1941 and 26 May 1941, Diary, and 28 March 1941 Ismay to Dalton, and 24 June 1941 general report on S.O.E. in Yugoslavia, *Dalton Papers*; Wavell to Dalton, 16 June 1941, *FO 898/113*.

12. 17 May 1941, Diary, and 27 March 1941, S.O.E. roster, *Dalton Papers*; R.A.F. report, 7–8 June 1941, AIR 14/835, Public Record Office, London; M. R. D. Foot, *SOE in France* (London: 1966), Chapter 7; S.O.E. plan, 9 April and 18 June 1941, *WO 193/623*, Public Record Office, London.

13. *Hinsley*, I, pp. 312–314; Donald McLachlan, *Room 39*, pp. 230–231 (since Admiral Godfrey apparently believed James Forrestal was then secretary of the navy, anything is possible); *Hyde*, p. 152–153; "History of the Military Intelligence Division" Chapter 31, p. 22 (Microfilm Copy, Hoover Institution).

14. *Wilkinson*, 21 July 1943; *Harold Smith*, 11 April 1941, Box 13.

15. Berle Statement, 10 February 1941, Carter File, Box 57, Berle Papers, Franklin D. Roosevelt Library; Henry Field Papers, especially Box 44, Franklin D. Roosevelt Library; Boxes 122–139, *PSF* (the quoted Carter statement is from March–October 1941 File, Box 122); 1 March 1971, Mrs. Kempner to R. Harris Smith, Europe File, Box 21, R. Harris Smith Papers, Hoover Institution.

16. 10 June 1941 Donovan memorandum, C.O.I. Folder, 1941, Box 141, *PSF*. Some published versions, including that of Donald McLachlan, *Room 39*, omit whole paragraphs of the memorandum).

17. 20 June 1941, Morgenthau–Donovan phone conversation, 411: 67–69, *Morgenthau*; Donovan memorandum, C.O.I. Folder 1941, Box 141, *PSF*.

18. 411: 67–69, *Morgenthau*.

19. 20, 22, 24 June 1941, Vol. 34, Roll 6, *Stimson Diary*.

20. 24 and 25 June 1941, Vol. 34, Roll 6, *Stimson Diary*; Secretary Knox to the president and reply, 25 June and 14 July 1941, O.S.S. File, *OF 4485*; Foreign Office comments, 25 June 1941, *FO 371/26231*.

21. 25 and 30 June and 1 and 2 July 1941, Vol. 34, Roll 6, *Stimson Diary*.

22. Joe Alex Morris, *Nelson Rockefeller. A Biography* (New York: 1960), pp. 164–167; 3 July press release and comments, O.S.S. File, *OF 4485*.

23. 10 July 1941, Box 13, *Harold Smith*.

24. C.O.I. Budget Records, O.S.S. File, *OF 4485*.

25. The R. and A. E. T. O. War Diary shows that as late as December 1941 only three C.O.I. people were in London and they were part of F.I.S. (Reference collection, no RG number, Modern Military Branch, National Archives). Admiral Leahy was at least a year off when he wrote of C.O.I. agents in Vichy in the early spring of 1941, William D. Leahy, *I Was There* (New York: 1950) p. 71. Board of Analysts report on Justice Department activities, 23 September 1941, Box 1, Entry 58, *RG 226*.

26. *Taylor*, p. 309–312.

27. Carter memo, 30 July 1941, March–October File, Box 122, *PSF*; Board of Analysts statement, 17 October 1941, Box 1, Entry 58, *RG 226*; Berle to Welles, 25 July 1941, 103.918/7–2541, *Diplomatic Branch*.

28. 9 and 15 October 1941, Conference with the President File, Box 13 and 23 October 1941, White House Memoranda File, Box 17, *Harold Smith*.

29. Board of Analysts meeting, 22 September 1941, Box 1, Entry 58, *RG 226*; 15 and 20 October 1941 Memoranda, O.S.S. File, *OF 4485*.

30. 20 October 1941, Sherwood to Donovan, O.S.S. File, *OF 4485*.

31. Whitney to Sherwood Poynter, 25 November 1941, 103.918/3A, *Diplomatic Branch*; C.O.I. Budget Papers, 5 November 1941, O.S.S. File, *OF 4485*.

32. *Langer*, p. 182.

33. Baxter report on R. and A., 20 October 1941, C.O.I. File, Box 141, *PSF*; 19 September list of Board of Analyst members and functions, Box 1, Entry 58, *RG 226*. Immediate post–Pearl Harbor summary of C.O.I., File 41–10, Box 41, *Hayden*.

34. *Langer*, pp. 181–182. For the process of Board of Analyst recruitment, correspondence 1941 undated file and July–December 1941 File, Box 8, *Hayden*. For contacts and

linkups, see especially *Hayden*, C.O.I. 1941 File, Box 44; Henry Field Papers, Franklin D. Roosevelt Library; and Carter papers, Box 122, *PSF*. Hayden's contacts extended as far as General MacArthur and Justice Murphy; Carter provided Donovan's group with a number of business and overseas connections; and Field had contacts with many individuals of interest, including Kim Philby's father, 1 April 1941, Navy Department File, Box 44, Field Papers. The references to Board of Analysts trouble with Treasury reports and successes with the State Department are 16 September and 5 November 1941, Box 1, Entry 58, *RG 226*.

35. 23 October 1941, Directory of Special Information Personnel, July–December 1941 Correspondence File, Box 8, *Hayden*.

36. Meetings of the Board of Analysts, 11 September, 3, 21, and 25 November 1941, Box 1, Entry 58, *RG 226;* 20 October 1941 Baxter report, C.O.I. File, Box 141, *PSF*.

37. Board of Analysts meeting, 13 March 1942, Box 1, Entry 58, *RG 226*.

38. *Langer*, pp. 181–189.

39. On the tone of the Board of Analysts, see the minutes of the meetings, September–November 1941, especially 11 September and 21 November, Box 1, Entry 58, *RG 226*. The process for making the disastrous choice of Dr. Gayle as representative for China may be followed in: 27 October 1941 memo, File 14, Box 41, *Hayden;* 10 October 1941, Box 1, Entry 58 and Chunking File, Box 1, Entry 3, *RG 226*. The origins of F.N.B. were surveyed in the unpublished paper kindly lent by James Miller, "Italian American Politics and the Future of Italy: Reports of the FNB, OSS, 1943." See also 16 and 17 September Board of Analysts meetings, Box 1, Entry 58, *RG 226*.

40. 12 September, 25 November and 3 December 1941 reports, Mowrer File, Box 17, *Dulles;* 11 September and 21 November Board of Analysts minutes, Box 1, Entry 58, *RG 226*. Mowrer's later account does not accurately portray the contents of the reports, Edgar A. Mowrer, *Triumph and Turmoil*, p. 327.

41. September–October 1941 Board of Analysts minutes, especially 19 September and 23/24 October 1941 plus 13 March 1942, Box, 1, Entry 58, *RG 226*. After the first report was read aloud to Donovan, he took John Morrison and Geroid Robinson along to explain it to Henry Stimson, 23 October 1941, Vol. 35, Roll 7, *Stimson Diary*.

42. *Langer*, pp. 84–89; Interview with Henry Cord Meyer (on M.I.S. and O.N.I. connections). See above, p. 121 on later R. and A. difficulty in finding a useful place.

43. Diary, 23–24 June, 1 August, 12 and 16 September, 1941, *Dalton Papers*.

44. Diary, 6 and 8 August, 1941, *Dalton Papers;* Notes on no. 16 G (R) mission, 9 August 1941, *WO 193*/623; George A. Hill, "Reminiscences of Four Years with N.K.V.D." (Manuscript, Hoover Institution).

45. The major material on the S.O.E. Cairo crisis may be found in *FO 898*/113 and 114, May–July 1941, *FO 954*/24 pt. 1, and *Sweet-Escott*, pp. 73–76. On Turkey and Spain, 1 August and 1 September 1941 reports (Knatchbull Hugessen and Hoare) *FO 954*/24 pt. 1; 7 September 1941, C. in C. Middle East to War Office, *WO 193*/623; 30 March 1942, Annex COS (42) 100, *CAB 79*/19; 5 December 1941 S.O.E. plans for Spain, DO (41), *CAB 69*/3.

46. *Hinsley*, I, pp. 312–314; Hugh Dalton, *The Fateful Years*, II, pp. 379–382; Diary, July–August 1941, *Dalton Papers;* Dalton to Bracken, 15 November 1941, *FO 954*/24A. General Spears described Bracken as "large, bespectacled, with shrewd slit eyes in ambush behind thick lenses." *Spears*, II, p. 152.

47. On S.O.E. maturity see 16 November 1941 memorandum, *FO 954*/24 pt. 1; December 1941 summary; *WO 193*/620; 31 August, COS (41) 536, *CAB 80*/30; November/December memoranda and 3 November 1941 "strictly confidential" paper, 18/2 *Dalton Papers;* and 15 August 1941, COS (41) 288th mtg., *CAB 79*/13. On the Iraqi tribe subsidies, 20 November 1941, War Office mtg., *WO 193*/620. Even though the organization was mature, Dalton was not tamed. On 19 July 1941, he referred in his diary to an S.O.E. man in Cairo "as a poisonous little blighter who is working against us out there." *Dalton Papers*.

48. Robert Paxton, *Vichy France. Old Guard and New Order*, Chapter 1; Hugh Dalton, *The Fateful Years*, II, pp. 372–377; Jozef Garlinski, *Poland, SOE and the Allies*, pp. 28–62; M. R. D. Foot, *SOE in France*, Chapter 7. S.O.E. had trained ninety-seven Free French parachutists by July 1941, *WO 193*/623. An interesting summary of early Free French activity is in a 3 June 1960 talk between Whitney Shepardson and André de Wavrin (Passy), Miscellaneous Correspondence File, Box 3, Shepardson Papers, Franklin D. Roosevelt

Notes

Library. As an example of poor exile government intelligence, note that Beneš told Dalton on 17 October 1941 that Hitler had merely become a "pawn" of the generals, Diary, *Dalton Papers.*

49. 9 August 1941, JP (41) 649. *CAB 79*/13; The COS 288 minutes of August 1941 are still closed, but part of the text is in a joint planners paper appended to COS (42) 141, 6 May 1942, *CAB 79*/20.

50. Diary, 25 August 1941, *Dalton Papers.*

51. Standard works on Yugoslavian issues are, in addition to *Barker* and Mark C. Wheeler, *Britain and the War for Yugoslavia,* cited above; Matteo J. Milazzo, *The Chetnik Movement and the Yugoslav Resistance* (Baltimore: 1975); Walter Roberts, *Tito, Mihailović and the Allies 1941–1945* (New Brunswick, New Jersey: 1973); Jozo Tomasevich, *The Chetniks* (Stanford, California: 1975).

52. Diary, 1/2 and 4 November, 1941, *Dalton Papers;* 31 October 1941 Foreign Office memorandum, DO (41) 24, *CAB 69*/3; notes by Colonel Sugden, 16 October 1941, *WO 193*/623.

53. Walter Roberts, *Tito, Mihailović and the Allies 1941–1945,* p. 44; George A. Hill, "Reminiscences, etc.," Hoover Institution.

54. *Hyde,* pp. 106–115 and 163–167; Ewen Montagu, *Beyond Top Secret Ultra* (New York: 1978), pp. 72–84; G. Jebb memorandum "Activities of S.O.E.," 16 November 1941, *FO 954*/24 pt. 1. On S.O.E. expansion in the United States, see July 1941 papers, *FO 898*/103.

55. 29 October 1941 plan, *FO 954*/24 pt. 1; July report on layout of S.O. 1 New York and 10 July 1941 memo, *FO 898*/103.

56. July 1941 report on S.O. 1 New York, memorandum of 12 September 1941, plus examples of instructions from London to S.O. 1 addressed to "Sherwood," 9 October and 14 November 1941 *FO 898*/103. Henry Field, who did liaison with WRUL, was serving in this role even before C.O.I. was created, White House File, Box 44 and unheaded File, Box 45, Henry Field Papers, Franklin D. Roosevelt Library. See also *Hyde,* pp. 157–167.

57. July 1941 report on S.O. 1 New York and 10 July 1941 report, *FO 898*/103. The comeback file is *FO 898*/71.

58. The shark rumor is filed under 26 September 1941 in this huge sib file, along with another marvelously farfetched one (15 August) about an Austrian anti-Nazi skier, *FO 898*/69.

59. Sibs dated 15 August and 5 and 26 September, 14 November, 5 December 1941, *FO 898*/69. The comeback note is in *FO 898*/71.

60. 5 September 1941 sib, approved by the J.I.C., 10 September 1941, *FO 898*/69.

61. Diary, 2 August 1941, *Dalton Papers;* October 1941 request for information on radio jamming, *FO 898*/113; 10 November 1941, P.W.E.–S.O.E. mtg. on U.S. requests, *FO 898*/27; 13 November, 1941 Donovan requests via the M.O.I. *FO 954*/24 pt. 1. This helped set off another raging battle between Dalton and Bracken, see especially 26 October and 15 November 1941, *FO 954*/24 pt. 1. The C.I.A. historian passes over all this activity in silence, *Troy,* Chapter 5.

62. Diary, 2 and 4 July, 25 August, 6 and 26 November 1941, *Dalton Papers;* 13 November, Bracken to Eden, *FO 954*/24 pt. 1. President Roosevelt to Winston Churchill, 24 October 1941, O.S.S. File, *OF* 4485.

63. *Hinsley,* I, pp. 312–314; *Hyde,* p. 167; B.S.C. statement, 26 April 1944, Box 1, Forgan Papers, Hoover Institution; Donovan to F.D.R., 6 August, 21 October, 24 November, 1941. C.O.I. File, Box 141, *PSF.*

64. Donovan to F.D.R., 7, 12, and 17 November and undated November–December, 1941, C.O.I. File, Box 141, *PSF.*

65. *Hinsley,* I, pp. 312–314; Donovan to F.D.R., 13 November 1941, C.O.I. File, Box 141, and 1 January 1942, Azors Report File, Box 167, *PSF;* 3 December 1941, Donovan to F.D.R., O.S.S. File, *OF* 4485; John Foster Dulles comment, 16 September 1941, Box 20, Roll 6, John Foster Dulles Papers, Princeton; 1 November 1941 Halifax to Secretary of State, *FO 954*/24 pt. 1; 31 October 1941 Halifax memo., *FO 954*/24A.

66. 17 November 1941, Donovan to F.D.R., C.O.I. File, Box 141, *PSF* shows that some of the schemes came from the president rather than Donovan.

67. 24 November 1941 James Roosevelt to F.D.R., C.O.I. File, Box 141, *PSF;* 12 and 18 November 1941, Vol. 36, Roll 7, *Stimson Diary.* In some cases, after Stimson checked, the

president approved Donovan's projects: 24 October 1941, O.S.S. File, *OF* 4485. The president to Frederic Delano, 1 September 1941, E. Roosevelt, ed., *F.D.R., His Personal Letters 1928-1945*, IV, p. 1203.

68. *Lee*, pp. 334, 336, and 438.

69. Henry Field Papers, Box 44, Franklin D. Roosevelt Library; 20 August 1941 Carter memo, March–October File and 11 November 1941 memo, November–December File, Box 122, *PSF*. See also *Hyde*, pp. 73–93.

70. *Lee*, p. 402; Spruille Braden, *Diplomats and Demagogues* (New Rochelle, New York: 1971), pp. 245–246.

71. Vol. 35, Roll 7, *Stimson Diary;* October 1941 report on 207 Military Mission (the Canadian S.O.E. school), *WO 193*/631. On the China guerrilla scheme, Hornbeck to Hull, 13 November and 12 December 1941, Donovan File, Box 150, Stanley Hornbeck Papers, Hoover Institution. For Colonel Goodfellow and his appointment, Biographical Material, Box 2 and Donovan order of 9 October 1941, O.S.S. Memoranda 1941–March 1942 File, Box 4, *Goodfellow; War Report*. pp. 80–84.

72. *War Report*, pp. 70–73; *Troy*, pp. 104–111.

73. *Ibid*. Donovan memorandum, 10 October 1941, C.O.I. File, Box 141, *PSF;* Donovan to W. Phillips, late 1941, O.S.S. Memoranda 1941–March 1942 File, Box 4, *Goodfellow*.

74. Carleton Coon, *A North African Story* (Ipswich, Massachusetts: 1980), pp. 5–7; Donovan memo, 10 October 1941, C.O.I. File, Box 141; *PSF;* Halifax to Foreign Office, 31 October 1941, *FO 954*/24A.

Chapter 3

1. Allen Dulles speech to the Cosmos Club, 3 April 1967, Speech File, Box 162, *Dulles,* Donovan to F.D.R., 6 January 1942, 22 December–15 January File, Box 163, and 20 January 1942, 15–24 January File, Box 164, *PSF*, Diary, 1 February 1942, *Dalton Papers*.

2. 16 January 1942, Box 13, *Harold Smith;* 13 December 1941, Carter budget discussion, Carter File, Box 57, Berle Papers, Franklin D. Roosevelt Library; Donovan to F.D.R., 18 December, 18–21 December File, Box 163, and 31 December, 1941, January–February File, Box 164, *PSF:* 9 January 1942, Warburg to McCloy, Stimson Papers, Roll 105, Yale University; 12 January 1942, Vol. 37, Roll 7, *Stimson Diary*.

3. 5 March 1942, Board of Analysts, Entry 58, Box 1, *RG 226*.

4. F.N.B. establishment, 16 January 1942, Conference with the President File, Box 13, *Harold Smith;* 20 December 1941, F.D.R. initial approval, 18–21 December File, Box 163, *PSF;* Donovan to F.D.R., 15 January 1942, 22 December–15 January File, Box 163, and 20 January 1942, 15–24 January File, Box 164, *PSF*. On the Communist Party, Donovan to F.D.R., 22 April 1942, 13–28 April file, Box 165, *PSF*.

5. 15 March 1942 Bern dispatch with F.D.R. note, CCS 000.51, Sabotage (3–21–42), *RG 218;* Donovan to F.D.R., 7 April 1942, 26 March–13 April File, Box 165, *PSF; RG 218*, 10 April 1942 entry, Fred L. Israel, ed., *The War Diary of Breckenridge Long* (Lincoln, Nebraska: 1966), p. 257; Donovan to F.D.R., 14 February 1942, 16–28 February File, Box 164, *PSF*.

6. 31 December 1941, Ickes to Donovan, July–December File, Box 8, *Hayden;* Donovan to F.D.R., 13–17 December 1941, 13–17 December File, Box 163, *PSF*. Donovan also worked to improve Hawaiian radio communication, 14 May 1942, Donovan to Marshall, Secretary Knox Papers, Entry 23, File 89–1–24, *RG 80*, Navy and Old Army Branch, National Archives.

7. Donovan to F.D.R., 12 February 1942, 16–28 February File, Box 164, 14 April 1942, 13–28 April File, Box 165, 8 June 1942, 8–13 June File, Box 166, *PSF*. Hayden to Aiton, Arthur Scott Aiton Papers, Correspondence File, Box 1, Bentley Library, University of Michigan.

8. Donovan to F.D.R., 15 December 1941, 13–17 December File, Box 163, *PSF*, and 17 February 1942, 16–28 February File, Box 164, *PSF*.

9. The reports of Curtis Munson are contained in the files from October 1941 to Febru-

ary 1942 (the quotation is in the January–February 1942 File). As early as 22 October 1941, Munson reported from the West Coast, "the Japs here are in more danger from us than we from them." Box 122, *PSF.*

10. 3 April 1942, fifth mtg. of the J.P.W.C., CCS 334 (3–18–42), *RG 218.*

11. Donovan to F.D.R., 16 December 1941, 13–17 December File, Box 163, 24 January 1942, C.O.I. File, Box 141, 18 February 1942, 16–28 February File, Box 164, *PSF;* Donovan to F.D.R., 14 December 1941, *The Conference at Washington 1941-1942, FRUS,* p. 11; Vol. 37, Roll 7, *Stimson Diary.*

12. Donovan to F.D.R., 20 December 1941, 18–21 December File, 24 December 1941 and 3 and 13 January 1942, 22 December–15 January File, Box 163, *PSF;* 26 January and 4 February 1942, 26 January–11 February File, Box 164, *PSF;* 14 March 1942, 28 February–26 March File, Box 165, *PSF;* 27 May 1942, 18–28 May File, Box 166, *PSF,* Errol Flynn to W. Deuel, 25 March 1942, Correspondence File, Box 1, Wallace Deuel Papers, Library of Congress. Obviously, this is not the point advanced by Charles Higham, *Errol Flynn* (New York: 1980.)

13. Donovan to F.D.R., 26 March 1942, 28 February–26 March File, 6 April 1942, 26 March–13 April File, 21 April 1942, 13–28 April File, Box 165, *PSF;* 31 March 1942, Welles (presumably) to F.D.R., C.O.I. File, Box 141, *PSF.*

14. 11 January 1942, Carter memo, June–July File, Box 122, *PSF;* The president routinely sent Donovan's and Carter's suggestions on to the respective regular government offices.

15. Donovan to F.D.R., 2 April 1942, 26 March–13 April File and 14 April 1942, 13–28 April File, both Box 165, *PSF;* 18 January 1944 conversation, Daily Reports of Major Activities File, Box 400, *Stettinius.* E. Roosevelt, ed., *F.D.R.: His Personal Letters* IV (to Donovan), p. 1258. On 4 May 1942, the president complained about "very rich or very influential individuals ... constantly ... injecting themselves into foreign policy matters." COI 1942 File, Box 141, *PSF.*

16. Beatrice B. Berle and Travis B. Jacobs, *Navigating the Rapids 1918-1971* (New York: 1973), p. 412; F.D.R. to Donovan, 9 February 1942, Confidential File, Box 12, and Donovan to F.D.R., 28 February 1942, 28 February–26 March File, Box 165, *PSF;* David Bruce letter to the *New York Times,* 9 February 1959. In fairness to Roosevelt, it must be conceded that Carter's secret report claiming that "Stalin's Strategy Board" consisted of six foreigners (including one German) and *no* Russians, runs a close second to the "bat project." 6 January 1942, January–February File, Box 122, *PSF.*

17. Donovan to F.D.R., 21 January, 15–24 January File, Box 164, 8 April 1942, 26 March–13 April File, Box 165, and Langer to F.D.R., 10 March 1942, filed in 13–17 December File, Box 163. *PSF.*

18. Donovan to F.D.R., 17 December 1941, 13–17 December File, Box 163, January 1942, 26 February–11 February File, Box 164, 15 April 1942, 13–28 April File, Box 165, *PSF.*

19. This material may be found in Boxes 164–165, *PSF,* provided at regular weekly or fortnightly intervals, though from Dalton's diary it appears that Stephenson and Donovan were not then as close as they had been (December 1941, *Dalton Papers*). The American Embassy in London was receiving much of the same material direct from British agencies, note by H. Freeman Matthews, 103.918/300–349, *Diplomatic Branch.*

20. Donovan to F.D.R., 15 and 17 December 1941, 13–17 December File, 24 December 1941, 22 December–15 January File, Box 163, and 22 January 1942, 15–24 January File, Box 164, *PSF.*

21. Donovan to F.D.R., undated, 18–21 December File, 7 and 15 January, 22 December–15 January File, Box 163, and 12 February 1942 (plus others), 16–28 February File, Box 164, *PSF.*

22. Donovan to F.D.R., 24 January 1942, 15–24 January File, 27 February 1942, 16–28 February File, Box 164, 8 April 1942, 26 March–13 April File, Box 165, 9 May 1942, 1–18 May File, and 18 and 26 May 1942, 18–26 May File, Box 166, *PSF.*

23. Donovan to F.D.R., 19 and 21 January 1942, 15–24 January File, Box 164, *PSF.* A later variant, focusing on a possible invasion of Britain, was also dropped in May. JPS 7/15, ABC 385 (3–4–42), *RG 165.* Donovan to F.D.R., 30 December 1941, 22 December–15 January File, Box 163, 19 February, 1942, 16–28 February File, Box 164, 7 March 1942, 28 February–26 March File, Box 165, *PSF.*

24. Donovan to F.D.R., 19 December 1941, 18–21 December File, Box 163, *PSF.*

25. Childs to F. O., 5 February 1942, *FO 371/30688/2487*; Carter to F.D.R., 19 January 1942, January File, Box 122, *PSF;* 20 April 1942 to all missions, 103.918/100–149 folder, *Diplomatic Branch;* 31 August 1942, Hibbard to Department, 103.91802/796½, *Diplomatic Branch;* 20 December 1941, Fred L. Israel, ed., *The War Diary of Breckenridge Long*, p. 234.

26. On Donovan's radio plan, 11 December 1941, C.O.I. File, Box 141, *PSF;* and Donovan–Knox–Mrs. Roosevelt correspondence, Entry 23, Frank Knox Papers, RG 80, Navy and Old Army Branch, National Archives. On the I.D.C.: 22 December 1941 entry, I.D.C. File, Box 8, Entry 1, *RG 226;* 14 January 1942, 485: 464–466, *Morgenthau;* Meeting Minutes, 4 March 1942, I.D.C. Papers, Hoover Institution. On censorship: Donovan to F.D.R., 25 December 1941, 22 December–15 January File, Box 163, *PSF;* and 26 May 1942 entry, Box 1, Entry 58, *RG 226.* For B.E.W.: 2 February 1942, 26 Janaury–11 February File, Box 164. *PSF.*

27. 22–23 January 1942 exchange on censorship, 15–24 January File, Box 164, *PSF.* 13 January 1942, Vol. 37 and 20 May 1942, Vol. 39, Roll 7, *Stimson Diary.* For C.O.I.'s continuing reputation as a center for oddities, see Adlai Stevenson to Donovan (and Langer's ponderous reply), 23 February 1942, O.S.S. memoranda, 1941–March 1942 File, Box 4, *Goodfellow.*

28. Diary, 6 and 22 February 1942, *Dalton Papers;* 31 March, 1 and 7 April, *Cadogan;* 23 February 1942, Eden to Churchill (2), *FO 954/24A;* Ewen Montagu, *Beyond Top Secret Ultra*, p. 94.

29. 3 March 1942, Selborne to Churchill, *FO 954/24A;* P.W.E.–S.O.E. meeting, 28 May 1942, *FO 898/26.*

30. F.O.–S.O.E. treaty, 3 March 1942, *FO 954/24A;* 19 and 20 March 1942, *Cadogan.*

31. 12 February, 21 March, 5 and 7 April, 1942, complaints to and from Eden, FO 954/24A. On military action, see material in 16 December 1941 COS (41) 423, *CAB 79/12;* 15 December 1941, DO (41) 72 *CAB 69/2;* 26 March 1942, JP (42) 321 attached to COS (42) 100, *CAB 79/87;* Ewen Montagu, *Beyond Top Secret Ultra*, p. 91. The spring and summer agreements followed a long series of probes and discussions, see especially 17 May 1942, *FO 898/28* and 5 June 1942, FO 898/26. Note that there is also a battle on which activities should be civilian and which military between S.O.E. and the War Office, just as there was between Donovan and the J.C.S., 2 February 1942, *WO 193/620.*

32. 22 April 1942, COS (42) 152, and 16 May, COS (42) 152. *CAB 79/87.*

33. George A. Hill, "Reminiscences of 4 Years with N.K.V.D.," Hoover Institution, pp. 84, 102, 129, 145, 160–165; *Sweet-Escott*, pp. 117–118; 29 December 1941, S.O.E.–P.W.E. minutes, *FO 898/27.*

34. 21 March 1942, COS (42) 180, *CAB 80/35;* 4 February 1942 rumor, *FO 898/71.*

35. On Belgium, 4 June 1942, *FO 954/24A.* On Yugoslavia, Dalton to Churchill, 14 December 1941, DO (41) 36, *CAB 69/3;* Churchill minutes, 10 April 1942, COS (42) 215, *CAB 80/36.*

36. H. J. Giskes, *London Calling North Pole* (London: 1953), pp. 68–122; Donovan to F.D.R., 21 October 1941, C.O.I. File, Box 141, *PSF;* Winston S. Churchill, *The Grand Alliance* (Boston: 1955), p. 656.

37. Donovan to F.D.R., 22 and 29 December 1941, 22 December–15 January File, *PSF;* Budget allotment, 10 January 1942, *OF 4485.* The basic paper on subversive warfare, which was prepared with little C.O.I. participation, was developed between early February and mid-March 1942, CCS 385 (2–8–42) part 1, Donovan Organization, *RG 218.*

38. Donovan to Stimson, 17 February 1942 and related materials, CCS 385 (2–13–42) Sec. 1, Recruiting of various nationalities for subversive warfare, *RG 218;* Donovan to F.D.R., 9 February 1942, 26 January–11 February File, Box 164, *PSF.* The 25 February authorization is cited in Donovan to Marshall, 27 March 1942, U.S. War Department File, Box 4, *Goodfellow.*

39. Donovan to F.D.R., 3 January 1942, 22 December–15 January File, Box 163, *PSF;* Solborg to Donovan, 19 January 1942, O.S.S. memoranda 1941–March 1942 File, Box 4, *Goodfellow.*

40. Donovan to F.D.R., 27 January 1942, 26 January–11 February File, Box 164, and 5 March 1942, 28 February–26 March File, Box 165, *PSF;* Donovan to Marshall 13 February and 4 March 1942, and Lee to Marshall, 10 March 1942, CCS 385 (2–13–42), Section 1, *RG 218.*

Notes

41. On British–Donovan ties in this period, Donovan to F.D.R. reports, 26 January–11 February File, Box 164, *PSF*; c. May 1942 P.W.E. report, *FO 898/104*; 24 March 1942, S.O.E. message, *FO 898/27*; 1 April 1942, Major Morton to David Scott, *FO 371/30688/3874*; Diary, 9 January 1942, *Dalton Papers*. But others also had close ties. Carter's unit was using Somerset Maugham's secretary as a source (10 June, 1942, June–July File, Box 122, *PSF*) and Henry Field, who was a cousin of Ronald Tree, was on a first-name basis with General Ismay. Henry Field Papers, 1942–43 Files, Box 45, Franklin D. Roosevelt Library. Although some State Department officials, especially in North Africa, had a low opinion of S.I.S. (see 19 January 1942, Childs to State, 740.00EW, 1939/20213, *Diplomatic Branch*, and 30 January 1942, Doolittle from Tangier, Algeria File, Box 2, *Goodfellow*), State received secret material directly from the British without going via Donovan (see 11 March 1942, 740.0011EW 1939/20340, *Diplomatic Branch*).

42. Diary, 10 February 1942, *Dalton Papers*, S.O.E.–P.W.E. mtg., 9 February 1942, *FO 898/27*.

43. The C.I.A. historian devotes a complete chapter to the bureaucratic battles over the C.O.I.–O.S.S. and though we reach rather different conclusions, much of the same documentary ground has been covered. Therefore, I will only cite documentary material not included in *Troy*, or materials on which we sharply disagree. On the F.B.I. controversy, see memos of 11 and 27 December 1941, November–December 1941 File (Carter), Box 122, *PSF*.

44. Donovan was nearly as eager to court the military as the president. See for example his expansive memo on outdoing the British on shadow warfare sent to the secretary of the J.C.S., Gen. Walter B. Smith (as well as to the president) 23 March 1942, CCS 385 (2–8–42), pt. 1, *RG 218*.

45. A report from the American Embassy in Mexico City, sent to the State Department on 31 March 1942, supports Donovan's statement that he was not dabbling in Latin American intelligence (103.918/3–3142 *Diplomatic Branch*) as does a Carter statement that suggests that some of the trouble lay in internal State Department confusion. 12 May 1942, March–May File, Box 122, *PSF*.

46. In light of the British connection, the emphasis on special service units in General Smith's work seems to be the key largely passed over by *Troy*. Donovan to Smith, 22 March and J.C.S. 7th mtg., 23 March 1942, CCS 385 (2–8–42) pt. 1, *RG 218*.

47. c. 2 March 1942 Donovan to F.D.R. on his special service combined operations plans, 28 February–26 March File, Box 165, *PSF*. Note Donovan showed some signs of pressure and warned the Board of Analysts about outside groups producing trouble within C.O.I. 10 March 1942, Box 1, Entry 58, *RG 226*.

48. The aid to Mihailović plan, 26 March 1942, Balkan Countries File, Box 2, *Goodfellow*; J.P.W.C. consideration, 26 March 1942, CCS 334 (3–18–42) J.P.W.C., *RG 218*; J.P.S. and J.C.S. consideration, 27, 28, and 30 March 1942, ABC 385 (Norway) (4–4–42), *RG 165*. Stimson's authorization, 25 March 1942, CCS 385 (2–13–42) pt. 1, *RG 218*.

49. There is an indication of military hope of securing some of the C.O.I. budget here, 18 May 1942, CCS 385 (2–8–42), pt. 1, *RG 218*.

50. Stimson was worried about the existence of an independent C.O.I.–O.S.S. intelligence organization, 26 May 1942, Vol. 39, Roll 7, *Stimson Diary*. A "demolition batallion" plan is in 11 May 1942, O.S.S. memoranda April–May 1942 File, Box 4, *Goodfellow*. For Donovan's and C.O.I.'s general connections with the British, see Donovan to F.D.R., 31 March and 1 April, 1942, 26 March–13 April File, 23 April 1942, 13–28 April File, Box 165, *PSF* (Though he admitted that some Norwegians were opposed to commandos because of German reprisals, 25 April 1942, 13–28 April File, Box 165, *PSF*); 16 April 1942, Billinghurst Correspondence File, Box 1 and 23 May 1942, January–May 1942 File, Box 3, *Goodfellow*. On the eastern Mediterranean and British–C.O.I. connections: Donovan to F.D.R., 13 April 1942, 13–28 April File, Box 165, 13 May 1942, 29 April–16 May File, 8 and 9 June 1942, 8–13 June File, Box 165, *PSF*; J.P.W.C. consideration, 16 and 30 April 1942, CCS 334 (3–18–42) *RG 218*; The McCloy plan before the J.P.S., 19 May 1942, ABC 385 (4–4–42), *RG 165*. May 1942, Bowes-Lyon to London, *FO 898/106*.

51. Eisenhower to Marshall, 2 April 1942, Bull to Marshall, 10 April 1942, J.P.S. memorandum 11 April 1942, McNarney to J.C.S., 19 April 1942, Horne to C. in C. U.S. Fleet, 29 April 1942, Smith to Donovan 6 May 1942, CCS 385 (2–13–42) Sec. 1, *RG 218*; McNarney

to Smith, 16 April 1942, *Eisenhower Papers*, I, pp. 253–254 (see the same volume, pp. 304–305, for a subversive warfare plan for Bolero that was rejected).

52. As early as 9 April 1942, Carter had recommended creating a Federal public relations organization with Elmer Davis in charge, March–May 1942 File, Box 122, *PSF*. c. 1 June 1942, Stimson to Donovan, ABC 334.3 OSS, sec. 1, (5-1-42), *RG 165*.

53. Childs to London, 5 February 1942, *FO 371/30688/2487*; *Sweet-Escott*, pp. 151–152; *Hoover*, pp. 196–197; 3 March 1942, Box 1, Entry 58, *RG 226*.

54. Board of Analysts mtgs., March–June 1942, especially 18 February, 6 and 10 March, 1, 17, and 22 April 1942, Box 1, Entry 58, *RG 226*; First Editorial Committee mtg., Editorial Committee File, Box 7, Entry 1, *RG 226*.

55. 8 January 1942, Box 1, Entry 58 and March 1942, Functional Directory of Personnel File, Box 10, Entry 1, RG 226; Summary of C.O.I., post–Pearl Harbor, File 41-10, Box 41, *Hayden*.

56. On Latin America, see especially Boxes 63 and 64, passim, *PSF*. 5 January 1942, Geography Division Report File, Box 3, Entry 1 and Administration E-1 File, Box 1, Entry 3, plus Board of Analysts mtgs., February–March 1942, especially 19 March, Box 1, Entry 58, *RG 226*. Donovan to F.D.R., 24 December 1941, 22 December–15 January File, Box 63, and 27, 30, 31 March 1942, C.O.I. File, Box 141, *PSF*.

57. 3 June 1942, Donovan to F.D.R., 29 May–8 June File, Box 166, *PSF*.

58. 9 December 1941 and 10 February 1942, Box 1, Entry 58, *RG 226*. For an example of time-consuming diversions by old-timers in R. and A., see Poole to Wiley, 9 December 1941 (on the War Council plan), File 41-4, Box 41, *Hayden*.

59. 5 March, 1942, Box 1, Entry 58, *RG 226*; 15 May 1942 entry, O.S.S. E.T.O. War Diary, Reference Collection, Modern Military Branch, National Archives; Interview with Henry Cord Meyer; C.O.I. and O.S.S. Files, Box 323, *Hornbeck*.

60. 17 December 1941, Sherwood to Hopkins, Container 213, Hopkins Papers, Franklin D. Roosevelt Library; Donovan to F. D. R., 13 April 1942, 13–28 April File, Box 165, *PSF*; 4 March 1942 Donovan memorandum quoted in *Troy*, pp. 123–124. The main flow of F.I.S. material may be seen in Boxes 163–165, *PSF* together with Box 1, Entry 3, *RG 226*. Ambassador Hayes, who would later be highly critical of Donovan, wanted propaganda help from C.O.I. in this period: Carlton J. Hayes, *Wartime Mission in Spain* (New York: 1946), pp. 74–75 and 27 May 1942, Hayes to Donovan, 103.918/219, *Diplomatic Branch*. See Kirk to State, 9 June 1942, for a typical F.I.S. plan for propaganda in the Middle East, 103.91802/506, *Diplomatic Branch*.

61. Statement by Gerald Mayer, 24 March 1947, Mayer File, Box 31, *Dulles*; 2 April 1942, Hopper to Donovan, Stockholm File, Box 1, Entry 3, *RG 226*; April–June reports, January–May 1942 and June 1942–1945 Files, Box 3, *Goodfellow*.

62. 27 May 1942 list of C.O.I. people abroad, Foreign Reps. Abroad File, Box 10, Entry 1, *RG 226*; Memoranda in January–May 1942 File, Box 3, and O.S.S. memoranda 1941–March 1942 File, Box 4, *Goodfellow*.

63. On the Philippines plan: Donovan to F.D.R., 19 and 21 February, 1942, 16–28 February File, Box 164, *PSF* and 21 February 1942, Vol. 37, Roll 7, *Stimson Diary*. On Yugoslavia: Donovan to F. D. R., 13 May 1942, 29 April–16 May File, Box 166, *PSF* and Walter Roberts, *Tito, Mihailović and the Allies*, p. 60.

64. See Administration File, Box 1, Entry 3, *RG 226*. For early overseas agent placement plans: Donovan to F. D. R., 27 May 1942, 18–28 May File, Box 166, *PSF*; Hayden to Aiton, January 1942, Correspondence 1940–42 File, Box 1, *Hayden*; 18 May 1942, Kirk message, Administration Extras File T–Z, Box 1, Entry 3, *RG 226*.

65. Early 1942, Administration Extras File, J–S, Box 1, Entry 3, *RG 226*; Abercrombie and Fitch to Tolstoy, 12 June 1942, June 1942–1945 File, Box 3, *Goodfellow*.

66. The VICTOR channel material coming to Washington was filed under the 103.918 State Department filing number, much of which I have now had declassified. See also 9 June 1942, Donovan order, Foreign Representatives File, Box 10, Entry 1, *RG 226* and 3 June 1942, State Department and C.O.I. liaison committee, CCS 385 (2-8-42), pt. 1, *RG 218*.

67. 1 and 4 February 1942, 491: 410 and 492: 26–28, *Morgenthau*; Donovan to F.D.R., 17 February 1942, 26 January–11 February File, Box 64, and 13 May 1942, 29 April–16 May File, Box 166, *PSF*. But Donovan saw the weakness of the British position in North

Africa and the Middle East, Donovan to F.D.R., 27 December 1941 and 3 January 1942, 22 December–15 January File, 8 February 1942, 26 January–11 February File, Box 163, *PSF.*

68. Donovan to F.D.R., 30 December 1941, 22 December–15 January File, Box 163, and 18 February 1942, 16–28 February File, Box 164, *PSF*; Hull to Moscow Embassy, 11 December 1941, 103.91802/22c, *Diplomatic Branch;* Timothy P. Mulligan, "According to Colonel Donovan," *The Historian* (scheduled for publication 1983).

69. Donovan to F. D. R., 21 December 1941, 18–21 December File, Box 163, 6 (2) and 12 March, 1942, 28 February–26 March File, Box 165, 30 May and 8 June 1942, 29 May–8 June File, Box 166, *PSF.* Yet Donovan was very dubious about the Free French in this period, Donovan to F. D. R., 23 December 1941, *Conferences at Washington 1941–1942. FRUS,* p. 404.

70. See Boxes 63–66, *PSF,* the 103.918 *Diplomatic Branch* series, and some scattered Donovan to Hull in February 1942 in the 740.0011EW 1939 series (*Diplomatic Branch*). The Bishop Galen sermons are filed under 6 January 1942, 22 December–15 January File, Box 163, and 19 February 1942, 16–28 February File, Box 164, *PSF.*

71. Boxes 163–165, *PSF; Hoover,* pp. 200–211, and 218–220.

72. Boxes 163–165, *PSF.* On MacArthur, 24 January 1942, 15–24 January File and 18 February 1942, 16–28 February File, Box 164, *PSF.*

73. Donovan to F. D. R., 10 and 11 February, 1942, 26 January–11 February File, Box 164, *PSF*; 3 March 1944 survey of Donovan's organization in India, *WO 208/792.* American–British relations in Asia are treated exhaustively and brilliantly in Chrisopher Thorne, *Allies of a Kind* (London: 1978).

74. 1942 report, Administrative extras J-O File, Box 1, Entry 3, *RG 226.*

75. Donovan's coolness on the Soviets in Asia, 20 December 1941, Donovan to F.D.R., 18–21 December File, Box 163, *PSF.* On Korean plans, see File 4 and 41–44, Box 41, *Hayden;* Hahn File, Box 1, *Goodfellow;* March and 7 April 1942, JPS 7/9, ABC 385, (3-4-42), *RG 165;* 23 March 1942, CCS 334 (3-18-42), and 24 March 1942, enclosure, CCS 385 (2-8-42), pt. 1, *RG 218.* 9 January 1942, Magruder to War, Donovan File, Box 150, *Hornbeck.*

76. 25 March 1942 memorandum on Kachin levies, Operations Journal 2, Frank N. Roberts Papers, Hoover; Gayle to Hayden, 13 December 1941, File 41–44, Box 41, *Hayden;* Donovan to F.D.R., 28 February 1942, 16–28 February File, Box 164, 20 April 1942, 13–28 April File, Box 165, *PSF.*

77. Donovan did send overly cheerful reports on China to F.D.R., see 6 March 1942, 28 February–26 March File, Box 165, *PSF.*

78. R. Harris Smith, *O.S.S.* (New York: 1972), pp. 242–244; Richard Dunlop, *Behind Japanese Lines* (Chicago: 1979), pp. 68–69; Gayle statement, 7 February 1942, File 41–44, Box 41, *Hayden;* 9 January 1942, Magruder to War, Donovan File, Box 150, *Hornbeck;* Donovan to F.D.R., 3 and 5 January 1942, 22 December–15 January File, Box 163, 24 January 1942, 15–24 January File, and 19 February 1942, 16–28 February File, Box 164, *PSF:* 24 February 1942, Eifler File, Box 1, 18 February 1942, U.S. War Department File, and 4 and 17 April 1942, O.S.S. memoranda April–May File, Box 4, *Goodfellow.*

79. 27 April 1942, Hornbeck to Hayden, C.O.I. File, Box 323, *Hornbeck;* 15 and 21 May 1942, State Department–Gauss exchange, 103.918/207, *Diplomatic Branch;* 28 March, 1942, Gauss to State, File 41–44, 20 April 1942, Mrs. Gayle to Hayden, and 6 May 1942, Gayle to Hayden, File 14, Box 41, *Hayden.*

80. R. Harris Smith, *O.S.S.,* pp. 244–246; 23 May 1942, O.S.S. memos April–May 1942 File, Box 4, *Goodfellow;* 9 April 1942, Vincent report, Chunking File, Box 1, Entry 3, *RG 226.*

81. Milton E. Miles, *A Different Kind of War* (Garden City, New York: 1967) passim; R. Harris Smith, *O.S.S.,* pp. 245–250; Miles appointment was arranged between 13 March and 8 April 1942, 740.00118EW 1939/1164 and 1247, *Diplomatic Branch.*

82. 23 October 1943, journal, *Wilkinson;* 18 May 1942, Donovan to Hull, 18–28 May File, Box 166, *PSF;* 29 May 1942, plan, C.O.I. File, Box 323, *Hornbeck;* 1 June 1942, JIC 23/1, CCS 350.05 (Japan) (6-5-42), and 6 June 1942, McNarney to Smith, CCS 385 (2-8-42) pt. 1, *RG 218;* 1 April 1942 plans, Chunking File, Box 1, Entry 3, *RG 226.*

83. Donovan to F.D.R., 21 December 1941, 18–21 December File, and 26 December 1941 and 5 February 1942, December–January File, Box 163, *PSF.*

84. Murphy reports of 2 and 10 December 1941 and 22 April 1942, are in 740.00118EW

1939/18428 and 17715 and 20863, also a long January report from I. D. Shapiro, 740.00118EW 1939/1042, *Diplomatic Branch.* Requests for specific intelligence begin 19 January 1942 on the Victor channel, 103.918, *Diplomatic Branch.* On Eddy, 18 December 1941, Box 1, Entry 58 and 24 January 1942, Administrative extras P-S file, Box 1, Entry 3, *RG 226;* R. Rives Childs, "30 Years in the Near East," (Manuscript, p. 159, Hoover Institution). See also Carleton S. Coon, *A North African Story,* passim. Note that it was Frank Knox who was championing Donovan's North African intelligence activities at the Washington Conference, 4 January 1942, *The Conference at Washington 1941-42, FRUS,* p. 165.

85. 18 March 1942, J.P.W.C. mtg., CCS 334 (3–18–42) *RG 218* and Murphy to State, 2 December 1941 and attachments, 740.0011EW 1939/17715, *Diplomatic Branch.*

86. Donovan to F.D.R., 9 January 1942, 22 December–15 January File, Box 163, 1 February 1942, 26 January–11 February File, Box 164, *PSF:* 26 March 1942, J.P.W.C. mtg. CCS 334 (3–18–42), *RG 218;* R. Harris Smith, *O.S.S.,* pp. 36–43.

87. 19 February 1942, Childs to State, *FRUS 1942,* II, pp. 256–257; Donovan to F.D.R., 6 March 1942, February–28 March File, Box 165, *PSF;* Eddy messages, 11 March and 8 April 1942, North Africa File, and 1 April 1942, O.S.S. correspondence January–May 1942 File, Box 3, *Goodfellow.*

88. The four cables, 10, 12, and 13 (2) April 1942, are in CCS 350.05, North Africa (4–14–42), *RG 218.*

89. Donovan messages of 12–14 April and Buxton to Knox, 17 April 1942, CCS 350.05, (4–14–42), *RG 218;* Donovan and Knox messages, 12–15 April 1942, in O.S.S. memoranda April–May File, and Canfield to Goodfellow, 15 April 1942, O.S.S. memoranda March–April File, *Goodfellow.*

90. 20 April 1942, Solborg to Donovan, CCS 350.05, (4–14–42), *RG 218.*

91. J.I.C. evaluation, 14 and 16 April 1942; Donovan to General Smith, 20 April 1942; J.C.S. decision, 20 April, CCS 350.05 (4–14–42), *RG 218.* Donovan to J.I.C., 14 April 1942, O.S.S. memoranda, March–April 1942 File, Box 4, *Goodfellow.* For those interested in the finance of espionage, a payment of $100,000 to Solborg was authorized by C.O.I.'s W. L. Rehm. The transfer was authorized via the VICTOR channel and was made by Howard J. Sachs of New York City: 25 May 1942, 103.91802/4240 and 740.00118EW 1939/1367, *Diplomatic Branch* and Donovan to F.D.R., 13 April 1942, 26 March–13 April File, Box 165, *PSF.*

92. Donovan to F.D.R., 21 April 1942, 13–28 April File, Box 165, *PSF;* Eddy at the J.P.W.C., CCS 334 (3–18–42), *RG 218;* and Eddy oral report, 11 June 1942, North Africa File, Box 3, and Solborg to Goodfellow, 10 June 1942, Solborg File, Box 2, *Goodfellow.*

Chapter 4

1. See CCS 111 (6–17–42), C.O.I. Budget, *RG 218.*

2. J.C.S. memo for Information, 20 June 1942, ABC 381 Russia (5–21–42), *RG 165.*

3. Solborg went to Lisbon in February with the understanding that he was not to go to North Africa. Donovan to Goodfellow, 23 March 1942, O.S.S. memoranda 1941–March 1942 File, Box 4. *Goodfellow.* On Solborg's trip: O.S.S. memos, June–July 1942 File, Box 4, *Goodfellow;* J. Rives Childs, "30 Years in the Near East," p. 163, Hoover Institution; Arthur L. Funk, *The Politics of Torch,* pp. 45–65; Elmar Krautkämer, "General Giraud und Admiral Darlan in der Vorgeschichte der Allierten Landung in Nordafrika," *Vierteljahrshefte f. Zeitgeschichte* 30, no. 2 (April 1982) 206–255.

4. Murphy Memorandum, 6 July 1942, *WO 204*/10100.

5. 17–23 June 1942, S.O.E.–O.S.S. deal, O.S.S. memoranda, June–July 1942 File, Box 4, *Goodfellow.* See confusion in J.P.W.C. and with JPS 35/1, 10 June and 14–29 July 1942, ABC 385 Norway (4–4–42), *RG 165.* On Eddy and M.I. 6, Eddy letter, 9 May 1954, File G., Box 1, Leland Rounds Papers, Hoover Institution. On special operations and seaborne arrangements, AFHQ History of Special Operations, Seaborne Operations Section, *WO 204/* 2030B.

6. Arthur L. Funk, *The Politics of Torch*, pp. 65–89. The C.C.S. go ahead for Torch established direction for S.O.E. but made no mention of O.S.S., 25 July 1942, CCS 33rd, ABC 381 (7–25–42), sec. 1, *RG 165*.

7. Much of the planning material is in CCS 350.05 (4–14–42), *RG 218*; and ABC 381 (7–25–42), *RG 165*. On the Free French, see Solborg to Donovan, 25 July 1942, O.S.S. memos, June–July 1942 File, Box 4, *Goodfellow;* Benson–De Chevigne talk, 30 July 1942, CCS 381, Torch, (7–24–42), *RG 218*. On 7 August 1942, Marshall wrote to the president that de Gaulle was being excluded because his "headquarters is very leaky." 80/34, *Marshall*.

8. Cover plans developed in the summer and fall are in ABC 381 (7–25–42) sections 1½, 4–A, 4–B, and 5, *RG 165*.

9. On the crashed courier ("the man who was"): *Hinsley*, II, p. 479; 28 September 1942 report. *WO 204/4499;* Bernard Fergusson, *The Watery Maze* (New York: 1961), pp. 205–206. On other security worries, Eisenhower to Handy, 1 September 1942, *Eisenhower Papers*, I, pp. 522–523. Ultra, Dakar, and the change in deception plan, 13 October 1942, *WO 106/2778;* Donovan message, 16 October 1942, CCS 350.05 (4–14–42), *RG 218*.

10. Eisenhower to War, 24 August 1942, CCS 381 (7–24–42), sec. 1, *RG 218;* 21 August 1942 G–2 summary and undated Mason Macfarlane memo, ABC (7–25–42) sec. 4–A, *RG 165;* 20 September 1942, *Butcher Diary;* 16 September 1942, Provisional Directive, *WO 204/4080;* 31 August 1942, D.M.I. estimate and 12 October 1942, Admiral Ramsay question, *WO 204/4128A*.

11. 21 September 1942, Patton to Handy, *WO 204/4591*. For recent appraisals of the Allied intelligence picture see *Hinsley*, II pp. 463–505 and David Kahn, *Hitler's Spies*, pp. 462–478.

12. 16 September 1942 Murphy talk (twelve pages), *WO 204/4128A;* 16 September 1942, *Butcher Diary;* See also Eddy to Gruenther, 30 August 1942, ABC 381 (7–25–42), sec. 4–B, *RG 165;* 31 August 1942, General Clark's conferences and decisions, Operation Torch File, Box 153, *Eisenhower;* September directive to Murphy, *WO 204/4595*. See also Robert Murphy, *Diplomat Among Warriors*, pp. 99–106; and Arthur Funk, *The Politics of Torch*, passim.

13. 31 August 1942, Mountbatten to Clark and 16 September 1942 report on Murphy's talks with the military, *WO 204/4128A*.

14. The files bulge with British and American items on these organizational questions. The C.C.S. orders to Eisenhower (14 August *WO 204/4080*) and Eisenhower to Marshall, 21 September 1942 (*Eisenhower Papers*, I, p. 573–574) are among the most important. Despite all the revision and stress on the mission appearing American, the psychological warfare section on 30 October had twenty-four American and forty-one British personnel. *FO 660/9*, Public Record Office, London.

15. 9 October 1942, Donovan to J.P.W.C. ABC 385 (8–4–42), *RG 165;* 12 October 1942, Clark Conferences and decisions, Operation Torch File, Box 153, *Eisenhower;* 13 October 1942, *Butcher Diary*. Eisenhower memorandum, 16 October 1942, ABC 381 (7–25–42), sec. 4–B, *RG 165*. Through the Torch and post-Torch squabbling, General Eisenhower's brother Milton, a high O.W.I. official, sometimes acted as a go-between.

16. See 1 and 10 October 1942 messages, CCS 350.05 (4–14–42), *RG 218;* 8 September and 27 October 1942, ABC 381, Mediteranian Area, (12–3–42), sec. 1, *RG 165;* 10 August 1942, Eisenhower to Marshall, *Eisenhower Papers*, I, p. 456.

17. Donovan to Deane, 9 October 1942, CCS 350.05 (4–14–42) *RG 218;* 2 October 1942, *Butcher Diary;* Eisenhower to Marshall, 2 October 1942, *Eisenhower Papers* I, p. 590; 5 October 1942 (General Wedemeyer's view), CCS 334 (5–18–42), *RG 218*.

18. From 7 October 1942 on, we can examine the composite intelligence picture in the First Army intelligence reports, *WO 204/10327*.

19. Intelligence items: 10 and 13 October, 4 and 5 November, 1942, CCS 350.05 (4–14–42), *RG 218;* 30 October and 1 November 1942, ABC 381 (12–3–42), sec. 1, *RG 165;* 15 August 1942, ABC 385 (8–4–42). *RG 165*. On direct landing support: Bolton to King, 10 December 1947, Correspondence File, David King Papers, Hoover Institution; and Eddy to Gruenther, 30 August 1942, ABC 381 (7–25–42), sec. 4–B, *RG 165*.

20. 10 September 1942, Eddy to Donovan, *WO 204/10100;* 15 September Eddy cable and 17 September 1942 Mark Clark comment, *WO 204/4128A;* Eddy to Donovan, 2 September 1942, ABC 381 (12–3–42), *RG 165;* 16 September 1942, *Butcher Diary;* 22 Septem-

ber 1942, Clark conferences, etc., Box 153, *Eisenhower*. A list of S.O.E. stocks (including 11,000 Stens), is in Mack to Gruenther, 31 August 1942. *WO 204/4586*.

21. Lemnitzer O.S.S.–S.O.E. instructions, 18 September 1942, ABC 381 (7–25–42), sec. 4–A, *RG 165;* Special operations summary, 22 September 1942, JCS (4) file, Box 63, *Eisenhower;* Special operations instructions to all O.S.S. units, 14 October 1942, Special Ops (2) File, Reel 6 D–I, *AFHQ;* 14 October 1942, General Smith orders to Eddy and to Central Task Force, and 23 October 1942 Eddy reply, File H, Box 1, L. Rounds Papers, Hoover Institution.

22. 25 October 1942, *Butcher Diary;* 29 October 1942, Eisenhower to Marshall, Marshall File, Box 72, *Eisenhower*.

23. David King material on personal data, and reports written 12 December 1947 and May (no day) 1949, personal data and correspondence files, David King Papers, Hoover Institution. Robert Murphy, *Diplomat Among Warriors*, pp. 126–127. George F. Howe, *Northwest Africa* (Washington: 1957), p. 212n. An S.O.E. official claims that three attempts were made to deliver arms but there were no recognition signals given on the ground. J. G. Beevor, *SOE Recollections and Reflections* (London: 1981), p. 135.

24. 6 November 1942, *Butcher Diary;* the code and communication system, 21 September–13 October 1942 memos., *WO 204/4589*.

25. 17 October 1942, *CAB 79/86*.

26. The basic source of most later accounts is *Taylor*, pp. 321–340. See a draft letter, undated, Knight to Murphy, File H, Box 1, L. Rounds Papers, Hoover Institution.

27. 18 December 1942, report by Colonel Hendrickson. *WO 204/4324*.

28. Much material on O.S.S. relations with State and the F.B.I. is in the June section of CCS 385 (2–8–42) pt. 1. *RG 218*. On the B.E.W., 28 August and 4 September 1942, CCS 385 (8–28–42) OSS and BEW, *RG 218*. For the State Department side of the story see the June 1942 to January 1943 section of the 103.918 series, *Diplomatic Branch*. There was a C.O.I.–O.S.S. office in Hawaii, Hawaii File, Box 17, Entry 1, *RG 226*. William Phillips claims that O.S.S. got on quite well with everyone in London, the troubles were in Washington. William Phillips, *Ventures in Diplomacy* (Boston: 1952), pp. 331–332. For O.S.S. turning the J.C.S. tie to advantage, see under July 1942 in the Grombach File, Box 2, and O.S.S. memos June–July 1942 File, Box 4, *Goodfellow*.

29. On S.O.E. and P.W.E., 17 July 1942, Embassy to Cadogan and 4 August 1942, New York to F.O., FO *898/107*, plus P.W.E.–S.O.E. coordinating meetings (as frequent as every other day), and the agreement of 13 January 1943, *FO 898/27*. For quotations, 24 February 1943, *Wilkinson* and 28 December 1942, *Cadogan*. S.O.E. and gas weapons: 20 July 1942, COS (42) 212th mtg., *CAB 79/22*.

30. Eden comments on an S.O.E. memorandum, 2 October 1942, *FO 954/24A*.

31. Diary, 10 February 1942, *Dalton Papers;* 4 March 1943, COS (43) 56th mtg., *CAB 79/26*.

32. 17 June–3 August 1942 records, CCS 111 (6–17–42) and "Bulky Package" *RG 218;* 6 August 1942 conference with the president, Box 13, *Harold Smith*.

33. Again, the C.I.A. history devotes two long chapters to these events (*Troy*, Chapters 7 and 8), therefore only supplementary material or points that underscore the differences of interpretation will be cited. The controlling attitude of the military is perhaps best shown in Woodnough to Wedemeyer, 24 June 1942, ABC 334.3., sec. 1, (5–1–42), *RG 165*.

34. 29 June 1942, Eisenhower diary, Box 1, *Eisenhower;* 26 June 1942 Blizzard memo and 4 July 1942 Hull to Wedemeyer, ABC 343.3, sec. 1, (5–1–42), *RG 165;* 14 July, 1942, Marshall to General Smith, CCS 385 (2–13–42), sec. 1, *RG 218*.

35. July–September 1942 memos. CCS 385 (2–13–42), sec. 1, *RG 218;* JPWC 21/2, 24 July, J.P.W.C. 21st mtg., 3 August, J.C.S. 29th mtg., 18 August, 1942, CCS (2–8–42) sec. 1, *RG 218;* 11 July–4 August papers, ABC 334.3, sec. 1, (5–1–42), *RG 165;* 18 July 1942 plan, O.S.S. memos June–July 1942 File, Box 4, *Goodfellow*.

36. 31 August 1942, pencil draft, O.S.S. memos August–December 1942 File, Box 4, *Goodfellow;* 31 August 1942 J.P.W.C. mtg. and Donovan to J.C.S. and Stimson; 7 September 1942, J.P.W.C., 11 September 1942 Donovan to J.C.S., CCS 385 (2–13–42), sec. 1, *RG 218*.

37. 10 September 1942, Ohthank memorandum up through 21 October 1942 McNarney to Secretary of J.C.S., in CCS 385 (2–13–42) Sec. 1. *RG 218*.

Notes

38. In addition to the two standard file series repeatedly cited above (CCS 385 [2–13–42] and [2–8–42]), this development may be followed in CCS 385 (3–16–42) (2), Objectives and Methods Employed by Psychological Warfare, *RG 218;* and ABC 385 (3–4–42), no title, *RG 165.*

39. Both *Troy* and I think this document is important, but he does not relate it to the operational achievements in North Africa, Deane to Marshall, 22 October, 1942, CCS 385 (2–8–42), pt. 1, *RG 218.*

40. On the Rogers–Stimson tie, see Vol. 39, Roll 7, *Stimson Diary* and 23 and 27 July, 1942, Stimson Papers, Roll 6, Yale. On Rogers activity, Rogers essay (undated) file FF-OSS, Box 8, J. G. Rogers Collection, Colorado State Historical Society. J.P.W.C. 44/2nd, 27 October 1942, CCS 385 (3–16–42) (2) and 4 November 1942, Chapman to Hammond, CCS 385 (2–13–42) sec. 1, *RG 218.*

41. Harold Macmillan, *The Blast of War 1939–1945* (New York: 1967), p. 352. The idea of basing O.S.S. on "psychological warfare" never had much chance. When in July 1942, Carter had volunteered to be psychological warfare coordinator under the J.C.S., the president's reply indicated that he was not keen on giving the military much control over such matters: "Admiral Leahy would have very little to do with psychological warfare." Carter to F.D.R. and attached, June–July 1942 File, Box 122, *PSF.*

42. December 1942–February 1943 Donovan requests for personnel in CCS 385 (2–13–42) sec. 1, *RG 218;* and especially Donovan request of 18 February 1943 CCS 385 (2–8–42) pt. 4, *RG 218.* Donovan note, 19 January 1943, CCS 311.1, (1–28–43) *RG 218 Postwar;* Donovan to commander army ground forces, 19 February 1943, CCS 353 (2–19–43), Course of Instruction in Parachute Training, *RG 218;* 13 February 1943, M.I.S.–O.S.S. exchanges, CCS 385 (2–8–42) pt. 4, *RG 218;* 27 March 1943, O.S.S. board to pass on military commissioning, Special Orders File, Box 9, Entry 1, *RG 226.*

43. David Bowes-Lyon to Bruce Lockhart, 16 August 1942 and R.H.S. Crossman's report, 2 October 1942, *FO 898/107.*

44. Two British reports on the O.W.I.–O.S.S. struggle are interesting: a second Crossman memorandum, 19 October 1942, *FO 898/107;* and a further P.W.E. report of 1 February 1943, *FO 898/105.* Troy has the main document references from military papers, pp. 191–209.

45. Aside from the materials in the main military files (CCS 385 [2–8–42] sec. 4 and [2–13–42] sec. 1, *RG 218*) see 5 and 19 February 1943 entries, Box 17, *Harold Smith;* Stimson to F.D.R., File 80/42, Box 80, *Marshall;* John Morton Blum, ed., *The Price of Vision. The Diary of Henry A. Wallace* (Boston: 1973), pp. 160–161.

46. J.C.S. 63rd. mtg., 23 February 1943, CCS 385 (2–8–42) pt. 5, and J.P.W.C. 19th mtg., 22 July 1942, pt. 1, *RG 218.*

47. 24 February 1943, Leahy to Deane, CCS 385 (2–8–42) pt. 5, *RG 218.*

48. Jonathan Daniels, *White House Witness, 1942–1945,* (Garden City, New York: 1972), p. 138.

49. *Troy,* Chapter eight, seems to feel this is much more the result of ignorance and dark motive.

50. 2 March 1943, J.C.S. minutes, CCS 385 Italy (10–19–42) sec. 1, *RG 218;* Heber Blankenhorn, "Psychological Warfare Report" 1945 (Manuscript, Hoover Institution).

51. March–May 1943 File, Box 72, *Map Room.*

52. 6 February 1943, 606: 178 *Morgenthau;* 1 March 1943, J.C.S. 230 and subsequent psychological warfare manual, CCS 385 (2–2–43), *RG 218.* The activities of Carter–O.W.I.–O.S.S. regarding Putzi Hanfstaengl provide a good example of the problems. Carter Papers, August–December 1942 file on, Box 123, *PSF.*

53. Chapman to Deane, etc., 5 March 1943, CCS 385 (3–16–42) (2) *RG 218;* 14 January 1943, (J.P.S. 104) and 29 September 1943 (J.C.S. 104), ABC 385 Norway, (4–4–43), *RG 165.*

54. On interviewing: 30 June and 1 July 1942, CCS 350.05 (6–30–42), *RG 218.* Photographic units: 13 and 24 August, 29 September 1942 and 25 February 1943, CCS 062 (8–21–42), Campaign for collection of pictures. *RG 218.* The British did collect photographs from the public, which was probably the source of Donovan's idea.

55. I.D.C. consideration, July 1942–March 1943, especially 23 September 1942, Galdieux to Onthank and 29 August Onthank to General Smith, CCS 385 (2–8–42) pt. 1, *RG 218;* I.D.C. materials, 1943–45, Box 6, Entry 1, *RG 226;* Fairbank message, 11 October 1942,

File 41–12, Box 41, *Hayden;* John K. Fairbank, *Chinabound* (New York: 1982), pp. 185–286.

56. 9 July 1942, de Kay to Donovan, June 1942–45 File, Box 3, *Goodfellow.*

57. 30 June–7 August 1942, O.S.S. memos June–July and August–December 1942 Files, Box 4, *Goodfellow.*

58. 16 July 1942, Billinghurst to Williams, O.S.S. memos June–July File, Box 4, *Goodfellow;* 22 June Solbert to Story and 27 July 1942, J.P.W.C. 20th mtg., CCS 000.51 (7-10–42) Sabotage; 30 September 1942, V. Bush statement, etc. CCS 385 (2–8–42) pt. 1 and 19 January 1943 J.C.S. 50th mtg., pt. 4, *RG 218.*

59. Memos of 9 and 10 June 1942, June notes by Goodfellow, and the basic 32-page O.S.S.–S.O.E. agreement, 17–23 June 1942, O.S.S. memos, June–July 1942 Files, *Goodfellow.*

60. Goodfellow later asserted that Williams was not with him in London, but the minutes of the meetings show that he was. Goodfellow to R. Harris Smith, Box 1, R. Harris Smith Papers, Hoover Institution. S.O.E.–O.S.S. equipment deal, 20 June 1942, O.S.S. memos, June–July 1942 File, Box 4, *Goodfellow.* The main texts of the agreement may also be found in CCS 385 (8–6–42) OSS–SOE Agreements, *RG 218.* Donovan did not submit them formally to the J.C.S. until 10 August 1942; ABC 334.3, sec. 1 (5–1–42), *RG 165.*

61. O.S.S. monthly report to the J.C.S., CCS 319.1 (9–15–42), *RG 218.*

62. Minutes of the 16 June COS mtg. are closed until 1993, *CAB 79/21.* Donovan to the J.C.S., 28 June 1942, covers the main points of his London intelligence arrangements, ABC 334.3, sec. 1, (5–1–42), *RG 165.*

63. 2 July 1942, Goodfellow to Donovan and 9 September 1942, Lowman to Goodfellow, O.S.S. memos. June–July and August–December 1942 File, Box 4, *Goodfellow.* These files indicate that despite formal denials some code decipherment effort had been made.

64. 21 June 1943 note, 103.918/11145, *Diplomatic Branch;* 23 October 1942, J.I.C. 37th mtg., CCS 334 (5–4–42), J.I.C. *RG 218.*

65. 13 February 1942, M.I.S.–O.S.S. exchanges, CCS 385 (2–8–42) pt. 4., *RG 218.*

66. *Hinsley,* II, pp. 52–53; Donovan to Deane, 6 March 1943, CCS 385 (8–6–42), *RG 218;* Donovan to Deane, 22 April 1943, CCS 385 (2–8–42), pt, 5, *RG 218.* In *Smith and Agarossi,* we concluded that O.S.S. was not directly privy to decoded material, but to the extent indicated here, that was not correct.

67. Deane messages of 12 February and 23 and 27 April 1943, and Price message of 10 March 1943, CCS 385 (2–8–42) pts. 4 and 5, *RG 218.*

68. The organizational picture: 25 January 1943 list of important O.S.S. personnel, CCS 385 (2–8–42) pt. 4, *RG 218.* On Magruder, September 1942, File 1855 (Microfilm 54, Marshall Library).

69. "From OSS with Love," December 1978, p. 99, *Psychology Today.* Projects Committee minutes, October 1942 on, especially 28 October 1942 and 8 February 1943, Box 1, Entry 59, *RG 226;* 2 November and 17 December 1942, Box 1, Entry 58, *RG 226.*

70. Mason to Buxton, 20 June 1942, CCS 385 (2–8–42) pt. 1, *RG 218;* June–December Board of Analysts mtgs. on relations with the military, Box 1, Entry 58, *RG 226;* 4 March 1943, Box 1, Entry 59, *RG 226.*

71. 19 June 1942, Wilson report on London R. and A, Mission to England File, Box 19, Entry 1, *RG 226;* 20 June 1942, Box 1, Entry 58, *RG 226;* 17 December 1942, Box 1, Entry 59, *RG 226;* 31 July 1942, O.W.I.–P.W.E. mtg., *FO 898/104;* Russell to Hall, January 1943, *FO 371/37634A/922.*

72. Trend memoranda in March–May 1943 File, Box 72, *Map Room;* Projects Committee minutes, 14 and 23 October, 3 November, 16 December 1942 and the overall count March to May 1943, Box 1, Entry 59, *RG 226.*

73. The shifts in S.I. placement and communications show up in the Victor channel, 103.918, *Diplomatic Branch.*

74. Carleton S. Coon, *A North African Story,* pp. 63–122; *Sweet-Escott,* p. 167; Special Seaborne Operations section of History of Special Operations, *WO 204/2030B.*

75. 24 November 1942, CCS 400 (11–24–42) Requisitions for O.S.S., *RG 218.* On persecution of pro-Allied Frenchmen, Patton to Eisenhower, 14 November 1942, *WO 204/4130;* Eddy to Knight and Rounds, 29 November 1942, File K, Box 1, L. Rounds Papers, Hoover Institution. 30 December 1942 report on Arabs, *WO 204/3987;* Donovan to Deane, 31

Notes

December 1942, ABC 381 (12–3–42) sec. 1, *RG 165*. A special allotment of $50,000 was sent to Eddy on 10 December 1942; 103.918/765A, *Diplomatic Branch*.

76. H. Blankenhorn, "Psychological Warfare Report," (Manuscript, Hoover Institution). On the psychological warfare system, 27 October 1942 and following, *FO 898/176*.

77. Kenneth Strong, *Intelligence at the Top* (Garden City, New York: 1968), pp. 116–119 and 135–136. On the J.I.C. Mediterranean, *WO 204/477* and 18 and 20 February 1943, *Butcher Diary*. The British were often equally critical of Washington G-2 reports, 6 January 1943, *WO 204/4128A*. For Donovan's Mediterranean intelligence hopes, see memo to Deane, 7 November 1942, CCS 385 (11–7–42) North Africa, *RG 218*.

78. 13 November 1942, Phillips to Heppner, Donovan specifically rejected combining O.S.S. with Massingham, Special Ops (2) File, Reel 6-D-I, G-3, RG 331, *AFHQ*. 10 December 1942, War to Eisenhower, Marshall (1) File, Box 7, *Eisenhower*. Washington's and Donovan's views, 30 November, 4 and 18 December 1942, (J.P.W.C. 53), ABC (12–3–42) sec. 1, *RG 165;* Styler to Deane, 7 December 1942 and Donovan to Deane, 28 December 1942, CCS 385 (11–7–42), *RG 218*. The Huntington mission: J.C.S. to Eisenhower, 24 December 1942, *WO 204/4683;* 1 February 1943 Huntington to W. B. Smith, CCS 330, Spain (3–26–43), sec. 1, *RG 218;* 3 February and 19 July 1943, layout of Special Ops. Hq., ABC 334.3, sec. 3, (5–1–42), *RG 165*. Gen. W. B. Smith in consequence called for a study of O.S.S. and "related" organizations in A.F.H.Q., 24 February, 1943, *WO 204/65* (based on Eisenhower approval, 4 February 1943, ABC 381 [12–3–42] sec. 1, *RG 165*.)

79. Donovan to Maddocks, 3 February 1943, ABC 381, (12–31–42), sec. 1, *RG 165*.

80. See especially JCS 139 (28 October 1942), JPWC 51/1 (16 November 1942) and 6 February 1943 O.S.S. psychological warfare plan for Italy, CCS 385, Italy, (10–19–42), sec. 1, *RG 218*.

81. On Rockefeller: 14 January 1943, CCS 385 (10–19–42) sec. 1 and 2, *RG 218*. S.O.E. to Cadogan, 12 February 1943, *FO 954/24A*; Report to London, 4 March 1943, *WO 106/3876*. On requests for personnel: Donovan to Deane, 28 December 1942, and 7 and 25 February 1943, and Eddy to Maddocks, 5 March 1943, CCS 385 (2–13–42), *RG 218*. On Keswick and British planning: 8 March 1943, *WO 204/1618* and 6 March 1943, *WO 204/6958*.

82. 1 October 1942, OSS monthly report to J.C.S., CCS 319.1 (9–15–42), *RG 218;* 2 and 17 November 1942, 103.918/646D and 688A, *Diplomatic Branch*.

83. The minister of state wanted to increase the 5,000 pounds per month for special intelligence, 27 October 1942, *WO 193/620*. The British were using many "Italian collaborators" as intelligence sources, 17 September 1942, Roseberry to Stevens, *FO 898/26*. On the Political Intelligence Center: 11 August 1944 report, *WO 204/798*.

84. "History of Air Support for SO Mediterranean," History of Special Operations, *WO 204/2030B*; C. M. Woodhouse, *The Struggle for Greece* (London: 1976), pp. 21–38.

85. Jozo Tomasevich, *The Chetniks*, pp. 284–290; Phyllis Auty and Richard Clogg, *British Policy Toward Wartime Resistance in Yugoslavia and Greece* (London: 1975) pp. 3–22 and 210–213; Mark C. Wheeler, *Britain and the War for Yugoslavia 1940–1943*, passim; O.S.S. monthly report, F.N.B. section, CCS 319.1 (9–15–42) *RG 218*.

86. *Sweet-Escott*, p. 162; Report of Colonel de Chevigné, CCS 350.05 (4–14–42), *RG 218*. On S.O.E. Middle East: August 1942, *FO 954/24A*; George A. Hill, "Reminiscences, etc.," pp. 222–225, Hoover Institution; *Barker*, p. 163.

87. 9 August, 1 and 18 September, 1942, ABC 000.24, Middle East, (7–27–42), *RG 165*.

88. 20 October 1942, Welles to Leahy, ABC 000.24, (7–27–42), *RG 165*.

89. See November 1942–February 1943, ABC 000.24, (7–27–42), *RG 165;* 15 February 1943, General Brereton message, ABC 334.5 (5–1–42), sec. 3, *RG 165;* November 1942–February 1943, CCS 385, Middle East (12–1–42), sec. 1, *RG 218;* Deane to Marshall 6 September 1942 and Donovan to J.C.S., 21 January 1943, CCS 385 (2–8–42), secs. 1 and 4, *RG 218; Sweet-Escott*, pp. 137–140.

90. O.S.S. monthly report to J.C.S., 1 October 1942, CCS 319.1 (9–15–42), *RG 218*.

91. 27 July 1942, JPWC 20th mtg., CCS 334 (5–18–42), *RG 218;* 2 December 1942, Morse to Victor, 103.918/741, 16 September 1942, Leopoldville to State, 103.918/490, 22 October 1942, Hull to Monrovia, for Victor, 103.918/581B, 26 December 1942, Taylor to State, 103.918/878, *Diplomatic Branch*.

92. O.S.S. monthly report to J.C.S., 1 October 1942, CCS 319.1 (9–16–42), *RG 218*.

93. On N.K.V.D.: 24 November 1942 meeting with "C" and the S.O.E. chief, *Cadogan;*

Notes

George Hill, "Reminiscences, etc.," p. 189, Hoover Institution. On S.O.E. successes and failures: 31 October 1942, Harman to Leeper, *FO 898/28*; Lord Gladwyn, *Memoirs*, pp. 107–108; Walter Schellenberg, *The Labyrinth* (New York: 1956), p. 367; 12 April 1943, COS (43) 89, *CAB 79/26*, gives S.O.E. credit in Norway, but *Hinsley* (II, p. 127) now says the main long-term damage to German atomic facilities there was produced by the American air force. On the beginnings of an O.S.S. establishment tied to the American military in Europe: *Eisenhower Papers*, I, p. 384; 5 October 1942, JPWC 28th mtg., CCS 385 (8–6–42), *RG 218*.

94. 16 November 1942, Deane to Donovan, ABC 336, France (11–16–42), sec. 1, *RG 165*; 8 October 1942, Carter report (note that all through the fall of 1942 Carter was also reporting in detail on prospects for beating the Republicans in New York), August–December 1942 File, Box 123, *PSF*.

95. On Nicol Smith, June 1942–1945 File, Box 3, 24 October 1942 memo, 1942–44 unidentified File, Box 1, late October 1942 memo, O.S.S. memos, August–December 1942 File, Box 4, *Goodfellow*. Donovan wanted McCloy to go to London to look at O.S.S. operations, but Stimson refused to authorize it: 4 September 1942, Vol. 40, Roll 7, *Stimson Diary*. On Norway: 12 March 1943, COS (43) 117 (0), *CAB 80/68*; 14 January 1943, ABC 385 (4–4–43), *RG 165*.

96. Donovan reports to Wedemeyer, 18 September, 28 October, 5 November, 1942, CCS 381, (12–3–42), sec. 1, *RG 165*; 6 October 1942, Phillips to Donovan, Diplomatic, Great Britain File, Box 53, *PSF*.

97. November 1942–February 1943, especially 3 January 1943 Kramer report, and 20 February Marecki to Wedemeyer, ABC 452.1 Poland (11–26–42), sec. 1, Poland, *RG 165*. On the Carter connection, see 21 May 1942 report, March–May 1942 File, Box 122, 20 November and 30 December 1942 reports, August–December 1942 File, Box 123, *PSF*.

98. 21 August 1942, J.P.W.C., CCS 000.5 (8–21–42), Subversive activity, *RG 218*; 21 August 1942 (JCS 92) and 5 September, following committee action, ABC 000.24, France (8–21–42), *RG 165*; 4 November 1942, Donovan to Deane, CCS 350.5 (11–4–42), *RG 218*.

99. Huntington to E.T.O., 5 March 1943 (in JPS 178D), CCS 385 ETO (4–12–43) and Donovan to Deane, 8 March 1943, CCS 385 (2–8–42) pt. 5, *RG 218*.

100. *Hoover*, pp. 205–220.

101. Monthly O.S.S. report to J.C.S., 1 October 1942, CCS 319.1 (9–15–42) *RG 218*.

102. Mtgs. of 22 and 29 October; 5, 12, 19, and 25 November, 1942, CCS 334 J.P.W.A.C., (10–22–42), *RG 218*.

103. 7 October 1942, Wilson to Victor and 2 July 1942, Hull to Madrid, 103.918 and 103.918/345A, *Diplomatic Branch*.

104. Hayes to State, 26 August 1942, 103.918/438, 13 November 1942, 103.918/666, Hayes to Donovan, 12 December 1942, 103.918/763, *Diplomatic Branch*, See below, p. 218.

105. Burns (Dulles's cover name on the Victor channel) to Victor, 10 November 1942, 103.918/651, *Diplomatic Branch*.

106. October 1942, S.O.E.–F.O. relations on peace feelers, *FO 898/28*. Burns to Victor, 24 December 1942, 103.918/810 and 6 March 1943, 103.918/1071. *Diplomatic Branch*. Postwar British accounts bristle with accusations that the United States tried to undercut the Gaullists inside France and frequently point a finger at Dulles; M. R. D. Foot, *SOE in France*, p. 230; and *Sweet-Escott*, p. 182.

107. 6 March 1943, March through May File, Box 72, *Map Room*, Burns to Victor, 31 January 1943, 103.918/944, *Diplomatic Branch*.

108. For the earliest indications of Dulles's contacts with, and attitude toward, the German resistance see Burns to Victor, 13 January 1943 and 4 February 1943, 103.918/879 and 968, *Diplomatic Branch*. 10 March 1943, Burns to Victor, is a partly accurate, partly confused, report on the killing of Jews in Berlin, 103.918/106, *Diplomatic Branch*. The Italian question is treated in Burns to Victor, 1 February 1943, 103.918/943, *Diplomatic Branch* and the group of reports in March–May 1943 File, Box 72, *Map Room*.

109. Burns to Victor, 6 December 1942, 103.918/744; 1 and 10 February 1943, 103.918/943 and 987, *Diplomatic Branch*.

110. 8 March 1943, Welles to Bern, 103.918/1141A and 20 March, Matthews to State, *Diplomatic Branch*, attached, ordered Dulles to stop reporting because Washington and London had learned that the Germans had "been able to decipher" one of his cables. Dulles claimed that he learned that the Germans had broken the code from Gisevius, and this story

445

has been followed by others. It is unclear whether by this he was trying to cover an Ultra source or inflating the importance of the German resistance. Allen W. Dulles, *Germany's Underground* (New York: 1947), p. 130.

111. *Taylor,* pp. 354–355.

112. O.S.S. report to J.C.S., 1 October 1942, CCS 319.1 (9–15–42), *RG 218.* William R. Peers and Dean Brelis, *Behind the Burma Road* (Boston: 1963), pp. 60–104.

113. R. Harris Smith, *O.S.S.,* pp. 296–300; August–September Files, ABC 000.24, Thailand (8–20–42), *RG 165;* Pramoj File, Box 1, O.S.S. memos August–December 1942 File, Box 4, *Goodfellow.*

114. 17 December 1942, Phillips to F.D.R., Diplomatic, Great Britain, O.S.S. File, Box 153, *PSF;* November–December 1942 files on Wavell's troubles, *WO 106/4632;* 16 January 1943 Donovan to Phillips and 28 January Phillips reply, 103.918/937A and 938, *Diplomatic Branch.* 11 March 1943, COS (43), 62 mtg., *CAB 79/26.*

115. Charles A. Willoughby and John Chamberlain, *MacArthur 1941–1951* (New York: 1954), pp. 144–156. Some marks of the early intelligence operations are in File 3/2, *Wilkinson.* 8 January 1943 J.P.S. recommendation, CCS 385 (1–1–43) Philippine Islands, *RG 218;* Ritchie to Roberts, 22 June 1943, ABC 385, Southwest Pacific (6–14–1943), *RG 165.* Marshall to MacArthur, 14 July 1942, ABC 334.3 (5–1–42) *RG 165.* On the Hayden mission: 15 January–9 February 1943, reports, on special microfilm, *Hayden;* Hayden–Victor exchanges, 1, 17, and 25 February, 1943, 103.918/958 and 1001 and 1040A, *Diplomatic Branch.* On 22 January 1943, Donovan declared that he had never been shown Hayden's crucial 16 January message reporting that Willoughby might allow O.S.S. in for work in the Dutch East Indies if it was totally under MacArthur's control. CCS 385 (1–1–43), *RG 218.*

116. 18 June 1942, Vanderbilt to Goodfellow, O.S.S. memos, June–July 1942 File, Box 4, *Goodfellow.* On Dragon: J.P.W.C. subcommittee mtg., 14 July 1942, CCS 334 (5–18–42), *RG 218;* 15 July 1942, Kroner to Stilwell, ABC 334.3 (5–1–42), *RG 165;* Montague to JPS, 31 July 1942, CCS 385 (2–8–42), pt. 1, *RG 218;* 23 July 1942, revised plan and 15 December 1942 summary, CCS 350.05, (6–5–42), *RG 218;* Hayden mission: R. Harris Smith, *O.S.S.,* pp. 246–247; 23 October 1942, CCS 350.05 (6–5–42), *RG 218;* Special microfilm, particularly appendix B–1, *Hayden;* Donovan to Hayden, 11 September 1942, 109.918/ 488D, *Diplomatic Branch.*

117. Special microfilm, appendix B–1, *Hayden.* Some suspicions were floating about that Donovan was operating a deep cover operation in China (i.e., the Starr network); see October 1942, Ernest B. Price resignation, Confidential File, Box 12, *PSF.*

118. 1 November talk with General Hearn, File 41–12 (other material on Chinese contacts is in Files 12 and 21) Box 41, *Hayden.* Claire Lee Chennault, *Way of a Fighter* (New York: 1949), p. 211.

119. Hayden's reports: 8 November 1942, to Victor, 103.918/644, *Diplomatic Branch;* to Board of Analysts, 13 March 1943, Binder 4, Box 1, Entry 58, *RG 226.*

120. Hayden's view is in File 41–44, Box 41, *Hayden.*

121. See Stilwell's caution, February 1943, CCS 385 (2–4–43) sec. 1, Exchange of intelligence reports prepared by the Chinese Mission, *RG 218.*

122. 8 July 1942, attaché report, *WO 208/254;* Kimbel–State talks, 11 February 1943, Box 323, *Hornbeck.*

Chapter 5

1. On O.W.I.–O.S.S.: Donovan to Deane, 16 March 1943, CCS 385 (2–8–42) pt. 5, *RG 218;* 13 January 1944 J.P.W.C. reports, CCS 385 (2–8–42) pt. 8, *RG 218;* Bureau of R. and A. of O.S.S. May–August File, Box 5, Philleo Nash Papers, Harry S. Truman Library; Bowes-Lyon view that O.W.I. was in trouble, 31 May, 1943, Kenneth Young, ed., *The Diaries of Sir Robert Bruce Lockhart* (London: 1980), II, pp. 238–240. Carter claimed (28 July 1943) that he, Dorothy Thompson, and Sumner Welles were unhappy about O.W.I. New York because of incompetence and because he alleged it was "highly pink" and "many of this group are Commies." January–July File, Box 123, *PSF,* but the military

insisted on keeping O.S.S. out of open propaganda, 20–30 April 1943, CCS 000.76 (4–20–43). *RG 218.* On relations with the Treasury: 19 May 1943, 635: 42 *Morgenthau* and B.E.W.: Donovan to Perkins, 23 March 1943, CCS 385 (2–8–42) pt. 5, *RG 218.*

2. 10 and 12 September 1943, *Wilkinson.* On housekeeping services (second quarter 1943) and revision of JCS 155/11/D, September–October 1943: CCS 385 (2–8–42), pts. 5, 7 and 8, *RG 218.* On communications and coding: 12 October 1943 and 21 April 1944, CCS 385 (2–8–42), pts. 8 and 9, and 22 April 1944, CCS 311.5 (3–29–44), Messages of O.S.S. *RG 218.* On weapons and research: May–October 1943 (JCS 268), CCS 385 (2–8–42), pts. 5–7, *RG 218.* On military government: Military Government File, Box 8, Entry 1, *RG 226.*

3. 21 October 1943, Royal to J.C.S., CCS 385 (2–13–42), sec. 1, *RG 218;* April–May 1944, McNarney–Cannon exchange, ABC 384 (4–29–44) and ABC 334.3, sec. 4, (5–1–42), *RG 165.*

4. For exaggeration, see 25 November 1943, Vol. 45, Roll 8, *Stimson Diary;* and 23 February 1944 Manual, ABC 334.3, sec. 4, (5–1–42), *RG 165.* On General Strong and navy hostility, 14 April 1943 J.I.C. 59th mtg. and 29 May 1943, J.I.C. 64th mtg., CCS 334 (10–15–43), *RG 218* plus Colonel Lincoln to Allen Dulles, 27 December 1966, Box 155, Wolff File, *Dulles.* Concern for the adequacy of O.S.S. combat training, 18 June 1943 (xerox item, 3471, Marshall Library). Berle and the F.B.I.: Berle, 20 November 1943, pt. 8, Magruder and Gridley, 1 and 3 May 1944, pt. 9, CCS 385 (2–8–42), *RG 218.*

5. June 1943 Halpern report, *FO 892/174;* 16 June 1943 State Department inquiry, 103.918/6–1643 and 9 March 1944, 103.918/2128A, *Diplomatic Branch;* 8 May 1943, Inquiry, CCS 385 (5–8–43) (2), *RG 218.*

6. 23 March 1944, *Butcher Diary;* Anthony Cave Brown, *Bodyguard of Lies* (New York: 1975), pp. 529–530. April 1943, Joint Strategic Survey Committee Report quoted in JCS 1682/7, 7 June 1946, CCS 334 (12–19–42), J.I.C., *RG 218 Postwar.*

7. May 1944, *FO 898/26;* 15 February 1944, Foreign Office–S.O.E. mtg., *Cadogan;* COS (43) 240, 7 October 1943, *CAB 79/65;* D.O. (44) 2, 11 January 1944, *CAB 69/6.*

8. 20 May 1944, Deane to Donovan, CCS 310.1 (5–20–43), Liaison between J.C.S. and O.S.S., *RG 218;* 26 May 1944, J.P.S. 76th mtg., Wedemeyer suggestion, ABC 385, India (4–8–43), *RG 165;* J.P.S. on O.S.S. Sardinia/Corsica plan, 29 May 1943, CCS 385 (5–8–43) (1), Plan for Psychological Warfare, Sardinia and Corsica, *RG 218.*

9. For the basic system of acquiring personnel, see the large number of items, between 25 March 1943 and 1 May 1944 in CCS 385 (2–8–42), pts. 5–9, *RG 218;* 13 November and 13 December 1943, CCS 385 (2–13–42), sec. 2, *RG 218.* On direct commissions and drafting of personnel: see 29 June and 11 August 1943, CCS 385 (2–8–42) pts. 6–7, *RG 218.* O.S.S. had less success in acquiring sophisticated radio equipment that it wanted because its agents were not perfect radio men: J.P.S. 178/3, ABC 381 (12–3–42), sec. 2, *RG 165.* Also no luck for O.S.S. on getting approval to use Italian P.O.W.s for labor or German P.O.W.s for any purpose, 6 May 1944, CCS 385 (2–8–42), pt. 9, *RG 218.* 8 December 1943, CCS 385 (11–28–43), German POWs for OSS, *RG 218.*

10. 28 June 1943, Cheston to adjutant general, 28 October 1943 list of personnel overseas, 9 December 1943, Corey to Gridley, 22 December 1943 (JCS 627) and 29 May 1944, Harrison to adjutant general are the most important items but other materials are also in pts. 6–9, CCS 385 (2–8–42), *RG 218,* plus JCS 406, 13 July 1943, CCS 385, ETO (4–12–43), *RG 218* and JPS 375/16, 8 June 1944, ABC 400.3295, sec. 2-A (8–2–43), *RG 165.*

11. June–November 1944, S.O.E. strength, *WO 212/209,* Public Record Office, London.

12. 8 and 19 April 1943, 28 February and 6 March, 1944, CCS 111 (6–17–42) *RG 218;* Memo for F.D.R., 8 May 1943, *OF 4485.*

13. 13 May 1943, memo, Special Orders File, Box 9, Entry 1, *RG 226;* 24 April 1944 memo, CCS 385 Middle East (12–1–42), sec. 2, *RG 218.*

14. Rumor lists, 31 December 1943, 7 January and 31 March 1944, *FO 898/69.* Carter was busy on the black propaganda front in 1943, working with Hanfstaengl and (partly with O.S.S. money) preparing the first Hitler study (by Henry A. Murray of Harvard) for covert propaganda use (Boxes 123–125 *PSF*). But the president began to turn cautious on Hanfstaengl by July 1943: F.D.R. memo, 23 July, January–July File, Box 123, *PSF.*

15. 7 January and 5 May 1944 rumor directives, *FO 898/69.*

16. Undated report, filed in September–December 1943 File, Box 72, *Map Room.*

17. August 1943 report in NATO Monthly Report File, Box 23, Entry 1, *RG 226;* 2 July 1943, British Embassy to F. O., *FO 371/34584/C8670.*

18. See *PSF* and *Map Room* files for this period.

19. 16 March, 25/26 June, 13, 21, and 29 July, 9 August, 11 and 20 September 1943, *Wilkinson.*

20. 30 September 1943, *Wilkinson.* Since nearly routine estimates of enemy intentions from Magic and Ultra sources went directly to commanders (see for example 16 March 1944, Marshall to Eisenhower, Folder 29, Box 56, *Marshall,*) exclusion tended to make O.S.S. look second-rate in combat theaters, too.

21. Jonathan Daniels, *White House Witness 1942–1945* (Garden City, New York: 1972), p. 206. 10 November 1943, 675: 1–4, *Morgenthau.*

22. 17 December 1943, Royal for J.C.S., pt. 8, 30 July 1943, Magruder to Deane, pt. 6, CCS 385 (2–8–42), *RG 218.* Under an Anglo-American agreement, S.I.S. people in the United States were banned from contact with representatives of governments other than those of the U.S. and the U.K.: 9 August 1943, *Wilkinson.*

23. *Langer,* pp. 187–188. 8 June and 17 September 1943, Miscellaneous File and "Grudge" File, Box 1; 11 May 1943, Morale File, Box 10; and 23 September 1943, Morrison to Langer, U.S.S.R. Division File, Box 5, Entry 1, *RG 226.*

24. 19 May 1943, Wheeler to Morse (2), Evaluation Committee File, Box 7; 22 May 1943 and 9 February 1944, Relations with S.I. File and 26 May 1943, U.S.S.R. Division File, Box 5, Entry 1, *RG 226.*

25. See projects committee Files, May 1943 on, Entry 59, Box 1, plus March 1944, Personnel Reports, Box 11, and Wilson to Langer, 22 April 1943, Middle East Expedition File, Entry 1, Box 19, *RG 226.*

26. 12 January 1944 mtg., *WO 204/827;* Conley to Langer, 1 April 1944, NATO File, Box 23, Entry 1, *RG 226;* 6 July and 4 September 1943, Hull–Stimson Exchange, Vol. 44, Roll 8, *Stimson Diary.*

27. 12 April 1944, (report), Box 2, Entry 59, *RG 226.*

28. 31 July–6 August 1943 exchange, Justice Department File, Box 1, Entry 1, *RG 226.* 10 November 1943 Projects Committee, S.O. File, Box 1, Entry 60, 20 September 1943, Kent to Schorske, Chief Europe–North Africa File, Box 1, Entry 1, *RG 226.*

29. Projects Committee, Boxes 1 and 2, Entry 60, 13 July 1943, Remer to Hall, F.E.T.O. File, Box 16, 12 July 1943 agreement, CAD File, Box 2; 20 January 1944, London File (2), Box 17, 10 February 1944, Brinton to Donovan, Brinton File, Box 21, all Entry 1, *RG 226.*

30. 12 April 1944, Director's Committee File, Box 7, Entry 1 and 9 March 1944, Box 1, Entry 59, *RG 226.*

31. On the Soviet Union, see chapter 7.

32. 10 February 1944 mtg., *WO 204/827.*

33. June–August 1943 (no date), 23, 27 July, 1943, June–August File, Box 72 and 29 July and mid–December 1943, MR 210 (3) File, Box 78, *Map Room;* 11 August 1943, Wiley to F.D.R., 1943 File, Box 167, *PSF;* 17 April and 18 August 1943, Box 6, Wiley Papers, Franklin D. Roosevelt Library.

34. On 25 February 1944, F.N.B. reported that the pro-Soviet press in the United States "vigorously" supported an American national service act, and on 2 March 1944, regarding the Polish–Russian border issue, concluded that American opinion was split with 57 percent having no opinion, while 22 percent were pro-Polish and 17 percent pro-Russian: January–May File, Box 73, *Map Room.* On a possible German–Soviet deal: 15 and 22 March, 30 April, 9 May, and pre-October 1943 (appropriate files for these dates), Box 72, *Map Room.* Bern to Victor, 24 September 1943, September–December File, Box 72, *Map Room.*

35. Pre-22 October 1943 (2 items), September–December File, Box 72, 11 January and 5 April 1944, January–May File, Box 73, *Map Room.* 11 October 1943, Donovan to F.D.R., 1943 File, Box 167 and Donovan to F.D.R., 20 May 1944, January–June File, Box 167, *PSF.*

36. 3 December 1943, Bern to Victor, 103.918/12–443 and 21 April 1944, Bern to Victor, 103.918/2227, *Diplomatic Branch,* 20 March 1944, Donovan to F.D.R., O.S.S. Safe File, Box 6, *PSF;* 18 February and 29 April 1944, January–May File, Box 73, *Map Room.* See also Donovan to F.D.R., 3 April 1944, O.S.S. Safe File, Box 6, *PSF.*

37. Pre-13 September, pre-28 October and pre-15 November 1943, September–December File, Box 72, and 2 and 22 February, 12 and 21 April, 1944, January–May File, Box 73, *Map Room.* Note on rules governing O.S.S. contacts: Donovan to Welles, 6 April 1943, *FRUS 1943,* I, p. 490.

38. 11 November 1943, Wiley memo, Box 6, Wiley Papers, Franklin D. Roosevelt Library.

39. For Poole's views, 18 September memorandum, Poole Papers, correspondence 1918–1952 File, Box 1, State Historical Society of Wisconsin. On Rogers, FF–Buxton File, Box 2, FF–OSS file, Box 8, and FF–Wilson File, Box 12, Rogers Papers, Colorado Historical Society. 20 September 1943 Wiley Memo, Box 6, Wiley Papers, Franklin D. Roosevelt Library.

40. 10 July 1943, uncatalogued correspondence, Horatio Smith File, Box 12, O'Brien Papers, Columbia University.

41. *Taylor,* pp. 349–351. Wallace Deuel, 4 September and 6 December 1943 letters, 1943 File, Box 1, Wallace Deuel Papers, Library of Congress.

42. 6 December 1943, Deuel to his parents, 1943 File, Box 1, Wallace Deuel Papers, Library of Congress; Wilson to Rogers, 10 and 27 January 1944, FF–Wilson File, Box 12, Rogers Collection, Colorado Historical Society; Heber Blankenhorn, "Psychological Warfare Report," p. 301, Hoover Institution. On rising British wariness of Donovan: 7 February 1944, Sporborg report, *FO 954/24A.*

43. 26 and 29 October 1943, Sherwood and Donovan to F.D.R., 1943 File, Box 167, *PSF;* Stettinius to Hull, 12 November 1943, Secretary October 1943–January 1944 File, Box 218, *Stettinius.*

44. *Taylor,* pp. 349–351; David Seifer to R. Harris Smith, 5 August 1971, Box 1, R. Harris Smith Papers, Hoover Institution; 21 October 1943 (2) Donovan to F.D.R. with F.D.R. comments, 1943 File, Box 167, *PSF.*

45. 3 March 1944, *Wilkinson.*

46. 25 October 1943, ABC 381 Germany (10–29–43), sec. 2–A, *RG 165;* 30 March 1944, January-May File, Box 73, *Map Room.*

47. 13 February 1944, *WO 204/1008.* An O.S.S. report that noted that despite the destruction in Berlin, an eyewitness reported that the railroads were still running and the population saw no choice but to fight to the end, bore a pencilled note from Admiral Brown, "please show to Admiral Leahy." 5 April 1944, January–May File, Box 73, *Map Room.*

48. 20 September 1943, *Wilkinson;* Marshall to Handy, 20 October 1943, 1893 File, (microfilm nr. 55, Marshall Library).

49. Hayes to State, 17 February and 8 and 18 March, 1944, ABC 381 (12–3–42), *RG 165;* Hayes to State, 6 March, and Berle to Deane, 26 March 1943, CCS 330 Spain (3–26–43), Sec. 1, *RG 218.*

50. See 18 February–10 April 1943, CCS 330, (3–26–43), sec. 1, *RG 218;* 13 March–8 April 1943, JCS 254, ABC 381 (12–3–42), sec. 2, *RG 165.*

51. McFarland to Donovan and 25 p. reply, 3 April 1943 and following, ABC 381 (12–3–42), sec. 2, *RG 165.*

52. J.C.S. 73rd. mtg., 9 April 1943, CCS 330 (3–26–43) sec. 1, *RG 218.*

53. 17 June 1943, Hayes to State, 103.918/1352, *Diplomatic Branch.*

54. 6 July 1943, Strong to Marshall, CCS 330, (3–26–43), sec. 1, *RG 218;* Selected documents concerning O.S.S. operations in Lisbon, spring 1943 SRH–113, Records of NSA, RG 457, Modern Military Branch, National Archives.

55. 17–27 July 1943, Peck-Donovan-Burton exchange, CCS 330 (3–26–43) sec. 1, *RG 218.* Donovan's 31 May 1943 reply to a J.C.S. question about his European plans skips over Spain, ABC 381 (12–3–42), sec. 2, *RG 165.*

56. Victor channel on Gridley mission, 6 August, 22 and 23 September 1943, 103.91802/1249 and 103.918/1803 and 1692, *Diplomatic Branch.* Gridley and Greenwood investigations, 17 September 1943, 6 February 1944, ABC 381 (12–3–42), sec. 3. Gridley conclusion and basis of "treaty," 27 October, 3 and 6 November 1943, CCS 330 (3–26–43), sec. 1, *RG 218;* George Kennan's view is in 19 June 1943, Leahy to Berle, CCS 383.4 (6–18–43), Coordination of Intelligence, *RG 218.* The treaty text is enclosed in JPS 386/2, 2 February 1944, CCS 385 (12–1–42), sec. 1, *RG 218.*

57. 19 July 1943, *Cadogan.* A 9 March 1944 British summary notes that at least six separate Allied agencies were running agents in Spain, *WO 204/1958.*

58. 24 August 1943, Special Ops. committee mtg., *WO 204/840;* July 1944 O.S.S. Operational Plans, pp. 2–3, ABC 350.05 (6–21–44), *RG 165;* 11 January 1944 Medusa personnel requirements, CCS 330 (3–26–43), sec. 2, *RG 218.* By 1 April 1944, some 750 agents and

subagents were operating: Medusa File, G–2 Message Center Reel, *AFHQ.*

59. 9 April 1943, JCS 73rd mtg., CCS 330 (3–26–43), sec. 1, *RG 218.*

60. JCS memo. of information 258, 28 June 1944, ABC 381 (12–3–42), sec. 3, *RG 165;* 6–29 April 1944, Donovan–Francis Perkins exchange, Francis Perkins Papers, Columbia; 28 April 1944, Hull to London for Stockholm, 103.918/1214A, *Diplomatic Branch;* Donovan to F.D.R., 20 March 1944 (on Kersten), O.S.S. Safe File, Box 6, *PSF;* 14 October 1943, 103.918/1752 (on Kersten), *Diplomatic Branch; The Kersten Memoirs 1940–1945* (New York: 1957), pp. 187–197 (these should be treated with great caution); *Hoover,* pp. 218–220.

61. G. Schulze Gaevernitz article, 1965, Gaevernitz File, Box 141, *Dulles.*

62. 17 February 1950 Dulles defense of Jung, Switzerland File, Box 47, *Dulles.* Letter of 15 September 1943 and scattered 1944 letters, J. Foster Dulles Papers, Princeton.

63. 6 January 1944, 103.91802/1–644, *Diplomatic Branch.*

64. 22 April 1943 (on U-boats), March–May 1943 file; pre-14 December (one on "window" and three on German rockets), September–December 1943 File, Box 72, *Map Room.*

65. 14, 22, and 27 April 1943, March–May File, Box 72, *Map Room* (note 21 April Stockholm report on gas in the same file). J.C.S. consideration of these problems, in which Bern O.S.S. reports are noted, are in CCS 385.2 (12–17–43), sec. 1, Chemical, Biological and Radiological Warfare, *RG 218.*

66. Four reports from Bern, late May–August 1943, June–August File, Box 72, *Map Room.* The original of the erroneous prediction of German intentions in the east is Bern to Victor, 27 May 1943, 103.918/1271, *Diplomatic Branch.*

67. On the Kolbe contact: Gerald Mayer statement, 24 March 1947, Mayer File, Box 31, *Dulles;* 15 June 1948, sworn Allen Dulles statement on Kolbe, Kolbe File, Box 36, *Dulles.*

68. Dulles frankly and rather bravely admitted after the war that his initial estimate of the effect of the bombing was wrong, Allen W. Dulles, *Germany's Underground,* p. 169. 4 August 1943, June–August File, October (2) and December (1) 1943 reports, September–December File, Box 72, and 6 and 11 March 1944, January–May File, Box 73, *Map Room.* 19 April 1944, Buxton to F.D.R., Naval Aide PF File, Box 171, *Map Room.* The flurry over Dulles comments on the Kolbe material: 12–19 April 1944, File 15, Box 66, *Marshall.*

69. 6, 22, 24 April 1943 reports, March–May File; June–August 1943 (3), June–August File; one pre-6 October 1943 report, September–December File; Box 72, *Map Room.* An erroneous report on Himmler, 26 August 1943, is in Burns to Victor, 103.918/1559, *Diplomatic Branch.*

70. Ten Bern reports on Italy, mid-June to mid-August 1943 are in June–August File, with two more in the September–December File, Box 72, *Map Room.*

71. 15 April 1943, Burns to Victor, 103.918/1155, *Diplomatic Branch*; 24 May 1943 report on Italy, March–May File and two summary reports in August, June–August File, Box 72, *Map Room.*

72. 7 May 1968, Swiss letter to Dulles, Switzerland File, Box 169, *Dulles.*

73. 14 and 21 April 1943, March–May File, a summary report is in June–August File and another summary report is in September–December File, Box 72, *Map Room.* A Dulles man in Rome dealing directly with Badoglio people concluded that the Germans were bluffing, 11 August 1943, Burns to Victor, 103.918/1495, *Diplomatic Branch.* Dulles reported on many other matters as well, such as Yugoslavia, including two reports in December 1943 on Mihailović's connections with the Germans, 3 and mid-December 1943, September–December File, Box 72, *Map Room.*

74. O.S.S. and S.O.E. numbers, May–June 1944 summary, *WO 212/208,* Public Record Office, London, and Cheston to adjutant general, 28 June 1943, CCS 385 (2–8–42), pt. 6, *RG 218.* On priorities and air power: C.O.S. (43) 255th mtg. (attachment) 16 October 1943, C.O.S. (43) 289th mtg. 26 November 1943, COS (44) 15th mtg., 19 January 1944, *CAB 79/69;* AFHQ History of Special Operations, *WO 204/2030B;* Dodds–Parker summary of S.O.E. operations, 16 July 1943, ABC 334.3 sec. 3 (5–1–42), *RG 165.*

75. On aircraft: Donovan request and J.P.S. consideration, 13 June 1943, ABC 381 (12–3–42), sec. 2. On psychological warfare: 25 July 1943 report by Makins: *FO 898/167;* 16 November 1943, Colonel Thornhill report, *FO 898/175;* 11 June 1943, Sherwood to Jackson, "Needed from War files" (3), Box 10, C.D. Jackson Papers, Eisenhower Library. On X-2 and S.I.: July counterintelligence reports, North Africa, *WO 204/808;* Special Ops. Committee mtgs. (especially 17 August 1943), *WO 204/840;* S.I. and Corsica, Spec. Ops. (2)

File, Reel 6-D-I, G-3, *AFHQ*. On R. and A.: October 1943–August 1944 reports, especially 28 November 1943, Kline to Robinson, NATO File, Box 23, Entry 1, *RG 226*. Praise by General Rooks, and Eisenhower's echo: JCS memo for record, 14 August 1943, ABC 381 (12–3–42), sec. 3, *RG 165*; 28 August 1943, *Eisenhower Papers*, II, pp. 1360–1361. On overall intelligence and special operations system Mediterranean, see AFHQ History of Special Operations, *WO 204*/2030B; fifteenth Army intelligence summaries, *WO 204*/7274; G-2 organization, 9 August 1943; *WO 204*/941; Intelligence distribution, 23 December 1943, *WO 204*/4179. Role of the theater intelligence section, 27 December 1943, *WO 219*/1661.

76. Smith to Eddy, 18 August 1943, *WO 204*/2030B; 17 August 1943 on the P.W.B., *FO 898*/176; 3 November 1943, on AMGOT, *WO 204*/9471E. On the long-lasting negative view of Glavin, Hyde to Dulles, 7 November, 1966, Wally File, Box 151, *Dulles*.

77. On organization: 13 October 1943 memo to Murphy, File K, Box 1, L. Rounds Papers, Hoover Institution; Glavin to King, 23 October 1943, Correspondence and Personal Data Files, David King Papers, Hoover Institution; 5 June 1944, 350.05 O.S.S. (6–21–44) sec. 1, *RG 165*. On counterintelligence in North Africa: 1–15 May 1944 report, *WO 204*/806; fortnightly reports, November–December 1943, *WO 204*/808; 17 January 1944, Childs to State, 103.918/2048, *Diplomatic Branch*; J. Rives Childs, "Thirty Years in the Near East," pp. 184–186, Hoover Institution; 16 March 1944, Wilson to C.C.S., CCS 385 (11–7–42), *RG 218*. On sub-saharan Africa: 8 and 26 September 1943, CCS 385 (2–8–42), pt. 7, *RG 218*; 5 June 1944, O.S.S. Operational plan, ABC 350.05 (6–21–44), *RG 165*.

78. Murphy to Hull, 30 June 1943 on Donovan's negative views of de Gaulle, File 49, Box 80, *Marshall*; 9 February 1944, Rounds to Boulton, File K, Box 1, L. Rounds Papers, Hoover Institution; Hughes to Langer, 23 March 1944, Algiers File, Box 15, Entry 1, *RG 226*.

79. On Italian resistance contacts, S.O.E. summary, 2 April 1943, *FO 898*/170; COS (43) 212 (0), *CAB 80*/69. On N.K.V.D.: *FO 371*/47709/N1109. (My thanks to Martin Kitchen for sharing this reference.) The operational intelligence in the files comes overwhelmingly from the British, especially I.S.I.S., not the Americans: *WO 204*/758, *WO 204*/6955, *WO 204*/6964. This was even true for American officers, Box 2, Walter J. Muller Papers, Hoover Institution.

80. 5 April 1943, *WO 204*/758; 3 May 1943, *WO 204*/1953; 18 June 1943, *WO 204*/7274.

81. On S.O. and S.O.E. in Husky: Special Ops. File, Reel 6 D-1, G-3, *AFHQ*. May–June exchange: CCS 385 (2–13–42), sec. 1, *RG 218*; General Rooks note, 4 May 1943, *WO 204*/1953. Beach Jumpers: 7 March 1944, *WO 204*/8425. On psychological warfare: British paper, 1 April 1943, *FO 898*/165; COS (43) 233 (0) 2 May 1943, S.O.E. paper attached, *CAB 80*/69; 20 May 1943, J.C.S. and Churchill anger at O.W.I., CCS 385, Italy, sec. 2, (10–19–42), *RG 218*; 21 May 1943, March–May File, Box 72, *Map Room*; June 1943 Eisenhower black radio plan, *WO 106*/3876.

82. Counterintelligence organization Sicily, 21 August 1943, *WO 204*/758. The American army official history sees some Mafia revival, Harry L. Coles and Albert K. Einberg, *Civil Affairs: Soldiers Become Governors* (Washington D.C.: 1964), pp. 208–210. The civil affairs reports are: fall 1943, *WO 204*/9736–9740; September 1943, *WO 204*/9741A; 1 September 1943, *WO 204*/9741C; 20–21 August 1943, *FO 371*/37237/R10218; 3 September, 1943, *FO 371*/37237/R10225; 6 October 1943, *FO 371*/37237/R11482; 29 October 1943 report on Mafia in Sicily, *FO 371*/37237/R11482. Release of Sicilians, 28 July 1943, *WO 204*/6894. Rodney Campbell, *The Luciano Project* (New York: 1977), pp. 175–181. Part of the confusion may have arisen from the fact that some in O.S.S. wanted to use partial self-government in Sicily as a propaganda weapon to weaken Fascist and Nazi morale (June–August File, Box 72) *Map Room* and that a July S.I. mission using Sicilian-born O.S.S. men, which was canceled, was code-named Mafia. Special Ops. File (2), Reel 6-D-I, G-3, *AFHQ*.

83. On 13 July 1943, the War Office ordered Eisenhower's British deputy chief of staff, Maj. Gen. J. F. M. Whiteley, to recover Lord Lilford's stuffed birds, *WO 204*/307. Some British officers, including General Wilson, had doubts about the soft underbelly idea, Kenneth Strong, *Intelligence at the Top*, p. 130. One of the elements in the early armistice talks with the Italians was to gain release of an S.O.E. man code-named Mallaby, captured in northern Italy. (Kenneth Strong, *Intelligence at the Top*, p. 152). This was the same man who, in a much later mission, would contribute to the Nazi idea that the West wished to

Notes

make a deal with the Nazis against the Soviets, *Smith and Agarossi*, p. 67. 10 September 1943, D.40 Directive, *FO 898/69*. Donovan was present as an observer during the Sicily and Salerno landings.

84. General Airey's estimate, 25 September 1943, *WO 204/7274*. Robert Murphy, *Diplomat Among Warriors*, p. 201.

85. 24 August 1943 orders to Special Force, 5th Army, *WO 204/1953*. 14 September 1943 document attached to 18 August 1943 entry, *Butcher Diary*.

86. Special Operations mtgs., 10 August 1943 on, *WO 204/840*. Support from Switzerland shows up in *FO 898/26*. Cooperation with Italian intelligence: 15 September 1943, W. B. Smith memo, *WO 204/2780*; 17 September 1943, *Butcher Diary*. On O.S.S.-inspired Italian O.G. units, Donovan to F.D.R., 1943 File, Box 167, *PSF*; 7 October 1943 Algiers to War, and 12 October Donovan to Royal, CCS 385 (2–13–42), sec. 1, *RG 218*.

87. Donovan to F.D.R., 23 October 1943, 1943 File, Box 167, *PSF*; 27 January 1944 Badoglio to F.D.R., *FRUS 1944*, III, p. 1011–1012. On Pazzi-Rossi, 26 May 1944 Stettinius memo, Secretary of State File, Box 218, *Stettinius* and Jonathan Daniels, *White House Witness*, p. 224–225. A cryptic reference to "the Italian matter," which may be related to this is in Donovan to F.D.R., 23 and 29 May 1944, Subject File, Box 167, *PSF*.

88. 19–29 August 1943, CCS 385 (5–8–43), pt. 1, Plan for Psychological Warfare, Sardinia and Corsica, *RG 218*.

89. 29 May 1943, JCS 337, CCS 385 (5–8–43), pt. 1, *RG 218*; 16 September 1943, COS (43) 218, *CAB 79/64*; 21 September and 5 October 1943, *WO 204/840*. History of Special Operations, April 1943 on, *WO 204/2030B*; 17 September 1943, Whiteley to Kennedy, *WO 204/307*.

90. On organization, 28 June 1944 report, ABC 381 (12–3–42), sec. 3, *RG 165*; History of Special Operations, *WO 204/2030B*; AFHQ minutes, 20 September 1943, *WO 204/65*; 30 November 1943 Special ops. mtg. shows that Eddy was out and Glavin was in, *WO 204/840*. The advance headquarters of the 2677th was ordered to Bari on 23 September 1943, *WO 204/7818*. By 20 September 1943, O.S.S. had twenty-four agents in Naples and approximately fifty-five officers and men attached to fifth Army, plus a courier service from Switzerland. Special Ops. 2 File, G-3 Division, Reel 6 D-I, *AFHQ*. On further input of agents, see file *WO 204/307*. The loss near Spezia appears in the 25/26th Sit. Rep., *WO 204/1964*. On O.G. action, 24 March 1944, *WO 204/6806* and a graphic account by Peter Karlow written 24 February 1945, History of O.S.S. File, Box 11, Entry 1, *RG 226*. On intelligence organization and distribution system, 13 November 1943, W. B. Smith instructions, *WO 204/840*, and 3 March 1944 distribution list, *WO 204/7032*.

91. The 2678th Headquarters Company was the C.I.C., 20 October 1943, *WO 204/4179*. X-2 report on Italian Communists, 14 January 1944, *WO 204/9741F*. For R. and A., see NATO File, Box 23, Entry 1, *RG 226*; and 10 January 1944, Glavin to Sloane, *WO 204/935*. On black propaganda, 24 February 1944 special directive on coordination with operations, *WO 204/1966*.

92. For "S" forces and P.O.W. recovery, *WO 204/907* and 14 December 1943 mtg., *WO 204/840*. Partisan numbers in History of Special Operations, *WO 204/2030B*; 10 April 1944 J.C.S. memo for Information contains the whole organizational layout in Caserta. CCS 385 (12–1–42), sec. 2. *RG 218*. For problems see, Peter Tompkins, *A Spy in Rome* (New York: 1962), passim.

93. Marshall put this case to F.D.R., 22 November 1943, File 5, Box 81, *Marshall*.

94. 20 March 1943, Hoskins report, ABC 000.24 (7–27–42), *RG 165*; 27 April 1943 report on Middle East O.S.S., Middle East Expedition File, Box 19, Entry 1, *RG 226*.

95. Part of the trouble in Turkey was whether use of military O.S.S. people would violate international law. For the Turkey issue: 30 April–16 June 1943, ABC 385 (12–7–42), *RG 165*; 29 July–9 August 1943, CCS 385, Turkey (6–13–43), *RG 218*. For the Middle East O.S.S. personnel authorization, 15 November 1943, Buxton memo., CCS 385 (2–8–42), pt. 8, *RG 218*.

96. *Barker*, p. 114. On Greece: 23 April–20 November 1943, History of Special Operations, *WO 204/2030B*; 21 May 1943, *FO 954/24A*. Albania: History of Special Operations, *WO 204/2030B*; *FO 898/26*; Deane to JCS and G-1, 13 May 1943, CCS (2–13–42), sec. 1, *RG 218*.

97. Matteo J. Milazzo, *The Chetnik Movement and Yugoslav Resistance*, pp. 131–164; Jozo Tomasevich, *The Chetniks*, pp. 191–195, and 279–368. 21 April 1943, *Cadogan;* Sar-

gent to Eden, 16 November 1943, FO 954/24A. On American participation: 19 April 1943, C in C Middle East, *WO 204*/8644; 3 July 1943, Kirkpatrick to Minister of State and attached, *FO 898*/69. On the O.S.S. view of British Yugoslav policy, 30 March and 8 and 13 April 1943, March–May File, Box 72, *Map Room*.

98. On. O.S.S. entrance into the Balkans and relations with the British: 11 June–4 July 1943, ABC 385 (12–7–42), *RG 165;* 26 July 1943 agreement, ABC 091.411 Greece–Yugoslavia (11–27–43), sec. 2, *RG 165;* 16 July 1943, *Cadogan;* 20 August 1943, Donovan to F.D.R., January–June File, Box 167, *PSF*, Jozo Tomasevich, *The Chetniks,* pp. 373–383; Robert Murphy, *Diplomat Among Warriors,* p. 221; *Sweet-Escott,* pp. 195–196. On O.S.S. views of Balkan policy: Donovan to F.D.R., 11 May and 25, 28, and 29 October 1943, 1943 File, Box 167, *PSF;* pre-20 September 1943, September–December File, Box 72, *Map Room;* 6–7 November 1943 report on Mihailović and 4 December 1943 General Strong opinion, CCS 381 (10–29–43), sec. 1, *RG 218.*

99. The statistics are in 14 October 1943, COS (43) 626, *CAB 122*/762. For British policy struggles on S.O.E.–O.S.S. and the Middle East: 31 July 1943, COS (43) 428 (0), *CAB 80*/72; 12 September–10 October 1943, minister of state–prime minister exchange, *WO 193*/620; 21–22 September 1943, DO (43), *CAB 69*/6; 30 September 1943, *Cadogan.* For later, less comprehensive O.S.S. Middle East statistics, see 6 June 1944, ABC 350.05 (6–21–44), sec. 3, *RG 218.*

100. 11 October 1943 mtg., *WO 204*/840 and *WO 204*/65; plus 12 October *WO 204/840.* 17 October 1943, seaborne delivery system reorganized, History of Special Operations, *WO 204*/2030B; and relations with Middle East group, 16 November 1943, *WO 204*/840. But the British wanted even more special operations activity, 15 October 1943, COS (43) 250, *CAB 79*/66 and 17 October 1943 COS to JSM, *CAB 122*/762.

101. JCS 484 and related documents, 20 August, 7 and 17 September 1943, ABC 019.411 Balkans (8–21–43), *RG 165;* 11 August 1943 comments, CCS 092 Bulgaria (8–2–43), *RG 218.*

102. *Barker,* pp. 118–119; 6 January 1944, Harriman to State, *FRUS 1944,* I, pp. 580–581; 25 November 1943 and 2 March 1944, CCS 092 (8–2–43), sec. 1, *RG 218.* 7 January 1944, Donovan to MacVeagh, John O. Iatrides, ed., *Ambassador MacVeagh Reports,* p. 424. Note that the first important item that the Soviets provided in the N.K.V.D. exchange (see chapter 7) was an extensive report on Bulgaria in 11 March 1944, Chronological File, *RG 334.*

103. 20 November–9 December 1943, on Hungary, ABC 384 Hungary (11–21–43), *RG 165.* General British suspicions of Donovan's activities: War Office note, 10 October 1943, *WO 204*/1953; 3 December 1943, *FRUS Conferences at Cairo and Teheran,* pp. 777–778. British views on Bulgaria and Donovan's activities: *Sweet-Escott,* p. 194; 31 December 1943, COS to Eisenhower, O.S.S. Ops. File nr. 1, Roll 17A, AFHQ; 15 January 1944, *FO 371*/43579 (again my thanks to Martin Kitchin for the reference); 3 March 1944, M.I. 3 appraisal. *WO 208*/111. Donovan's general appraisal of the situation in the Balkans: 26 November 1943, CCS 381 (10–29–43), sec. 1, *RG 218,* and his report on Jadwin to F.D.R., 24 March 1944, Safe File, O.S.S. Box 6, *PSF.* The policy issues involved in Jadwin, relations with the British and Soviets, and bombing policy are covered in a huge file ranging from 6 January to 24 March 1944, CCS 092 (8–2–43), *RG 218.* Note too that J.I.C. Cairo concluded on 3 May 1944 that bombing and propaganda would help convince Balkan states that they would have to deal with the Soviets as well as the West, *WO 204*/8564.

104. *Loewenheim,* pp. 385–386; Ilija Jukić, *The Fall of Yugoslavia,* pp. 213–215; JCS 603, 27 November 1943, general materials on Yugoslavian policy, CCS 381 (10–29–43), sec. 1, *RG 218;* two late November–early December reports, September–December File, Box 72, *Map Room.* The Farish report is readily available in *FRUS, Conferences at Cairo and Teheran,* 29 October 1943, pp. 606–615.

105. 5 December 1943, CCS 387/3, *WO 204*/480.

106. 11 January 1944, Wilson to Marshall, CCS 385 (12–1–42), sec. 1, *RG 218;* 19 January 1944, Annex A to JCS 714, ABC 322.01, Yugoslavia, (11–5–1943), sec. 5, *RG 165;* 20 January 1944, *Butcher Diary.*

107. The original Donovan disagreement with the British may be followed in: 17 January 1944 mtg., *WO 204*/840; 18 January 1944, Donovan to General Gammell, O.S.S.–S.O.E. Policy File nr. 2, Reel 38-A, Spec. Ops. *AFHQ;* 19 January 1944, Donovan to JCS, CCS 381 (10–29–43), Sec. 1, *RG 218;* 16 and 22 January 1944, Macmillan to F. O., *FO 954*/24A; 4

Notes

February 1944, Macmillan to Prime Minister, *WO 106*/3965B; 25 January 1944, COS (44) 23rd. mtg., *CAB 79*/69. The parallel mission plan and its approval; 26 January 1944, *FRUS 1944*, IV, pp. 1339–1340 and 1369–1370; 28 January–3 March 1944, CCS 385 (12–1–42), sec. 1, *RG 218;* 2 February 1944, Gridley to Donovan, ABC 091.411 (11–27–43), sec. 2, *RG 165;* 5 March 1944, Churchill report and 18 March, MacLean report, *WO 204*/1967; 20 April, Caffey report, *WO 204*/1968.

108. 4 March–May 1944, on a Mihailović mission (much just declassified), CCS 381 (10–29–43), sec. 2, *RG 218*. Donovan to F.D.R., 1–2 March 1944, January–June File and Subject File, Box 167, *PSF;* 22 March, 10 and 22 May, O.S.S. Safe File, Box 6, *PSF*. Donovan even sent a Mihailović letter to Eisenhower, 31 March 1944, Donovan File, Box 35, *Eisenhower,* but the latter refused to reply, 9 April 1944, *Eisenhower Papers*, II, p. 1815. British prompted MacVeagh protest about pro–Mihailović activities; 21 February 1944, *FRUS 1944*, II, pp. 1349–1350; and a Churchill protest, 6 April 1944, *Loewenheim*, pp. 482–483. The British also had some balmy ideas. When the commanders of A.F.H.Q. and Middle East met on 5 February 1944, one of their conclusions regarding Yugoslavia was that "the King is to be encouraged to fly over to Yugoslavia as a fighter pilot." A member of Wilson's staff wrote on the margin, "Blimey!!!" O.S.S./S.O.E. policy File no. 2, G-3 Spec Ops., Reel 38-A, *AFHQ*.

109. January–June 1944 reports, CCS 381 (10–29–43) sec. 2 and bulky package. *RG 218*. Donovan forwarded a Tito message to F.D.R., 15 March 1944, confidential file, OSS Files, Box 12, and on 5 May 1944, Major Weil's sympathetic report on the partisans, O.S.S. Safe files, Box 6, *PSF*. It should also be noted that Eisenhower was highly impressed by partisan sacrifices and achievements and sought to send additional aid, 16 May 1944, 11 May on file, Box 145, *Eisenhower*.

110. In early 1944, O.S.S. told Ambassador MacVeagh that it was sending no warlike stores to the E.A.M. John O. Iatrides, ed., *Ambassador MacVeagh Reports*, p. 430.

111. 30 October 1943, Special Ops. to G-3, *WO 204*/840. The move and the base in Italy were codenamed "monkey puzzle" and "jungle" respectively. Formally, between March 1944 and February 1945 O.S.S. was responsible to the senior American officer (General Devers) who was in turn responsible to the theater commander. In February 1945 this contrivance was abolished, and O.S.S. was placed directly under the theater commander. O.S.S. Ops file no. 7, Reel 17A *AFHQ*.

112. History of Special Operations; *WO 204*/2030B; January–March 1944 Special operations mtgs., *WO 204*/840; February–March 1944 report on force 133, *WO 204*/1967, and 18 March 1944, *WO 106*/3965B. On "Z" Mission: March 1944, *WO 204*/1970. On supply to Tito: 26 November 1943, COS (43) 289, *CAB 79*/67. On the main bases: 17 February 1944, CCS 381 (10–29–43), sec. 2, *RG 218;* and 29 May 1944, *WO 204*/1957. On the overall mission denotation: April 1944, *WO 193*/620; Interview with Hans Tofte.

113. 11 January 1944 Spec. Ops. mtg., *WO 204*/840; 15 February 1944, February–May air sorties report, *WO 204*/870; 14 February 1944, COS (44) 163 (0), *CAB 122*/762; January 1944 report, CCS 381 (10–20–43), sec. 2, *RG 218*. Aircraft distribution: History of Special Operations, *WO 204*/2030B. May 1944 tonnage allotments, *WO 204*/1978; Major Morton report to Churchill; 26 April 1944, *Prem 3*/185/1.

114. The quote comes from February–March 1944 planning paper, Appendix A, *WO 204*/1967. On American complaints: 24 March and 24 April 1944, CCS 385 (12–1–42), sec. 2, *RG 218;* 21 April 1944, Madison to Langer, Cairo File, Box 15, Entry 1, *RG 226;* 7 May 1944 comment, *WO 204*/1968. On air supply and the Poles (and British efforts to control them): 19 January 1944, COS (44) 15th mtg., *CAB 79*/69 and 22 March 1944, Algiers to Washington, CCS 385 (12–1–42), sec. 2, *RG 218*.

115. On P.O.W. rescue: Airey Neave, *Escape Room* (New York: 1970), M. R. D. Foot. *M.I. 9*, (London: 1979); and 10 and 27 March 1944, CCS 381 (10–29–43), sec. 2, *RG 218*. Chrome operations: 10–13 April 1944, ABC 384.5, Sofia, (10–23–44) sec. 2, *RG 165;* SAC conference, 20 April 1944, *WO 204*/1969. Hungary, Bulgaria, Albania, Rumania: 16 March and 9 June 1944, CCS 383.4, Hungary (3–25–44), *RG 218;* 29 February 1944, *WO 204*/840; 28 April 1944, *WO 204*/4043; 15 May 1944; *WO 204*/1982; 7 June 1944, (Albania), COS (44) 502 (0), *CAB 80*/84; 22 March 1944 (Rumania), *WO 106*/3166. Raider forces: 15 March 1944, *WO 204*/8425; 19 March 1944, *WO 204*/7818.

116. On money sent into Yugoslavia: 19 April 1944, *WO 204*/1968. Intelligence collected

about the partisans: May–November 1944, *WO 204*/1977. Mission names: 27 May 1944, *WO 204*/1945. The Game Book, entry of 8 April 1944, *WO 204*/1971.

117. 16 March 1944, J.I.C. mtg., CCS 381 (10–29–43), sec. 2, *RG 218. Barker*, pp. 122–123. S.O.E. wanted to "dampen down" Greek resistance (Noah's Ark) because it feared—rightly—that it could not control it, 25 January 1944, COS (44) 23rd. mtg., *CAB 122*/762 and June 1944 O.S.S. operational plan, ABC 350.05 (6–21–44), *RG 165*.

118. History of Special Operations, *WO 204*/2030B; and 20 May 1944 report, *WO 204*/1957.

119. Free French organization for Overlord and Anvil, 4 November 1943, *WO 204*/935; c. May 1944 (Noce report) and April 1944 appraisal, *WO 204*/1957; 25 May 1944 history of Special projects center, *WO 219*/4968; 8 June–August 1944, intelligence inflow, *WO 204*/1947; March 1944, jurisdictional system, *WO 204*/485. On Sussex and its problems, File F-12, Box 4, Francis Miller Papers, Marshall Library.

120. 9 May 1944, SAC conference (44), 41st, *WO 204*/89; 12 May, Macmillan to Wilson and 13 May 1944, Wilson to Eisenhower, *WO 204*/1957.

121. 16 May 1944, *Butcher Diary;* May 1944 plan, History of Special Operations, *WO 204*/2030B.

122. Harold Macmillan, *The Blast of War*, p. 436. For Churchill's unfair blast at the S.O.E., *Barker*, pp. 141–142. Bruce Lockhart complaint about "trouble-makers," 20 May 1944, *FO 898*/171.

123. 14 June 1944, Wiley to Grace Tully, 1943 File, Box 167, *PSF*. The inflow of reports may be seen in Box 72, *Map Room*. There was some O.S.S.–Irish contact via David Bruce in early 1942, Carolle J. Carter, *The Shamrock and the Swastika* (Palo Alto, California: 1977), p. 81.

124. ETO File, Box 21, Entry 1, *RG 226*, especially 29 February note, 1 March and 11 April Deutsch messages, and 26 May 1944 Morse message. Also June 1944, CCS 334 (6–12–44), Combined Intelligence, *RG 218*.

125. 5 July–4 September 1943, CCS 385 (4–12–43), Sec. 1, *RG 218*; 13 July–27 September 1943, ABC 381 (12–3–42), sec. 2, *RG 165*; April 1943, ABC 385, Norway, (4–4–43), *RG 165*; 20 March 1943, COS (43) 143 (0) and 4 April 1943, COS (43) 167 (0), *CAB 80*/68; 24 March 1943 COS (43) 75th mtg., *CAB 79*/26. On Sussex trouble, File F-10, Box 4, Francis Miller Papers, Marshall Library.

126. 7 October 1943–45 April 1944 (much just declassified), CCS 385 (4–12–43), *RG 218*.

127. *Les Allies et la Resistance en Europe*, (Milan: 1961), II, p. 16; Files 5–8, Box 4, Francis Miller Papers, Marshall Library; 27 November 1943 ETOUSA Directive, *WO 204*/4179; 28 September 1943, British intelligence plan, CCS 350.09 (10–8–43), Spheres of Responsibility, *RG 218*. The British were most anxious to control, and were most successful in controlling, all O.S.S. contact and support for Poland: 2 July 1943–11 February 1944, ABC 452.1, Poland (11–26–42), sec. 1, *RG 165*; 7 November 1943, Eisenhower–Sosnokowski conference, *WO 204*/551.

128. Arthur L. Funk, "Churchill, Eisenhower, and the French Resistance," *Military Affairs*, 45, no. 1 (February 1981) 29–33. The basic documentation is in *PREM 3 185*/1 (January–June 1944). See also 28 January 1944 P.W.E.–S.O.E. mtg., *FO 898*/206; and 19 January 1944, COS (44) 15th mtg., *CAB 79*/69.

129. The main American documentation is in ABC 400.3295, sec. 2-A (8–2–43), *RG 165*. The British side is again in *PREM 3 185*/1.

130. April–May 1944 (especially 6 May 1944, Eisenhower report on comparative British and American aid to the resistance), ABC 400.3295, sec. 2-A (8–2–43), *RG 165*; 28 April–10 May 1944, White House–Marshall exchange, Files 14 and 15, *Marshall*; 27 May 1944, Matthews to Murphy, 103.918/2346, *Diplomatic Branch*; 17 May 1944, Eisenhower to War on increasing aid, *WO 106*/4320. See also Gordon A. Harrison, *Cross Channel Attack* (Washington: 1951), and Marcel Vigneras, *Rearming the French* (Washington: 1957), pp. 300–304. None of the heretofore published sources have shown the overwhelming British aid preponderance revealed by these inquiries.

131. 19 and 25 May 1944, ABC 400.3295, sec. 2-A (8–2–43), *RG 165*. On 3 March 1944, there was even a composite O.S.S. report playing down the political threat of the communist resistance, January–May File, Box 73, *Map Room*.

132. On legal questions: 4 May 1943, General Rooks, *WO 204*/1953; 23 October 1943

Culbertson memorandum, July–December 1943 File, Box 24, Culbertson Papers, Library of Congress. On air support: Forrest C. Pogue, *The Supreme Command* (Washington: 1954), p. 155. 8 and 17 April 1944, *Butcher Diary.*

133. A long 24 April 1943 S.O.E. survey of the state of resistance, country by country: COS (43) 212 (0), *CAB 80/69;* 23 October 1943 history of French resistance aid to invasion, *WO 219/4967.* The Netherlands investigation: 1 December 1943, CAB 79/88; 4 January 1944, AIR 14/3474, Bomber Command, Public Record Office; 5 January 1944, Ismay to prime minister, *FO 954/24A;* 14 January 1944, DO (44) 2 (0), *CAB 69/6.* M. R. D. Foot, *SOE in France,* Chapter 10; H. J. Giskes, *London Calling North Pole,* passim. On reimbursing plant owners, 25 April 1944, Selborne to Eden, *FO 954/24A.* The rumor plan, Directive 102, 5 May 1944, *FO 898/69.* Churchill was ready to go with pocket incendiaries for foreign workers in Germany as early as 21 April 1943, but there was Free French opposition: COS (43) 207 (0), *CAB 80/69.*

134. 22, 24, and 31 March and 4 April 1944, *FO 898/25 and 27.*

135. On Sussex, Files F-6, 9, 10, and 20, Box 4, Francis Miller Papers, Marshall Library.

136. Files F-5, 8 and 9, Box 4, Francis Miller Papers, Marshall Library; O'Brien to Donovan, 15 November 1946, Donovan File, Box 2, and O'Brien to Lucy B. Waters, Waters File, Box 13, O'Brien Papers, Columbia University; 11 April 1944, Hughes to Langer on anti–de Gaulle tendencies in North Africa, Algiers File, Box 15, Entry 1, *RG 226.*

137. Donovan to F.D.R., 6 April 1945, Box 167, *PSF;* Bernard Fergusson, *The Watery Maze,* pp. 303–304.

138. W.P. (44) 570, 13 October 1944, S.O.E. Assistance to Overlord, *CAB 66/56;* May–August 1944, Heber Blankenhorn, "Psychological Warfare Report," pp. 303–307, Hoover Institution.

139. File F-16, Box 4, Francis Miller Papers, Marshall Library; Forrest C. Pogue, *The Supreme Command,* p. 153; History of Special Operations, *WO 204/2030B;* 8 May 1944, JCS Memo 228, ABC 381 (12-3-42), sec. 2, *RG 165;* 17 December 1943 and 12 May 1944, special force plans, *WO 219/4967.*

140. March to May 1944, especially 9 May planning review, *WO 219/4967;* 1 June 1944 Eisenhower message, *WO 204/1958;* Forrest Pogue, *The Supreme Command,* p. 155.

141. "A Short History of F.F.I.," *WO 219/4968;* 13 October 1944, WP (44) 570, *CAB 66/56;* Donovan to President Truman, 4 May 1945, O.S.S. File, Box 15, Misc., *Truman;* Cheston to J.C.S., 15 March 1944, CCS 385 (2-8-42), pt. 9, *RG 218;* 27 March 1944, SOE/HQ. to G-3, ABC 400.3295, sec. 2-A (8-2-43), *RG 165.*

142. On Korea: 12 November–16 December 1943, ABC 385, (4-4-42), *RG 165;* Goodfellow to Hayden, 10 July 1942, Files 4 and 11, Box 41, *Hayden.* On the Thais: 26 October 1943, 103.918/11–843 and 26 February 1944, Wilson to Donovan, 103.918/2–2644, *Diplomatic Branch.*

143. 16 June–25 July 1943, 27 April and 3 May 1944, CCS 385, Pacific Theater (6-16-43), sec. 1, *RG 218;* 14–30 June 1943, ABC 385, Southwest Pacific (6-14-43), *RG 165;* 25 June and 15 July 1943, CCS 385 (2-8-42), pt. 6, *RG 218;* 17 April 1943, Box 1, Entry 1, Entry 58, *RG 226;* 26 February, 21 March, 19 April, 1944, *Wilkinson.* There are traces of R. and A. material in Hayden's files, Boxes 4, 8, 21, and 41, *Hayden,* but MacArthur's headquarters even had its own research section, Box 2, Bonner F. Fellers Papers, Hoover Institution.

144. 31 August 1943, Sherwood to Davis, CCS 385 (1-1-43), *RG 218.* Some British officers speculated that Donovan was going to Australia to offer MacArthur a deal if he would not be a presidential candidate! *FO 898/26.* 2 November 1943, *Wilkinson.*

145. William R. Peers and Dean Brelis, *Behind the Burma Road,* pp. 104–132.

146. Christopher Thorne, *Allies of a Kind,* pp. 338–339; 29 March 1943, COS (43) 79, *CAB/26;* 8 April–14 May 1943, ABC India (4-8-43), *RG 165.*

147. 5 May June and 5 August 1943, Bowes Lyon messages, CCS 385 (4-8-43), *RG 218;* 31 May and 18 June 1943, *WO 208/792;* 20 April 1943, Butler to Sayers, *WO 106/4632.*

148. 21 June and 10 July 1943, CCS 385 (4-8-43), *RG 218.*

149. Donovan to F.D.R., 10 June 1943, OSS Safe File, Box 6, *PSF;* 6 August 1943, Heppner to Victor, 103.918/1102; *Diplomatic Branch;* 7 August 1943, COS (43), 450, *CAB 79/72.*

150. 9 August–3 September 1943, ABC 385 (4-8-43), *RG 165.* At Quebec the British

specifically protested about O.S.S. activities in India, *FRUS. Conferences at Washington and Quebec*, 1943, p. 424.

151. 7 and 11 September, 3 and 12 October, 15 November, and 15 December 1943, *Wilkinson*. On S.A.C.O., Chinese weakness and inactivity: Davies to Donovan, 6 October, 20 September 1943 Wilson to Hoffman, FETO File, Box 16, Entry 1, *RG 226;* 15 April 1943 SACO agreement, ABC 384 China (12–15–43), sec. 1-D, *RG 165;* Milton E. Miles, *A Different Kind of War*, pp. 291–306. On plans: Langer to Donovan, 2 May 1943, FETO File, Box 16, Entry 1, *RG 226;* Fairbank to Langer, 5 April 1943, 103.918/1132, *Diplomatic Branch*.

152. Remer to Langer, 30 August 1943 (2), FETO File, Box 16 and 14 October 1943, Remer File, Box 3, Entry 1, *RG 226;* Heppner to Donovan, 29 July 1943, 103.918/17580, *Diplomatic Branch*; 6 November 1944, Donovan to F.D.R., November File, Box 170, *PSF;* Milton E. Miles, *A Different Kind of War*, pp. 169–174; *Taylor*, pp. 346–347.

153. 16, 18, 19 February 1944, CCS 385 (2–8–42), pt. 9, *RG 218;* 16 December 1943, Buxton to F.D.R., 1943 file, Box 167, *PSF;* 4 May 1944, Donovan to F.D.R., OSS Safe File, Box 6, *PSF;* 12 and 24 January 1944, SO File, Box 1, Entry 60, *RG 226;* 10 October 1943, Fairbank to Langer, 103.918/1740, *Diplomatic Branch;* 24 January 1944, M.I. 2 appraisal, *WO 208/254*.

154. Clam project, 2 March–10 May 1944, *Wilkinson*. O.S.S. and fourteenth Air Force, 13 October 1943, Donovan to Heppner, 103.918/1742, *Diplomatic Branch;* 27 January 1944, Hall to Donovan, SEAC File, and February–August 1944 reports, FETO General File, Box 20, 28 March 1944, Lockwood to Hall, FETO–Lockwood File, and 28 April 1944, FETO–Hall File, Box 22, Entry 1, *RG 226*.

155. Hall and Spencer reports on the situation, 28 February and 20 June 1944, FETO–Spencer File; 20 April 1944, Wiens to Hall, FETO–"W" File, Box 22, Entry 1, *RG 226*. In this shadowy era, Tolstoy wanted to supply China by pack mules through Tibet, the French were already building up a force within China for operating into Indochina, and various factions (one led by Joseph Alsop) were intriguing against Stilwell: *FRUS 1944*, VI, pp. 960–963, Donovan to Stettinius, 6 March 1944, Strategic Services File, Box 745, *Stettinius*, Folder 21, Box 56 *Marshall*.

156. December–January 1943–44, especially 13 December orders to Taylor, 20 December Heppner plan, and 29 January 1944 Hall to Langer, SEAC Command File, Box 20, Entry 1, *RG 226; Taylor*, pp. 342–346.

157. On American anti-imperialism: *Taylor*, pp. 352–353; John Davies, 17 April 1944 report, ABC 385 (4–8–43), *RG 165*. 7 November 1943, Mountbatten to Foreign Office, *WO 208/792;* 18 December 1943, Mountbatten order, SEAC Command file, Box 20, Entry 1, *RG 226*.

158. 4 February 1944, *Wilkinson;* O.S.S. trouble in Ceylon, 1 and 22 October 1943, 103.918/1724, *Diplomatic Branch;* 28 October 1943, Langer to Donovan, New Delhi File, Box 18, and 5 June 1944, Langer to Heppner, SEAC Command File, Box 20, Entry 1, *RG 226*. There was even a legal problem over the rights of non–United States citizens in O.S.S. stationed in India, 28 August 1943, Naturalization File, Box 21, James Donovan Papers, Hoover Institution.

159. 24 May 1944, Overall O.S.S. plan S.E.A.C., ABC 350.05, (6–21–44), sec. 2, *RG 165;* William R. Peers and Dean Brelis, *Behind the Burma Road*, pp. 132–220.

Chapter 6

1. 18 June 1944, Donovan to F.D.R. on O.S.S.–O.W.I. cooperation, OSS Safe File, Box 6, *PSF;* 17–20 July 1944 exchange on personnel acquisition, CCS 385 pt. 9, (2–8–42), *RG 218;* Donovan–Marshall exchange, 17 July and 9 August 1944, ABC 334.3, sec. 4 (5–1–42), *RG 165*.

2. See Box 73 *Map Room* and Boxes 168–170 (especially 25 October 1944 Donovan to F.D.R. on Dulles report, October File), *PSF*.

Notes

3. June 1944 reports (3), OSS Safe File, Box 6; July reports (especially 12 July 1944) (5), Box 168, *PSF*; 9 July 1944, Donovan to Marshall, ABC 400.3295 sec. 2-A (8–2–43), *RG 165*; Donovan to F.D.R., 21 October 1944, October File, Box 169, *PSF*; Matthews telephone conversation with McCloy, 15 June 1944, State Department Misc. June 1944 File, Box 741, *Stettinius.*

4. 4–24 July 1944 (6) reports, July File, Box 168 and 11 October 1944, October File, Box 169, *PSF*; 24 July 1944, July–December File, Box 73, *Map Room*; 11 July and 4 August 1944 reports, ABC 385.2 Germany, sec. 1, (12–20–43), *RG 165*; 2 October 1944, 103.918/ 10–1044, *Diplomatic Branch*; 1 December 1944, Deutsch to Bruce, ETO–Deutsch File, Box 21, Entry 1, *RG 226*; 7 December 1945 report, Alsos Missions, p. 20, Alsos Chronological File, Box 1, Boris T. Pash Papers, Hoover Institution; 15 November 1944, Stephenson to Donovan, Box 1, Forgan Papers, Hoover Institution.

5. 5 July–3 August 1944 (7) reports, July and August Files, Box 168, and 21 November 1944, file, Box 170, *PSF*; Donovan to Marshall, 3 and 8 August comment, ABC 381 Germany (1–29–43), sec. 2-A, *RG 165.*

6. 6–29 July 1944 reports, July File, Box 168, *PSF*; 18 July 1944, July–December File, Box 73, *Map Room*; 26 June 1944, Johnson to State, 103.918/6–2644, *Diplomatic Branch.*

7. 15 July 1944, July File, Box 168, *PSF*; 18 July 1944, July 1944–1945 File, Box 73, *Map Room*; Allen W. Dulles, *Germany's Underground*, pp. 134–139 (also see sources in footnote 38, chapter 5, below).

8. 14 July 1944, Bern to Victor, 103.918/1423, sec. 2 (the 103.918 series has many instances of satellite contact efforts in the fall of 1944) *Diplomatic Branch.* On G-2 rules on contacts: 23–24 August 1944, ABC 384 (11–21–43), *RG 165.*

9. 26 July 1944, Walter Langer to Donovan, Box 24, Entry 1, *RG 226*; 21–26 July 1944 (5), July File, 2–7 August (3), August File, Box 168, 27 January 1945, January File, and 1 February, February File, Box 170, *PSF*; 17 August 1944, July–December File, Box 73, *Map Room*. The 1 February 1945 report (originating with Gisevius) also went to the *Map Room*, Box 73, and to Henry Morgenthau, 816: 220–226, *Morgenthau.* Other O.S.S. reports on 20 July include: 11 August, 6 September, 6 October, June–December File, Box 73, *Map Room.* The State Department and J.I.C. were worried that the Germans might try a unilateral surrender either East or West: 4 August 1944 Berle note and reply, CCS 334 (10–15–43), *RG 218.*

10. 27 November 1944, COS (44) 381 mtg. (0), *CAB 79/83*; 13 February and 5 March 1945, CCS 111 (6–17–42), *RG 218.*

11. This file shows much British worry over the collapse of O.W.I.: *FO 898*/105. 9 December 1944, Langer to Morse, London File, Box 18, Entry 1, *RG 226.*

12. 16 November 1944, Box 14, *Harold Smith*; 17 January 1945, F.D.R. to Stettinius, Memos for sec. File, October–February, Box 733, *Stettinius.*

13. Hayes to State, 13 July 1944, 103.918/7–1344, 25 August 1944, 103.918/8–2544, 15 September 1944, 103.918/9–1544, 13 September 1944, Donovan to Hayes, 103.918/11–244, *Diplomatic Branch*; 31 August 1944, Thayer–Matthews talk, Memo of Conversations File (2), Box 724, *Stettinius* and 6 September 1944, Cheston to Hull, 103.918/9-1144, *Diplomatic Branch.*

14. See Boxes 123–126 for Carter's general activities in this period (Boxes 126–139 contain the Nazi Party membership project papers). On the Hanfstaengl project and its problems, 24 June 1944, Special Memos to the President December 1944–March 1945 File, Box 232, and 14 July 1944, Division of Central European Affairs File, Box 216, *Stettinius.*

15. X-2 reports welcomed by the Foreign Correlations Division range from 6 July 1944 to the end of the year (103.918 series, *Diplomatic Branch*). This division has recently become notorious because of alleged smuggling of Nazi war criminals into the United States. On the F.N.B. and the State Department: 30 November 1944–25 January 1945 exchanges, 103.918/11–3044 and 20 January 1945, 103.918/1–2045, *Diplomatic Branch.* Note that the American Consul in Palermo protested against removal of the O.S.S. from Sicily, 17 September 1944, 103.918/–2744, *Diplomatic Branch.*

16. 29 January 1945 directive, General ETO File, Box 20, Entry 1, *RG 226.* Much of this keyed on the role of O.S.S. in German occupation, see 22 November 1944, CCS 350.05, ETO (8–4–44), sec. 1, *RG 218*; 10 and 15 December 1944, Germany 3 File, Box 16, 1944–45, Paris Office File, Box 19, 18 December 1944, G. Overton File, Box 21, Entry 1, *RG 226*;

18 November 1944 State to Murphy (103.918/11–344) and 1 December 1944 Stettinius to Murphy, (103.918/11–2544), *Diplomatic Branch*.

17. 1 October–25 November 1944 exchanges, Strategic Services File, Box 745, *Stettinius*; 7 November 1944, 103.918/11–744, *Diplomatic Branch*.

18. May–June 1945 F.O. summary, *FO 371/51022/U3925*.

19. Constantine Fitzgibbon, "Spying for the Yanks," *Sunday Telegraph Magazine*, 4 August 1979. Donovan and Langer were on an outpost tour from 25 July to 17 August 1945, one of the most critical times (V.J. Day) for the survival of O.S.S. Executive Committee Mtg. File, Box 16, Entry 1, *RG 226*.

20. On de Wavrin-Passy, 13–26 December 1944, Memos for sec. October–February File, Box 733, *Stettinius*; Donovan to F.D.R., 6 April 1945, Donovan File, Box 167, *PSF*; Hall–O'Brien exchange, 2–7 October 1946, Uncatalogued Papers, Hall File, October 1946, J. O'Brien papers, Columbia. On the Ciano Diaries: 16 March 1945, 103.918/3–1645, *Diplomatic Branch*. A 24 August 1944 general survey of O.S.S.–State Department relations is in State Department File, Box 2, Entry 1, *RG 226*. In such a secret, complex, and rapidly changing organization, people could get lost (see Jenkins to Hayden, 1945 File, Box 8, *Hayden*) but the undercover mechanisms continued to function. As of 21 October 1944, Emerson Bigelow was acting as an O.S.S. secret paymaster via P.O. Box 1929, main post office, Washington D.C.: 103.918/10-2144, *Diplomatic Branch*.

21. 12 December 1944, 103.918/12-1244 and 16 December 1944, 103.918/12-1644, *Diplomatic Branch*.

22. The original exposé of Scattolini was made by Father Graham in the *Washington Post*, 3 August 1980. At my request, "Black" reports of 8, 13, and 30 November 1945 were declassified. In addition to the "Vessel" reports declassified at the same time, ten more "Black" reports of 8 December 1944 and one of 16 February 1945 in the Roosevelt Library Files are not presently marked as fakes, although they are. November 1944 and February 1945 Files, Box 170, *PSF*.

23. Dunn's comment 13 February 1945, 103.918/2–145, *Diplomatic Branch*. For Glavin: OSS Ops. no. 6 File, Reel 17 A, *AFHQ*; Donovan to Dunn, 8 March 1945, 103.918/3–845, *Diplomatic Branch*.

24. 5, 17, and 27 October 1944 reports, October File, Box 169, 2, 16, and 19 November 1944, November File, 1 December 1944, December File, 22 January 1945, January File, Box 170, *PSF*; 8, 16, 20, and 28 November and 13 December 1944, July–December File, Box 73, *Map Room*. The curious reference to the consul in Zurich is in Donovan to Stettinius, 13 December 1944, 103.918/12–1344, *Diplomatic Branch*. Note instances of Washington O.S.S. being more skeptical than overseas representatives about dealings with the Axis: 29 September 1944 and 2 December 1944, July–December File, Box 73, *Map Room*.

25. Rumor Directive 115, 18 August 1944 and revised directive 29 August 1944, *FO 898/69*; 15 and 27 November reports on Walter Langer, Naturalization File, Box 21, James Donovan Papers, Hoover Institution.

26. 2, 3, and 4 August estimates and 8 November 1944, ABC 381 (1–29–43), sec. 2-A, *RG 165*; 31 August 1944 conference with the President; Box 14, *Harold Smith*. At MacArthur's headquarters, Joseph Hayden thought it "extremely unlikely" that the war with Japan would end before June 1946. 21 November 1944 letter to E.S. Brown, Correspondence Files, Box 8, *Hayden*.

27. Reports of 2 September, September File, 10 (2), 12, 13, 25, and 30 October, October File, Box 169, and 18 December 1944, 16–30 December File, Box 170, *PSF*; 26 August and 8 November 1944, June–December File, Box 73, *Map Room*; 11, 12, 16, 18, 22, 26, and 27 January and 3 February 1945 reports, Books 809–816 (indexed at Hyde Park) *Morgenthau*. Bradley F. Smith, *Road to Nuremberg*, p. 271. 16 August 1944, J.I.C. 208/1, ABC 381, (1–29–43), sec. 2-A, *RG 165*; 29 December 1944, December (4) File, Box 34, *Eisenhower*.

28. Donovan to F.D.R., 2 September, September File, 31 October, October File, Box 169, 1 and 5 December 1944, December File, Box 170, *PSF*; Donovan Directive, 23 August 1944, OSS Ops. no. 6 File, Reel 17A, *AFHQ*; 2 and 4 September 1944, Donovan proposals, JCS 1047, and 11 September King memo, CCS 384 (4–12–43), sec. 1, *RG 218*; 12 September 1944 JCS memo 325, ABC 334.3, sec. 4 (5–1–42), *RG 165*; Admiral King on JCS 1047, 11 September 1944, ABC 381 (12–3–42), sec. 2, *RG 165*; 18 December 1944 Donovan request on German capabilities, November–December File, Box 3, Entry 59, *RG 226*.

Notes

29. 6 October 1944 Directive no. 123, and 8 December 1944 directive no. 129, *FO 898/* 69. Donovan's plans show up in: 7 November 1944 Donovan to Murphy, 103.918/11–844, *Diplomatic Branch* and 11 December 1944 Donovan to Stettinius *FRUS 1944*, I, pp 567–570.

30. Donovan and Buxton to F.D.R., 23, 24, and 29 November, November File, 5, 6, and 9 December, 1–15 December File, 14 and 16 December 1944, 16–30 December File, Box 170, *PSF*; 6 December 1944, 103.918/12–644, *Diplomatic Branch*; 23 and 24 November, 5 and 11 December 1944, ABC 381 (1–29–43), sec. 2-A, *RG 165*. See below, chapter 7.

31. Donovan and Buxton to F.D.R., 21, 22, 26, and 28 December 1944, 16–30 December File, Box 170, *PSF*.

32. 13 July–7 August 1944, ABC 452.1 (11–26–42), sec. 2-A, *RG 165*; 5 October 1944 (2) Donovan to F.D.R., October File, Box 169, *PSF*; 1 August 1944, Strategic Services File, Box 745, *Stettinius*. A General Walter B. Smith note of 12 June 1944 says that the sabotage orders to be given to the Poles in support of D Day were actually to assist the Soviet advance, but the Poles were not to be told that! COS (44) 516 (0), *CAB 80/84*.

33. On tying down Axis forces: 16 June 1944, Gammell order, *WO 204/1982*; 17 October 1944 appreciation, *WO 204/1969*. For British complaints about O.S.S., 21 August 1944, PREM 3/212/2. Donovan had peculiar ideas about what was going on in Greece. In July 1944, he reported to the president that 90,000 Jews were being "expatriated," when they were actually being shipped to the death camps, Donovan to F.D.R., 20 July 1944, July File, Box 168, *PSF*.

34. Donovan and Cheston to F.D.R., 18 and 28 July, July File, 3 and 9 August 1944, August File, Box 168, 24 September 1944, September File, Box 169, *PSF*; Donovan to Hull, ABC 091.411 (11–27–43), sec. 2, *RG 165*; 10 January 1945, MacVeagh mixture of praise and blame for O.S.S. Greece, 103.918/1–1045, *Diplomatic Branch*. On Churchill's anger and S.O.E.: 23 August 1944, *FO 954/24A*. The British prime minister and General Smith on Donovan and O.S.S.: 24 and 26 August, 3 and 9 September, 1944, *PREM 3/212/2*.

35. 24 September 1944, *PREM 3/212/2*; 26 October 1944, MacVeagh message, 103.918/ 10–2644 and 29 December 1944, X-2 report, 103.918/12–2944, *Diplomatic Branch*; 3 January 1945 report, Cairo File, Box 1, Entry 60, *RG 226*; September–December 1944 M.I. 6 file on Greece contains O.S.S. reports, *WO 204/8858* and another file has material from "UNRRA Intelligence," *WO 204/9363*. 14 March 1945, Donovan to F.D.R., March File, Box 170, *PSF*; Thomas M. Campbell and George C. Herring, eds., *The Diaries of Edward R. Stettinius, Jr., 1943–1946* (New York: 1975), p. 205. 2 January 1945 (2 memos.), S-Secretary, 1-7 January 1945 file, Box 222, *Stettinius*.

36. The British were now pleased to draw a line between their policy and that of O.S.S., Gammell order, 22 June 1944, *WO 204/1970*. General Wilson was happy to see Tito not too powerful, but he was also impressed by him. 27 June 1944, Donovan to F.D.R., January–June File, Box 167, *PSF*; 12 August 1944, *WO 204/1971*.

37. 28 June 1944, 103.918/7–444, *Diplomatic Branch* and 8 July 1944, Subject File, Box 167, *PSF*.

38. JPS 504/1 and related materials, 15 August, 3, 7, and 11 September and 6 October 1944, CCS 381 (10–29–43), sec. 2, *RG 218*; 1 June–17 August, 1944, ABC 091.411, sec. 2, (11–27–43), *RG 165*; 19 August 1944, Markham to Murphy, *WO 204/1972*; 1–3 September 1944, Churchill–Roosevelt exchange, *Loewenheim*, pp. 570–571. 8 September 1944, Cheston to F.D.R. and 9 October 1944, Donovan to F.D.R. (the stamp item), Subject File, Box 167, *PSF*. This was not an unusual phenomenon, for Donovan provided the president with a worldwide stamp and map delivery service.

39. Donovan to F.D.R., 15 and 22 September, September File, 20 October, October File, Box 169, and 9 November 1944, November File, Box 170, *PSF*. 2 October 1944 on McDowell contacts with the Germans, *FRUS 1944*, I, p. 557, 9 September 1944 Cheston to Murphy, 103.918/9–144; McDowell material, 1 December 1944, 103.918/11–3044, Donovan report, 4 December 1944, 103.918/12–444 (see 103.918/12–2644 for the reports themselves), *Diplomatic Branch. Smith and Agarossi*, chapter 3. Milazzo's contention that O.S.S. was purely antipartisan is too simple: Matteo J. Milazzo, *The Chetnik Movement and Resistance*, pp. 170–184.

40. 17 November 1944, MacMillan message, Special information for the President File, Box 740, *Stettinius*. Maclean was trying to get Kupi out of Albania at the same time, 25 October 1944 message, *WO 204/1982*. Countless O.S.S. reports on Yugoslav politics are in

Boxes 168–170, covering August 1944–January 1945, *PSF.* See also, Ilija Jukic, *The Fall of Yugoslavia,* pp. 234 and 271.

41. Donovan to J.C.S., 3 November 1944, CCS 381 (10–29–42), sec. 3, *RG 218;* 31 January 1945, Cheston to F.D.R., January File, Box 170, *PSF.* Supply cut off: 24 September 1944, *FRUS 1944,* IV, p. 1412. December 1944 intelligence files, *WO 204*/1973 and *WO 204*/9673A. On 29 November 1944, the N.A.T.O. R. and A. chief referred to Belgrade as the "most important" intelligence location in the Balkans: Nato-Hughes File, Box 23, Entry 1, *RG 226.*

42. Dozens of reports from September to December are in Boxes 169–170, *PSF.* X-2 reports 18 and 24 November 1944, 103.918/11–1844 and 2444, *Diplomatic Branch.* The British—due to their Palestine fears—were reluctant to use Jewish agents in Hungary, which may have contributed to the informational muddle and delay when Eichmann crashed into Hungary in the fall. Wilson to C.C.S., 26 July 1944, *WO 204*/1831.

43. 20 October 1944, Donovan to F.D.R., October File, Box 169, *PSF;* 29 November 1944, Poole to Berle, 103.918/11–2944, *Diplomatic Branch;* 20 June 1944, Neumann Paper, Director's Committee File, Box 7, Entry 1, *RG 226.*

44. In the 1945 O.S.S. operational plans, there was a routine reference that their activities were aimed "at the enemy" but this phrase was not included in the O.S.S. plan for Egypt and Turkey, ABC 350.05 (6–21–44), *RG 165.* Donovan to Deane and Harriman, 24 October 1944, 103.918/10–2444, *Diplomatic Branch.* See chapter 7, p. 352.

45. 12 October 1944, Donovan to F.D.R., October File, Box 169, *PSF;* Donovan to State, 20 October 1944, 103.918/10–2044 *Diplomatic Branch* (both on Kleist's effort to contact the Soviets). 11 January 1945, R. and A. paper, Director's Committee File, Box 7, Entry 1, *RG 226.* See chapter 7, p. 352.

46. 15 January 1945 conference record, conference with Stalin File, Box 26, W.B. Smith Collection, Eisenhower Library.

47. Donovan to Miss Conway, 19 April 1945, Donovan secret intelligence File, Box 15, Misc., *Truman;* Donovan to Byrnes, 17 June 1945, 103.918/6–1745, *Diplomatic Branch.* The problem for intelligence flow to the White House occasioned by Mr. Roosevelt's death is indicated by the fact that General Marshall did not explain the Ultra system to President Truman until five days after he took office. 17 April 1945 Marshall to President Truman, File 33, Box 81, *Marshall.*

48. The final phase of reports to President Roosevelt are in Boxes 170–171, *PSF,* and those to his successor in Box 15, Misc., *Truman.* On 5 April 1945, Donovan raised the possibility of dealing with Grand Ludwig of Hesse, but the State Department quickly rejected the idea, 103.918/4–545, *Diplomatic Branch.* Rumor Directives 9 and 16 February and 13 April, 1945, *FO 898*/69.

49. *Smith and Agarossi,* passim, plus Sunrise and Donovan Files Box 21, Sunrise File, Box 29, Edge File, Box 141, *Dulles;* Forrestal Diary, II, Princeton. On Austrian approaches, *FRUS 1945,* III, p. 561f and Fritz Molden, *Exploding Star* (New York: 1979), passim. On North German arrangements: Goerdeler File, Box 204, *Dulles.*

50. *Smith and Agarossi,* chapter 5.

51. The reports to F.D.R. are in Boxes 170–171, *PSF,* see especially 21 February, 1945, Donovan to F.D.R. on Polish intelligence people, February File, Box 171. The reports to President Truman are in Box 15, Misc., *Truman.* An 8 May 1945 anticommunist message from Caserta was considered extreme by O.S.S. Washington, 103.918/5–845, *Diplomatic Branch.*

52. Donovan to F.D.R., 9 and 14 March 1945, March File, Box 170, *PSF;* 13 May 1945, Donovan to President Truman, Box 15, Misc., *Truman.* 11 January 1945 paper, Director's Committee File, Box 7, and 20 January 1945, Hartshorne to Read and Sweeney, Projects Committee File, Box 9, *RG 226.* Note, however, that Donovan's suggestions of "spying" activities at the United Nations San Francisco conference were rejected by Stettinius, Thomas M. Campbell, and George C. Herring, eds, *The Diaries of Edward R. Stettinius, Jr.,* p. 303.

53. 5 May 1945, Box 15, Misc., *Truman.*

54. Donovan to President Truman, 21 June 1945, tried to set up an O.S.S.–White House liaison arrangement, Box 15, Misc., *Truman;* 4 July 1945 effort to get approval for Balkan S.I. and X-2 operations is in NATO File, Box 20, Entry 1, *RG 226;* 25 August 1945, Donovan pushing for continuation of S.I. and X-2 in the Middle East, CCS 385 (8–25–45), O.S.S.

Notes

in Africa and Middle East, *RG 218;* Undated, unsigned, mid-summer 1945 memorandum accusing O.S.S. of being anti-Soviet and supportive of German cartels, Donovan secret intelligence file, Box 15, Misc., *Truman.*

55. May-August 1945 Files, Box 15, Misc., *Truman.* A most interesting Japanese account of the Dulles dealings is in Japan File, Box 53, *Dulles.* Intelligence on Japan was collected by O.S.S. in Europe, see N.A.T.O.–Hughes File (16 March 1945), Box 23 and ETO–London File, (16 May 1945), Box 21, Entry 1, *RG 226.* For occupation and war criminal prosecution activities, see especially War Crimes File, Box 2 and Germany 3 File, Box 16, Entry 1, *RG 226.* At least Judge Rosenman was impressed by one R. and A. study related to war crimes problems, 18–21 May 1945, OSS File, Box 3, Rosenman Papers, Truman Library.

56. 18 May–17 September 1945, OSS Files, Box 15, Misc., *Truman;* 26 April 1945, cited in Eban A. Ayers Papers, Intelligence Service File, Box 7, Truman Library.

57. For an example of a subsequent use of an R. and A. report, see 21 November 1945 item, *FRUS 1945,* III, p. 908. Reports of 20 and 25 June and 4 (2) and 5 September 1945, OSS Files, Box 15, Misc., *Truman.* The most interesting of these is a "sanitized" one of 4 September, which, if one counts the spaces of the deleted section, points to cooperation with "Israeli" intelligence in the Middle East.

58. Morton and Selborne to Churchill, 17 and 22 June 1945, *PREM 3/185/1;* Donovan to F.D.R., 14 and 16 June 1944, January–June File, Box 167, OSS Safe File, Box 6, *PSF.* Note that the 14 June report stresses naval gunfire and air power and does not exaggerate the role of resistance.

59. 10 July 1944 *Butcher Diary;* Donovan report, 9 July 1944, ABC 400.8395 (8–2–43), sec. 2, *RG 165;* Selborne to Churchill, 20 June 1944, *PREM 3/185/1.*

60. Files F-6 and F-9, Box 4, Francis Miller Papers, Marshall Library; 19 August 1944, SHAEF report message, *WO 204/1963;* 30 August 1944, *Butcher Diary* (Butcher had been one of the doubting Thomases).

61. 13, 21 and 29 June 1944, JLC 134, ABC 400.3295 (8–2–43), sec. 2-A, *RG 165;* 17 July and 16 September 1944, *Butcher Diary;* 26 June 1944, Directive, *WO 204/1930.* On reprisals; 23 July 1944, SHAEF to AFHQ, *WO 204/1958.*

62. M. R. D. Foote, *SOE in France,* p. 408; Daily SCAF reports, 1–26 July, 1944, *WO 219/4970;* Donovan to F.D.R., 4 July 1944, July File, Box 168, *PSF.*

63. 28 June 1944, J.C.S. Memo of Information 250 (on O.S.S. operational problems from the U.K.), ABC 381 (12–3–42), sec. 3, *RG 165;* 22 July 1944 discussion, *WO 219/4967.*

64. Post-V.E. Day appraisals, the E.T.O. and Mediterranean theaters: Eisenhower to War, 24 May 1945, Folder 54, Box 9, *RG 218 Leahy;* 15 June 1945, *WO 204/4364;* 17 June 1945 report, OSS no. 7, File 1, Reel 17A, *AFHQ;* 3 August 1945, *WO 204/1554;* 2 and 10 August 1945, *WO 204/10247.* Wartime tactical support organization of O.S.S: 30 September 1945, SHAEF G-3 to AFHQ, *WO 204/1960;* 21 December 1944 and 31 March 1945, Fifteenth Army Group to AFHQ. *WO 204/1931.* The quotation comes from September 1944, Hq. AAI to no 1, Special Force, *WO 204/7295.*

65. On Operation Cadillac, *Eisenhower Papers,* III, p. 1932. Supply statistics: 5 September 1944, *WO 204/1963.* A map of missions sent in dated 3 September 1944 is in *WO 219/4972.*

66. Reviews of the week for 29 July, 5 and 12 August 1944, *WO 204/1817;* Special Ops. center established 29 June 1944, SPOC File, Reel 37A, *AFHQ;* de Gaulle–Wilson mtg., 20 July 2944, *WO 204/5847;* 16 August SHAEF report on post–D Day total of resistance aid, *WO 204/1963;* 1 September 1944, Special Projects Center totals for Anvil, *WO 204/1946.* On supply and Vercors plateau, see especially AFHQ history of Special Operations, *WO 204/2030B.*

67. Resistance plans for Anvil, AFHQ History of Special Operations, *WO 204/2030B;* W. Duff to R. Harris Smith, 21 July 1970, R. Harris Smith Papers, Hoover; 30 October 1944, Colonel Hitchens report, 103.918/11–2244, *Diplomatic Branch.*

68. 19 August 1944 review of the week, *WO 204/1817;* Week of 9 September 1944, SPOC Weekly Review File, Reel 17–A, *AFHQ.*

69. 12 and 16 November 1944 orders, 1–15 November and 16–30 November 1944 File, SHAEF War Diary, Box 34, *SHAEF.*

70. Daily SCAF report, 13 August 1944, *WO 219/4971;* 25 and 27 September 1944 Special Force Reports, *WO 219/4972.*

71. September–October reports on Dutch resistance, *WO 219*/4972 and 4973; Daily SCAF report, 13 August 1944, *WO 219*/4971 and 15 September 1944, *WO 219*/4972.

72. November–December 1944 Special Force reports, *WO 219*/4973.

73. *Les Allies et la Resistance en Europe*, II, p. 33.

74. 23 August 1944, Donovan directive, File OSS Ops. no. 6, Reel 17A, *AFHQ*; Eisenhower to Donovan, 30 August 1944, *WO 204*/1960; Special Force reports, 25 and 27 September, and 2 October, 1944, *WO 219*/4972.

75. 5 December report and 10 December 1944 mtg. minutes, December (1) File, 18 December 1944 plan, December (4) File, 31 December 1944 report, December (5) File, Box 34; 10 January 1945 mtg. minutes, January (1) File, 16 January 1945 report, January (2) File, Box 35, *SHAEF* (the V–2 specialists such as Werner von Braun were only secured after the war). Casey to Donovan, 12 October 1944, Germany File, Box 17, Entry 1, *RG 226*; Donovan to F.D.R., 1 December 1944, 1–15 December File, Box 170, *PSF*: 8 November 1944 General Bull report, SHAEF War Diary, Box 34, *SHAEF*. Note also that O.S.S. studied Nazi antiresistance measures: 24 March 1945 report, Paris File, Box 19, Entry 1, *RG 226*; Donovan to F.D.R., 3 April 1945, April File, Box 171, *PSF*.

76. 10 December 1944 mtg. minutes, December (1) File, 18 and 20 December 1944 memoranda, December (4) File, Box 34; 16 January 1945 memo, January (2) File, 7 February 1945 memo, February (1) File, 9 and 22 (2) February 1945 memoranda, February (4) File, and 14 February 1945 mtg. minutes, SHAEF War Diary (1), February File, Box 35, *SHAEF*. 7 October 1944 memo, McClure (1) File, Box 7, C. D. Jackson Papers, Eisenhower Library. Donovan to President Truman, 4 May 1945, Box 15, Misc., *Truman*.

77. 29 January 1945 directive, January (3) File, Box 35, *SHAEF*.

78. On resistance support the following reports: 22 August 1944, *WO 204*/80; 15 August 1944, *WO 204*/1817; 25 October 1944, *WO 204*/1931; 8 July 1944, *WO 204*/1971, and Charles F. Delzell, *Mussolini's Enemies* (Princeton: 1961), p. 423. A sample O.S.S. report, 30 June 1944, is in *WO 204*/7290, while the Daily special operations "sitreps" from 10 August 1944 to 27 April 1945, are in *WO 204*/1965. For efforts to incite mutinies among Axis forces, 27 July 1944, *WO 204*/1831.

79. *Smith and Agarossi*, chapter 3; Chief of Staff to G–3, 21 January 1945, File No. 1, Special Force, G-3, Special Ops., Roll 38A, *AFHQ*.

80. 25 November 1944 instructions, *WO 204*/7296; 15 and 27 November 1944 area reports, *WO 204*/7305 and 7296; 30 December example of an action "Sitrep," *WO 106*/3947.

81. April 1945, S.O.E. operations, *WO 106*/4805; Appendix A, AFHQ History of Special Operations, *WO 204*/2030B; 22 and 30 March and 14 April 1945 operational reports, *WO 204*/7289; 12 and 17 April 1945 (misassessment of partisan chances in Genoa), *WO 204*/7299; 11 February 1945 box score of S.O.E. missions, *WO 204*/7297; April supply drop for Italy *WO 204*/1931; Charles F. Delzell, *Mussolini's Enemies*, pp. 455 and 479; 16 April 1945 report, 2671st Sp. Rec. Bn. Weekly Reports File, G-3 Spec. Ops., Reel 38-A and 18 April 1945 report, OSS G-3 Report File, Roll 17A, *AFHQ*.

82. 7 March, 15 and 18 April, reports, *WO 106*/3948. On overlap and confusion: 19 February 1945 report, *WO 204*/7301. 18 June 1945, Fifteenth Army Group report on S.O.E. *WO 204*/4364. On the case of Colonel Hall: 31 May 1945 report in AFHQ History of Special Operations, *WO 204*/2030B. On the case of Major Holohan: Charles F. Delzell, *Mussolini's Enemies*, pp. 436–439.

83. AFHQ History of Special Operations, *WO 204*/2030B.

84. Reports on Austria: 26 September 1944, *WO 204*/80; 17 October 1944, *WO 106*/4018; 5 November 1944, *WO 204*/6839; October–December 1944, *WO 204*/1954; January 1945 on, AFHQ History of Special Operations, *WO 204*/2030B; 30 December 1944, 23 January and 17 April 1945, *WO 204*/1554; 11 March 1945, *WO 204*/10186B; 18 February 1945, SHAEF to AFHQ, February (4) File, Box 35, *SHAEF*. On Austrian resistance: Prince Otto and F.D.R., *FRUS 1945*, III, pp. 559–565.

85. G-2 appraisal by Twelfth Army Group, Box 43, W. B. Smith Collection of World War II Documents, Eisenhower Library; Forrest Pogue, *The Supreme Command*, p. 361. For the line crosser system: 12 December 1944 order, December (1) File, Box 34, *SHAEF*.

86. 23 September and 25 December 1943 OSS Ops. reports, OSS Ops. File no. 1, and November–December 1944 and March 1945 reports, OSS G-3 Reports File, Reel 17A, *AFHQ*: 1 February 1945 report, *WO 204*/1931; 18 February 1945 *WO 204*/7297. On the

Notes

Joint Army–Navy Intelligence Collection Agency: AFHQ History, *WO 204*/489. On the problems of dealing with intelligence from S.O.E. type operations: "Intelligence Value of S.O.E.," *WO 204*/1554.

87. 28 June 1944, JCS memo. 258, ABC 381 (12–3–42), sec. 3, *RG 165*; 17 July 1944 program, ABC 350.05 (6–21–44), sec. 6, *RG 165*; July 1944 Normandy study, 103.918/6–844, *Diplomatic Branch*; Intelligence notes, *WO 204*/863; *Smith and Agarossi*, chapters 4–6.

88. 1944–45 reports, NATO–Conley File, Box 23 and 23 November 1944, Burckhardt to Corey Ford, O.S.S. History File, Box 11, Entry 1, *RG 226*.

89. 19 April 1945, Report on intelligence training, *WO 204*/994. 16 February 1945 Nice, France item, *WO 204*/7297.

90. 27 February 1945, Hoover and Meyerhoff to Deutsch, ETO File, Box 21, Entry 1, *RG 226*; 3 February 1945 Stone to G-5, *WO 204*/2781.

91. For S.O.E.: December 1944 and 4 February 1945, *WO 204*/1931. For the October 1944 size and personnel allotment of O.S.S.: OSS reports no. 6 File and OSS Ops. no. 6 File, Reel 17A, *AFHQ*: January 1944, OSS File, Reel 37A, *AFHQ*. On R. and A.: Hite to Langer, 23 October 1944, NATO–Hite File, Box 23, Entry 1, *RG 226*. Marshall did ask for a cut of 323 O.S.S. personnel in North Africa on 10 October 1944. CCS 385 (2–8–42), p. 9, *RG 218*.

92. February 1945, "Penetration of Germany" memo., ETO–Paris File, Box 21, *RG 226*. Allan Evans to R. H. Smith, 21 May 1970, Box 1, R. Harris Smith Papers, Hoover Institution. On 13 November 1943, General Rooks wanted an order issued forbidding O.S.S. personnel from dabbling in Italian politics. OSS Policy File, Reel 38-A, G-3 Special Ops., *AFHQ*. Duff Cooper complaint about O.S.S.: 24 June 1944, *FO 954*/24A.

93. Gerald Mayer statement, 25 April 1947, Germany File, Box 21, *Dulles*.

94. On counterintelligence: Donovan to F.D.R., 27 July 1944, July File, Box 168 and 30 March 1945, 15–30 March File, Box 171, *PSF*: 17 July 1945, Donovan to President Truman, Box 15, Misc., *Truman*. Counterintelligence reports, North Africa, *WO 204*/806; 28 August 1944 (2), Military Orders, File, and 1/3 November 1944, King–Bolton exchange, Correspondence File, David King Papers, Hoover Institution; 5 January 1945, ETO–Overton and Starr File, Box 21, Entry 1, *RG 226*. See also chapter 7 below.

95. 17 September 1944 Hughes report, *WO 204*/1960, and undated report, NATO–Hughes File, Box 23, Entry 1, *RG 226*. Quotations: 15 and 29 January 1945, *WO 204*/7301 and 1554. *Smith and Agarossi*, pp. 43–48. On Rankin conditions: 28 August 1944, CCS 449/2, CCS 385 (4–12–43), *RG 218*; 11 December 1944 O.S.S. plan, ABC 350.05 (6–21–44), sec. 2, *RG 165*; 20 Septembr 1944 orders, *WO 204*/7293. On worry regarding Italian partisans: 24 and 31 January 1945, *WO 204*/1554 and 6839. Field reports on Communists: November 1944, No. 1 Sp. Force reports from the field no. 2 File, G-3 Special Ops., Reel 38-A, *AFHQ*. On northeast Italy: 25 and 31 January 1945, *WO 204*/6839; and 9 September 1944, *WO 204*/1972 northwest Italy: AFHQ History of Special Operations, *WO 204*/2030B and 17 November and 28 December 1944 War Diary, Box 34, 6 December 1944 report, December 1944 (1) File, 18 December 1944 memo, December (4) File, Box 34, 4 January 1945 SHAEF to Sixth Army, January (1) File, Box 35, *SHAEF*.

96. May 1945 reports on aftermath of Sunrise, AFHQ History of Special Operations, *WO 204*/2030B; 20 August and 17 September 1945 reports, *WO 204*/2781. 7 November 1944, War Diary, Box 34, *SHAEF*; 22 November 1944 British initiative, ABC 384, Indochina (12–16–44), sec. 1A, *RG 165*.

97. Reports on Danish and Norwegian special force action, January-May 1945, *WO 219*/4974. On the Yugoslavs and Operation Bearskin: 29 June 1944 report, *WO 204*/1971. By July 1944, O.S.S. claimed to be sending 1,000 "kits" per week to Yugoslavia to assist in producing propaganda, including copies of the *Reader's Digest!* Donovan to F.D.R., 8 July 1944, July File, Box 69, *PSF*; SHAEF and the War Department watered down last minute O.S.S. plans for Norway, see the sprinkle of materials, 27 November 1944–42 February 1945, Boxes 34–35, *SHAEF* and William Colby and Peter Forbath, *Honorable Men* (New York: 1978), chapter 1.

98. On Bulgaria: 15 July 1944, *WO 204*/1966; 27 August and 20 September 1944, *WO 204*/1982; O.S.S. and Bulgarian bridges: 18 June 1944, Donovan to F.D.R. OSS Safe File, Box 6, *PSF*: 24 June 1944 report, *WO 204*/1982. On political aspects of central European resistance: 9 November and 21 December 1944, *WO 204*/1554 and SHAEF/Bradley exchange, 25/27 April 1945, on Czechoslovakia, *WO 204*/10186B and *WO 204*/1554.

99. Intelligence situation of O.S.S. in the Balkans as of 28 June 1944, JCS memo 258, Appendix G, ABC 381 (12–3–42), sec. 3, *RG 165*. On Yugoslav partisan reports: *WO 204/ 1969* and *1978*. On Hungary: 29 September 1944, Donovan to State, 103.918/9–2944, *Diplomatic Branch* and November 1944 and subsequent file sequence, *RG 334*. See also chapter 7, p. 350.

100. Donovan to F.D.R., 25 October 1944, October File, Box 169, *PSF;* 28 June 1944, JCS Memo. 258, ABC 381 (12–3–42), sec. 3, *RG 165;* report of 1 October 1944, File 24, Box 81, *Marshall;* 6 August–14 September 1944, CCS 0911, (8–21–43), sec. 1, *RG 218*. See also chapter 7 below.

101. 24 May 1945, McNarney to War, and 26 May 1945, Eisenhower to War, Folder 54, Box 9, *RG 218 Leahy*.

102. 27 January 1945, Spencer to Langer, China File, Box 16, Entry 1, *RG 226*.

103. On the failures: 11 August 1944, Donovan request, CCS 385 Japan (4–27–42), sec. 3, *RG 218;* 25 August–16 October 1944, CCS 385 (6–16–43), sec. 1, *RG 218*. Atherton Richards: 103.918/1–2545, *Diplomatic Branch*. On Sumatra–Java: 28 June 1944, JCS Memo 258, ABC 381 (12–3–42), sec. 3, *RG 165;* 1944–45 operational plan, sec. 5, ABC 350.05 (6–21–44), *RG 165*. On the Twentieth AAF: 14 March 1945, India–Burma File, Box 17, Entry 1, *RG 226*. On S.O. in the Philippines: 6 December 1944 mtg., Philippines File, Box 19, Entry 1, *RG 226*. On Hayden: 4 September, 30 November, 6 and 20 December 1944, and 8 February 1945, 1944 and 1945 Files, Box 8, *Hayden*. Yet someone on General Feller's staff covered the O.S.S. psychological warfare plan for the Pacific with critical and sarcastic comments. Basic Plan File, Box 3, Bonner F. Fellers Papers, Hoover Institution.

104. 9 November 1944, instructions to Colonel Fertig, Correspondence File, Box 8, *Hayden;* 8 May 1945 report on SOA, COS (45) 322 (0), *CAB 80/94;* 23 May 1945, MacArthur to War, folder 54, Box 9, *RG 218 Leahy*.

105. 16 October–13 December 1944, CCS 385 (6–16–43), sec. 1, *RG 218;* 11 June 1944, *Wilkinson*.

106. William Leahy, *I Was There*, p. 338. On Operation Dart: 27 July 1944, Box 2, Entry 59, *RG 226;* 1 January–2 April, 1945, CCS 385 (6–16–43), secs. 1 and 2, *RG 218*. On Triangle: 2 April 1945, ABC 334.3, sec. 4, (5–1–42), *RG 165;* 29 March and 9 April, 1945, CCS 385 (6–16–43), secs. 1 and 2, *RG 218*.

107. On Korea: 17 April–26 May 1945, ABC 385 (4–4–42), *RG 165;* Special program and implementation study, 23 January 1945, sec. 10 and 1945 operational plan, 15 May 1945, sec. 15, ABC 350.05 (6–21–44), *RG 165* (quotation from the latter item).

108. 23 April 1945, Study no. 15, ABC 385 (4–4–42), *RG 165;* Napko project, June–August 1945, (JPS 688), ABC 350.05 (6–21–44), *RG 165;* 18 July 1945 Donovan recommendation, CCS 385 (6–16–43), sec. 2, *RG 218*.

109. 28 June 1944 and 11 January–20 March 1945, CCS 385 (6–16–43), sec. 2, *RG 218;* John Zuckerman to R. Harris Smith, Box 1, R. Harris Smith Papers, Hoover Institution.

110. Donovan to F.D.R., 23 March 1945, 15–30 March File, Box 171, *PSF;* 31 May–9 August 1945, Cheston, Buxton, Magruder, and Donovan to President Truman, Box 15, Misc., *Truman; FRUS 1945*, VI, pp. 486–495; Friedrich W. Hack, one of the people who was working on the O.S.S. Bern–Tokyo connection, had been used by Ribbentrop to open the way for the anti-Comintern pact in the 1930s! F. W. Deakin and G. R. Storry, *The Case of Richard Sorge* (London: 1966), p. 162. The quotation and much other interesting, and unpublished, material is in a 11 July 1945 report and related papers, Japanese Surrender File, Box 21, *Dulles*.

111. 2 and 16 February 1945, February File, Box 171, *PSF*.

112. 11 January–11 April 1945 "Vessel" reports, January and February Files and Donovan File, Boxes 167, 170, and 171, *PSF;* 30 January 1945, Ballantine to Grew approves of the reports ("should be given some credence"), *FRUS 1945*, VI, pp. 475–476. 11 January–11 April 1945 in State Department Files, 103.918/1–1145 to /4–1145, *Diplomatic Branch*. The G-2 rebuttal, 3 February 1945, File 82, Miscellaneous messages, *RG 218 Leahy*.

113. 18/25 August 1945 Donovan–President Truman exchange, no box number, OSS Files, C. F. Collection, *Truman*.

114. 27 January 1945, Spencer to Langer, China File, Box 16, and 25 April 1945, Colonel Whitaker report, Kunming File, Box 17, Entry 1, *RG 226*.

115. Donovan to F.D.R., 1 July 1944, July File, Box 168, 6 November 1944, November File, and 12 December 1944, 1–15 December File, Box 170, *PSF;* 15–29 March 1944, (JCS

1290), ABC 384 China (12–15–43), sec. 2, *RG 165;* John K. Emmerson, *The Japanese Thread* (New York: 1978), p. 212. Miles's memoir deviates sharply from the documentary record, Milton E. Miles, *A Different Kind of War,* pp. 437–452.

116. The quotation is from Spencer to Langer, 27 January 1945, China File, Box 16, Entry 1, *RG 226.* Donovan to F.D.R., 19 June 1944, OSS Safe Files, Box 6 and 17 November 1944, November File, Box 170, *PSF;* Donovan to President Truman, 12 May 1945, Box 15, Misc., *Truman.* The British were concerned about the rivalries among American organizations in China (July 1944 report, *WO 208/471)* but R. and A. and S.I. actually seem to have cooperated rather well there. 16 February 1945 report, Far East File, Box 3, Entry 1, *RG 226.* See also Miles "Secret" Memorandum on conditions in China, 17 May 1946, "Secret Memorandum" File, Box 3, Miles Collection, Hoover Institution.

Donovan to F.D.R., 28 September 1944, September File, Box 169, *PSF;* 1944–45 O.S.S. operational plans, secs. 12A and 13, ABC 350.05 (6–21–44), *RG 165.* Davies memo, 4 January 1945, China File, Box 16, Entry 1, *RG 226.* On expectation of an S.O.E. move, see Donovan to F.D.R., 17 October 1944, October File, Box 169, *PSF.* At this time the American military thought there were "several thousand" (!) British agents in China, while eighteen months earlier, British Naval intelligence had bemoaned the lack of Chinese M.I. 6 sources. Charles F. Romanus and Riley Sunderland, *Stilwell's Command Problems* (Washington: 1956), p. 159, 13 July 1943, *Wilkinson.*

117. 16 January 1945 plan, China File, Box 16, Entry 1, *RG 226;* 1 February 1945, File 136, National Intelligence Authority, *RG 218 Leahy;* Charles F. Romanus and Riley Sunderlund, *Stilwell's Command Problems,* pp. 251–252.

118. 1 February 1945 Wedemeyer report, File 136, National Intelligence Authority, *RG 218 Leahy.*

119. 10 June and 5 July 1945, China File, Box 16, Entry 1, *RG 226;* 24 May 1945, Wedemeyer to War, Box 9, Folder 54, *RG 218 Leahy;* 1944–45 report, sec. 10/23, Gilbert Stuart Papers, Box 1, Hoover Institution. Note though that on 6 April 1945 Spencer reported to Langer that R. and A. Chunking about ready to really function at a time when only four months of war remained. Kunming File, Box 17, Entry 1, *RG 226.*

120. 27 August 1945 report, no. 2494, *Marshall.* On not accepting Tai Li's intelligence: 11 June 1945, 103.918/6-845 *Diplomatic Branch.* On adverse effect of association with Tai Li: July 1945, memoir, pp. 95–96, Ivan D. Yeaton Papers, Hoover Institution and 17 July 1944 from Chunking, 103.918/7–1744, *Diplomatic Branch.* On the marine general, 30 October 1944, Donovan to F.D.R., October File, Box 169, *PSF.*

121. 25 April 1945, Whitaker report, Kunming File, Box 17, Entry 1, *RG 226.*

122. 1944–45 operational plans, sec. 12, ABC 350.05 (6–21–44), *RG 165;* Charles F. Romanus and Riley Sunderland, *Stilwell's Command Problems,* pp. 352–393. As late as 16 July 1945, O.S.S. China was trying to get the legal counsel's office to approve poisoning of enemy draft animals in China but was refused. International Law File, Box 21, J. Donovan Papers, Hoover Institution.

123. Donovan to President Truman, 23 August and 18 September 1945, Box 15, Misc., *Truman.*

124. Miles, "Secret memorandum," 17 May 1946, Secret Memorandum File, Box 3, Miles Papers, Hoover Institution.

125. 19 November 1944 item on Dutch recruiting, War Diary, 16–30 November File, Box 34, *SHAEF;* 27 October 1944, October File, Box 169, *PSF.* Thorne's conclusion that this report increased F.D.R.'s belief that a colonialist compact existed has no basis in the available documentary record, Christoper Thorne, *Allies of a Kind,* pp. 594 and 628.

126. 20 July 1944, *Wilkinson.*

127. 7 September 1944, Mountbatten to F. O., *WO 106/4633.*

128. April–August 1945 sorties and supply records, *WO 106/4805;* S.O.E. strength, 14 April–May 1945, *WO 212/211,* 212, 213, Public Record Office, London.

129. On wireless sets, (no file name), Box 11, Entry 1, *RG 226.* On cooperation in the field: 6 April–8 July 1945 reports, *WO 106/4805; Sweet-Escott,* p. 235.

130. 7 April 1945, Fahs to Donovan, Far East–Fahs File, Box 24, Entry 1, *RG 226;* 28 April 1945, State Department to American representatives in India, *FRUS 1945,* VI, p. 1241; consul in Ceylon to State, 17 February 1945, 103.918/2–1745, *Diplomatic Branch;* 29 May 1945, Sultan to War, Folder 54, Box 9, *RG 218 Leahy.*

131. 1944–45 operational plans secs. 2, 4, and 14, ABC 350.05 (6–21–44), *RG 165;* 19

June 1944, Donovan to F.D.R., January–June File, Box 167, *PSF;* 28 June 1944, JCS Memo 258, ABC (12–3–42), sec. 3, *RG 165.*

132. O.S.S. activity covered in British field reports, 6 April–3 July 1945, *WO 106*/4805.

133. R. Harris Smith, *O.S.S.,* pp. 290–318; Donovan to F.D.R., 4 and 15 December 1944, 1–15 December File, Box 170, 22 February 1945, February File, 23 March 1945, 16–31 March File, and George Summer to F.D.R., 8 March 1945, March File, Box 171, *PSF;* 24 and 26 February 1945 (JPS 615D and 7637D), CCS 381 Thailand (2–22–45) *RG 218.*

134. 26 March–2 April 1945 (JCS 1034 and 1304/2), CCS 381 (2–22–45), *RG 218;* Donovan to F.D.R., 16 and 26 March 1945, 16–31 March File, Box 171, *PSF;* Dubois to Fahs, 22 August 1944, SEAC File, Box 20 and 7 June 1945 report, FETO–Kates File (so George Kates was the likely author), Box 22, Entry 1, *RG 226.*

135. Buxton to J.C.S., 14 April 1945, CCS 381 (2–22–45), *RG 218;* Donovan and Cheston to President Truman, 14 June 1945, 27 and 30 August, 6 and 10 September, 1945, Box 15, Misc., *Truman.*

136. 25 August mtg., *FRUS, The Conference at Quebec 1944,* p. 248; Donovan to F.D.R., 10 and 18 July 1944, July File, Box 68 *PSF* (note that the Donovan estimate of July that the Japanese would immediately move against the Vichy administration was nine months premature). An important recent article, though based largely on different material, reaches many of the same conclusions as those in the following paragraphs; Ronald Spector, "Allied Intelligence and Indochina, 1943–1945" *Pacific Historical Review,* 51, no. 1 (February 1982) 23–50.

137. 13 October 1944, Donovan to Hull and reply, *FRUS 1944,* III, pp. 776–777; 15 and 28 December 1944 and 8 and 11 January 1945 (related to JCS 1200/2), ABC 384 Indo China (12–16–44), sec. 1A, *RG 165.*

138. 9 and 21 January and 9 February 1945 reports, ABC 384 (12–16–44), sec. 1A, *RG 165.* In the 16 January 1945 SWNCC mtg., McCloy raised the French Indochina issue, p. 122, Forrestal Diaries, Princeton.

139. 12 March 1945, Donovan to F.D.R., March File, Box 171, *PSF;* 13 (2), 15, 17, and 29 March 1945 exchanges regarding JCS 1200/7 and CCS 644/21, ABC 384 (12–16–44), sec. 1-B, *RG 165.*

140. 8 April 1945, Mountbatten to COS, *WO 106*/3483; 30 March 1945, Wilson–Marshall exchange and 11 April 1945 Churchill message, ABC 384 (12–16–44), sec. 1-B, *RG 165.*

141. On French anger about being "let down" by O.S.S. in Indochina, 2 June 1960 Shepardson–Passy talks, Misc. Correspondence File, Box 3, Shepardson papers, Roosevelt Library; 7 November 1944, War Diary, 1-15 November File, Box 34, *SHAEF.* In 1947, O'Brien was trying to get medals for Frenchmen who had worked with O.S.S. in Indochina in the late summer of 1945 even though he did not know them. Donovan File, Box 2, O'Brien Papers, Columbia.

142. 13 April 1945 Draft reply, ABC 384 (12–16–44), sec. 1-B, *RG 165.*

143. Exchanges between Wedemeyer, Mountbatten, Marshall, and Wilson, 17 April–5 June 1945, (JPS 687), ABC 384 (12–16–44), sec. 1-B, *RG 165.*

144. 4 June 1945, Marshall to Wedemeyer and 7 June 1945 State Department to Hurley, ABC 384 (12–16–44), sec. 1-B, *RG 165.*

145. 18 August and 19 October 1945 reports, *WO 106*/4805, Donovan and Cheston to President Truman, 21 August–28 September 1945, Box 15, Misc., *Truman.*

146. September 1945 memoir, W. G. Cheshire Papers, Churchill Library, Cambridge.

Chapter 7

1. 27 December 1944, Hayes to State, 103.918/12-2744, *Diplomatic Branch;* 31 August 1945, Frechtling to Langer (quoting MacVeagh), Cairo 2 File, Box 15, Entry 1, *RG 226.* During hostilities and even in the British–Greek fighting, however, MacVeagh reported no sign of O.S.S. tipping to the left, John O. Iatrides, ed., *Ambassador MacVeagh Reports,* pp. 591–679. A splendid right-wing diatribe is James Burnham, *The Web of Subversion* (New York: 1954), pp. 118–124.

Notes

2. On pre-22 June activities: 14 January 1941 *Cadogan* and 9 April–18 June 1941 planning meetings, *WO 193/623*. For the SAM code name: 29 April 1944, *FO 954/24A*. Diary, 23–24 June 1941 (for quotation), 8 August, 12 and 16 September 1941, *Dalton;* George A. Hill "Reminiscences of four years with N.K.V.D.," pp. 133 and 214, Hill Papers, Hoover Institution; 1 August 1941 note, *WO 193/623*.

3. Diary, 1 and 6 August, 1941, *Dalton Papers;* George A. Hill, "Reminiscences, etc.," pp. 1–33, Hoover Institution; Reports of January 1945, *FO 371/47709* (my thanks to Martin Kitchen for this reference); and 12 January 1945, *FO 204/1931*. The various sabotage plans for use *inside* Russia were continued by S.O.E.: 1 July 1941 (the source of the quotation), 6 and 9 August, 1941, *WO 193/623;* and 1 July 1941 *WO 208/1579*.

4. Minutes of S.O.E.–P.W.E. meetings, 17 November 1941 and 17 December 1943, *FO 898/27;* Peter Calvocoressi, *Top Secret Ultra* (New York: 1980), p. 94; *Hinsley*, II, pp. 59–66. The statement that no work was done on Soviet codes after 22 June comes from *Hinsley*, I, p. 199.

5. George A. Hill, "Reminiscences, etc." pp. 67–217, Hoover Institution; 24 November 1943, *Cadogan;* Walter Roberts, *Tito, Mihailović and the Allies*, pp. 44 and 58; *Barker*, p. 163.

6. 12 January 1945 report, *WO 204/1931;* Deane to Marshall after a talk with Hill, 17 November 1943, CCS 385 USSR (11–4–43), *RG 218;* George A. Hill, "Reminiscences, etc.," pp. 189, 222–225, Hoover Institution.

7. June 17–23 1942, O.S.S.–S.O.E. agreement, OSS Memos, June–July 1942 File, Box 4, *Goodfellow*.

8. January 1944 report, Mission to Moscow File, Box 19, Entry 1, *RG 226*. That the initial prompting came from the I.D.C. is indicated by a 13 July 1943 memo (103.91802/1146A) and the November 1943 materials (103.918/1850–1899), *Diplomatic Branch*. Deane–Marshall exchange, 13-17 November 1943, CCS 385 USSR (11–4–43), *RG 218;* Memos, 9, 13, 18 November 1943, ABC 385 USSR (11–9–43), *RG 165*.

9. Deane to Marshall, 17 November 1943, and 1 and 21 February, and 30 March 1944 versions of the Donovan–Molotov talks), CCS 385 (11–4–43), *RG 218;* 3 January 1944, Donovan to Buxton, 103.918/1978, *Diplomatic Branch;* Haskell to R. Harris Smith, 4 April 1970, Europe File, Box 1, R. Harris Smith Papers, Hoover Institution; 6 January 1944, Harriman to Department, *FRUS 1944*, I, pp. 580–581; John R. Deane, *The Strange Alliance* (New York: 1947), pp. 50–58.

10. Conference record, 27 December 1943, and 5 January 1944, Donovan to Harriman, Subject File, OSS, *RG 334;* 1 February 1944, JPS 387/D, CCS 385 (11–4–43), *RG 218;* Donovan to Buxton, 3 January 1944, 103.918/1978, *Diplomatic Branch;* Haskell to R. Harris Smith, 4 April 1970, Europe File, Box 1, R. Harris Smith Papers, Hoover Institution; John R. Dean, *The Strange Alliance*, pp. 50–58.

11. Reports of 28 December 1943, 6 and 21 January and 15 February (on shipping) and 13 February (personnel list), 1944, Subject File OSS, *RG 334;* 1–10 February (JPS 387) and 15 February 1944 Deane message, CCS 385 (11–4–43), *RG 218; Hoover*, p. 221. W. Averell Harriman and Elie Abel, *Special Envoy to Churchill and Stalin* (New York: 1975), pp. 291–295. On R. and A. preparations: January 1944, especially 15 January 1944, Fahs to Langer (2)—source of quotation—Mission to Moscow File, Box 19, and 20 January 1944 Hartshore to Applebaum, Europe–Africa Division File, Box 3, Entry 1, *RG 226*.

12. 1–3 February 1944, JPS 387/D, CCS 385 (11–4–43) *RG 218*. 10 February 1944, Hoover to Harry Hopkins, ABC 385 (11–9–43), *RG 165*.

13. 14 and 15 February 1944, Royal to Leahy and J.C.S. 146th mtg., CCS 385 (11–4–43), *RG 218;* 16 February 1944, Haskell to Deane, Subject File OSS, *RG 334*.

14. Hoover to Biddle, 15 February 1944, ABC 385 (11–9–43), *RG 165;* Biddle to F.D.R., 16 February 1944, CCS 385 (11–4–43), *RG 218*.

15. J.P.S. 128th mtg., 16 February 1944, CCS 385 (11–4–43), *RG 218*.

16. J.P.S. 129th mtg., 17 February 1944, CCS 385 (11–4–43), *RG 218*.

17. *Ibid.* Only a phrase indicating that the military advantages outweighed the disadvantages (a standard J.P.S. phrase) was cut.

18. 18 and 19 February 1944, CCS 385 (11–4–43), *RG 218*.

19. Royal to McFarland and a penciled note, 19 February 1944, plus an additional note of 22 February. CCS 385 (11–4–43), *RG 218*.

20. J.C.S. 148th mtg., 21 February 1944, CCS 385 (11–4–43), *RG 218*.

21. 18 February–14 March 1944, O.S.S. messages to Deane, Subject File OSS, *RG 334;* Memo for record 15 March 1944, CCS 385 (11–4–43) *RG 218;* 15 March 1944 memo for Marshall, King, Arnold and Donovan, Miscellaneous Memoranda File, *RG 218 Leahy;* 20 March 1944, J.P.S. 387/3/D (enclosing the Deane and Harriman cables), CCS 385 (11–4–43), *RG 218;* 23 March 1944 Haskell to Deane, Subject File, OSS, *RG 334;* John R. Deane, *The Strange Alliance,* pp. 50–58.

22. 21 March–4 April 1944, consideration of J.C.S. 708/2 and the Hull letter, including post–4 April 1944 OPD memo for record, CCS 385 (11–4–43), *RG 218;* 21 March 1944 G-2 report, ABC 385 (11–9–43), *RG 165;* W. Averell Harriman and Elie Abel, *Special Envoy to Churchill and Stalin,* pp. 291–295; John R. Deane, *The Strange Alliance,* pp. 50–58.

23. 21 April 1944 memo for record, CCS 385 (11–4–43), *RG 218.* On 30 April 1944, General Wilson notified all O.S.S. and S.O.E. offices in the Mediterranean theater that information to be given to the Soviets would be handled by the War Department and the War Office and not directly, or via A.F.H.Q. OSS/SOE Policy no. 3 File, G-3, Spec. Ops., Reel 38-A, *RG 331, AFHQ.*

24. Deane–Buxton–War Department exchange, 4–8 April, 28 April, and 28 June, 1944, Subject File OSS and 3 March 1944, chronological file, outgoing, *RG 334.*

25. 11 March 1944, Deane transmissions of the Bulgarian report, chronological outgoing file, *RG 334.* For Robert L. Wolff's 9 May comment: Balkan Section File, Box 2, Entry 1, *RG 226.* Ironically, in May 1944 the Americans were getting detailed intelligence data on conditions in Bulgaria from the Bulgarian minister in Switzerland. 8 May report, 103.918/5–1845, *Diplomatic Branch.* On queries and the dispatch of O.S.S. reports: 11–21 April 1944, Haskell to Deane and transmission of 9–10 May and 22 May, 1944, Subject File OSS, *RG 334.* See also John R. Deane, *The Strange Alliance,* pp. 50–58.

26. Memos of 6, 7, 16, and 22 December 1944 and 2 January 1945, Germany File, OSS, *RG 334.* Note that these shipments did not include O.S.S. material for embassy use, which went via another channel, for example, 103.918/3–2145, *Diplomatic Branch.*

27. Donovan to Christ, 20 July 1944 and Donovan to Fitin 23 August 1944, Subject File OSS, and Fitin to Deane, 27 September 1944, Germany File, OSS, *RG 334.* Note that from 17 March 1944, O.S.S. used many more hand couriers, so fewer document references remain in the files: memo, 17 March, CCS 385 (2–8–42), *RG 218.* On published Russian Soviet material, Thomas P. Whitney of the industrial unit of the U.S.S.R. section of R. and A. was assigned to the Moscow Embassy to handle this by 30 January 1945, Cheston to Harriman, Moscow File, Box 19, entry 1, *RG 226.* For an earlier transmission, 19 July 1944, 103.918/7–1944, *Diplomatic Branch.* On material gained from the Russians, see also John R. Deane, *The Strange Alliance,* pp. 50–58.

28. On naval intelligence: Deane messages, 29 February and 19 June 1944, 350.05 USSR (3–3–44), *RG 165;* 30 March 1944, General Christ report, ABC 452.1, Poland (11–26–42) sec. 2-B, *RG 165.* Note also Donovan to Deane, 10 January 1945, Moscow File, Box 19, entry 1, *RG 226.*

29. 12 April 1944 message, Subject File OSS, and 10 and 25 November Deane messages, Germany File, OSS, *RG 334;* Memo for record of 21 April and 14–19 May 1944 messages, CCS 385 (11–4–43), *RG 218.* Donovan also sought to establish M.O. coordination, but with what results is not clear from the records, Ruggles to Robinson, 2 January 1945, USSR Division 1945 File, Box 5, Entry 1, *RG 226.*

30. Donovan exchanges with Deane and Fitin, July–September 1944, especially 22 July, 2 August (naming Col. I. Chichayev and claiming that there was no N.K.V.D. representative in Stockholm) and 29 August 1944 (in which Donovan reported the London O.S.S.–N.K.V.D. connection in operation), Germany, OSS file, *RG 334.*

31. 22 April 1944, Deane to War Department, 091.411 Balkans (8–21–43) sec. 1, *RG 218; Barker,* p. 234.

32. Donovan was preparing Balkan air crew rescue operations as early as May 1944, and had been alerted to Soviet sensitivity by Deane: 29 May 1944, Donovan to Deane, Subject File, OSS *RG 334.* J.C.S. preparatory authorization (6 August 1944) and delay for Soviet authorization order (30 August 1944); CCS 091.411 (8–21–43) sec. 1, *RG 218.* Orders to prepare such missions were issued by Balkan Air Force, 28 August 1944, and on 16 September A.F.H.Q. ordered that the missions remain in Bulgaria and Rumania "for collection of intelligence" *WO 204/1982.*

33. On the activities of the missions: Burckhardt to Langer, 23 September 1944, NATO

Notes

Burckhardt File, Box 23, entry 1, *RG 226*. On the expulsion and the use of the Donovan–Fitin connection to reverse it, 25–30 September 1944, CCS 091.411 (8–21–43) sec. 1, *RG 218*. A full summary of the affair (thirty pages) is in 1 November 1944, O.S.S. to State, 103.918/11–144, *Diplomatic Branch*. An O.S.S. representative in Istanbul reported that the expulsion was caused by deep Soviet suspicion of the head of the S.O.E. mission, Lieutenant Colonel Gibson, CCS 091.411 (8–21–43), sec. 1, *RG 218*.

34. The names for Bulgaria, Rumania, and Yugoslavia–Czechoslovakia went across on 29 September and 3 and 6 October 1944 respectively: Germany OSS, and Rumania OSS, files, *RG 334*. On N.K.V.D.–O.S.S. Balkan cooperation: Deane to Donovan, and coordination meeting, 11 November 1944, Subject File, *RG 334*. Deane–Donovan exchange 10 and 23 November 1944, Germany OSS File, *RG 334*. In December 1944, the Soviets wanted the existing O.S.S. team in Bulgaria to be replaced by another, and this was done, *WO 204/ 1982*.

35. On transmission of material on Rumania 10 October and 4 and 11 November 1944 (Subject File OSS) and 30 October (Rumania OSS File) *RG 334*. Regarding Wisner: 12 December 1944 report, 091.411 (8–21–44), sec. 1, *RG 218;* and 31 October 1944, 103.918/ 10–3144, *Diplomatic Branch*. The information on the anti-Soviet plot is in 31 December 1944 Donovan–Fitin message, Subject File OSS, *RG 334*.

36. Donovan to F.D.R., 29 September 1944 (source of the quotation) and 30 September 1944 (in which he talks of "cover"), September File, Box 169, *PSF*. On limiting the flow of material related to Germany: 12 December 1945 memorandum, Europe–Africa Division File, Box 3, Entry 1, *RG 226*. There was considerable concern about American oil property in Rumania; 10 November 1944, 103.918/11–1044, *Diplomatic Branch*, 2 November 1944, June–December File, Box 73, *Map Room*.

37. J.C.S. 1084 Enclosures B and C, 2 October 1944, CCS 091.411 (8–21–43) sec. 1, *RG 218;* 10 October 1944 Donovan to Fitin, Subject File OSS, and to Deane, 20 February, 1945, Germany OSS file, *RG 334*. On the Czech mission: 1 September 1944 Deane to J.C.S., CCS 091 (8–21–43), Sec. 1, *RG 218;* Donovan to F.D.R., 23 September 1944, September File, and 20 October 1944, October File, Box 169, *PSF;* 30 December 1944–2 January 1945 messages, Subject OSS File and Czech OSS File, *RG 334*. Since in the subsequent investigation of the mission, Howard Chapin was afraid of "undue interest" in the mission, its S.I. elements were certainly primary, 29 January 1945 and following, *WO 204/10184*.

38. January 1945 reports, *FO 371/47709* and 12 January 1945, *WO 204/1931*; George A. Hill, "Reminiscences, etc.," p. 250–251, Hoover Institution. On the pull back by the Soviets, messages of 4, 9, and 13 April 1945 (9 April is the withdrawal of Chichayev), Subject File OSS, and 20 April message, Rumania OSS File, *RG 334*. On Donovan and Drew Pearson: May–June 1945 exchange, Subject File OSS, *RG 334*.

39. 18 December 1944, Dunn to Stettinius, 103.918/12–1844, *Diplomatic Branch; Hoover*, pp. 218–220; 3 March 1971, Calvin Hoover to R. Harris Smith, Europe File, Box 21, R. Harris Smith Papers, Hoover Institution.

40. 11 December 1944, Donovan to F.D.R., 1–15 December 1944 File, Box 170, *PSF;* Dunn to Stettinius, 18 December 1944, 103.918/12–1844, *Diplomatic Branch*.

41. 23 December 1944, Stettinius record, Memos sent to the President File, Box 734, *Stettinius*. Confirming evidence that F.D.R. ordered the codes sent back comes from combining *Hoover*, pp. 218–220 and Calvin Hoover to R. Harris Smith, 3 March 1971, Europe File, Box 21, R. Harris Smith Papers, Hoover Institution. Buxton to Deane, 5 January 1945, Subject File OSS, *RG 334*. Donovan to F.D.R., 11 December 1944, 1–15 December File, Box 170, *PSF*.

42. 9 January 1945 Harriman message, 103.918/1–945, *Diplomatic Branch;* 9 January and 15 February 1945 (2) messages, Subject File OSS, *RG 334*.

43. On Reseda: 16 April 1945, Minutes of Radio Advisory Committee File, Box 8, Entry 1, *RG 226;* 16 May 1945 message, Subject File OSS, *RG 334*.

44. Robinson–Deane exchange, 31 May–6 June 1945, Subject File OSS, *RG 334*.

45. Donovan to Deane, 11 July 1945 and Eisenhower to War, 3 August 1945, Subject File OSS, *RG 334*.

46. Messages of 11, 23, and 30 July 1945, Subject File OSS, *RG 334* and 26 July 1945 (In J.C.S. 1084/1), CCS 091.411 (8–21–43) sec. 2, *RG 218*.

47. Messages of 31 July and 1 August 1945, Subject File OSS *RG 334*.

48. Messages of 1 and 3 August 1945, Subject File OSS, *RG 334;* 3 August 1945 message (in J.C.S. 1084/1), ABC 091.411 Balkans (8–21–43), *RG 165.*

49. 18 August 1945, (J.C.S. 1084/1) and 24 August 1945 Donovan message, CCS 091.411 (8–21–43), sec. 1, *RG 218;* Donovan to Deane, 30 August 1945, Subject File OSS, *RG 334.*

Chapter 8

1. I believe that I appropriated some form of this remark from Colin Young of the National Film School, Beaconsfield, Buckinghamshire.

2. 26 June 1945 conference record, Germany 3 File, Box 16, Entry 1, *RG 226.*

3. See projects committee records: Entry 59, and also especially Langer to Donovan 23 August 1945, OSS Director's Office File, Box 2, Entry 1, *RG 226.*

4. 11 May 1943 memorandum to Lieutenant Applebaum, Morale File, Box 10, and 23 August 1945, OSS Director's Office File, Box 2, Entry 1, *RG 226.* See also Richard Dunlop, *Donovan* (New York: 1982), p. 309.

5. Box 3; 3 March 1945, James to Langer, Europe–Africa Division File. 5 May 1944 "Guide to Preparation of Political Reports," Political Reports File, Box 9, January–December 1945 reports, Executive Committee File, Box 6; 28 November 1944, Hartshorne paper and huge 15 March 1945 "Analysis of Major Transfers of German Territory from the Standpoint of International Security (rather late!), Director's Committee File, Box 7. Only Hartshorne's side of the July 1945 squabble is here, 23 July 1945 Hartshorne memorandum, Europe–Africa Division File, Box 3, Entry 1, *RG 226.*

6. Morrison to Langer, 14 June 1945, OSS History File, Box 11. In a post–O.S.S. Morrison report to Langer (10 October 1945), the evils of "Prediction" and reports with "considerable interpretation" are decried. USSR Division File, Box 5, Entry 1. In June 1945, H. Stuart Hughes referred to the "journalistic and now outmoded approach to Italian reporting" of a former R. and A. man. Hughes to Langer, 1 June 1945, MEDTO Office File, Box 20, Entry 1, *RG 226.*

7. 31 July 1944, Langer to Morse, London 2 File, Box 8, Entry 1, *RG 226; Langer,* pp. 181–187. Interview with H. Stuart Hughes.

8. *Langer,* p. 187; *Hoover,* p. 196; Langer to Hughes, 26 February and 3 March 1944, Hughes to Langer, 6 November 1944, Algiers File, Box 15; May 1944 reports, N.A.T.O. File, Box 23, 19 December 1944 Fahs report, Spencer File, Box 22, Entry 1.

9. The "burying" reference is in Morse to Langer, 20 May 1944, ETO London 2 File, Box 21. Donovan could also be very gentle in dealing with subordinates; see, for example, 6 December 1944 to Bruce, London 3 File, Box 18. On cooperation during combat with other O.S.S. units, Seeley to Langer, 2 January 1945, NATO Seeley File, Box 23. The system of processing captured enemy records is described in Burckhardt to Langer, 3 January 1944, NATO Burckhardt File, Box 23, Entry 1. *RG 226.*

10. Hall to Langer, 28 February 1944, FETO–Spencer File, Box 22 and 6 November 1944, Algiers File, Box 15, Entry 1, *RG 226.*

11. Langer to Hughes, 26 February and 3 March 1944, Algiers File, Box 15. On the maneuvering ability of Kent and Langer, see 17 April 1945, Kent to Langer, Europe–Africa Division File, Box 3. On Cora DuBois and Crane Brinton: Langer to Heppner, 5 June 1944, SEAC File, Box 20 and Langer to Bruce, 26 February 1944, London 2 File, Box 17. Langer to McCulloch, 25 May 1944, Cairo 3 File, Box 15, Entry 1, *RG 226.*

12. Some of the fortnightly R. and A. progress reports, mimeographed, were thirty-five pages long. The Outpost Memos File, Box 14, Entry 1, *RG 226* is a good indicator of the amount of paper, and supervision, in the R. and A. system.

13. Langer to Hall, 17 February and Hall to Langer 13 May, 1944 New Delhi File, Box 18. 9 January 1944–June 1945 Langer Hughes correspondence, NATO, Hughes File, Box 23. The Neumann letter, 9 November 1944, London 3 File, Box 18, Entry 1, *RG 226.*

14. Schorske to Deutsch, 4 January 1944, London 2 File, Box 17, Entry 1, *RG 226.*

15. Brinton to Langer, 22 January 1944, London 2 File, Box 17, Entry 1, *RG 226.*

16. Langer to Brinton, 7 February 1944, London 2 File, Box 17 and Schorske to Deutsch 4 January 1944, in the same file. This was not the only case in which overseas R. and A. people were burned. In December 1944–January 1945, Langer and Neumann went after Morse, who admitted that his first reaction was a "defensive" one. London 3 File, Box 17, Entry 1, *RG 226*.

17. 22–30 May 1944, Hughes–Langer exchange, Algiers File, Box 15, Entry 1, *RG 226*. Ten months later when Langer wanted a man from the same theater and Glavin resisted, Langer turned to Donovan who sweetly ordered Glavin to send him to Washington. 20 March 1945, Donovan to Glavin, MEDTO Office File, Box 20, Entry 1, *RG 226*.

18. 29 June 1944, Langer to Hughes, Algiers File, Box 15. For Hughes manner, see 19 June 1944 to Langer in the same file. For Hughes position in the theater, 23 October 1944, Hite to Langer, NATO–Hite File, Entry 1, *RG 226*.

19. Interview with H. Stuart Hughes.

20. Personnel: March 1944, Personnel Reports File, Box 11; 1944–45, Branch Summary of Personnel File, Box 9; May 1945 (R. and A. Overseas), General ETO File, Box 20. Reports and R. and A. ETO library: 13 March ETO Becchio File, Box 21; 28 March 1944 report, Office File, Box 4; 23 August 1945, Langer to Donovan, OSS Director's Office File, Entry 1, *RG 226*.

21. On foreign experts survey: 15 December 1943, Branch Orders File, Box 9, and Interviews File, Box 10. Woodruff to Wolff, 12 April 1944, MEDTO File, Box 20, Entry 1. On shift of people out of specialties: 11 December 1943, Central Europe File, Box 1, Entry 60. On collecting materials on Japan in Europe: 16 March 1945, NATO–Hughes File, and 16 May 1945, ETO London File, Box 21, Entry 1, *RG 226*.

22. 2 November and 17 December 1942, Board of Analysts mtgs., Box 1, Entry 58. There was an interesting tie of R. and A. and Princeton University and the Council of Learned societies to produce a glossary of Arabic, 8 January 1943, Box 1, Entry 59. On outside contracts in general: SF Miscellaneous File, Box 20 and contracts projects file, Box 10; 22 October 1945 Report on Relations with universities, Director's Committee File and 24 October 1945, Executive committee action, Executive Committee File, Box 7, Entry 1, *RG 226*. On Cal. Tech.: 23 February 1945 memorandum, ABC 334.3, sec. 3 (5–1–42), *RG 165*.

23. 1 June 1945, MEDTO Progress File, and 1 February 1945, North American Office File, Box 20; 22 September 1944, ETO Evans File, Box 21; August 1945 Hawaii File, Box 17, Entry 1, *RG 226*. 6 June 1944 on, History of OSS File, Box 11 and 25 July 1944 OSS History Committee establishment, Special Orders File, Box 9, Entry 1. On access to State department cables: Holmes to Langer, 22 May 1943, 103.918/1347 and Dreier–Hussey exchange, 103.918/8–845, *Diplomatic Branch*. On Kent's deft touch: 29 August and 6 September 1944, Europe–Africa Division File, Box 3, Entry 1, *RG 226*.

24. Embassy to F.O. January 1943, *FO 371/37634A/922*; 31 May 1943 memo, *WO 208/ 792*; 1 June 1944, *Wilkinson*; 21 May 1945, Rosenman note, OSS File, Box 3, Rosenman Papers, Truman Library; 19–20 March 1945, Morgenthau note on R. and A. Paris Intelligence Weekly, no. 831, *Morgenthau*.

25. F.N.B. complaint that it was getting the wrong reports and desire for internal distribution papers, Kranthal memos of 3 August 1943 and 8 February 1944, FNB File, Box 1, Entry 60, *RG 226*. 8–22 June 1945, Langer–Schorske exchange on improper circulation of reports, Europe–Africa Division 1945 File, Box 3, Entry 1. On Sweezy: 2 February 1945 Committee report, EPR File, Box 23, Entry 1. Donovan to F.D.R., March 1945, March File, Box 170, *PSF* (for a postwar view of the Himmler speech treated in this issue of the European Political Report, see Bradley F. Smith and Agnes F. Peterson, eds., *Himmler Geheimreden* [Frankfurt/M: 1974], pp. 213–237 and accompanying notes). Morse to Wilson on European Political Report, 9 April 1945, London 3 File, Box 17, Entry 1, *RG 226*. For Sweezy's views, see his essay "Economic Problems of the Peace Treaty," 6 March 1944, Sweezy Report File, Box 24, Entry 1, *RG 226*. Note that on 11 July 1944 the O.S.S. counsel, James Donovan, ruled that no one could be excluded from government employment simply because of "mere membership" in the Communist Party. Naturalization File, Box 21, James Donovan Papers, Hoover Institution.

26. John H. Backer, *The Decision to Divide Germany* (Durham, North Carolina: 1978). R. and A. reports, May 1944–April 1945, Box 73, *Map Room*. A copy of the second part of R. and A. report 1899 (a document that plays a major role in the argument of the Backer

book) was "destroyed by burning" three days after it arrived in the Map Room: June–December 1944 File, Box 73, *Map Room.*

27. On output: January–July 1945, R. and A. Reports Distribution File, Box 24, Entry 1. On maps: 13 December 1944, November–December 1944 File, Box 3, Entry 59, *RG 226*; 20 April 1945, Achievements File, Box 12, Entry 1, Joint War Plans Committee praise, 2 January 1946, CCS 200.6 (9–13–44) Application of Donovan Circular, *RG 218*. On distribution of R. and A. work and coping with short deadlines: 14 October 1942, Box 1, Entry 59; 1 January 1945, Langer to Ream, Deputy Director File, Box 2, Entry 1, *RG 226*. On special projects: 21 and 22 October, 16 November, 9 December 1942, 8 March, 10, 11, 20 May, and 23 September 1943, Projects Committee Minutes, Box 1, Entry 59; 4 March 1942, Board of Analysts, Entry 58; Langer to Donovan, 6 October 1944, Rumania Documents File, Box 3, Entry 1, *RG 226*.

28. On the Justice Department: F.B.I. and Latin America issue, 5 April and 22 November 1943, Box 1, Entry 59; 31 July–6 August 1943 exchange, Justice Department File, Box 1, and Neumann and Kent to Langer, 27 March and 12 April 1945, Europe–Africa Division 1945 File, Box 3, Entry 1, *RG 226*. Donovan offered to take responsibility for a 7 January 1943 study of the American armed forces that teetered on the edge of the O.S.S. authorized activity area; Box 1, Entry 59, *RG 226*. Wilson to Berle, 7 June 1944, 103.918/6–744, *Diplomatic Branch* and 8 July 1944, Wilson to Clayton, July 1944 File, Box 167, *PSF.* 2 February 1945, Langer–Treasury luncheon, no. 816, *Morgenthau.*

29. 27 January 1944 report, Central Europe File, Box 1, Entry 60; Projects Committee Minutes, Boxes 1–2, Entry 59, March and July 1945 reports, no file name, Box 11, Entry 1, *RG 226*. The basic agreement between R. and A. and General Hilldring: 12 July 1943, CAD File, Box 2, Entry 1, *RG 226*. Arrangements with the State Department: 20 August 1943, 103.918/1863, *Diplomatic Branch*. Appointment of liaison men: 4 May 1944, Box 2, Entry 59, *RG 226*. On the general importance of postwar work for R. and A.: Langer to Donovan, 11 June 1945, Memos to Donovan File, Box 2, Entry 1, *RG 226*.

30. O.S.S. to State, 30 August 1944, 103.918/9–3044, *Diplomatic Branch*. R. and A. did not want the Soviets to know of its role in preparing reports sent to Moscow: Lyon to Durbow, USSR File, Box 5, Entry 1, *RG 226*. Martin to Hartshorne, 21 May 1945, Far East File, Box 3, Entry 1, *RG 226*.

31. On R. and A. and F.N.B.: 21 February–3 March 1944 Schorske–Langer exchange and 8 August 1945, Poole to Langer, FNB File, Box 3. R. and A. and M.O., 16 February 1944, Deutsch memo, ETO–Deutsch File, Box 21. R. and A. and S.I., 16 February 1945 memo, Far East File, and 17 April 1945, Casey–Morse deal on Germany, London 3 File, Box 17. For the overall problem, 14 October 1944, Hughes to Langer, Algiers File, Box 15, Entry 1, *RG 226*.

32. The R. and A. ETO War Diary gives a fine, single source, over view of the kind of assistance R. and A. provided to other organizations, Modern Military Branch Reference Collection, National Archives.

33. 2 November 1944 report, Box 3, Entry 59; Sparks to Langer, 6 July 1945, London 3 File, Box 17, Entry 1, *RG 226*.

34. Donovan to F.D.R. (no day), 22 December 1941–15 January 1942 file, Box 163, *PSF.*

35. Langer to Heppner, 5 June 1944, SEAC File, Box 20, Entry 1, *RG 226*.

36. 22 March 1945 report, Alien File, Box 9, Entry 1, *RG 226*.

37. 22 January 1945, Martin to Langer, Far East File, Box 3, Entry 1, *RG 226*.

38. 10–27 July 1945 exchanges, Far East File, Box 3, Entry 1, *RG 226*.

39. 15 November 1944, Robinson to Bohlen, 103.918/11–1544; 25 November 1944, Kennan to Bohlen, 103.918/11–2544; 11–22 November 1944, 103.918/11–1144, *Diplomatic Branch.*

40. R. and A. reports 1899 and 2060; 14 October 1944 Langer to Acheson and attached, 103.918/10–1444, *Diplomatic Branch*. A summary of the report was sent by Donovan to F.D.R. on 30 October 1944, October File, Box 169, *PSF.*

41. John L. Gaddis, *The United States and the Origins of the Cold War* (New York: 1972), chapter 6; Adam B. Ulam, *The Rivals* (New York: 1971), chapters 3–5.

42. Charles F. Romanus and Riley Sunderland, *Stilwell's Command Problems*, p. 16.

43. 17 August 1944, Langer to Morse, London 2 File, Box 18, Entry 1, *RG 226*.

44. 13 July 1943, Remer to Hall, FETO File, Box 16; 2 April 1944 study, NATO–Hughes

File, Box 23; 20 January 1944, Langer to Bruce and 11 August 1944, O.S.S. plan for occupied Germany, London 2 File, Box 18; 17 August 1944, General Lewis to General Wickersham, ETO–Morse File, Box 21; 17 August 1944, Langer to Applebaum, London 2 File, Box 18, Entry 1, *RG 226*.

45. 17 August 1944, Langer to Morse, London 2 file, Box 18, Entry 1, *RG 226*.

46. *Ibid*. 22 September 1944, Langer to Ream, Demobilization File, Box 10, Entry 1, and Holborn to Langer, 6 November 1944, Fort Ord File, Box 14, Entry 1, *RG 226*.

47. Langer to Morse, 9 December 1944, London 2 File, Box 18, *RG 226*.

48. *Ibid*.

49. 29 January 1945 draft and finished version, General ETO File, Box 20, Entry 1, *RG 226*.

50. Hartshorne–Langer exchanges, May 1945, Burma–India File, Box 17; 7 June 1945 report, FETO–Kates File, Box 22, *RG 226*.

51. The map issue bounced along from February to July 1945: 103.918/2–545 to 103.918/7–2445, *Diplomatic Branch*. Sawyer to Langer, 21 May 1945, Paris Office File, Box 19, Entry 1, *RG 226*.

52. Langer to Donovan, 11 June 1945, Memoranda to Donovan File, Box 2, Entry 1, *RG 226*.

53. 14 June 1945, Morse and Deutsch to Neumann (after a talk with Donovan), Germany 3 File, Box 16, Entry 1; Evans to Langer, 1 September 1945, London 3 File, Box 18, Entry 1; Spencer China Outpost letter, China File, Box 16, Entry 1, *RG 226*.

54. Byrnes to Rome, 18 October 1945, 103.918/10–2245, *Diplomatic Branch*. H. Stuart Hughes interview quoted in Martin Weil, *A Pretty Good Club* (New York: 1978), p. 244f. A number of O.S.S. specialists participated in such short-term projects as the Strategic Bombing Survey.

55. Gregory Bateson to William Donovan, 18 August 1945, India–Burma File, Box 17, Entry 1, *RG 226*.

Chapter 9

1. *Taylor*, p. 350; 13 October 1943, Rounds (?) to Murphy, File K, Box 1, Rounds Papers, Hoover Institution; Wilson to Rogers, 10 January 1944, J. G. Rogers Collection, Colorado Historical Society.

2. 24 February 1943, *Wilkinson;* Dulles to Robert Murphy, 11 September 1951, Murphy File, Box 50, *Dulles*.

3. Especially Corey Ford, *Donovan of O.S.S.*, book three, and *Troy*.

4. 1 October 1945, *Wilkinson;* Henry L. Stimson and McGeorge Bundy, *On Active Service in Peace and War* (New York: 1947), p. 455; Kenneth Young, ed., *The Diaries of Sir Bruce Lockhart*, p. 232 (quoting Hopper) and p. 175 (quoting Scott); 18 January 1946, Miller to O'Brien, uncatalogued papers, O'Brien Collection, Columbia; *Hoover*, pp. 200–221; Rogers statement (undated), J. G. Rogers Collection, Colorado Historical Society. On old irritants see such items as Spencer to Langer condemning Donovan's boosterism; 27 January 1945, China File, Box 16, Entry 1, *RG 226*; Army investigation of an O.S.S. complaint about black market operations in North Africa: 20 May 1944, OPD 430, Case 10, *RG 165*. On rare occasions, Donovan could turn down business for O.S.S., such as an administrative role on a technical intelligence project: 9 February 1945, J.I.C. mtg., 125, CCS 334 (10–13–44), *RG 218*. On budget making: General Richards telephone message, 28 May 1945, CCS 111 (6–17–42), *RG 218*.

5. Merger discussions, 6 December 1942 on, CCS 334 (12–6–42), *RG 218;* and 11 October 1943, Vol. 45, Roll 8, *Stimson Diary*. Donovan to Deane, 4 September 1943, CCS 385 (4–12–43), *RG 218;* Margruder to Deane, 30 July 1943, CCS 385 (2–8–42), pt. 6, *RG 218;* 6 August 1943, Donovan to Eddy and 17 September 1943, Donovan to W. B. Smith, File OSS-A, Roll 37A, *AFHQ*.

6. Donovan plan and 23 September 1943 critique by Lt. Col. James O. Curtis, File OSS-A, Roll 37A, *AFHQ*.

7. See chapter 6, p. 268. *Troy.* (chapters 9–12) covers the abolition of O.S.S. story with a rather different interpretation than the one presented here.

8. Carter memo, 31 August 1944, no file name, Box 125, *PSF;* 27 November 1944, COS (44) 381 mtg. (0), *CAB 79/83.*

9. Memoranda, 21 August and 29 September 1944, Foreign Intelligence File, Box 731, *Stettinius.* 23 October 1944, JIS 89, CCS 334 (12–6–42), sec. 1, *RG 218.*

10. Barton to Hicks, Monthly Reports File, Box 24, Entry 1, *RG 226.*

11. Donovan to F.D.R., Subject File, Box 167, *PSF.*

12. J.I.S. 89 and 96, 15 November–12 December 1944, CCS 334 (12–6–42), *RG 218.* Carter to F.D.R., 26 October 1944, Subject File, Box 167, *PSF;* Carter memo, 2 January 1945, unnamed file, *PSF.*

13. Russell memo, 14 December 1944, Foreign Intelligence File, Box 731, *Stettinius;* J.I.C. 239 and J.I.C. 121st mtg., 20 December 1944–January 1945, CCS 334 (12–6–42), sec. 2, *RG 218.*

14. Donovan to F.D.R., 7 November 1944, November File, and 26 December 1944, 16–30 December File, 169, *PSF;* Stephenson to Donovan, 15 November 1944, Stephenson File, Box 1, Forgan Papers, Hoover Institution; Constantine Fitzgibbon, "Spying for the Yanks," *Sunday Telegraph,* 4 August 1979; 13 December 1944, Vol. 49, Roll 9, *Stimson Diary;* 15 December 1944, Stettinius to F.D.R., memos. Secretary to the President File, Box 734, *Stettinius.*

15. 16 November 1944 conference, Box 14, *Harold Smith;* F.D.R. to Stettinius, 17 January 1945, memos for the Secretary File (October–February), Box 733 *Stettinius* (compare with Troy, p. 274).

16. A. R. K. Mackenzie to the F.O., 23 February 1945, *FO 371/44542/AN683;* The main anti-Donovan clippings from February 1945 may be found in Donovan Secret Intelligence File, Box 15, Misc., *Truman.*

17. Lord Halifax to the F.O., 17 February 1945, *FO 371/44535/AN685;* 15 and 28 February 1945 memoranda, Donovan Secret Intelligence File, Box 15, Misc., Truman; Marshall and Leahy memoranda, 22 February and 6 March 1945, CCS 334 (12–6–42), *RG 218.*

18. 27 March and 3 April 1945 memoranda, File 131, N.I.A., *RG 218 Leahy;* 29 March 1945, Forrestal Diaries, II, p. 237, Forrestal Diary, Princeton.

19. Harold Smith to F.D.R., 2 March 1945, White House memos., Box 17, *Harold Smith.*

20. Donovan to F.D.R., 20, 21, and 23 February 1945, February File, and 6 March 1945, March File, Box 170, *PSF;* Lately Thomas, *When Even Angels Wept* (New York: 1973), pp. 53–57.

21. 5 April, 1945, Donovan to J.C.S., CCS 334 (12–6–42), *RG 218;* 6 April 1945, Donovan to F.D.R., 16–31 March File, Box 171, *PSF;* 12 April 1945, Morgenthau to Donovan, 836: 222–225, *Morgenthau;* Francis Biddle, *In Brief Authority* (Garden City New York: 1962), p. 359.

22. 30 April and 4 May 1945, Donovan to President Truman and 20 April 1945, Biddle to President Truman, Donovan, Secret Intelligence File, Misc., Box 15, *Truman.* Apparently, Donovan saw the President during the week of 14–21 June, but there is no indication of what transpired. Donovan to President Truman, 21 June 1945, Donovan, Secret Intelligence File, Misc., Box 15, *Truman.*

23. 26 April and 4 May 1945 conferences with the president, Box 15, *Harold Smith.* Bradley F. Smith, *The Road to Nuremberg,* chapter 1.

24. 26 April 1945 conference with the president, Box 15, *Harold Smith;* 18 June 1945, Rosenman–Vinson–President Truman exchanges, memos to the President File, Box 2, Rosenman papers, and Donovan, Secret Intelligence File, Misc., Box 15, *Truman.*

25. John Morton Blum, ed., *The Price of Vision, The Diary of Henry A. Wallace,* pp. 444–445. The newspaper clippings were sent to the F.O., *FO 371/44543/AN 1962;* 9 and 21 May 1945, questionnaire exchanges, CCS 111 (6–17–42), *RG 218;* Cutter to Settle, 22 May 1945, ABC 384 (4–29–44), *RG 165.* The sounding of the theater commanders and their replies is in Folder 54, Box 9, *RG 218 Leahy.* On Leahy's reply and Cannon's attitude, 28 and 29 May 1945, CCS 111 (6–17–42), *RG 218* and ABC 384 (4–29–44), *RG 165.*

26. June section, Misc., Box 15, *Truman.* An example of O.S.S. men exiting is O'Brien to H. Smith, 27 August 1945, H. Smith File, Box 12, O'Brien Papers, Columbia. 28 Aug.–11 September 1945, CCS 385 (2–8–42) pt. 10, *RG 218 Postwar;* 7 September 1945, Marshall memo, CCS 334 (12–6–42), sec. 1, *RG 218.*

27. 25 August 1945, Donovan to Truman, Donovan, Secret Intelligence File, Misc., Box 15, *Truman*. O.S.S. was in fact closing down. Belmont radio monitoring center was already closed and Reseda was closing by 4 September. Minutes of Radio Advisory Committee File, Box 8, Entry 1, *RG 226*. 17 August and August–September 1945 Deuel letters (one to Fred Oechsner and one presumably to Deuel's parents), 1945 File, Box 1, Wallace Deuel Papers, Library of Congress; Allen to John Foster Dulles, 20 August 1945, Roll 6, Box 26, John Foster Dulles Papers, Princeton.

28. 10 September 1945, Balfour to F.O., *FO 371/44538/AN2820;* Donovan to President Truman, 4 (2) and 5 September 1945, Box 15, Misc., *Truman;* conferences with the president, 5 and 13 September 1945, Box 15, *Harold Smith.* Anthony Panuch's 1945 summary of events, State Department R. and I. File, Box 7, Panuch Papers, Harry S. Truman Library (this is vital for unraveling the O.S.S. dissolution process). JCS 965, 10–20 September 1945, CCS 385 (2–8–42), pt. 10, *RG 218 Postwar.* A convenient chart showing O.S.S. structure at its end is in August Howe Ransom, *The Intelligence Establishment* (Cambridge, Mass.: 1970).

29. 13 September 1945, Conference, Box 15, and Daily Record, Box 10, *Harold Smith;* Donovan to President Truman, 13 September 1945, Donovan, Secret Intelligence File, Misc., Box 15, *Truman;* Donovan order of 13 September 1945, Organizations and Individuals File, Box 21, James Donovan Papers, Hoover Institution; 14 and 18 September 1945 U.S.I.S. releases, FO 371/44543/AN1962; 14 September 1945, R. Cecil to F. O., *FO 371/44545/AN2963;* 10 September 1945, Balfour to F. O. *FO 371/44538/AN2820.*

30. Sours to Dulles, 23 February 1964, Donovan File, Box 123, *Dulles;* 20–21 September 1945, CCS 385 (2–8–42) pt. 10, *RG 218 Postwar;* 19 and 20 September 1945 preparatory papers, OF 128–B, OSS File, *Truman;* Intelligence service file, Box 7, Eban A. Ayers Papers, Harry S. Truman Library; 20 September 1945 Conference, Box 15, *Harold Smith.*

31. Admiral Leahy would not even agree to a special letter of commendation for Donovan (8 October 1945) and General Lemnitzer failed in his effort to get the Unit Citation for the 2671st Recon. Bn. (the O.S.S.–O.G. unit in the Mediterranean). CCS 200.6 (9–13–44), *RG 218.* 31 December 1945 report, Singapore File, Box 19, Entry 1, *RG 226.*

32. 10 October 1945, Magruder memo, 103.918/10–1045, *Diplomatic Branch.* 25 October 1945 Shepardson to Miller, folder F-3, Box 9, Francis Miller Papers, Marshall Library. As an example of the change note that the M.O. unit in S.S.U. in December 1945 totaled 8 people while in September 1945 O.S.S. had in the relative backwater of the Middle East 115 people in R. and A., X-2, and S.I., 8 December 1945, Herbert Little memo, 103.918/12–845, *Diplomatic Branch;* September 1945 report, NATO File, Box 20, Entry 1, *RG 226.*

33. Colombo to State, 24 September 1945, and Rangoon to State, 8 November 1945, 103.918/9–2455 and /11–845, *Diplomatic Branch;* 17 May 1946 Miles memorandum, Secret Memorandum File, Box 3, Milton E. Miles Collection, Hoover Institution. On an O.S.S. history: 31 August 1945 report, Box 2, R. Harris Smith Papers, Hoover Institution; 26 July–17 September 1946, CCS 385 (2–8–42), pt. 10, *RG 218 Postwar* (M.I.D. opposed any such history—even if secret—because "a history or compilation of records of any intelligence agency invites compromise of its methods and sources"). On Rhee: 12 October 1945 note, June 1942–1945 File, Box 3, *Goodfellow.*

34. Reports of 20 September and 30 November 1945, State Department R. and I. file, Box 7, Panuch Papers, Harry S. Truman Library. For sample S.S.U. contacts see Richard Helms File, Box 30, *Dulles.* December 1945–February 1946, materials, Kesort Code File, Box 10, Entry 1, *RG 226.*

35. 16 October 1945 SWNCC mtg., Forrestal Diaries, III, pp. 547–548, Princeton; 20 September 1945 Bureau of the Budget report, State Department R. and I. File, Box 7, Panuch Papers, Harry S. Truman Library; 16 October 1945, Lord Halifax to F.O., *FO 371/44545/3168;* 17 October 1945 entry, John Morton Blum, ed., *The Price of Vision,* p. 492; 10 January 1946, Smith to Rosenman, Intelligence File, Box 7, Rosenman Papers, Harry S. Truman Library; 22 January 1946 President Truman order and 18 April 1946 list of Truman's statements on intelligence, Intelligence Service File, Box 7, Ayers Papers, Harry S. Truman Library; *Troy,* chapters 13–16.

36. 26 September 1945, McCloy to Magruder, ABC 334.3, sec. 4, (5–1–42), *RG 165;* 1 October 1945, *Wilkinson;* Donovan to President Truman, October 1945 (no day), Donovan, Secret Intelligence File, Misc., Box 15, *Truman;* Donovan–Rosenman exchange, 13–16 January 1946, Alphabetical File, Box 10, Rosenman Papers, Harry S. Truman Library.

37. 1 October 1945, Buxton to Rogers, FF-Buxton File, Box 2, J. G. Rogers Papers, Colorado Historical Society; 10 October 1948, Donovan to Forgan, Donovan File, Forgan Papers, Hoover Institution; Dulles speech at Maxwell Air Force Base, 9 December 1946, Box 26, *Dulles;* Lemnitzer to Dulles, 23 November 1946, JCS File, Box 26 and Dulles to Lemnitzer, 25 November 1946, Oppenheimer File, Box 17, *Dulles.*

38. 13 December 1945, Bruce–Dulles exchange, Bruce File, Box 21, and Dulles to Hugh Wilson, Wilson File, Box 27, *Dulles.*

39. 30 July 1946 letter, "Washington, George-O.S.S. operations" File, Box 27, *Dulles.*

40. V.V.S. Files, Boxes 47, 107, 129, 175, *Dulles;* Donovan to Eisenhower, 5 May 1948, Donovan File, Box 35, *Eisenhower;* Arnold A. Rogow, *James Forrestal* (New York: 1963), pp. 334–335; 25 August 1960, Dulles to Lemnitzer, Lemnitzer File, Box 45, *Dulles;* 1951 letters, Donovan to Dulles, Donovan File, Box 49, *Dulles;* 5 February 1953, O'Brien to Ostheimer, uncatalogued correspondence, O'Brien Papers, Columbia; Wiley to Dulles, 24 February 1958, Box 6, Wiley Papers, Franklin D. Roosevelt Library; Princeton Associates signatures, 19 October 1961, Langer File, Box 96, *Dulles;* Dulles speech to V.V.S., 22 January 1962, speech-role of CIA File, Box 107, *Dulles.*

41. Poole to Dulles, 8 February 1946, Poole File, Box 26, *Dulles;* Stanley Lovell, *Of Spies and Strategems* (New York: 1963), p. 77; 18 January 1946, Miller to O'Brien, uncatalogued correspondence, O'Brien Papers, Columbia.

42. 1945 memorandum, File F-7, Box 8, Francis Miller Papers, Marshall Library; Dulles to Donovan, 16 July 1955, Box 66, Helms to Dulles, 16 September 1965, OSS File, Box 143, *Dulles.*

43. 14 July 1945, *Wilkinson;* 25 October 1945, Shepardson to Miller on the "George" project, File F-3, Box 9, Francis Miller Papers, Marshall Library; 30 December 1964, Wisner to Dulles, Wisner File, Box 137, *Dulles.*

44. 16 September 1963, Benton–Dulles exchange on drawing a sharp line between C.I.A. and propaganda activity, OSS File, Box 114, *Dulles.* In 1947, Bruce did suggest a system closer to that of C.O.I. in 1941, 9 October 1947 memo to Marshall and Forrestal, Folder 23, Section 13, David Bruce Papers, Virginia Historical Society.

45. David Atlee Phillips, *The Night Watch* (New York: 1977), p. 111.

Bibliography

A complete bibliography of works on the history of World War II and the history of American intelligence would greatly exceed the size of this volume. The bibliography has therefore been limited to works cited in the text plus those that I have recently read (or reread) or from which I have gained important insights. See also the bibliography in Bradley F. Smith and Elena Agarossi, *Operation Sunrise*, New York: 1979, and the recent comprehensive work by Myron J. Smith, Jr., *The Secret Wars: A Guide to the Sources in English*, Santa Barbara, California: 1980.

Unpublished Documents

Great Britain

Winston S. Churchill Library, Cambridge University
  Sir Alexander Cadogan
  W. G. Cheshire
  Gerald H. Wilkinson
British Library of Political and Economic Science, London School of Economics
  Hugh Dalton
Public Record Office
  AIR 14: Bomber Command
  CAB 65: War Cabinet Minutes
  CAB 66: War Cabinet Memoranda
  CAB 69: War Cabinet Defense Committee
  CAB 79: Chiefs of Staff (COS) Minutes
  CAB 80: Chiefs of Staff (COS) Memoranda
  CAB 122: Joint Staff Mission
  FO 371: Main Diplomatic Files
  FO 660: Minister Resident's Papers
  FO 892: British Mission to the French National Committee
  FO 898: Political Warfare Executive
  FO 954: Lord Avon's Papers
  PREM 3: Operations
  PREM 4: Confidential Papers
  WO 106: Directorate of Military Operations and Intelligence
  WO 193: Directorate of Military Operations

WO 204: A.F.H.Q. Files
WO 208: Directorate of Military Intelligence
WO 212: Order of Battle
WO 219: S.H.A.E.F.

United States
Colorado State Historical Society, Denver, Colorado
  James Grafton Rogers
Columbia University
  Julien O'Brien
  Francis Perkins
Hoover Institution, Stanford University
  Heber Blankenhorn Psychological Warfare Report
  J. Rives Childs
  James Donovan
  Delos C. Emmons
  Bonner F. Fellers
  The Fight For Freedom Committee
  James Forgan
  Henri Giraud, "The Causes of the Defeat: Military Causes." Report to Marshal Pétain.
  Millard P. Goodfellow
  George A. Hill
  Stanley Hornbeck
  Interdepartmental Committee for the Acquisition of Foreign Periodicals
  David King
  Milton Miles
  Walter J. Muller
  Boris T. Pash
  Frank N. Roberts
  Leland Rounds
  Geo. von Schulze Gaevernitz
  R. Harris Smith
  Gilbert Stuart
  Ivan D. Yeaton
Library of Congress
  W. S. Culbertson
  Wallace Deuel
  Archibald MacLeish
George C. Marshall Library, Lexington, Virginia
  George C. Marshall
  Francis Miller
Bentley Library, University of Michigan
  Arthur Scott Aiton
  Joseph R. Hayden
National Archives Federal Record Center, Suitland, Maryland
  RG 331: A.F.H.Q. Records.
National Archives, Washington, D.C.
  Diplomatic Branch
    RG 59: General Diplomatic Files
  Modern Military Branch
    RG 165: ABC Files
    RG 218: JCS Files
    RG 226: Research and Analysis Branch of O.S.S.
    RG 334: Mission to Moscow Files
    RG 457: Records of N.S.A
    Reference collection (no RG number)
  Navy and Old Army Branch
    RG 80: Frank Knox

Bibliography

Dwight D. Eisenhower Library, Abilene, Kansas
  Eisenhower Papers, 1916–1952
  C. D. Jackson
  Selected Records of S.H.A.E.F.
  Walter B. Smith Collection of World War II Documents
Franklin D. Roosevelt Library, Hyde Park, New York
  Adolf Berle
  Henry Field
  Harry Hopkins
  Map Room
  Henry Morgenthau
  OF (Official File)
  PSF (President's Secretary's File)
  Whitney Shepardson
  Harold Smith
  John Wiley
Harry S. Truman Library, Independence, Missouri
  Eban A. Ayers
  Philleo Nash
  J. Anthony Panuch
  Samuel I. Rosenman
  Harry S. Truman
Princeton University
  Allen W. Dulles
  J. Foster Dulles
  James Forrestal
Virginia Historical Society, Richmond, Virginia
  David Bruce
State Historical Society of Wisconsin
  Dewitt Poole
Yale University
  Henry Stimson

Published Documents

Berle, Beatrice B., and Travis B. Jacobs. *Navigating the Rapids 1918–1971. From the Papers of Adolf A. Berle*. New York: 1973.

Blum, John Morton, ed. *The Price of Vision. The Diary of Henry A. Wallace 1942–1946*. Boston: 1973.

Campbell, Thomas M., and George C. Herring, eds. *The Diaries of Edward R. Stettinius, Jr., 1943–1946*. New York: 1975.

Chandler, Alfred D., Jr., and Stephen E. Ambrose, eds. *The Papers of Dwight David Eisenhower. The War Years*. 5 vols. Baltimore and London: 1970.

Ciano, Galeazzo. *The Ciano Diaries 1939–1943*. Garden City, New York: 1946.

Dilks, David, ed. *The Diaries of Sir Alexander Cadogan 1938–1945*. London: 1971.

Foreign Relations of the United States 1940–1945. Washington, D.C.: 1957-1965.

Foreign Relations of the United States. The Conferences at Cairo and Teheran 1943. Washington, D.C.: 1961.

Foreign Relations of the United States. The Conference at Quebec 1944. Washington, D.C.: 1972.

Foreign Relations of the United States. The Conferences at Washington 1941–1942 and Casablanca 1943. Washington, D.C.: 1968.

Foreign Relations of the United States. The Conferences at Washington and Quebec 1943. Washington, D.C.: 1970.

Iatrides, John O., ed. *Ambassador MacVeagh Reports. Greece 1933–1947*. Princeton, New Jersey: 1980.

Ickes, Harold L., ed. *The Secret Diary of Harold L. Ickes. The Lowering Clouds 1939–1941.* Vol. III. New York: 1954.

Israel, Fred L., ed. *The War Diary of Breckinridge Long.* Lincoln, Nebraska: 1966.

Leutze, James, ed. *The London Journal of General Raymond E. Lee 1940–1941.* Boston· 1971.

Liddell Hart, B. H., ed. *The Rommel Papers.* Trans. Paul Findlay. New York: 1953.

Loewenheim, Francis L., Harold D. Langley, and Manfred Jonas, eds. *Roosevelt and Churchill. Their Secret Wartime Correspondence.* New York: 1975.

Roosevelt, Elliott, ed. *F.D.R.: His Personal Letters 1928–1945.* Vol. IV. New York: 1950.

Shirer, William L. *Berlin Diary.* New York: 1941.

Smith, Bradley F., and Agnes F. Peterson, eds. *Himmler Geheimreden.* Frankfurt/M.: 1974.

Smith, Jean Edward, ed. *The Papers of General Lucius D. Clay. Germany 1945–1949.* 2 vols. Bloomington, Indiana: 1974.

Young, Kenneth, ed. *The Diaries of Sir Robert Bruce Lockhart. 1939–1965.* Vol. II. London: 1980.

Interviews

Gordon Craig
William Cunliffe
Harold Deutsch
William Emerson
H. Stuart Hughes
Barry Katz
Sherman Kent
Henry Cord Meyer
Reginald Phelps
Carl Shorske
Hans Tofte

Articles and Pamphlets

Donovan, William J., and Edgar Mowrer. *Fifth Column Lessons for America.* Washington, D.C.: 1941.

Fitzgibbon, Constantine. "Spying for the Yanks." *Sunday Telegraph Magazine.* 4 August 1979.

"From the OSS with Love: The Rise of a Testing Method." *Psychology Today,* December 1978.

Funk, Arthur L. "American Contacts with the Resistance in France 1940–1943." *Military Affairs* 34, no.1 (February 1970) 15–22.

Funk, Arthur L. "Churchill, Eisenhower and the French Resistance." *Military Affairs* 45, no. 1 (February 1981) 29–33.

Kramer, Paul. "Nelson Rockefeller and British Security Coordination." *Journal of Contemporary History* 16, no. 1 (January 1981) 73–88.

Krautkämer, Elmar. "General Giraud und Admiral Darlan in der Vorgeschichte der Alliierten Landung in Nordafrika." *Vierteljahrshefte für Zeitgeschichte* 30, no. 2 (April 1982) 206–255.

Miller, James Edward. "Italian American Politics and the Future of Italy: Reports of the Foreign Nationalities Branch, Office of Strategic Services, 1943–1945." (Unpublished.)

Mulligan, Timothy P. "According to Colonel Donovan: A Document from the Records of German Military Intelligence." *The Historian.* (In press.)

Spector, Ronald. "Allied Intelligence and Indochina, 1933–1945." *Pacific Historical Review*, 41, no. 1 (February 1982) 23–50.

Stafford, David A. "The Detonator Concept: British Strategy, SOE and European Resistance After the Fall of France." *Journal of Contemporary History* 10, no. 2 (April 1975) 185–217.

Stafford, David A. "Britain Looks at Europe, 1940: Some Origins of SOE." *Canadian Journal of History* 10, no. 2 (August 1975).

Stafford, David A. "SOE and British Involvement in the Belgrade Coup d' État of March 1941." *Slavic Review* 36, no. 3 (September 1977) 399–419.

"U.S. Blessing: OSS Agent in Vatican." *Washington Post,* 3 August 1980.

Memoirs and Secondary Volumes

Alcorn, Robert Hayden. *No Bugles for Spies.* New York: 1962.

Les Allies et la resistance en Europe. Milan: 1961.

Alsop, Stewart, and Thomas Braden. *Sub Rosa, the OSS and American Espionage.* New York: 1946.

Arnold, Henry H. *Global Mission.* New York: 1949.

Backer, John H. *The Decision to Divide Germany.* Durham, North Carolina: 1978.

Baer, George. *Test Case.* Stanford, California: 1976.

Barker, Elisabeth. *British Policy in South-East Europe in the Second World War.* London: 1976.

Beaufre, Gen. André. *1940. The Fall of France.* Trans. Desmond Flower. London: 1965.

Beesly, Patrick. *Very Special Intelligence.* London: 1977.

Beevor, J. G. *SOE: Recollections and Reflections.* London: 1981.

Bennett, Jeremy. *British Broadcasting and the Danish Resistance Movement.* Cambridge: 1966.

Benoist-Mechin, Jacques. *Sixty Days That Shook the West. The Fall of France: 1940.* Trans. Peter Wiles. New York: 1963.

Biddle, Francis. *In Brief Authority.* Garden City, New York: 1962.

Bloch, Marc. *Strange Defeat.* Trans. by Gerard Hopkins. London: 1949.

Boyle, Andrew. *The Climate of Treason.* London: 1979.

Braden, Spruille. *Diplomats and Demagogues.* New Rochelle, New York: 1971.

Brown, Anthony Cave. *Bodyguard of Lies.* New York: 1975.

Bry, Gerhard. *Resistance: Recollections from the Nazi Years.* West Orange, New Jersey: 1979.

Burnham, James. *The Web of Subversion.* New York: 1954.

Butler, J. R. M. *Grand Strategy.* London: 1957.

Butler, J. R. M. *Lord Lothian (Philip Kerr) 1882–1940.* London: 1960.

Calvocoressi, Peter. *Top Secret Ultra.* New York: 1980.

Campbell, Rodney. *The Luciano Project.* New York: 1977.

Chadwin, Mark Lincoln. *The Hawks of World War II.* Chapel Hill, North Carolina: 1968.

Chennault, Claire Lee. *Way of a Fighter.* New York: 1949.

Churchill, Winston S. *Blood, Sweat and Tears.* New York: 1941.

Churchill, Winston S. *The Second World War.* 6 vols. Boston: 1953.

Ciechanowski, Jan M. *The Warsaw Rising 1944.* Cambridge: 1974.

Colby, William, and Peter Forbath. *Honorable Men.* New York: 1978.

Coles, Harry L. and Albert K. Weinberg. *Civil Affairs. Soldiers Become Governors.* Washington, D.C.: 1964.

Collier, Richard. *1940: The World in Flames.* London: 1979.

Cookridge, E. H. *Inside SOE.* London: 1966.

Coon, Carleton S. *A North Africa Story.* Ipswich, Massachusetts: 1980.

Cruickshank, Charles. *The Fourth Arm. Psychological Warfare 1938–1945.* London: 1977.

Dalton, Hugh. *The Fateful Years. Memoirs 1931–1945.* London: 1957. Vol. II.

Daniels, Jonathan. *White House Witness 1942–1945.* Garden City, New York: 1972.

Deakin, F. W. *The Brutal Friendship. Mussolini, Hitler and the Fall of Italian Fascism.* Garden City, New York: 1966.

Deakin, F. W., and G. R. Storry. *The Case of Richard Sorge.* London: 1966.

Deane, John R. *The Strange Alliance.* New York: 1947.

Delmar, Sefton. *Black Boomerang. An Autobiography.* London: 1962. Vol. II.

Delzell, Charles F. *Mussolini's Enemies. The Italian Anti-Fascist Resistance.* Princeton, New Jersey: 1961.

Divine, Robert A. *The Reluctant Belligerent.* 2nd ed. New York: 1979.

Dixon, Piers. *Double Diploma. The Life of Sir Pierson Dixon.* London: 1968.

Djilas, Milovan. *Tito.* Trans. Vasilije Kojic and Richard Hayes. New York: 1980.

Dulles, Allen W., and Hamilton Fish Armstrong. *Can We Be Neutral?* New York: 1936.

Dulles, Allen W. *Germany's Underground.* New York: 1947.

Dulles, Allen W. *The Craft of Intelligence.* New York: 1965.

Dunlop, Richard. *Behind Japanese Lines with the OSS in Burma.* Chicago: 1979.

Dunlop, Richard. *Donovan, America's Master Spy.* Chicago: 1982.

Emmerson, John K. *The Japanese Thread. A Life in the U.S. Foreign Service.* New York: 1978.

European Resistance Movements 1939–1945 First International Conference on the History of the Resistance Movements. New York: 1960.

Fairbank, John K. *Chinabound.* New York: 1982.

Farago, Ladislas. *The Game of Foxes.* New York: 1971.

Fergusson, Bernard. *The Watery Maze.* New York: 1961.

Field, Henry. *Trail Blazers. Chicago to Moscow.* Miami, Florida: 1980.

Foot, M. R. D. *M.I. 9.* London: 1979.

Foot, M. R. D. *Resistance.* London: 1978.

Foot, M. R. D. *SOE in France.* London: 1966.

Ford, Corey. *Donovan of O.S.S.* Boston: 1976.

Franklin, Jay. *The Catoctin Conversation.* New York: 1947.

Fuller, Jean Overton. *The German Penetration of SOE. France 1941–1944.* London: 1975.

Funk, Arthur Layton. *The Politics of Torch.* Lawrence, Kansas: 1974.

Gaddis, John Lewis. *The United States and the Origins of the Cold War 1941–1947.* New York: 1972.

Garlinski, Jozef. *Poland, SOE and the Allies.* Trans. Paul Stevenson. London: 1969.

Giskes, H. J. *London Calling North Pole.* London: 1953.

Gladwyn, Lord. *Memoirs.* New York: 1972.

Goudsmit, Samuel A. *Alsos.* London: 1947.

Green, Martin. *Children of the Sun.* New York: 1976.

Grew, Joseph C. *Turbulent Era. A Diplomatic Record of 40 Years 1904–1945.* Boston: 1952.

Guderian, Heinz. *Panzer Leader.* Trans. Constantine Fitzgibbon. New York: 1952.

Hamilton-Hill, Donald. *SOE Assignment.* London: 1973.

Harich-Schneider, Eta. *Charaktere und Katastrophen.* Berlin/Frankfurt: 1978.

Harriman, W. Averell, and Elie Abel. *Special Envoy to Churchill and Stalin 1941–1946.* New York: 1975.

Harrison, Gordon A. *Cross Channel Attack.* Washington, D.C.: 1951.

Hayes, Carlton J. N. *Wartime Mission in Spain 1942–1945.* New York: 1946.

Higham, Charles. *Errol Flynn.* New York: 1980.

Hilton, Stanley E. *Hitler's Secret War in South America 1939–1945.* Baton Rouge, Louisiana: 1981.

Hinsley, F. H., E. E. Thomas et al. *British Intelligence in the Second World War. Its Influence on Strategy and Operations.* New York: 1979–81. Vols. I and II.

History of the Military Intelligence Division, United States Department of the Army. Microfilm Copy, Hoover Institution, Stanford University. 1959–61.

Hoare, Sir Samuel. *Ambassador on Special Mission.* London: 1946.

Holmes, W. J. *Double Edged Secrets.* Annapolis, Maryland: 1979.

Hoover, Calvin. *Germany Enters the Third Reich.* New York: 1933.

Hoover, Calvin. *Memoirs of Capitalism, Communism and Nazism.* Durham, North Carolina: 1965.

Bibliography

Horne, Alistair. *To Lose a Battle. France 1940.* Boston: 1969.

Howarth, Patrick. *Undercover. The Men and Women of the Special Operations Executive.* London: 1980.

Howe, George F. *Northwest Africa. Seizing the Initiative in the West.* Washington, D.C.: 1957.

Hyde, H. Montgomery. *Room 3603.* New York: 1962.

Hyde, H. Montgomery. *Secret Intelligence Agent.* London: 1982.

Hymoff, Edward. *The OSS in World War II.* New York: 1972.

Ind, Allison. *Allied Intelligence Bureau.* New York: 1958.

Irving, David. *The War Between the Generals.* New York: 1981.

Jones, R. V. *Most Secret War.* London: 1978.

Jong, Louis de. *The German Fifth Column in the Second World War.* Trans. C. M. Geyl. Chicago: 1956.

Jukic, Ilija. *The Fall of Yugoslavia.* Trans. by Dorian Cooke. New York: 1974.

Kahn, David. *The Codebreakers.* New York: 1967.

Kahn, David. *Hitler's Spies.* New York: 1978.

Kennedy, Maj. Gen. Sir John. *The Business of War.* London: 1957.

Kersten, Felix. *The Kersten Memoirs 1940-1945.* Trans. Constantine Fitzgibbon and James Oliver. New York: 1957.

Koskoff, David E. *Joseph P. Kennedy. A Life and Times.* Englewood Cliffs, New Jersey: 1974.

Langer, William L. *In and Out of the Ivory Tower.* New York: 1977.

Langer, William L., and S. Everett Gleason. *The Challenge to Isolation 1937-1940.* New York: 1952.

Leahy, William D. *I Was There.* New York: 1950.

Lewin, Ronald. *Ultra Goes to War.* New York: 1978.

Liddell Hart, B. H. *The German Generals Talk.* New York: 1948.

Liss, Ulrich. *Westfront 1939-1940.* Neckargemünd: 1959.

Lockhart, Robert Bruce. *Comes the Reckoning.* London: 1947.

Lovell, Stanley. *Of Spies and Strategems.* New York: 1963.

McLachlan, Donald. *Room 39.* New York: 1968.

Macmillan, Harold. *The Blast of War 1939-1945.* New York: 1967.

Masterman, J. C. *The Double-Cross System in the War of 1939 to 1945.* New Haven, Connecticut: 1972.

May, Gary. *China Scapegoat. The Diplomatic Ordeal of John Carter Vincent.* Washington: 1979.

Milazzo, Matteo J. *The Chetnik Movement and the Yugoslav Resistance.* Baltimore: 1975.

Miles, Milton E. *A Different Kind of War.* Garden City, New York: 1967.

Molden, Fritz. *Exploding Star.* Trans. Peter and Betty Ross. New York: 1979.

Montagu, Ewen. *Beyond Top Secret Ultra.* New York: 1978.

Moravec, Frantisek. *Master of Spies.* London: 1975.

Morris, Joe Alex. *Nelson Rockefeller. A Biography.* New York: 1960.

Mowrer, Edgar A. *The Nightmare of American Foreign Policy.* New York: 1948.

Mowrer, Edgar A. *Triumph and Turmoil.* New York: 1968.

Murphy, Robert. *Diplomat Among Warriors.* Garden City, New York: 1964.

Neave, Airey. *Escape Room.* Garden City, New York: 1970.

Neumann, Franz. *Behemoth.* New York: 1942.

Page, Bruce, David Leitch, and Phillip Knightley. *The Philby Conspiracy.* Garden City, New York: 1968.

Paxton, Robert O. *Vichy France. Old Guard and New Order 1940-1944.* New York: 1972.

Pearson, John. *The Life of Ian Fleming.* New York: 1966.

Peers, William R. and Dean Brelis. *Behind the Burma Road.* Boston: 1963.

Persico, Joseph E. *Piercing the Reich.* New York: 1979.

Pertinax, Andre Geraud. *The Gravediggers of France.* New York: 1944.

Philby, Eleanor. *Kim Philby. The Spy I Loved.* London: 1967.

Philby, Kim. *My Silent War.* New York: 1968.

Phillips, David Atlee. *The Night Watch.* New York: 1977.

Phillips, William. *Ventures in Diplomacy.* Boston: 1952.

Pogue, Forrest C. *The Supreme Command.* Washington: 1954.

Popov, Dusko. *Spy/Counter Spy*. New York: 1974.
Porter, David L. *The Seventy-sixth Congress and World War II 1939–1940*. Columbia, Missouri: 1979.
Powers, Thomas. *The Man Who Kept the Secrets*. New York: 1979.
Ransom, Harry Howe. *The Intelligence Establishment*. Cambridge, Massachusetts: 1970.
Read, Anthony, and David Fisher. *Operation Lucy*. New York: 1980.
Roberts, Walter. *Tito, Mihailović and the Allies 1941–1945*. New Brunswick, New Jersey: 1973.
Rogow, Arnold A. *James Forrestal. A Study of Personality, Politics and Policy*. New York: 1963.
Romanus, Charles F., and Riley Sunderland. *Stilwell's Command Problems*. Washington: 1956.
Roosevelt, Kermit, ed. *The War Report of the OSS*. New York: 1976.
Roosevelt, Kermit, ed. *The War Report of the OSS. The Overseas Targets*. New York: 1977.
Rostow, Walter W. *Pre-Invasion Bombing Strategy*. London: 1981.
Schellenberg, Walter. *The Labyrinth*. Trans. Louis Hagen. New York: 1956.
Sherwood, Robert E. *Roosevelt and Hopkins*. New York: 1948.
Smith, Bradley F. *The Road to Nuremberg*. New York: 1981.
Smith, Bradley F. and Elena Agarossi. *Operation Sunrise*. New York: 1979.
Smith, R. Harris. *OSS. The Secret History of America's First Central Intelligence Agency*. New York: 1972.
Spears, Sir Edward. *Assignment to Catastrophe*. 2 vols. New York: 1955.
Stafford, David A. *Britain and the European Resistance 1940–1945*. London: 1980.
Stevenson, William. *A Man Called Intrepid*. New York: 1976.
Stimson, Henry L., and McGeorge Bundy. *On Active Service in Peace and War*. New York: 1947.
Strong, Kenneth. *Intelligence at the Top*. Garden City, New York: 1968.
Sweet-Escott, Bickham. *Baker Street Irregular*. London: 1965.
Taylor, Edmund. *Awakening from History*. Boston: 1969.
Taylor, Telford. *The March of Conquest*. New York: 1958.
Thayer, Charles W. *Diplomat*. New York: 1959.
Theoharris, Athan. *Spying on Americans*. Philadelphia: 1978.
Thomas, Lately. *When Even Angels Wept*. New York: 1973.
Thorne, Christopher. *Allies of a Kind*. London: 1978.
Toland, John. *The Last 100 Days*. New York: 1967.
Tomasevich, Jozo. *The Chetniks*. Stanford, California: 1975.
Tompkins, Peter. *A Spy in Rome*. New York: 1962.
Tree, Richard. *When the Moon Was High. Memoirs of Peace and War 1897–1942*. London: 1975.
Troy, Thomas F. *Donovan and the C.I.A.* Central Intelligence Agency: 1981.
Tuchman, Barbara. *Stilwell and the American Experience in China*. New York: 1970.
Ulam, Adam B. *The Rivals. America and Russia Since World War II*. New York: 1971.
Vigneras, Marcel. *Rearming the French*. Washington: 1957.
Weil, Martin. *A Pretty Good Club*. New York: 1978.
Weinstein, Allen. *Perjury. The Hiss-Chambers Case*. New York: 1978.
Westphal, Siegfried. *The German Army in the West*. London: 1951.
Wheeler Bennett, John W., and Anthony Nicholls. *The Semblance of Peace*. New York: 1974.
Wheeler, Mark C. *Britain and the War for Yugoslavia 1940–1943*. Boulder, Colorado: 1980.
Whitehead, Don. *The FBI Story*. New York: 1956.
Willoughby, Charles A., and John Chamberlain. *MacArthur 1941–1951*. New York: 1954.
Winant, John G. *Letter from Grosvenor Square*. Boston: 1947.
Winterbotham, F. W. *The Ultra Secret*. London: 1974.
Woodhouse, C. M. *The Struggle for Greece 1941–1949*. London: 1976.

Index

"C," *see* Menzies, Sir Stewart
Cadogan, Sir Alexander, 14, 18
Caffey, Benjamin F., 241
Cairo Conference, 337
Cal Tech, 373
Calder, Ritchie, 95, 117
California, University of, Berkeley, 105, 175, 372
Canaris, Adm. William, 22
Canary Islands, O.S.S. in, 188
Cannon, Clarence, 201
Cape Verde Islands, 105
Carter, John Franklin, 63–64, 74, 85, 93, 185, 186, 271, 416, 431n34, 434n16, 436n41, n45, 437n52, 442n41, 446n1, 447n14; Donovan and, 90–91, 105; and internment of Japanese-Americans, 100; post-Pearl Harbor activities of, 97, 101; and postwar intelligence plans, 396, 398, 400–401
Casablanca (submarine), 227
Casey, William J., 296
Catholic Church: politics of, 32; *See also* Vatican
Censorship Board, 106
Central Intelligence Agency (C.I.A.), 106, 167, 191, 266, 296, 329, 349, 351, 361, 394, 403; academic recruiting for, 388; Board of Estimates of, 209; charter of, *xiv;* creation of, *xiv;* 391, 409–11, 417; Dulles and, 223; history of O.S.S. by, 399; influence of O.S.S. on, 414–15, 417, 419; and O.S.S. veterans, 411–13; remnants of R. and A. in, 387; repressive methods of, 331; support for reactionary regimes by, 240
Century Group, 56
Ceylon: O.S.S. operations in, 261; S.E.A.C. headquarters in, 319
Chamberlain, Neville, 15, 17
Chapin, Howard, 470n37
Chennault, Gen. Claire, 197, 259, 325
Cheshire, Air Chief Marshal W. G., 327
Cheston, Charles, 204, 273
Chetniks, 83
Chiang Kai-shek, 130–33, 196, 199, 317, 326, 330, 332
Chicago Daily News, 25, 31, 33, 41
Chicago Tribune, 270
Chicayev, Col. I., 334, 336, 341, 349, 353
China, 256; Allied victory in, 307, 310; Board of Analysts representative in, 76; California College in, 105; C.O.I. opera-

tions in, 130–33; Free Thai army bases in, 194–95; French interests in, 324, 325; guerrilla warfare in, 92, 414; N.K.V.D. operations in, 337; S. I. and, 127; O.S.S. operations in, 171, 196–99, 207–8, 257–62, 310–12, 314–19, 325, 328; postwar operations in, 410; R. and A. in, 366, 367, 377, 386; S.O.E. and, 44; S.S.U. in, 408; U.S. policy and, 331–33
China-India-Burma Theater (C.B.I.), 257, 258, 310, 314, 316
Churchill, Winston, 7, 38, 40, 62, 89, 164, 182, 239, 334, 349, 428n61, 429n78; and Allied invasion of France, 246, 249, 251; and Balkan front, 45–49, 51; and Battle of Britain, 19–20; and British colonialism in Asia, 319, 323, 325–26; cabinet shuffling by, 109; at Casablanca conference, 178, 191; and defense of imperialism, 158; designated leader of war cabinet, 17; Donovan and, 52, 53; and entry of U.S. into war, 113–15, 134; after fall of France, 14–15; on fifth column, 13; Hopkins and, 28; and invasion of Russia, 82, 334; and losses to Japan, 107; Maclean and, 240; North African strategy of, 135, 146–48; on O.S.S. and communism, 330; postwar Balkan policy of, 280–82; Quebec meetings with Roosevelt, 236, 257, 281; S.O.E. and, 43; Stephenson and, 29; Stimson on, 58; Tito supported by, 282–83; and Trieste incident, 287; and Yugoslav revolt, 83, 112
Ciano, Count Galeazzo, 274
Civil Affairs Office, 304
Clam project, 259, 314
Clark, Grenville, 24, 56
Clark, Gen. Mark, 150, 153, 155
Clay, Gen. Lucius, 413
Clopet, C. V., 151
Code and Cypher School, 36
Cohen, Ben, 66–68
Colby, William, *xiv*
Cold War, *xiv, xvi,* 351, 354–56, 409; C.I.A. operations during, 413; Dulles and, 214; intensification of, 412
Coleridge, Baron Richard, 200
Colombia, German activities in, 84
Colonna d'Istria, Maj., 232
Columbia University School of Law, 31
Combined Chiefs of Staff (C.C.S.), 113, 245, 260, 350, 440n6; and need to control special operations, 158, 159; and North Afri-

Index

Index

Index

Index

Index

United States: Aid to Britain *(continued)* 56, 58, 61, 63; aid to French resistance by, 249–50; attempt to control special operations in, 158; attitude toward Soviet Union, 212–15; British attempt to influence intelligence activities of, 61–62; China and, 130–31; deterioration in relations with Japan, 78; early victories of, 141; entry into war, 95–96, 113–14; European strategy of, 142; in European war, 264; and fall of France, 20–21, 23, 24; fifth column myth and, 21–23, 29–30, 38–39, 56–57; and German invasion of Russia, 79; in Italian campaign, 229–30; losses of, 143; M.I. 6, operations in, 208; and North African invasion, 147; North African policy of, 134–35; official World War II policy of, 331–33; in Pacific war, 307, 309–10; postwar interests of, 211; rearmament of, 24; relations with de Gaulle, 156; relations with Soviet Union, at end of war, 288–89; Vichy France and, 185; and Yugoslav revolt, 83

Uruguay, German intelligence operations in, 22

Ustachi regime, 83

V-1 flying bomb, 223, 266
V-2 rockets, 223, 266, 296
Van Deman, Gen. Ralph, 99
Vanderbilt, William, 174
Vansittart, Robert, 88
Vatican: false reports on, 274; Japan and, 313; N.K.V.D. and, 340
V.E. Day, 285, 304, 396, 407
Vendôme tragedy, 245–46
"Vessel" memoranda, 313–14
Veterans of Strategic Service (V.S.S.), 410–12
Vichy France, 9, 10, 40, 104, 219, 232; C.O.I. and, 28; Donovan and, 47, 58; Donovan's plan for attack on, 100; German occupation of, 180; Indochina and, 322–23; Langer's report on, 210; North Africa and, 52, 58–60, 135–38, 145–50, 153–56; S.O.E. operations in, 109, 146; U.S. relations with, 185
Victor communications channel, 127, 437n66, 438–39n84, 439n91
Viet Minh, 327
Vietnam, 323

Vietnam War, 328, 388, 419
V.J. Day, 285, 307, 322, 327, 329, 380, 386, 396, 405, 407
Vinson, Fred, 404
Volkesdeutschen, in France, 12

Wainwright, Gen. Jonathan, 317
Wake Island, fall of, 95
Wallace, Henry, 404, 409
War Department, U.S., 55, 57, 66, 67, 97, 119, 135, 166, 168, 314, 326, 353–54, 362, 406; and abolition of O.S.S., 386–87; and Allied invasion of France, 246; and Chennault-Stillwell conflict, 197; Civil Affairs Division of, 223, 376, 384; conservatives and, 212; disputes with C.O.I., 105, 118; Dulles reports to, 279; good relations with O.S.S., 201; and Hoettl affair, 357, 358; intelligence machinery of, 92; and Jedburgh plan, 187; N.K.V.D. and, 341, 349; Operations Division of, 120, 186; and postwar intelligence plans, 393, 394, 398, 399, 403, 405, 406; R. and A. and, 76, 78, 123, 175, 376, 377, 384; Strategic Services Unit of, 408, 410
War Office, British, 15, 61, 451n83; and Allied invasion of France, 246; "sibs" approved by, 86; S.O.E. conflicts with, 109
War Shipping Board, 411
Ward, Barrington, 255
Warren Commission, 414
Warsaw Ghetto, 86
Washington, George, 411
Washington Times Herald, 270
Watson, Hugh Seton, 61
Wavell, Gen. Archibald P., 48, 60, 195
Wavrin, André, 273, 431n48
Wedemeyer, Gen. Albert C., 263, 307, 312, 314–16, 324–27, 332, 377, 404
Wehrmacht, 108, 141, 142, 246; blitzkreig strategy of, 4–5; C.O.I. report on, 122–23; defeat of, 292, 294, 303; invasion of France by, 8, 10; in Italy, 321, 299; in Norway, 305–6; reprisals against, 291; in Russia, 80
Weinberg, Stanley, 337
Welles, Sumner, 70, 101, 117, 127, 183, 446n1
West, Mae, 302
Westphal, Gen. Siegfried, 5
Weygand, Gen. Maxime, 9, 19, 59, 134

506